DATE DUE		AUG 26	
MAR 1 5 1984			
NOV 1 9 1987			
FEB 2 2 1989			
NOV 1 3 1993			

STANDARD HANDBOOK OF
STAMP COLLECTING

STANDARD HANDBOOK OF

STAMP

COLLECTING

❖❖❖❖❖❖❖❖❖❖❖❖❖❖❖❖❖❖❖❖❖❖❖❖

RICHARD McP. CABEEN

Stamp Editor, *Chicago Tribune*

New Revised Edition

THOMAS Y. CROWELL, PUBLISHERS

NEW YORK   ESTABLISHED 1834

To my wife,

Blema,

for her patience

and encouragement

HE
6215
C2
1979

STANDARD HANDBOOK OF STAMP COLLECTING, NEW REVISED EDITION. Copyright
© 1965, 1957 by Richard McP. Cabeen. Copyright © 1979 by the Collectors Club of Chicago. All rights reserved. Printed in the United States of America. No part of this book may be used or reproduced in any manner whatsoever without written permission except in the case of brief quotations embodied in critical articles and reviews. For information address Thomas Y. Crowell, Publishers, 10 East 53rd Street, New York, N.Y. 10022. Published simultaneously in Canada by Fitzhenry & Whiteside Limited, Toronto.

LIBRARY OF CONGRESS CATALOG CARD NUMBER: 78-3297

ISBN: 0-690-01773-1

80 81 82 83 10 9 8 7 6 5 4

PREFACE

A stamp collection is a number of stamps systematically mounted.

A mere accumulation, stored in envelopes or boxes, is not a collection, for the owner has little to show, and he cannot tell easily what he has or what he needs. His stamps should be arranged in a logical way: by countries and issues, or by subjects.

Many of us have an inborn desire to collect things, and that is what makes collecting fun for us. Some are looking for quick profits, and they miss much of the pleasure. Others put aside stamps for their children to treasure; very often they are wasting their effort, unless they become converted themselves.

The collecting desire is stirred up in all sorts of different ways. More often than not the fascinating stamps on foreign letters are enough to touch it off. Sometimes it is the cleaning out of an old attic. There may be letters of the Civil War period, or even an abandoned collection. Special events and organizations have started off many. The issues of the American Medical Association and of the American Society of Civil Engineers undoubtedly made many an enthusiast.

The beginner, young or old, should realize that as a hobby stamp collecting is fun. It will bring hours of pleasure, and relaxation. It should never turn into work. Some collectors become so engrossed that they have to find second hobbies as relief from the first!

Of course I am often asked the question, "Why do you collect stamps?" I could point to the knowledge I have gained, the profit, the other benefits, but the real answer is the answer given by the philatelic authority, the late Mannel Hahn: "Because I like it." That is sufficient!

The collector is bound to learn a great deal in a pleasant manner. It is hardly possible to handle stamps of Oltre Giuba, an Italian colony, or Ifni, a Spanish possession, without wondering about their locations. A stamp of Pitcairn Island will likely lead to an investigation of this British possession, and the collector will learn that the *Bounty* mutineers of 1790 settled an island of only two square miles; that the population is now about 140; and that her postage stamps, first issued over a decade ago, are the island's chief source of revenue.

In order to classify his stamps the collector will learn something of perforations, paper, and watermarks, and often he will want to know how to determine the printing process that was used.

The educational opportunities in collecting cannot be over-emphasized, but the least importance should be placed on the profit possibilities. Strangely, of all hobbies, stamp collecting is the only one that is expected to pay its way. There is always a chance that the collector may have stamps that will increase in value while he holds them, but it is nonsense to assume that more than a small proportion of collections can be sold at a profit.

Soon after the beginner buys his first packet he will be asked if he is a philatelist or a stamp collector. *Philately* was coined by a French collector, Georges Herpin, from two Greek words, *philos*, meaning "fond of," and *atelia*, "freedom from tax." Since further payment is not required when letters bear the proper postage stamps, M. Herpin used *atelia* as a synonym for stamp. A philatelist, therefore, is one who engages in philately, or the collection and study of stamps—in short, he is a stamp collector. It might be added that in recent years the term philately has been broadened to include the study of postal-history items, with or without stamps, and it now also embraces fiscal stamps and other nonpostal material.

While gathering information for this book the author had access to nearly all the English-language books on the subject of general philately published during the past thirty years, and a large number of the earlier period. Files of important magazines covering a period of more than sixty years were consulted, as well as a clipping file maintained by the writer for many years. English, French, German, and Spanish catalogs were used, with particular attention given to Scott's *Standard Postage Stamp Catalogue*, as this is the basis for most of the collections formed in the United States.

Society publications as well as commercial have aided. Important titles in the first category are *The American Philatelist*, *The Collector's Club Philatelist*, *The Bureau Specialist*, and *The Stamp Lover*. In the second are *The American Journal of Philately*, *Philatelic Journal of America*, *Philatelic Gazette*, *Mekeel's Weekly Stamp News*, *Stamps*, *Weekly Philatelic Gossip*, *Linn's Weekly Stamp News*, *Western Stamp Collector*, *Scott's Monthly Journal* and *Gibbon's Monthly Journal*.

Other publications consulted include those concerned with limited fields, such as aerophilately, postal markings, etc., and the *Stamp Specialist* series, published by H. L. Lindquist, the yearbooks of the American Philatelic Congress, and the occasional publications of the National Philatelic Museum.

The author has been glad to accept matter from other sources, the main criterion being whether the source was considered accurate or the opinion was that of an authority.

PREFACE TO THE NEW REVISED EDITION

The author of this book, Richard M. Cabeen, was a valued member of the Collector's Club of Chicago during his life and the benefactor of it at his death. We, the members of the Committee on Publications of this club, have been happy to revise this edition of his work in his memory. We were helped greatly by George W. Brett of the Bureau Issues Association with the section on Intaglio Printing and the United States Printing Methods and wish to acknowledge our thanks to him. Principal revisions have been done by Alfred Diamond, Charless Hahn, Dr. Harvey Karlen and Fred P. Schueren.

COMMITTEE ON PUBLICATIONS
Charless Hahn, Chairman
Alfred Diamond
Joseph L. Eisendrath, Jr.
Dr. Harvey Karlen
Michael Laurence
Rev. George C. Muresan
Paul C. Rohloff
Fred P. Schueren
Harold Stral
Raymond Vogel
Morrison Waud

CONTENTS

Part IV Technical Matters

Part V Classification and Identification

LIST OF ILLUSTRATIONS

PART I

Introduction to Stamp Collecting

❖❖

CHAPTER ONE

STARTING A COLLECTION

ADVANTAGES OF A GENERAL COLLECTION

Beginners should start a general collection in order to learn something about many kinds of stamps. If a collection is limited to a single country, the collector learns few methods of producing stamps.

The general knowledge gained will make new collectors aware of the many phases of the hobby, and a collector with a little imagination can develop a collection that differs from all others.

FIRST PACKET AND ALBUM

When starting a general collection, buy as large a packet of stamps as you can afford. After this packet has been arranged in the collection, some other source of stamps must be found, for a second large packet will duplicate the first to a great extent. A better way to start is to buy one of a series of non-duplicating packets.

If the stamps are for a youngster, they should be parceled out, a few at a time, the number depending on the ability of the child to classify and mount them. It is easier to find your way out of a clump of trees than out of a forest.

The starting album should have printed spaces and many illustrations to assist in identifying the stamps. Such albums are available in several styles and with various capacities, and may be solidly bound or loose-leaf.

A desirable album might have spaces for at least five thousand stamps, but there will be some disappointments, for no album will show many of the stamps on current letters—stamps issued after the album was prepared. The starting album will probably not be permanent but rather a temporary shelter for some stamps which later will be transferred to another book.

TOOLS NEEDED

Stamp hinges and tongs will be needed from the first since the beginner should learn to mount the stamps correctly and neatly and never to handle them with his fingers. Proper habits formed at the start will prevent damage to valuable stamps later on.

Albums are described in detail in chapter 4, and hinges and tongs in chapter 6.

Long ago collectors stuck unused stamps in their albums with the gum of the stamps, and used glue to hold the used copies, but that day has passed and the beginner should use stamp hinges. Do not use odd pieces of gummed paper for hinges, as some are thick and will mark the stamp, or are so weak that they will break after a few folds. Some will stick too tightly and cannot be removed, or they may have a kind of gum that will harm the colors of the stamps.

Various kinds of hinges are described in chapter 6. Ways of preserving stamps without hinges will be found in chapter 5.

A beginner is usually most concerned with stamp designs. He pays little attention to perforations, watermarks, and other details and so will not need a perforation gauge or a watermark detector. Until he begins to fill all the spaces of a large album or tries to find all the listed varieties, he will see no differences except in designs.

A small magnifying glass is very useful in studying designs

and reading inscriptions. This may be about one and one-half inches in diameter and the strength of an ordinary reading glass.

The proper way to remove stamps from paper and the precautions that must be observed are so important that this book has a chapter entitled "Preparing Stamps for Mounting."

IDENTIFYING STAMPS

When stamps are examined the beginner will find some with the names of the countries in English. Others will have the names in a foreign language so like the English equivalent that only a little imagination is needed to identify them. Examples are Danmark for Denmark, Nederland for Netherlands, Norge for Norway, Belgie or Belgique for Belgium. There will also be some names in Latin letters, such as are used for English words, which bear no resemblance to the names we use for the countries. Examples are Helvetia for Switzerland, Magyar for Hungary, Oesterreich for Austria, Lietuva for Lithuania, and Suomi for Finland.

Many stamps will have the names in Greek, Cyrillic, Arabic, or other Oriental letters. These will give the beginner trouble until he has memorized the characters or designs used by each country, or has access to the information included in chapter 33 of this book.

The stamps of China and Japan will not be difficult to separate from others as they have little characters, called ideograms, each of which is the equivalent of a word or more in English. Many stamps of these two countries bear inscriptions in English, in addition to the ideograms.

Finally, there are numerous stamps that show nothing but abbreviations to indicate their origin, and still others that show only a design, with or without numerals of value.

After the stamps at hand have been identified, nothing remains but to mount them correctly in the album. When the first packet of stamps has been mounted, the beginner should adopt some plan to increase the size of his collection without obtaining too many duplicates. Some of the methods to use are outlined in the following chapters.

❖❖❖

EXPANDING THE COLLECTION

APPROVALS

A collector may begin to fill spaces in his album by obtaining packets of countries from which he has very few stamps. Eventually he will gather too many duplicates. At this point he arrives at the stage where he asks dealers to submit stamps on approval.

The term "on approval" indicates one of the most important methods used in buying and selling stamps. The collector examines the stamps before paying for those he wants to keep. The approval business is not limited to beginners but is the normal method used in buying and selling by mail.

Stamps sent to beginners on approval are mounted on sheets or in small books, with the stamps priced singly or by sets, in some cases at a reduced price if the entire lot is taken. If a stamp is removed from an approval lot, and later remounted, it is a good idea to note this fact alongside the stamp, so that there will be no question of a trade or substitution.

When asking a dealer to send stamps on approval, a collector should specify the kind of stamps he wishes to see, used or unused or both, naming the countries in which he is interested and the price range desired.

Beginners and mature general collectors may obtain many new stamps for their collections from what are called "penny approvals." These are put up by dealers who buy quantities of stamps by weight and mount them on sheets at one cent each. Such dealers cannot spend the time necessary to catalog the stamps. They remove from their bulk purchases only those which they recognize as valuable. Many stamps are found on these sheets which could be priced at five cents or more if identified.

These dealers depend on a quick turnover. They make a better profit selling at one cent each than could be had at even half-catalog value if the time of listing the stamps is taken into account.

UNSOLICITED APPROVALS

Soon after starting to collect, and especially if he joins a stamp club, a collector may begin to receive selections of stamps on approval even though he has not asked for them. This practice of sending unsolicited approvals is decried in better stamp circles.

If the approvals are not desired, and if return postage has been included with the lot, it will be a simple matter for you to mail the shipment back to the dealer with a note stating that you are not interested in unsolicited stamps. If return postage has not been provided, you are under no obligation to return the lot at your expense. The dealer may threaten all kinds of dire consequences, but cannot take any legal action. Keep his lot intact and wait for him to supply the postage, or better, ship it back to him as a valuable package, express charges collect.

However, unsolicited approvals are not always undesirable for many beginners, particularly those in rural communities and small towns, receive their first knowledge of stamp dealers through these offerings.

STAMP CLUBS

If a beginner lives in a city it will be to his advantage to join a club, where stamps can be shown and traded. The new collector will learn more from associating with other collectors than from any amount of reading. There are clubs for boys in connection with many schools, churches, libraries, YMCA's, and other organizations. Adult stamp clubs will be found in almost every city, and there are also intercity clubs.

If one lives where there is no possibility of belonging to a club, or of forming one, it will be necessary to follow the hobby through reading and correspondence.

STAMP NEWS

There are several stamp newspapers published weekly, and one semiweekly. The subscription rates are nominal. There may also be a weekly stamp column in your local newspapers, and there is stamp news in most boys' and girls' magazines. Many public libraries have stamp books, catalogs, and periodicals on their shelves, or they will be obtained if the demand is sufficient.

MISSION MIXTURE AND KILOWARE

Among the advertisements that a collector will see in his stamp paper are some which call attention to mission mixture and kiloware. A mission mixture consists of mixed stamps collected by church organizations and sold to dealers by weight. Dealers sell these stamps without careful sorting, and there may be some scarce items in any package.

Kiloware is usually sold in sealed packages weighing a kilogram or more. The seals indicate that the mixture has not been opened since it was packaged in some foreign country. The stamps all come from one country and are current stamps taken from parcel post cards, money order forms, and the like. In certain foreign countries stamps are not affixed to parcel post shipments and money orders, but are attached to a card or form retained in the original post office until the shipment has been completed or the order paid. When the stamps have finished their use the postal authorities clip them from the forms, package them, and sell them to dealers, or at auctions. All are on paper and nearly all are in the finest condition possible. Mission mixture stamps are also generally on paper, but they are not as clean and free from wear as kiloware.

Either type of mixture often yields a good return to the beginner in new stamps for his collection and duplicates to trade. Prices of mixtures are reasonable and many advanced collectors enjoy an occasional hunt through one of the packages in the hope of finding a "sleeper," a scarce stamp which has passed through a dealer's hands without being recognized.

WANT LISTS

When a collector decides that he must complete a certain set, it may be advisable for him to send a want list, containing the catalog numbers and other data, to some dealer who solicits this business. He should mention whether used or unused stamps are wanted and if they must be select copies or just average. When the stamps are received, the collector is at liberty to return any which do not suit him.

STAMP DEALERS

Some readers may feel that too much importance is given to dealers in this book. However, the dealers have done much to make stamp collecting the fascinating hobby it is. They publish catalogs, albums, and other accessories, and their advertisements make the publication of stamp periodicals possible. Without their priced catalogs and lists the hobby would be in a chaotic state, with every collector fixing the prices on his duplicates or trading them stamp for stamp. Dealers have accumulated the data on which values are based, and while these are questionable in some cases, they stand up very well through the years, since they reflect the law of supply and demand. Stamp auctions provide an accurate check on list prices, and are the reason for the subsequent raising and lowering of many items.

National societies have collected data on stamps and some association of those societies might produce a far better catalog than is available now, but it would be a labor of love. The cost of illustrations and the tons of type matter standing ready for additions, price changes, and the like are beyond the financial horizon of collector's societies.

PRIVATE SOURCES

The beginner collecting in a general way will make contacts with friends who receive foreign letters or know where they may be found. Business houses often have stamps which may be had for the asking. Although the large mail-order houses have had outlets for their stamps for many years, there are smaller houses and various organizations of an international character which have not been approached by any collector.

Numerous collectors would like to buy all their stamps in the countries of origin, but many countries do not sell stamps by mail. In such cases, a friend must be found who will undertake the task while living abroad. Unless this friend is a collector, it may be an imposition to expect him to watch for new issues.

Usually the purchase of small lots abroad by correspondence is relatively expensive, as the various service charges may amount to several times the face value of the stamps. The procedures are explained later in this chapter.

EXCHANGE AND CORRESPONDENCE CLUBS

Exchange relations may be opened with collectors in foreign countries to obtain stamps merely by sending the equivalent in used or unused United States issues. When attempting to arrange contact with foreign collectors it is usually more satisfactory to join an exchange or correspondence club than to act as a lone ranger. The fact that you and your correspondent are members of the same club gives each more confidence in the other. References are necessary when joining such a club, and those who do not follow its rules will lose their membership and find it difficult to join another club.

SOCIETY SALES DEPARTMENTS

Members of the national philatelic societies and of some clubs are able to buy, sell, and exchange through the sales and exchange departments of their organizations. Duplicates are mounted in sales books provided by the department at a nominal cost, listed according to a standard catalog, and priced by the owner. These books are then circulated among the club members. Those who buy stamps remove the stamps from the books, sign the empty spaces, and itemize their purchases on sales slips. Slips and remittances are sent to the organization's sales superintendent, who deducts a small percentage of the sale price for insurance and handling costs.

AUCTIONS

Stamp auctions are frequently conducted here and abroad, and the material sold over a period of years includes almost every item listed in the standard catalog.

Since World War I, beginning with the sales of the famous Count Ferrari collections, which France sequestered during the war as enemy property, nearly all of the great rarities have been seen at auction sales. In June, 1921, in one section of the Ferrari sale, the unique British Guiana one-cent magenta stamp of 1856 was sold to Arthur Hind, an American collector, for $37,500, plus a tax of 20 per cent imposed by the French government. Mr. Hind's bid was above that of Britain's King George V, who had hoped to complete the royal collection of British Empire stamps by adding this specimen.

Many medium-priced stamps are seldom available except at auctions, and while low-priced stamps are not put up for sale individually, many choice items are offered with other stamps.

The catalogs of auction sales are mailed to all regular bidders and to others who request them. The stamps and covers offered are described concisely and often illustrated. Dealers are sometimes criticized for inadequate descriptions, but the cost of listing a lot is such that often it exceeds the commission on the sale.

As a collector learns to know values he will be able to judge how lots will sell and can bid accordingly. He enters the lot number and his maximum bid on a bid sheet and sends it to the dealer. New bidders should give references with their first bids or send a cash deposit. In theory, at least, a successful bidder is supposed to obtain his lot at one raise above the second high bid. He should examine his purchases at once to see that they were correctly catalogued, since he may return any which do not agree with the descriptions.

A collector who lives in the city where a sale is to be held may examine the stamps before the sale. Out-of-town collectors may have lots sent them for inspection, but must undertake to return the lots on the day of receipt. When a very important sale is to be held, the dealer often visits the larger cities to show the collection.

Stamp auctions are of two kinds, the public sale, which combines mail and floor bidding, and the mail sale, which is not open to the public. The first is the more highly considered, as the bidding is conducted by a licensed auctioneer, under state supervision, and the prices realized are the result of open competition.

The mail sale is under the sole control of the dealer and he may withhold lots if he feels the bids are inadequate. There is no way to check on his agreement to sell at one raise above the second high bid, and more frequently than not the lot is billed to the collector at his maximum bid. The dealer may also sell several identical lots under one number if the bids are sufficient. However, this practice does not injure a collector and saves the dealer listing many similar lots.

In a public sale the first bid is made by the auction dealer in an amount at one raise above the second high mail bid. The next bid is made from the floor by some collector or dealer. Again the auction dealer bids, and again the floor, the cash amount of the raises depends on the price range in which the lot is selling. These bids alternate until either the auction dealer stops from lack of higher mail bids, or the floor bidders drop out.

In stamp auctions the dealer's commission is deducted from the amount realized for the seller.

At one time "daily auctions" had large followings, for collectors could buy or sell with little trouble. Stamps mounted on the dealer's sheets were placed in loose-leaf binders. When a collector entered a bid on a sheet it became eligible for sale at the end of two weeks, providing a second bid was entered. Bidders enrolled as members of the auction club, removing the necessity of having a licensed auctioneer. A collector seriously interested in buying returned on the final day to make a last bid.

A lack of sufficient first-class material—probably the result of unsatisfactory bids—caused a decline in popularity and these auctions are now replaced by consignment stamps.

In one city a variation of the daily auction idea is to put the lots on display on a bid board. Bids are entered on the sheets and the lots are sold after two weeks have elapsed. These lots attract customers to a stamp shop but require a great deal of wall space.

CONSIGNMENT SALES

Dealers often handle stamps on consignment for collectors and other dealers, with the stamps mounted on sheets and housed in binders. The lots are catalogued and priced by the owner, and a customer who finds a lot he needs may buy it at once. The dealer keeps his record by removing a stub which contains the code number of the owner and the price of the lot. This simple system enables a dealer to handle a consignment stock of many thousands of stamps.

THE UNITED STATES PHILATELIC AGENCY

A philatelic agency is a government bureau that supplies collectors with current unused stamps of select quality. The

United States Philatelic Agency was the first such bureau, and it is still the most important one. It opened in December, 1921. Since that time it has supplied stamps at face value to hundreds of thousands of collectors and dealers.

In addition to all current stamps, numerous commemorative issues are available after they are no longer on sale at post offices. The agency also sells stamped envelopes, and migratory bird hunting stamps. A list of stamps on hand and instructions and order blank may be obtained by sending a stamped, self-addressed envelope with your request to Philatelic Sales Unit, U.S. Postal Service, Washington, D.C., 20026. Postage and fees vary with the number of stamps ordered; full instructions are on the instruction sheet.

FOREIGN PHILATELIC AGENCIES

Following the success of the United States Philatelic Agency, numerous foreign countries introduced similar services, but many were terminated by the Second World War.

Canada maintains an agency which may be addressed as Philatelic Service, Canada Post, Ottawa, Ontario, KIA OB5 Canada. This country usually pays the postage on orders for mint stamps but charges a fee per cover on lower value stamps for first day service at the same address.

The United Nations sells stamps to collectors by mail and across the counter at the Secretariat building in New York. They are also available at its agencies abroad. When writing for information, address the United Nations Postal Administration, United Nations, New York, N. Y., 10017.

The Crown Agents Stamp Bureau, of London, supplies current stamps of about 65 colonies and former colonies to stamp dealers only.

Other foreign governments provide monthly, bi-monthly, quarterly or annual information publications for collectors, but their schedules and availability are continually changing.

Several foreign countries have offices in the United States

for the distribution of their stamps, but as some of these sell only in quantity or to dealers, and as the locations of their offices are not permanent, no purpose would be served by listing them.

Foreign philatelic agencies operate in various ways but all require payment in United States dollars. Some make a service charge, and all require the purchaser to pay the postage on his order, which usually is sent by registered mail. Payment must be made as prescribed by the country, usually by international money order. When a bank draft is required the bank will convert the foreign sum to dollars.

When a remittance is to be made through the post office you must figure the amount to send in dollars to equal the foreign sum. Do not send United States currency or that of the foreign country, as nearly every country has restrictions on the return of obligations which are outside its boundaries. No remittance should be sent unless registered, for otherwise there is little recourse if receipt of your money is denied.

Many collectors do not understand the relation between United States money and that of other countries, and for this reason the assistance of a bank is recommended. In one case, an American collector who had learned that a foreign commemorative set had a face value of $20 sent that amount for the stamps. He later learned that the value was actually in pesos, abbreviated and that his dollar was worth six pesos, but he was never able to obtain a refund.

In past times some foreign agencies, although completely honest, were somewhat ignorant of collectors' wants. Sheets were folded without regard to perforation lines, stamps were torn out in a careless manner, and no protection was given against moisture, so that stamps often stuck together during transit by ship. Today agencies are better informed, and shipments by air usually preclude sticking, but there is still no recourse if the arrival condition is unsatisfactory. Many enterprising foreign countries accept deposit accounts, send all their new stamps as they are issued, and notify the collector when his deposit is nearly spent. Collectors using this method will miss no new issues and will receive selected stamps, carefully wrapped.

Some foreign countries have laws against selling their stamps to collectors by mail, but many are happy to engage in the business because of the considerable profit involved. The stamps may cost ten or twenty-five cents a thousand to produce, and the difference between this and the face value, which the collectors pay, is sometimes great.

You may not know the exact name and address of a foreign philatelic agency, but since it is always an official, not a private concern you may write your letter of inquiry to the Post Office Department or the Director of Posts of the capital city. If you cannot write it in the language of the country in question write it in French or English.

Generally speaking, stamps bought in the country of origin will cost more than when purchased from dealers in the United States, unless the order amounts to a substantial sum. The charges for money orders or bank drafts, air mail postage both ways, registration of the shipment, and perhaps a service charge, may increase the cost to several times the stamps' face value.

COOPERATIVE BUYING IN FOREIGN COUNTRIES

When a group of collectors pools its purchase orders, foreign stamps may be bought more cheaply. The expenses for the entire group will hardly be greater than for a single purchase, since many of the routine charges will amount to the same minimum in either case.

The cooperative buying plan will not be successful unless all the buyers are satisfied. No person should receive the pick of the shipment, since the copies will not be equally good. The stamps should be distributed by lot so that each person in the pool receives a share of the poorer ones.

NEW-ISSUE SERVICE

A collection may be kept up to date through a new-issue service offered by many dealers. The service may be a complete service, covering the world, or it may be limited in any way the collector desires. For example, one may ask for the stamps of a single country, or a group of countries, or one may want stamps of limited face value, say British Colonial issues under ten shillings. The commission charge for this service is reasonable and the stamps will not cost as much as individual sets purchased at retail. The collector has the privilege of returning unsuitable copies within a certain time.

ORIGINAL FINDS

In addition to the usual ways of adding to a collection there is a chance of making a find of old letters. When a business closes down or is absorbed by another or moves to a new location it may abandon its older files. This happens often but seldom does a collector see the material. The papers may go to a paper mill or be auctioned at the site; sometimes they may be obtained from the wrecker who is removing the building.

Regardless of dates, the material should be carefully examined, for some envelopes may show interesting and valuable postal markings even though the stamps have no philatelic value. There are letters of all wars with markings of camps, prison camps and naval vessels. Some may be pictorial or special envelopes of the service groups. Exposition envelopes, some pictorial, with exposition station cancels are desirable, and often there are postal cards with views of the fair.

Late in the nineteeth century the hand-stamp cancels, some hand-cut, gave way in the cities to machine cancels and it is worth while to find one with an eagle's head and sun rays. Next came flag cancels, at first vigorously waving, next undulating, and finally only straight lines. Soon station names were inserted and then slogans of the postal service and, finally, of events.

There may be postal markings of the territories and those of railroads and other special carriers. Envelopes may have pictorial corner cards and these are eagerly sought by collectors. The finder of a hoard of letters should ask for help if he is not sure that he can identify all of the important covers.

❖❖❖

CHAPTER THREE

WHAT TO COLLECT

The first stamp enthusiasts were general collectors; that is, they collected the stamps of all countries, not only the adhesive postage but stamped envelopes and postal cards, either as entires or cut squares, and often revenue and telegraph stamps and many labels which resembled postage stamps. As the number of stamp-issuing countries increased and new issues were added for special purposes, collectors found it difficult to keep up. The result was that they stopped collecting the nonpostal items and finally the stamped envelopes and cards.

In time some of the small nations learned that they sold more stamps for collections than for postage, and new issues began to appear more frequently and in more denominations. Again it became impossible to keep up with the flood, and the next step was to form a "limited general" collection. Many collectors speak of this as "specialization" but the correct name is as given.

LIMITED COLLECTIONS

Limited collections were at first defined by geographical or political boundaries, later by a date limit. Thus we find collections of the stamps of a continent, a hemisphere, a group of related countries, such as the British Empire, or of a single nation. After 1900, we find collections limited to the nineteenth century, while others contain twentieth century stamps only.

Beginners of more recent years, on finding that the older stamps command high prices, may fix their limits by recent events and collect only those stamps issued between the two World Wars. Actually there is no logic in limiting a collection to one of the two centuries, since the date 1901 is not critical in the history of any country, and the observance of that date as a starting point often divides a nation's stamps in a grotesque manner. More appropriate dates for closing a collection seem to be those of the World Wars as they are reflected in the stamps of nearly all countries, and are the starting or ending dates of many countries and colonies.

Many collectors with patriotic motives build collections of their native countries, but even this limit may be too great, and a single political period is selected. Thus, a collection of British stamps may be held to the reign of a single sovereign. A collection of United States stamps may be limited to either of two logical sections, the dividing point being 1894, the date when the private bank-note printing companies ceased printing United States stamps and the Bureau of Engraving and Printing took over their production.

Other limited collections may be those of such regional groups as British North America, or the British West Indies. One of the most instructive collections which can be assembled is that which starts with the German states and progresses through the North German Postal Union into the German Empire.

Many collectors, who like to work in fields with their limits clearly marked, select countries which no longer issue stamps. Although many are older countries with very high-priced stamps, there are also recent but now defunct states whose stamps can be collected without great expense.

Another demarcation line is available to those who like the older classical issues. There is no rigid date which applies to all countries, but 1870 seems to apply to many. The end of the period sees some change in the character of the stamps, a change from engraving to typography, or to a standard design; in any case, something of sufficient importance that the collector of the classics may stop his collection at that point.

Perhaps a word of caution should be given those collectors who limit not only their collections but their appreciations. Every collector worthy of being known as a philatelist should know enough about all stamps to be able to enjoy the work of another collector, no matter how different from his own.

MINT OR USED

Mint is a philatelic term to describe a stamp in the condition as sold by a post office. In nearly all cases it indicates that the stamp has its full original gum (o.g.) and is without hinge marks. Unused is a term which may designate mint stamps but usually means no more than that the stamp has not been canceled. Used stamps are those which have seen postal service and have been canceled.

Every collector faces the question of whether to collect mint or used stamps, and periodically this subject is debated with considerable spirit in stamp papers. Those who argue in favor of unused stamps rest their case on the fact that the stamps, having no disfiguring cancellations, make a finer collection because the designs are clear. Those who favor used stamps contend that mint stamps are only receipts, or evidences of money paid for services to be rendered, and that they cannot be classed as postage stamps until they are used as such. Many collectors ignore the argument and mix the two kinds in their sets.

The face value of mint stamps usually determines a minimum selling price, while used stamps are priced according to the supply, with a minimum somewhat above the value of waste paper. However, there are many foreign stamps of extremely low face value which are traded in mint condition at a lower figure than for used stamps, since the latter must be soaked off the paper and sorted before they go into packets, while the mint stamps are ready as soon as the sheets can be separated into single stamps. These low-value stamps, together with others made obsolete by currency inflation, account for a large percentage of the mint stamps found in cheap packets. Such stamps are scarcer canceled than unused.

In Europe it has long been customary to save every stamp received on mail. These find their way into the market through the efforts of churches, schools, and societies, as mission mixture. So many stamps have been available through these sources that there has been little increase in their market value. In other countries, where this intensive method of saving stamps was not used, canceled stamps have appreciated in value, and some that once were common have become moderately scarce.

Since stamp collecting became popular on the basis of saving used stamps, no collector or dealer put aside quantities of mint stamps for future trading. In many cases an entire issue was sold for use on mail, or the stock on hand when a new series arrived would be destroyed, with the result that no mint examples were available except those in collections. These things account for the extreme rarity of unused stamps of early issues.

At various times remainders of stamp issues reach the market. Prices then usually are depressed, but unless the supply is enormous, they will recover when the remainders have been distributed and the incident forgotten. Remainders are discussed in chapter 31.

It has been mentioned that the face value of stamps enters into the basic valuation placed on unused stamps. It should also be noted that nearly all countries from time to time demonetize their past issues. This destroys the stamps' face value and prevents their being offered to pay postage, but has little effect on prices in the stamp trade. Great Britain, for example, has invalidated all her stamps up to the end of the reign of George V. The United States has done the same for all stamps issued prior to the Civil War, but even if it should invalidate its stamps up to 1894, it is doubtful if there would be any change in list prices.

Collectors of mint stamps may point out that many used stamps are "canceled to order," and often with postmarks or devices not used on regular mail. In some cases a country does this to provide collectors of used stamps with clean fresh copies, charging the same price as for mint stamps. Other countries cancel the stamps in wholesale lots and sell them at a figure somewhat below face value. Actually, no face value is being destroyed and the entire sum charged for the stamps is profit, except for the few cents per thousand it costs to print the stamps. When post offices prepare souvenir cards or sheets bearing sets of stamps nicely postmarked, they are engaging in another canceled-to-order practice. They collect full face value or more and render no postal service whatever.

At one time anything which had the appearance of being "philatelically used" was carefully avoided. The term indicates any postal item which has been made for or by a collector to secure a particular cancellation or to obtain a used stamp not normally available. Such items are generally considered not so desirable as others which have been found in ordinary business or personal use of the mails.

First-day covers, discussed at length in chapter 14, are included in this group by some authorities but their collection is an established custom and they have historical interest. However, they should come to a collector in the open mail. When they are transmitted under wraps, with or without name and address, they fall into the status of canceled-to-order material. However, when a name and address have been added later it may be very difficult to classify such a cover correctly.

Were collections limited to used stamps, commemorative and semi-postal issues would be reduced or eliminated in many countries. Those which depend upon the revenue gained by selling quantities of unused stamps to dealers and collectors would have little incentive to change their designs. The general public cares little about postage stamps.

MINT SINGLES, BLOCKS

A collector desiring an extensive collection will buy single stamps only. There seems to be little excuse for collecting blocks of duplicates. They make impressive spots on an album page but the design of each copy is no easier to see. It is seldom possible to mount a complete issue or set of blocks on a single page and an arbitrary division of the set often proves unsatisfactory.

A collection of blocks costs four times as much as one of singles and usually is started by beginners for no reason except that it is the current fashion. Block collecting has been stimulated by the very high prices at which some older blocks are sold, on the theory that the current issues will someday be valuable. However, the older blocks bring high prices because only a few collectors bought them when the stamps were current. The late A. B. Slater, of Providence, Rhode Island, was mentioned under the nickname "Blocks of Four" Slater by a periodical early in 1893, in a story which stated that he had 2400 blocks of United States stamps at the close of 1892.

Very few blocks of the dollar values of the Columbian issue (1893) and the 1894 and 1895 regular issues were saved by collectors at the time. The maximum domestic postage rate was $1.28 and collectors were slow to invest in expensive stamps that could not be used for postage if they were rejected from collections.

The collecting of multiple examples became necessary when the United States began to issue imperforate stamps for the makers of affixing and vending machines. As single imperforate stamps could be forged by trimming oversize copies of the perforated issue, pairs or preferably blocks were needed to guarantee authenticity. Imperforate sheets and private coils are treated in chapter 11.

The collection of the various position blocks found in imperforate sheets led some collectors to save similar perforated blocks. These include plate-number, corner, and margin blocks and in some cases, particularly in bi-colored issues, it was possible to obtain the line, crossed-line, and arrow blocks.

In current rotary-press issues the position blocks are limited to corners, and perhaps margin blocks, although the latter largely duplicate the detail found on corner blocks. In all block collecting those showing imprints and plate numbers, or plate numbers alone, are of prime interest and are the subject of the next section.

The discussion of plate number blocks applies equally to used and unused blocks, the former being scarcer except in recent commemorative issues. Another subject of much interest is found in the "Tab" stamps of Israel and the United Nations and in the "Zip Code" tabs now appearing on the margins of some United States stamps.

PLATE-NUMBER BLOCKS

Although a few blocks with plate numbers were saved in the early days it was unusual for a collector to invest in the number of stamps needed to show the full imprint and number. When the Bureau of Engraving and Printing began producing United States stamps, the small imprint and number occupied the margins of only three stamps and many collectors attempted to gather the entire series in strips of three.

These imprints and numbers appeared on the four margins of the sheets as printed and on two margins, at least, of the panes prepared for post-office use, the preferred position being at the bottom of the sheet. Some collectors were satisfied with plate-number singles and collected these used and unused. They could acquire them rather easily as the only scarce numbers were those on the dollar-value plates.

The block-of-six size was adopted by those who favored blocks, since the margins of three stamps were required to show the full imprint and number. When the use of the imprint was stopped the only change made by collectors was to pick the block with the number opposite the central stamp. Soon after the introduction of rotary-press printing the plate number was given a position opposite one corner stamp of each pane in the sheet the numbers being located on the side margins. This form is now standard in all types of United States stamp printing. Since centered numbers cannot be obtained collectors have reduced the plate block size to four stamps.

In the days of flat plate printing two plates were used for every bi-colored stamp, but with the adoption of the Giori press for multi-color stamps it was hoped that several colors might be printed from a single plate. However it soon became evident that the use of more than one plate would prevent wet colors from mixing and in such work there are two numbers or more in different colors on the margins of plate blocks.

Few early collectors tried matched plate block sets, that is, one block from each margin of the full sheet, but were content with a single block for each number, the favorite being the bottom marginal block. Today with chrome plating, fewer plates are needed and it is not too difficult to obtain the four blocks of four each from the four or six plates used for single color commemorative stamps.

Matched plate blocks can hardly be obtained at a single post office since each book of 100 stamp panes contains only two numbers, alternating in the book, and all from the same corner of the sheet. However a search of other offices and stations will reveal some and others can be ordered from the Philatelic Sales Agency.

A matched set of plate blocks is usually mounted as a miniature sheet with margins outside and numbers at the corners.

SHEETS

Full sheets of early commemorative issues, and of the early twentieth century regular issues of United States stamps, have brought such high prices when offered at auction that many beginners believe they will reap a harvest if they lay aside a few sheets of each new issue. But had only a moderate number of the early sheets been saved, their present auction prices would be far different.

The issues which are scarce in sheets are also scarce in blocks, for multiple pieces were not saved by many collectors, and few dealers tied up money in unused stamps. In addition, many of the stamps which were laid away were so poorly centered that some would be difficult to sell at a profit today. There seems to be no certainty of making profits in mint sheets, but a collector of United States issues need lose nothing unless he is compelled to sell his sheets in a hurry. The stamps are good for postage, and at worst may be used or sold at face value if a little time is allowed for such transactions. In a forced sale the only customers are stamp dealers or stamp brokers. The latter discount stamps received as remittances by mail-order houses and retail them at face value, usually to fellow tenants of a building. The broker may be a public stenographer, notary public, or in a small business.

Neither the stamp dealer or the broker will pay more than 95 per cent of the face value, for dealers usually have a stock which they purchased at face value when the stamps were current, and stamp brokers, who sell a few stamps at a time at face value, must be able to make a little profit.

As a rule, the centering of stamps is nowadays very good, but collectors who put aside mint sheets should be satisfied with nothing less than extremely fine, and all others should be used for postage. The sheets must be preserved in perfect condition. Appropriate albums and files are described in chapter 5.

STAMPS TO AVOID

Every collector would like to know what stamps he might collect most advantageously, but a list of them would not be possible without being unfair to some countries or to some part of their stamps. In 1900 such a list might have been prepared, but now that the use of commemorative and semi-postal stamps has become so general, some countries which once rated very high lack a passing grade.

Almost all countries have made some missteps in issuing stamps for collectors, with the exception of those that stopped issuing stamps before 1900. The most notorious example of misconduct was that of four countries which contracted with N. F. Seebeck to supply their stamps. He agreed to furnish stamps free each year for the privileges of taking back unsold stamps at the end of the year and using the plates of each issue to print stamps for collectors.

These Seebeck issues gave the countries such a bad name that it has affected their earlier stamps as well as those issued after the contract was canceled. It is possible that the value of all Central and South American stamps suffered through this unfortunate affair. The story is told in greater detail in chapter 31.

Great Britain perhaps heads the list of countries with high philatelic standards, with a single lapse in over a century. This occurred when a £1 stamp was issued for the Postal Union Congress in London in 1929. There was no need for this high-value in the commemorative set unless to impress the visiting delegates or to sell to collectors. However, the stamp has now become a most desirable item and only one regular British postage issue since 1900 has had a higher listing.

Stamps nearly always live down bad publicity and finally are much sought after. The famous S.S.S.S., or the Society for the Suppression of Speculative Stamps, was founded in 1894 or 1895 to work against unnecessary issues and to outlaw all stamps not intended primarily for postage. The society was organized so soon after the Columbian issue appeared that it seemed to have been formed to prevent a recurrence of such an affair.

The American Philatelic Society and the International Philatelic Federation blacklist stamps which seem to have been issued solely for collectors. Some new countries appear to be under the control of philatelic agents and issue stamps for many foreign events in which they have no direct interest. These countries have been advised to curtail such issues or at least to keep the values within reasonable limits and to issue sufficient quantities to fill all orders. (See S.S.S.S. page 441.)

Until there is some change in the methods used by the Iron Curtain countries to exploit collectors, it is advisable to avoid all their current stamps except those that have been used in the international mails. This, of course, does not apply to the stamps of Imperial Russia nor to those issued during the first years of the communist regime. Nor is this advice directed against the stamps that Albania, Bulgaria, Czechoslovakia, Hungary, Jugoslavia, Poland, and Roumania issued before they accepted the communist doctrine. But their recent issues and those of East Germany, North Korea, the People's Government of China, and the communist regime in Tibet, are to be avoided, particularly the three last mentioned, since importation from these countries is prohibited by federal order.

All Iron Curtain countries have abolished stamp dealing, and perhaps nearly all collecting, and control the export and import of stamps through state agencies.

For a few years after the first World War there was an all-Russian philatelic society which functioned in quite a democratic fashion. However, Russian participation in the International Philatelic Exhibition in New York in 1926 led to extensive correspondence between Russian and foreign collectors, with the result that Russians learned that their country was somewhat less a paradise than claimed. Within a short time the hobby was suppressed, several prominent philatelists were liquidated, and a state monopoly on the export of stamps was set up. Since that time Russia's beautiful stamps have been produced mainly for foreign collectors, and very few have ever been sold in post offices. Ordinary issue stamps are used for general correspondence, and the Soviet philatelic agency, mailing out parcels of stamps to collectors or dealers, often omits postage and marks the shipments "postage paid" (Taxe Percue).

The decorative Russian issues began to appear in 1927 and have increased in number year by year. During the four years ending in 1951 almost six hundred issues were produced with an average face value of about sixteen cents. When buying these stamps from the Soviet agency, one pays an additional tax of 20 per cent. The stamps are also available in used condition at something like one-third less than mint issues. It is said that the cancellation on these "used" stamps is printed on the full sheets as the stamps are being produced and differs from that of any Russian post office.

Avoid canceled-to-order stamps wherever possible. These often are canceled in blocks with one impression to reduce the work of hand stamping, and the mark used may differ from any in use in ordinary postal work. The stamps of North Borneo and Labuan were thus canceled with an oval grid and are easily recognized. Some collectors include certain stamps of St. Helena in the canceled-to-order group but they are actually remainders the colony sold to stamp dealers after defacing them with a purple, diamond-shaped grid.

Only a few years ago leftovers were discovered in Italy's post office vaults which dated back to the first issues of the kingdom. They were priced to collectors in some relation to today's values rather than at face value. In 1952 this sale was discontinued and the remaining stock was destroyed.

Pen cancellations are a source of trouble for many collectors but should not be avoided unless found on the stamps of a country which uses the same stamps for postage and revenue. Many stamps of the British Commonwealth serve this double purpose, and pen cancellations and bank hand stamps, usually in colored ink, indicate revenue use. In the United States, on the other hand, postage stamps have never been legal for revenue payments, and pen cancellations though common for the first twenty years were always postal markings.

❖❖

CHAPTER FOUR

ALBUMS

PRINTED, BOUND, AND LOOSE-LEAF

The first piece of equipment that a collector must have is an album. These may be printed or blank page, the former bound or loose-leaf, the latter loose-leaf only.

Printed albums of the simpler kind have pages with lined spaces, and nearly all contain pictures of common types of stamps. Ordinarily, spaces are provided for stamps on both sides of the pages. These albums range from booklets selling at twenty-five cents or less up to large volumes selling for several dollars.

The next grade of printed album has a more detailed layout with spaces assigned to various sets and printed data relating to them. Such albums provide space for from fifteen to sixty thousand stamps and contain about half as many pictures as stamp spaces. The better albums of this type are loose-leaf, so that leaves may be added where desired, and annual supplements will bring them up to date. The great objection to any bound printed album is that it quickly goes out of date.

The pages of better albums are printed on one side only, so that there are no stamps facing each other to interlock and be torn when the album is opened. The only cure for the double-face hazard is to interleave the pages with glassine or acetate and this may cause the album to bulge.

When printed albums are desired of greater capacity than those described, it is advisable to obtain a sectional album with spaces for all stamps listed in the standard catalog. These have pages printed on one side only and are arranged by political divisions, and in some cases by continents. One or more sections are required for the stamps of Great Britain, another for those of France and her colonies, and so on. Publishers of such albums do not expect many collectors to buy the entire series of sections and it may be possible to limit your purchase to those of any country or countries you desire. Although no spaces are provided for minor varieties or shades, blank pages with matching borders are available and can be inserted in these albums where desired. A complete set, with pages to house all the world's stamps, runs to about forty volumes, more if interleaves are provided.

Printed albums are available for such limited collections as airmail issues, commemorative stamps, blocks, and plate-number blocks, to mention but a few. All the loose-leaf albums described here were once made in the spring-back type, with pages crimped at the binding edge to prevent slipping. Today, nearly all are post binders with pages punched to slip over the posts. Pages are easier to insert in a spring binder but it is difficult to keep the edges even.

BLANK-PAGE ALBUMS, LOOSE-LEAF TYPE

Blank-page albums are useful to collectors who make no attempt to collect all the stamps of any country and want no unfilled spaces on a page, but they are also used by the collector who wishes to make his own arrangement of stamps, with space for notes, or because he does not like the crowded effect of most printed albums. Needless to say, nearly all the important collections which are exhibited at stamp shows are mounted on blank pages.

These pages may be found in a variety of makes and prices. They may be completely plain or with printed borders. They may have a quadrille background to assist in lining up the stamps. The paper ranges from heavy writing paper to very fine grades of drawing paper. The cheaper grades are rigid sheets, punched or crimped, depending on the binder, or they may have a single cloth hinge at the binding edge. The better grades made for post binders are double linen-hinged for greater flexibility, and binders with these pages will lie perfectly flat, but the very fact that these albums flatten out causes more rubbing between the stamps and the overlying page. Such pages should be interleaved. Pages with glued-on tissue backs appear soft and harmless but they actually wear the color off a stamp very fast.

Page size is standardized to a large extent and measures about 11½ by 11 inches, including the binding margin, though smaller and larger sizes can be obtained. Some pages in the finer grades have the names of the countries engraved at the top.

Covers are available in many grades, from simulated leather to padded covers with full morocco binding. The cover selected should be in keeping with the pages used and perhaps with the type of collection to be mounted. Binders accommodate about fifty pages with interleaves, but a few more may be added if the album does not bulge.

Albums should be stored on the bottom edge. They should not be crowded on the shelf as pressure may cause unused stamps to stick down on the pages in humid weather. Dust covers will keep collections clean and help prevent pressure. They are of cardboard, covered to match the album, and are lined with a soft material to protect the album cover.

THREE-RING BINDERS

Another variety of album is the three-ring binder with standard 8½-by-11-inch pages, ranging from cloth-covered boards to metal-hinged, simulated leather, often with zipper closures. Printed pages are available for popular countries and for many block and similar specialty collections, and blank pages, with or without borders and quadrille ruling. Acetate folders to protect pages of this size are standard for these binders, and are obtainable at stationery stores.

Work books used during stamp study will require nothing heavier than the standard pages made for such binders, and these are often used for lesser collections, for cancellation study, and the like. Some collectors prefer smaller work books and may use the same type of binder with pages about 5 by 7¾ inches.

HINGELESS MOUNTING

Most pages are suitable for the hingeless mounting so often desired by collectors. See chapter 13, under Pochettes and Protective Mounts. However, a new type of album page is now sold which is equipped with acetate devices to hold unhinged stamps. Pages are available for certain countries and for block and some other specialties.

BLACK PAGES

These have been standard for certain albums for many years but are not extensively used. It is claimed that colored stamps show up better on black, but unfortunately there are some colors that look washed-out. The pages cause no glare under a strong light, and show off well-centered stamps to the best advantage. The defects of off-center stamps are exaggerated.

When considerable write-up is necessary, black pages are inadvisable, for it is very difficult to write captions in white ink on any material. Black pages also require interleaving, as the dye will otherwise transfer to the stamp faces.

LEFT-PAGE ALBUMS

Album pages are customarily made so that the binding margin is at the left. When these pages are turned to the left, because of the way stamps dangle, it is difficult to prevent occasional damage. Stamps hinged near their centers will not dangle from the page so much but are more apt to warp than when the hinge is correctly applied at the very top.

The obvious solution to this problem occurred to P. M. Wolseiffer, veteran stamp dealer and inventor of the stock-book page and approval card, and he at once published a line of left-hand stock pages with the binding margin at the right. Stamps no longer were damaged. His idea could also be applied to ordinary pages so long as they had no inscriptions or printing other than a border. All that was necessary was to turn the pages bottom edge up and mount the stamps with the binding margin at the right. The albums worked perfectly and a collector's worries vanished for he could see the stamps were in order before the next page was turned.

The method is seldom used today, probably because so many pages have definite tops and cannot be reversed. Another solution to the problem has been used by the author almost from the time left-hand pages were invented. Since his pages have write-ups and cannot be turned upside down, the necessary last look at the pages is obtained by reversing their order in the album. Page one is placed where the last page occurs in a normal album, the succeeding pages in order above it. This album is opened by placing it on a table with the spine at the right. The top cover turns to the right. Each page of stamps is fully visible as the next page is closed down upon it.

BOXLIKE ALBUMS

In recent years a boxlike album has come into use for fine collections. This may be used with existing pages but new pages should be simple sheets with or without borders and without punching or hinge strips. This album is a box with a cover of equal depth which is not separable but hinged to the box along a common side corresponding to the spine of a book. The ends of box and cover are free from this spine and when open the album lies perfectly flat upon a table. In showing the contents the pages are turned one after another, from one section to the other. The utility of this album is readily apparent for any page may be removed with a minimum of effort.

❖❖❖

CHAPTER FIVE

STORAGE OF DUPLICATES AND OTHER UNMOUNTED STAMPS

Collectors usually store duplicates in stock pages. These are rather stiff pages on which horizontal strips of material have been fastened to form pockets. The better grades are made of black cardboard with clear acetate pockets. Manila pages are available at less cost, but these do not display the stamps as nicely.

Stock pages are made in several sizes ranging from small cards with two or three pockets up to eight and one-half by eleven inches, perhaps larger if desired, with ten or twelve pockets. The smaller sizes may be provided with an acetate flap to cover the stamps. Pocket-size books with one or two pages are useful to carry new purchases or stamps to sell or exchange. The larger pages are punched to insert in post or ordinary three-ring binders, and a stock page placed at the back of an album will provide storage space for new stamps until they can be mounted.

In using any stock page you must be careful not to damage stamps on the edges of the pockets. As a precaution place valuable stamps in envelopes before filing them. This is cheap insurance against stamps sticking to a page, and will prevent damage to perforations and edges.

When filing used or unused perforated blocks, precautions must be taken to prevent them from breaking along the perforations. Individual envelopes are used by many, but as transparent envelopes are not stiff enough to prevent mint stamps from curling, it is suggested that a thin card be included in each. Two blocks may be filed in a single envelope, stamp faces out, with a card between. Several blocks may be filed in a single envelope if they are alternately faced, interleaved, and stiffened with one or more cards. The alternate facing helps counteract the tendency to curl. Filled envelopes should be stored so there is not enough pressure to cause them to stick down. Envelopes for mint stamps should have gum lines at the ends only. Use large enough sizes so that there will be no contact between your stamps and the gum lines. Avoid those which have X-flap formation, a central seam, or gum on the loose flap.

To prevent sticking, many collectors in the tropics and other high-humidity places dust the gum side of all stamps with pure talcum powder. Some new-issue dealers place a little powder in all envelopes containing mint stamps. Avoid face powder which has any medicinal or aromatic additives, as these may harm the stamps.

Mint sheets are the most difficult of all philatelic items to preserve. The accepted practice is to place them in glassine or acetate pockets or folders, but this will not be fully effective if the humidity is high or the stamps are under pressure. Pressure should be very light, only sufficient to prevent curling. A collector should periodically allow air to get at his stored mint stamps, and he should note their condition inasmuch as no storage material on the market at this time is guaranteed harmless to colors or to stamp gum under pressure, although harmless to stamp paper.

❖❖❖

CHAPTER SIX

ACCESSORIES AND THEIR USE

HINGES

Stamp hinges are rectangular pieces of gummed paper about half an inch wide and three-fourths of an inch long with the corners rounded. They are die-cut from various thin papers to which gum has been applied in two coats. This double gumming makes the hinges peelable, allowing them to be removed from stamps or album pages without damage to either.

The peelability exists only when the gum is dry. Do not attempt to remove a hinge while it is moist. There are some poor-grade hinges on the market that will hardly stick to anything, and others that are not peelable.

A hinge should not be too narrow, as it is called upon to support a stamp in all positions. Little support is required while the page lies flat, but as it is turned the stamp tends to twist. Large stamps or blocks may tear off if the hinge is too weak. The length is not so important but should be sufficient that the stamp may be turned up to examine the back without pinching the top perforations. Some collectors prefer long hinges and will use any length that can be hidden by the stamp. A long hinge permits the stamp to be remounted several times.

Nearly all the process of hinging a stamp should be done with the stamp tongs alone. Grasp one end of a hinge with the tongs and fold it. Pinch the fold with the tongs and moisten half the folded end, the part farthest from the fold, and apply the hinge lightly at the top of the stamp with the fold line slightly below the tips of the perforation teeth. Iron the hinge

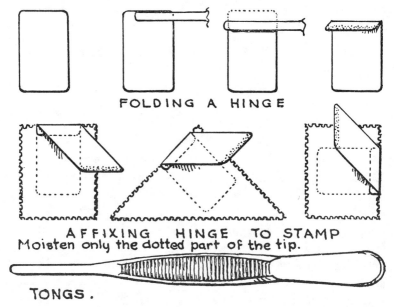

FOLDING A HINGE

AFFIXING HINGE TO STAMP
Moisten only the dotted part of the tip.

TONGS.

FIG. 6–1. Hinges and Hinging.

down on the stamp lightly with the tip of the tongs, very lightly if the stamp has gum. Do not allow the moistened gum of a hinge to come in contact with the perforation teeth or it may be very hard to peel off later.

Now use the tongs as a guide and expose about ⅛ inch of the free end of the hinge. Moisten this with the tip of the tongue and mount the stamp on the album page. Iron the hinge slightly to fix it firmly and when the moisture has dried a little, press the stamp flat on the page with one finger. If the fingers are moist place a slip of paper over the stamp. Do not press with the tongs as they may leave a slick mark and mar the appearance of the stamp.

Some collectors oppose the licking of hinges and use a sponge or similar device. However, there is no way of judging how wet a hinge becomes on a sponge. It even takes practice with the tongue to keep from removing all the gum, or making the hinge so wet that moisture squeezes out from under it. If any moisture is visible around a hinge it should be allowed to dry before pressing the stamp down on the page. The gum on good hinges has little taste and there are no records of harm resulting from licking hinges.

When a collector wishes to remount a stamp hinged as directed he has only to lift it a little and cut the hinge with his tongs close to the page. A long hinge will allow several mountings, and then a second hinge may be attached to the stub of the first. Avoid peeling hinges from stamps whenever possible as this is the source of many thin spots. The end of the hinge that is left on the page usually peels easily, but may be removed with water on a small brush. Then blot the page.

Blocks or long strips of stamps may require more than one hinge and care must be taken to avoid stretching the piece or fixing it so rigidly that it will break along the perforations when the page is bent. Long hinges will provide more flexibility and less chance of damage, but better success will be had if strips are premounted on mats which in turn are mounted in the album.

It is advisable to mount some stamps at their sides instead of their tops, particularly those near the binding margin of a page. All unused stamps may curl a little on dry or moist days and unless interleaving is provided some may fold when a page is turned. Side-hinged, these trouble-makers near the margin will flatten automatically. Triangular stamps with point up should likewise be hinged at the side. In top-hinging such an item, if the hinge is placed low to conceal it, the top point may be damaged; if not placed low, the hinge will be visible and unsightly.

Various improvements in hinges appear from time to time,

one being the prefolded hinge. This takes a lot of the work out of stamp mounting. Though there is a tendency to make the folded end a little too long, on the whole these hinges are very satisfactory. Another type of hinge has gum on the upper side of one end, the lower of the other, and requires no folding, one end being attached to the stamp, the other to the page. This type has more of a spring than a hinge action and it is difficult to examine the back of a stamp so attached.

When you make a mistake and attach a hinge to either stamp or album page, do not attempt to remove it right away, which will ruin the stamp or page, but let it dry completely, and then it will peel off harmlessly.

A handy gadget is available which does away with the trouble occasioned by loose hinges curling up in a box. This is a holder from which the hinges may be removed one at a time with one finger. The hinges are held flat and require less manipulation.

TONGS

Stamp tongs should not be confused with tweezers equipped with serrations on the blades. The blades of stamp tongs must have smooth inner faces to avoid marring stamps.

The most useful tongs are those with straight parallel-edge blades about ⅛ inch wide. The blades should be thin and flexible and the ends should have slightly rounded corners. This shape will assist in folding hinges, and the thin blades may be used as a knife in cutting off a hinge when a stamp is to be remounted. The blade will slip under a stamp easily, even on a polished surface, and not require one to play shuffleboard before picking up a stamp.

Use the tongs for all stamp work: soaking, pressing, mounting, placing in envelopes or stock books, and passing stamps around for examination. If anyone starts to finger your stamps, you should overcome any timidity and say, "What, no tongs?" Collectors need a word to cover the situation, like the golfer's "Fore!"

PERFORATION GAUGE

A perforation gauge is needed by every collector who is making a complete or a specialized collection of a country, for there are many varieties which differ only in the gauge of the perforations. Topical collectors and others concerned only with designs have little use for a gauge since one stamp of each design fills all their needs.

The best gauges are engraved on stiff paper or a thin, tough card. A paper gauge is more suitable because it will expand and contract under high and low humidity conditions at about the same rate as the stamps. Paper gauges are not affected by heat or cold, but when it is hot and dry, the heat will cause a metal gauge to expand, while the dryness shrinks the stamps, and the reading may show too large a number in the case of fine perforations.

Plastic gauges respond both to temperature and humidity changes and there is no certainty that such gauges ever return to the original size, and the changes in size may be progressive. Metal gauges, however, can be depended upon to give the same reading at a given temperature, regardless of the number of changes undergone. The need for an accurate gauge is apparent when working with such stamps as the recent British issues, in order to separate those with perforation 14 from others which are perforated 14½ × 14.

Loose stamps may be placed on a gauge and moved along until the perforations match with a row of dots. When they cannot be matched the user must fix the gauge as a number between those nearest to matching. An opaque gauge is not very satisfactory when working with stamps on envelopes or those mounted in an album. If possible match the mounted stamp with a loose stamp of known gauge, and keep a set of such samples in gauges suitable to your stamps. A United States collector will find that five stamps gauging 12, 11, 10½, 10 and 8½ will take care of everything issued since 1861, with the exception of the Rossbach 12½ experimental perforation of 1919.

A useful gauge for loose United States stamps shows all perforation varieties of sheet and coil stamps as white shapes on a black sheet. The stamps being checked are placed beside the white stamps on the gauge. When there is a perfect match, nothing shows between the stamps and the gauge except a row of clean round dots.

Another gauge has converging lines limited at the sides by parallel lines 20 millimeters apart. At the reading 10 there are 10 spaces between the limiting lines, at reading 12, 12 spaces, etc. Gauge numbers and half numbers show on the margins. The stamp is moved along the gauge until the teeth of the perforations coincide with the converging lines.

The Roto-Gage is another of the convenient gadgets of philately. This has a perforation gauge mounted on a cylinder. The stamp is placed on a platform overlapping the gauge, which is rotated until its dots match the perforation holes of the stamp. There is also a magnifying glass mounted in a position to check the reading or for use in any stamp examination. In addition this device includes a watermark detector and a millimeter scale.

MILLIMETER SCALE

A millimeter scale is usually printed on every perforation gauge but unless it is located at the edge of the card it will be difficult to use. For accurate measurements, collectors at one time used bow dividers, transferring the size of the thing being measured to a millimeter scale where the reading was made. The sharp points of the divider were adjusted by a screw and held the setting until the screw was moved.

A millimeter scale must be placed directly upon the stamp with the zero mark set at one end of the space being measured. The setting and reading should be made under a magnifying glass, and it is important to look squarely at the scale, for a view at the slightest angle will give an incorrect reading. All readings should be outside measurements and not to centers of lines.

The scale for stamps need not be more than 10 centimeters (about 4 inches) long and should be of boxwood with celluloid edges. One edge usually reads in millimeters and the other in half-millimeters. There may be finer graduations in the first millimeter but these will be of little use as it is easier to estimate quarter-millimeters than to count the finer lines. Readings in quarter-millimeters are necessary when measuring some of the United States rotary-press stamps issued between 1916 and 1923.

MAGNIFYING GLASS

A magnifier enables the collector to read many inscriptions which are indecipherable to the naked eye, and he can see the small differences in stamps which identify varieties or mark the work of different printers.

Magnifiers are available in many styles and sizes but the one recommended is about 1½ inches in diameter and magnifies three times (3x).

The usual glass of this size has a protective case which becomes a handle when in use. Larger glasses of the same power are much heavier and soon become tiresome.

When finer detail must be studied stronger magnifiers are available in great variety. As the power increases the field which can be seen is reduced. A suitable maximum power is reached at about 6.5x. One common type consists of a pair of lenses mounted so that either may be used or the two combined to give a 6.5 power. Another type of pocket glass contains a triple lens cemented to form a single unit, in which there is no distortion. In a diameter of about 1 inch the magnification is 6.5x, and in a diameter of less than ½ inch, at least 12x. The latter is of little use to a collector for at 12x a dot $\frac{1}{32}$ inch in diameter will fill the field almost completely.

Stands or holders are available for many glasses and will enable a collector to work with both hands. There are illuminated glasses also, for use with standard electric current or with batteries. These concentrate a flood of light where it is needed. The usual glass of this type has a magnification of 6x.

WATERMARK DETECTOR

Watermarks are about as important as perforations in the identification of stamps, and some issues have varieties which require that both be determined. Watermarks are impressions which thin the paper while it is being made, and while some may be seen and identified without aids, others are faint and often obscured by the stamp design. The usual method of ascertaining such a watermark may be is to put the stamp face down in a shallow black dish containing a liquid which will quickly penetrate the stamp without damaging it.

Most watermark trays are made of glass and have a cover to prevent evaporation of the volatile liquid when not in use. Almost any solvent of the naphtha, benzine, or cleaning-fluid class may be used. Cigarette lighter fluid is also good but it evaporates rapidly. The danger of fire when using these liquids has led to the use of carbon tetrachloride, a noncombustible fluid, but there is a very serious objection to this chemical. If its fumes are inhaled, even for brief periods, it may cause severe organic injury. Its effect is cumulative and is not avoided by taking a breath of fresh air between periods of watermarking.

None of the liquids mentioned will affect the gum on unused stamps but all will destroy a stamp printed by photogravure, as these or similar solvents are used to dilute the ink in this kind of printing.

When testing a stamp, place it face downward in the tray and watch it closely while the liquid is penetrating the paper, since it will strike through the thinner paper at the watermark before the remainder. As the stamp remains in the liquid it will all become somewhat transparent and the watermark will vanish. If the first test fails, dry the stamp and repeat the process.

As your experience increases it will not be necessary for you to tray-test all stamps, for usually there are but two possibilities, such as large crown or small crown, and very slight indications may give you the answer. In other cases it is only necessary to know whether a stamp is watermarked or not, and any slight indication of a watermark will permit identification.

Some watermarks may be seen if the stamp is placed face down on a black card and held at reading distance, then tipped this way and that to allow the light to strike it at various angles. Another method is to hold the stamp and black card in a half-light where it is tipped and twisted to present various angles to the light. Half-light may be obtained by holding the card below the edge of a fully lighted desk where only reflected light can strike it.

Various watermark detectors are made which depend upon glass or plastic filters of various colors to neutralize the stamp color and render the watermark more visible. One of these has three filters in the lid of the watermark dish. If there is no success when the stamp is tested with the filters alone, it is immersed in the liquid and again viewed through the filters.

While nearly all watermarks can be identified, a few resist almost every effort to make them visible. Unfortunately, United States stamps have difficult examples in the later types of paper with the single-line U.S.P.S. watermark. It is not difficult to identify the double-line U.S.P.S., but quite often it is all but impossible to determine whether a stamp has a single-line U.S.P.S. or no watermark at all.

The watermarks of some stamps may become more visible under ultraviolet rays, and others may be discovered clearly by x-ray photography even though the stamps are on cover.

COLOR GUIDES

The difficulty of defining colors accurately becomes more apparent when color charts are examined; for example, two guides made by a leading publisher and stamp dealer. One printed about forty years ago has pasted-on labels of the size and character of typographed stamps while the second, printed a few years ago, has the samples printed on the guide in solid colors. The older guide has not been exposed to sunlight but nevertheless some colors have changed a little. It has matching colors for the British stamps of that time but none which even approximate the bright colors of British photogravure issues, or of the engraved issues of Bosnia and Austria just prior to the First World War.

The new guide uses many of the color *names* which appeared on the earlier guide but the color samples have little relation to the earlier ones. Some of the old names, such as "solferino," which never should have been used, have been dropped for the more understandable "light purple," but it is hardly possible to compare solid patches of color with stamps that have colored lines with white paper showing between. However, the new guide is useful for photogravure stamps, as they are more nearly solid in color and are usually printed in strong colors.

It is apparent that no simple guide can be prepared that will be entirely successful. Most beginners will classify their stamps as red, blue, yellow, orange, green, violet, or brown, and look to friends for advice in naming the elusive colors. Experience and a good memory for shades seem to be the only solution at present.

ACCESSORIES TO BE AVOIDED

When Scotch tape was introduced it seemed a cure-all for the collector's mounting problems. It has proved to be the exact opposite. It discolors with age and penetrates and stains everything with which it comes in contact. The nondrying adhesive creeps out from the edges of the tape and sticks to and stains whatever it touches. For these reasons it should not be used for anything connected with stamp collecting. If used by mistake, the adhesive is at least partially soluble in benzine, carbon tetrachloride, and some other solvents. If a stamp is soaked and gently manipulated with tongs or a thin blade, the tape can be removed. If the spot where the tape was affixed appears a little transparent this may be improved by a thorough soaking in the solvent.

Rubber cement is an adhesive to shun unless you know that it contains nothing but pure rubber in a solvent. It is not a permanent adhesive and two sheets of paper cemented with it will separate as soon as the solvent and rubber have dried out completely. The length of time this takes depends on the character of the paper. Rubber cement usually sold in art-supply shops contains ingredients to increase its sticking qualities, its chief use being for temporary mounting of art work where water would expand and wrinkle the paper. Under normal conditions pure rubber cement can be removed from stamps and covers by soaking in benzine.

Above all other things, avoid using indelible pencils and ink to mark your stamps. Old timers who used these mediums are nearly all gone but their work still shows up in collections. It may not be evident until someone tries to soak off an old hinge. Then the marks bleed through the stamp to show in bright purple on the face.

If you acquire stamps that you think may be marked with indelible pencil, test one before going further. Soaking a stamp in strong brine will sometimes fix the color of indelible pencil so that it will not spread.

An instance of the damage caused by such careless marking occurred at a New York auction many years ago. A full imperforate sheet of the two-cent stamp showing the three five-cent errors was sold for $2500, but when the successful bidder was about to take possession he found that someone at the sale had circled the three errors lightly with an indelible pencil. He withdrew his bid and the damaged sheet was sold later at a greatly reduced price.

Indelible pencil marks may be very faint when applied but may become prominent if the paper absorbs a little moisture from the air.

Do not allow stamps to remain very long in contact with waxed paper as the wax will soften in warm weather and soak into the stamps to give them a semitransparent appearance. The interleaves of stamp booklets should be examined. If of waxed paper, they should be removed or additional interleaves should be provided.

❖❖

CONDITION

Condition is a word which collectors use to define the quality of a stamp. Quality and scarcity coupled with demand establish values. Condition ranges from below poor to above superb, and stamps that are equal in scarcity and demand may vary tremendously in value, depending on the condition of the copies. Those who demand superb condition are known as "condition cranks" by persons who have other than superb stamps to sell. Catalog values usually are based on average condition, and a collector pays a premium for stamps of better quality. In addition he may have to wait a long time before he finds the superb examples he wants, but when he has made a collection of this kind he will have little trouble in selling it if the need arises. There are many collectors willing to pay half or two-thirds list price for stamps in mediocre condition, few who will pay the premium for a perfect copy. A collector who insists on perfection should know enough to avoid seeking the unattainable. Few collectors who set out to buy only superb stamps ever succeed, for there are varying qualities in impression, centering, and can-

48

cellations, and relatively few stamps are of the highest class in all these features.

When attempting to decide whether a stamp is superb, very fine, or only good, it is necessary to have a clear idea of what constitutes perfection. Standards are not the same for all countries and some have never issued superb stamps of the quality found in early United States issues. In such cases it may be necessary to qualify a description by saying, for example, "Very fine for Nonamia," or whatever country is involved.

Standards vary for different kinds of stamps, since there are imperforate, part perforate, and fully perforated issues, coils, etc. As a simple example, booklet panes are not penalized for having straight edges but can be down graded if off center.

Many early perforated issues are so closely spaced that there are no margins and the perfectly centered copies are touched by the perforation holes on all sides. These must be given as high a grade as later stamps with ample margins. In the early imperforate stamps conditions are about the same but there is a little more chance of having margins as the scissor cuts did not reduce the width of the paper.

An argument made against collecting fine stamps is the one that a battered, dog-eared copy shows proof of its use to carry mail. However, few stamps become worn-looking in transit unless there has been a wreck or mail robbery. Those that show evidence of wear and water have probably been on letters stored in a basement or attic, or have been handled by careless collectors. Stamps in the finest possible condition come from envelopes that were carried in the ordinary mail.

In unused stamps condition is a four-part problem, with impression, color, centering, and gum to be considered. The first three factors and cancellation are important in used stamps. In the first case three of the factors are immediately visible, in the other all four affect the appearance. Impression is the most important but the others follow so closely that all must be associated in an analysis of a stamp.

A collector who has learned to recognize a really fine impression, and knows the full, fresh colors of a certain stamp, can easily grade copies. If a survey of everything visible on the face is not satisfactory, he turns the stamp over to examine the back. If this passes he will examine the stamp with a glass and look through it toward a light. A dip in benzine may show up repair work, and there may be an examination under ultraviolet light if the stamp is an old unused copy or if anything suspicious has been noticed in the examination.

A condition collector should require that every factor be up to a certain standard, and he should not accept a stamp just because it is perfectly centered when the other factors are below grade. Defects of a very minor nature are given too much importance, for a tiny closed tear, or a hinge mark, does not detract from the appearance of a stamp. The desire for never-hinged mint stamps often causes a collector to select copies which obviously are inferior in all other respects.

As time goes on more and more stamps with unobtrusive defects will be placed in fine collections for the simple reason that no other copies will be available. The supply of superb old stamps diminishes year by year. Some are destroyed, others wear out or acquire minor defects.

IMPRESSION

This quality in stamps is not fully appreciated and only a few collectors make it the primary consideration. In line-engraved issues the first or early impressions usually are much finer than later printings. The depth of impression is evident and all lines and minute details are clearly visible. When such a plate is not cleaned regularly the lines fill with dried ink and the impression appears flat and all lines may be fuzzy.

Sly-wiped plates—plates not fully cleaned and polished before the impression is made—produce overinked stamps on toned paper and the fine lines of the engraving are lost.

Overwiping is just the opposite: so much ink is removed from the plate that the impression is weak and detail is missing.

Wear on engraved plates has the effect of lightening the impression; the lines become thinner and the spaces between lines wider. Very poor impressions sometimes are the result of dirty, worn plates, but when such plates are well cleaned the impressions will be of good quality even though there will be a continuous loss of depth and detail as the wear progresses. In typographed and lithographed work there is never as much difference between early and late printings. The quality may also be maintained nearly uniform by frequent renewal of the relatively inexpensive plates.

COLOR

Nearly every stamp may be found in a full, fresh color that probably represents an early printing. In nearly all stamp printing there has been a tendency to allow colors to lighten or darken through the life of the issue. Sometimes the color may take on a muddy appearance as though some other pigment or material had been added to extend or cheapen the ink.

Usually there will be examples showing too much or too little ink. In the case of engraved stamps the person or mechanism that wipes the plate is at fault, while in the case of typographed stamps the trouble is in the inking fountain and rollers. The fountain may feed too fast or too slow or may be supplied with an ink too thick or too thin to work properly.

Various shades may be the result of fading or of changing under atmospheric conditions. Nearly every colored ink will fade more or less when exposed to direct sunlight. Some will be ruined in one or two hours. Others still less permanent will fade even though never exposed to full light.

CENTERING AND PERFORATIONS

The amount of margin, that is, the border of paper around the stamp design, that stamps should have varies with different times and issues. Many early closely spaced stamps rate as superb, so far as margins are concerned, if the design is not cut into on any side. In modern issues, with much wider spacing, the margins should be equal to half the space between the stamps. When stamps are slightly off center any excess or deficiency of margin should be at the bottom. Stamps are down graded for poor centering but this does not count as an actual defect until the perforation holes cut the stamp design.

Poorly perforated stamps that have some of the little disks of paper adhering do not look as well as those with clean perforation teeth.

GUM

Since collectors of never-hinged stamps like to have the full original gum, damage to it or lack of it results in a reduced grade. However, minute traces of a hinge on an otherwise superb stamp should not lower the grade. Other deficiencies in the gum lower the grade progressively to a bottom that is reached when the stamp is without gum or has been regummed.

CANCELLATIONS

When forming a cancellation collection some stamps will be included for the cancellation alone. However, in a regular collection of used stamps an attempt should be made to obtain the finest copy with suitable cancellation within the collector's means.

The usual goal of a collector is a clearly impressed townmark, not too heavy and not too light, and one that does not obscure the eyes of a portrait or the feature point of the design. There are many other kinds of cancellations that will qualify for superb stamps, or enhance their value, but none will increase the condition grade. Some of these are the straight-line and fancy townmarks, the "Paid," "Free," "Way," "Ship," and similar marks, numerals, and slogans.

Very faint cancellations are not as desirable as legible marks but on some of the older issues any marking not smudged should be accepted. On modern issues where machine cancellations are in use a slogan or other device should be preferred to a straight- or wavy-line cancellation or killer.

OTHER FACTORS

In addition to the four main factors that determine the condition of sound stamps, there are numerous defects which lower the grade. Superb stamps have none of these but they are permitted in varying degree in all other grades. These defects include scuffed and rubbed spots on the face, open or closed pinholes, tiny tears or cuts, thin spots, folds, breaks, thinned gum, nibbed perforation teeth, and soiled and faded colors.

GRADING

It is seldom possible or desirable to limit the description of a stamp to one word. When a stamp is superb and has a special cancellation, that fact should be mentioned; if an otherwise perfect stamp has a minute closed tear, that detail must be included.

There is no question but that the terms used to define condition relate more to the visible parts of a stamp than to hidden features such as gum and paper defects. As an example, there is no regular term to indicate that an unused stamp is without gum. Unless the fact is mentioned, a collector may claim misrepresentation no matter how low a condition grade has been assigned to the stamp.

It is a simple matter to grade modern unused stamps for the centering is apparent and impression, color, and gum usually are uniform. The trouble that arises when an attempt is made to grade miscellaneous stamps can be lessened by a point system. This suggestion may strike dealers and many of the older collectors as ridiculous, but it still may have the merit of calling attention to the drastic reduction in value charged to trivial faults. Experienced collectors grade stamps by instinct, while others may not have the slightest idea how to distinguish between a fine and a very fine stamp.

Grade names are a necessity in the stamp business, since a large part of it consists of mail order and auction sales, where the collector must depend on written descriptions.

Schedule A is based on sound, undamaged stamps of varying

condition. The scores obtained from it are to be reduced by the percentages shown in Schedule B before referring to the table of grades in Schedule C.

SCHEDULE A

The first column applies only to unused stamps, the fifth only to used

Gum	Impression	Color	Centering	Cancellation	Points
Full original gum (O.G.)	Early, very fine	Fresh, full	Centered	Sharp, legible	25
Slight hinge mark			Slight extra or less at bottom		23
Strong hinge mark	Fine	Fine	Off, slight to one side	Same, but obscures feature	20
Near full— or surface altered	Good	Good	Off, slight in two directions	Faint, slightly heavy or machine	15
Half O.G. or thin	Ordinary	Dull or slight fade	Off, more, two directions or touched top or bottom	Heavy, or slight smudge	10
Some O.G. or very thin	Underinked or dry or dirty plate	Faded	Touched one side	Worse than last or pen cancellation	5
None or regummed	Heavily overinked	Badly faded	Touched two sides	Heavy smudge	0

DEDUCTION FOR DEFECTS

Since defects have more serious effect on high-priced stamps it is reasonable to subtract a percentage for each defect, reducing for defects in the order given below. When there are major defects no attention need be given minor defects of the same nature. For example, when the perforations cut the design on two sides, do not consider other perforation or centering defects; if there is a fold breaking the paper fibers, do not consider any minor paper defects.

SCHEDULE B

Percentages to be deducted progressively from the rating obtained from Schedule A

Scuffed, stained, or soiled, entire surface	75%
Same, medium portion	50%
Same, small portion	25%
Fold breaking paper fibers, or visible tear	75%
Fold, prominent but not breaking fibers	50%
Slight fold, hardly visible	25%
Design cut two sides by scissors or perforation holes	50%
Design cut on one side by scissors or perforation holes	30%
Straight edge or reperforation	25%
Corner perforation or two or three perforations nibbed	20%
One perforation nibbed	10%
Open pin- or worm-hole, or small visible tear	25%
Closed pinhole, closed small cut or tear	15%
Thin all over, as peeled or split	75%
Thin, not over half the surface	50%
Thin, as from hinging	25%
Thin, very slight, 2 or 3 sq. mm.	10%

An examination of Schedules A, B, and C shows that a stamp must be nearly perfect to be rated as superb. It can have none of the defects listed in Schedule B but may be slightly off center toward the bottom. An unused copy, if perfectly centered, may make the grade with a slight hinge mark. Any additional faults will drop the grade to very fine (88-95), where the stamp may be slightly inferior in impression or color, or in centering or gum, or may have a single nibbed perforation.

Fine stamps (76-85) may have still more of the deficiencies indicated in Schedule A, or may have one of the defects listed in Schedule B. Additional defects continue to lower the grade until the zero point is reached.

Two examples may serve to clarify the system. Assume a stamp with early impression and good color, slightly off center in two directions and a slightly heavy cancellation. Color and impression give 40 points with 15 each for centering and cancellation, or a total of 70 points, or very good. If there is a small visible tear the figure will be reduced by 25 per cent to a rating of 52, or fair. If in addition there is a minimum thin spot it will be reduced by another 10 per cent to 47, but still fair.

Assume a similar-looking stamp, perfectly centered but with a straight edge and only half the original gum and the paper thinned where the gum is missing. Color and impression again give a rating of 40, to which will be added 25 for centering and 10 for gum, or a total of 75 points. The straight edge will deduct 25 per cent, leaving 54 points and the thinned paper will take away another 50 per cent, leaving 27 as the final score, or very poor.

VALUE AS AFFECTED BY CONDITION

The value of stamps has a direct relation to condition and increases rapidly above a certain grade which appears to be in the "fine" group at about the 80-point score. Unfortunately the catalog value is not the true value but is based on average condition for the stamp listed. Dealers apply various discounts to list prices (or premiums when the stamps are above average).

The older United States stamps may be assumed to be worth list price at the 80-point level, middle period stamps to be worth 75 per cent of list, and recent and current stamps, 50 per cent of list, all at the same level of condition. Middle United States stamps are assumed to lie in the period between about 1900 and the adoption of electric-eye perforating.

Foreign stamps do not demand the relatively large premiums for finer condition that old United States stamps do but this may be because the best market for stamps is in the country of origin. This condition is leveling off due to more rapid international communications and may vanish when all currency and export restrictions are removed.

SCHEDULE C
Valuations

Condition	Rating	Early U.S.	Middle U.S.	Recent U.S.
Superb	96-100	List, plus	Full list	75-80% list
Very fine	86-95	List, plus		
Fine	76-85	List value	75% list	50% list
Very good	66-75	75% list	50% list	40% list
Good	56-65	50% list	⅓ list	⅓ list
Fair	46-55			
Poor	36-45	⅓ list	¼ list	¼ list
Very poor	26-35	¼ list	⅙ list	⅙ list
Bad	16-25	10% list	10% list	10% list
Very bad	6-15	5% list	5% list	5% list

List price means the current quotations in *Scott's Standard Catalogue* and the *United States Specialized Catalogue*.

❖•❖

CHAPTER EIGHT

PREPARING STAMPS FOR MOUNTING

Stamps should be put in the best possible condition before they are mounted in a collection. The first step is to free them from undesirable paper, such as envelope corners or old hinges. Following this there may be a few creases to smooth out, or dirt or stains to remove.

SOAKING

Paper is removed from stamps by soaking, except under very unusual circumstances, when a form of peeling may be undertaken. Before soaking, separate your stamps into two lots, putting aside all that are on bright-colored envelopes, envelopes with colored tissue linings, wrapping paper, corrugated box-board, or heavy or colored cardboard. Also put aside all poster stamps, and stickers, such as air-mail etiquettes and registry labels, and all stamps with colored cancellations.

Nearly all the remaining stamps may be soaked without risk, especially if they are stamps in current use. Some of the earlier issues require special attention and some may not be soaked at all. Until you are adept at soaking do not place more stamps in water than you can handle in a few minutes. Use warm water. Allow the stamps to soak ten or fifteen minutes, then slip them off the paper and place them in clean warm water until their gum is completely dissolved. As long as any gum remains on a stamp the paper will feel slick and more soaking is required.

Free of gum, the stamps may be placed face down on colorless blotters or clean newspapers to remain until nearly dry. Any that curl badly should either have more soaking or, when fully dry, they may be drawn with a sharp bend across a smooth edge, such as that of a ruler. This breaks the gum slightly. When nearly dry, stamps may be shifted to fresh blotters or newspapers and pressed until completely dry.

Collectors who do a lot of soaking may have a letter press or heavy metal plate to put pressure on the drying stamps. Some who soak only a few stamps at a time use a stamp press made for the purpose. A miniature letter press, this is large enough to handle blocks of the large commemorative issues.

Stamps that are thoroughly dried under pressure nearly always lie perfectly flat on the album page, and this is helped to a very great extent if the minimum amount of hinge is affixed to the stamp.

If any of your stamps change color or fade during soaking, make a list of them for future reference. Some of the troublesome varieties will be mentioned later.

After soaking the first group of stamps, examine those in the second group before putting any of them in water. Remove colored envelope linings, split the cardboard and boxboard, and try to pop the stamps off the colored envelopes and wrapping paper by bending and manipulating the paper a little, or loosen them with a fifteen-minute chill in a deep-freeze compartment. It is often possible to peel the paper off stamps, or at least to remove most of it, if the work is done carefully with fingers and tongs, taking care not to bend the stamp but only the paper.

These stamps that were on potentially harmful paper may be floated one by one on the surface of the water, face up, taking care that they don't bunch together and damage one another. A little salt added to the water will prevent color from spreading. Soaking these stamps in running water is an even better way.

Oversoaking and hot water are to be avoided, for the glue sizing that gives the paper its printing surface may be dissolved with a partial loss of stamp color and a general softening of the paper itself. Line-engraved stamps are the exception to this rule, for they are printed on a variety of paper that has little or no sizing.

Some stamps were purposely printed with fugitive ink that, when wet spreads or bleeds, or changes color, or in some cases washes away. Others were printed on coated or chalk-surfaced papers, to prevent the removal of cancellations. All such stamps are difficult to soak and some must be left on the paper. Here are a few examples with some general suggestions.

The few United States stamps that water harms are printed in deep reds, such as the lakes, carmine lakes, and deep clarets of the standard catalog. Examples are found in the 2-cent stamps of the issue of 1890, in a few of the 2-cent values of the Famous Americans issue of 1940, and in the postage due stamps from 1894-1917. The two groups of regular postage stamps should be floated off the paper but the postage due stamps, if they are to show the full color, must be left on the paper.

The pale lilac and pale green stamps of Great Britain from 1880 to 1887 will not stand much soaking as there is a fugitive element in the ink, and the bicolored values of the next two issues usually have one fugitive color which fades or changes color at the slightest touch of water. All these should be left on the paper.

Many British and British colonial issues are on chalk-surfaced paper. While some may be floated off, it is advisable to leave all of them on paper for the chalk washes off and carries away some of the design. The doubly fugitive varieties, that is, those printed in fugitive colors on this coated paper, are more easily damaged than any other stamps.

From 1858 to 1875 Russia used paper to which a thin coating or network of glue size had been applied. During the later years of this period pigment was added to the glue size to improve the printing quality of the paper. All are damaged by soaking and the surface of these stamps should not be moistened. Some of the last issues of the Dutch East Indies were printed on a very tricky paper that had a striped coating of soapy material which would dissolve in water and at once reveal an attempt to remove the cancellations.

Many red stamps were printed in an analine ink that bleeds. Among these are some of the 20-lepta Greek stamps of 1882, the 1-krona of Hungary (1900), the 1-yen of Japan (1888), the 10-centimes of Switzerland (1889), and all the 20-paras stamps of Turkey from 1901 until 1913.

A few photogravure stamps have been printed in water-soluble ink. Examples include those of the Dutch East Indies, the 1939-1946 issue of Egypt, and the 1935 War Heroes' Day issue of Germany.

REMOVAL OF OBSTINATE GUM

Some stamp gum does not dissolve in plain water but may yield if a little vinegar or dilute acetic acid is added. After any gum has once been softened in water, it should be removed if possible. Otherwise there is a greater tendency for the stamps to curl than before soaking was attempted. The gum on some of the early printings of the 3-cent 1851 issue of the United States adheres strongly and must be scraped off the wet stamps with the blade of a dull knife, after which the stamps should be washed a little to remove the last traces.

Stamps from which the gum has been removed in this manner should be allowed to air-dry a little. Then place them face up on a plastic sheet, cover with a blotter, and press until dry. Some may stick so tightly that they cannot be popped off the plastic by bending it, and must be soaked off. Floated stamps may also be dried on plastic. Whatever gum remains on them will receive a glasslike finish, but a trace of gum is preferable to a stained or faded stamp.

Austrian stamps of 1890-1908 are often troublesome to beginners. The gum resists dissolving and when the thin paper starts to dry it coils up tightly. Those with varnish bars should be soaked in a warm vinegar solution and scraped to remove the gum. Those without the bars may be soaked in a hot vinegar solution. The bars, which would turn white in hot water, may be detected before soaking by holding the stamps so that light is reflected from the shiny bars.

Fortunately, beginners of today will not handle such stamps as those of Hanover that bothered collectors years ago. From 1850 until 1860, or near the end of issue for that country, the stamps were provided with a rose-colored cement that could neither be dissolved nor scraped. It was axiomatic that a stamp without gum had thin spots for there was no way of removing the gum that did not take away some of the paper.

STUCK-DOWN STAMPS

Mint stamps often stick to one another or to an album page so strongly that they cannot be separated without damage. Several methods have been tried but none is wholly effective and some of the gum will be lost or altered in appearance.

If the stamps are subjected to high humidity for a few seconds, they can be separated with a loss of somewhat less than half the gum. If the lost gum is on the face of another stamp it will be difficult to save its entire original gum. A humidified stamp must be handled with care to prevent it from curling tightly. Allow it to become partly dry in the open air, then place it gum side down on a plastic sheet and allow it to finish drying under pressure. The gum should then be broken to minimize the curling effect.

A small metal box with a cover can be used for a humidity bath if several layers of moistened blotting paper are placed in it and covered with a wire screen or perforated plate to prevent the stamps from coming in contact with the water. A few experiments will show how long the stamps should remain in the box. The process will be speeded if the box is warmed a little. Outfits of this nature are available at stamp stores under such names as Stamp Lift and Gonmet.

Another method of removing stamps from paper involves the use of dry ice. The refrigerant must be handled with tools, or the hands must be protected by heavy gloves, as serious burns may result from contact with it. The stamp face is placed in contact with the dry ice, which has been scraped to remove frost. Moisture is transferred to the paper stuck to the stamp by breathing on it, or by making use of an atomizer. When this moisture is seen to enter the paper, the stamp is taken up and an attempt made to peel off the paper. More than one treatment may be necessary, and the stamp should not be allowed to thaw out between trials. The kind of paper involved will affect the time required and some impervious paper may defeat the work entirely. Incidentally, there seems to be no reason against using this process to remove stamps printed in fugitive inks, as no moisture reaches the face of the stamp.

A quick freeze in a deep freezer or in the freezing compartment of a refrigerator has been suggested to assist in separating stamps from paper. This method may be successful when handling single stamps, but full sheets are too fragile to stand the strong pull required, and will separate along the perforations.

Another long-familiar method is to use an electric iron to melt the stamp gum, causing the stamp to curl so that it can be lifted off the paper. This method has the advantage of leaving the envelope or other paper undamaged.

A little experience will show that it is easier to free stamps that have stuck down accidentally than it is to loosen those on which the gum has been thoroughly moistened.

IMPROVEMENT OF STAMPS

This is a delicate subject, since some collectors view any attempt to improve the appearance of stamps as some sort of fraud. Of course nothing should be done that will alter a type or variety, nor should anything be painted or drawn on a stamp to strengthen a weak impression. These matters constitute faking and, together with various improper mending operations, must be watched for by collectors.

The restoration of stamps differs from similar work on paintings. A work of art is unique and its restoration is desirable to preserve it as long as possible. Stamps, however, are produced in quantity, and even in the case of rare examples restoration of one stamp might make it appear better than a copy not so treated.

In the following suggestions there is no idea of altering a stamp but only of overcoming, in a small way, the harm it may have suffered through careless handling, and of preventing further damage. No collector should hold the opinion that a lightly creased or dirty stamp must be left in such condition, or that pencil marks should not be removed. Stamps should look as fine as possible and any improval treatment is legitimate so long as it does not conceal flaws or alter variety.

Removal of Creases

Light folds or creases that do not break the paper fibers may be removed completely, but when the fibers are broken the line of the fold will always show. Soak the stamp in warm water until it is thoroughly softened, place it face up on a hard, smooth surface, cover with blotters, and press until dry.

Some collectors use an electric iron to press out creases. After this treatment the stamp should be pressed between blotters to avoid any warping or curling.

Removal of Dirt and Pencil Marks

Usually all that dirty stamps need is a light wash with a mild soap. Place the stamp in the palm of the hand and with one finger or a stubby brush—a worn shaving brush is excellent—wash with a little suds, taking care to brush toward the edges so as to not damage the perforation teeth. If the dirt is obstinate add a drop of ammonia to the suds. In every case soak the stamp in clean water before pressing.

Light pencil marks may be removed with a soft rubber

eraser. Confine the work to the pencil marks by using an erasing shield with a very narrow slit. Do not continue to erase obstinate marks or the result may be less desirable than the pencil mark.

Restoring Color of Sulphuretted Stamps

The pigments of certain orange, orange-brown and red-brown stamps are darkened by exposure to sulphur in the atmosphere. The altered color may appear natural in the 3-cent 1851 stamps of the United States, or artificial in the 6-cent orange stamps used in this country from 1908 to the present time. Both will be restored to their natural colors if immersed in hydrogen peroxide.

Allow the stamps to remain in the chemical only long enough to remove the rusty effect and then wash them in clean water to stop the action. On-cover and mint stamps may be restored by careful painting with peroxide, using a camel's-hair brush, but the mint stamps must be kept as dry as possible as the chemical will dissolve the gum as readily as water does.

Prior to 1892 or 1893 sulphuretted (often called oxidized) stamps were frequently classed as color errors and about that time the 2-cent orange registration stamp of Canada was discovered in a brown "error." Almost at the same time an English dealer placed an expensive fluid on the market, claiming that he had developed it to restore the original color of such changelings. Within a few months a second English dealer announced that this magic fluid could be purchased at any drugstore under the name hydrogen peroxide.

Removal of Mildew

Mildew (sometimes called rust spots) and stains caused by tropical fungus may be removed or bleached by painting the stained places with a very weak solution of Clorox. Try a solution containing one or two drops in a teaspoonful of water. If this is not effective, increase the Clorox a drop at a time until the bleaching action is obtained. Then wash or soak the stamp to remove all traces of the chemical. This bleaching will give an unnatural whiteness to the paper and may lighten the color of the stamp, and is not recommended unless the stamps so treated are almost worthless otherwise.

A less-known and without doubt less harmful treatment is to soak the affected stamp in a hot bath of salted milk. This has been declared to be very effective in removing brown stains from early engraved issues of United States postage and revenue stamps.

Removal of Grease, Oil, and Wax

Spots caused by oil or wax may be removed in several ways, but for some stamps any treatment is too severe. What to do depends on the type of printing, the color of the inks, and the paper.

Dipping two or three times in boiling water will usually clean a line-engraved stamp. The paper for this type of stamp contains little or no glue sizing and should not be harmed. However, do not put early blue and violet stamps in boiling water—they may fade. Stamps with an analine red base, used only since about 1880, will be greatly damaged.

Any dry-cleaning solvent will remove grease and oil to a greater or less degree and generally harms no stamps except those printed by photogravure. Place the stamp on a blotter and wet the entire surface with the fluid. Then blot up the liquid and repeat without allowing the stamp to dry out between the treatments. After removing as much of the oil or wax as possible place the stamp in a bath of the fluid in a watermarking dish.

Ether is the most active solvent that collectors use in removing grease, but this very activity makes it dangerous to certain printing inks.

Another method is to vaporize the grease or oil with a very hot iron. The stamp must be protected with blotters to prevent scorching and to absorb the oil vapor. With proper care this treatment should not damage a stamp or fade or change any paper.

Removal of Sealing Wax

In a few cases a collector will find stamps affixed to envelopes with a spot of red cement. If this is a wafer, such as was used to seal folded letters and some envelopes before the days of gummed flaps, it will dissolve readily in water. If it is sealing wax, a mixture of pigment and shellac, it will dissolve in alcohol.

Resizing

Now and then a collector has an old stamp which has been soaked and handled so it is as limp as a wet rag. It may be restored by replacing the glue sizing that washed away in repeated soakings. Dip the stamp in a weak solution of animal glue, made by diluting the commercial glue with about ten times its bulk of water. Air-dry the stamp and press flat. Household starch or library paste may also be used. Dilute them to about the consistency of skim milk and apply to the back of the stamp only, as these materials may slightly whiten the face of the stamp.

Reinforcing Pairs or Blocks

When a pair or other multiple piece becomes fragile or starts to separate along the perforations, it is permissible to reinforce the weak spots. Use strips of peelable hinge about two millimeters by ten and apply them carefully. There will be little tendency to warp the piece if the strips are moistened as little as possible.

Closing Small Cuts and Tears

Use the procedure outlined above, but have the strip of hinge no larger than necessary to cover the cut or tear.

Reconstructing Pieces

Collectors often find stamps that originated as neighbors in a sheet. It is customary to join such stamps as a reconstructed pair. Imperforate stamps usually are matched by the scissors cuts or torn edges, perforated stamps by the unequal lengths of the perforation teeth. The joining procedure is the same as described for reinforcing pairs.

Lacquering

Some collectors have experimented with a coating of water-clear lacquer as a preservative. The lacquer is made by two or more manufacturers and is used, among other purposes, to spray-coat fine wall paper block-printed in soluble colors. After coating the paper may be washed like an ordinary painted wall. The lacquer does not change the colors or the opacity of the paper. Its presence on stamps is not apparent except that the stiffness is increased. It preserves them from finger and pencil marks. The lacquer may be removed at any time if the appropriate solvent is used.

Recently a similar treatment was developed by Heinze Grubbe, a German stamp authority. Grubbe coats the stamps at a fixed charge per copy and agrees to remove this coating at any time for a similar fee. This process, called *grubbieren*, is said to have no effect on color, gum, or paper, and does not prevent the usual watermarking procedure. The treated stamps are marked *grubbiert* on the back and are said to be washable with mild soap and water.

Straightening Margins and Cleaning Perforations

Philatelic writers generally advise against altering the margins of imperforate stamps, but so many copies of the early issues were cut irregularly with scissors or knife, or were just torn apart without any guide, that a collector is justified in correcting some faults. A specialist may keep all stamps with irregular margins in the hope of finding matching neighbor copies, but a general collector will often improve the looks of a stamp by cutting off the rough edges.

Stamps of the same design that were issued both imperforate and perforated are an exception to this rule. Nothing should be removed from the imperforate copy that would help in identifying it as a true imperforate and not a trimmed copy. Such evidence might include portions of the sheet margin or other irregular margin showing parts of adjoining stamps. Usually in later issues the only acceptable proof of an imperforate stamp is to show it in a pair, for the vagaries of perforation are such that some copies may be deperforated and still show ample margins and parts of one or two adjacent stamps.

Another small improvement that will benefit the appearance of stamps is to "pick the teeth" of the perforations. Impacted perforations should be removed so that all the teeth will show, and overlong teeth should be trimmed back to the normal line.

INVESTIGATION OF STAMPS

When buying a scarce stamp a collector should inspect it carefully to see that there are no repairs or alterations. No reflection on dealers is intended, and they nearly always will refund for stamps that are not as described. However, dealers do not always have a chance to examine each stamp carefully before selling. Many times when collections are purchased the dealer is importuned to sell certain stamps at once. If one happens to be repaired the purchaser demands a refund without considering the circumstances of his purchase.

Unfortunately, it is not unusual for a collector to purchase a superb stamp and damage it while placing it in an approval card or stock book. He may close the cut or tear and later, after his collection has been sold, someone discovers the repair work. Sometimes the face of a stamp is touched up with watercolor to conceal a scuffed spot or a slight fold, or to strengthen a faint line. Such repairs are not made to change the variety of the stamp, and often not to increase its value, but rather to make it more presentable.

Similar drawing and painting may be done to change the variety. This is, of course, faking. Small thin spots may be filled in with cement and wood-pulp fibers so expertly that the stamps appear perfect to a casual observer. Nibbed perforation teeth have been extended in this manner, and many an old, closely trimmed imperforate stamp has been given an entire new set of margins by mounting it on a piece of paper, or by adding the margins one at a time, with any missing parts of the design painted on in watercolor.

Ordinarily a collector will be satisfied with a stamp that passes inspection under a magnifying glass and in a look-through inspection before a strong light. As the rarity of the stamp increases so must the buyer's inspection. It is good business to test expensive stamps in a benzine bath, under an ultraviolet lamp, or by x-ray.

The benzine will show nearly all repairs, for the foreign material will retard the penetration of the fluid and such spots will appear more opaque than the remainder of the paper.

Ultraviolet Examination

When pen cancellations have been removed to make a stamp appear unused, or when another cancellation has been added to cover the traces of a pen cancellation, or when the designs have been touched up with ink or watercolor, the benzine bath may be insufficient. Better results will be had by examining the stamp in ultraviolet rays.

Many collectors now own inexpensive examination lamps. Under their black light, as it is sometimes called, a stamp often looks better than in natural light, but any chemical alterations stand out plainly. "Removed" pen marks are almost as clear as when first placed on the stamp, and added materials appear in slightly different tones or shades, unless the faker was able to match everything in chemical composition.

When an entire cancellation has been added it may be necessary to compare the suspected stamp with a genuine copy of the same period. Collectors are gradually learning the dates when new kinds of ink were put into use and of course any appearance of an ink prior to the proper date is evidence of fraud.

Chemicals and pigments show up differently and some fluoresce under the lamp, glowing in unsuspected colors. These effects make it very difficult for fakers to alter stamps or to add stamps to old covers and "tie" them on by extending the cancellations out onto the cover.

X-Ray Investigation

Within recent years the use of x-rays in the study of stamps has been developed simultaneously by Dr. H. C. Pollack, a radiologist of Chicago, in collaboration with Mr. C. F. Bridgman, an x-ray research worker of Rochester, New York, and by Mr. W. H. S. Cheavin of London.

Previous to taking up the study of stamps Dr. Pollack had made use of some of the techniques in the examination of old prints for the Art Institute of Chicago. Dr. Pollack and Mr. Bridgman both collect stamps and are able to appreciate and evaluate phenomena which might appear inconsequential to a noncollector.

The apparatus required is very expensive but it appears that x-ray laboratory technicians can be instructed in making the necessary pictures on a commercial basis, which then can be analyzed or diagnosed by an x-ray specialist who also is a stamp collector.

It is possible to photograph the paper and watermark alone, or the cancellation, or the stamp design, without interference of the other elements, and also to photograph the watermarks of stamps on cover. Such factors as differences in ink composition make these studies possible. They are most successful when the elements are mixed, organic and metallic, or when the metallic elements are not closely related in the atomic scale.

Repairs show up quite clearly for it would be hardly possible that a forger selected materials exactly matching those in the original paper. Even the adhesive used to cement added fibers in filling a thin spot shows plainly. Pictorial counterfeits that are perfect to the eye can be readily exposed by radiographing a genuine stamp and a suspected copy together.

Three techniques have been used in studying stamps: the low-voltage radiograph, the x-ray autoelectronograph, and the x-ray electronograph. In the first the image is obtained by the absorption of the low-penetration rays by the materials in the stamp, and the consequent variation in the rays that reach the film. In the autoelectronograph the image is created by electrons emitted by metallic elements in the printing ink under bombardment by x-rays of extremely short wave length made with very high voltage.

The electronograph is used to study paper structure without interference from the stamp design or cancellation. The stamps are covered with a thin sheet of lead and the image is produced by the electrons emitted from the lead sheet while under bombardment. In this technique the stamp design and cancellation produce no image even though they may be of metallic composition, but watermarks and paper texture and the like show up clearly even if the stamps are on cover. This technique makes it possible to study watermarks on stamps that cannot be immersed in any watermarking fluid.

Stamp hinges show up clearly in both the low-voltage radiograph and the electronograph, due to increased absorption of the rays by the thicker paper. Also, stamps printed in metallic ink and cancelled with a carbon black ink appear to be uncancelled, while stamps printed in organic ink and cancelled with a metallic ink—red, for example, is usually metallic—appear to be photographs of a cancellation only. An interesting result is obtained when a bicolored stamp in organic and metallic inks is radiographed, for only the color printed in metallic ink will show.

X-ray investigation may well become a court of last resort for stamps that have been bandied about, first as genuine, then as forgeries, as was the case with the Grinnell find of Hawaiian missionary stamps.

The illustrations and captions used in Plate IV were made available by Dr. Pollack and Mr. Bridgman.

❖❖

SPECIALISM

After a period spent with a general collection one may find a series of stamps or a single issue that he would like to study in detail. This may be his introduction to the field of specialism. Any collector in a limited field may extend his work in greater detail and become a specialist to any extent that his time, capacity for work, and his resources allow.

Beginners who announce that they are specializing are likely to be forming a very limited collection. Plate blocks, blocks of four, and similar items do not constitute a specialized collection.

Budding specialists should not overlook anything in their particular field and should try to show the entire history of the stamps being handled. Dated cancellations will help to fix the years when various shades were used and the complete sequence may be established if sufficient material is available.

Designs should be memorized so that new copies can be examined for variations without the need for comparison with other stamps. It is not possible to tell a collector what to look for when he is working on an unstudied stamp except to look for anything out of the ordinary.

A specialist must know enough of stamp manufacture to be able to identify engraving, typography, and lithography, and to distinguish between flat-plate and rotary-press engraved stamps of the United States if he is at all concerned with these issues.

In engraved issues he should look for shifted transfers, evidences of recutting or re-engraving, short transfers, long transfers, re-entered designs, slips of engravers' tools, cracked plates, worn plates, scratches, damages caused by articles falling on a plate, and numerous little varieties inherent in line engraving.

In lithographed stamps he will look for transfer varieties characteristic of this work. When designs are being transferred from die to plate, the fragile paper is often torn or wrinkled, or incorrectly positioned so that the stamp spacing is affected. The collector may be able to determine that a plate is made up of several nearly identical groups of stamps, and this will show that the transfers from the original die were not placed directly on the plate but on a secondary block from which transfers of groups of a dozen or more subjects were made to the plate. Consistent varieties regularly located on a plate will determine the size of the group transfers, and when the workman did a careless job there may be enough variation in each transfer to allow plating (see pages 78-82).

In typographed stamps the student will find varieties caused by accidental damage, or by wear. The upstanding lines of the plate may wear or break off, those at the edge of the plate may be flattened by pressure, and there may be printings from dirty plates that have filled up between lines to make large areas print in solid color. There may be underinked or overinked prints. Some of the latter will have lettering and designs in a paler color with dark outlines.

During the study of a stamp the paper must be watched for abnormalities. It may be too thick or too thin, it may be double or show a paste-up between webs in certain kinds of printing. Watermarks may be found where normal watermarks do not occur, or there may be errors or omissions of watermarks due to some damage to the dandy roll.

Perforations will come in for study. If the collector is working with stamps that have numerous gauges he may have difficulty in locating all varieties. Also there may be imperforate and part-perforate varieties of perforated stamps, and trial perforations or roulettings in early imperforate issues.

Cancellations and the use of the stamps will take up a large part of the student's time and may become the major interest. In such a specialized collection completeness is never attained for new postal markings are found as well as new rates on covers, mixed frankings, and numerous other desirable items.

Specialists who collect covers cannot make a full study of their subject without a fairly complete knowledge of postal rates at the time the cover was mailed. In early days the rates to foreign lands were complicated. Now and then a cover is suspected of being fraudulent because the postage prepaid or collected on delivery cannot be reconciled with the known rates. In some cases such a cover must be judged by the stamps, postal markings, and various other factors. If everything seems correct except the actual postage paid, there is little reason to condemn the cover. Many covers show overpaid or underpaid postage, overpaid because the mailer did not have the exact stamps to pay the rate and preferred to overpay rather than buy additional stamps, underpaid through a clerk's error in computing the rate. Clerks in early days had a more difficult task in determining rates than those today, but errors are still made. There are other reasons, too, why the postage may not match with the known rates. For example, some people purposely underpay postage in the hope that it will pass unnoticed. And a few people of more than ordinary honesty, may do the reverse. Some years ago, back when the basic rate was 3 cents an ounce, two friends of the author, one being the wife of a prominent specialist of Evanston, Illinois, and the other a resident of Cassopolis, Michigan, always placed a 1-cent stamp beside the 3-cent value whenever they suspected their letters of being overweight, even by a fraction of an ounce.

HOW SPECIALISM HELPS PHILATELY

Through his study the specialist is able to solve many problems that seem to lack any explanation. When freak stamps are studied by a person who has a knowledge of the printing process used, their true status usually is revealed. A situation of this kind arose when a collector produced a full sheet of bureau-print precancellations without stamps of any kind on the sheet. There were enough flecks of orange ink on the perforated sheet to indicate that it had been in contact with sheets of ½-cent or 6-cent stamps, perhaps of the presidential series. A theory was advanced that precancellation preceded the printing of the actual stamps, but this was not plausible for stamps printed in dark colors would have obscured the precancellation. The true explanation was found when the operation of a two-color web-fed press was studied, for the web is threaded through the entire press before the work starts and when printing is begun each color or other operating unit starts up at the same time.

When the "leader," as the leading end of the web is called, begins to issue from the press, it shows only the final operation, which in this rotary press is the gumming operation. After an interval the web will show the next-to-last operation, that is, the precancellation on gummed paper. Finally the precancelled stamps arrive, completing the starting operation. The intervals between the various stages of the work run several minutes because the stamp ink must be fully dried before the precancellation is applied, and after gumming the web must pass along a lengthy dryer so that it can be made into a roll for the perforating machines.

The leader up to the point where the fully finished product appears is printers' waste. Under normal conditions it is discarded by the operator of the perforating machine when he finishes perforating this starting roll. Only during a change from one value to another does the web appear at the finished end without stamps.

Even more difficult problems perplex collectors but are finally solved by specialists with or without the help or, in some cases, the hindrance of the stamp printers. One of the most extraordinary cases of this kind occurred in the famous plate of

2-cent stamps containing three 5-cent stamp subjects. The story is told in chapter 29.

SPECIALIZED COLLECTION OF A SINGLE STAMP

One of the most outstanding subjects for a specialized collection is the United States 3-cent stamp of 1851. No other stamp has so many possibilities in combination with a rather large supply of low- and medium-priced stamps. Since all the subjects on the various plates were finished by hand engraving, and many were re-entered with the transfer roll to make worn plates useful, it is possible to reconstruct all the plates. The problem is treated in greater detail in the discussion of plating.

A specialized collection of early stamps should include historical material relating to the issue, for new rates were being put into effect, and during the period before prepayment became obligatory the postage was less if prepaid in stamps or money. Under these conditions postmasters were required to figure the postage at 5-cent rates if unpaid, 3-cent rates if prepaid. The larger offices were equipped with hand stamps to mark ratings as in the stampless days, to mark ratings paid in money, and to cancel the stamps when affixed.

A collection of a single stamp should include essays and any other suggestions for the stamps, proofs of the die and plate when available, as well as the actual copies as issued. Plating is not a requisite for this sort of collection but there should be typical shades and typical examples from any plate or group of plates from which the stamps can be identified. There should be examples of shifted transfers, re-entries, and all the various types of recutting and re-engraving that abound in most any issue. Copies showing wear in the plates and cracks will add to the varieties which can be assembled.

Cancellations and uses of a stamp are sufficient to require a separate collection. Stamps came into use during a period when transportation extended far beyond the limits of the postal system, and the postal markings include those of private carriers, express and steamboat companies, and authorized public carriers.

Many of the most interesting United States postal markings come from the territories and the frontier army posts. There was no standardization of markings and a postmaster was at liberty to use whatever was at hand, and in any color available. If the income of the office was low, little money was spent for equipment and the postmaster often made his handstamps. More often he used a pen and ink to indicate the office name, date, and cancellations.

It was a strenuous and exciting period, clouded with the possibility of civil war, and the presidential elections were highlighted with pictorial envelopes praising the candidates and propaganda envelopes for various important causes.

Since stamps of this time were imperforate, the collector will be able to show multiple pieces in a great variety. He may be able to obtain copies showing the experimental perforation of 1857 and others having traces of the roulettes used in an occasional large office.

If the collection is extended into the perforated issue of 1857 there will be examples of the earlier plates which now are perforated and in addition two new types from new plates will be found. The latter are more uniform and show less hand engraving and varieties are limited. Any loss of variety, however, is made up in the field of cancellations and covers.

At this time patriotic covers came into use, and with the outbreak of the war there are examples of late use in the South, and of the rare postal markings indicating that the issue had been demonetized and the stamps could no longer be used for postage.

In the cover and cancellation field the task of collecting everything available may be so great that a collector usually limits himself to one or more states, or the territories, or perhaps to railroad or steamboat covers.

PLATING

This term applies to the intensive study that enables a collector to identify the positions of the stamp subjects on a printing plate and to reassemble copies into sheets. These sheets duplicate original sheets except that they may be composed of stamps in a variety of shades. Such a study can be made only with stamps that have enough peculiarities to allow positive identification. The early line-engraved stamps lend themselves most readily to plating as many issues required some hand engraving or retouching before they were placed in use. In addition, after the plates had begun to show wear, it was customary to retouch the poorest subjects, to re-enter the positions with the transfer roll, or to re-engrave the entire design.

On account of the restoration work performed on a plate it may be possible to plate a stamp in its second or restored state, although the various subjects cannot be identified in the original state. In somewhat the same manner it is possible to plate some overprinted stamps through the varieties in the overprints although the basic stamps are identical in all respects.

Lithographed stamps printed from plates made by the old process, using paper transfers to produce the multiple designs, frequently have enough variety to enable a collector to reconstruct an entire plate or in some cases a transfer unit if the subjects were laid down on the plate in groups.

Typographed stamps made from individual clichés, and the duplicate plates made from assembled clichés, may be plated in some cases, but when the actual printing was made from a plate of movable clichés that were separated and cleaned between printings, it becomes a hopeless task to trace the various states of the plate.

Many collectors think of the British stamps with corner letters as suitable stamps for plating, but this is hardly the case for it requires little work to plate the Penny Blacks and none at all to plate stamps with four corner letters. After a collector has learned to identify the alphabets used for the several plates of Penny Blacks, he has only to arrange the stamps according to the corner letters starting with stamp AA in the upper left corner of the plate. Plate numbers are included in the design of stamps with four corner letters such as the Penny Reds, and a good magnifying glass is the only requisite for plating.

The plating that a serious student undertakes is not so simple. The stamps must be examined very carefully for peculiarities that will identify each subject, and duplicates must be found to prove that the varieties are constant and not printing variations from careless inking and the like. To record their findings it is not unusual for collectors to procure printed enlargements of the stamp in some light shade that will show pen or pencil marks. Such mats, as they are called, if four times normal stamp size will save a large amount of examination and comparison.

Plating should be an original piece of work, not just matching stamps that were first plated by someone else. There may be cooperation among collectors working on the same stamp, but it should not become an out-and-out copying job.

A plater usually makes a start when he finds a copy that can be identified as coming from the corner of a plate, that is, a stamp with sheet margins at two sides. Next he needs a pair showing this corner stamp with another attached at the side or above or below. Thus, step by step, he will be able to progress throughout the plate. Sometimes the plating will move inwardly from both sides or from all four corners, and it is a time for jubilation when the groups meet, hardly less memorable than the moment when a collector determines the plate size, if he is working on an unknown plate. Sometimes there are gaps in the plate that remain unfilled for months or even years.

When working with a stamp from a single plate the task is not too hard but if there are an unknown number of plates the problem may be extremely complicated unless the plater can discover some means of identifying the stamps from various plates. Shades and dated copies are of great help, for it may be assumed that the early dates identify the early shades and that certain plates will be found only in early shades while other plates appear only with late dates and late shades.

A collector may find that he has two differing stamps which nevertheless must come from the same position on the same plate. This may seem a major setback until he realizes that he has found stamps from two states or conditions of the plate, and that the differences are the result of retouching or perhaps of completely re-entering the design with a transfer roll.

This might have been the experience of Dr. Carroll Chase,

who began to investigate certain extra-line varieties of the United States 3-cent stamp of 1851 while a convalescent, and succeeded during the next twenty years in completely reconstructing the thirteen plates used for this stamp. Actually only nine plates were involved but the first was worked over twice, and two others were given a single restoration each. In spite of extensive re-entry and re-engraving, there were certain unchangeable characteristics of each plate, such as the horizontal spacing of the vertical rows, that proved very useful in the identification of stamps from the various states.

Considering that each plate contained 200 subjects, this student had to determine the characteristics of 2600 varieties of one stamp, and this was accomplished in spite of a complete lack of official information regarding the number of plates.

Another striking example of original plating was performed by Charles Lathrop Pack on the Sydney Views, as the first stamps of New South Wales are called. These, unlike Dr. Chase's stamps, were fairly expensive and it was difficult to find enough copies to do the job. At the start it appeared that every 2-pence stamp issued by New South Wales in 1850 and 1851 differed from every other copy, and this was not far wrong for when the task was finished Mr. Pack had identified 144 varieties of his single stamp, all printed from one plate of 24 subjects.

In solving the problem he soon found that there were certain characteristics which appeared very often on stamps that otherwise were quite different. Dates of use were of great help and it must have been apparent almost from the start that the early dates were on stamps in fine impressions and late dates on stamps which appeared quite worn.

This plater encountered identical stamps attached to other stamps that did not match. He soon determined that 12 positions of the 24 had been retouched when they began to show signs of wear, thus providing the mixed pairs mentioned. When the plate showed excessive wear it was entirely re-engraved, making the second state, but cataloged as plate II. When this began to wear 12 positions again were retouched, and again after excessive wear the plate was entirely re-engraved to become the third state, cataloged as plate III, and so on until the fifth state had been reached.

Except for the scarcity and cost of the stamps, it is doubtful if this plating is comparable to that done on the United States 3-cent of 1851, since only 144 and not 2600 varieties were involved.

A lithographic stamp recommended to anyone who would like to investigate plating is the 1-cent value of the Guy issue of Newfoundland of 1910. This is the stamp with the NFW variety caused by a broken E in the transfer. Almost every subject on the plate of 200 shows some differences in the form of broken letters or misplaced letters and ornament, and it is apparent that the lithographic transfers were put down on the stone in fragments.

There are many collectors who believe that this intensive work is a waste of time and energy and a detriment to stamp collecting, but there is evidence that it is of value in many cases. Through ability to identify the plates of the United States 3-cent, 1851, it is possible to detect frauds, including stamps on covers dated prior to the printing from a certain plate. A packet-boat cover of great rarity bore a plate No. 4 stamp with a cancellation dated two years before the first printing from that plate, and was thus a forgery. Another cover with an orange-brown stamp of the same issue bearing the July 1 date easily could have been sold as a first-day cover without intentional fraud, as stamp dealers cannot learn the pedigrees of all stamps, but the stamp was from plate 0 (a plate without number), which was not used until some time after the date mentioned. Actually this cover was cancelled on July 1, 1852, and showed a very late use of an orange-brown stamp.

There are a few modern stamps that can be plated or partly plated on account of numerous shifts and irregularities, but it is safe to say that no amount of work would result in the plating of a United States 2-cent stamp, series 1922-1923, as the plater would be confronted with almost 1500 plates of 400 subjects each, all identical except under a microscope.

✤✤✤

TOPICAL COLLECTING

During recent years topical collecting, or themately, as it is called in England, has attracted many people. The terms indicate that the collection is made up of stamps related to each other by their designs or by some other feature. While the names are new the idea is as old as collecting and fascinates many people who never could have been induced to make a complete collection of the stamps of any country.

Topical collectors seldom confine their attentions to one subject unless it is quite large, such as Religion on Stamps, but take up one after another. Although many never take up regular collecting, it is well known, according to Edwin Mueller, that many of the most studious specialists are able to have some of the fun of general collecting by making topical collections of some attractive subject. Some critics call topical collecting superficial, but such a collection will never be as boring to an outsider as a complete showing of British colonial key and duty plate stamps of the late nineteenth century.

In its simplest form a topical collection consists of pictures with no attention paid to denominations, perforations, paper, or watermarks. Portraits form one of the largest groups but can be

83

broken down into various categories: men, women, rulers, scientists. An interesting collection might be and probably has been formed showing all members of some one of the old royal families of Europe, with its relationships scattered over a dozen lands.

Flags, maps, and arms of countries are of interest but the last mentioned are usually reproduced in such a small space that they are difficult to identify. Some of the other large divisions include agriculture, archeology, architecture, art, astronomy, commerce, construction, engineering, ethnology, exploration, history, industry, invention, literature and language, machinery, medicine, music, natural history, religion and mythology, scenery, transportation. Each may be broken down into sections. In transportation, for example, there are the three major divisions of land, sea, and air, with further logical divisions into railroads, motors, wagons, carts; naval vessels, steamships, sailing vessels; airplanes and airships.

Here are a few additional subjects, but fewer are mentioned than omitted, for nothing of importance has escaped the stamp designers:

Athletics, authors, battles, buildings, children, Christmas, costumes, dams, dragons, education, electricity, fountains, gates, gods, harbors, heraldry, idols, inscriptions, jails, jewels, knaves, liberators, lighthouses, martyrs, monuments, navigators, natives, oceans, orators, palaces, pottery, quotations, radio, ruins, saints, symbols, temples, towers, uniforms, universities, viaducts, volcanoes, walls, waterfalls, x-rays, yachting, youth, zoos.

Several topical collections have been limited to stamps of a single color, but some secondary classification must be followed to keep some sort of order. A collection of such a category as air mail, commemorative, semipostal, postage dues, or precancels is topical in a sense, but these must be mounted in some logical sequence.

Topical collections with a national aspect are quite common. Almost everyone is interested in Americana or foreign stamps, and some make a companion collection showing foreign subjects on United States stamps. Events or anniversaries of world-wide importance are commemorated by various countries and the stamps for each occasion will make an interesting collection. Among these are the recent observance of the seventy-fifth anniversary of the Universal Postal Union, and the earlier anniversary of the ratification of the Constitution of the United States. Collectors are always partial to stamps commemorating the hundredth anniversary of postage stamps in various countries, to those issued to honor philately, and those showing stamp collectors and collecting. Equally important subjects for collections are stamps issued in special form as souvenir and miniature sheets, in booklets, and in official and private coils.

HISTORICAL AND EDUCATIONAL COLLECTIONS

Special-subject collections can be of great value in teaching beginners the rudiments of collecting. One may show all the technical aspects and would include examples of the various types of paper, printing, and perforations used to produce stamps, with typical examples of watermarks and perhaps a few types of gum. This would include also examples of overprints, showing the various ways in which they are used to alter stamps. There would be errors and printing varieties and copies, perhaps, from plates restored to improve the printing quality.

Another collection with historical and educational aspects might consist of the first stamp issued in various technical subjects, and shape categories. Following are lists of such "firsts."

TECHNICAL ASPECTS

Printing

Engraved, black, 1 penny	Great Britain	1840
Engraved, color, 2-pence	Great Britain	1840
First engraved, in multicolor	Basle, Switzerland	1845
Engraved and embossed	Great Britain	1847
Photogravure	Bavaria	1914
Typographed	France, Bavaria	1849
Lithographed	**Victoria**	1850

Typeset, as a handstamp	British Guiana	1850
Typeset in printing plate	Hawaii	1851
Embossed without color	Sardinia	1854
Lithographed and embossed	Sardinia	1854
Typographed and embossed	Sardinia	1855
Typewritten	Uganda	1895
Blueprint, Mafeking	Cape of Good Hope	1900
Offset lithography	United States	1918

Overprinting

To change value, semiofficial carrier	United States	1846
To change value, manuscript 5	Hawaii	1853
Overprint to indicate value	Mauritius	1854
To change value, "Y ¼," printed	Cuba, *et al.*	1855
To change the country, overprint on India	Straits Settlements	1867
To indicate the use, postage	Natal	1869
For special user, officials	Luxembourg	1875

Separation

Experimental roulette, Archer	Great Britain	1848
Experimental perforation, gauge 16	Great Britain	1850
Official perforation, gauge 16	Great Britain	1854
Perforation outside England	Sweden, India	1855
Serpentine and serrate roulettes	Victoria	1855
Roulette, and pin roulette	Victoria	1856

SUBJECTS

Sovereign, Victoria	Great Britain	1840
Numeral design, 30-60-90	Brazil	1843
Illustrious person not in office, Franklin; Washington	United States	1847
Allegorical design { Ceres	France	1849
{ Minerva	Mauritius	1849
Arms in design	Austria, Hanover, Switzerland, Schleswig-Holstein	1850
Seal of a state, view of Sydney	New South Wales	1850

Member of royalty not a sovereign, Prince Albert	Canada	1851
Animal, part of arms { beaver	Canada	1851
{ Tuscany lion	Tuscany	1851
Heraldic symbols, British flowers	New Brunswick	1851
Inscription as design motif	Denmark	1851
President in office, Louis Napoleon	France	1852
Ship, part of arms	British Guiana	1852
Foreign notable, Columbus	Chile	1853
Bird, part of arms, black swan	Western Australia	1854
Locomotive	New Brunswick	1860
Scene, mountains	Nicaragua	1862
Marine animal, seal	Newfoundland	1865
Fish, cod	Newfoundland	1865
Painting as a subject, landing of Columbus	United States	1869
Statue of a ruler, Kamehameha	Hawaii	1882
Map	Panama	1887
Sports design, Olympic games	Greece	1896
First stamp complete with country, value, and use	United States	1847
First stamp without value indication	Mauritius	1849
First bilingual stamp	Hawaii	1859

SHAPES

Normal shape, vertical rectangle	Great Britain	1840
Horizontal rectangle	Brazil	1850
Rectangle, decorated	Brazil	1844
Rectangle, sides curved	Roman States	1852
Square, normal	Bavaria	1849
Square, on corner	Nova Scotia	1851
	New Brunswick	1851
Triangle, right-angle isosceles, on hypotenuse	Cape of Good Hope	1853
Triangle, right-angle isosceles, on point	Latvia	1921
Triangle, right-angle, on hypotenuse	Colombia	1869
Triangle, equilateral, on side	Colombia	1865
Triangle, equilateral, on point	Austria	1916
Diamond, long axis horizontal	Somali Coast	1894

Diamond, long axis vertical	Lithuania	1923
Octagon, elongated vertically	Great Britain	1847
Octagon, elongated horizontally	Roman States	1852
Octagon, true	Portugal	1853
	Tasmania	1853
Octagon, true, perforated as octagon	Thessaly	1898
Circle	Roman States	1852
Circle, die cut to shape	Tonga	1963
Ellipse, vertical	New South Wales	1856
Map of the country, die cut	Sierra Leone	1964
Heart shape, die cut	Tonga	1964
Ellipse, vertical	New South Wales	1856
Shield	Argentina	1867
Star, six points	Colombia	1865

❖❖❖

CHAPTER ELEVEN

SPECIALTY AND SIDELINE COLLECTIONS

BOOKLETS AND BOOKLET PANES

An interesting collection can be formed of stamp booklets or panes of stamps from such booklets.

Although booklets of telegraph stamps were issued by the California State Telegraph Company, in 1870, and by the Western Union Telegraph Company, in 1871, the Post Office Department took no notice until many years later. After application on April 17, 1884, Mr. A. W. Cooke, of Boston, obtained patent No. 306674, October 14, 1884, for a stamp booklet. He offered the idea to postal authorities without success, and so far as known abandoned it.

In 1900, Mr. P. C. Blanc, a binder in the Bureau of Engraving and Printing, showed the director a small booklet he had made for his own convenience. Third Assistant Postmaster General Edwin C. Madden was impressed and on March 26, 1900, ordered a supply for experimental use.

However, similar booklets of 5-centime stamps were on sale in Luxembourg as early as 1895, and booklets of 5- and 10-ore stamps had been on sale in Sweden since 1898.

The first United States booklets appeared April 2, 1900, in three sizes, containing 12, 24, or 48 2-cent series 1898 stamps, to be sold at face value plus 1 cent. On January 24, 1903, the 2-cent flag-type stamp, series 1902-1903, appeared but soon was replaced by the new shield type, series of 1903. At the end of six years the profit on booklets after deducting production costs, amounted to almost half a million dollars.

On March 6, 1907, booklets were issued containing 1-cent series 1902-1903 stamps. These and the first two types of 2-cent booklets are the rarities of United States issues. Combination booklets with 1- and 2-cent stamps were placed on sale October 25, 1913, and 3-cent booklets October 17, 1917. All booklets up to 1926 contained flat-plate stamps; all subsequent ones, except the Lindbergh air-mail booklet, contained rotary-press issues.

The booklet idea spread around the world. Initial supplies were made out of regular sheet stamps, but later booklets were usually made from specially printed sheets.

In some countries novel ways were found to fix the sale price at an even multiple of the coinage. Great Britain omitted a halfpenny stamp on each pane and substituted a large X, similar in purpose to the St. Andrew's crosses used in Austria a half century before. This X label in the British booklets is called the kiss stamp.

Several countries have mixed the values in booklets or on single panes, while others have sold unwanted spaces for advertisements. These ads often are used on cover, "se-tenant" with the stamps. In a few cases the perforations between ads and stamps have been omitted to force their use.

The mixing of values on panes produces se-tenant pairs that are of great interest but hardly to be compared with these se-tenant pairs resulting from the use of a wrong cliché in the plate. The latter pairs are in a single color, while those of booklets are in differing colors.

Certain plate arrangements have part of the panes inverted with respect to others. Were all sheets made into booklets this would not be noticed except when watermarked paper is used. For this reason inverted watermarks in booklet stamps are not as collectible a variety as in ordinary sheet stamps. When sheets prepared for booklets are made available to collectors, as has been done in several countries, *tête-bêche* or top-against-bottom and various se-tenant combinations may be obtained.

Switzerland is responsible for a large list of these varieties and Germany has produced combinations of two or three values on a single pane of eight or ten stamps, with some omitted stamps replaced by labels. In France the margins of the panes and the covers of the booklets are sold as advertising space. One French booklet had extra pages outlining the history of shirts, and these were embellished with small swatches of shirting material.

The usual booklet panes are cut from sheets with all stamps straight-edged on one or more sides, but there are a few perforated all around, an indication that the panes were separated by tearing. Still others show evidence that the panes were cut along the perforated lines to separate them.

Booklet panes are of two general kinds, being bound at the end (short dimension) of the stamps, or at the side. United States booklets, excepting the air-mails, are bound at the end. Some booklets may be found with binding at any side, but these usually are of a provisional nature and have been made by selecting marginal blocks of stamps and binding them at their natural margins. One example is found in the Canal Zone issues and in all such cases the stamps are fully perforated.

Panes with six stamps predominate, but there are many other sizes. France uses a double pane of twenty stamps, the two halves separated by a gutter and affixed to the covers with its own gum at the gutter. Panes have contained as few as three stamps. One Canadian issue of this size had two sheets of 1-cent stamps and one sheet each of 2-cent and 4-cent values, to bring the selling price to 25 cents. United States booklets of large-size air-mail stamps have three stamps on a pane but as these stamps are double size, the covers are normal.

When Sweden began to use Stickney presses, booklet panes

contained ten subjects and were accordion folded to fit in a normal cover for a six-stamp pane. With the new Goebel presses the panes were increased to eighteen or twenty stamps, similarly folded to fit small covers, and the pane was attached to the cover with its own gum. Early Swedish booklet stamps were fully perforated but now all have straight edges at the sides. They are not interleaved but give no trouble in the cold, dry climate, even though folded gum to gum.

Nearly all booklets are wire stapled, but those of Japan and Great Britain, and some of Canada, are stitched with thread. Cuba, with excessive humidity, covers the wire staples with tape to prevent rust.

MOUNTING BOOKLETS AND BOOKLET PANES

Booklet collections may consist of panes only, or may show the complete booklets as bought at the post office. Those who mount the complete booklets will have better albums if they indent the pages or provide mats all round, to compensate for the thickness of the material being displayed.

One accepted practice is to "explode" the booklet and mount all parts separately, including even the thread or staple. At the minimum there should be two covers, one stamp pane, and an interleaf, or two panes, if a combination cover. Covers often change even though there may be no change in the stamps, and there have been changes in stamps without alterations of covers. Collectors who seek completeness must be on the lookout for new items.

Some collectors who do not wish to show all booklets complete, both in covers and panes, mount only the changes as they occur. They may show several covers with a single pane of stamps, or more than one pane with the same cover.

Collectors should watch for plate varieties and for plate markings on the margins. In United States stamps the early booklet plates showed center lines, arrows, and plate numbers, but the current rotary-press issues show little except the plate number. The early center lines crossed the panes or showed at one side, while the plate number and arrow could be found on the binding margin. Today, partial plate numbers are found at the side of some poorly centered panes.

Collectors should not attempt to preserve booklets intact if they have wax-paper interleaves, as these will in time cause the stamps to become transparent. Though in exploded mounting the only damage will be to the album pages, it is suggested that the interleaves be covered with glassine or acetate.

IMPERFORATE STAMPS

This term includes all stamps issued without a means of separation, either intentionally or by accident. Accidental imperforates are classed as errors. They are discussed in chapters 25 and 29.

Intentional imperforates include: (1) stamps issued before a means of separation was available; (2) stamps issued imperforate in a period of normal perforation, because of a lack of time or a breakdown of perforating machinery; (3) stamps issued imperforate for special use; and (4) stamps issued for philatelic purposes.

Imperforate stamps that normally are available in perforated form must be collected in pairs, multiple pieces, or pieces with sheet margins, to prove that they are not trimmed copies. Blocks are preferred, and great attention is paid to marginal pieces showing plate numbers, imprints, etc. Corner blocks with two wide margins are most desirable.

Imperforate stamps of the first group mentioned above are becoming scarce and it is not easy to obtain pairs and larger pieces, but singles are acceptable in nearly all cases. In cases where the stamps were never perforated, or where the subjects were so closely spaced on the plate that trimming will not make a four-margin copy (as in the case of early issues of Great Britain and the United States), or where the perforated stamps are more valuable than the imperforate, there is little reason to suspect an imperforate single.

The stamps of the second group may appear in any country. Bonafide examples are found in the first issue of United States revenue stamps and result from the haste to collect revenue to pay the cost of the Civil War. Shipments of the stamps included whatever was ready at the time, not only imperforates but part perforated in either direction and fully perforated copies.

The imperforate stamps of the third group were made for use in affixing and vending machines. The manufacturers of these machines had tried to use coils made from ordinary sheet stamps but they separated too easily along the perforated lines. (Coils with special perforations are described later in this chapter under Private Coils.) The imperforate sheets made for machine use were available to the public and the examples now owned by collectors and dealers were purchased at the wholesale windows of large city post offices, or in the case of the last issues, at the Philatelic Agency in Washington. The stamps were printed from the regular plates, which for ordinary stamps were laid out in four panes of a hundred subjects each, marked by lines ending in arrows to guide the operators when perforating the stamps. Imprints and plate numbers were centrally located on two margins of each hundred-stamp pane.

From 1906 until about 1912 experiments were made to compensate for the cross-web shrinkage of the paper during the wet-paper intaglio printing process. Among the ideas tried was a varying horizontal spacing of the stamp subjects. Plates with this spacing were marked by adding a star near the plate number. Ultimately a wider spacing between vertical rows was adopted and these were marked with the letter A. At about the same time the use of the imprint was stopped and only the plate number remained on the margin.

Collectors who bought these full sheets usually broke them up and held only the important blocks: one with crossed center lines, one with horizontal line, one with vertical line, four arrow blocks, four corner blocks, four margin blocks, four plate-number blocks, and one normal block without special features. The plate-number blocks contained six stamps, the others were blocks of four. When the spacing was varied, it required at least one more block to show it.

At the end of the period when imperforate sheets were available the printing process changed from flat plate to rotary press. There had been no intention of issuing any rotary-press stamps in imperforate sheets as the gutters which had been provided between panes to do away with straight-edge stamps made them useless for machine coils. However, one order for 1½-cent stamps was inadvertently filled with the rotary-press Harding issue. When these sheets were returned by the affixing-machine company, they should have been perforated but instead they were placed on sale at the Philatelic Agency.

The Lincoln centennial issue of 1909 and two large-size commemoratives were among the stamps issued imperforate. There was some excuse for having the normal-size Lincoln stamp in this form, since it could be used in the machines, but none for the large Hudson-Fulton and Alaska-Yukon-Pacific commemoratives.

Imperforates issued for coils and vending machines include:

Series 1902-1903   1-, 2-, 4-, and 5-cents.
Series 1908-1909   1-, 2-, 3-, 4-, and 5-cents.
Series 1909   2-cent Lincoln, Hudson-Fulton, and Alaska-Yukon-Pacific.
Series 1911   1- and 2-cent, single-line watermark.
Series 1912   1- and 2-cent, single-line watermark.
Series 1916-1917   1-, 2-, and 3-cent, (and 5-cent in sheets of 2-cent), unwatermarked.
Series 1918-1920   1-, 2-, and 3-cent, offset lithography.
Series 1923-1925   1-, 1½-, 2-cent, and 2-cent Harding.
Series 1926   1½-cent, rotary-press printed.

The issuance of imperforate sheets began October 2, 1906, and continued until 1927, when the sole remaining producer of private coils adopted standard government coils.

The 4-cent stamp, series of 1902-1903, was not available to collectors in sheet form, as all sheets had been punched with

Schermack III perforations before collectors knew of them. See Private Coils.

In spite of the fact that nearly all of the imperforate 5-cent stamps of this issue were purchased by dealers or collectors, this value is the scarcest of all in this form. It should be remembered that sheets converted into coils by the various companies automatically ceased to be available except as coil singles or pairs with punched holes to fit some machine.

The imperforate stamps of the fourth group include the souvenir sheets of the United States and other countries, the imperforate varieties of the so-called Farley Favors or Farley Follies (described in chapter 31), and various stamps now being issued in imperforate form to sell to collectors. The first of these souvenir sheets was issued at the American Philatelic Society convention in 1933. The two varieties were sheets of twenty-five stamps of Century of Progress Exposition issues, with marginal inscriptions. Other smaller sheets have since been issued at philatelic meetings, the most recent being four different sheets of the U.S. Bicentennial Celebration and the INTERPHIL stamp exhibition. Others include a 3-cent Byrd-Little America, a 3-cent National Parks, a 1-cent National Parks, a block of four 3-cent stamps in four designs, a 10-cent National Parks, reproductions of the 5-cent and 10-cent 1847 stamps in 1947, 3- and 8-cent Statue of Liberty in 1956, and a 5-cent SIPEX sheet in 1966.

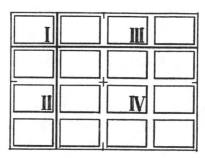

Fig. 11–1. Diagram for Cutting a Large Block from Imperforate Sheets. *I*, center-line block; *II*, vertical-line block; *III*, horizontal-line block; *IV*, plain block.

Many foreign countries issue two varieties of each souvenir sheet, one being imperforate. There has been some criticism of the practice, but it is hardly warranted as the country could have issued a single higher-priced sheet and raised the same amount of money.

An interesting way of cutting an imperforate sheet is shown in the accompanying diagram. It enables a collector to mount a large block on his album page showing four of the principal block varieties attached. These may be separated at some future time without loss of value. Had the large block been taken from the exact center of the sheet, no future division into special blocks would be possible. This method of cutting sheets was used by the author for all sheets of the Farley Favors, as the crossed gutters were necessary in many cases to prove that the stamps were not from the ordinary sheets.

PRIVATE COILS

Soon after 1900 several makers of vending machines began to sell postage stamps through their machines in drugstores and similar localities but failed to attain permission to place them in post office lobbies for use after hours. These machines sold four 1-cent or two 2-cent stamps for five cents. The coils used were made by pasting up strips of sheet stamps, but they were so weak at the perforations that they tore apart and clogged the machines. The postal authorities were asked to supply unperforated sheets that might be made into suitable coils. The request was granted, and in addition the Post Office Department began to produce coils from partly perforated sheets. These are known as government coils.

A committee was appointed under an order of November 24, 1905, to examine the suggestion of having vending machines in post offices. It reported unfavorably due to the experimental nature of both the machines and coils. However, Postmaster General George B. Cortelyou expressed interest in his report for 1905 and recommended further study to perfect the machines.

The vending and affixing machine companies began to perforate some series 1902-1903 stamps and certain values are found with the punchings of the Brinkerhoff, Mail-O-Meter, Schermack, United States Auto Vending, and International Vending Machine companies. Several of these had altered their machines during development and now were furnishing two or three types of punchings to various customers.

Only the last-mentioned company was able to use the first government coils by converting its machines to handle perforations gauging 12 instead of 12½. At once the other manufacturers demanded that they be supplied with their own distinctive punchings, but the authorities countered with the suggestion that the companies redesign their machines. A compromise was reached when the coils were furnished in imperforate form.

All except the International Vending Machine Company continued to make private coils for many years In 1911 the John V. Farwell Company, a Chicago wholesale dry goods house, began to make coils for its own use. These were perforated with two groups of holes known as the Chambers perforation, after the Farwell mechanic who built the machinery. The coils were made for use in a Schermack machine to eliminate the extra cost of fifty cents for each coil purchased from the company.

The Schermack Company after various name changes became the Mailometer Company in 1909 but continued to punch coils for the various machines manufactured under various names. The only private coils after 1912 had the Schermack III punchings made by Mailometer for various old machines. This continued after Mailometer had been acquired by the Postage Meter Company but was ended December 1, 1927, when the postal authorities began to supply coils of three thousand stamps with the gum side out.

All private coils, except those of Brinkerhoff and the first type of the United States Auto Vending Company, had the stamps side to side. One or two of the companies applied their perforations to the Lincoln, Hudson-Fulton, and Alaska-Yukon-

Pacific commemorative issues, but it is doubtful if the two over-size commemoratives were made for business use. Some of the United States Auto Vending stamps were put up in a folded strip of paper that received the distinctive separation slits of that firm.

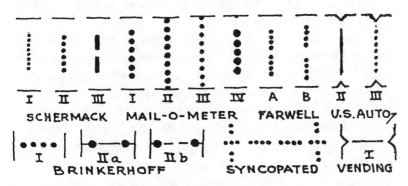

Fig. 11–2. Coil Perforations.

Many varieties may have been issued to please stamp collectors and those who wrote to the perforating companies were usually able to obtain unused stamps, often in blocks or larger pieces from companies that punched the entire sheets before slitting and winding the coils. Stamps in this category show the Schermack III, Mail-O-Meter I, and Chambers perforations.

One of the great rarities of the private-coil group is the 4-cent stamp, series 1902-1903, in the Schermack III type. Only ten thousand were issued in imperforate form and all were punched in Detroit. Karl Koslowski, a collector of that city, had the opportunity to purchase an imperforate sheet but did not take advantage of it. When he reconsidered and stopped at the Schermack office on the following morning, the entire lot had been punched. He obtained eighty copies and sent thirty-five out on mail. When the scarcity of this variety became known, about twenty-five used copies were recovered.

All of these private perforations are desirable on cover and many are still available on old correspondence. Some are so scarce that they have not been listed or priced on cover. Unused stamps are collected in pairs and strips, and the varieties include the paste-ups, perhaps with plate number or imprint, and the guide lines. Used copies that have not been soaked should be examined for paste-ups.

One other private perforation, although arbitrarily denied catalog listing, is worthy of that recognition. This is the Attleboro perforation, applied to the 1-cent stamps, series 1908-1909, and to the 2-cent Alaska-Yukon-Pacific issue, and used only by the Attleboro Stamp Company. The Chambers perforation had but a single user also, and the fact that the Attleboro was used by a stamp company should not condemn it. In addition there were no so-called experimental varieties or any unnecessary values.

UNITED STATES GOVERNMENT COILS

Flat-Press Coils Perforated

The first coils produced at the Bureau of Engraving and Printing were made by pasting sheets of stamps end to end, or side to side, after they had been perforated 12 in one direction. The pasted webs were then put through machines that slit them into strips and coiled them in rolls of five hundred or a thousand stamps. They were weak at the perforation lines and not much better than coils made by tearing up fully perforated sheets, except that the smooth, straight edges eliminated one source of trouble.

The first issue, February 18, 1908, was of the 1- and 2-cent values, series of 1902-1903, in coils with the stamps end to end or side to side, and the 5-cent value in endwise coils. Soon the series of 1908-1909 replaced these with endwise coils in 1-, 2-, 4-, and 5-cent values, and sidewise coils in 1-, 2-, 5-, and 10-cent values.

When the single-line U.S.P.S. watermarked paper was introduced in 1910 the 12-gauge coils continued but only in 1- and 2-cent endwise and 1-, 2-, and 3-cent sidewise coils. Within a few weeks the perforation gauge was changed to 8½ in the hope that it would please all users. The 1-cent value appeared in endwise and sidewise coils December 12, 1910, and soon both types of 2-cent coils followed. After a year the 3-cent value was issued in sidewise coils followed by the 4-cent in 1912 and the 5-cent in 1913.

The new 1- and 2-cent stamps, with numerals of value, were available in endwise coils and the 1-cent in sidewise coils March 18, 1912, and the 2-cent sidewise March 21, 1912.

Complaints were made that the coils were too strong and tore as easily across the stamps as along the perforations, and beginning April 25, 1914, the gauge was changed to 10. This has proved satisfactory and is still in use.

In 12-gauge coils, care must be taken to avoid frauds for the endwise coils can be faked by trimming overwidth strips from booklets panes. However, the watermark in booklet panes reads up and down, and not across the stamp. Guide lines across a pair are not proof of genuineness for these occur in booklet panes also. Another possibility is that a faker may use imperforate stamps and falsify all perforations. Sidewise coils cannot be faked from booklet panes, but perforations may be added at the straight edges, although it is more difficult to match the central line of perforations than it is to supply all perforations on imperforate stamps.

The usual varieties of paste-up, perhaps with imprint or plate number, should be looked for as well as pairs with line between.

The great rarity of the flat-plate stamps is a 3-cent sidewise coil issued January 24, 1911. This has a single-line watermark and is perforated 12, vertically. The one small issue went to the Bell Pharmaceutical Company, of Orangeburg, New York, and was used in mailing samples. It was noticed at once and a few unused copies were obtained from the company and some used copies from sample packages. At one time the recorded total consisted of a mint strip of four, three mint pairs, and three or four mint and used singles, but now there is reason to believe that double this number of copies exist.

All coil stamps of the 1902-1903 series are extremely scarce, and any perforated 12 are worth having, even the latest issued on single-line U.S.P.S. paper.

Imperforate Coils

Beginning with the 1902-1903 series, the United States issued imperforate coils in sidewise and endwise types. Both 1-cent and 2-cent values were available in this series as well as the 1908-1909 designs in both watermarks and in the new design with numerals of value. The 4-cent and 5-cent values, series 1908-1909, were sold only in endwise coils, but the 2-cent Lincoln commemorative appeared in both types.

These stamps are difficult to identify, and those that have been scissored apart provide little on which to base an identification. Those placed on cover by an affixing machine show peculiarities due to the type of cutter used, and these may be considered as a positive identification. Rare varieties should be accompanied by a certificate of genuineness.

Rotary Press Coils

So much hand work was required in the production of coils that Benjamin Stickney, the mechanical engineer of the Bureau of Engraving and Printing, was assigned to find a solution. Also involved were complaints that the paste-ups jammed some machines. Experiments were made with offset printing on pre-gummed paper, with perforating performed by the same machine. The advantages of this process were that the paper was dry and therefore there was no shrinkage problem, spacing was uniform, and there were no paste-ups as the press was web fed and could produce coils of any size.

However, offset printing was rejected on account of the real or imaginary danger of counterfeiting and Mr. Stickney was directed to seek other means. Eventually he produced a web-fed rotary press that printed stamps from cylindrical intaglio plates on paper only slightly dampened. This was the Stickney Press as announced in the report of the Postmaster General, June 30, 1914.

The first stamps from this press appeared June 30, 1914, when the 2-cent value was issued imperforate in sidewise coils on single-line U.S.P.S. watermarked paper. This was the only imperforate rotary-press coil. By March 1916, the 1- and 2-cent values were on sale in endwise coils, the 1-, 2-, 3-, 4-, and 5-cent values in sidewise coils, all perforated.

Late in 1916 the change to unwatermarked paper was made and by 1919 the 1-, 2-, and 3-cent values were on sale, in endwise coils, the 1-, 2-, 3-, 4-, and 5-cent values in sidewise coils. Early in 1922 the 10-cent value was added in the latter type.

When the series of 1922-1925 came into use coils were produced in sidewise form in the 1-, 1½-, 2-, 3-, 4-, 5-, and 10-cent values, endwise form in the 1-, 1½-, and 2-cent values. Other coils during this period include the Edison commemorative, the 1½-cent full face Harding, and the 4-cent value picturing Taft.

In 1932 a new 3-cent stamp, showing Washington instead of Lincoln, came into use and was issued in both coil forms, and in the same year the current 6-cent value was issued in sidewise coils to handle double-weight letters.

The Presidential series of 1938 brought a complete change and January 20, 1939, the 1-, 1½-, 2-, 3-, 4-, 4½-, 5-, 6-, and 10-cent values were issued in sidewise coils. January 27 the 1-, 1½-, 2-, and 3-cent values went on sale in endwise coils. These were superseded by the 1954 series and these, in turn, by the 1966-73 series.

On December 1, 1927, the post office began to furnish coils of three thousand stamps with the gum side out, for use in machines which previously had required private coils or rewound government coils. With this change all imperforate sheets and private perforations were eliminated.

The United States has issued air mail regular size stamps in endwise and sidewise coils which are called vertical and horizontal coils by the stamp collector. On horizontal coils there are joint lines between the stamps which occur every 17 stamps, and pairs with joint lines between them are prized by the collector more than ordinary pairs.

Rotary-press stamps may be distinguished from flat-plate stamps by appearance or by dimensions, the latter method being the most definite. Stamps in the rotary-press endwise coils are taller than normal but the width is normal, while stamps from sidewise coils are wider than normal but the height is unchanged. The normal measurements are those of the flat-plate stamps. The reason for these differences is evident, for the rotary-press plates are flat when made, and then are curved to fit the press cylinders. This bending stretches the outer surface of the plate in the direction of the curve, and the stamps become longer or wider depending on how they are placed on the plate. Stamps for the endwise coils are placed heads up on the horizontal cylinder, while those for sidewise coils lie on their sides.

About the only constant variety in rotary-press coils is produced by the joint line between the plates on a cylinder. These joints receive ink just as any other recess in an intaglio plate and print as lines of various widths. They occur seventeen stamps apart on sidewise coils and fifteen apart on endwise coils. Partial plate numbers may be found on the margins of badly centered coils but they are usually difficult to identify.

The Stickney press made an important contribution to the stamp-printing industry and several foreign governments were allowed to buy presses or working drawings. Among those using the presses were Canada, Sweden, Poland and Czechoslovakia. Although none may have continued long with Stickney presses, the invention spurred others to build presses for the same type of printing, and the results are largely due to Stickney's work.

FOREIGN GOVERNMENT COILS

Although many foreign countries have issued coils, few can be identified as they usually were made from sheet stamps and not printed from special plates.

Canada has issued coils continuously since 1912 and these separate into three groups identified by changes in the printing companies and the processes used.

Those from 1912 to March 31, 1930, were printed by the American Bank Note Company, of Canada (which became the Canadian Bank Note Company on November 30, 1922), and all coils were made by pasting together partly perforated sheets of regular stamps which then were slit and coiled into rolls of five hundred, as a rule. Two gauges of perforations were used: 12 for endwise coils in 1-, 2-, and 3-cent values and 8 for endwise coils in 1- and 2-cent values, sidewise coils in 1-, 2-, and 3-cent and 2-plus-1-cent war tax, all of the 1912-1924 series, and sidewise coils in 1- and 2-cent values of the 1928 series. All have paste-ups at intervals of twenty stamps and all except the perforation 8, endwise coils occur in all the colors of the sheet stamps.

The British-American Bank Note Company held the contract from April 1, 1930, until March 31, 1935, and printed continuous coils on Stickney presses. These were without paste-ups and show a joint line at intervals of twenty-five stamps. All were sidewise coils, perforated 8½ in 1-, 2-, and 3-cent values of both the George V Maple Leaf and Medallion types of 1930-1931 and 1933, and in all the colors used for the sheet stamps.

Since April 1, 1935, the Canadian Bank Note Company has printed the stamps and has produced sidewise coils on a modified cylinder press equipped to use a web instead of sheets. The curved printing plate occupies only a portion of the cylinder surface and the web of paper advances and then stops to await the plate at the next revolution of the cylinder. This is a slow process and while it produces a continuous web, theoretically without paste-ups, there are many "jumps" or gaps between impressions and much misalignment of rows, and it is frequently necessary to cut the web to remove them. Thus, there are paste-ups at irregular intervals. There are no joint lines in this method of printing.

All these stamps were perforated 8 until 1948, the list including the 1-, 2-, and 3-cent values of the George V, 1935 series, the George VI, 1937 series, and the 1-, 2-, 3-, and 4-cent values of the George VI, 1943 series. In 1948 the gauge was changed to 9½ and stamps so perforated included the last four mentioned above, the same four values of the 1950-1951 series, including the 1- and 3-cent values with "Postes-Postage" omitted, and the 2-, 3-, and 4-cent Elizabeth, 1953 series, and the 2-, 3-, and 5-cent Elizabeth, series 1954. In all cases these stamps appeared in all the colors used for sheet stamps.

Sweden, another purchaser of a Stickney press, now issues practically all her stamps in coil form. The first coil was issued in 1920 and since then every issue except four commemorative sets has been available in coil form. All are of the sidewise type except some oversize varieties that are turned so that the short side of the large stamp is equal to the longer side of the normal issues. These large stamps are on a band of paper of the same width as the regular postage issues and are vended or handled in the same machines.

Sweden's booklet stamps are actually coil stamps in a double-width band separated by a row of perforations. After some use of Goebel presses, Sweden now prints all stamps on Wifag presses in coil form, but the change from sheets to coils should be credited to the Stickney press.

Czechoslovakia used a Stickney press for a number of years and first issued coils in 1926 or 1927. Only a few values and types were issued in this form up to 1931 when the idea appears to have been abandoned.

In The Netherlands, German affixing machines came into use in 1920 and the first coils were made by pasting up strips of the regular sheet stamps. Some of these stamps can be identified by the punched initials of the user made with an auxiliary device provided for the purpose. The coils were unsatisfactory for the usual reason and the postal authorities soon altered the horizontal perforation of the sheets used for coils by removing part of the pins. The only perforations left at the ends were two groups of four holes separated and bounded by bridges of paper without holes. These were called "syncopated" or "interrupted" perforations.

Stamps with this perforation, cataloged as type A, were ready for sale in 1925 in values below 1 gulden and were first used on October 25. All values except the 35-cent were issued that year and in 1936 the new 9-cent value was available. In addition to those used in affixing machines, others were sold to the public in post office vending machines.

Late in 1927 the 7½-cent value was issued in sidewise coils made from sheets with a special perforation on all four sides. There were two groups of three holes at the ends and two groups of four holes at the sides. The issue was limited to three coils of a thousand stamps each for an Amsterdam banking house.

In February, 1928, this perforation was modified to two groups of four holes at each side (listed as type B), and all values then current were issued except the 10-cent red, the 22½-cent olive-brown, and the 35-cent olive-brown. Additional values issued later in 1928 and others issued in 1929 were also perforated in this type. It proved to be too strong for the machines and was abandoned. Type C, with a single pin omitted on the short sides near the corners, was tried about 1930. The values of 6 cents and under and the 10-, 20-, 21-, 30-, and 50-cent values were given this perforation. New values issued in 1935 and later had no syncopated perforations, so the idea probably was abandoned about 1934.

All values in all types of perforations, except the 7½-cent experimental type issued between types A and B, were sold in sheet form to collectors at post offices.

Some semi-postal stamps of 1925, 1926, and 1927 have type A perforations; those of 1929 have type B, and those of 1930 to 1933 type C. So far as known no semi-postal stamps were issued in coils, these varieties being made solely for collectors.

Those collecting the syncopated perforations of The Netherlands should keep a sharp watch for "perfins," or punched stamps, as these were used by about sixty-five firms only and identify the early coils of that country.

SOUVENIR AND MINIATURE SHEETS

Small sheets of stamps that could be mounted entire on an album page were attractive to collectors long before the first souvenir sheet was issued. It may be news to many that large numbers of the world's stamps were issued in small panes, rather than in the panes of fifty or a hundred to which we are accustomed.

One method used to distinguish between souvenir and miniature sheets is to class as souvenirs all that have inscriptions and decorations calling attention to some event or reason for the sheet. The others may have imprints, plate numbers, and the like, but nothing more than would be standard for the regular sheets.

It is possible to make a complete collection of souvenir sheets but quite impossible to gather all the miniature sheets that have been issued since 1840. The usual limit for both kinds of sheets is placed at twenty-five stamps.

When a person begins to accumulate miniature sheets he will meet some of the rarer stamps, many of which were issued in panes of fifteen, ten, or even less, as were the famous St. Louis postmaster's provisionals. Sheets of twenty-five are not unusual because some countries issue high-value stamps in small panes to facilitate distribution to their smaller post offices.

Many souvenir sheets have been issued in connection with philatelic exhibitions and conventions. These have a double attraction for collectors and may constitute a separate collection. The sheets may have a single stamp, or a pair or block or strip, and the stamps may be alike or all may differ. At first they were limited to the regular postage issues but soon they appeared among the semipostal issues, and Czechoslovakia has issued a souvenir sheet of newspaper stamps.

The same country issued one of the most famous sheets in its national-anthem souvenir of 1934. This contains fifteen stamps with appropriate titles and borders and the musical score and words of "Kde domov muj," the national anthem, and is as expensive as it is impressive.

The sheets of six stamps in bilingual pairs issued by South Africa for the Johannesburg Philatelic Exhibition of 1936 are perhaps the only sheets with postal and commercial advertising tabs on the stamps. The side margins bear inscriptions concerning the exhibition. One very unusual sheet was issued by Belgium in 1941. It had nine different value stamps, each depicting a different Belgian city's coat of arms in full color.

While it is now customary to issue sheets in both perforated and imperforate form, there was little complaint until Roumania found a new way to exploit collectors. This country was not content with sheets of regular postage sold at over double face value with the excess assigned to charity, and turned to semipostals selling them at prices as high as six times the stated value.

PRECANCELLED STAMPS

The word precancel is applied to a cancellation that has been placed on a stamp on outgoing mail before it reaches the post office. Today adhesive stamps are precancelled before they are affixed, but in the very early period they often were placed on the envelope and cancelled along with some other printing operation. Stamped envelopes and postal cards are similarly precancelled today but the latter usually are handled by a job printer who has other work to print on the cards at the same time.

Precancelled stamps form one of the largest groups in topical collecting. The cancellation is all important and the stamp secondary. In many collections no attention is paid to varieties, the stamp being considered only a medium to show a cancellation.

United States Precancels

United States precancels are classified as pioneer, classic, city types, city coils, and bureau prints.

The pioneers date back to the earliest stamps, perhaps to

1847, although the 5- and 10-cent stamps of 1847 with a portion of a grid, as applied at Wheeling, Virginia (now West Virginia), appear to have been given a control marking by a postmaster rather than a precancellation.

There are examples of 1-cent 1851 stamps with the printed precancellation "Paid," and of the 1- and 3-cent stamps of 1857 precancelled at Cumberland, Maine. Other examples are the Glastonbury, Connecticut, "G" on the 3-cent stamps of 1869, the Glen Allen, Virginia, star on various stamps from 1873 to 1883, and the full town name of Burlington, Vermont, on the 1-cent stamps of 1887. In some other examples the precancellations consist of bars or lines made with a brush or pen, or by printing, and were evidently applied to entire sheets at one time.

The use of precancels spread rapidly between 1890 and 1900. While there had been no governmental sanction, the practice must have been looked on with favor on account of the labor saved in post offices. Early in 1890 the *Youth's Companion* used large quantities of 1-cent stamps precancelled "Boston" in mailing that magazine. This was the first precancel similar to the later accepted types. It showed the city and state names separated by a horizontal bar, with two additional bars at top and bottom and short thin bars at either end of the words.

The precancels of this early period are usually called "lines and bars" in the catalogs. In precancel nomenclature lines are continuous across the sheet of stamps and any ends that show are at the margins of the sheet. The bars were designed to be contained on the face of a stamp and not overrun the margins. Under this definition bars include all manner of designs such as the Glen Allen star, the Glastonbury "G," the Menominee "M," the New York monogram in an oval of pearls for postage due issues, and many others.

With the spread of precancellation cities began to compete in original designs, and in this classic period appeared the Lansing spider web of railroads, the Fort Wayne tombstone, the Jackson, Michigan, oval, and the Indianapolis circle with "USA."

Chicago, Boston, Minneapolis, Racine, Binghamton, Attica (Indiana), and several other cities began to use simple designs that included the month and year of use. These had their start in 1901 and were soon discontinued, but it is of interest that in July, 1939, the Post Office Department ordered the use of dates and the initials of the user to prevent fraud in the reuse of precancels.

On May 23, 1903, the department advised postmasters that precancelling stamps was permissible, but suggested a standard form. It recommended including the city and state names in two lines with a plain line above and below. Since that time precancels have been more or less uniform, although some postmasters have been very free in their interpretation of the standard.

Precancels of the period 1903-1923 are city types and these still are used in many places. They were locally applied by postal employees, or were printed by local printers when larger quantities were needed. Almost all categories of stamps were precancelled in this manner—regular issues, postage due, commemoratives, parcel post, air post—both in flat-plate printings and in the later rotary-press issues. The cancellations were applied by machine or by hand. The machine processes included ordinary printing, multigraphing, mimeographing, and a special coil printing. The hand processes included rubber stamps, rollers, and hand electros.

All such processes are dependent on the human equation and numerous errors and varieties are found. Workmen feel that it is not important for the job to be of the finest quality, for after all they are cancelling stamps, not printing them, and a little more cancellation will do no harm if the design is still legible.

MACHINE PRECANCELLATION

There may be considerable difference in printed precancellations for it takes a quantity of type to set up a hundred identical units, and a few wrong-font letters may be found in the designs. For this reason the usual precancelling plate has only fifty subjects and the sheets of stamps are put to press twice. If the postmaster has no objection the plate will not be reversed after the first printing. Instead the sheets will be turned, thus inverting half the precancels.

When stereotypes or electrotypes from typeset forms are used there will be as many errors as in the typeset group, with double prints, diagonal prints, and missed marginal rows. None, obviously, can be discarded as printer's waste, and the gummed and perforated sheets can be very cranky in a job press.

Multigraph machines using electros produce precancels that often cannot be distinguished from printed work unless the inking is done with a ribbon that shows its texture.

Mimeograph precancels are made with a stencil that has the whole number of subjects typed on it, with various rows of characters to simulate the precancel lines or bars. There is almost certain to be variation, for it is hardly possible to type a hundred identical subjects.

A device to precancel early stamp coils took the form of a rewinding machine with a printing roller to put one precancel subject on each stamp. These precancels at first copied the local city types, but since they could not be spaced regularly they were superseded by a type showing a band of subjects, each in a box, closely spaced so that almost two fell on each stamp. This change also enabled a coil printer to handle both sidewise and endwise coils with the same cancelling roller.

HAND PRECANCELLATIONS

Cities with a limited demand for precancelled stamps were provided at first with a flat rubber stamp, carrying from one to twenty-five subjects. The larger sizes generally used a black indelible ink that appeared gray when applied. The hand method is subject to more errors of application than printing, for nothing is fixed and the handstamp may be applied in any position or at any angle. The rubber deteriorated badly and when cleaned with certain solvents it swelled, producing wavy lines and fuzzy letters. When the user had a heavy or nervous hand, the results were far from legible. About 1932 such conditions caused a change to electros of twenty-five subjects curved slightly to allow the impression to be rocked on with less pressure and more legibility than possible with a flat handstamp.

Another form of handstamp was a cylindrical rubber roller with several precancelling units on its perimeter. These were used in various widths with one or more rows of units. A special roller bearing several staggered rows of units was used by mail-order houses that had permission to precancel stamps received as remittances.

The general revision of the regulations governing precancels that was made effective in July 1938, reduced the number of precancels with city names only by requiring that the initials of the user and the month and year of use be shown, or added in a line above the town name. This caused a reduction in the height of all forms to allow space for the added line. The modified designs are called "narrows."

BUREAU-PRINT PRECANCELLATIONS

This term indicates that the precancellation is applied in the Bureau of Engraving and Printing. Excepting only the "experimental bureau prints," the mark is applied as the stamps are printed. In 1916 the Post Office Department made a survey to learn if precancels could be printed more cheaply by the bureau than by local post offices or local contract printers. All offices that estimated a need of four million or more precancels during the year were asked to submit printing costs. Of the twenty that reported, only three showed excessive costs, and during 1916, precancels were furnished for New Orleans, Augusta, Maine, and Springfield, Massachusetts. These were the "experimental bureau prints." Evidently little money was saved for the idea was dropped until the bureau's rotary presses were in full operation, printing nearly all of the low value postage issues. Then it was suggested that a small printing unit be added to the rotary press, just in advance of the gumming unit, and the precancellation applied at minimum cost. This is the process now used. The press combines engraving and typographic units, and the precancelling unit may be disengaged, fitted with plates for another city, and again put to work without the necessity of stopping the main press, which continues to print uncancelled stamps while the change is being made. The first precancels of this type, on the 1-cent value of the 1923 issue, appeared May 3, 1923. In general, bureau prints may be distinguished from similar city types by the following points. All have lines, not bars, that run across the entire sheet, except at the extreme side-row margins. They are never found on stamps perforated 11 or 12, but only on those perforated 10, or 11 by 10½ (10½ by 11 in the case of stamps in horizontal format). They have never been applied to commemorative issues. They always have a single line above and below. They always read normally on stamps of vertical format, and should read down on those of horizontal format, but three orders of 20-cent stamps for Dallas, Denver, and Detroit were printed reading up and are classed as errors. All printed precancellations on rotary-press coil stamps are bureau prints.

To obtain bureau-printed precancels a post office must order at least 500,000 copies of any value in sheet form, or half that number in coils, but orders of less than half a million have been accepted for values above ten cents.

Very few other bureau-print errors have been recorded and all appear to be misspelled names. Broken letters and misalignment of names are classed as varieties rather than errors.

UNITED STATES REVENUE PRECANCELS

Almost from the start in 1862, the proprietary and private proprietary revenue issues were precancelled before being affixed to the taxed bottles or packages. These are very popular with collectors, not only as precancellations, but because of their neatness in comparison to the handstamped or pen-cancelled copies.

Documentary stamps also have been precancelled, particularly those in use at the time of the Spanish-American War. In recent years playing-card stamps have been issued in coil form by the Bureau of Engraving and Printing and precancellation during the original printing is now the usual procedure. These are collected by precancel collectors as well as by revenue enthusiasts.

Foreign Precancels

CANADA

Canadian post offices began to precancel stamps in 1889 using any of proper denomination that were on hand. They included the 15-cent of 1868, the 1- and 2-cent values of 1869, the 6- and 10-cent of 1872, the 5-cent of 1875, and the issue of 1882.

The first precancellations consisted of various straight, wavy, or broken lines, and were applied to sheets with rubber rollers. There is reason to believe that some rollers were locally made, while others were supplied by the postal authorities at Ottawa. Unless these stamps are on cover it is almost impossible to discover where they were used.

Presently a more or less standard design of three lines was adopted, the central line being wavy, and in 1903 the design showed the city and province names separated by two closely spaced bars. In 1922 a design with three pairs of closely spaced bars was authorized, but perhaps for the smaller offices only. There were three varieties of this type and some of these and also some of the 1903 designs continue in use at the present time.

When a new post office accounting system was instituted in 1931, it was decided to discard the city names and substitute numerals, using those which had been assigned to various cities under the money-order system. These now account for nearly all the precancels in use.

FRANCE

The first French precancels (*préoblitérés* or *préos*) were made by affixing stamps to newsprint intended for newspaper use. When the paper was printed, the text or title precancelled the stamp at the corner of the sheet.

The first stamp to be precancelled thus was the 1-centime value of 1853, but in 1868 special newspaper stamps were introduced and used until 1870. Following the proclamation of the republic in that year, the Bordeaux issue came into use, and from that time until 1893 nearly all the French issues were precancelled throughout France to some extent, though after 1893 until 1908 they were used only in Savoy and the south of France. The non-Parisian issues of this period are quite scarce.

In 1893 the Paris post office began to use hand rollers bearing a repetition of the words "Paris—Impr.," in two lines with the day and month in two more. A variant roller included the year in a fifth line. These were experimental and the stamps are quite rare.

Printed precancels were introduced between 1920 and 1922, with one type for Paris, with "Postes—Paris—France- 1922," in three lines. These also were little used and the stamps are not common. Both types were replaced in November 1922, by a double half-circle, with the words "AFFRANCHts—POSTES" in two lines. These were also placed in use in Algeria (1924), Tunis (1929), and Monaco (1943).

Postage due stamps were precancelled with a roller in 1929 and for a time regular postage stamps at high value were overprinted with a large "R" for use as due stamps. Various stamps that were not may appear to be precancels; for example, those with the overprints "Annule" (cancelled) and "Specimen," which were used by students in the postmen's school.

Also there are tax and due stamps overprinted with triangles, either blank or inclosing one of the letters A, B, or R, or with circles containing a Roman numeral representing a Parisian sub-

I (top). Examples showing that well-centered stamps may be affected by cancellations, from very fine to very poor. II (above). Various grades of centering, from well centered to badly off center in two directions. All with average to fine cancellations. III (below). A range from extremely sharp early impression down through various grades to a dull impression from a worn plate.

IV (above). X-ray investigation. *Netherlands, 1852 issue, 15 c. orange:* (1) Photograph. (2) Low-voltage radiograph shows the stamp image due to metallic printing ink, while the cancellation of organic material is absent. Watermark is faintly outlined. (3) Autoelectronograph shows the metallic ink design clearly, while the cancellation of carbon and grease is not reproduced. (4) Electronograph shows the watermark clearly, but little else. *El Salvador official stamp. Printed in blue, gold, rose, and green, with black overprint:* (5) Photograph. (6) Autoelectronograph reproducing only the metallic base inks. *Bremen, 1866 issue, 10 grote black:* (7) Photograph. (8) Low-voltage radiograph which shows that all four margins were added, the black dots being caused by mineral filler in the modern paper. (Courtesy Dr. H. C. Pollack and Mr. C. F. Bridgman.) V (below). Issue to commemorate the Girl Scout Jamboree at Gödöllö, Hungary, in 1939. VI (bottom). Left and center: Stamps honoring the Boy Scouts. (Acme Photos.) Right: Australian topical issue. (Australian News and Information Bureau.)

post office. The numerals I, VII are those of the main post office and were not used on any stamps.

On several occasions during rush periods a small "T" in a triangle has been used in precancelling. Examples must be on cover to have any particular value, since the "T" is the usual indication of postage due. France has issued several stamps which were never available except in precancelled form. One was issued in 1926 with the precancellation altering the value of the stamp. The 60-centime light violet issue of 1924 was altered by printing the new value, 55 centimes, with bars to obscure the original value while the sheets were being precancelled.

A 90-centime dull green stamp of 1946 and a series of four stamps of 1954 are other examples which do not exist in uncancelled form.

BELGIUM

Belgium began to precancel stamps on December 2, 1893, using an oval design with "Bruxelles," the full date, "Journaux" in three lines. Soon a bilingual style was adopted, the inscription in French above the date, in Flemish below. This was in use until May, 1911.

For printed matter only, Belgium in 1894 began to use a frame with the name of the locality in French and the year, but in 1910 this was replaced in various places with a bilingual form in which the date separated the town names in French and Flemish.

The precancellation "Belgique—Belgie" with date was current from 1929 to 1938, and until 1937 it sometimes included numerals to alter the value of the stamps being precancelled. New 5-centime values were made in 1929 by overprinting values no longer in use. Similar value changes appeared during the following years.

A large hexagon with the same inscription was used only in 1938, then a smaller hexagon with post horn in 1939, and a small rectangle with post horn from 1939 to 1951 or later.

LUXEMBOURG

This country began to use precancels in 1900, with a design similar to that of Belgium, with the word "Luxembourg" and the date. In 1900 this was replaced by an unframed design which was used until 1925.

THE NETHERLANDS

The precancels of this country are scarce and recent listings are far from complete. The design was on a roller and shows two continuous parallel lines with small circular cachets spaced around the roller. Three short bars are placed between the circles, and within each circle is the town name and a smaller circle which may have the date or be blank.

There are no records to show how the dated and undated cancellations were assigned, but it has been noted in one or more cases that the dated cachets alternated with the undated on a roller. The range of dates extends from 1912 to about 1923.

AUSTRIA

The newspaper tax stamps of Austria from 1858 until 1890 are found overprinted with newspaper text or the masthead of a paper. There is no regularity of position and the language of the overprint may be almost any, as the stamps were used only to collect a tax on foreign papers.

The stamps are not rare off the paper but are scarce on piece and almost unknown on entire papers. There were some forgeries made to evade the tax, but it is odd that a publisher would run such a risk for the small amount involved.

Newspaper wrappers with imprinted stamps with designs of current adhesives were precancelled from 1910 to 1920 with a design of three compartments surrounded by inscriptions. The cancellation was applied to the wrappers by the same printer who produced the stamps but at a second printing. These precancels were made for the exclusive use of the German—Austrian Alps association. From 1910 until September, 1914, the wrappers were valid for only two weeks; they then were valid for one month.

The place and date of precancellation and the period of validity are indicated in the compartments. This cancellation is found on stamps of the 2-heller Mercury type, 3- and 5-heller 1908 Jubilee, 3- and 5-heller Crown, 20- and 40-heller Arms, and on the 2-, 6-, 9-, and 18-heller values of the new Mercury type.

HUNGARY

The most common Hungarian precancels are the printed forms used for newspapers from 1900 to 1914. They show the name of the paper, the year, and date, in four lines without frame; for example, "Budapesti—Hirlap—1908—Okt. 10." They were printed by the publications using them. Occasionally the papers made use of handstamps, of similar design but in larger type. These are easily identified by their careless application to the stamps.

A three-line form in smaller type was used for the "Pesti-Hirlap" precancel from the end of October, 1913, until October 9, 1914.

On occasion a newspaper made use of a circular handstamp like a townmark with a newspaper name instead of the town name. These may have been used after the supply of precancels printed for that day had been exhausted. One newspaper only, *Pesti-Naplo-Budapest*, used an oval handstamp. The rectangular handstamps used by the smaller papers and by some foreign papers are scarcer than the printed precancellations. Examples include those of *Pesti-Hirlap-Budapest* among others.

As a general rule all precancels are dated, those of the *Pester-Lloyd-Budapest* being an exception, and all are framed except those of the *Budapester-Tagblatt, Kiadohivatala* which is in three lines above the date.

The handstamps usually were made of rubber with only a few in metal.

Precancel Collections

For a general collection, a large unmixed lot should be sorted first by states, then by cities, and finally by precancel types and stamp issues. Special albums are available for general and limited collections, but since an almost-empty album is very uninteresting, it is wiser to start with plain pages in a ring binder. This has an additional advantage in that the growing collection may be grouped in various ways. If good peelable hinges are used, you may later transfer your collection to a permanent album without using new hinges.

Limited collections may be made of a state, group of states, or single cities, in all of the type categories or a single type. The commemoratives, postage dues, or parcel post issues suggest other limits. Collections of one stamp or one color have a tendency to become monotonous if very extensive.

Synoptic or simplified collections appeal to some people. In these an attempt is made to show a single example of every stamp which has been precancelled. Other collections may show every type of precancellation which has been used, or an example from each city which has used precancelled stamps. The last mentioned goal is not too difficult when only bureau prints are collected, for here the form is standard and varieties are limited. Other collections may be of coil stamps only, or they may extend back into the classic period and show ornamental designs or dated types.

METERED MAIL AND METER IMPRESSIONS

With metered mail approaching the point where it now accounts for almost half of the postage paid in the United States, some collectors are trying to gather all types and varieties. The experimental types and those used when meters were first approved are very scarce.

A postage meter was patented in England in 1884, and soon another patent was granted for a coin-operated machine, but the author can find no record of the use of either. The earliest records seem to point to the antipodes as the birthplace of franking machines, as they were called, with experiments in Australia and New Zealand. Trials were made in Brisbane in 1903, and in other Australian cities soon after. Attempts to amend the Australian postal laws to permit the use of machines met with defeat, and the subject was not considered again until 1920.

Meanwhile a machine had been placed in use in New Zealand in 1904 and this may have been the first to operate officially. After a few months it was withdrawn when it became apparent that washers and slugs would serve as coins to operate it. When machines were placed in use in several Bavarian post offices in 1910, the American press predicted that postage stamps soon would become extinct.

The first use of a machine in England was in the London post office, January 25, 1912, but this was removed on August 31 of that year, perhaps on account of misuse as in New Zealand.

The installation of meters or rate printers commenced in Germany in 1919 and in Wurttemberg in 1920. Germany soon allowed the machines to be installed in business offices, realizing their economy over postage stamps. These had a counting device to lock after a certain number of impressions. This was controlled by a punched card paid for at the post office and inserted in the machine. The users of German meters were allowed to include a slogan, name or trademark in the printing device. One make of machine was designed to print values from one to 9999 pfennigs, but usually a machine printed only a few rates and large packets required several impressions to make up the required postage.

In America inventors had difficulties in getting machines approved for use and not until 1921 were they able to proceed. In the previous year the Universal Postal Union had authorized the use of meter impressions in international mails.

The growth of metered mail has been rapid and there has been a constant improvement in the machines. Starting with a single-rate printer which would handle nothing but identical pieces of mail, they were developed to use interchangeable rate printers and finally to the type which prints any value from one-half cent upward.

The metering unit is set at the post office to equal the amount of money paid in, and the machine will operate until the meter registers zero, when it again must be taken to the post office. The meter unit is nowadays usually part of a machine which also seals the envelopes as it prints the indicia.

Fig. 11–3. United States Meter Impressions
(courtesy Philometer Society).

The multirate machines will print on envelopes or on a tape intended for parcels. Although several companies have manufactured meters, the Pitney-Bowes company is now well ahead of its competitors and has installed machines in post office parcel-post sections, where they greatly simplify the clerical work.

At first the meters had both permit and serial numbers but those in business offices today have only a serial number to identify the user. Impressions may be in any one of several colors.

The original idea of duplicating the color of a certain stamp had to be abandoned when the multirate machines were placed in use.

Strict regulations govern the use of meters. Mailing cannot be postponed without loss or inconvenience. Ninety per cent of the face value of incorrect or spoiled impressions may be recovered. Mail may be posted after the date of the impression, subject to the approval of the post office, which then overprints the meter mark to show a new date. In addition, metered impressions may be used for prepaid reply envelopes if properly accounted for.

At present over twelve hundred varieties of United States meter impressions are available, without including slogan or serial-number differences. When a new type of meter printer is introduced collectors soon learn its first serial number and attempt to obtain it or a number closely following and with as early a date as possible.

Collections are made of entire envelopes or of clippings measuring two by four inches (two by six if slogans are involved). Sometimes it is desirable to clip the entire top of an envelope to preserve the corner card to identify the user. When single-rate printers were in use multiple impressions often occupied large spaces on envelopes.

Meter tapes may be collected in any of the forms mentioned or may be soaked off the cover and mounted as stamps. Some must be folded as long tapes, for fifteen or more impressions are not uncommon. Almost every collector will try to show all possible marks from $0.00 up.

PERFINS

This coined word is the American name for stamps with perforated initials, monograms, or other devices to identify the user and render the stamps less liable to be stolen by employees. In England they are called "punch-perforated stamps" or "spifs," a word made from "stamps punched with initials of firms." Usually included are all punched stamps, such as the

"OS" ("on service") stamps of Australia, and the various specimen stamps provided for the Universal Postal Union by some countries.

The first official permission to mutilate stamps by punching was given by Great Britain following Joseph Sloper's patent on a machine in 1868. Belgium followed in 1872, France, Germany, Denmark, and Switzerland in 1876, and Austria in 1877. The practice later spread to nearly every country, and some have marked stamps for official use in this manner.

At least two countries have issued punched stamps as a regular postal issue. British Guiana brought out a locally printed typeset issue of two values in 1882 and punched it with the word "Specimen" to prevent counterfeiting. Both values and a subtype of each are found without the punched word, due to accidental omission. Later, in 1893, Paraguay issued a 10-centavo value in violet-blue which is available only in punched form.

United States regulations require that the punched design must not exceed a half-inch square with perforations not larger than $\frac{1}{32}$ of an inch in diameter.

Perfins may be collected in various ways. Some collectors try to obtain all possible stamp varieties with each design, but many more limit their collections to one or two stamps for each design. Those who collect in the first way have at least one page for each type of perfin and may never obtain a complete collection. Those who collect by designs may show the earliest and latest use obtainable, or may show two copies, one with the reverse exposed to show the design more clearly. Some collectors make contact photographs to mount beside the stamps instead of using a turned-over copy. Black album pages will accentuate the perforations. Perfins are also collected on cover and on two-inch strips from the tops of envelopes in order to show the postmark and corner card.

Collectors are not fully agreed on a classification system, but nearly all agree on a grouping by single letters, row letters, monograms, designs in circles or squares, ornamental designs, etc. Other collectors arrange the perfins according to the user:

that is, by states, cities, colleges, railroads, insurance companies, and the like. This latter arrangement may appeal to beginners more than the grouping by designs.

There is no record of the number of designs which have been used, nor of how many have become obsolete for various reasons, but collections exist containing upward of 3,500 types. This count does not include variations purposely incorporated into designs to indicate the actual place of use at branch offices, etc. One collector has reported 170 office identifications in the stamps used by a large life insurance company, and nearly as many in the case of a large electrical manufacturing company.

Postage meters are replacing punched stamps at a rapid rate, since the companies which had the greatest need for the stamps are able to solve their problems more easily with the machine. However, there are many small branches of large concerns that do not have sufficient mail to warrant the use of a meter, and they keep the use of punched stamps alive.

RED CROSS STAMPS

An interesting topical collection may be formed of stamps issued to raise funds for the Red Cross or to honor the organization and its founders. The International Red Cross came into being as the result of the distressing conditions witnessed by Jean Henri Dunant, a native of Switzerland, during and after the battle of Solferino. This indecisive action was fought on June 24, 1859, between the Franco-Italian troops under Napoleon III and the Austrian army under Franz Joseph. The retiring armies abandoned their wounded on the battlefield, and it has been reported that 22,000 Austrian soldiers and almost as many troops on the other side were lost in the engagement.

Dunant determined to prevent another such scene. In 1862 his pamphlet *A Souvenir of Solferino* presented an account of the ghastly affair. In a series of lectures before *La Société Genevoise d'Utilité Publique* he suggested a permanent committee to adopt an international code for the treatment of wounded in battle. This committee was formed and it drafted a basic code and called an international meeting in Geneva, October 26-29, 1863. This was attended by delegates from fourteen countries. The fundamental principles of the Red Cross were established at this meeting and the delegates returned home to make personal appeals. At a second meeting August 8, 1864, the Geneva Convention was adopted. Unfortunately, not all countries yet observe its terms.

The emblem of the Red Cross was devised from the Geneva cross and field of the arms of Switzerland with colors reversed. Dunant's life was consecrated to the alleviation of suffering and in 1901 he was awarded the Nobel Prize. He died in 1910 but was not honored on stamps until 1928, when his portrait was used in the Swiss "pro juventute" issue on the centenary of his birth. In 1939 Belgium honored Dunant in an issue commemorating the 75th anniversary of the Red Cross.

Portugal, in 1889, was the first country to recognize the Red Cross in a postal manner when it made a substantial contribution by issuing the Cruz Vermelha franchise stamps which gave free postage to its national organization.

During the First World War France issued semi-postal stamps to raise funds for Red Cross work, and since that time its issues and those of its colonies number about 110. The use of such stamps spread throughout the countries affected by the war until there were at least 230 issues by 47 countries. Spain and its colonies have nearly 150 issues for Red Cross funds, but this country and many others use postal tax stamps for the purpose.

Up to the present about 150 countries have issued more than 1100 varieties of stamps for the Red Cross, many being commemorative and not intended to raise money. Three stamps have been issued by the United States to honor the organization or its local founders. The Netherlands and the Dutch East Indies have issued Red Cross stamps. The first issues of Surinam were for the Groene Kruis (Green Cross), the title changing in 1941 to match the others.

The Red Crescent stamps of Turkey should be included in

the collection, as the purpose is identical. The crescent substitutes for the cross, an unwelcome symbol in a Moslem country. Turkish issues were postal tax stamps and first appeared in 1928, with frequent issues in recent years.

Collectors of these stamps have an international society, the Red Cross Stamp Study Circle, which fixes standards to which the stamps must conform to be acceptable to it. Its existence discourages unnecessary issues and "basket" issues which raise funds for many purposes with just enough assigned to the Red Cross to give the issue a charity rating.

CHRISTMAS SEALS

These colorful stickers, which now are in use throughout the world to raise money for the battle against tuberculosis, are the subject of a sideline collection for many stamp collectors. Their only postal significance is in their form and the fact that great numbers are used on greeting cards. One of the principal sources of early examples (1908–1914) is on Christmas cards of the period. The rule against their use on the face of covers was then seldom enforced and some postmarked copies are found.

At first the designs followed no standard but within a few years nearly all displayed the double-barred or Lorraine cross, the international symbol of the antituberculosis societies.

The Christmas seal was conceived by Einar Holboell, a Danish postal employee, and the sale of seals began in Denmark, Norway, and Sweden in 1904. They appeared in the United States in 1907, through the efforts of Miss Emily P. Bissel after a suggestion by Jacob Riis, a social service worker. The first sale was conducted by the Delaware chapter of the American Red Cross, and its success induced the national society to conduct a nationwide sale in 1908.

Until 1917 the annual sales were conducted by the Red Cross, but in 1918 and 1919 seals provided by the Red Cross were sold by the National Tuberculosis Society, and after 1919 the latter organization handled the entire work.

The Danish West Indies also issued seals in 1907, and yearly thereafter until the islands were bought by the United States in 1917. Renamed the Virgin Islands, the territory again issued seals, beginning in 1934. Other countries to make an early start in selling seals were Finland, Italy, and Canada, all in 1908; and Iceland and Switzerland in 1913. No others issued them until after the First World War, when the new Republic of Czechoslovakia brought out seals in 1919.

Since that time nearly all the nations have adopted this rather painless method of raising money to fight tuberculosis.

REVENUE STAMPS

This title, or the term fiscals, is intended to include all stamps used to collect taxes or fees. They have been required on a large variety of legal documents, commercial papers, luxuries, liquor, tobacco, proprietary and other articles that insure a constant source of revenue. Each country has its own list of taxable items. Today, stamp taxes are largely replaced by withholding at source, or hidden by taxing the dealer. This saves the cost of printing and distribution of the stamps.

In the early days of stamp collecting, revenue stamps had a status equal or superior to that of postage stamps, for they were available in greater numbers and in many countries were more interesting in design. However, as stamp-issuing countries grew in number it became necessary to limit collections and revenue stamps were soon eliminated. Another factor which prevents a modern renewal of interest in old revenue stamps is the lack of a general catalog, none having been published since the Forbin Fiscal Catalog expired about the time of the First World War.

Revenue stamps printed or embossed on the sheets of paper used for documents and other purposes antedate postage stamps by almost two centuries. The nearest approach to an adhesive fiscal stamp was made by attaching a small piece of colored paper to a document with a thin metal strip, after which it was embossed with a device similar to a notarial seal. The impression appears on the document, the slip of paper, and the metal strip and the attachment prevent removal for a second use.

Adhesive revenue stamps first appeared in 1854 in issues for Austria and her Italian province of Lombardy-Venice. By 1880, Great Britain, Belgium, Spain, France, and Switzerland had followed this lead and today there probably is no country which has not issued fiscal stamps. Some countries have a distinctive variety for each purpose, while others make use of one set of values for all taxes.

The specialized catalogs of a few countries, including the United States, list revenue stamps, and this may help postage-stamp collectors to understand certain things about their stamps, particularly when both postage and revenue stamps are produced by the same printers.

This condition did not exist in the United States until 1894 but the connection between postage and revenue stamps was always close for the former were printed from 1851 until 1861 by Toppan, Carpenter, Casilear and Company, and its successor Toppan, Carpenter and Company, while the same organization operating as Butler, Carpenter and Company and later as Joseph R. Carpenter Company, printed the revenue stamps from 1862 until 1875.

After 1875 the regular revenue issues were printed by the National Bank Note Company, which had printed the postage stamps from 1861 until 1873. In 1862 the Bureau of Engraving and Printing, which had been set up by the Treasury Department, began to print currency and various tax stamps, and in 1894 took over the production of all stamps. Knowing that the bureau produced both postage and revenue stamps makes it easier to understand how some values of the 1895 and the one-dollar value of the 1938 postage issue happen to be printed on revenue paper.

It is unfortunate for collectors that some countries issue a single set of stamps which are used both for postage and revenue. Undoubtedly there is a great saving in costs and since all money reaches the treasury, there is no reason for separate issues. The combination use, however, leads to very high values that cannot be used for postage but must be purchased to complete the set.

Collectors of these double-purpose stamps must be on the alert to avoid stamps with fiscal cancellations if they are collecting postage stamps. Some denominations may be scarce with postal cancellations and quite common with fiscal. It is not difficult to avoid pen-marked copies but there are handstamps used by banks and business firms which may be hard to detect.

When revenue stamps are found with postal cancellations it may be due to a shortage of proper postage stamps, but more than likely the stamp was used by mistake and slipped past a clerk. In a few countries this incorrect use is allowed and specialists might consider them to be provisionals. There also may be some postage stamps with revenue cancellations which could be included in either postage or revenue collections.

The so-called postal-fiscals of New Zealand and Victoria are examples in which the date of use is important. In 1881, New Zealand ordered that all fiscal stamps having a face value of one shilling or more were to be made available for postage. Similarly, Victoria, on January 1, 1884, began to honor all fiscals on hand or thereafter issued for the payment of postage. In either case a collector must have postally used copies.

Perhaps there would be more revenue-stamp collectors if there were not so many pen-marked copies. This was the usual method for cancelling stamps on checks and notes and there are perhaps a dozen such copies for every one with a handstamp cancellation.

In spite of the scarcity of handstamped revenue copies it is possible to make a complete collection of them, or as near complete as with pen-marked stamps. In addition a representative showing may be made of proprietary issues with printed cancellations—precancels without a doubt.

The first stamp taxes in America were levied by the Massachusetts Bay Colony in 1755 and by New York Colony in 1757. The first was in force two years, the second, four years. In 1765 the British introduced the famous "tea party" stamps in three categories, namely, for almanacs, newspapers, and for general purposes, but never to tax tea for that levy was not made until 1767 and the tax was not paid with stamps.

The federal government's first issue of revenue stamps for documents was placed in use July 1, 1798, and withdrawn February 28, 1801. These stamps were embossed and show the name of the state so that sixteen sets were required for the thirteen original states and Vermont, Kentucky, and Tennessee. The second issue omitted the state name and was in use only from March 1, 1801, until June 30, 1802. A third and final issue was made in 1814 to help pay the expenses of the War of 1812.

There were a few federal stamps for liquor licenses and other purposes late in the eighteenth century and again after the War of 1812. Documentary revenue stamps were issued by the states of Delaware, Virginia, and Maryland.

Following the outbreak of the Civil War a large series of adhesive stamps was issued to help defray the expenses of that conflict. The stamps were placed on sale in 1862. There were many titles—mostly documentary—to indicate the use and the numerous denominations increased in size according to the face value. After less than a year it was ordered the documentary values could be used indiscriminately.

Counterfeiting and stamp washing, a treatment to remove cancellations, caused a change in 1871. All values were now issued in bicolor designs on chemically treated paper that would expose tampering. All were in blue with black portraits and this caused so much confusion that about half of the denominations were changed in the frame color in 1872. Shortly after this issue appeared the tax was repealed for the most part, the remainder being modified so that only low values were required.

Proprietary issues were continued for some time with new values appearing as late as 1881. During the preceding period the Treasury Department granted users of proprietary stamps the privilege of having individual stamps bearing their names and trademarks. Those who took advantage of the offer were required to pay for the dies and printing but were allowed a discount of 5 to 10 per cent of the face value of all stamps printed.

These revenue stamps are known to collectors as "match and medicine" stamps, or "private-die proprietary stamps," and were used by a large number of concerns manufacturing matches or proprietary medicines, a few others making perfumes or playing cards, and one firm which canned fruit.

During all the period when adhesive stamps were required on documents, imprinted stamps were also in use on a great variety of checks, bonds, insurance policies, and other commercial papers, in denominations from two cents to one dollar.

About the only adhesive revenue stamps in use during the last decade of the nineteenth century were those on packs of playing cards, but when this country went to war with Spain in 1898, new series of documentary and proprietary stamps appeared. Before these could be printed, provisional stamps were made by overprinting postage and newspaper issues and a few ordinary postage stamps were used, after precancellation, by a proprietary medicine manufacturer.

During the war period the private-die proprietary issues came into use again but in only a few varieties. The last such stamps were issued in 1902.

When it became apparent in 1914 that this country should arm defensively, a revenue act was passed and stamps were issued to provide funds. The taxes ordered at that time have continued almost without interruption to the present day. There have been changes and dormant periods for some taxes but there has been no period when some stamps were not in use.

In addition to revenue stamps with stated face values, there is a very large group of issues which are called "tax paids." These state that the tax has been paid on the article or container to which it is affixed. By avoiding a stated face value, the same stamp may be used through many changes in tax rates. All these stamps indicate the amount of the product on which the tax has been paid, either by weight or volume, or by the number of units within the package.

Tax paid stamps are found on alcoholic beverages and on

some tobacco products. Today the tax on cigarettes is paid on the gross product. Other federal stamps have been used on stock transfers, consular fees, cotton and potato sales, as lock seals and hydrometer labels, and to collect other excise taxes.

Numerous state taxes have been imposed in addition to those collected for the federal government, some being levied on the same items and others on items not previously taxed. State tax stamps in many instances must be collected upon the container or a piece, or not saved at all because of their fragile nature.

MIGRATORY BIRD HUNTING STAMPS (DUCK STAMPS)

The duck stamps are a favorite subject for collectors who go outside the postage field for sidelines. Much of their appeal lies in the beautiful subjects used and the large size at which they are presented. The designs are by known artists, whereas most of our postage stamps are designed by the Bureau of Engraving and Printing.

These are tax stamps to provide funds for refuges where migratory waterfowl may be safe from slaughter. When the revenue measure was passed only an estimated 27,000,000 waterfowl were within the country. Ten years later the number had grown to over 125,000,000. The act provides that every hunter over sixteen must have a current hunting stamp affixed to his license before shooting geese, duck, or brant. A single stamp permits hunting anywhere in the United States. At least 90 per cent of the proceeds of the stamp sale must be applied to the refuges and the remainder may be used to provide the stamps and enforce the act.

The stamps are produced by the Bureau of Engraving and Printing and are sold at all first- and second-class post offices and at the Philatelic Agency in Washington. The first issue was placed on sale August 14, 1934. Succeeding issues appeared July 1 of each year, except that the 1949 stamp was delayed until September 1.

The first stamps had a face value of one dollar, but this has gone up to five dollars to offset rising costs in all wild life activities. Those issued prior to 1939 were inscribed "U.S. Department of Agriculture." After transfer of the service in 1939 all issues were inscribed "U.S. Department of the Interior."

In 1945, when it was found that the stamps were being transferred from one hunting license to another to avoid the fee, a warning was printed on their backs by offset lithography stating that it was illegal to hunt unless the stamp had been signed.

Sales of the stamps have ranged from a low of 448,204 copies in 1935-1936 to a high of over 2,000,000. Recent issues may top the latter figure, but as the stamps remain on sale for some time at the Philatelic Agency, the final results are not yet available.

TELEGRAPH STAMPS

These are not tax but service stamps, indicating the payment of charges on telegrams. They are very generally in use in countries which operate their telegraph and telephone lines as units of the governmental communications system. When a message with the proper stamp affixed is dropped in a mail box, it is collected and dispatched without further bother.

In some countries where a single set of stamps is used for all purposes, telegrams are prepaid with postage stamps, and some of these may be identified by the cancellations.

In certain countries—Belgium is an example—special delivery letters with limited area destinations are delivered by telegraph messengers, and telegraph stamps may be used to prepay them.

In the United States the telegraph lines have never been owned by the government and the stamps issued by the companies to prepay or frank telegrams are locals in a sense, or at least private issues. In many instances they were distributed as gratuities which could be used to frank messages.

❖•❖

CHAPTER TWELVE

CANCELLATIONS ON STAMPS
OFF COVER

Cancellations are one of the most interesting features of stamp collecting. Although beginners of all ages seem to concentrate on mint stamps, there is an impressive movement among more experienced collectors toward stamps with interesting cancellations. At exhibitions, many visitors will examine cancellation collections carefully, but will walk quickly past the commemorative issues. The relative merits of mint and used stamps were discussed in chapter 3. Here it might be noted that cancellation collections can be completely individual while two collections of mint stamps of the same period can hardly be distinguished from one another.

The used stamps which have the greatest interest are not those with the least cancellation but those with clear-cut town names or other inscriptions, or with well-defined and recognizable marks. A summary of the development of postal markings in the United States may help collectors understand why some cancellations are so desirable.

The markings found on stamps are usually either town marks or the actual cancellation, or "killer" as it has been dubbed.

The first is now normally circular in form. Other shapes, including straight-line marks, were formerly in use. When postmasters first were required to cancel stamps the townmark and the killer were separate and two operations were necessary to mark a letter.

This was a natural development when the stampless period was coming to an end, for the postmaster had been required to postmark the letter, figure the charges, and apply a rate mark, and also mark the letter "Paid," if this were the case, or send it unpaid. All this information could be written or handstamped and at least some markings were in manuscript even in large post

Fig. 12–1. Rate and Miscellaneous Markings.

offices. Only the most important office had handstamps for all purposes, and the postmaster himself usually furnished them. In Chicago, for example, during the 1847 to 1851 period, the post-master had a townmark, a "Paid" handstamp, a "Free" hand-stamp, a "5" and a "10" as rate marks, and perhaps one or two other marks. But even in Chicago if a letter required fifteen cents postage, it was necessary to write the amount in ink.

When the new rates went into effect in 1851, the postmas-ter's job became more complicated, for the low rates were only for letters paid in stamps or money, and collect letters were charged at a higher rate. Now the postmaster needed all the

Fig. 12–2. Killers and Townmarks.

handstamps of stampless days, with additional marks for rates paid in money, and a killer for the stamps. Quite often the postmaster never provided a killer but cancelled the stamps with his townmark or put a pen mark on them. During this period the majority of post offices had no handstamps at all and used pen and ink for everything, but fortunately for collectors, these offices handled only a little of the mail matter.

Even in larger offices the use of a special killer was delayed for some time, and the clerks used whatever was at hand, including rate marks, which give us the numeral cancellations so highly prized, or "Paid" or "Free" marks. The special killers, when finally obtained, usually were a grid of parallel lines within a circle, and a little later a target of concentric circles.

Post office regulations, then as today, were not taken too seriously and while there may have been orders to use black ink, or to place the townmark where it would be legible, the clerk used his own judgment. Many of our interesting cancellations would never have appeared had everyone followed instructions.

During the period when the townmark and killer were separate, different colors were used in many cities for each, in combinations of red, blue, and black, with an occasional green or magenta.

About this time many postmasters began using bottle corks for killer handstamps. The round blob at first produced was too much of a killer and it was lightened by a cut across the center to give two semicircular blobs. A second cut produced the familiar "country pie" of four segments, and two additional cuts produced the "city pie" of eight segments. Often the country pie was lightened by cutting a notch in each segment. The resulting mark is known as a "crossroad." Knives were now sharpened and clerks and postmasters began to turn out all kinds of fancy killers. Geometrical forms, examples of plant and animal life, fraternal emblems, shields, flags, stars, and all kinds of things received attention.

The most inventive carvers were located in the Waterbury,

Connecticut, post office. They kept up with all holidays and special occasions, national and local, and put some killers into use for which no reason is now apparent. This office produced mugs and barrels, plain and arrow-pierced hearts for St. Valentine's Day, mortars and pestles, the famous Shoo Fly, inspired by a popular song, running chickens, pumpkin heads, skull and bones, padlocks, and other forms too numerous to list.

About 1861 the New York post office began to use special killers on foreign mail. These included interlaced rosettes, geometric forms, multipointed stars, and other intricate designs, usually within a circle. While some may have been produced by amateurs, most of the designs are so delicate and accurate as to indicate the hand of a professional wood engraver. These killers were used until about 1880 with a few continuing until near the end of the century for letters that could not be run through a cancelling machine.

It took time to postmark letters and cancel stamps with separate handstamps and some postmasters obtained new types combining the operations, while others improvised such handstamps by fastening the two parts together. However, collectors are grateful that these were not furnished at the start or the choice killers of 1860-1880 never would have been seen.

About thirty years after stamps appeared the duplex handstamp combining townmark and killer on one handle was in general use. The townmark usually was circular, and the killer oval, the latter made up of horizontal bars in most examples, with a circular space at the center for an initial, or numeral, or some special monogram or device. In some cities the number or letter placed in this space identified the postal station or district, but in general it simply identified the work of the clerk to whom it was assigned. The abbreviations or double letters generally identified stations, and special devices such as a star indicated a particular kind.

Soon after 1880 the cancelling machine, which had been invented a few years before, began to replace hand work in the larger cities, and postmarks began to look alike. Except for a vigorously waving flag, called the involute flag, there was little to attract attention. This soon was replaced by a stiffer flag, which in turn gave way to a band of parallel lines. A box was often placed at the left end of the killer as a location for station names.

The first use of this box for a slogan appears to have been to advertise the Universal Postal Union Congress in Washington in 1897, and examples of the postmark are eagerly sought by collectors. In a short time postal officials realized that this was an ideal spot for various notices to the public and such service slogans as "Have Your Mail Addressed to Street and Number" began to appear.

Various local, national, and international exhibitions and fairs were advertised in this box and in some cases it was extended to occupy the entire killer portion. In recent times slogans have been authorized for various local and national events and the postal authorities have provided the dies which are substituted for the normal killer for a certain period. These slogans have quieted many requests for special stamps and collectors have accepted them as another interesting feature.

In addition to these normal markings, it is possible to find stamps with a partial impression of almost every handstamp a post office owns. Some of these are carelessly applied by clerks while others overlap stamps when there is no other space to impress them.

Foreign receiving and transit marks, special handstamps of railroads, steamship lines, express companies, and similar carriers are all interesting subjects for cancellation collection when the marks are legible.

It is not possible to include the long story of foreign markings in a book of this size, but the collector who examines his stamps carefully will find much of interest in the postmarks of every country, in spite of the fact that only a few ever learned to cut corks.

Revenue cancellations on United States postage stamps are unusual, but one common use of this kind occurred at the start of the Spanish-American War, when 50-cent Trans-Mississippi stamps were used for revenue purposes in Chicago stockyards transactions.

Generally speaking, stamps which are available both for revenue and postage are worth less with revenue cancellations. Some collectors prize revenue stamps used by mistake for postage. Even though they bear a normal postage cancellation, they must be considered as freaks. When off cover there is no evidence that the stamp paid the postage, for the letter may have been rated as unpaid with postage to be collected from the addressee.

Another unusual cancellation is to be found on letters carried outside the postal service by a private delivery company or an express company acting under the provisions of the Express Carriers Act. This allows private carriers to deliver letters when the full postage is paid by stamps, and the stamps are cancelled by the mailer or the carrier when transferred to the latter.

Markings on covers rather than on stamps are discussed in chapter 14.

CANCELLATION COLLECTIONS

One may arrange a collection of cancellations either by the stamp varieties or by the cancellations. The former usually will work to advantage for the older issues, the latter for the more recent.

It is not easy to duplicate postal markings on the older stamps and a better collection will result if a page is devoted to a single issue or variety with differing cancellations.

Many countries assigned a killer number to each post office. Interesting collections may be formed of these with a notation showing the name of each city. Early foreign stamps with townmarks are often scarce, as the regulations in many cases required the mark to be placed on the envelope for better legibility.

Stamps of the ordinary letter rate usually have a great variety of cancellations while other values of the same issue show nothing out of the ordinary. In such cases one page may be assigned to the complete set while the following pages show the differing marks on the values most often used.

Certain slogan cancellations have continued in use for years and are found on a great variety of issues. Here it is logical to use the cancellation as the page subject and show as many stamps as possible with the same marks. The large commemorative may show the full slogan, while the small stamps may show only some distinctive portion of it.

At the present time collections may be made with stamps showing the initials of the R.M.S., the R.P.O., and the H.P.O., but the stamps will not be available long for all are being replaced by the initials P.T.S.

Legible townmarks are always desirable and today are being picked up by collectors who are trying to obtain all possible types from a single city, county, or state. These marks are more highly prized when the cancellation is centered on the stamp, or "socked on the nose," in philatelic parlance.

Some collectors assign separate pages to colored cancellations and to fancy designs, or perhaps to those applied on naval vessels or at forts or military stations. All these may be collected on or off cover.

CURIOUS SUGGESTIONS FOR CANCELLING STAMPS

Soon after the introduction of stamps many ingenious ideas were suggested to prevent their second use. One tried out in the United States was a handstamp provided with a sharp ring which would cut a little circle of paper when impressed. Another handstamp had several projecting points which rotated under pressure and effectively roughed up the stamp at the center of the cancellation. An envelope was tried with a small window at the stamp position. This allowed the stamp to be attached to the letter as well as to the envelope with the result that the stamp was destroyed when the enclosure was taken out. A variation of the window had small bars.

In 1870, Postmaster General John A. J. Creswell listed some of the cancelling devices which had been suggested. These included a rasp, a small branding iron, and saws and cutters in the handstamps. Another thought was to incorporate a thread in the paper. This would be pulled by the postal clerk and divide the stamp in two pieces.

Another suggestion was to gum the stamps at one end only so that the cancellation would be made by pulling off the un-gummed portion. A variation of this idea was used in Afghanistan from 1871 to 1891, the postmaster tearing off a small piece of each stamp before affixing it to the envelope.

The grill device adopted by the United States and used for several years to prevent stamp cleaning was effective as long as the dies were not worn flat by use. The grill broke the paper with numerous points and allowed the ink to penetrate deep into the fibers.

The most amazing idea of all was submitted to the French postal authorities, and appears to have been a serious suggestion. The inventor would have placed a small wafer of fulminate of mercury on the back of each stamp. Application of a handstamp would explode it, removing a portion of the stamp. The inventor made no statement concerning the envelope or its contents.

◆∗❖∙

ARRANGING AND WRITING UP COLLECTIONS

These suggestions are for collectors who mount their stamps on the blank pages of loose-leaf albums, especially those who add written data.

Since accidents may happen during writing up, whether with pen and ink or typewriter, it is safer to do it before the stamps are mounted. The sheet arrangement should be studied with the actual stamps or with dummy slips of paper. When the layout is settled, the spaces are marked and the write-up made.

It is not important to present the stamps in numerical sequence and often there are reasons for some other arrangement. A better layout may be possible if the stamps are grouped according to shape and size. In some cases the clashing of two colors may be avoided by separating the unharmonious pair.

ARRANGEMENT OF A GENERAL COLLECTION

On completely blank pages the country name and the issue description will occupy from 1½ to 1¼ inches at the top of the page and an additional half-inch space will separate the text and stamps. After allowing for margins at sides and bottom, there will be a working space of about 7 by 7½ inches on a 9½-by-10-inch page. When the pages have printed border lines the space may be a little less.

The best collections have the stamps in a somewhat standard pattern, with no attempt made to make a new and startling arrangement on each page. Fanciful designs with the stamps in various geometric forms are not as pleasing as some collectors believe.

Unless the collector is artist enough to obtain balance in other ways, he will do better to arrange his stamps symmetrically about the vertical center line. The focal point should be a little above the center and in general the stamps should be grouped about it with the rows growing shorter toward the top and bottom, the bottom row being the shortest. An arrangement of this kind will not appear top-heavy or bottom-heavy, and will be more pleasing than one with short rows of stamps near the center. Some collectors oppose checkerboard layouts, with the stamps lining up vertically as well as horizontally, but as a rule this arrangement is difficult to better.

The stamps should not be placed too close together horizontally, two quadrille spaces or six millimeters being about the minimum. The vertical spacing usually is greater for in many cases lettering may be required under a stamp. If possible the same spacing should be used throughout a collection, even though the layout will vary when the stamp sizes differ.

It is good practice to block out the page arrangement several issues in advance so that long sets will not be broken when it is possible to place all examples on one page. To accomplish this it may be necessary to stretch some sets a little or even to move a short set out of chronological order. Such a move should not be made if it conflicts with some important feature of the issue. For example, it is not desirable to place a set with a different watermark between sets with earlier or later watermarks.

Two or more short sets may be mounted on a single page when the general data is the same and can be placed in a single note at the top of the page. When a set has mixed sizes or shapes, it usually is advisable to forget the numerical order and mount the stamps in a pleasing layout.

In the present condensed versions of the general catalogs, the actual order of issues has been abandoned to some extent and all stamps of one design are grouped if they have the same paper and perforations. Thus, some countries which have not changed designs in several years will have stamps listed under the design, even though some appear in advance of stamps issued many years before. In such cases it is better to mount the basic set as it first appeared and follow with the color changes, etc. Sets of this kind when mounted according to the list may appear very uninteresting, as several copies of the same stamp in different colors will be mounted side by side.

The question of providing spaces for stamps not now owned is one that bothers many collectors. If the missing stamps may never be obtained, it is better not to leave spaces that call attention to them. Ordinary high values that will be obtained when the money is available may be provided for.

A few minor varieties in an issue may be grouped together at the bottom of a page with special notations, but if there are many such stamps it may be better to mount them on an additional page.

WRITING UP A GENERAL COLLECTION

A novice should realize that he is making a collection of stamps, not a display of ornamental penmanship, and that a write-up which is more attractive than the stamps defeats its purpose. Whatever is written on the album pages should be legible and subdued, not garish or laudatory. Do not stress the high value of some stamps or their rarity. These matters can be pointed out modestly. The lettering (freehand or guided or even typewritten) should be kept in a single color, not accented with red notes or underscores, but it is permissible to have some notes in bolder lettering than others. Ornamental frames around stamps and other embellishments are excessive. The artistic effort could be put to better use in drawing a frontispiece for the album, or a map and title page for each country.

Each stamp page should display the name of the country in larger letters than those used elsewhere. Some collectors obtain pages with the country name engraved at the top, but there seems to be no good reason for having the initial letter in a different color from the others.

Name and date of issue, particular reason for issue, design subject, designing and printing information, paper and watermark, perforation and gum—these points are practically all the philatelic information necessary in either general or limited collections. The date of the issue should be given to the day if possible. When the subject of a stamp is taken from a portrait or statue, the artist's name, date of the work, and its location may be given, but there is no reason for adding a biography of the artist. A reference to his masterpiece, if he has one, or to another of his works used as a stamp design should be sufficient. Some collectors place such information at the bottom of the page, separating it from their philatelic notes.

The paper description may be only the watermark, or it may be necessary to note such details as "chalky paper" or "surface-colored paper." Designing and printing information will include names of designers and engravers, if known, the kind of printing, and the company or office that produced the stamps. Perforation data is usually abbreviated in this form: "Perf. 14."

SPECIALIZED COLLECTIONS

Each page of a special collection will present a different problem for the collector who is concerned with engraving varieties, cancellations, and similar details. Space may be required for illustrations, as these will convey the information much better than any amount of description.

A collector working on a single stamp often has an enlarged cut made, and mats printed on which to indicate varieties. Such a cut should be about four times the stamp size by linear measurement, and the printing should be pale so that the points of interest may be drawn over in black ink. In most cases an entire mat need not be mounted but only the portion which shows the variety.

In write-ups of this kind only the object of the specialization need be mentioned, for the usual philatelic information is of little concern. Notes regarding the varieties should be concise and not narrative, and all should be lettered in a single color. A more pleasing effect is produced when the lettering is in a gray ink rather than a full black, as this gives the stamps more importance. Small adhesive arrows sometimes are used to point out varieties, particularly when no illustrations have been provided.

TOPICAL COLLECTIONS

In these collections greater write-ups under individual stamps require that they be more widely spaced on the pages. None of the routine information is of much importance except the subject of the design, and since all stamps on a page are usually related by subject, this will replace the country name at the top of the page. In extensive topical collections, subheadings are usually required. Thus, in a collection of Religion on Stamps, the section may be concerned with churches and the page with French cathedrals. Individual captions will be located below or near each stamp, for it is almost necessary to explain each one if the collection is to serve as a reference album.

Commemorative stamps may be handled in the same manner. When properly separated into groups, they may present an outline history covering the important events of their country. Such an outline for the United States would include its settlement, the colonies, the Revolution, the establishment of the United States, its expansion, new states, wars, and its statesmen and famous citizens.

LETTERING TOOLS

For hand lettering, in addition to pen and ink, one needs pencils, erasers, an erasing shield, and perhaps a blotter. Other

VII (top). Americana on foreign stamps. A series issued by Iceland
in 1939 to call attention to the New York World's Fair. VIII (above).
Israel New Year issue of 1952 (5713), of interest to topical collectors
as well. The subjects are nuts, dove and cattail, lily, and figs. IX
(below). An early example of precancelled stamps.

X (top). United States precancels. Top row shows three Chicago Buroprints and two examples of double-line electros. Bottom row shows four city types and a mail-order-house type of Denver, Colo. XI (above). Foreign precancels. Examples from Luxembourg, France, Canada, and Belgium. XII (below). Slogan in use in Canada during early days of World War II. Slogan "V" shows also in code. (Courtesy Bernard D. Keenan.)

useful things include a bottle of pen cleaner, a lettering guide, and an electric erasing machine. A soapstone crayon is useful in restoring an erased surface, and a little ammonia or ox gall will help in dry seasons when using India ink.

The ink used is usually black or one that will turn black after a few days. Most draftsmen prefer a waterproof ink since it does not penetrate the paper to any extent but dries on the surface and errors may be removed by light erasing or scraping. If watered or diluted with ammonia this ink will be harder to remove as it will penetrate the paper to a greater degree. Ox gall is used to make the ink flow more freely.

Nonwaterproof or general purpose drawing ink penetrates paper freely. It may be diluted with water when gray ink is desired.

Accidents sometimes happen and every ink bottle should be placed in a large rubber base or in a metal rack to prevent upsets. An important rule that will save you grief is: never write with ink on any page that contains stamps. Bottles of drawing ink are equipped with a quill or dropper. This should be used to fill the pen, as it helps avoid the overloading that may cause it to leak or letter too broadly.

In recent times fountain pens have come into use for work with drawing ink, and are very satisfactory. Interchangeable points are available for them.

Lettering with a Mechanical Guide

Lettering outfits such as the Leroy or Wrico are very satisfactory after the user has achieved a certain facility and learned the proper spacing of letters. Complete outfits are not needed as all a stamp collector's lettering can be handled with two or three of the smallest guides and points for two widths of lines. The machines consist of guides and a scriber that will produce vertical, slanting, or italic lettering by simple adjustments. Small amounts of lettering can be handled with a special pen and a guide without resorting to the scriber. Since the points must be kept clean to produce uniform lettering, a bottle of pen cleaner is essential.

Although the letters produced by these machines may be perfect the effect is very often ruined by uniform spacing. Good spacing is never uniform but depends on the character of the adjoining letters. A novice should consult a book on lettering and study inscriptions and other examples of fine composition.

Jig for Album Pages

It is advisable to set up a jig on a drawing board to hold pages securely while lettering. The drawing board if small should be clamped to a table or provided with suction cups. A piece of plywood will answer if one edge is trued up for use with a T-square. The jig is a sheet of illustration board to which are glued cardboard guides slightly thicker than the album pages. These guides form a snug pocket for the pages. A bottom strip or two corner pieces hold the lower edge of the page, while the upper edge is held by a movable top strip fastened with thumb tacks, masking tape, or spring clips.

When page layouts have been determined, the position of horizontal rows and lettering lines should be marked on the side guide strips so that all pages may be uniform without measuring. Several page arrangements can be handled if the marks on the guides are identified. The vertical center line and the end limits of titles, notes, etc., may be marked on the top guide and will be of great help when laying out the lettering.

HAND LETTERING

In hand lettering it is necessary to draw lines to mark the top and bottom limits of letters or they cannot be held to a uniform size. These guide lines are usually drawn in sets of three except when block capitals are used alone. The center line may then be omitted. The lines may be drawn along a T-square or a lettering guide may be used. These guides have small holes in groups of three and arrange to provide for any height of letter. A very sharp pencil is placed in a hole and a line drawn as the guide moves along the T-square. Next, the matching hole in the group of three is selected and another line drawn. All lines drawn through a set of holes will be uniform in spacing, a result that cannot be duplicated when they are measured individually.

The lines should be drawn with a fairly hard pencil and should be just strong enough to follow and never strong enough to indent the paper. Pencil grades H, 2H, and 3H are recommended for trial. The one used will depend upon the character of the album pages.

ABCDEFGHIJKLMNOPQRSTUVWXYZ&·12345
abcdefghijklmnopqrstuvwxyz·Lower case text is legible.
VARIATIONS MAY ADD INTEREST IF NOT OVERDONE.
Roman letters are more legible than sans serif or gothic..
All pen strokes required for BLOCK CAPITAL LETTERS are
contained in the word "SOAP" thus SOAP. 10 strokes.
Copper plate script should be lettered and not written

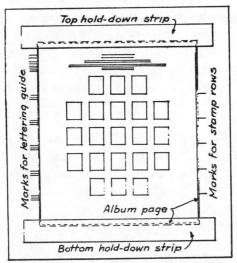

JIG TO HOLD ALBUM PAGES

FIG. 13-1.

Titles and notes should be penciled carefully before they are inked in. Some draftsmen letter both directions from the central point. Write out the note on scratch paper and count the letters to find the center, and make allowance for the broad *m*'s and *w*'s, the narrow *i*'s, and the spaces between the words. A transparent scale graduated both directions from a central zero point is an ideal spacing tool. It is standard equipment in some mechanical lettering outfits, but can be drawn on a piece of tough paper and mounted on the T-square.

The lettering should be made with a medium pencil so that it will erase easily with art gum or kneaded rubber. Grades H, F, and HB are recommended for trial. It is much easier to letter with a soft pencil; the effort required to make marks with a hard pencil affects the lines and curves.

The pen points used will depend on the width of line desired and the amount of pressure normally used by the letterer. For block or gothic letters a beginner will have the most success with a stiff pen that makes a certain width line in spite of varying pressure. Gillott's No. 202 is a point of this character.

Script or copperplate lettering will need a pen with a fine, flexible point, as the down strokes in this work are broadened by pressure. Gillott's Nos. 170 and 303 are examples of this type. Script can be made with facility only on a very smooth paper and with ink which flows freely. If the pen picks at the paper on the upward strokes, it will be impossible to produce thin, neat letters.

Lettering pens are available in sizes and styles almost without number, and a beginner should try out several to find one which works easily for him. One difficulty is to keep the ink flowing for it dries quickly on the very fine points. A drop of ammonia or ox gall helps.

The arm should be fully supported on the drawing board and not overhang the edge or rest on anything irregular. Nearly all lettering requires that the arm move freely on the drawing board. It usually helps if the arm is bare to the elbow.

No album page will lie perfectly flat. It should be held

down at the point of lettering with some instrument such as a brush handle or reversed penholder. If the paper springs up and down between pen strokes the lettering will be irregular.

When slight errors occur with India ink, do not erase but add the strokes necessary to correct the work, and when fully dry, remove the unnecessary lines with a steel scraper. This will avoid the necessity of inking over an erased spot, always a hazardous undertaking. Confine the scraping to the minimum area by using one of the small steel erasers which fit a pen holder and are sharpened diagonally at the end.

When ink must be removed with a rubber eraser, use a metal erasing shield to prevent damage to the surrounding paper. Never use an abrasive eraser (an "ink eraser") but a medium-hard grade such as the Ruby or a similar brand. This grade is available in a paper wrapping, looking like a pencil, and it will provide a small point combined with stiffness.

A beginner who spends a lot of time correcting mistakes should go back to the practice pad or obtain an erasing machine. A small power tool equipped with a chuck to hold pencil erasers will remove the mistakes in a moment. Always work through the smallest openings of an erasing shield, to limit the work and to hold the paper down tightly. After erasing, particularly spots which must be inked over, the surface should be restored with an agate burnisher, or by rubbing with a soapstone crayon. There is no effective eradicator for India ink, and it is likely that the pigment cannot be bleached. Any chemical strong enough to affect the ink probably would ruin the paper either at once or by latent action.

Most collectors will use block capital letters. Having selected the sizes, they should practice on similar paper, such as a discarded album page. It is necessary to learn only ten strokes for block lettering and all of them, and no more, will be found in the practice word SOAP. When the letters can be made without a waver in the vertical lines the job is half done, the other half being the ability to join strokes such as those in the letter N without allowing them to run together for some distance.

After the letters can be formed it is necessary only to learn how to space them. In some cases they must be altered slightly, particularly when two open letters such as L and A come together. In this case the L is often narrowed or it may touch the second letter, as in the case of certain stamps of Queensland.

Some notes may be lettered in lower-case form. The letters belonging with block capitals are not hard to make. In very small letters trouble may be found with *a* and *e* for it is difficult to keep the small loops from filling with ink. This may be solved by using a modified *a* and by enlarging the loop of the *e*.

Script should be handled as drawing, each letter being separate with connecting strokes to reach the next letter. Upper and lower case letters must be used, for a sentence in script capitals would not be legible.

When a page has been lettered it should be cleaned with art gum, kneaded rubber, or a dry, clean pad of gum particles, and guide lines removed with a Ruby eraser.

FRAMES AROUND STAMPS

Ornamental and decorative frames around stamps detract from the stamp display. However some collectors desire a simple single-line frame around each stamp, particularly for exhibition purposes. When carefully drawn a single ink line may be as neat as if engraved.

The page should be secured in the jig and the stamp spaces outlined in pencil using T-square and triangle. The frame should be only large enough to allow a one-millimeter border around the stamp. The frame lines are inked in with a right-line or ruling pen. Care must be taken in this work to avoid turning the pen for it will empty if the space between the nibs comes in contact with the guide.

STAMP MOUNTS

These improve the appearance of an album and serve the same purpose as a frame line if made of black paper. They are neat only when they project not more than a millimeter beyond the stamp edge. They should be thin, hard, and smooth and cut true with full square corners. Hinge the stamp firmly to the mat and make future changes by moving the assembled stamp and mat.

In specialized collections with the stamps all one color, it may be advantageous to use a tinted rather than a black mat. Strong colors are not suggested but a gray or pale cream may show off the stamps to advantage. When a special variety is mounted, attention can be directed to it by using a mat of a deeper shade.

Engraved mats in white or cream with a single frame line have been used for many collections. These mats usually have a panel below for a drawing of the cancellation or a note on the variety shown.

One great objection to mats of any kind is that the stamps are raised and subjected to more rubbing than if mounted directly on the page. There is a great amount of lateral movement between the pages of better-grade albums, which nearly always are double-hinged, and smooth, hard interleaves are the best solution. The older pages backed up with tissue usually show spots of color where they have been in contact with the stamps of the next page.

DEPRESSED SPACES FOR STAMPS

A very few albums for particularly valuable stamps have been made with recesses for each stamp. This is a tedious job for a collector and should be used only for collections which are complete or are to be placed in a museum.

The pages can be Whatman drawing paper and the recesses made by pressing copper bits into the paper in a letter press. The bits are cut about two millimeters larger in each direction than the stamps and are finished with rounded corners and edges so that they will not cut the page under pressure.

After the page layout has been determined and marked, the paper is soaked and placed on the press bed. The copper bits are placed, covered with a blotter and a hard press board, and pressure applied. When fully dry, each page is trimmed and hinged as are other pages. Placed in the depressions the stamps either lie flush or below the surface of the page.

POCHETTES AND PROTECTIVE MOUNTS

Pochettes are pockets or coverings of transparent material to protect stamps and to provide a method of mounting without hinges. Surface protection of all stamps is important but mounting without hinges is of value only for unused stamps.

In theory pochettes seemed to be a perfect solution and many collectors remounted their stamps or used them for all new acquisitions. Prior to the introduction of fully transparent sheetings glassine had been used but so much visibility was lost that it was never satisfactory.

The first of the new materials was cellophane but soon it was found that this changed size rapidly and damaged closely wrapped stamps through its shrinkage. Cellulose acetate sheeting next became available but in some cases was no better for it was hygroscopic and had a shrinkage factor almost as great as cellophane. It appears that these materials may shrink when moistened and again when they dry but they never return to their original size.

Complaints were made to the manufacturers and after tests cellophane was pronounced unsatisfactory for the permanent storage of paper but cellulose acetate was found to be safe for that purpose.

To overcome the undesirable effects both materials were produced in moisture-proof form by adding a film of cellulose nitrate. Tests of the coated materials revealed that both were dangerous to paper and color on account of the fumes given off by the coating. Since this coating is actually celluloid the effects were the same as though the stamps had been placed in the dangerous celluloid envelopes of an earlier day. When complaints began to arise about the glassy appearance of stamp gum after storage in pochettes it was learned that the "harmless" tag applied only to the effect on the paper. New tests indicated that the gum, softening in high temperature and humidity, took an impression from the surface of the transparent material, and in some cases stuck fast.

The reports also stated that the plasticizers used in making the materials differed from time to time, and that it would be impossible to guarantee that a kind of sheeting found harmless would be so when another later lot was tested. In fairness, it should be stated that a similar gum effect occurred when stamps were encased with glassine except to a lesser degree. Any stamps closed tightly with any of the materials will suffer gum damage unless the gum is of a variety known as "tropical" or "summer."

It appears that cellulose sheeting may be used for pochettes with reasonable safety if there is a free passage of air when the albums are opened. This is accomplished by having the pochettes open at the sides or at the top. There will be less distortion if the thinner grades of material are avoided. The glazing effects on gum will be minimized if a paper mat is placed in the pochette, or if a mat is a part of its construction. However, the sticking down may be increased unless the mat has a smooth, hard finish. The use of nondrying cements in the construction of pochettes, or to attach them to album pages, should be avoided. These adhesives have a tendency to penetrate everything and have altered the character of paper, color, and gum. Manufacturers of sheetings will supply the names of safe adhesives to be used with their products.

Collectors should obtain the sheetings from dealers who will guarantee at the very least that the material is plain and has not been moisture proofed. Stamps should be examined frequently, page by page, to allow air to dissipate any accumulating gases or moisture. Examine particularly the stamps printed in the least permament colors, violet and green, to see if any change is taking place. Slit any coverings which seal stamps in tightly.

The use of pochettes does not improve the appearance of any collection as the reflections make it difficult to examine the stamps. The usual excuse for them is that they preserve the stamps in "unhinged" condition. This word adds to the cost of a stamp but does not help its looks. A hinge mark may lower the value of a stamp very slightly, but if the stamp is wrinkled, or if the color is altered or the gum glazed, the value may be lost completely. Interleaves protect stamps sufficiently from rubbing and careless handling, and there will be no danger to gum or color. If a collection is being made hingeless simply to make a profit, it would be safer to invest in the older used stamps of established value. These produce much more and require less attention and cultivation than any other vegetables in the garden of philately. When current commemorative issues must be embalmed to preserve face value, the game is not worth the effort.

PART II

Postal History and Cover Collecting

❖❖❖

CHAPTER FOURTEEN

COVERS AND POSTAL MARKINGS

The study of postal history includes the investigation of all material relating to the postal services of a country or group of countries in which a collector is interested. Although particular attention is given to covers, there is also a study of postal laws and treaties and everything which may have a bearing on postal rates or account for the way mail is handled.

The word *cover* applies to any postally used item, whether stampless, or with adhesive or imprinted stamps, and whether fully enclosing, as folded letter sheets, envelopes, and wrappers, or nonenclosing, as cards. It includes items with written or printed advice, applied directly or by labels, to indicate that the mail so marked is carried without charge. These free items may be official mail, that of military forces in service, or that of individuals or organizations.

When speaking of envelopes, letter sheets, and cards with imprinted stamps, a collector usually calls them *entires* to distinguish the complete items from those trimmed either to *cut square* or to *shape*, as was customary in early days. Occasionally the term *face of cover* is used to indicate that condition, or *on piece* when a stamp exists on a fragment of the original cover.

MOUNTING A COVER COLLECTION

Covers may be mounted on any blank album pages of the post-binder or spring-back type; ring-binder pages will need reinforcements at the holes to keep the pages from tearing. One of the easiest ways to mount the covers is with transparent corners, similar to those sometimes used for photo prints and post cards. These are available in various sizes and they allow the covers to be removed for examination.

Some collectors provide a thin cardboard mat for each cover, making a slight attachment between the cover and mat with hinges and fastening this assembly to the album page with the transparent corners. Covers so mounted are not readily removable. Since many of the postal markings are on the backs of covers, collectors have taken to using transparent sheeting in various forms. This eliminates the work of cutting windows through the album page and mat where the back markings occur.

One handy transparent protector comes in flattened tubular form, in lengths which will handle at least two covers. It may be cut down as desired and hinged at the top on the album page, allowing lifting.

Special albums are available with fifty transparent pockets. Each pocket holds two covers, placed back to back, and turns up so that either face may be examined. The pockets are open on one or more sides to allow air to reach the contents, and they are arranged to permit indexing.

POSTAL MARKINGS

Some explanation of postmarks has already been given, but these items are only a part of the whole group of postal markings met with on covers. Others include any written marks, handstamps, or labels showing when and where the piece entered the mail, whether paid or part paid or collect, what route it was to follow, air mail, registration, insurance, special delivery, customs inspection, possible fumigation, military censorship, transit markings, date of arrival at destination, forwarding marks, addresses unknown, return to sender, reason for nondelivery, advertising.

Stampless Period

Postal markings antedate adhesive stamps by several centuries. Henry Bishop, postmaster general of Great Britain, announced in 1661 that "a stamp has been invented which is to be put on every letter." The "Bishop mark," as this handstamp came to be called, gave the date of mailing so that a delay in answering could not be charged to slow delivery by the post office. The mark was a small circle divided by a horizontal line, with the date in one half and the month, abbreviated to two letters, in the other. When William Dockwra was operating the Penny Post in London in 1681, need was felt for a more definite time of mailing and his heart-shaped Bishop mark indicated morning and afternoon as "Mor." and "Af." with the hour of mailing below. An additional triangular handstamp was inscribed "Penny-Post-Paid" at the sides with a letter in the center to show at which station the letter had been deposited.

Out of such small beginnings grew the vast array of handstamps that show town names and dates. At an early date other handstamps appeared to indicate whether a letter was "Free" or "Paid" or "Part Paid" and the like. These often had only the initial letters of the words. As the mails increased, rate stamps with numerals were provided to indicate the charges. Letters brought by ship and not in a closed pouch were given special markings since the captain of the vessel was entitled to a fee for his trouble. Transit marks showing the passage of a cover across a country add interest. Often they are accompanied by handstamps showing the points of entry and exit.

Stampless covers of the United States may be separated into two groups, the first for the prestamp covers, the second those mailed after stamps were introduced, but before the payment of postage or use of stamps was obligatory. These differ little except in the postage rates, letters sent unpaid being charged a higher rate.

Postage Stamp Period

When postage stamps were introduced some handstamps became obsolete as the stamp itself indicated the rate, but the townmark and date were still needed as well as a new handstamp to cancel the stamp. In England, such a handstamp, standardized as a small Maltese cross with curved arms, was placed in use with the first stamps.

In the United States many years passed before handstamps were furnished to postmasters, who thus were left to their own resources. Many foreign countries provided all offices with uniform handstamps and killers which differed only in the town name and number in the killer. This number often was an office number used in general accounting and as a number on forms used at that office. Killers of this kind usually were impressed directly on the stamp while the townmark was placed on the cover in a position where it would be legible.

After the adoption of uniform rates and the compulsory prepayment of postage, it no longer was necessary to deliver letters to the post office. They could be dropped in a letter box. Under such conditions many overweight letters were mailed with insufficient prepayment and it became necessary to establish a procedure for handling them. "Postage Due" handstamps came into use, with a figure to indicate the deficiency and sometimes a penalty in addition. A clerk handling letters to foreign countries had to be an expert in foreign exchange to convert the deficiency into the proper currency. After the organization of the Universal Postal Union and the adoption of uniform foreign-letter rates, covers from foreign lands lost much of their variety and interest.

POSTAL HISTORY IN COVERS

All the cancellations described as being collectible on stamps off cover are even more desirable on the original cover, for they are more completely identifiable and are usually accompanied by other markings. About the only disadvantage in cover collecting is in the amount of space required and the difficulty of bringing related items together on album pages.

No one has the stamina or resources to collect the postal history of the entire world, but many narrow the field to a country or group of countries related by geography or political connections. The more intensive the study, the narrower the field, for it requires a vast amount of research to handle the least of the nations.

Early United States Period

In order to show the extent of a postal-history study of the United States it may be useful to outline the field to be covered. There are three periods, determined by the form of government: the colonial, the pre-Constitutional up to 1789, and the national from that year on. Philatelically, the first two periods have little complication but the material is excessively scarce. The preliminary goal is a cover from each of the colonies during each period.

The third period becomes very complicated due to territorial expansion, and the division of these areas into territorial governments and eventually into states. Again the preliminary goal is to show something from each in every stage of development and perhaps from the acquired regions before they became a part of the United States. In a few cases the collector must be content to show letters or documents without postal markings since some of the areas had no postal facilities.

Following is a list of the political divisions of the United States existing in 1784, or organized between that date and 1812. The dates are of the organization, or of the entire time the division existed.

In 1784 the colonies were operating under authority of the Continental Congress, the Vermont region was disputed territory, and Maine was a part of Massachusetts. These were the successive changes and additions: State of Franklin (or Frankland), unofficial, now a part of Tennessee, 1784-1788; the thirteen original states, 1789, Vermont unorganized; District of Maine, 1789-1803; Southwest Territory, 1790-1796; State of

Vermont, 1791; Kentucky, 1792; Tennessee, 1796; Mississippi Territory, 1798-1817; Indiana Territory, 1800-1816; District of Louisiana, 1804-1805; Orleans Territory, 1804-1812; Michigan Territory, 1805-1837; Louisiana Territory, 1805-1812; Illinois Territory, 1809-1818; State of Louisiana, 1812; Missouri Territory, 1812-1821.

With this start the list continues through the territories and states formed in the Northwest Territory and the Louisiana Purchase, and on through the new regions acquired by the Florida Purchase of 1821, the annexation of Texas in 1845, the treaty acquisition of the Oregon country in 1846, the Mexican cessions of 1848 and 1853, the Alaska purchase in 1867, the annexation of Hawaii in 1898, the cession of Puerto Rico and Guam in 1898, the discovery of Wake Island in 1899, the treaty acquisition of Samoa in 1900, the acquisition of the Canal Zone in 1904, and the purchase of the Danish West Indies in 1917.

An outline cannot show the full extent of the postal history involved for there are intermediate steps to be accounted for. Kaskaskia, finally an Illinois post office, might be shown in Virginia, Northwest Territory, Indiana Territory, and Illinois Territory, all of which political divisions claimed it before the state of Illinois was organized. Detroit might be shown as a British post office in 1798 (in spite of the Treaty of 1783), and then successively in Northwest Territory, Indiana Territory, the eastern division of the Northwest Territory, Michigan Territory, and finally in the state of Michigan.

Another interesting example of the changes in government is indicated by the postmarks of Dubuque, Iowa, which show it first as Dubuque Mines, Michigan Territory; Dubuque, Wisconsin Territory; Dubuque, Iowa Territory; and Dubuque, Iowa. There is a possibility that it was a post office in Spanish Louisiana, and perhaps it may have had one or two other addresses in the period before Michigan Territory was extended west of the Mississippi.

A summary of this character makes no mention of methods used in carrying the mail but a collection of the period would contain examples carried by packet boats, stage coaches, and perhaps by western express companies.

At an early date it was realized that patrons would pay extra for faster service and an official express mail was organized under an act of 1836, carrying letters at three times the normal rate. This extended from New York to New Orleans, with branches or other routes reaching St. Louis, Charleston, South Carolina, and other points. This has been called the "first pony express," in an attempt to borrow a little of the fame of the overland route to California, but it might better be named a "horse express" for no ponies were used.

Any outline of United States postal history must include sections showing the effect of war on the handling of mail. The War of 1812 would disclose increased postal rates. The Mexican War would be indicated by covers originating in the Gulf coast ports and interior cities of Mexico and the Republic of Texas. The Mormon troubles resulted in army mail being carried overland from such frontier posts as Fort Bridger and Camp Floyd and from Salt Lake City, the capital of the unofficial Mormon state of Deseret.

Civil War Period

The Civil War provides the most interesting group of covers of any period. The seceded states were never a foreign country and their postal history is that of a section of a country in rebellion. Had the rebellion succeeded the postal history could have been that of a separate country, with forerunners under another government.

There are covers which show the discontinuance of service to the southern states, the new issue of 1861 to prevent the use or sale of stamps in Confederate hands, and the demonetization of the issue in use when secession took place. Covers will show the attempted use of the old stamps and their rejection after the official deadline dates.

There are soldiers' letters from training camps and from the battle lines, and from southern regions occupied by federal forces, as Port Royal, New Orleans, Ship Island, etc. There are early covers carried into southern territory by Adams & Co.'s Express, and later ones by flag of truce, and a few covers from Union soldiers in prison camps. Throughout the conflict there are numerous northern patriotic covers.

The Confederate covers will show the use of United States postal facilities as long as possible, months after secession in many states. Others will show the opening of the Confederate service without stamps, the covers marked as in the prestamp days, with postage paid in money. In many cities the postmasters supplied provisional issues until regular stamps were available. There are trans-Mississippi covers carried at special rates and blockade covers sent out of the country in spite of the watchful United States Navy. Covers dated after April 19, 1861, which show evidence of foreign receipt, are in this category. As the shortage of materials increased envelopes were turned and used a second time, and others were made of wallpaper and of ledger paper from old account books.

In addition to the mail carried into the North by the express companies and later by flag of truce, there are rumors of messages sent across the Potomac attached to kites, or carried by "wetbacks" who swam the river with instructions for the Confederate spies in the capital. Southern patriotic covers are less common than in the North.

Covers from the camps where Confederate prisoners were held are more numerous than those from southern camps and all show markings of the camps. They fall into two groups, the first consisting of covers mailed to regions behind the advancing Union lines, the second of letters mailed to points deep in the South. The covers of the first group had no special treatment and were carried by the United States post directly to the addressees. Those of the second group were carried by a flag of truce to an exchange point, usually via Fortress Monroe to City Point, Virginia, thence to Richmond and onward to destination. These showed the payment of two charges, the United States charge being paid by stamps, the Confederate charge by money or stamps. The closing phase of the Civil War may be indicated by covers with United States stamps used in the southern states soon after the surrender of the Confederate armies.

Spanish-American War Period

Except for Indian disturbances, which provide covers with marks of frontier posts and Indian agencies, the country was at peace until 1898, when war broke out with Spain. Patriotic covers appear again, but seem to have been used more by soldiers than the public. There are also covers with the marks of military postal stations established in Cuba, Puerto Rico, and the Philippines soon after the islands were occupied. Troop transports stopped at Honolulu *en route* to Manila, and a lucky collector may obtain a soldier's letter with a cover bearing Hawaiian stamps. Among the Philippine covers will be mementoes of the Aguinaldo insurrection and the battles fought to put it down. Other patriot covers of the period trace the participation of American troops in quelling the Boxer rebellion in China, the reoccupation of Cuba, the occupation of Santo Domingo and Nicaragua, and even the Mexican disturbance of 1914 when Vera Cruz was occupied.

The World Wars

Covers from the military forces during World War I show censor labels. The location of army units was concealed by using station numbers. There were few pictorial envelopes but many showing the insignia of the nonmilitary service groups looking after soldier welfare. Prisoner-of-war letters were common but the location of prisoners was hidden so far as possible by all powers. Troop sailings were secret but the arrival of troops at a foreign port released a flood of "safe arrival" cards notifying family and friends.

World War II found the posts operating in much the same way but on a much larger scale. There were more patriotic covers, thanks to stamp dealers. Postal stations abroad, which at first operated under a number, soon concealed their identity completely. The amount of space required on airplanes for soldiers' and civilians' letters led to the use of V-mail. Letters were microfilmed at central stations and enlargements, made after the film had been flown home or abroad, were delivered in special envelopes to the addressees. This process was first used by the British to handle mail from the Middle East Command to England.

The participation of American troops with those of the United Nations' forces in Korea provides a number of interesting postal history items in the 1950s. Similarly, American involvement in Vietnam, Cambodia, and Laos in the 1960s adds another dimension to U.S. postal history. Patriotic covers were seldom used in these years but the methods of handling the mails were much the same as in World War II.

RECORDING DATA

In recent years collectors have recorded information about new postal developments much more completely than in the past and the specialist of the future will not face so many mysteries. Among the groups performing this service are the Bureau Issues Association, which publishes detailed information concerning designs and production of all new United States stamps, and societies devoted to air-mail, railway and highway postal services, and to naval and sea post cancellations.

The failure to record current events while the material is available accounts for the lack of information about various items, one of them Allen's City Despatch, a local post that started up in Chicago late in 1882. Little is known except the date when the post was suppressed by postal inspectors. Allen's conviction appears in court records.

All the information could have been written for the stamp papers by members of the Chicago Stamp Collectors Union, now the Chicago Philatelic Society, to whom Allen delivered copies of *The Stamp Collector's Bureau*. After Allen had been restored to society he was engaged by the Chicago Telephone Company to deliver its bills, and later he operated a handbill distributing agency, marking all the material with a handstamp of Allen's City Despatch.

POSTAL HISTORY OF CHICAGO

In order that a collector may not take too large a bite of postal history it may be useful to show what is involved in the case of a single city.* Chicago's history includes almost every phase except the colonial and pre-Constitutional. A collector would endeavor to indicate the prepostal history of Fort Dearborn in Indiana and Illinois Territories, with communications over army roads to Niles, Fort Wayne, Green Bay, Galena, Dubuque, and Vincennes; the establishment of the post office in 1831; the successive locations and the list of postmasters; changes in post office classifications; growth of the city by annexations, with the names of post offices absorbed, and their final incorporation into the city system as neighborhood stations, for the most part; the establishment of branch post offices, later to be known as stations; and the periodic renaming and moving of the rented stations.

Other basic features would include the introduction of such special postal services as the collection of mail from street boxes, carrier delivery, advertisement of mail, supplementary mail on east-bound trains, direct foreign mail in closed pouches, railway mail service, street railway service, pneumatic tube service, rural free delivery, air mail, and highway post offices.

Special features would include the treatment of Confederate prisoner-of-war mail at Camp Douglas, the temporary exhibition stations at the Columbian Exposition, A Century of Progress Exposition, and at philatelic conventions.

Additional matters to be covered include the private carriers which served Chicago from the east, with or without approval of postal authorities: Pomeroy & Company, Wells & Company, American Letter Mail, etc.; the local posts and expresses such as Allen, Brady, Bronson & Forbes, Chicago Penny Post, Floyd, Whittlesey, and others; the experimental use of perforated

---

* For an interesting and authoritative study to 1892, see Dr. Harvey M. Karlen, *Chicago Postal History* (Collectors Club of Chicago: 1973).

stamps in 1856 and early 1857; Chicago's connection with counterfeit United States stamps; the private coil perforation used by the John V. Farwell Company, and the first-day sales of stamps, first trips, and first flights.

Nearly every item in this long list provides postal markings, some in great variety. The handstamps of the North Branch and West Branch post offices are most desirable and may be unique. The peculiar supplementary mail, for which no extra charge was made, provides four types of markings, and there is no scarcer marking in the United States than the "Old Stamps Not Recognized" applied to covers bearing the demonetized stamps of 1857, or to the old envelope stamps.

The townmarks applied to covers between September 15 and November 15, 1863 (both dates approximate) differ from those used at any other period, for the year has been removed and letters have been substituted. Covers going out of the city show "GA," "RA," "SB," or "X," while those for local delivery show "KB," "KM," "PB," and perhaps others. No reason whatever has been discovered for their use.

All the usual markings appear on Chicago covers, including carrier backstamps, machine backstamps, and special backstamps to indicate that the fast mail trains were late. In addition the street railway markings are numerous enough to make a separate collection, and one which will be difficult to complete.

Another collection can be formed of the patriotic covers used in the city, and still another of the pictorial covers printed in Chicago. When one adds to these the slogan cancellations and the multitude of machine cancellations it can be seen that a complete postal-history collection of Chicago is a project for a society of collectors rather than an individual.

LOCAL POSTS

This term is used by collectors for two entirely different mail-carrying agencies. The first is a government agency carrying mail in a limited area or along a definite route. The stamps of such carriers are official and should be given recognition in catalogs of government issues. The local issues which include the Zemetvos and other official posts are discussed in chapter 32.

The second type of local post was a private concern, operated solely to make a profit. Many had official sanction when they complemented the regular postal service and did not compete with it. As a general rule the private local posts served a definite need or they could not have been profitable, but as soon as one began to prove its usefulness, it was suppressed and its field of operation taken over by the regular postal facilities.

Private Local Posts

Private local posts have been used in the following countries, among others: British Columbia, Brunei, Colombia, Cuba, Denmark, Egypt, France, Germany, Great Britain, Greenland, India, Mexico, Morocco, Newfoundland, New Hebrides, Norway (here called by-posts), Poland, Russia, Spain, Sweden, and Turkey. Undoubtedly some of these posts were sanctioned by the authorities while others operated in direct competition with the government posts.

Stamps were issued for several Chinese cities which were open to foreign trade by treaty, and at first were given full catalog recognition. When it became apparent that the stamps had no standing in the international mails, and that many had been issued for collectors only, the catalogs dropped them from their general lists.

Those of Shanghai were used at Shanghai sub-offices in other treaty ports and were accepted throughout the world, and therefore are listed in standard catalogs. The other principal treaty ports were Amoy, Chefoo, Chinkiang, Chunking, Ichang, Hankow, Foochow, Tientsin and Wuhu.

Companies engaged in delivering circulars, and using stamps, operated without restraint in England and Scotland. England produced the college stamps of Oxford and Cambridge Universities which were used from 1871 to 1886. Switzerland contributed several issues of hotel stamps which paid for conveying mail of hotel guests to the nearest post office. Local posts operated on various steamship lines, among them those of the Danube Steam Navigation Company, the Hamburg American Packet Company, the St. Lucia Steam Navigation Company, the Lady McLeod of Trinidad, the Royal Mail Steam Packet Company, the Suez Canal Company, the Turkish Steamship Company, the Tevastehaus and Helsingfors Steam Packet Company, the St. Thomas, La Guaira and Pto Cabello Company of Venezuela, and the Russian Company of Navigation, Commerce and Railroad, of Odessa.

Other carriers which have operated between cities or across the water include British railways with their railway letter stamps, the pigeon posts of New Zealand and the Lake Lefroy Cycle Post of Western Australia.

Collecting Locals

The collecting of local stamps is usually a matter for specialists or postal-history collectors covering all phases of a country, but there is no reason why an advanced collector should not specialize in locals only. In every case local stamps are more valuable on cover than off. The stamps were moderately scarce at the start and those which could not be reprinted were counterfeited without fear since they were not government issues. The on-cover state largely rules out the possibility of fraud.

Information is rather meager on the entire subject of locals and there are many pitfalls for an inexperienced collector. The best protection is to obtain these stamps only from reliable dealers who will guarantee them without reservation.

United States Private Local Posts

In the larger cities a demand arose for a service which would save a trip to the post office to deposit letters or to receive them and local posts were established to provide these services. The postal authorities could not object to the delivery of parcels of all kinds, but when the carriers began to deliver local letters without passing them through the post office, measures were taken to stop the practice. Soon Congress passed an act declaring all public thoroughfares to be post roads upon which the Post Office Department had the sole right to carry mail.

This act was broad enough to include all highways and by-ways, rivers and railroad routes, and to lessen further the need for any local service, a carrier system for home delivery was instituted in the larger cities and was extended as rapidly as possible to all but the smallest post offices. Any companies remaining in business after this time had to confine their operations to parcel delivery and express business, or to the distribution of handbills, and could deliver letters only after complying with strict regulations.

The local posts usually had stamps to show payment of charges and nearly all indicated the face value, but there were a few companies that based their charges on the volume of mail carried and charged varying rates, omitting any denomination from their stamps.

INDEPENDENT MAIL ROUTES

These may be considered the equivalent of the local posts but their service was between towns rather than within a city. They were established, as a rule, in direct competition with the government service, and gave a much faster service by providing a messenger who carried the letters, usually as an adjunct to an express package service.

These carriers operated on railroad, stage and steamboat lines, and finally were joined by others organized to carry mail only. In the 1840's letters were arriving in such out-of-the-way places as Chicago after passing through the hands of several of these companies. While some of them provided stamps to indicate the payment of charges, others relied on handstamps to indicate the route over which they traveled.

Overland and Western Express Companies

As settlement extended to California and Oregon the gold seekers demanded a faster service with the East than could be given by vessels sailing around the Horn. Soon, mail was being taken off Atlantic steamers at Central American ports and transported across the Isthmus of Panama or Nicaragua, to be placed aboard the first northbound ship which appeared.

FIG. 14–1. Postal Markings: inland waterways and Western express marks.

These routes were also used to reach the west coast of South America and the Panama transit marking is familiar to all cover collectors. Still faster service was needed; in 1858 a group of express company proprietors obtained a subsidy from the government to carry mail from St. Louis to California. A southern route was selected as the most suitable for year-round service and supposedly was through lands occupied by less hostile Indians. The mail carried on this route was handled by the postal authorities throughout the trip.

The freighting companies which had opened the central routes to the West during the Mormon trouble followed the Oregon Trail into what is now Wyoming and there branched off to the Great Salt Lake. Mail was carried on this route and on the Sante Fe Trail leading to Sante Fe and the new settlements of New Mexico. When gold was discovered in Colorado, then a part of Kansas territory, there were increased demands for a central mail route which could handle passengers and supplies and bring out gold.

The freighters organized stage routes, following old trails in some cases, and establishing new short routes in others, all converging on the area where Denver now stands. The Sante Fe route was extended farther up the Arkansas River with a turn north to reach the same place. To meet the demand for even swifter communication between the Missouri River and the West Coast, Russell and Majors, of the freighting company of Russell, Majors and Waddell, began to operate a fast pony express, April 3, 1860, between St. Joseph, Missouri, and Sacramento and San Francisco.

At first a rider left each terminal once a week but soon two were leaving. Letters of minimum weight were charged five dollars, plus the United States postage, and telegrams were charged by the number of words, at fees established by the leading telegraph companies. After a short period the fees for letters were reduced greatly but the company was never able to show a profit.

During this period the eastern and western telegraph companies were toiling across the prairies and on mountain slopes to join their lines into a transcontinental system. This was accomplished in October, 1861, and the need for the pony express was ended. The end had been anticipated for many months, during which the pony riders had carried messages only between the advancing ends of the line.

When it became apparent in 1860 that a war between the

North and the South could not be averted the great southern overland express was abandoned and a new line set up in a more central location. This followed the Oregon Trail in a general way and then went through Utah and Nevada over the route used by the pony express. The two services complemented each other to a great extent for the pony carried nothing but letters and telegrams, while the slower mail went by stagecoach. There was no extra charge for letters carried by the stages but they required more than twice the time to make the trip.

When the eastern and western railroads were joined at Promontory Point, Utah, on May 10, 1869, there was no longer any need for a transcontinental stagecoach line and this too was abandoned. However, for many years branch stage lines were used to reach Denver, the Oregon settlements, and other points.

Although very few western express companies provided stamps for the letters they carried, all had distinctive markings, and these were often used to cancel the United States stamps which were required on all mail privately carried, the express charges being additional. Envelopes bearing these markings are among the most interesting and valuable items connected with United States postal history.

INLAND WATERWAYS

Postal service on eastern and southern inland waterways antedated the express service described above. In some cases it was official, on carriers operating over definite routes: more often it was casual, the mail being picked up en route, and turned over to the first post office. For this handling of the mail the master of the boat was entitled to a fee fixed by postal regulations.

Many letters carried by packet boats belong in another category, these being the waybills which accompanied the shipments of freight. The envelopes nearly always were marked with a handstamp giving the name of the vessel and required no postage so long as the contents related exclusively to the freight shipment. However, if there were other communications in the envelope, or if it became necessary to post the waybill to the owner, full postage was required.

OTHER DEVELOPMENTS IN POSTAL SERVICE

The last quarter of the nineteenth century saw the rapid development of the Railway Mail Service and a great improvement in postal service. The organization of the Universal Postal Union and the adoption of nearly uniform foreign rates brought

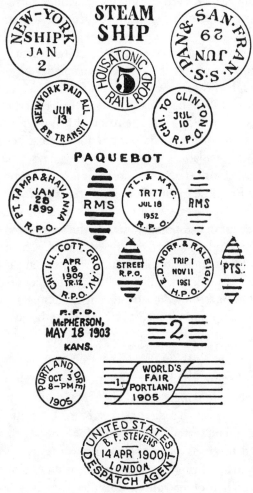

FIG. 14–2. Postal Markings: ocean mail, railroad, RMS, and R.F.D. marks.

a vast increase in correspondence, but unfortunately for collectors, a corresponding decrease in the variety and attractiveness of covers.

Near the end of the century the Rural Free Delivery added another milestone in service but marked the end of thousands of small post offices which had supplied many interesting covers. However, the R.F.D. used distinctive markings for a few years, and these now are sought by many collectors of state and local postal history.

The most revolutionary change in postal service came after the end of the First World War when airplanes began to carry mail. Although this service is only about forty years old it has provided more philatelic records than any other method of transportation and it has not even yet reached full development.

Air mail has brought the continents so close together that new stamps are available everywhere a few days after they are issued, and collectors are able to correspond with foreign friends as easily as with those in an adjoining state. With jet propulsion foreign letters may be expected on the day after they are written.

Other recent developments include the short-lived Highway Postal Service, and the distribution of mail by helicopter. In 1976, the Postal Service, no longer a department in the executive branch of the federal government, but an independent government corporation, stopped using air mail stamps for domestic use and began shipping all mail between cities by air or surface means, whichever was most convenient and available.

RAILWAY MAIL SERVICE

Mail has been carried by railroads since the day that postal officials became convinced that the cars would stay on the tracks. At first it was handled as freight to be unloaded at the terminal and there sorted for distribution. Soon, route agents were assigned to trains and to steamboat routes to sort the tied bundles of mail and bring together those for cities along the way or for transferal to other routes. Bundles for cities beyond the terminus were not sorted.

These route agents could accept mail en route and post-mark it with a distinctive handstamp, varying from the straight-line Baltimore Railroad to ornamental forms like that used on the Housatonic Railroad. The usual mark was circular, with an inscription including an abbreviation of the railroad name or the mail route. Some included the route agent's name or title.

Records show that mail in Great Britain was first carried by train in 1830 on the Manchester and Liverpool Railway. It was carried as freight. In 1838 a post-office surveyor on the Grand Junction Railway, connecting Birmingham with the Manchester and Liverpool Railway, suggested working the mail on the train. At about the same time an arm and net device was invented to pick up bags of mail at full speed.

The first regular sorting was begun in September, 1838, on the London and Birmingham run. This operation was studied by a United States postal employee named Plitt in 1839. Other cars were added on various trains and on January 1, 1855, one was operating between Dublin and Cork, in Ireland.

French railway service was in full operation at the same time and was described and illustrated in *Harper's Magazine* in 1854, in an article entitled "Life in Paris." This reads in part, "But where the French post office is unequaled perhaps by any other, is in the elegance and convenience of its ambulatory ar-rangements. The moving post office is an elegant car attached to the express trains, in which the postal service goes on as quietly and as uninterruptedly while traveling at the rate of 40 miles per hour, as if stationary in the Rue Jean Jacques Rousseau. The mails are made up, letters received, weighed, stamped and dis-patched en route."

In the United States a friendly argument continues between those who believe that the Burlington railroad had the first sort-ing car and those who credit the North Western Railway. In some cases it is claimed that one or the other invented the service. Actually, it was the Chicago, Burlington and Quincy, through its ownership of the Hannibal and St. Joseph Railroad, that had the first sorting car. The idea was proposed by a post-office clerk, W. A. Davis, in order to avoid a delay at St. Joseph when the mails arrived for the overland express. The service began July 28, 1862, but soon was interrupted by rebel raiders in northern Missouri.

An order of the Post Office Department, September 24, 1863, recognized the services of Mr. Davis in speaking of him as "superintendent of overland mail distribution on the cars of the Hannibal and St. Joseph Railroad Company from 26th July to 31st of August, 1862," and ordered that he be paid a hundred dollars. In addition, Third Assistant Postmaster General A. N. Zevely is quoted in the *Centennial History of Missouri* as saying, "I talked with Mr. Davis in St. Joe during my visit there . . . and believe that the idea of assorting mail on the cars . . . was entirely original with himself."

In spite of these facts, credit for the Railway Mail Service usually is given to George B. Armstrong, Assistant Postmaster of Chicago. He had the aid of Samuel B. Bangs, of his office, and with the assistance of Schuyler Colfax and Assistant Postmaster General Zevely, obtained authorization to test the idea.

A sorting car was placed in service on the Chicago and North Western Railway, August 28, 1864, on the Chicago and Clinton, Iowa, run. It was such a success that by 1867 the service was well established on many mail trains in the Middle West. In 1869, Colonel Armstrong became superintendent of the Railway Mail Service and proceeded to extend it throughout the country.

A bronze bust of Colonel Armstrong was unveiled in the Chicago post office in 1881, and both he and Mr. Bangs were honored after death by monuments in Rosehill Cemetery, in Chicago, indicating their contributions to the service.

A replica of the car used on the Hannibal and St. Joseph Railroad on the run between West Quincy and St. Joseph was exhibited at A Century of Progress Exposition in Chicago in 1933 and 1934. It was equipped as an operating postal car and covers were postmarked in it. The car now is preserved as a historical exhibit of the railroad and bears a plaque presented by the Railway Mail Association (now the National Postal Transport Association) on the seventy-fifth anniversary of the first run. In none of the literature is any mention made of an earlier railway mail service.

By 1872 the postal cars were in operation on 57 railroads over almost 15,000 miles of track, and 50 years later there were more than 1700 routes in service, but by 1942 the number had shrunk to a little more than 1000 with some hundreds of branch routes. At that time three highway post offices had been placed in service. In mid-1978, there was only one railway mail service route—between Washington and New York—while the highway service has been eliminated.

The usual markings of the Railway Mail Service show the route designation in abbreviated form and the letters R.P.O. in the townmark, while the letters RMS appear in the killer. On November 1, 1949, the service's name was changed to Postal Transportation Service and the letters PTS were substituted in the killers as new handstamps were provided. For some time both varieties were used by different employees on the same route. Those in use on the Broadway Limited and the 20th Century Limited show the train names in the townmark and the letters PTS in the killers. These handstamps were placed in use June 15, 1952, the fiftieth anniversary of the maiden runs of each train from New York to Chicago.

RAILWAY MAIL SERVICE ON BOATS

Railway post offices were operating on the inland waterways in the 1870's and on vessels running between the United States and Alaska as early as 1892. This was the Port Townsend and Sitka route but no postmarks are known before 1899.

In 1898 railway post offices were established between Tampa, Florida, and Cuba to handle soldiers' mail, and in 1900 the route name Port Tampa & Havanna was altered to Port Tampa & Havana, and in 1912 to Key West & Havana. Mail to Puerto Rico was carried by the New York & San Juan R.P.O., but in 1912 this service and that of the New York &

Canal Zone R.P.O., established in 1907, were changed to sea post offices.

The American Mail Line had five ships in service starting November 11, 1922, with sea post offices but all used the Railway Mail Service handstamps until 1925. The townmarks read "U.S. Sea Post TRANSPACIFIC," but the killers had the RMS device. In 1929 there were some twenty railway post offices operating on boat lines on interior and coastal lines, the latter to Alaska, Puerto Rico, the Canal Zone, etc.

The final run of the last "round the year" mail boat of the Railway Mail Service was on February 28, 1953. This route started as the Cape Charles & Norfolk R.P.O. (by steamer), but its recent history was of a combination railroad and steamboat run of the Phila. & Norfolk R.P.O., the vessel being the *Elisha Lee*. In 1953 there were four summer R.P.O.'s on boats, three in New Hampshire and one in New York. These were the Asquam Lake R.P.O. on Squam lake, the Alton & Merrymount R.P.O. and the Lake Winnepesaukee R.P.O., both on the lake of that name, and the Inlet & Old Forge R.P.O., on the Fulton chain of lakes in Herkimer County, New York. These four were not ordinary R.P.O.'s for they acted as carriers and delivered mail to individuals along the routes, as well as to post offices.

It may be mentioned that the floating postal station that operates out of the Detroit post office to serve ore boats which touch no port between the Soo and Cleveland, at least, is not connected with the Railway Mail Service.

Collectors may wonder at the use of R.P.O. markings on vessels but the confusion arises only through the use of the title Railway Mail Service for the entire operation division of the Post Office Department. This was cleared up when the title Postal Transportation Service was in full use.

POSTAL TRANSPORTATION SERVICE

The Postal Transportation Service now includes the railway, highway, terminal railway, and air-mail field post offices. In other words, it handles the transportation of mail by land, sea and air, in and around the United States, except within the areas served by local post offices. The latter have jurisdiction over Rural Free Delivery routes originating in the post offices.

At present the air service is limited to the sorting of mail and the cancellation of stamps at air-mail field post offices, and the dispatching of mail by appropriate planes. Should the service undertake to transport all first-class mail by planes, clerks may be put aboard to work the mails en route to make the best use of the time saved. Then it may be necessary to find a new title. Flying Post Office has been suggested.

STREET RAILWAY POSTAL SERVICE

The street car service, one of the most interesting divisions of mail service, was originally a part of the Railway Mail Service, but after a few years city routes were placed under the control of postmasters.

Street cars were first considered for mail service in St. Louis in 1891, when the Lindell Avenue Electric Company negotiated with the postmaster to pick up mail at letter boxes and deliver it to the post office, and on outbound trips to transport bags of mail to carriers for distribution. This contract was not completed but a similar agreement was entered into by the St. Louis and Suburban Railroad in 1892. Several extensions were made to the suburbs and by December 5, 1892, all routes were in operation with sorting, cancelling, and distribution on the cars.

On February 3, 1893, the Post Office Department officially recognized the service and the provisional use of a cancellation reading "Street R.P.O. No. 1." This was changed to "St. Louis & Florissant R.P.O." in 1896. Altogether about fourteen Street Railway Post Office lines or routes were in operation in St. Louis and its suburbs.

The second unit of this service began operations on August 8, 1894, when Brooklyn, New York, established a route to Coney Island. In 1895, Boston began service on May 1, Philadelphia on June 1, New York City on September 23, and Chicago and Cincinnati on November 11. In 1896, Washington,

Baltimore, San Francisco, and Rochester, were added, and Pittsburgh in 1898. After that year the only additions were Seattle in 1905, Cleveland in 1908, and Omaha in 1910. The service in all these cities covered about seventy routes, counting new names and new cancellations as new routes. Although the intention had been to process the mail completely on the cars, this often was not possible due to the volume of mail and the shortness of the route, especially in cities like Chicago where the entire system was within the most populated sections. In some cities with service to suburban areas there was ample time to sort and pouch the mail and deliver it direct to mail trains.

In 1899 much of the service was transferred to the jurisdiction of the postmasters in the cities where the routes operated, the date in Chicago being July 1. In this city it was contended that the service should not be under the R.M.S., as it operated wholly within the city limits, and on that basis it was transferred to the postmaster.

In Chicago the cancelling devices had "R.P.O." in the townmark as a general rule. The old handstamps in use before the R.M.S. period were provided with a cut cork killer, while handstamps issued during the R.M.S. period had "RMS" in the killer but retained the "R.P.O." in the townmark. Cancellers issued after the end of R.M.S. jurisdiction were provided with killers containing numerals of a two-line inscription "Street R.P.O.," but old handstamps with "RMS" killers continued in use for many years and perhaps until the end of service on some routes.

Because the postal cars caused many delays in other transportation while halted to pick up mail, the service operated at its best in non-rush-hour periods. With the coming of automobiles, the service was doomed for the trucks could avoid congested streets by altering their routes.

Service ended in New York in 1900, in San Francisco in 1905, in Seattle and Washington in 1913, in Boston, Chicago, Philadelphia, and St. Louis in 1915, in Pittsburgh in 1917, and in the other cities by November 9, 1929, when the Baltimore service was discontinued.

Due to the limited amount of mail that could be postmarked on some routes, the markings are scarce when compared to the volume of mail carried. A large number of the postmarks are not recognized at a casual inspection since they include two city names and appear to be ordinary Railway Mail Service markings. These postal markings should be collected on covers and close attention be paid to varieties, as each handstamp is unique in some respect. On some routes, Doremus cancelling machines were carried in the street railway cars to speed the handling of mail. More than five hundred varieties are now listed; many are recent discoveries as collectors have been focusing on these marks for only a short time. Any sizable bunch of personal or business mail from Chicago during this period will provide some covers with postmarks of the street railway service.

The service in Chicago underwent considerable curtailment and alteration in 1904 when a pneumatic tube service was installed between the main post office and railway stations and postal stations. Some routes ceased to deliver mail to the main post office and handled it only to a tube station on the route.

COLLECTION AND DISTRIBUTION WAGON SERVICE

This service began in Washington and New York City on October 1, 1896, and appears to have complemented the street railway postal service for areas without streetcar lines. The wagons were fitted much like the street cars, with pigeonholes and other furniture for handling and sorting mail. Mail was picked up at street boxes and postmarked, and time permitting, was sorted and tied up for direct delivery to trains and to the post office. It provided a faster service than had been available before, and commercial firms, particularly in New York, went out of their districts to place mail in the wagon route boxes.

This custom practically nullified the time saving for it was not possible to work all mail and much of it was delivered in bulk to the post office. The New York service was replaced, August 2, 1897, by pneumatic tubes.

The New York wagon was put to use in Buffalo and handled mail in that city until June 30, 1899, when its equipment and that of Washington, which had last been used on the same day, were shipped to St. Louis. Here the wagons were used to carry pouches of mail between the main post office and the railroad stations, or to postal stations, until sometime in 1903 or 1904.

MARYLAND EXPERIMENTAL WAGON SERVICE

On April 3, 1899, a two-horse postal wagon began to operate in Carroll County, Maryland, over a thirty-mile route, collecting mail from boxes set up at half-mile intervals, and postmarking and sorting it in transit. This service was a success and on December 20, 1899, three additional wagons were put in service in Carroll County, and two more in Frederick County. Additional wagons were commissioned in Washington County, Pennsylvania, and Jackson County, Missouri, and some of these probably continued in service as late as 1905.

HIGHWAY POST OFFICE SERVICE

This service, designated by the initials H.P.O. is the most recent addition to the Postal Transportation Service, and one of the most short-lived. The work performed en route on the buses was identical with that in the railway mail cars, except that mail was delivered directly to post offices, while in the Railway Mail Service it was delivered only to the railway stations.

The new service was designed to improve mail deliveries in regions without railroads, or on railroads where service was inadequate, and perhaps in some cases to allow railroads to discontinue trains, or service on uneconomical lines. The H.P.O. usually improved service by reducing the time between post offices or by including post offices which had no previous Railway Mail Service. In addition the buses had the great advantage of being able to select a new route when it becomes necessary to bypass a temporary trouble area.

The first suggestion for this service appears to have been in 1925, when the railway postal clerks were unable to handle the altered schedules of the railroads around Stockton, California. Also, the roads between the cities involved were shorter than the railroads, and in some cases the estimates showed that a highway schedule would require but half the railway time.

After local discussion, the matter was presented to the Sacramento branch of the Railway Post Office in 1927, by James F. Cooper, and later he took it before the Eighth Division convention in San Francisco. It was then presented to the National Convention of the Railway Mail Association, where it was approved after a hard struggle against Post Office Department opposition.

A bill passed by Congress was vetoed by the President, but the Railway Mail Association continued to press the matter and eventually a new bill was approved, July 11, 1940. The Post Office Department now claimed full credit for originating the service and obtaining the legislation.

The first H.P.O. was placed in operation on February 10, 1941, on a route covering the 148 miles between Washington and Harrisonburg, Virginia. Two other routes, one between South Bend and Indianapolis, and the other between San Francisco and Pacific Grove, were established on May 3 and August 4, 1941.

During the Second World War no additions were made until 1946, when three routes were opened in Alabama and Michigan. After a dormant period of two years an intensive program was started in 1948, and by the end of the year 16 routes were operating. In the following year 39 additional routes were established, not including two old routes under altered names, and in 1950, 26 were added, again not counting one with an altered name.

In 1951 the Korean War slackened the pace and only three

routes were opened, with two additional new names for existing routes, but in 1952, 31 routes were added and since that time there has been a steady increase in this service.

New names for routes were the result of changes in one or both of the terminal points. Internal changes were frequently made on a route, and post offices were added or detached, without any change in the designation. The first name change affected the Middletown, N.Y. & Newark, N.J. route only two months after its inauguration, when the New York terminal was moved to Goshen on January 23, 1949, and the route became the Goshen, N.Y. & Newark, N.J. route. The short periods during which some names were in use make those postmarks very desirable.

By the mid-1950s, two-thirds of the H.P.O. routes were equipped with government owned and operated buses with the remainder under contract. No distinction whatever was made between the two methods of operation so far as postal employees and postmarks were concerned. Included in the contract group for a number of years were several routes operated by the railroads.

One of the longest of these R.P.O. bus routes was inaugurated by the Gulf, Mobile & Ohio Railroad (Alton route) on February 1, 1952, over the 320 miles between Chicago and St. Louis. Prior to that date this railroad had R.P.O. bus routes in operation in Tennessee, Mississippi, and Alabama, and early in 1953 the link between St. Louis and Jackson, Tennessee, was added. The G.M. & O. provided R.P.O. bus service almost the entire distance from Chicago to Mobile.

All H.P.O. bus routes became H.P.O. routes Jan. 1, 1956, with an eventual change in postal markings.

The postmarks show the letters "H.P.O." at the bottom of the circular postmark and now have the letters "PTS" in the oval killer. Those of the R.P.O. bus routes have the letters "R.P.O." in the circular postmark and "RMS" in the killer, just as do the marks of the railway post offices on trains. However, the R.P.O. bus marks may be identified by the word "TRIP" and numeral in the postmark, whereas the railway mail service uses the train abbreviation "TR," and the number of the train.

All regular postmarks were placed on the mail by postal clerks working the mail on the buses, using metal handstamps. First-trip postmarks are placed on collectors' covers by the postmasters at the terminals, and not by a clerk on a bus. This is done, according to Hershel E. Rankin, editor of *Transit Postmark*, to insure a clear impression of the postmark and cachet, which might be difficult on a moving bus. These postmarked covers were carried by bus to the other terminal and dispatched to destination.

The first-trip postmarks were made with a rubber stamp having long lines to cancel the blocks which some collectors place on their covers. The literature of the H.P.O. collectors gives the impression that regular postmarks applied on the bus are more important than first-trip cancellations.

The Highway Post Office service was finally terminated in 1972 so that there no longer were either H.P.O. or (later) R.P.O. markings available to collectors except on special occasions when routes may be opened up for old time's sake and for special use of stamp and cover collectors. Though the period of the H.P.O. was brief it was a most interesting section in the history of the Post Office Department. The reminders of that history can still be seen today in the albums of the cover collector.

RURAL FREE DELIVERY

The first experiment with this service was made on October 1, 1896, in West Virginia, the home state of Postmaster General William L. Wilson. The routes selected were based at Uvilla, Hallstown and Charlestown, and each was about 20 miles long. The first vehicles were horse drawn and probably were buggies or spring wagons. These were soon replaced by little R.F.D. wagons with postal equipment so that mail could be delivered from pigeonholes without delay, and business could be transacted en route.

By June 30, 1897, this rural service had been extended to 29 states and 82 routes were in operation. Automobiles were introduced in 1912, the first official use of one being made on August 7 in Bennington County, Vermont.

At the present time there are more than 32,000 routes covering more than 1,500,000 miles in the United States and its territories. The routes average a little less than 50 miles. In spite of their impressive number and the mileage, this service extends to only a little more than half the 3070 counties in the United States.

In the period up to about 1902, the mail posted on each route was postmarked by the carrier with a rubber handstamp which indicated the town where the route originated and the number of the route. The normal postmark was a straight-line type with a four-line inscription as the townmark and a four- or five-bar killer. The usual form had the letters "R.F.D." at the top, the state at the bottom, and the town and date in the other lines. The bars of the killer form a regular rectangle but two or three are interrupted at the center to leave a space for the route number. Various sizes and styles of type were used in the handstamps but all appear to have been made of rubber.

The marking "Mailed on Rural Route" is found in both straight-line and circular forms, the former as a simple endorsement. The latter, which had a killer attached, must have been intended as a cancelling device. The law covering these markings provided that the postage on fourth-class matter mailed on rural routes would be at less than standard rates, by two cents per parcel if for local delivery, otherwise by three cents. If parcels prepaid at the reduced rates were shipped without the marking any postal clerk might have checked the postage and put on a due notation.

There seems to have been no fixed rule concerning the use of these rural marks. A majority of those found by collectors are on first-class mail to which the discount did not apply, and it is apparent that the rural carrier often postmarked more than the parcel post matter.

This law was entirely political and in line with a recent enactment which allows patrons on rural routes to send and receive merchandise by parcel post in amounts almost double the size and weight allowed other patrons. This puts a double burden on city dwellers, who must take their parcels of forty pounds or less to the post office, while the post office sends out a truck to pick up the rural patron's seventy-pound load.

SEA POST OFFICES

Sea post offices are official postal stations on board vessels and have the equipment for the transaction of postal business of every kind. Before the Second World War the United States had a large number in operation between this country and Germany, France, South America, the Far East, and other places. In nearly all cases the sea post offices were on vessels with regularly scheduled trips.

Those offices which were conducted jointly with a foreign country, as with Germany, for example, were United States post offices on the outgoing run and German post offices on the return trip. The postmarks read "U.S. Ger. Sea Post" in the first case; the order of the country names is reversed in the other.

Nearly or perhaps all sea post offices of the belligerent nations were discontinued during the Second World War and have not been re-established. The great increase in air services may be responsible for this, and there is a possibility that they will never be revived.

The postmarks which were in use to the Orient usually had a mark which included the letters "U.S.T.P. Sea Post," the "T.P." meaning trans-Pacific. One of the first sea posts in operation from the United States had a standard machine cancellation with "U.S. Sea Post No. 1" in the townmark space and the vessel name, "Coamo" or "Cristobal" in a flag killer.

French sea posts have an octagonal townmark which usually gives the terminals of the trip, as "New York—au Havre," "Le Havre à New York," "Yokahama à Marseille," or the reverse. Germany operated many sea posts, including coastal lines touching at African and Oriental ports, with inscriptions such as "Deutsche Seepost—Australische Hauptlinie," "New Guinea

Zweiglinie," and "Deutsche Seepost—Hamburg—Sudamerika."

Italy had post offices on various lines and used postmarks showing the name of the vessel and such inscriptions as "Agenzia Postale," "Navigazione Generale Italiana—Piroscafo Postale Italiano," and "Soc. Italiana di Servisi Marittimi—Piroscafo." Italian lake service used postmarks without vessel names but with such inscriptions as "Servicio Postale sul Lago d'Iseo."

Belgian sea post offices serving the Congo used the inscription "Courier de Haute Mer," and perhaps this mark was also used in services to other places. Postmarks applied to mail on Spanish vessels have the words "Vapor Correo" with the name of the country and the vessel. One Swedish postmark reads "S.J.P. 7-Göteborg—New York—Svenska Amerika Linien—Drottingholm."

The Netherlands sea postmarks show the name of the operating company and the vessel. Thus, the Royal Packet Navigation Company's postmark reads "Konink. Paket vaart Maatschappig," around a circular mark containing the name of the vessel.

Japanese vessels have a postmark with the words Imperial Japanese Post abbreviated to "I.J.P.," followed by "Sea Post" and the name of the vessel.

New Zealand uses a cachet on all covers with the words "Marine Post Office" at the top and the name of the vessel below. The stamps on these covers are cancelled "Packet Boat" in several styles. Since these Pacific Ocean ships stop at various islands and colonies, many varieties of foreign stamps may be found with this cancellation.

Ocean mail marks made before sea posts were placed in operation bear such legends as "Hamburg Packet" or "Ham. Pkt." These belong in the category of paquebot markings rather than sea post markings.

PAQUEBOT MARKINGS

Although only a few vessels had sea post offices almost every vessel that plies the seven seas carries mail under certain conditions. Mail may originate with passengers or may be put aboard at a port of call. The master of the vessel is obligated to put it ashore and into the regular mail when he reaches an appropriate port and he receives a fee for each letter handled.

Such mail matter usually is given the cancellation "Paquebot," and the townmark of the post office receiving it. These often are incorporated into a single hand or machine marking. As a rule, the separate paquebot marks are straight line, some framed, others not.

Australia favors the mark "Loose Ship Letters" in various forms and Mauritius has made use of the words "Ship Letter." Other countries use the words "Posted at Sea" in the townmark.

Various steamship lines place a cachet on all letters of this sort, using the purser's handstamp. This advertises the company and includes the name of the vessel, date, and the words "Posted on the High Seas." In a few cases a similar mark but without the purser's indicum is used to cancel the stamps, but this is hardly official and probably is done for philatelic reasons.

A great variety of stamps may be obtained with foreign paquebot cancels. For example, British stamps are accepted on any British ship, even including colonial stamps. It is doubtful if any sort of legitimate stamp on an incoming letter would be refused at the post office where it is put ashore.

Prior to the use of paquebot markings such letters reaching the United States were usually handstamped "Steamship," "New York Steamship," "New York Ship," etc.

NAVAL POSTAL MARKINGS

The first post office placed aboard a United States naval vessel was commissioned on July 1, 1908, and during that year 69 navy ships were so equipped. These have made use of various types of rubber and metal handstamps and in a few cases machines have been needed to handle the mail.

The first marks appear to have been made with rubber handstamps, with killers of four closely spaced bars. The townmark portion carried the name of the vessel at the top. Later came a handstamp with wider-spaced killer bars, the letters "U.S.S." at the top of the townmark, the vessel name below. This was followed by a three-bar killer spaced to permit type to be set between the bars, showing the name of the port or perhaps the object of the cruise. Some use was made of the standard metal handstamp with the upright oval killer of horizontal bars, the date located between the townmark and the killer. Machine marks were of the flag type and wavy-line types in use ashore at the same time. During World War II, the identities of naval units were concealed and postmarks simply read "U.S. Navy." Since then, ship names, often accompanied by the ship classifications, have been re-inserted in postmarks. From its commissioning date as a rocket cruiser on May 2, 1964, the postmark of the U.S.S. Chicago bears the designation (CG-11).

Cachets have had a great deal to do with the popularity of naval cover collecting. They are sponsored for every phase of a ship's career. There will be one for keel-laying, another for launching, and others for the trial run, shakedown cruise, first day in commission, first day of postal service, last day in commission, and even one if the ship is recommissioned. Some collectors attempt to show the complete life history of a vessel; others regard these items as purely philatelic.

FIRST-DAY COVERS

This phase of collecting is almost exclusively American, but has been extended to some countries interested in catering to United States collectors. Cancellations showing the first day of use have been sought since the first stamp was issued on May 6, 1840, and among the United States issues the 3-cent stamp canceled on July 1, 1851, is a most desirable item.

However, collecting first-day covers alone made little progress until the United States Post Office Department began to sell the new issues at selected cities. The first issue to be so sold was the Pilgrim Tercentenary of 1920, placed on sale in Plymouth, Massachusetts, Philadelphia, and Washington, D.C., December 21, 1920.

Since that time the initial sale of commemorative issues has been limited to selected cities only, but Washington has been the choice for many issues. Several values of the regular postage issue of 1922-1926 were released at appropriate cities, the others at Washington. All values of the presidential issue of 1938 had their first-day sale in Washington but the new ordinary issue of 1954-1955 is being placed on sale in various cities. The 24-cent air-mail stamp of 1918 was placed on sale in Washington, Philadelphia, and New York, May 14, not as a philatelic gesture but to provide stamps at the three points served by the initial flight.

The first use of the slogan "First Day of Issue" was at the sale of the 3-cent Northwest Territory issue, July 13, 1937, at Marietta, Ohio, New York, and Washington.

Obtaining United States First-Day Covers

New issues usually are announced far enough in advance to permit the special envelopes to be printed and distributed, and the notice gives the date and place of first-day sale. Those who collect these covers may send their prepared envelopes to the postmaster at the city named, with cash or a postal money order to cover the exact cost of the stamps to be affixed. Money orders should be made payable to "Postmaster," without naming him.

Today, pictorial envelopes on excellent paper are prepared for each issue and are available at stamp shops or at the publisher's office. Unless these are used, a collector should buy high-grade envelopes which will not yellow or become brittle. The envelopes should be of standard size, about 3½ to 3¾ inches high by 6½ to 6¾ inches long. Neither high-back or long envelopes should be used as they will not fit in regular albums, are likely to be damaged when tied up in bundles in the mail, and are difficult to sell.

The instructions today state that a "reasonable number" of prepared envelopes may be sent with each order. Ten would be considered reasonable; if more are desired, another order may be sent. Each envelope should have a filler—cardboard or letter paper—to ensure a good impression of the cancellation.

The flap must be sealed or tucked in to prevent entanglement in the machine and damage to it and to all that follow it until the machine can be stopped. Each cover should be addressed in ink or by typewriter, or a removable address slip may be fastened to the envelope with rubber cement. Ample space must be allowed above the address for the stamps ordered, especially if blocks are requested. Place a pencil notation on each envelope, where it will be covered by the stamps, stating how many stamps are to be affixed.

It is permissible to order singles, pairs, and blocks, but not plate-number blocks. There seems to be no reason for having first-day covers with blocks, unless several stamps are needed to make up a single first-class postage rate. There is also the danger that blocks will crowd or overlap the designs on pictorial covers.

Covers must have the postage paid at the first-class rate to obtain a dated cancellation. When blocks or high-value stamps are ordered it is permissible to ask for registration, special delivery, or air-mail service. A brief note may be written to the postmaster asking for first-day service, and this should accompany the prepared envelopes and remittance in a single envelope. Place a notation on the face of the envelope: "First-Day Covers, —Stamp." Be sure that your postage is fully prepaid for the postmaster will not accept packages on which postage is due.

Collectors may obtain first-day covers with plate-number blocks through dealers and other operators of first-day cover services. They attend the sale in person, buy the stamps and affix them to envelopes in quantity, for the post office will not handle wholesale orders.

'Self Service' Covers

The Postal Service has begun the self-servicing of certain selected first day covers. Collectors may buy the new stamp for an announced number of days, apply it as desired to their own covers, and send them to a designated address at the first day city, where the first day cancellation will be applied (late) and the covers returned through the mailstream. No money changes hands except at each local post office.

Foreign First-Day Covers

Although notices of foreign first-day sales appear in the stamp journals, there seldom is time to order except by air mail. Since many foreign commemorative stamps are of low value, designed for domestic use, a first-day cover mailed to the United States may need several copies. The cost of money orders or bank drafts and air-mail postage will make a first-day cover, bearing a few cents worth of stamps, very expensive. Where first-day service is available at all in foreign countries, it seldom is necessary to send envelopes or addressed covers. The foreign postal agency includes the cost of an envelope, addressing it, and affixing the stamps, in a service charge. Dealers, who order in quantity through an agent, spread the expense over the entire lot and are able to sell the covers rather more cheaply. ·

Members of international exchange clubs obtain first-day cover service through their foreign members at very little over cost, as the service usually is free and only the stamps and envelopes must be purchased abroad.

The announcements of new Canadian stamps usually appear in ample time to be of value. This country requires a service charge except when high-value stamps are being issued, and there is no designated first-day city other than the capital, Ottawa.

Instructions for addressing letters to foreign post-office departments will be found in the discussion of foreign philatelic agencies in chapter 2.

UNITED STATES CACHETS

The first cachets were rubber-stamped impressions placed on covers to call attention to events having definite relations to the date and place indicated in the postmarks. Some were type-set but when time permitted it was customary to reproduce a special design on a rubber stamp.

Cachets for first-day covers and other important events have been developed until they now are pictorial envelopes with a design reproduced, as a rule, by line engraving. The most important, perhaps, are the official cachets supplied by postal authorities or approved by the Post Office Department. These are supplied for various air-mail events, and for new Highway Post Office Service.

Events of national importance, such as the Washington Bicentennial, may bring a deluge of cachets on dates and from places having a connection with the event or person who is honored. These covers have a place in collections, particularly when the stamps used tie in with the event.

Covers with cachets marking philatelic conventions and exhibitions also may deserve a place in a special collection of similar material, but in too many cases the cachets are issued only to finance the event. Some cachets have been gotten out by individuals to boost home towns and to obtain a little personal publicity, but few of them have any interest for the more experienced collectors.

None of the cachets receive any particular listing except those issued in connection with air mail or other official events, and then only in the specialized lists of the interested groups of collectors. Pictorial envelopes are a decided improvement over handstamped cachets, but in spite of the different designs, a collection becomes a little monotonous when an album contains nothing else. Nevertheless, many philatelists still find a lot of satisfaction in collecting cachets.

PATRIOTIC, CAMPAIGN, AND PROPAGANDA ENVELOPES

It may be assumed that pictorial envelopes grew out of the short-lived Mulready stamped envelopes of 1840 in England. The many caricatures which appeared at that time hastened the demise of these decorated envelopes but they had lineal descendents in the propaganda stationery gotten out for universal penny postage, temperance, and other subjects.

Propaganda envelopes also appeared in the United States and it was but a short step to the presidential campaign types.

When the Civil War broke out the designs carried patriotic messages and pictures. The sentiments which they expressed often lacked good taste and in the North attempts were made by southern sympathizers to have them barred from the mail.

At that time good illustrations required the use of woodcuts or lithography and this accounts to a certain extent for the poor presentation of some excellent ideas. Of the few printers who were willing to risk the expense, Charles Magnus perhaps was the foremost with his lithographs in black and white, and in full color.

Envelopes were published in the southern states to present the Confederate views, but none had the Magnus quality. Among the most interesting are those which show the Confederate flag in its various stages as new stars were added for the states joining the rebel cause.

Numerous well-designed pictorial envelopes were used during the Spanish-American War but were scarcely recognized by collectors until some thirty years later when the Civil War envelopes began to command fancy prices. Scarcely any pictorial covers were in use during World War I and those of World War II were due in a large measure to the work of a well-known stamp dealer.

Campaign envelopes were in use in the two presidential campaigns before the Civil War and in the campaign during the war, during both the convention and election periods, but those of later campaigns are very scarce, and probably no complete collection exists.

ADVERTISING ENVELOPES

Advertising envelopes were in use in the United States as early as the 1850s. They were used to attract settlers to some particular region, and maps of various states and territories are frequently seen. One of the earliest groups pictures life in the gold fields of California and is quite scarce in spite of the number that must have been mailed to relatives back east.

Hotels and business concerns have adorned their envelopes, front and back, with views of their buildings, and manufacturers have shown their products. Railroad and steamboat companies have pictured engines, trains, and boats, and so many stock raisers advertised their businesses that a collection of the latter would include every animal, fish, and fowl which has been raised or sold in the United States.

College covers include some with views of the buildings and others prepared for the use of a class or social organization. Although direct-mail advertising may be considered a modern idea, a study of covers will show that it was well established in the 1850-1860 period. Almost every cover collection includes an example of an envelope used to promote phonography, later to be called shorthand, and another relating to phrenology, the science of determining character by the shape of the skull.

Today a pictorial cover is a rarity and a company that may buy space in national magazines and on billboards often uses a plain envelope with only a street address or box number, on the theory, perhaps, that this envelope will be opened and the contents read, while an identifiable envelope will be thrown away unopened.

MAXIMUM CARDS

One of the newer sidelines of philately, gaining many followers during the past twenty years, is the maximum card, the name for a picture post card mailed with a stamp showing the same subject, the stamp being affixed and tied by the postmark on the view side, the postmark being that of a place closely related to the subject. The stamp picture and card picture should be identical if possible, though the card will of course, illustrate the subject more clearly than a stamp can. The stamp should be more or less contemporary with the card, although the card should not be one published to match the new stamp.

The date of postmarking should be one of importance in connection with the stamp. It might be the first day of use, which usually is a commemorative date, or it might be the birth or the death date of the person who is the subject. The place of postmarking may require some latitude when there is no post office at the actual scene.

The requirements were formulated by the Maximum Card Society of America (MACSA) and formed a basis for listing and sale. One stipulation is for a single stamp on the card, but where one stamp will not pay the postage, or where there are two or three stamps in a commemorative set differing only in value, a card should be acceptable with two or three stamps.

When a stamp design has many elements, the principal subject should be the subject of the card. When there are subjects of equal importance, as on the Yorktown stamp, or the Army and Navy issues, maximum cards may be made for each subject, and if possible, a card for the combination of subjects.

Rulers, national emblems, and arms, may be postmarked at any place in the country. Cards with portraits of persons noted for their work or attainments may be postmarked at the scene of their success, as well as at their place of birth or death.

Foreign postal authorities appear to have no objection to postmarking cards on the view side but the United States has not allowed this until recently and under certain restrictions. At present there is an order to all postmasters to postmark cards on the view side when presented in person or by mail in lots of twenty-five or more. Some of the smaller post offices will postmark a lesser number, but only as a favor. To help in this situation, the Maximum Card Society of America, MACSA as it is called, has provided a service for members in order to accumulate a sufficient number to meet the post-office ruling.

BISECTS AND OTHER STAMP FRACTIONS

Bisects or splits, although meaning half-stamps, are terms used to describe all portions of stamps that have been used to pay postage. The postage value of the split is a portion of the value of the original stamp.

In addition to half-stamps there are thirds, quarters and eighths, used as these portions of the original. There are also two-third stamps, used for either two-thirds or three-fourths of the value. Bisects, when half-stamps, have been cut diagonally, vertically, and horizontally; the thirds, vertically; the fourths and eighths rectangularly.

United States Bisects

Though it is stated in *Scott's Specialized United States Catalogue* that only authorized bisects are listed, the present author has not seen any postal order or law giving such authority. Very recently Philip H. Ward, Jr., in *Mekeel's Weekly Stamp News*, quoted some old letters from postmasters requesting rulings on the matter. These letters of August and September, 1853, may have brought the ruling of November 10, 1853, in which the Post Office Department stated that stamps cut from envelopes were not valid for postage and that the law does not "authorize the use of parts of stamps in prepayment of postage." From this it appears that United States bisects were passed through the ignorance of postal clerks, except in those few cases where a temporary shortage of stamps of certain low values was found and the local postmaster authorized the use of bisects to meet postal needs.

The 10-cent stamp of 1847 is listed as bisected in all three ways, with the parts serving as 5-cent stamps. The 12-cent stamp of 1851 is bisected diagonally for a 6-cent rate and quartered to make 3-cent stamps, and the 12-cent value of 1857 is known bisected diagonally. The Scott catalog lists the 2-cent Black Jack issue of 1861-1866 with an "F" grill with a diagonal half, a vertical half, and a horizontal half—each found on cover used as 1-cent. In the revenue series of 1862 the 2-cent proprietary stamp was bisected horizontally while the 2-cent U.S.I.R. was bisected vertically and diagonally, all being used as 1-cent values. In the 1871 series the 4-cent stamp was bisected horizontally and used as 2-cent values.

Foreign Bisects

Neither *Scott's Standard Catalogue* nor *Gibbons' British*

Empire section makes any general statement regarding the listed bisects. In specific cases they are listed as "authorized" but generally there are no remarks.

In the British Commonwealth hardly a country or colony of the western hemisphere is missed and nearly all appear to have been used before 1885. Often the bisect was necessary to provide halfpenny stamps before that denomination was available. Most of the West Indian colonies and British Honduras provided halfpenny stamps in this manner. In addition Barbados bisected a 2-pence, Montserrat a 6-pence, Turks Islands a 5-pence value. The halves of the Montserrat 6-pence value were used as 2½-pence stamps.

British North America was more prolific in its bisects, Canada having 3- and 6-pence, and 5- and 10-cent bisects between 1851 and 1859; Newfoundland, 4- and 6-pence and 1-shilling bisects between 1857 and 1862; Nova Scotia, 1-, 3-, and 6-pence and 1-shilling bisects, 6-pence and 1-shilling quarters in the 1851 issue, and 1- and 10-cent bisects in 1860-1863; New Brunswick 3- and 6-pence and 1-shilling bisects and 1-shilling quarters in the 1851 issue, 10-cent bisects in 1860; Prince Edward Island 2- and 3-pence values in 1861, 1-, 2-, 3-, 4-, 6-, and 9-pence bisects in 1863-1868, and 2-, 3-, and 6-cent bisects in 1872.

Single examples of bisects are noted in Gibraltar, Egypt, Sierra Leone, and Transvaal, with three examples in Niger Coast. India produced several bisects in the 1855-1860 issues, but all are listed for use only in the Straits Settlements.

Bisects of European stamps are rather uncommon but nearly all values of the Roman States issue of 1852 were cut in some fashion. The ½-, 2-, 4-, 5-, 6-, 7-, and 8-bajocchi values were bisected, the 3-bajocchi was cut into one-third and two-thirds for use as 1- and 2-bajocchi values, the 6- into thirds to serve as 2-bajocchi values, and the 4- and 8-bajocchi stamps into quarters to be used as 1- and 2-bajocchi values.

Two Sicilies have splits in the 1851 and 1861 issues and Romagna in several values of the 1859 issue. San Marino bisected the 2-centesimos value of 1871 and Sardinia provided four examples in the 1855-1863 issue, also quartering the 80-centesimos stamp and bisecting the newspaper stamp of 1861. In 1867 Turkey needed a 1½-piastre value and made two-thirds of a 2-piastre value valid for that rate.

Many examples of fractional stamps are found in the issues of Mexico, among them being the only eighths noted. These fractions generally occur in the earlier issues but a few were used as late as 1884 and 1895. Other Latin American countries listed as users of bisects are Brazil, Chile, the Dominican Republic, Ecuador, Guatemala, Peru, and Uruguay, with the last mentioned furnishing quartered stamps in addition.

Cuba bisected some issues between 1882 and 1885, and the Danish West Indies authorized the bisecting of the 4-cent value in 1900 to provide 2-cent stamps. In Hawaii a shortage of stamps was the excuse for bisecting the 2-cent value of 1864 to obtain 1-cent stamps.

It goes almost without saying that these fractions of stamps must have been affixed to letters at the post office in the presence of a postal clerk, for otherwise it would have been a simple matter to obtain and reuse parts of stamps showing no cancellation.

Full covers are needed for proof of genuineness as fractions "on piece" may have been cut down to remove postage due marks or other postage stamps.

A pair of diagonal bisects connected by perforations is almost certain to be an example of philatelic use.

❖❖❖

CHAPTER FIFTEEN

AEROPHILATELY

The conquest of the air opened a new field to collectors not only of stamps but of items of postal history and associated material showing the development of the service. The glamor of aviation and its specially designed stamps have induced beginners as well as collectors of long standing to enter this branch of the hobby. The entire development of aviation is so recent that many have been able to follow it from the start and build their collections as the service progressed from experiments to its present stature.

Some pioneer flights before the First World War carried mail, either privately or by postal authority. Examples of this belong in the category of forerunners. The history of the air post is similar in many countries, with pioneer flights, experimental flights, and finally scheduled service. However, countries entering the field late profited from the experience of others, and soon it was necessary only to prepare landing fields, buy planes, and hire pilots to start a complete service.

ZEPPELINS

Count Ferdinand von Zeppelin's introduction to aeronautics took place in the United States, where he had been sent during the Civil War as an official observer for the German army. His first balloon ascent was made at Fort Snelling, near Minneapolis. Zeppelin retired from the army in 1891 and at once tried to raise capital for his experiments with lighter-than-air machines. Finally, William II of Wurttemberg advanced the money and in July, 1900, the Z-1 made its maiden flight. After a few trials this ship was abandoned as unsafe and work was started on a smaller ship with three times as much engine power. The new ship, the Z-2, was completely destroyed in a storm on her maiden voyage.

In spite of these setbacks, Zeppelin was able to finish the Z-3, and in October, 1906, he took eleven passengers for a 2½-hour cruise covering seventy miles. After a much longer flight in the following year, Zeppelin was acclaimed a national hero. In 1908 he organized the Zeppelin Company and built a plant and landing field at Friedrichshafen.

Between 1910 and 1915 several Zeppelins were in use and the most notable, the *Viktoria Louise*, or LZ-11, made over a thousand flights.

Ultimately transoceanic, round-the-world, and polar flights were made and the dirigibles became well established in aviation. However they were particularly vulnerable in electrical storms as their buoyancy depended on hydrogen. This fault could have been overcome by using nonexplosive helium but the United States, which alone had a supply of this gas, had scarcely enough for its airships.

Some mail was carried on nearly every Zeppelin trial or flight but covers from the period before 1910 are classed as rarities. After a series of catastrophes in Germany and the United States, rigid airships were abandoned for mail and passenger carrying purposes.

THE WRIGHT BROTHERS

Although airplane designs date back to the time of Leonardo da Vinci in the fifteenth century it was not until December 17, 1903, that anyone was able to demonstrate that a heavier-than-air machine could be made to fly. On that date Orville and Wilbur

Wright made a flight of a few hundred feet at Kitty Hawk, North Carolina. Within a few years airplanes were being built and operated by adventurous pilots.

The first flights were exhibitions at county fairs with pastures as landing fields, but soon the flights were extended from one pasture to another and eventually they increased to the limits of the fuel capacity of the plane. Soon a continent became too limited for daring aviators and transoceanic flights were made by hopping from one island to another, or from the closest point of one continent to another. In many of these experimental and historic flights the pilots were deputized as special carriers and covers were handled for collectors.

Prior to World War II, some countries were sending all letter mail to colonial possessions by air but this ended with the beginning of hostilities. After 1945, however, airmail service was reconstituted and expanded. The great development of aviation during the war and the vast number of planes and pilots available at its end provided the means to blanket the globe with a network of air routes. In Europe, several countries began giving airmail service to all minimum weight first-class mail without extra charge. Since 1975, the U.S. Postal Service also has been giving such handling to inter-city first-class mail on a when-available basis.

AIR POST STAMPS

The first stamps for air mail were issued by Italy in 1917, for the experimental flights between Rome and Turin and between Naples and Palermo. These were provisional and were made by overprinting the current special delivery stamps.

On March 31, 1918, Austria overprinted the word "Flugpost" on her regular postage stamps for an air-mail flight from Vienna to Kiev, in the Ukraine via Cracow and Lemberg.

On May 13 of the same year the United States issued the first definitive air-mail stamp, the famous 24-cent red and blue, for use on the Washington–Philadelphia–New York experimental service. This value paid for special delivery service as well as the air-mail charge.

Since that time air-mail stamps have been issued by most countries and usually these have been well designed, utilizing subjects which indicate flight by air and the speed of the service.

There also are numerous semiofficial stamps in this category used in countries where an operating company has been authorized to carry mail and to collect the postage. The S.C.A.D.T.A. issues of Latin-American countries are examples. Still other countries have allowed private concerns to operate outside the regular postal limits and to collect postage by means of stamps.

In addition to adhesive stamps the aerophilatelist collects the air post stationery of the country in which he is interested. There are envelopes, letter sheets, and postal cards, and recently a somewhat standard air-letter sheet called an aerogramme has been adopted in the international mails with a uniform charge of postage somewhat below the air-mail letter rate. Aerogrammes make an interesting special collection and have attracted sufficient collectors to make a special society possible.

AIR POST ETIQUETTES AND OTHER LABELS

Perhaps nearly all aerophilatelists also collect etiquettes, as they call the labels fixed to ordinary envelopes to indicate air-mail service. These are printed in nearly every foreign language, and those for international use nearly always show a second inscription "Par Avion," as suggested by the Universal Postal Union.

Some collectors include the colorful labels affixed to baggage, freight, and express shipments by the operating companies. The connection of these items with postal service is a little vague but, as in other phases of philately, there is no set course and few would follow even if there were.

SHIP-TO-SHORE FLIGHTS; CATAPULT COVERS

As early as 1927 ship-to-shore flights were suggested as a way to speed the arrival of foreign letters, and on July 31 of that year Clarence D. Chamberlin sailed from New York on the *Leviathan* with the service plane of the Wright Aeronautical

Corporation on board. Next day he flew the plane from the deck at 8:14 A.M. Fog forced him to land at Curtiss Field, on Long Island. As the skies cleared he again took to the air and reached Teterboro Airport in New Jersey at 10:51 A.M., carrying 916 covers franked with 10-cent Lindbergh and 2-cent White Plains stamps.

In 1928 a similar flight from the S.S. *Conte Grande* on an eastbound voyage was scheduled to land passengers and mail in Spain. When the passengers learned that Spanish planes were to be substituted for the Lufthansa planes promised, they refused to make the trip. The mail, however, was landed at Barcelona and the covers, previously postmarked in New York, were back-stamped on June 4.

On August 8, 1928, the *Ile de France* sailed from Le Havre with a plane on board to be catapulted when nearing New York. This trial was successful and brought mail to New York eighteen hours ahead of the ship.

Some trials were being made at this time to put late mail aboard outbound ships, but this was much more difficult and never passed the experimental stage. Catapult mail was brought to a high point of efficiency by the North German Lloyd line, using the *Europa, Bremen*, and *Columbus*. The *Bremen* was equipped in 1929 and the other vessels soon after and the service was fairly regular on both sides of the ocean, shortening the passage time by eighteen to twenty-four hours.

CRASH COVERS

A small section of an aerophilatelic collection may be devoted to crash covers, salvaged when mail planes have been forced down. A premium is placed on damaged items—those partly burned, or water-soaked at sea or during a winter on some mountainside. A rubber-stamped impression usually tells of the accident and explains the condition of the covers. Often the collector accompanies the crash cover with a newspaper clipping giving an account of the mishap.

AIR COVERS WITH CACHETS

From the start some inscription or rubber-stamped identification was placed on covers carried on experimental or special flights, and out of this grew the practice of placing cachets on airmail of various kinds. These may be inscriptions only or a combination of pictures and words which explain the nature of the flight or of the event taking place. Such covers often are autographed by pilots or officials as an indication of genuineness.

When a new air-mail route is inaugurated the interested collectors obtain covers posted at every stop on the route, in both directions, and often from point to point. These covers must have a cachet to indicate the new service and should be backstamped at the route's terminal point.

Another source of ornamental cachets is found in the covers which usually are available when a new airport is opened. These may be official, or sponsored by the local chamber of commerce or other quasi-official body, or they may be of private character.

BALLOON MAIL

Sir John Franklin was one of the first who used a balloon to carry mail and the messages he sent aloft are highly prized by collectors. These were marked "Dispatched Sept. 9, 1850, by a balloon from H.M.S. *Assistance*, 74, 30 N., Long. 96 W. John Franklin."

In 1859, John Wise undertook to carry mail from St. Louis to New York for the United States Express Company. His balloon *Atlantic* carried a pouch containing a bag of overland newspapers and a number of letters from residents of St. Louis to friends in the east. The bag was marked for the express company office at 32 Broadway. Begun July 1, 1859, the trip was uneventful until Lake Ontario was reached. There a violent storm was encountered and to avoid foundering everything was thrown out except the four balloonists. After skimming the waves the balloon reached the shore in Jefferson County, New

XIII (above). This much-forwarded cover received a lot of service for a two-cent stamp. It shows the stamp of B. F. Stevens, U. S. Despatch Agent at London. Below: XIV (left). Unusual design for airmail stamp, 1951. XV (center). Airpost stamp in honor of the centenary of the birth of Count Zeppelin. (Acme Photo.) XVI (right). Stamp issued to mark the flight of the Swissair passenger plane from Geneva to New York, May 2, 1947, to participate in the International Philatelic Exhibition. St. Pierre Cathedral at Geneva at right; Statue of Liberty at left. (Courtesy Swiss PTT.)

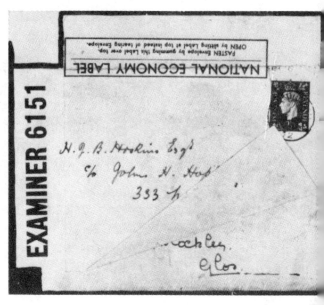

XVII (above). Economy stationery
World War II. Strips of paper, gumme
at ends, were pasted over original nam
and address. Simpler than the turne
covers of an earlier day. (Courtesy H.
B. Hoskins.) XVIII (left). First stan
design and source, the Wyon med
XIX (below). Confederate prisoner-o
war cover used from Camp Dougl
Chicago, which entered the South b
yond the Union line, via flag of tru
through City Point, Va. (Courtesy E
Antrim.)

York, where it knocked over several small trees and came to rest in a large tree near Henderson. The express pouch washed ashore and was picked up two days later at Oswego. Its careful preparation had saved the contents from damage and when it reached New York the letters were put into the post office for distribution. No example of this mail is known, but collectors should examine any letters dated at St. Louis, June 30, 1859.

Samuel Archer King, a professional aeronaut with years of experience, began using a new balloon, the *Buffalo*, on September 16, 1873, at Buffalo, New York. During the following two years he operated around Buffalo and Cleveland, and in 1876 he made ascents at the Centennial Exposition in Philadelphia. The following year he was in Nashville, Tennessee, providing private stamps for letters to be carried on flights. The stamp design included a view of the *Buffalo* and the inscription, "Balloon Postage—Five Cents," with numerals at the sides. King arranged to drop letters bearing the private stamp and a regular United States stamp, with a request on each envelope that it be placed in the nearest post office.

An ascent was made at Nashville on June 18, with a landing at Gallatin, 26 miles distant, and on the following day the balloon reached Taylorsville, Tennessee. One cover is known from this trip with the balloon stamp and a 3-cent green United States stamp of 1873. It was postmarked at Gallatin, June 18, and bears the request mentioned. This cover remained hidden until 1933, which should convince new collectors that it is not too late to make stamp finds.

A collection might well show an example of a cover carried on a stratosphere flight of Auguste Piccard in 1932 or 1933, or on one of the flights made by the United States Army and the National Geographic Society in the Black Hills of South Dakota in 1934 and 1935. In 1934 an altitude of 60,000 feet had been reached when the bag ripped and the crew were forced to bail out. In 1935 a similar accident occurred during the inflation of the balloon, but on November 11 of that year the *Ex-*

plorer II ascended to 72,395 feet and drifted south to land in Nebraska. The balloon and pigeon posts used in Paris during the Franco-Prussian War are described later in this chapter.

PIGEON POSTS

Pigeons have been used to carry mail to residents of remote places and to others needing a swift service. One such post was established in 1897 between New Zealand and Great Barrier Island, 65 miles northeast, and private stamps were provided for the service. Pigeons were able to fly from the island to the mainland in any weather, but fog and other obstacles made the outbound flight almost impossible. There was insufficient use of the service to require any photographic reduction to save space and the original messages on thin paper were placed in a waterproof carrier attached to one leg of the pigeon. The first private stamps were held to be illegal and the inscription was altered to "Pigeongram" instead of "Special Post." Competition brought a second pigeon post, also with private stamps, but both were abolished by the government after about two years of operation.

There are records of many other pigeon posts, including the story that Nathan Rothschild of London started his fortune through the early advice received by pigeon post from agents following the army of Napoleon. It is said also that pigeons were in regular use between Holland and France and between Belgium and London about 1840 to transmit stock market news.

German lighthouse keepers used pigeons in 1876 to announce the arrival of ships and to summon aid in time of storms, and as recently as 1949 pigeons were used at Herm, one of the Channel Islands, to communicate with England. The owner of Herm used local stamps but the covers required a British stamp to obtain delivery in England and elsewhere.

Other pigeon posts have been used at one time or another in the United States, Poland, India, and Australia.

ROCKET POSTS

This term applies to mail dispatched in a carrier propelled at great speed by the combustion of fuel within the rocket. All the early experiments with such rockets were to explore their use in carrying mail. These trials were always subject to explosions at the take-off, in flight, or during the landing, but with improved fuel and radio guidance, it became possible to control the rockets and to release the mail capsules to parachute to the ground, thus removing much of the hazards of the early flights.

Dr. Robert H. Goddard of the physics department of Clark University in Worcester, Mass., was perhaps the first person to experiment with mail-carrying rockets, and soon after 1914 obtained his first patent in that field. Altogether he held 214 patents on rockets and related subjects. On March 16, 1926, Goddard fired the first rocket using liquid fuel as a propellant. His rocket tests annoyed his Massachusetts neighbors and at the suggestion of the state fire marshal, he selected a desert site near Roswell, N.M., for further experiments. With a grant from the Guggenheim Foundation, Goddard began to devote full time to rocket research. During these tests, which lasted until 1941, with a break in 1932-34 because of the depression, Goddard developed nearly all of the features of the V-2 rockets used by Germany against England toward the end of World War II. Goddard, who was in charge of research in the Naval Bureau of Aeronautics during the war, died on August 10, 1945, just before the fruit of his research began to ripen. He is honored on a U.S. air post stamp issued in 1964.

Mail was first carried by rocket in the United States in 1935, but most of it was lost when the rocket exploded in flight. At Greenwood Lake, N.Y., firings were made in 1936, but with little success although the second rocket, after a flight of 50 feet, fell to the ice and, rebounding, continued on for almost 2,000 feet. Mail-carrying flights across the Texas-Mexico border were the most successful in the United States but meanwhile intensive work was under way in Austria and Germany.

Experiments were begun near Graz, Austria, in February

1931 by Friedrich Schmiedl when he fired the V.7 rocket from the top of the Schöckel to Radegund with 102 covers bearing Austrian stamps canceled with a private handstamp showing the mark "V.7." In later trials 79 and 84 covers were carried.

On Sept. 9, 1931, public service was started from the Hochtrotsch to Semriach with the "R.1" rocket, carrying 333 covers bearing an approved special stamp of which 500 copies had been issued. During the next two years 11 flights handled 3,135 covers using rockets V.9 to 18 and S.1. The usual cargo was 380 covers in the last five trials, the minimum being 28 on V.11.

In April 1931, Reinhold Tiling began trials with a rocket firing directly upward. The 188 cards carried on the first shot were then consigned to the regular mail at nearby Dielingen. This rocket was demonstrated at the Templehof in Berlin in the following year, but in 1933 Tiling was killed in a premature explosion. Gerhard Zucher's first scheduled flight in 1933 was halted by the authorities and the 420 covers were held over and carried from Hasselfelde to Stiege, in the Harz mountains, on Aug. 31. These bore special stamps, as did the 370 covers placed on a night flight at Hasselfelde later. Of these only 38 were saved when the rocket exploded in flight. Later two night flights bore 700 covers and in early 1934 700 covers were carried on a flight for German United Relief. Zucher made firings in England, Italy, Trieste, Switzerland, and the Netherlands in 1934 and 1935. In the latter year he fired a rocket from Ostend toward the British coast but this fell into the sea short of its goal.

Experimental mail flights were made in India by Stephen Smith, and several rockets carried medicine and food to flood-isolated districts. Smith made almost 160 firings before the Second World War and during the same period the Queensland Air-mail Society was making flights in Australia. Later these were continued by the Australian Rocket Society successfully.

Since civilian enthusiasts performed all of this ground work without government aid, they should be credited with making a valuable contribution to society when they converted the high-flying, pyrotechnic toy into something of lasting value.

These experimental models were appropriated by the world powers and soon converted into military weapons capable of carrying high explosives instead of letters.

KITE MAIL

There is a story, unverified by this writer, that kites were used to convey letters across the Potomac River from Virginia rebels to Maryland sympathizers during the Civil War. When the winds were favorable the kites were flown back to Virginia. The letters are said to have been used in making the kite tails. Since Maryland was largely sympathetic to the South there seems to have been no necessity for the kites except within the fortified area of the District of Columbia.

THE PARIS BALLOON POST

Paris was besieged by the Prussian Army in September, 1870, and attempts to carry messages out of the city proved futile. At that time ballooning was popular and soon a balloon had been requisitioned and was ready to leave the city. In the haste of releasing it the fabric was torn and the flight had to be abandoned, but on September 23, a second, the *Neptune*, took off under the guidance of Jules Durouf and landed safely 65 miles away.

Other balloons followed, *La Ville de Flora* on September 25, *Les Etats Unis*, a twin balloon, on the twenty-ninth, and the *Celeste* and an unnamed balloon on the thirtieth. The stock of balloons was now exhausted but a factory set up in the Gare d'Orléans soon finished two more and these ascended October 7.

Sixty-five balloons were sent out before the siege ended January 28, 1871, and a large proportion of the flights were successful. Two were lost at sea, two landed in Germany, three were captured by the enemy in France, six landed in Belgium, four in the Netherlands, one in Norway, and the remaining 47 landed in France.

The *Ville d'Orléans* left Paris at midnight on November 24

with a 600-pound load and made the long flight of 185 miles to Norway in 14 hours and 40 minutes. *Le Jacquard* left Paris November 28, and was sighted off England the next morning. It then vanished into the sea but some of its mail was picked up by a British ship and conveyed to Plymouth, where it was postmarked and sent on to destination.

The other balloon lost at sea was the *Richard Wallace*. It set out January 27, the day before the armistice, and passed over Niort, almost touching the ground. When citizens called out for them to land, the balloonists became alarmed, threw out ballast, and soared out to sea and oblivion beyond La Rochelle. Mail from this balloon was recovered all along the nearby coast.

La Ville de Paris, released December 15, and *Le General Chanzy*, released five days later, landed in Germany, at Wertzler, Prussia, and Rotenburg, Bavaria, respectively, where the crews were made prisoners of war.

The balloons carried out a total of 238 passengers and aeronauts, 21 tons of mail, 6 dogs, and 384 pigeons. The number of letters has been estimated at about four million. The postage rate was fixed on September 23, 1870, at 20 centimes for domestic letters, all weighing over 4 grams to be confiscated. Foreign rates were not raised, and post cards of small size were charged 10 centimes.

Letters were not registered and the postmarks are normal but many may be recognized by the inscription "Par Ballon Monté." It is almost certain that all letters postmarked "Paris" during the siege and addressed to points outside were carried out by balloon whether they bear the inscription or not. A balloon under the guidance of an aeronaut was known as a *ballon monté* while an unmanned balloon was called a *ballon non-monté*.

THE PARIS PIGEON POST

Although balloons enabled the citizens to send out messages during the siege of Paris in 1870-1871, there would have been no means of return communication except for the foresight of postal officials. In August, when a siege seemed likely, a dovecote was set up at the post office and stocked with pigeons already in Paris and with others brought in by one of the officials.

The government moved to Tours as the Germans advanced and from this city the first communications were sent to Paris on small slips of pelure paper inscribed by hand in minute characters. Such as reached the city were in small quills attached to a tail feather of a pigeon. They were read under a magnifier and transcribed, and after censoring were delivered as addressed.

Each balloon leaving Paris carried pigeons out. The returning pigeons were taken by locomotive as close to the city as practical before release. As the volume of messages grew they were photographed to save space and to render them less vulnerable to rain. In this operation at Tours the messages were first written in large letters on cards which were then assembled into sheets one meter by 65 centimeters, about 40 by 26 inches, and reduced on film to 6 by 4 centimeters, about 2.4 by 1.6 inches. Several positive prints were made of each group and several birds carried identical dispatches. In spite of this duplication many messages never reached the city, but on the other hand many pigeons eluded all enemies on several trips, the famous Gambetta making at least four flights into the city.

On November 4, 1870, this service was opened to the public, at a charge of 50 centimes for 20 words, with no guarantee of delivery. The right of censorship was reserved, and the right to deliver by any means without extra charge, with no refunds for any cause. It soon became evident that typeset messages would be more legible after reduction, and it was discovered that both sides of the positive print could be used for messages if one side was finished before the other was sensitized and printed.

The typeset cards measured 37 by 23 centimeters, about 14½ by 9 inches, and between November 10 and December 11, 1870, when the government was moved to Bordeaux, 64 cards of private messages were set up and photographed. These were in groups of four, making a total of 16 negatives which were printed on 8 positives front and back. These carried 9800 dispatches averaging 16 words. During the same period the official messages required 43 negatives, all of which were said to have been received in Paris.

On November 10, the director of posts in Paris contracted with René Dagron, a specialist in microphotography, to handle all dispatches. Dagron was the man responsible for the tiny transparencies which were mounted on the flat undersides of minute magnifiers and placed in penholders, knife handles, jewelry, and other souvenirs. These little lenses were slightly over one millimeter in diameter and were ground flat at the focal point of the opposite spherical face, giving magnifications of a hundred diameters or more.

Dagron, with his crew and a part of his equipment, left Paris on November 12, at 9 A.M., on the balloon *La Niepce*, while the remainder of the apparatus set out at the same time on the *Le Daguerre*, accompanied by three travelers leaving the city. *Le Daguerre* was shot down and captured and *La Niepce*, on descending near Vitry-le-Français, was also captured with a large part of the equipment. Dagron and his assistants, after exchanging clothes with some peasants, were able to escape with some of the apparatus, although most of that was captured later.

Dagron was coolly received in Tours when he presented credentials authorizing him to take charge of the photo dispatches and to establish himself at Clermont-Ferrand. Leon Gambetta was angry that any minor official in Paris should order him to send official messages and private correspondence to a point sixty leagues from Tours, to people entirely unknown to him. François-Frédéric Steenackers, Director of Posts, then notified Dagron that any attempt to send dispatches from Clermont-Ferrand would result in his court martial and subsequent shooting.

In view of this Dagron accomplished little at Tours but when the government moved to Bordeaux he began operating there within five days. Messages were transmitted on pellicles, or thin films each having a capacity of about twenty-five hundred messages. The first pigeon carrying these pellicles reached Paris on January 8, 1871, with over forty thousand messages. Another on January 19, brought eight pellicles of official dispatches, two of reply cards, and two of orders, or about thirty thousand messages in all. On January 28 a third brought eighteen pellicles with better than forty thousand messages. Although every shipment was made in multiple, the severe winter and the increasing distance of the release point caused losses of about 95 per cent. All cards were numbered consecutively so that the Paris authorities could reorder missing numbers when higher numbers arrived. Some messages were dispatched again and again, and there is a record that one series was shipped no less than thirty times. The last pigeon flight carried a notice written on pelure paper to inform the city that an armistice had been signed.

THE *PAR MOULINS*

While this method of carrying mail has no connection with aerophilately, it has interest here as a "forerunner" of the Paris pigeon post. An attempt was made to send messages into Paris in hollow zinc balls, dropped in the Seine above the city. The balls were weighed to float below the river's surface and the intention was to intercept them with nets. Fifty-five balls were started but all but one, it is said, were lost or captured by the Germans. Some reappeared years later, flushed to the surface by high water. One was recovered forty years after the war, and another was reported in the press in the fall of 1955. The children who found and opened the latter scattered and lost most of the letters before anyone recognized the ball as a priceless relic of the siege of Paris. Another ball has been fished out of the Seine at Paris, according to a Reuters' Despatch which was published in the *New York Times* on October 1, 1956. In this case, the contents were recognized and saved.

❖❖

POSTAL STATIONERY

A collector who expects to make a complete study of the postal history of a country must include the stamped envelopes, letter sheets, and other postal stationery. These are collected used, unused, and as cut squares, but for postal history the entire items are usually necessary to identify varieties and to study postal markings.

Postal cards are not collected as cut squares since a large number are meaningless without the inscription and full design. The other items may be trimmed to a standard 2 by 2 inch size, or to 4 by 2 if the postmarks are to be preserved. A collection of cut squares will be much smaller in numbers than one of entires, since each stamp design is used on several sizes of envelopes and often on paper with various watermarks. Usually some sizes of envelopes are quite scarce and these at least should not be mutilated.

UNITED STATES POSTAL STATIONERY

The United States has issued envelopes for ordinary mail and for official and air mail, newspaper wrappers for ordinary and airmail. The envelopes include denominations from 1-cent to 90 cents, and there is one compound variety with 1-cent and 3-cent stamp impressions. There have been many commemorative issues of envelopes in connection with expositions, sports, the

United States Bicentennial, honoring the writer Herman Melville, the Pony Express Centennial, the White House Youth Conference, the Postage Stamp Centennial, the 5th International Philatelic Exposition, Human Rights Year, the 25th Anniversary of NATO and others. Probably the most important was the first which was issued in connection with the Centennial Exposition in Philadelphia in 1876 as it was not only the first commemorative envelope but the first commemorative issue of any kind.

ENVELOPE FREAKS

During the early period there were few oddities among the envelopes, due to the slower hand processes used and the ability to inspect for defective items. With the advent of improved machines, some of which are fully automatic, there is little chance for inspection and everything is counted and boxed.

Stamps that are embossed but not inked are called "Albinos" and are the result of feeding two sheets of paper through the printing press at one time. Only the top sheet receives the printed impression, and if no one is watching when the sheets pass through a folding machine, the albino sheet is made into envelopes.

Another freak is inked inside the envelope as well as outside but the inner impression is little more than a smudge. This occurs when the press is allowed to close without a sheet of paper in place. The inked die prints on the counterpart pad and the next sheet of paper receives the impression on front and back. This smudge on the reverse will appear on succeeding sheets until the counterpart pad is clean.

If an automatic feeder misses a sheet and takes two the next time, the top sheet will be normal while the under sheet will be an albino with a smudge on the reverse.

Envelopes with perfect impressions inside are the result of feeding printed sheets to the envelope machine wrong face up, and those with stamps in incorrect locations occur when printed sheets are fed to a machine making a different size of envelopes.

These latter have also been found with the stamps inside, indicating a double mistake.

Double envelopes occur when two printed sheets are fed at the same time. The machine attempts to turn out finished envelopes and the closed flaps usually are sealed down, but the loose flap is double and is gummed on the inner flap only. There also are mutilated or partial envelopes that have been counted and boxed through oversight.

All types of freaks cannot be produced on any one type of envelope machine but with a combination of three processes almost anything is possible. The rotary presses printing on a web of paper cannot produce albinos, or envelopes with colored blobs inside, under normal conditions, but misplaced stamped and wrong-side-out envelopes may occur when this material is later fed to envelope machines. The automatic machines which print the stamp impressions and then fold the envelopes cannot produce envelopes with stamps inside or in wrong positions, but may be the source of double envelopes, albinos, and those with smudged impressions inside.

It should be mentioned that in all methods of envelope making used in recent times, each sheet of paper receives several impressions of the stamp. When there is an albino or similar freak, it will be repeated at regular intervals in the boxed envelopes. If twenty-four envelopes are made from a sheet it may be assumed that there will be twenty-four freaks distributed through the run.

All the printing on "return" envelopes is performed at one operation before folding, and a low price is charged since no second handling is required.

OFFICIAL ENVELOPES

Envelopes were issued for the Post Office and War Departments when the franking privilege was abolished by an act effective July 1, 1873. The envelopes were discontinued on July 5, 1884. In 1910, stamped envelopes were issued for the Postal Savings Division by Act of June 25, and discontinued October 5,

1914, with the remaining stocks overprinted as "penalty" envelopes.

LETTER SHEETS

Several kinds of letter sheets have been issued by the U.S. A blue 3-cent letter sheet appeared in August, 1861, but was withdrawn in 1864. Letter sheets bearing the likeness of U.S. Grant were issued August 18, 1886, but discontinued June 30, 1894. All the early forms were unpopular and soon discarded. The first were shaped like a fully opened-out envelope, with square top and bottom flaps. Later ones were perforated around three margins, to be torn off to disclose the contents. An aerogramme or air letter sheet is a recent addition to this group.

All letter sheets should be collected in the entire form.

WRAPPERS

United States wrappers usually follow the designs of the stamped envelopes, and in cut-square form some can be distinguished only by the laid lines or watermarks in the paper. The laid lines in envelopes always run diagonally, while those in wrappers run across or up and down. The same Manila paper used for wrappers also was used for a cheap grade of envelopes for third-class matter. These were usually without gum on the flap.

Some wrappers are not easy to mount entire in albums as they may measure as much as 9 by 12 inches.

AIR POST STATIONERY

The stamp designs for this stationery are usually related to the service and in nearly all cases there is a border in red and blue to call attention to the type of service. The paper is generally light in weight but strong and durable.

Commemorative air-mail envelopes have been issued in connection with the hundredth anniversary of United States postage stamps in 1947 and for the Fifth International Philatelic Exhibition in New York in 1956. The aerogramme for international service was mentioned in the chapter on aerophilately.

POSTAL CARDS

A postal card is a government stamped card, a *post* card is a private mailing card, picture post card, or other card requiring an adhesive stamp. Postal cards must be collected in entire form as many of the designs are incomplete or meaningless when cut-square. The first United States cards of 1874 were printed on watermarked cardboard but this was not necessary and soon a plain card was substituted.

United States cards have varied greatly in size, from 117 by 75 millimeters up to 155 by 95 millimeters, both these sizes being issued late in 1891. This last card was larger than permissible for the Universal Postal Union uniform rate of two cents, and had to be trimmed when sent abroad or prepaid at the letter rate. It was used in quantity for official views of the Columbian Exposition of 1893, printed in colors on the back of the cards after a chalk surfacing had been applied. Later a cheaper set of views was printed directly on the Manila cards in black ink. Sets of the official view cards were prepared for foreign use by trimming them and affixing a 1-cent Columbian stamp to make the 2-cent rate. The added stamps were usually cut from sheets with scissors.

The U.S. issued a commemorative postal card in connection with the Fifth International Philatelic Exhibition in New York in 1956. Since 1962, commemorative postal cards have been issued annually, honoring government services, tourism, or Revolutionary War heroes.

Postal cards are available in values for domestic and foreign use, the latter having the appropriate inscriptions in French to conform to Universal Postal Union regulations. Double cards with paid reply are also provided for foreign and domestic service. The reply portion, when returned to the United States, will show foreign cancellations on United States stamps. It should be mentioned that the average foreign postal clerk is not familiar with these reply cards and seldom passed them without marking the card "Unpaid," or "Postage due."

Although outside the category of postal cards, attention is called to private mailing cards with paid reply. These are acceptable in international mails if they have the proper inscriptions in French, and the reply portion may be prepaid with United States stamps. Collectors who have attempted to use these cards as a means of obtaining foreign cancellations on United States adhesive stamps find foreign postal clerks very reluctant to pass them as fully paid.

Large users of postal cards obtain them in uncut sheets in order to reduce the cost of printing forms or advertisements. Collectors and stamp dealers often obtain these sheets and cut them to show stamps in wrong positions, etc., but these freaks have little standing.

REVALUED ITEMS

More than once a change in postal rates has left quantities of stamped envelopes and postal cards on hand with obsolete values. Many of these have been made usable by overprinting, the usual method being to run them through a cancelling machine equipped with a suitable die to raise or lower the value as the case may be.

This overprinting has been conducted at numerous places in the United States and has resulted in many minor varieties. In some cases cards and envelopes of wrong type have been revalued, or proper items have been revalued in a wrong ink color.

PENALTY ENVELOPES

The official mail of all United States government departments was sent free under personal signatures until 1873, when official stamps were introduced in an effort to cut down the amount of mail. Much of the franked mail was not requested or wanted by the addressees, and considerable private mail was being franked. Members of Congress continued to frank their official mail but from 1873 to 1879 all other departments were required to purchase special stamps, or to a limited extent envelopes, bearing the department name. Within six years it was determined that the savings were hardly enough to pay for the special stamps, and in 1879 the idea of the "penalty" envelope was advanced and adopted.

Penalty envelopes bear the statement, "Penalty for Private Use to Avoid Payment of Postage—$300." Their use required less effort than a personal signature for franking and did not deter anyone who wanted to mail his personal letters without postage. There was no control whatever and any department could make penalty envelopes, labels, or stickers, or type, print, or write the penalty clause on the envelopes.

During World War II the immense volume of free mail caused Congress to investigate, and it was learned that in 1943 some two billion pieces were carried at a net cost of thirty million dollars. The same bulk would have cost private mailers about four times this amount. And the amount of free mail carried in 1943 was almost three times as great as it was in 1935. Congress now ordered that all penalty envelopes be provided by the Post Office Department. Stocks were inventoried and some government departments were found with enough envelopes to last for years.

The new envelopes bore code letters to indicate the origin and use and the departments were required to pay the postage cost as billed by the postal authorities. The letters PMGG indicated that the envelopes were furnished by the Post Office Department, GPO indicated that they came from the Government Printing Office, and PN or Permit No. —— showed that they were privately printed or obtained under special permit. The immense stocks on hand were also marked with code letters.

Within four years it was found that the auditing cost was greater than the savings and the Eightieth Congress eliminated the provision that departments and agencies pay their postage. Other features of the 1943 act were retained and departmental heads were still required to certify quarterly that all mail sent out was official or had been requested by the addressee.

In the fiscal year 1951 this mail added about eighty-four million dollars to the postal deficit, while Congressional mail added but a million. At present, agencies pay for air mail, and for registered mail, except from Washington, and parcels are limited to four pounds except special shipments originating in the Government Printing Office, or those containing post-office supplies. Business conducted with private citizens, such as between collectors and the Philatelic Agency, must have the postage paid by stamps or meter impressions, or figure notations on parcels, and under some conditions such mail must bear a dated post-mark.

When large stocks of stamped envelopes have been made useless by a change in postal rates, it has become customary to run them through a cancelling machine equipped with a penalty indicium to convert the envelopes to penalty type. This costs less than to provide new envelopes. Some of the overprinted envelopes are as interesting to collectors as the ordinary penalty types.

In addition to the usual rectangular forms of the indicia, there are some unusual and ornamental designs, of which the oval post-office form is the best example. There is scarcely any hope of making a complete collection of penalty types, but a reasonable showing should include those used by the major departments, with some coded-letter and permit-number varieties, and a few showing the payment of the special fees by means of stamps, although the penalty clause covers the normal postage on the shipment.

FOREIGN POSTAL STATIONERY

Many nations issue the same range of postal stationery as the U.S., and some have additional issues such as registered-letter envelopes and pneumatic tube stationery. Formerly at a disadvantage because few lists were available, collectors in this field have been helped considerably by publication of the catalog of postal stationery of the world by Higgins and Gage.

Postal cards are the commonest examples, many of them being small works of art. Commemoratives are not unusual. An early example is the card issued by Great Britain in 1890 for the jubilee of penny postage. This card also rates as a semi-postal.

The postal cards of Italy from 1874 until 1884 were unusual in that the postage stamp was impressed in the upper left corner, with a circular space provided at the upper right for the postmark. When handled like ordinary mail, these cards were passed with the stamps uncancelled.

Several foreign countries provide view cards with imprinted stamps, and in some cases their extensive number makes it difficult to form a complete collection.

The registered-letter envelopes of Great Britain and a number of her colonies and dominions are usually in normal form but in other cases have the stamp impressed on the end flap on the reverse of the envelope. The envelopes are ordinarily lined with a tough, open-weave fabric, and show crossed blue lines on the face to indicate registration.

Among the unusual items used by foreign countries were the special stamped envelopes for railroad postal service and river postal service. There also were stampless, postage-free war service cards used by German soldiers in 1870. These no doubt were similar to cards used in later wars. In 1868, following the formation of the North German Confederation, the stock rooms of Brunswick, Mecklenburg-Strelitz, Oldenburg, Prussia, and Saxony were filled with obsolete stamped envelopes of those states. These were salvaged by pasting a North German Postal District stamp over the envelope stamp, then overprinting stamp and cover with a rectangular area containing a pattern of closely spaced lines of type reading "Nord Deutscher Postbezirk." About 36 varieties of envelopes were treated in this manner, and examples of the overprinted stamps turn up cut-square or off cover in old mixtures.

BRITISH COMPOUND ENVELOPES

Prior to 1900 English post offices stocked only four values of stamped envelopes, but any value could be obtained on special order, or the regular values could be obtained in special colors. All the special values or special colors were printed from dies that had three small changeable date plugs. In some cases the little date plugs are the only identification of the special printing. Special dies were available from halfpenny to tenpence, and a user who wished a distinctive or a high-value envelope could have it with one or more dies, in different colors, to make up the required denomination.

These compound envelopes are recorded with as many as four stamp dies, and in values from twopence up to fifteen pence, by halfpenny steps, and from eighteen pence to twenty-four pence or two shillings, by twopence steps. The user could select any values which would produce the desired denomination and had almost the same liberty in selecting colors. At some extra cost the stamp office at Somerset House would provide a colored band surrounding each die which could show the name and address of the user. These advertising bands were available at least as late as 1888 and were in the color of the stamp frame. Other similar frames could be placed on the envelopes by private printers but were required to be in a color differing from that of the stamp.

Excepting the frames, there was no additional charge for the special dies or colors but there was a minimum requirement in the number of envelopes ordered.

PNEUMATIC POST STATIONERY

At one time four countries, France, Germany, Austria, and Italy, provided special stationery for pneumatic tube service in their capital cities. France provided envelopes, letter cards, and cards for use in Paris, with charges, at first of 75 centimes for the two first mentioned and 50 centimes for a card. A little later these were reduced to 60 centimes for a letter, 50 centimes for a letter card, and 30 centimes for a card. The corresponding charges for ordinary mail by carrier were 15 centimes for letters and letter cards and 10 centimes for cards.

❖❖❖

CHAPTER SEVENTEEN

THE UNIVERSAL POSTAL UNION

THE MEETING OF 1863

The first movement for an international understanding on postal rates and service was made in 1862 by Montgomery Blair, Postmaster General in Lincoln's cabinet. His suggestion applied to all nations having diplomatic relations with the United States, and the delegates met in Paris, May 11, 1863, and drew up a memorandum of thirty-one articles designed to simplify the postal service. Since none of the delegates had authority to ratify an agreement, the memorandum was simply a record of their ideas.

Since 1850 a postal union had been operating in Germany and Austria, greatly facilitating the handling of mail passing among the sixteen member states. Following the Paris meeting Heinrich von Stephan, Superior Privy Councilor of Posts of the North German Confederation, outlined a similar organization that would take in all nations with international posts. He suggested an international conference to consider his proposals but the meeting was delayed by the outbreak of the Franco-Prussian War.

THE GENERAL POSTAL UNION

Following the Franco-Prussian War Germany emerged as a world power. With the support of Belgium and the Netherlands, she requested Switzerland to sponsor a congress on postal affairs. Switzerland invited all European nations and the United States and Egypt to send delegates to Berne for a meeting on September 1, 1873. Russia could not be present until the fifteenth, and on that day the representatives of twenty-two countries assembled.

These were Austria, Belgium, Denmark, Germany, Hungary, Luxembourg, the Netherlands, Norway, Portugal, Russia, Spain, Sweden, and Switzerland (the delegates of all these countries had full power to act), and Egypt, France, Great Britain, Greece, Italy, Roumania, Serbia, Turkey, and the United States. Delegates of the latter countries were required to report back to their respective countries. The United States delegates were delayed and did not reach Berne until September 21.

The last of fourteen sessions, held October 9, 1874, completed the discussion of a proposition presented by Germany The lengthy debates of the congress centered around the propositions for uniform rates and gratuity of transit.

Twenty articles were included in a Treaty of the General Postal Union, and the document was signed by all except France. The French delegate stated that his country would adhere to the treaty, subject to the approval of the national assembly, providing that the treaty did not become applicable to France until January 1, 1876. This proviso was approved by the other delegates and a space was reserved for the French signature. The treaty was ratified by the United States on March 8, 1875, and went into effect on July 1.

The important provisions were an international letter rate between the signatory countries of twenty-five centimes or equivalent, based on a unit weight of fifteen grams, with similar uniform rates for other mail matter. These rates insured transmission throughout the member countries, with delivery at the address where carrier service was in operation or would later be instituted, or to the local post office in case carrier service was not available.

Under the treaty each country retains all of the postage collected, thus eliminating the involved and detailed accounting systems formerly in use. Transit charges were not abolished but were to be paid by the country of origin in amounts depending on the bulk weight of mail and how it was handled, to be determined between the two countries involved, by a weighing and counting of mail during a selected two-week period.

The United States Official Postal Guide of January, 1876, refers to the agreement as the "International Postal Treaty concluded at Berne, Switzerland, October 9, 1875, which went into operation July 1, 1876." This is one of the first uses of an incorrect title for the postal union or the treaty, but in spite of a later change of name, the incorrect title is the only one used in the *Encyclopedia Britannica*.

Prior to the treaty, postal rates were very involved, and depended on weight and distance between each two countries, the nationality of the vessel carrying the mail, whether it went direct or was transshipped en route, and whether it was prepaid or sent collect, etc. All these factors were negotiated between each two countries and since much of the mail was sent collect, each letter required some bookkeeping. The rates usually included three to five factors—the domestic rate in the country of origin, sea rate, domestic rate in the country of delivery, and transit rates, etc. The charges for a letter from Chile to Germany by the shortest and fastest route might include Chilean postage, sea postage to Panama, Panama transit charges, sea postage to New York, sea postage to England, transit charges from Liverpool to Southampton, sea postage to Bremen, and German domestic rates.

Soon after the General Postal Union began operating, a meeting was called in Berne in January, 1876, with the result that many additional countries and colonies signed the agreement. By 1900 practically all the major or significant countries were members.

THE UNIVERSAL POSTAL UNION

The original treaty called for a meeting in Paris in 1878 to amend or continue the pact. At this meeting some changes were made, and the name was altered to Union Postale Universelle. Under the Convention of Paris, signed June 1, the countries forming the union became a single postal territory with provision for the admission of members at any time and for the withdrawal of members upon a year's notice. Switzerland was named as chief executive of the union and the provisions of the Convention of Paris became effective January 1, 1879.

Another congress meeting in Paris in 1880 attempted to establish an international parcel post, but this was found to be impractical.

Although the Convention of Paris provided for regular meetings, the schedule was interrupted at times. Congresses were held in Lisbon, 1885, Vienna, 1891, Washington, 1897, Rome, 1906, Madrid, 1920, Stockholm, 1924, London, 1929, Cairo, 1934, Buenos Aires, 1939, Paris, 1947, and Brussels, 1952.

POSTAL UNION SUGGESTIONS

Few changes have been made in the basic agreement during the past seventy-five years but suggestions to improve the service have usually been adopted. One important recommendation was for member nations to use Arabic (conventional) numerals of value on all stamps.

The author has not checked to find countries which neglected this but two issues of Canada and two values of United States stamps have been noted. The Canadian Jubilee issue of 1897 came and went without numerals but the maple-leaf Victoria design, issued between November 9, 1897, and January, 1898, was being replaced by a modified design with numerals in the lower corners early in June of that year.

In the United States the new series of 1908-1909 appeared

without numerals on the 1- and 2-cent values, which were issued December 2, and November 16, 1908. Succeeding values
issued between December 12, 1908, and January 29, 1909, have
numerals. The series continued in use without change until
1912, when these two values were replaced with others showing numerals on February 12. Much comment was made about
the U.S. stamps that lacked numerals, but the International
Postal Union doesn't seem to have objected to them or to the
Canadian issues. Some confusion did arise when the U.S. issued
its Christmas stamps of 1975. The stamps had to be printed
before the question of raising the first-class rate to 13 cents was
resolved, so no numeral was printed on them. While it was
decided that these issues bore the value of 10 cents, some foreign
postal systems refused to handle letters bearing this issue. The
"A" denomination stamps of 1978, printed for just such an
emergency, were called into use with the same foreign problem
when the rate became 15 cents rather than 16 cents as the
Postal Service had expected.

Another suggestion, followed until recently, was that stamps
for the basic unit rates in international mails be printed in standard colors throughout the postal union. This was adopted at
the Washington congress of 1897 and provided that the stamp
for the first-class letter rate of 25 centimes, 20 pfennigs, 2½
pence, or 5 cents be dark blue, the stamp for the postal card
rate of 10 centimes, 1 penny, or 2 cents be red, and the stamp
for a unit of printed matter, 5 centimes, a halfpenny, or 1 cent
be green. This resolution required changes in one or more
stamps of every country except Germany, which had made the
suggestion. The U.S. changed the color of its 1-cent and 5-cent
stamps and brightened the red of its 2-cent stamp. The standard
color scheme was abandoned in 1952 because changing rates of
many countries required too-frequent color changes.

An important service adopted at the 1906 congress in Rome
was the international reply coupon. See pages 238-239.

The Universal Postal Union has made no attempt to extend
uniform rates to international airmail for the cost of this service
depends almost entirely upon the distance covered. So far as
rates from the United States are concerned, the world is sep-

arated into three zones with 10-, 15-, and 25-cent unit rates.

In 1947 the postal union became an agency of United Nations, effective July 1, 1948.

STAMPS HONORING THE UNION

Many stamps have been issued in honor of the union, the first being the three-value set with which Switzerland celebrated the 25th anniversary of the Berne treaty. Starting with the Madrid congress of 1920 each host country has issued stamps for the meeting and in 1924, Switzerland observed the 50th anniversary of the original meeting. Perhaps the most extensive group of commemorative stamps is made up of the sets and stamps issued by the member nations for the 75th anniversary of the union in 1949 and 1950.

As the time approached the Councilor of Posts of Poland proposed to the union secretary that the anniversary stamps be uniform throughout the world. He suggested that the set contain three values in the three colors of the standard rates, green, red, and blue, and that they differ only in the country names and in the value designations.

This same Polish official proposed that the union open a philatelic agency at the Swiss headquarters, where the stamps of all member nations would be available to dealers and collectors. This idea was opposed by American stamp dealers and was not adopted, but such an agency might be beneficial to philately for it would centralize sales and provide a place to obtain those issues which some countries appear to sell out on the day before the stamp is supposed to go on sale.

OTHER POSTAL UNIONS

During the latter part of the nineteenth century some rates to remote countries were far above the uniform standard, that from England to New Zealand and Australia being sixpence, to India, fivepence and to South Africa fourpence. At the congress in Washington the delegates approved a proposition that countries might lower their rates below the postal union standards for political reasons. Accordingly, representatives of the British dominions and colonies met with those of the United Kingdom in 1899 and established a rate of one penny for letters passing among all British possessions except from the United Kingdom and western points to Australia and New Zealand. In 1901 this rate was extended to New Zealand, in 1905 to Australia, and in 1908 the United States was invited to enter the penny postage group.

This cheap rate was maintained until after the First World War and was not changed until domestic rates within some of the British units began to rise. This had the effect of also raising the foreign rate from those countries, for the penny postage agreement was based on the use of the domestic rate to other members of the group.

Other similar postal agreements were in force in France, her overseas territories and associated states; in the central European group composed of Austria, Germany, Czechoslovakia, and Hungary; in the Balkan group of Greece, Turkey, Roumania, Bulgaria, Albania, and Jugoslavia under a treaty of 1931, and at present in the domestic rate group composed of the United States, Canada, and Mexico.

A South American postal union was formed February 2, 1911, at a Latin-American congress in Montevideo, and negotiations for a Pan-American postal union were opened at the congress of the postal union in Madrid. As a result the Spanish-American Postal Convention was signed November 13, 1920. At a later meeting of this group in Madrid in 1931, the name was changed to the Postal Union of the Americas and Spain, and it now includes all autonomous countries of South and Central America, Mexico, Canada, the United States, and Spain. Domestic letter rates of each country apply throughout the union for surface mail.

INTERNATIONAL REPLY COUPONS

Reply coupons were adopted at the Rome congress of 1906 and were placed in use in some countries the following year. This idea is one of the best ever developed by the postal union, even though the coupons have been manipulated as a racket in a few instances.

A coupon may be purchased in any U.P.U. country and after being postmarked at the place of sale, may be mailed to any other member country where it will purchase a stamp to pay a single rate of ordinary postage on a letter to a foreign country. Some speak of these as receipts but they seem to be more like sight drafts.

The amount charged for a coupon seems to be arbitrarily fixed by the country selling it, for the charges have little relation to the foreign letter rate or to the coupon prices of other countries. In 1930 a coupon cost nine cents in the United States, fourpence in Australia, threepence in Great Britain, and even less on the continent. At present a coupon costs about fifty per cent more than the foreign letter rate and is redeemable, if not used, at about the foreign letter rate. This deters anyone from using the coupons for remittances, or from sending large sums of money abroad in this form.

When coupons bought in the United States are not used they may be redeemed at ten cents each.

There are also reply coupons for the Spanish-American Postal Union, exchangeable for a stamp to pay the postal rate within the union. These coupons are not sold in the United States, but are honored here toward purchasing stamps. Similar limited-use coupons have been provided within the British Commonwealth, and within some other political groups.

The Ponzi Episode

Currency fluctuations may have great effect on the value of reply coupons, a circumstance that in 1919 led Charles Ponzi, of Boston, to embark on a swindling career, by promising quick returns to those who trusted their money to him. Supposedly coupons were to be purchased in Spain, where they cost about one cent, and redeemed in the United States at six cents in postage stamps. Investors were promised a 50 per cent profit in forty-five days.

Ponzi founded the Securities Exchange Company, and investors during the early life of the company were paid the promised profits, but out of the new capital being invested in the bubble. Bankers who knew that something was wrong brought in postal inspectors to see whether or not the mails were being used to defraud. The inspectors who came to investigate remained to invest their savings, but a Boston newspaper made an independent inquiry and soon learned that the total amount of reply coupons sold in Europe during the preceding six months came to a few thousand dollars only.

This was sufficient proof that Ponzi was not using the coupons to make a profit but was relying entirely on new money to remain solvent. At the time it was estimated that he had taken in about eight million dollars from his customers. In 1921 he was convicted of operating a confidence game. After serving seven years, he was deported to Italy. During World War II Ponzi moved to Argentina, where he died penniless January 15, 1949.

Since that time several changes have been made in the sale and redemption prices of coupons and the present high price may be due in a measure to Ponzi's operations.

INTERNATIONAL STAMPS

The question of international stamps is frequently raised at postal congresses. Such a stamp would seem to be the logical solution for a paid reply. While it would deprive the country in which the answer is mailed of any share in the postage, there would be an averaging out of correspondence from year to year that would offset any minor inequities. The details seemed so near solution in London in 1929 that the proposition was put on the agenda of the Cairo congress of 1934 for serious study. As before, it stalled on the currency question, the slight differences between 25 centimes, 20 pfennigs, 2½ pence, and 5 cents, to say nothing of the dozens of other coinages, providing the stumbling block.

Today there is still less relation to the original currency and it would be more difficult to reconcile the rates. A smart operator could find a profit by buying the stamps in one country and selling them in another.

Collectors who have feared uniformity in stamps throughout the world need not worry about a shortage of stamps to collect. The international stamps might make a poor general collection, and might stop topical collecting entirely, but would make specialists of everyone. Since the same number of stamps would be needed, uniform or not, it would require all of the printing plants now in use to produce them, and it would be possible to identify the work of each plant. Those who refuse to work with "flyspeck" varieties could be content with gathering a collection of cancellations of the world on a uniform stamp subject.

The idea of an international stamp has great merit, for a person could send the actual stamp for reply, whereas with the coupon it is necessary to go to a post office to trade it for a stamp.

One of the earliest proposals for such a stamp was made by a Swedish philatelist, Albert Hallberg, who read a paper on the subject before the Philatelic Association of Göteborg, Sweden. The paper was printed in *"Tidning for Frimarksamlare,"* and a translation was published in the *Halifax Philatelist*, August, 1888. Hallberg suggested that each country in the postal union issue a special stamp to send abroad for the return postage on a letter. This stamp would have inscriptions in the language of the country and in French, the official language of the union. Thus a Swedish stamp would be inscribed "Sverige—Suede, Frimarke for Svaret—Timbre pour la Response," and "Tjugofem öre," with a central number "25."

Such a stamp sent abroad would be honored only on a letter addressed to Sweden, and this would eliminate nearly all manipulations. The use of reply stamps on original messages between countries with an advantageous differential in foreign rates was to be prevented by fixing the price sufficiently high to discourage this illegal use.

Here is an example of how the stamps could be used to

defraud a country of its legitimate postage unless the cost was raised. The international rate from Austria was 18 kreutzer, which equalled 16 öre, while the Swedish rate was 20 öre. Austrian reply stamps might be shipped to Sweden for use on original correspondence to Austria, saving 20 per cent of the postage cost and defrauding Sweden of the entire postage. But by fixing the value of the reply stamp at 25 öre for Sweden and at equivalent values for other countries there would be no profit in the illegal use. And the danger of counterfeiting was not more important than for regular postage stamps.

Nothing came of Hallberg's suggestion but the adoption of the reply coupon was a step in the same direction, though it too was subject to similar abuses.

❖❖❖➤

EARLY POSTAL HISTORY

The post in one form or another dates from the dawn of history and may have started when man first learned to write. The Bible contains many references, such as that in II Samuel, XI: 14, in which it is related, "And it came to pass in the morning, that David wrote a letter to Joab, and sent it by the hand of Uriah." On reading further it is found that this was Uriah's last appearance as a postman. In II Chronicles, XXX: 6, will be found "So the posts went with letters from the king and his princes throughout all Israel and Judah, and according to the commandment of the king," and in Esther III: 15, in connection with Haman's plot against the Hebrews, "The posts went out, being hastened by the king's commandment." In the book of Esther mention is made of the impression of the king's signet ring in wax on the message. This made the document inviolable and was a forerunner of the frank and the postage stamp.

There is evidence that Sargon the First had a postal system in Babylon about 3800 B.C., and the Louvre in Paris has a collection of clay seals which served as stamps on the messages carried at that time. A letter carrier pictured in the tomb of

243

Amen-Hotep II dates from about 1500 B.C., and indicates that the post was known in early Egypt.

Herodotus, the historian from whom we learn so much of ancient peoples and customs, describes an early Persian method of transmitting secret messages. He states that these were impressed upon the shaven heads of couriers, who were dispatched only after the hair had grown enough to hide the message, and that answers were returned in the same manner. This historian also describes the horse posts of Cyrus, in Persia, which were operated by his son Darius. Horses and men were stationed at regular intervals to receive messages and relay them to the next station. From Herodotus' description comes the idea expressed in the inscription on the New York post office, "Neither snow, nor rain, nor heat, nor gloom of night stays these couriers from the swift completion of their appointed rounds." The sentence is not a literal translation from Herodotus but was adapted by William Mitchell Kendall, of McKim, Mead and White, architects of the post office.

Herodotus also mentions that the Greeks employed runners to deliver messages and that the hundred and fifty miles between Athens and Lacedaemon could be covered in a day and a night.

The Romans under Augustus and succeeding emperors maintained similar posts, and from the Latin word *positum* comes the Italian *posta* and the English *post*. The word now occurs in many forms, in posts planted in the earth and in words relating to postal affairs.

The early posts were not open to the public but were for the private use of the ruler or the government, and, in fact, public letter writing was forbidden in the Roman Empire except by express permission of the Emperor.

Posts are seldom mentioned during the Middle Ages and about the only means of communication was by private courier if the message was urgent, or by traveling monks or the infrequent travelers who ventured across the bandit-infested areas between the fortified cities.

XX (above). A combination cover from the Knapp collection, showing use of U.S. and Samoan stamps on a single cover. (Philatelic Research Laboratories, Inc.) XXI (left). Cover showing use of a local stamp in Chicago long after such carriers had been outlawed. XXII (below). An essay for a United States message and reply card which passed through the mail in both directions without any question being raised.

XXIII (top). The superscription indicates that this cover was the first to be postmarked on Guam, when the United States Navy took possession in August, 1899. Autographed by the Acting Postmaster on board the U.S.S. *Yosemite*. Above: XXIV (left). A fine example of a maximum card. XXV (right). Typical foreign first-day cover. (StanGib, Ltd.)

There was, however, a postal system in Sweden about this time for a papal bull of 1262, now in the Vatican Museum, gives blessing to a new post office set up in Stockholm by Earl Birger, a Swedish statesman. Service between this city and Rome was maintained, with stops at important cities on the route, and in some cases monks acted as the couriers.

THE POSTS IN EUROPE

Shortly after the middle of the fifteenth century, Maximilian I, desirous of supplementing the courier service of the Holy Roman Empire with a regular delivery of official matter, brought Janetto Tassis from Italy to operate the service. As his indebtedness to Tassis grew the emperor granted him several fiefs, including the Pamkirchner Thurn in Carinthia. Out of this beginning grew the Thurn and Taxis postal monopoly which covered western Europe until the middle of the nineteenth century. Horse posts were established between the Tyrol and Italy, and from Innsbruck to Mechlin, in Flanders, over a route that served Augsburg, Bingen, Coblenz, and Cologne. Relays were at intervals of four or five miles and the couriers traveled day and night. Ultimately this service grew until it embraced most of central Europe.

Louis XI is credited with establishing the first postal system in France. Post houses were established on the main roads at intervals of four leagues and were equipped with relays of four or five horses, all under the supervision of a postmaster. During the reign of Charles VIII, son of Louis XI, the post, which had been solely for the use of the king and court, was opened for other purposes and couriers were allowed to carry any messages or parcels that could be readily handled. In 1477 this postal system employed 230 couriers.

Under Louis XIII, the offices of postmaster and carrier were sold at auction in the various cities and provinces, but in 1676, Louis XIV brought all offices under one head and leased the organization to Lazarus Petit for the present-day equivalent of $240,000 per year.

Meantime in 1653, while Jean Baptiste Colbert was in charge in Paris, stamps were conceived. They are described in a royal announcement which reads, according to Philip Hensberger's translation:

"We, Louis XIV, by the Grace of God King of France, bring to the knowledge of the people that letters and parcels will be safely delivered from one part of the City of Paris to another part, and also the answers will be brought back, if such letters and parcels have pasted on (each) a billet issued by our Government and bearing the inscription 'Port-payé.' But this official billet must be attached in such a way that the royal mail carrier can easily notice it and remove it as the letter or parcel is delivered. No mail matter will be delivered unless it bears the 'Billet de port-payé,' also the date, the day and the month (which must be done by the people). Further we inform the people that in our Royal Castle a post office is established and a general clerk is by us employed for the public sale of such 'Billets de port-payé,' to those who call for them. The price for each Billet is one sou, and the people can buy as many as they please."

Jean Jacques Renouard, Sieur de Villayer, is credited with the operation of this local post, in which boxes were set up throughout Paris, and letters and packets were taken up by the postmen on their regular rounds and delivered as addressed within the city.

The "Billets de port-payé" which were attached to this mail were the first postage stamps of which there is any record. Since they were removed by the carrier when the article was delivered, probably to prevent reuse, not a single specimen exists, so far as known. Following the death of Renouard this post fell into disuse and after a few years was forgotten.

No other French post is mentioned until 1758 when Claude-Humbert Piarron de Chamousset established "la petite poste" in Paris. This used 117 carriers and made deliveries three times daily. It was so profitable that the government cancelled the franchise and paid de Chamousset a pension of twenty thousand francs per year for his interest. But again government operation was a failure and the post soon was abandoned.

Spain, by a decree of December 7, 1716, granted the franking privilege on official correspondence between certain government officials, requiring that each piece be identified on the cover or wrapper by an impression in ink of the seal of Castile and Leon. This type of official franking was used well into the nineteenth century.

EARLY POSTS IN ENGLAND

Although a simple post had been started in England in the thirteenth century it had little in common with the post office of today. The duty of the master of the post of that time was to furnish horses for messengers carrying letters, at a fixed fee of 2½ pence per mile.

In 1644, Edmund Prideaux was appointed Master of the Posts by Parliament and established a weekly postal service to all parts of England. He maintained the system at his own expense and was allowed to retain whatever profit he could make. Within a few years this amounted to £5000 a year. The government, desiring some share in this revenue, but unwilling to assume the management and responsibility, leased out the system in 1650 for £5000 per year. The system continued to be farmed out for many years and when Henry Bishop became postmaster general in 1660 the annual rental amounted to £21,500.

A penny post for London was established in 1680 by William Dockwra, and for three years he had a very efficient system of collecting and delivering letters and parcels. He installed almost five hundred receiving offices and made deliveries six to eight times each day in the business district and four times daily in the city outskirts.

He was sued on the ground that he was infringing on the Crown's monopoly. His business was taken over and conducted as the Penny Post until 1801, when the rates were doubled and it became known as the Twopenny Post.

THE AMERICAN COLONIES

In the British possessions of North America the first mention of letters or posts appears in the Massachusetts General Court records of November 5, 1639:

> For the prenting [preventing] the miscarriage of letters; &ᶜ, it is hereby ordered that notice bee given that Richʳᵈ Fairbanks his house in Boston is the place appointed for all letters, which are brought from beyond the seas or are to be sent thither;—are to be brought unto; & hee is to take care, that they bee delivered or sent according to their direction; & he is allowed for every such letter a ld, & must answer all miscarriages through his owne neglect in this kind; pvided that no man shalbee compelled to bring his letters thither, except hee please.

During the next thirty years little attempt was made to extend the post throughout the colonies and it was not until 1672 that New York and Boston had a regular service. In 1692, Thomas Neale obtained a patent for the post office of America, and for the next several years sent agents to the colonial legislatures in an effort to establish a system from New Hampshire to the Carolinas.

In 1710, during the reign of Queen Anne, Parliament passed an act regulating the posts throughout the dominions. A chief letter office was established in New York and other offices were set up in each colony. Post routes were laid out from Piscataqua, New Hampshire, to Philadelphia and after a few years were extended to Williamsburg in Virginia. This last called for a postman to leave Philadelphia whenever sufficient mail had accumulated to pay the expense.

In 1753 Benjamin Franklin and William Hunter were appointed Joint Deputy Postmasters General for all the colonies. Franklin was removed by the Crown in 1774, and his successor, William Goddard, had little success in continuing the system.

Following the breach with England there was no postal establishment until July 26, 1775, when the Continental Congress provided for a Postmaster General for the United Colonies, and a chief letter office at Philadelphia with post routes from Falmouth in the north to Savannah in the south and as many cross routes as were necessary.

Benjamin Franklin became the first postmaster general, and he and his successors carried on until the Constitution became effective. Under that document Congress was given exclusive control of postal affairs.

Postal rates were high and were based on distance as well as the number of sheets of paper in a letter. Extra sheets doubled or tripled the rates, while the size of sheets did not matter. Consequently some were very large. The high charges encouraged private carriers to compete with the government post and these took away much of the revenue for they carried mail only over routes where quantities made it profitable.

The first real reduction in United States rates came only after the British one-penny rate had proved successful. In 1845 the minimum rate was reduced to five cents for distances under 300 miles. The preceding minimum of six cents had applied only to distances under 30 miles, and the cost of carrying a letter 250 miles was 25 cents.

In 1847 postage stamps were introduced in the United States and a few years later the rate was again reduced. Within a short time private carriers were prohibited from carrying mail and the service became a hard and fast government monopoly.

ORIGIN OF THE ADHESIVE POSTAGE STAMP

In the period just prior to 1840 the British post office was in dire circumstances for the high rates forced the average citizen to patronize illegal carriers or forego writing at all. All members of parliament had the franking privilege and many misused it by franking letters for friends and others for a fraction of the regular postage rates. Thus the cost of maintaining the post fell upon those poor wretches who had no friends to frank their letters.

Since postage was not prepaid but collected on delivery,

letters were often refused. The cost to the government was very large for in addition to the full service already given, it was necessary to return an unclaimed letter to the sender.

In 1835 Rowland Hill, a retired schoolteacher, known as somewhat of a busybody and reformer, entered the postal field with the avowed intention of changing the system. As a result of investigations completed in 1837 he published a pamphlet, *Post Office Reform; Its Importance and Practicability*. In this he proved that the cost of carrying mail was negligible, perhaps as little as $\frac{1}{36}$ of a penny per letter, and that the major expense was in computing rates, collecting postage, keeping books, and above all in transporting free of charge all sorts of matter, even cattle and servants, for those who had the franking privilege.

He proposed the complete abolition of the franking system, the adoption of a uniform rate of postage for letters regardless of distance, but dependent on weight, and the prepayment of all postage or the collection of double the rate if sent collect. His program did not include the radical reduction to one penny as finally adopted. Had the government, which opposed Hill's program, made a reasonable reduction, perhaps to fourpence per letter, it would have quieted the public and eliminated the private carriers, as they could not have cut below such a rate.

However, nothing was done to improve the service or lower the rates and the public finally forced the adoption of Hill's program. A minimum rate was fixed at one penny for each half ounce if prepaid, twopence if sent collect. The franking privilege was abolished except for petitions to the queen through members of Parliament, and petitions to members themselves, none exceeding 32 ounces in weight. One of the provisions was for the registration of letters at a prepaid fee of one shilling.

In order to avoid the confusion that might result if the program were put into effect as a whole, a temporary flat rate of fourpence per letter was put in force November 22, 1839. On January 10, 1840, the one-penny rate by weight became effective. To implement the program the government set out to furnish stamped envelopes and wrappers, and adhesive stamps in onepenny and twopenny denominations. The stamps were more or less an afterthought and were provided so that letters already in envelopes or wrappers could be brought to the post office for mailing by servants incompetent to address the government envelopes.

WHO WAS THE INVENTOR?

Although Rowland Hill is known as the inventor of the adhesive stamp, he may have had little to do with it. His preference was for the stamped paper. It is possible that suggestions made during the debates on postal reform were responsible for adhesive stamps. There were several claimants to the invention and no less than three were in England.

There were two or three earlier stamps of sorts, such as the "billets de port-payé" used in Paris in 1653, the Sardinian stamped letter sheets of 1818-1836, and some other prototypes of this nature, but the adhesives of 1840 could have been evolved from the existing embossed British revenue stamps as well as from any other source.

FIG. 18–1. The Sardinian Letter Tax Stamps.

The embossed stamps of the Sardinian letter sheets did not pay postage but were a tax on letters delivered privately, outside the Sardinian postal system. (The Kingdom of Sardinia then included provinces on the mainland in what are now Italy and France.) Sardinia held that all mail carrying was a government prerogative and required all letters that were to be delivered privately to be first presented at the post office. The charge collected varied with the distance to the place of address. To expedite such letters the postal department introduced the letter sheets marked "Carta postali bollata," in denominations of 15, 25, and 50 centesimi. Private communications wrapped with one of these sheets of the proper denomination did not need to go to the post office before delivery. As an indication that the stamps were a tax and not a postage fee, it is of record that when such stamped paper was used on a letter and forwarded through the post office, the stamp was disregarded and full postage collected.

The 1819 issue consisted of the three values mentioned, printed in blue on white paper, while the 1820 issue included the same values embossed without color on white paper.

Only a few years after the Sardinian stamped paper came into use, Lieutenant Curry Gabriel Treffenberg introduced a bill in the Swedish Riksdag, March 3, 1823, for the use of stamped paper as an indication of postage paid. He called attention to the complicated method of collecting postage and rendering accounts, and the ease of embezzlement. The new system, Treffenberg maintained, would eliminate the expense of collecting and accounting and a cheaper rate might be charged. His bill outlined a complete postal system, with registration, and provision for the collection of short-paid postage. It was debated in committee and returned to the division for further study but the three other divisions of the Riksdag voted against the bill and it was lost; otherwise Sweden would have had a cheap uniform postage system many years before Great Britain, but with imprinted stamps.

On the Grecian island of Parus, letters posted in 1831 bore what most collectors would call adhesive postage stamps. This label was printed in sheets and had inscriptions giving the value as 40 lepta, and the name of the governor, G. Glarakis. The fact that covers with this stamp have been found and that full sheets of the stamps are known may enable some specialist in Greek postal history to transfer the laurels from Rowland Hill to some Greek, now unknown.

In 1838 New South Wales issued a letter sheet with an embossed one-penny stamp for local use. The sheets were priced at fifteen pence per dozen and the extra three pence probably paid for the paper. As little demand arose, the price was cut to one shilling per dozen. When the response was no better, the sheets were removed from sale.

Between 1794 and 1809 the Dutch Indies made use of letter sheets with imprinted postage stamps, and numerous examples are in existence today.

One of the most valid claims concerning the adhesive stamp was presented by Robert Ripley in 1944, when a "Believe It or Not" cartoon contained the categorical statement that the adhesive stamp was invented by Henry Bessemer. The records show that Mr. Bessemer in 1833, at the age of twenty, proposed adhesive stamps of delicate structure to replace embossed revenue stamps and thus prevent counterfeiting and the resultant loss in revenue. To strengthen his argument Mr. Bessemer demonstrated to British treasury and Stamp Office officials that he could make a die from one stamp to emboss others which could not be detected. The officials were so impressed that Mr. Bessemer was appointed Superintendent of Stamps in lieu of other rewards. When he conveyed this news to his fiancee, she observed that the same result—the prevention of counterfeiting—might be obtained by dating the revenue stamps. The idea was adopted postponing the use of adhesive stamps for several years. The stamp dies were drilled so that plugs bearing dates could be inserted and changed daily if desired.

Perhaps his fiancee's simple suggestion saved Henry Bessemer from being buried in the Stamp Office, where he might not have had the time and freedom to invent the Bessemer process of making steel.

In the early 1880's Patrick Chalmers, a resident of Dundee, made the claim that his deceased father, James Chalmers, was the true inventor of the adhesive stamp, and witnesses swore under oath that they had seen adhesive stamps printed in 1834. It was claimed that the elder Chalmers had undertaken negotiations with the government but could make no headway against Rowland Hill and abandoned the idea. Examples of the actual stamps accompanied the petition.

Patrick Chalmers received so much publicity and his claims appeared so plausible that for a time the honor was transferred from Rowland Hill. The *Encyclopædia Britannica* revised its story and collectors throughout the world rallied to Chalmers' cause. He was made an honorary member of the Chicago Philatelic Society, ranking with such men as John K. Tiffany, Theodore Cuno, and other philatelic leaders. A Chalmers Philatelic Society was organized in Chicago but this appears to have been but a select group of the society mentioned.

The American Philatelic Association, now the American Philatelic Society, in convention in Chicago in 1887, passed a resolution acclaiming Chalmers as the true inventor of the stamp and spread it upon the minutes for the world to see. When it developed that no correspondence between James Chalmers and the British Government could be produced which dated prior to the proposal of Rowland Hill, the excitement died away, and scarcely any collector today remembers this threat to Rowland Hill's fame.

The claim to the first postage stamp is a continuing operation and almost yearly something new is produced. In 1952 an Austrian produced a stamp on cover dated February 20, 1839, of such "value" that only a selected group of experts were allowed to see it. Later it was indicated that this lone copy was not entirely "of the period" but had been worked over to a certain extent, and further that it could be only a local stamp issued by the postmaster at Spittal without the sanction of the Austrian government.

The question of whether a stamp is a regular government issue or a local issue seems to be beside the point when trying to locate the first adhesive postage stamp. The argument seems to indicate that adhesive locals were common before 1840, but this is not the case.

Still more recently an even earlier stamp was discovered at

Obervellach, in Austria. The claim is that it was mailed at Klagenfurt, June 26, 1838, thus antedating the Spittal stamp by about eight months. This stamp is bicolored and Ferdinande Mille, the finder, has asked the Austrian Philatelic Society to have its expert committee examine the stamp and cover.

In 1954, L'Union Postale, official organ of the Universal Postal Union, published documents placed before the first congress in 1874 by Lavrenc Kosir, or Laurenz Koschier as he signed in German, who claimed to be the inventor of the postage stamp. He alleged that his idea was conceived in 1836 and presented to the Austrian government, which returned it with a polite refusal and stated that the idea was impractical. Kosir claimed in his memorial to the Universal Postal Union that he had discussed the matter with G. Galway, a British commercial representative in Croatia, and that the latter had no doubt informed Rowland Hill. The memorial was noted and filed and Rowland Hill did not honor the claims with a denial. When Austria finally began to issue stamps, credit was given to Baron Bruck and Dr. Johann Jakob Herz, and no mention was made of the minor official in Croatia.

THE FIRST POSTAGE STAMP

Following the passage of the Postal Reform Bill, the British Treasury, in September, 1839, asked for suggestions and offered prizes of £100 and £200 for the most useful ideas submitted by October 15 for handling the prepayment of postage. Over 2600 entries were received and four £100 prizes were awarded, but few practical ideas were found and the final selection may have been a composite of the better suggestions as developed by Rowland Hill.

Stamped paper was considered to be the best solution and this had the preference of Rowland Hill. Only secondary consideration was given to adhesive stamps, which were to be used only when a patron brought a letter to the post office already in a wrapper. The design for envelopes submitted by William Mulready, R.A., was approved and provided in envelope and wrapper form, in 1-penny and 2-penny values, six items in all. However, it soon became evident that the envelopes and wrappers were less practical than the stamps. The stamps could be affixed to any letter or packet while the envelopes were too small for any bulky packets.

POSTAGE ONE PENNY.

FIG. 18–2. The Mulready Letter Sheet (from a reproduction by Stanley Gibbons, Ltd.).

Through the efforts of Rowland Hill, now employed in the treasury, negotiations were entered into with Perkins, Bacon & Petch, bank-note engravers, December 2, 1839, and this firm was commissioned to engrave dies, prepare plates, and print stamps upon paper furnished by the government for a fee of 7½ pence per thousand. When it became evident that sufficient quantities of stamps and stamped paper would be available, a date was announced for their sale to the public. This was May 6, 1840, a date which should be remembered by every stamp collector. The stamps at once became an unqualified success but Mulready's envelopes were never popular and were ridiculed out of existence within a short time.

About December 16, 1839, Perkins, Bacon & Petch engaged Henry Corbould to prepare drawings to be used by the engravers of the stamp dies. He made a portrait of Queen Victoria, copying William Wyon's commemorative medal of the Queen's first visit to the "City of London," November 9, 1837.

When the design had received final approval and royal assent, Charles Heath, a noted engraver, was engaged to cut the portrait on the original die. It is now believed that this work was done by his son Frederick, whose ability in portrait work is said to have exceeded his father's.

The background suggested by Joshua B. Bacon was a pattern of rose-engine work and was transferred to the stamp die from a stock roll which had been made on another order. When the inscription and corner ornaments had been added the die was in readiness for use in making the plate. The corner letters which show on each stamp were punched into the individual corner blocks of each stamp on the plate.

The successful production of intaglio stamp-printing plates was made possible only by the duplicating process invented by Jacob Perkins, an engraver of Newburyport, Massachusetts. His work included the production of notes for a large number of banks in the United States and he had perfected a process in which a steel die was annealed for engraving and then tempered to a hardness suitable for transferring the design by pressure to a transfer roll and then to a steel plate, thus producing exactly duplicated stamp subjects, a condition that was not possible by hand engraving.

At the height of his career, Perkins went abroad in an attempt to obtain the Bank of England as a client. That venerable institution was not interested but other banks were and Perkins remained to establish the engraving company of Perkins, Fairman & Company, later Perkins, Bacon & Petch.

Thus, at the time stamps were invented there was an engraving firm available to produce them. Had Perkins not taken the transfer process to England, the Penny Black might have been lithographed or typographed, for certainly the 240-subject plate would not have been hand engraved.

It has been stated that the production of the first stamps took considerable time due to the slow process used. When it is considered that the postage act was passed August 17, 1839, that a competition was held to bring out ideas, and that Perkins,

Bacon & Petch was awarded a contract as late as mid December, it is unreasonable to claim a waste of time between that date and May 6, 1840, when the stamps were placed on sale. During this period the designs were made and approved, a die was engraved and rejected, another die was made and approved, and finally the engraving company was allowed to proceed with the actual plates. On April 8 plate No. 1 had been completed and the day of issue announced for May 6. Today this work could proceed much faster. A stamp can be produced in quantity in a month if necessary, instead of three months, but it usually looks like a hasty job, while the Penny Black looks as if a lifetime of work had been put into the design, engraving, and production of the actual stamp. It is an interesting fact and not wishful thinking on the part of Penny Black collectors that this, the first stamp ever issued for postage purposes, has never been excelled in design or execution since it was issued.

The marginal inscriptions on the first plates refer to the stamps as "labels" and some writers believe that this usage continued for some time. There is some evidence to the contrary, for an article entitled "Postage and Post Office" in a general compendium of British Industry published at the end of 1844 refers in every instance to "adhesive stamps" and not "labels."

THE PERKINS PROCESS

This process begins with the softening or annealing of a cast-steel block perhaps two inches square and one-half inch thick so that it can be engraved more readily than untreated metal. On this die block the stamp design is hand engraved, though some portions of the design may be transferred from other dies.

When the die has been finished and a proof print approved, it is subjected to a heat treatment in charcoal in a closed cast-iron box. It is then removed and quenched in cold water, and again heated and quenched to increase the surface hardness without the danger of cracking.

The next step is the preparation of a transfer roll, a short cylinder of cast steel, three inches or more in diameter, with a thick integral axle or shaft. The roll is annealed, then mounted above and touching the die, which is secured to the bed of a transfer press. The press bed moves back and forth under the transfer roll and the pressure is increased, forcing the roll into the engraved lines of the die, thus making a positive impression in raised relief. The finished roll is now hardened.

Meanwhile a cast-steel plate of suitable size has been polished to a mirror-like surface and annealed in preparation for the transfer of stamp designs. This plate is secured to the transfer press and by successive operations the entire number of stamp subjects is transferred to it by means of the roll. Layout lines or guide dots lightly engraved on the plate control the spacing and alignment.

Proof impressions are taken from the soft plate and inspected for faint impressions and other defects. Faint impressions are corrected by a second application of the transfer roll known as a re-entry, but this requires most careful adjustment for any slight error in setting will result in a shifted entry and show as thickened lines or at the worst as doubled lines.

Following the final approval of the stamp subjects in the Penny Black plate the corner letters were added to each subject, the marginal inscriptions were engraved or entered with a transfer roll, and the plate was hardened as previously described.

Mr. Perkins had used this process for many bank notes and had built up a large stock of dies and rolls bearing portraits, ornaments, numerals and similar details. These could be used as often as desired in various combinations when making new plates. The amount of original engraving was thus so much reduced that Perkins was able to underbid less ingenious engraving companies.

Today the Perkins process, which is used whenever line-engraved stamps are mechanically transferred to printing plates, differs little from that of 1840. There have been minor improvements but that is all.

THE ROSE ENGINE

The rose engine was a device for engraving interlacing circular patterns on any smooth plate whether flat, convex, or concave. A common use was to decorate watch cases.

Perkins added eccentric cylinders and wheels and gears of various sizes to vary the number and extent of the movements. The engine now engraved not only the regular interlacing forms, but also ribbons of continuous ornament. Lines that were simple curves in the work of the original engine could now be produced in wavy or looped form in extremely intricate patterns.

The operator of the rose engine could work in a definite space but had little control of the design. The slightest change in the setting of one variable component might change it completely, and a duplication could be made only if the operator had recorded the setting of every adjustment. Engravers stated that they would prefer to make a thousand new designs rather than attempt to duplicate an existing pattern. However, duplication was not a problem when the original design was repeated by means of a transfer roll.

Rose-engine work is found on United States currency, though less on current small notes than on earlier issues. The work was considered proof against counterfeiting. To be doubly certain it was customary to use it in reverse, thus giving a pattern of colorless lines on a colored ground. It is generally conceded that this cannot be duplicated by hand.

This reversed type of design was used on the Penny Black and later on the 3-, 5-, and 12-cent values of the United States issue of 1851-1857.

THE FIRST UNITED STATES STAMP

This was not a governmental issue but a local stamp for use in New York City. Its introduction stems from the Penny Black and the local post of London. Such a post for New York was suggested by Henry Thomas Windsor, a London merchant, while visiting the city in 1841. He found such poor service that he seriously considered establishing a post himself, but he decided it would be better patronized if headed by an American. Alexander Greig, a business friend, agreed to manage the organization.

The City Despatch Post, as it was named, began operations February 1, 1842, and was the first local post to use stamps. The delivery rate was three cents, but stamps were sold in quantity at $2.50 per hundred. The response was so great that the post was swamped and its prestige suffered greatly.

After about six months the government complained that this post was infringing on its monopoly but offered to take it over rather than force it to close. Greig sold out to the Post Office Department, ceasing to operate August 13, 1842. Three days later the post reopened as the United States City Despatch Post. It used the same personnel and offices, and for some time, the same stamps. When new stamps appeared they were of the same design with the name changed.

It was not until 1847 that the United States provided stamps for general use. The 5-cent and 10-cent values of that issue were the first stamps to have the three elements considered necessary in stamp design; i.e., the name of the country, the use of the stamp (postage in this case), and the denomination. Great Britain had the second and third elements in the Penny Black but Brazil, which issued postage stamps in 1843, revealed nothing but the denomination in the designs of the famous "bull's eyes."

PART III

Miscellaneous Subjects

❖•❖

CHAPTER NINETEEN

COLLECTORS AND COLLECTING

Stamp collecting began almost as soon as the Penny Black was issued, for in 1841 a young lady advertised in the *London Times* for the assistance of strangers in her effort to secure enough stamps to paper her dressing room. In 1842 *Punch* mentions the mania of stamp collecting in which the young ladies of England have engaged, saying that they "betray more anxiety to treasure up Queen's heads than Henry VIII did to get rid of them."

In Belgium, J. B. Moens began collecting in 1848, became a dealer in 1852, and published his first philatelic work ten years later. Oscar Berger-Levrault, of Alsace, is said to have been the first collector in France, and in September, 1861, after three years in the hobby, he had collected 673 varieties. At the start of the Franco-Prussian War he had 10,400 varieties and 1,400 essays, and his collection lacked less than 50 stamps of being complete.

Dr. J. A. le Grand, another French collector, started in 1862, and writing under the pen name of Dr. Magnus, coined the word "timbrology" for stamp collecting. However, his greatest contribution was the system still used for measuring perforations.

In England, Stanley Gibbons, the founder of a famous stamp firm, had a small collection in 1854, and began dealing in stamps in his father's store in Plymouth about two years later. William Lincoln, also of England, had 210 varieties in 1854 and later became a full-time stamp dealer. In June, 1862, in the magazine *Young England*, Dr. John Edward Gray, of the British Museum, began publishing a series of articles entitled "The Postage Stamps of Europe." In the first number Dr. Gray stated his belief that he was the first—even before Rowland Hill—to propose a low uniform postage rate prepaid by stamps, but that he did not have time or energy to devote to the subject.

John Walter Scott was an early collector in the United States. He came from England and after a few years in the West returned to New York in 1867 and started the business that became the Scott Stamp and Coin Company. Ferdinand Marie Trifet started collecting in New York but moved to Boston in 1864 to engage in the stamp business. John K. Tiffany, of St. Louis, was one of the most prominent American collectors and his fine collection of stamps and literature was sold to the Earl of Crawford in 1901.

In the early 1860's collectors began to meet in the parks of Paris to exchange stamps and this has been perpetuated in the famous open-air stamp bourse of that city. This sort of exchange spread to London and New York, where street corners became the usual location of traders.

Justin Lallier, of Paris, provided printed albums for collectors in 1863, and many of the old stuck-down collections were housed in these. Hinges were unknown and mint stamps were stuck with their own gum, while used stamps required fish glue. The printed spaces were small and stamps usually were trimmed to the lines to avoid overlapping.

The first club on record was the Société Philatelique de Paris, organized in 1865, and the second was a club organized in New York in 1867. English collectors organized the Philatelic Society of London in 1869, but its members changed the name to the Royal Philatelic Society in 1906.

Alfred Potiquet appears to have originated the stamp catalog in Paris in December 1861, and was followed by A. C. Kline of Philadelphia, who published an American catalog in December, 1862. The first stamp periodicals and advertisements were issued in Paris. Next came the *Stamp Collectors' Review and Monthly Advertiser,* in Liverpool in December, 1862, while the first American journal was the *Stamp Collectors' Record* published by S. Allan Taylor in December, 1864.

Stamp collecting and dealing was accepted as an honorable calling at an early date and a listing of the occupation appeared in the London city directory for 1861. Stamp auctions appear to have originated in Paris, for there is a record of a sale held there in 1865, but in spite of all this early activity there is no record of a stamp exhibition open to the public until the Vienna Exhibition of 1881.

The first official or governmental recognition of stamp collecting is found in the special postal card issued by Italy in 1894 for an internationl philatelic exhibition.

SOCIETIES AND CLUBS

This hobby more than any other owes its development to the societies that have guided its course through the years and to the dealers who have provided catalogs and handbooks without which one would be lost in a jungle of uncharted stamp issues.

Societies might have handled the entire service but it is doubtful that a single group could have covered the world's stamps on a uniform basis, although a society in each country could have taken care of its part. However, the determination of values rests largely with dealers and auction houses and no one today believes that stamp collecting would be better off if conducted on a stamp-for-stamp trading basis.

In order to bind collectors more closely the national societies have enabled local clubs to become branches and to enjoy the sales department and other facilities of the society. The branch club pays ordinary dues as a corporate member and it is not necessary for all members to belong to the national society.

Largely through the efforts of Mr. Harry L. Lindquist, a national federation of stamp clubs was formed about thirty years ago for the general welfare of local clubs and societies. By mere numbers this federation has been able to influence postal officials and legislative bodies more than would have been possible by individual collectors or clubs. Since this first federation was formed the idea has spread and now there are city, state, and regional organizations which help in the promotion of stamp exhibitions and conventions. The publicity about these events attracts numerous beginners, and when there is a bourse where dealers may sell stamps many collectors have their first chance to buy stamps across the counter.

Local clubs are the real school for collectors. At their meetings stamps may be bought or traded, collections are shown, and sometimes a paper is read. Here one may learn the answers to his questions and solve the problems of mounting and writing up a collection and learn why the stamps of certain countries are more desirable than those of others.

In some cases the collecting habits of an entire club are influenced by a member who is an advanced specialist, or perhaps a postal history enthusiast. An outstanding example of members working together exists in a Chicago surburban club. The members resolved to obtain relief from the sameness of general collections and those of United States commemoratives, and picked the not-too-popular stamps of Mexico as a subject for specialization. Now each member collects some period of Mexican stamps according to his liking or perhaps in some cases according to his budget allowance.

One fault of many local clubs lies in their prolonged discussion of business matters and club politics at the expense of philatelic subjects. A club managed by a board of directors generally offers more to a collector than does the usual form that partakes of the nature of a debating society.

In addition to city or area clubs, there are institutional clubs made up of collectors who are employed by one concern. They exist in large banks, insurance companies, public utilities, and manufacturing establishments. There is one in the Pentagon, near Washington, and another in the Hawthorne works of the Western Electric Company.

Near the top of philatelic organizations are a number of associations and societies that may be spoken of as service groups, since their chief concern is in the general welfare of the hobby, and the relations between collectors, collectors and dealers, and of both to the general public.

Here are some of the more prominent stamp organizations of the United States.

Service Organizations

American Stamp Dealers Association (A.S.D.A.), 116 Nassau Street, New York 38. Limited to stamp dealers.

The Association for Stamp Exhibitions, 22 East 35th Street, New York 16. Sponsors international events.

Philatelic Foundation, 22 East 35th St., New York 16. Expertizing and appraisal facilities.

Philatelic Press Club, 220 West 42nd Street, New York 36. A society of professional philatelic editors and writers.

National Societies of General Character

American Philatelic Society (A.P.S.), P.O. Box 800, State College, Pennsylvania. Largest membership, publishes *American Philatelist*. Has an extensive list of branches and special study units.

Society of Philatelic Americans. Publishes *S.P.A. Journal*. Has many branches.

National Philatelic Society. Publishes *National Stamp News*.

Collectors Club of New York, 22 East 35th St., New York 16. Publishes *Collectors Club Philatelist*. Wide membership.

American Philatelic Congress. An annual meeting for the presentation and publication of papers on selected subjects.

Trans-Mississippi Philatelic Society. Membership for the most part is drawn from the middle west in the Mississippi-Missouri Valley area.

National Limited Societies

American Air Mail Society. Publishes *Airpost Journal.*
Aero Philatelists, Inc. Publishes *Aero Philatelist's News.*
Jack Knight Air Mail Society. Publishes *Jack Knight Log.*
Essay-Proof Society. Publishes *Essay-Proof Journal.*
Philatelic Literature Association. Publishes *Philatelic Literature Review.*
American Topical Association. Publishes *Topical Time.*
Bureau Issues Association. Publishes *The Bureau Specialist.*
U.S. Philatelic Classics Society. Publishes *Chronicle of U.S. Classic Issues.*
Confederate Stamp Alliance. Publishes *Confederate Philatelist*
Postal History Society. Publishes *Postal History Journal.*

Others in This Group

American First-Day Cover Society
American Metered-Postage Society.
American Naval Cancellation Society.
American Revenue Society.
Amerpo—R.P.O., H.P.O., T.P.O., and Sea Post Society.
Collectors of Religion on Stamps—COROS.
Maritime Postmark Society.
Maximum Card Society.
National Highway Post Office Society.
Perfins Society.
Philometer Society.
Precancel Stamp Society.
Reply Coupon Society.
Rocket Mail Society.
United Postal Stationery Society.
United States and State Revenues Society.
Universal Ship Cancellation Society.
War Cover Club.
Western Cover Society.

Several of those listed are units of a national society, while others, notably the American Topical Association, have many unit groups within the membership.

There are groups of collectors whose interests lie in the stamps of a single country or group of related countries. All principal countries are represented. Most United States groups and societies are not limited to American membership, and many foreign societies are associated with the American societies.

The thorough training a young collector receives in a Boy Scout stamp club is illustrated by the following examination.

BOY SCOUT REQUIREMENTS FOR A MERIT BADGE

Effective January 1, 1952

To obtain a Merit Badge for Stamp Collecting, a Scout must:

1. Mount and exhibit in a commercial album or one of his own making:

a. A collection of 750 or more different stamps from at least 30 countries, or

b. A collection of 150 or more stamps from a single country or group of related countries, or

c. A collection of 75 or more different stamps on some special subject such as birds, trees, railroads, music, aviation, etc. The stamps may be from any number of countries, or

d. A collection of 200 or more special items such as precanceled stamps, postage meters, revenue stamps, covers, postal stationery, etc.

2. Demonstrate the use of the *Standard Postage Stamp Catalogue*, or a catalog particularly related to his collection in Requirement No. 1, to find at least five items selected by the Counselor.

3. Show stamps to support brief definitions of the following terms: (a) perforation, (b) imperforate, (c) roulette, (d) cancellation, (e) cover, (f) mint stamp, (g) coil stamp, (h) overprint, (i) surcharge (overprint), (j) engraving, (k) printing process other than engraving.

4. Exhibit one stamp in each of the following classifications and explain the purpose of each: regular postage, commemora-

tive, semi-postal, air mail, postage due, envelope, special delivery, precancel, and revenue.

5. Explain the meaning of good condition of a stamp and show one stamp that is well centered, fully perforated, clearly canceled, clean and undamaged by tears or thin spots.

6. Demonstrate a knowledge of the following stamp collectors' tools:

a. Use a perforation gauge to determine, on a stamp supplied by the Counselor, the perforation measurement in accordance with the accepted standard.

b. Use a magnifying glass for careful examination of design and condition.

c. Use the watermark detector to show how a watermark may aid in identifying a stamp.

d. Use stamp tongs and stamp hinges correctly in mounting a stamp in an album.

Under the broadened requirements, it is now possible for Boy Scouts and Explorers to achieve this Merit Badge regardless of individual preferences in collecting.

PHILATELIC LITERATURE

Space will not permit any extensive listing of the many books and periodical publications on stamp collecting and philately in general. Many of the books are printed in small editions and soon go out of print. A new collector must wait for new books or watch the secondhand market. Some of the older books may show up at dealers' and auction sales, and some may be obtained by advertising or through the facilities of the Philatelic Literature Association.

One of the first requisites is a complete catalog of the stamps being collected. This may be a Scott *Standard Postage Stamp Catalogue* of the world's stamps, or either of the two volumes of this catalog—if the collector's limited field is completely covered by the information found in one of the volumes, then the other is unnecessary.

Collectors of United States stamps who go beyond the limits of a general collection and wish a listing showing cancellations, varieties, multiple pieces, etc., find the Scott *Catalogue of United States Stamps, Specialized,* a necessity. Similar specialized catalogs of some foreign countries are available but usually they are in the language of the country whose stamps are listed.

Some collectors may prefer the Stanley Gibbons catalogs and many collectors of British Commonwealth stamps use the single volume that contains detailed information and listings of all British stamps. The Gibbons catalogs are in several sections and only the needed sections have to be purchased. The catalogs are not brought up to date each year. Both Scott and Gibbons publish monthly magazines listing new issues.

Minkus Publications has three catalogs which are published annually. These are the *New American Stamp Catalog* covering the United States and possessions in detail, and the *New World-Wide Postage Stamp Catalog* in two volumes. The Minkus catalogs serve as handbooks for they show dates of issue, numbers issued, subjects, sources of designs, and other data where known.

Catalogs covering single countries or groups of related countries have been published at various times by Scott and by Minkus, and these may be the solution for collectors who have no use for world-wide catalogs.

Periodicals are available in great variety with material ranging from highly specialized articles down to the current chatter about club affairs. The journals published by the national and specialist societies have already been mentioned. These are sent to all members and may be obtained by nonmembers on subscription.

Every collector should subscribe to one or more stamp newspapers in order to keep up with events and news of stamps in which he may be interested. The leading papers are the *Western Stamp Collector* published in Albany, Oregon; *Linn's Weekly Stamp News,* Sidney, Ohio; *Stamps,* 153 Waverly Place, New York, N.Y., and *Mekeel's Weekly Stamp News,* Portland, Maine.

Many newspapers in the large cities have weekly stamp columns and while these usually are no more timely than the stamp newspapers, they do have the advantage of reaching several million people who have never heard of a publication devoted to stamps alone. Many other daily and Sunday papers carry philatelic items and pictures furnished by a news service such as the Associated Press.

BUILDING A PHILATELIC LIBRARY

A person with a limited field of collecting who subscribes to several magazines will find it easier to refer again to items in which he is interested if he clips the magazines and files the clippings alphabetically. Many collectors oppose clipping and believe that complete files should be kept. This idea is all right for magazines printed on good paper, but clippings of the newsprint papers can be preserved much longer than can the entire journals.

The clipped material can be filed in envelopes or mounted on letter-size sheets in loose-leaf notebooks. Bound scrapbooks are of little value for sooner or later the material will be out of order no matter what system is used. Loose-leaf sheets will be satisfactory only when the clippings pasted on a sheet have identical subjects. The best all-round file is a flapless envelope or pocket. When a new article appears that is an improvement over one previously filed, the old one may be discarded without trouble. Collectors intending to write up a country or some particular stamp subject can also file clippings of text, pictures, and maps relating to the subject.

Clippings should be marked to identify source and date. Only when it happens that two equally important articles are printed front and back on the same clipping will it be necessary to provide a cross index. The clipping is put in one envelope and a reference slip in the other.

Collectors who preserve their magazines entire must provide their own indexing, but can limit them to the subjects covered in their collections. The usual magazine indexes do not appear until the end of the year and at best are not very thorough.

A collector's file should be principally concerned with subject matter. The title of the article and the author's name are generally of less importance. Articles by an authority may be cross indexed under the author's name, but when a writer is not a recognized authority, perhaps the clipping should be questioned before it is given storage space.

PERMANENT STAMP EXHIBITIONS

Perhaps the greatest permanent exhibition of stamps in this country is the government collection in the Smithsonian Institution in Washington. This is a "live" collection, increasing constantly and being improved by modern methods of mounting and display. Here also is a large philatelic library. All the material is under a curator who is a competent collector and philatelic writer.

Another fine collection is in the New York Public Library, having passed to that institution upon the death of its owner, Benjamin K. Miller. Although this is prominently displayed it is a closed collection and ends abruptly at the point reached by its owner. There has been no attempt to add missing specimens and probably no desire to do so.

The most recent permanent stamp exhibition of a private nature to be established is in the Cardinal Spellman museum at St. Regis College at Weston, Mass. Here, in a building planned for this special use, is displayed the collection formed by Cardinal Spellman together with exhibits formerly shown in the National Philatelic Museum in Philadelphia and other material donated since the idea of this museum was first suggested.

Collections donated to museums, libraries, historical societies, and universities, when properly displayed, may be instrumental in acquainting many people with various aspects of stamp collecting, but those who have the best interests of the hobby foremost in their minds are opposed to this "burial" of great collections.

The scarce stamps in such collections are permanently off a market which already has too few copies and their inability ever to possess certain stamps deters collectors from starting a country in which there is no chance of ultimate completion.

VALUE AND APPRAISAL

Collectors who are interested in knowing the value of their collections should keep inventories as the stamps arc acquired. It is hardly possible to make a complete inventory at a later time unless the costs have been set down. An inventory should show the number of stamps, the cost, the catalog value, and the estimated cash value, all broken down by countries.

This information is not static for there will be changes in the stamps themselves as well as in the catalog and cash values. If the collector is a cautious buyer, it may be assumed that the cost price was the true cash value at the time of purchase, and a comparison with the present cash value will reveal the profit or loss.

Current quotations for complete sets of stamps, either mint or used, may be found in the lists of some of the larger dealers, and the same is true for medium- to high-priced single stamps, but it is impractical to note quotations on cheap stamps. There are companies handling United States stamps in sheets on a brokerage basis and their quotations offer some help, for it is doubtful if singles and blocks are worth more than the proper fractional part of the sheet.

The prices realized at auction sales usually give a true picture of market conditions, and sooner or later all varieties of stamps show up at the sales. In some cases very large collections are offered as single lots, a recent example being a 100,000 variety collection which realized about $8000.

An inventory will enable a collector to sell his stamps easily. In selling to a dealer, he will have to discount the value to enable the dealer to resell at a profit, but such a direct sale will net approximately the same amount as a sale at auction, after deducting the commission.

Many collectors keep inventory records, or the current value at least, on the binding margin of each page with a summary at the end of the album. This provides a ready reference and is available in case the collection reaches a noncollector's hands for disposal.

When offering a collection for sale, the owner should call attention to defective stamps. It is possible that the collection will bring a higher price if the damaged items are thrown out before the collection is shown to a dealer. Such stamps, together with stamps purposely mismounted in spaces belonging to higher-priced issues, cause a dealer to suspect others and to discount the value to take care of such mistakes.

In trying to arrive at a valuation it should be remembered that the common stamps are common stamps. It is well to count them and place a value on the lot not greater than the same number would cost in a packet. The wholesale price of packets containing under 5000 varieties is so low that a dealer can hardly afford to consider them in his valuation of a collection.

Valuation, however, is not always based on some fraction of list price and some collections of very fine used stamps are worth full catalog and several times that amount when they have exceptional cancellations. Full catalog is about the best that can be expected of a collection made up of exceptional copies of unused stamps.

Specialized collections are much more difficult to appraise, especially when they show original research. Unless there are auction records of similar material both the collector and dealer are handicapped and an auction sale is about the only solution.

The need for an appraisal often arises when a collection has been acquired by gift or inheritance or when an executor is settling an estate. In earlier times collections often were consigned to the furnace with old books but today there is a better appreciation of their possible value. How a collection is considered after the death of an owner depends largely upon how much he confided in his family or what instructions he may have given for its disposal.

When a collection passes into the hands of someone who has no knowledge of stamps, it may be shown to a friend, also a noncollector who, trying to be helpful, says that it appears to be valuable. The collection may be nearly worthless but the remark of the friend will carry more weight than the verdict of a jury of dealers and if no substantial offer is received the new owner will be convinced that stamp dealers are crooked and that collectors are crazy. Such an impasse would have been avoided had a valuation been noted in the album.

Now and then a collection is made up largely of defective stamps. Some collectors buy every lot possible that is selling at auction at less than 10 per cent of list price. When showing such a collection the owner mentions nothing about condition but emphasizes the value represented. A collector should not be blamed for trying to fit a collection to his purse but sometimes it would be easier for his heirs or assigns if he had placed an inventory in the album.

Appraisals are of two general kinds: to determine a value for tax purposes or for a division of property among heirs where an actual sale is not involved, and to determine the cash value prior to a sale. The first kind should be arranged, if possible, for a flat fee, or one based on the number of stamps to be examined, rather than on a percentage of the valuation. This will deter an appraiser who might be tempted to increase the valuation to raise his commission.

Once a collector without ability to appraise was entrusted with a valuable collection on which a state tax was to be paid. The inflated valuation given increased the tax and the appraiser's fee but when a sale was finally decided upon, the realization scarcely covered the tax and fee.

An appraisal made with a sale in mind constitutes an offer on the part of the dealer to purchase. The figure may be stated as the fair cash value, with the dealer offering to purchase at that figure, less a 15 to 20 per cent commission, or the dealer may agree to sell at auction and advance the owner the appraisal figure, less the 15 to 20 per cent auction fee, with a further provision to share any additional money realized. When a collection is sold to a dealer making an appraisal there is no charge for that work, but if taken elsewhere or withdrawn from sale the person making the appraisal is entitled to a fee for his work.

SELLING DUPLICATES

The various sources of stamps were mentioned in chapter 2: club or society sales departments, consignment services, and floor and mail auctions. All of these may also serve as outlets for duplicates. Other methods of disposing of stamps are by direct sale and by advertisements in collectors' journals. The method used may depend upon the kind and value of the stamps. There is little demand for stamps of low catalog value excepting the new issues.

All stamps placed in sales circuits must be identified by catalog number and value, and should be priced a little less than current offerings to quicken the sales. In some club circuits a credit allowance is given when stamps are entered, and purchases can begin at once, up to the extent of the credit, with a final settlement when the sales books are retired.

Exchange circuits use the same general procedure as sales circuits, but exchange is on the basis of net values and no money changes hands unless a collector takes more stamps out of the department than he is able to balance with stamps entered.

Exchange with other collectors can be on a stamp-for-stamp basis for cheaper stamps, or a catalog basis when the stamps are of the same or equally desirable countries, or on a net basis where condition may be reflected in the prices.

The finest duplicates may be mounted in small books to show to friends at the local club or to send to out-of-town collectors. In all cases it is better to mount the stamps by countries and then according to the catalog listing. Since many collectors limit themselves to certain countries it is better to use a booklet for each country, or for a related group of countries, but if there are only a few duplicates they may be mounted in alphabetical order in a single book.

Carefully identify each stamp with catalog number and value and point out any defects for it is better to miss a sale than to lose a customer who bought a damaged stamp which he thought was perfect.

INSURANCE

When a collection begins to assume importance and contains some stamps of value it is wise to consider insurance. For many years there was no thought of theft, for a burglar would not have been caught dead with a stamp collection. Today there are many reports of thefts from collectors and dealers and it is apparent that stolen stamps are often disposed of in some foreign country.

There are several forms of policies and a casualty insurance agent will supply the details. One form will insure any number of stamps at some estimated cash value and give full coverage and payment in case of total loss but limit payments to a certain maximum for the loss of single stamps. Another policy requires a detailed list of the stamps to be insured, with the net worth of each copy, and will pay the insured value of any stamps which mysteriously disappear or are stolen.

The American Philatelic Society provides for its members a stamp insurance program which cannot be cancelled on an individual basis, which is an obvious advantage.

❖❖

UNUSUAL USES FOR STAMPS

STAMPS USED AS MONEY

Perhaps the first use of stamps as money occurred during the Civil War when all minor coin vanished from circulation. As a medium for making change, F. E. Spinner, Secretary of the Treasury, suggested pasting stamps on cards, singly or in groups, to provide values up to fifty cents. The result was unsatisfactory for the stamps wore out and fell off the cards, and even though replaced without cost, the cards were a source of annoyance.

On July 17, 1862, an act was passed to allow stamps to be printed on cards, and the National Bank Note Company, the United States stamp printer at the time, was authorized to prepare plates for this postage currency, as it was called. The obverse designs showed one 5- or one 10-cent stamp, or five 5-cent or five 10-cents, both of the latter overlapping, with an appropriate border and background. The National Bank Note Company printed the obverses of the notes and delivered them to the Treasury Department. Meanwhile obverses had been designed and engraved by the American Bank Note Company, and these were printed on the unfinished notes. The work of this company is identified by the letters "A.B.N.Co." on the backs.

After a short time the Bureau of Engraving and Printing began to print the reverses, their work being without the initials mentioned above. All values and printings were issued perforated as well as imperforate. The issue of this currency began August 21, 1862, and ceased May 27, 1863, being replaced by a new series known as fractional currency, in designs not related to postage stamps.

ENCASED POSTAGE STAMPS

Encased postage stamps for small change were conceived by John Gault, of New York, in July, 1862, and patented August 12. A small brass case with mica front was used to protect the stamps. This "metallic postage currency" provided space on the reverse for an ad to recompense the person or firm who paid to have the stamps encased.

Gault's factory worked on a twenty-four hour basis to supply about thirty companies with currency and all values of the current stamp series were encased, although half of the companies used nothing above the 12-cent value. No actual use was made of encased 2-cent "black jacks" except by the inventor, and this type is very scarce.

In addition to his United States clients, Gault encased 1-, 3-, 5-, and 10-cent stamps for Messrs. Weir & Larminie, of Montreal. Although most of the firms which made use of the metallic currency have ceased operations, J. C. Ayer, of sarsaparilla fame, and Lord & Taylor, of New York, still survive. One of the important Chicago users was Gage Bros. & Drake, proprietors of the Tremont House.

After World War I several countries encased postage stamps when inflation made minted coins obsolete. Cases were of metal or paper, celluloid or other plastic, and in a majority the backs bore the name of a bank or commercial house. Encased stamps were common in Germany and Austria, but rather scarce in France, Algiers, Belgium, Denmark, Norway, Italy and elsewhere.

Rhodesia reverted to Spinner's suggestion during an emergency and used postage stamps pasted on small cards.

Russia used stamps for money in 1915, 1916, and 1917, but made special printings on thin cardboard. All were perforated but only those of 1915 were gummed for use as stamps. The 1915 issue of 10-, 15-, and 20-kopeck value had an inscription printed on the back attesting parity with coin. The 1916 issue, at first in 1- and 2-kopeck values with large numerals overprinted on the face, and later in 1-, 2-, and 3-kopeck values without numeral overprint, bore the royal arms and an inscription on the back.

The preceding were made under the czarist regime but the issue of 1917 by Kerensky's Provisional Government used the 1- and 2-kopeck values with the large numeral on the front, and the 3-kopeck without numeral, all with large numeral and inscription on the back. Although issued expressly to provide small change during the wartime shortage of metal, these stamps were available for postage and are listed in catalogs.

ADVERTISING AND STAMPS

An interesting collection can be made of stamps or covers showing forms of advertising. For the most part private advertising seldom appears in the designs of stamps or in cancellations, but such matter has been printed on the backs of stamps, on the margins, interleaves, and covers of stamp booklets, and on labels substituted for stamps in booklets.

It might be difficult to determine which country first pictured its natural recources and scenic wonders to promote exports or to attract tourists. Nothing of the sort was evident in the United States pictorial issue of 1869, but the Columbian issue and all subsequent exposition stamps were issued, partly at least, for advertising purposes. The New South Wales centenary issue shows no attempt to attract tourists, but the New Zealand issue of 1898 has several scenic designs.

The Cabot issue of Newfoundland of 1897 may have been one of the first intended to attract visitors for, along with monarch and explorer, the designs picture natural resources and such tourist attractions as caribou hunting, salmon fishing, and a view of ptarmigan. The various Olympic Games issues, national park and scenic issues are all advertising stamps as also are many individual stamps designed to call attention to current events. The first United States stamp devoted to advertising a commodity was the one of 1948 that pictured a hen.

South and Central American countries have waged a stamp war over their produce during the past 25 years. It started when Costa Rica celebrated the centenary of coffee cultivation in 1921. Brazil was the next country to follow this lead, but in 1929 a stamp appeared with the inscription in English "Guatemala Produces the Best Coffee in the World." What effect this had on coffee sales is unknown but the stamps were disliked in that Spanish-speaking country. To appease the citizens an issue of the following year bore the same inscription in Spanish and English on a stamp issued to call attention to an ancient monument. In 1928, Haiti advertised coffee and flowers, in 1930 Ecuador tried cacao, tobacco, fruit, and sugar, and in 1932 Colombia topped all countries with the Wealth of Colombia series showing emeralds, oil, platinum, gold, and coffee. This contest went on and on until nearly all Latin-American countries were engaged and the end is not yet in sight.

Colombia, on May 16, 1955, made a most unusual move by issuing stamps showing a view of the Tequendama Hotel in Bogota. This privately owned unit of Intercontinental Hotels, designed by the architects, with whom the author is associated, was opened in 1953 and the stamp issue marks the second anniversary of the opening.

Another method of making a stamp assist an advertiser has been tried in several countries. Its origin is obscure but might be traced to the propaganda envelopes used soon after the advent of penny postage. In an early form used with the stamps of the 1851-1857 issue, an ad was typeset to surround the stamp. This never appealed to the United States postal authorities and eventually it was banned by law, but at intervals the ban is forgotten and some young advertising man invents the idea anew and has envelopes in the mail before the postal authorities know anything about it. There have been at least six or seven revivals of the idea.

The idea of elliptical bands or collars around envelope stamps was tried out by George F. Nesbitt, the envelope manufacturer who held the government contracts for the 1864 issue. He prepared essays with bands for the United States Senate, the House of Representatives, and his own envelopes, but they were not placed in use. Later, similar bands were used by N. F. Seebeck and S. Allan Taylor, two thorns in the philatelic rosebush, and at about the same time a dozen or more mercantile companies from New York to San Francisco via Butte, Montana, made extensive use of government stamped envelopes with oval or rectangular frames around the stamps.

This form of advertising was usually stopped when the law of 1872, which prohibits any printing upon stamped envelopes except the return request, was cited to the users. Few such infractions were committed in the twentieth century.

In Great Britain the idea was encouraged and a customer who ordered envelopes at Somerset House, the British envelope printer, could have his name and address added in a narrow band around the stamp, at an extra charge.

Since the law of 1872 covering United States stamped envelopes did not apply to commercial envelopes and postage stamps, printers at once began to supply envelopes with a printed design surrounding the stamp space. This might include only the return card or a full advertising campaign. These examples also went down to defeat before the postal inspectors for the regulations indicate a free space around and near the stamp to permit a legible cancellation.

Stamp frames come and go and at various times expand to cover almost the entire envelope with just enough space for the stamp and the name and address. These last are a true throwback to the temperance and ocean penny postage propaganda envelopes of the 1850's.

One form of frame permitted by United States postal authorities deserves special mention. With the patenting, January 9, 1895, of the Neostyle envelope, which appears to be fully sealed but has a flap to pull out for postal inspection, large numbers of the envelopes were treated as short-paid first-class matter by clerks who were not familiar with them, and it became necessary to give them a prominent identification. This was in the form of a frame around the stamp space with the inscription "Neostyle" and some statement of the rate of postage at two cents for two ounces of third-class matter. While the frame occupied some of the space required for the postmark it was not very important as the envelopes were not intended to receive a dated cancellation.

Some liberties were taken with the neostyle frames and the user's name was often substituted for or added to the other inscriptions. Soon a competitor to the neostyle appeared and his envelopes were identified by solid patches of color where stamps normally would be placed.

France, Belgium, Mexico, and perhaps other countries, and the United States to a limited extent, have made use of gummed and perforated stickers of about four times the stamp area, bearing designs and inscriptions around the space for the stamp. These seldom bore private advertising but were used as a rule to carry propaganda for some religious or temperance cause. One very odd example, used in republican France, agitated for the return of royalty in the person of Philippe VII, the pretender to the throne, and bore his portrait in the area to be covered by a stamp. All other examples seen by this writer have been blank in the space for the stamp.

BOOKLET PANE ADVERTISING, AND STAMP MARGIN ADVERTISING

Many countries have sold advertising space on stamp margins but this reaches its greatest development in stamp booklets where margins, interleaves, and covers, inside and out, are sold to various concerns or all to a single concern. Some booklets have alternate ads and stamps imperforate between to force the use of the pairs on cover. Italy was the first country to use booklets of this nature.

ADVERTISEMENTS ON STAMP BACKS

This idea may have originated in the United States but the information on the subject is limited. Several ads are known on 3-cent green stamps. This would place the date before 1883, when that value was replaced by the new 2-cent rate. Some of the exhortations were, "Read the New York Ledger," "Buy Radway's Ready Relief," and similar notices for "Odonto" and "Devlin."

A little later the one-penny stamp of Great Britain appeared with an experimental ad for Pear's Soap but this was rejected by the postal authorities.

Both the United States and British examples antedate the well-known New Zealand stamps with ads on the back, now known as "adons." The ads were printed on the backs of nine denominations from one penny to one shilling in 1893, and called attention to nineteen firms. Since the stamps were printed in sheets of 240 subjects and issued to post offices in panes of 60 stamps, and inasmuch as there were several settings of the ads, it is difficult to assemble a complete set. The short contract for this work was not renewed but in later years the New Zealand authorities began to sell ad space on sheet margins and in stamp booklets.

Nicholas F. Seebeck made a futile attempt to sell space on the backs of the stamps he printed. Examples—now considered essays—are known with English-language ads on stamps of Ecuador. These appear to be copied from the New Zealand issues, but it is possible that Seebeck may have been the originator of the idea and may have been responsible for the ads on the three-cent green stamps.

One may question an attempt to sell English language ads on stamps of a Spanish-speaking country, but this may have been a specimen printing in which he used some of the stamps on hand without any regard for the language they bore.

CANCELLATION ADVERTISING

The use of cancellations to advertise national affairs began with the slogans for the 1897 Universal Postal Union meeting in Washington, and later extended to the various international expositions. Soon the post office began to use such service slogans as "Mail Early," "Have Your Mail Addressed to Street and Number," and later donated this space to the Red Cross, the Christmas Seal sale, and to other charitable groups.

There also were slogans of national interest, such as "Prevent Forest Fires," and the like, and now a gradual lessening of restrictions permits cities, counties, and states to call attention to local matters. It is not apparent that any individuals benefit from this advertising, although nationwide industries have been promoted. In some foreign countries the advertising seems to be a little more commercial but no individual or concern has been mentioned by name.

Foreign countries have made use of propaganda in postmarks to encourage the improvement of health. France, with pictures and inscriptions, has advised children to use toothbrushes and mothers to nurse their infants. Denmark has suggested that radios be tuned down and Britain has advised her people to confine purchases to Empire products.

METER ADVERTISING

When permission was given for slogans to be added to meter impressions an important field was opened to advertising. Ads in the bright colors of the meter mark attract more attention than a corner card and add little to the cost. These slogans are under some restrictions, particularly when used on foreign mail, and there has been some censorship. Generally speaking, they are institutional ads alterable at will, or they may call attention to the season, show trademarks, or convey a variety of messages.

WHAT APPEARS ON THE BACKS OF STAMPS

The backs of some stamps are worth as much attention as the faces for they show a variety of things in addition to gum and watermarks. Latvia became a stamp issuing country during a paper shortage and her first issue was printed on the backs of German military maps. These stamps can be replated by assembling them to reconstruct a map. Her 1919 issue was printed on paper with ruled lines, and some stamps of 1919 and 1920 were on unfinished Bolshevik and provisional government banknotes.

In 1872 Mexico used paper with a faint moire back-print to prevent counterfeiting, and used foolscap in 1887 and for one value of a revolutionary issue of Oaxaca.

In the St. Anthony of Padua issue of 1895, Portugal printed Latin prayers on the stamp backs. New Zealand, in 1925, printed a pale-blue pseudo-watermark, "N.Z.," on ordinary paper. Fiume, in 1919, printed "Poste di Fiume" on its stamp backs, and the "star and serpent" insigne on the high values of the Reggenza Italiana del Cornero issue of 1920. Some Hungarian semi-postals have back-inscriptions to increase the value 100 per cent.

Some Brazilian issues are on a paper with a band of three green lines to identify them as sold under special conditions.

TAGGED STAMPS

The word *tagged* is applied to stamps designed to actuate machines to sort mail and face letters for cancelation. The United States tried to build machines that would use the spot of color of the stamp to incite electric eyes, but other printing and labels had as much effect, and dark envelopes and light stamps nullified the work.

England tested machines with letters bearing "Naphthadag" stamps, that is, stamps with lines of colloidal graphite on the back, but dropped the experiment without explanation and turned to printing phosphorescent bands on the stamps. At first these were designed to glow green and later blue, but in all cases the inherent glow of the paper interfered with the test. Now they are searching for a completely neutral white paper.

Fluorescence and phosphorescence were next tried by the United States. Materials to induce those effects may be incorporated in the paper pulp, added in a finishing process, or printed on finished paper. Fluorescence appears only while the paper is in the direct field of ultraviolet rays, while phosphorescence continues for an appreciable time after passing the source of the rays. This afterglow is not affected by fluorescent materials in the paper.

Canada, in 1962, tested phosphor-band stamps in Winnepeg with a "Sefancan" (selecting, facing and canceling) machine. In 1961 West Germany and West Berlin used paper containing "Lumogen" as an additive to the pulp. This glowed yellow-orange, a color not found in any white paper. Later this paper was duplicated by inducing a chemical reaction in the pulp. All stamps since Jan. 1, 1962, are on the second type. The Netherlands began using the German paper late in 1962 but also printed the entire series on the regular watermarked paper. This country also made some trials with postal cards tagged with a phosphor band.

Denmark, on Nov. 1, 1962, issued stamps on the West German paper but continued with her standard watermarked variety. Switzerland, on Oct. 3, 1963, issued stamps made luminous by a zinc sulphide coating on the paper and also tried ordinary paper overprinted with that chemical. Russia has issued glow-print stamps using luminous ink but only as novelties with no value in sorting mail.

The presence of fluorescent or phosphorescent properties in stamps may be detected by exposing the stamps to ultraviolet light in equipment capable of producing both short-wave and long-wave rays. When using short-waves the eyes must be protected from direct exposure, but sunglasses usually suffice.

PART IV
Technical Matters

❖❖❖

CHAPTER TWENTY-ONE

PAPER

Although the technical aspects of paper manufacture are outside the scope of this book, certain details are of enormous importance to philatelists. A collector should have enough knowledge and experience to recognize the varieties of paper commonly or rarely used.

It is often necessary to distinguish between machine-made and handmade papers to determine a stamp issue. As a general rule, handmade paper is thicker and not so uniform. It may have small thin or thick spots, due to uneven distribution of the pulp, affecting the printing quality. Machine-made paper may also have thin spots (less often it will show thick spots) and may show defects caused by foreign matter introduced from the felt on which the wet pulp traveled. Embedded in the finished paper, this foreign matter may later fall out, leaving blank spaces in a stamp design.

Also important in the differentiation of the two papers is the variance in shrinkage during manufacture. Handmade paper has no initial stress and shrinks equally in both directions while passing from wet stage to dry. Machine-made paper is stretched lengthwise during most of its making and therefore has a greater shrinkage across the web than in the direction of stretch. This fact enables collectors to determine the web direction by measuring stamps wet and dry. Engraved stamps, wet printed, show great variation in size unless all sheets are cut with the grain in one direction. The United States 1934 stamp showing Whistler's portrait of his mother is an example of a stamp printed on machine-made paper cut in both directions.

An example of a stamp printed on both handmade and machine-made paper is found in the first issue of Austria and Lombardy-Venetia. Specialists separate the two varieties without trouble by the rough texture of the former.

Although stamps on handmade paper are more esteemed by collectors, stamp printers were pleased when they saw the last use of that uneven paper. Today, stamps are produced almost exclusively on machine-made paper.

WATERMARKS

A mold for handmade paper prior to 1750 consisted of a bed of parallel wires which produced the patterned thinnesses called laid lines. The wires were tied together at intervals with fine wire which produced chain lines crossing the laid lines. After 1750 much of the handmade paper was made on a bed of fine wire mesh producing what is called wove paper.

Metal designs, called bits, at first were attached to the wires of either type in such a way that they would show in the paper of each stamp. These bit marks are the true watermarks. The term "papermark" was in use in England before 1790. The French term is *filigrane*, the Dutch *papier marken*, and the German *Wasserzeichen*.

True laid lines and true watermarks occur only in handmade paper, and they are impressed on the under surface. Similar marks are impressed on the upper surface of machine-made paper by a roller, called a dandy roll. Strictly, these marks are only watermark effects. Stamp collectors, however, speak indiscriminately of watermarks in both types of paper and reserve the term "watermark effect" for imitations or pseudowatermarks.

Batonne Paper

Either machine- or handmade, this paper shows lines a little less than a half inch apart. It was devised as a writing paper. Some philatelic writers confuse the batonne lines with the chain lines of laid paper, but in laid batonne there are usually two or three batonne lines between the chain lines. In some stamps batonne lines show in two directions, some varieties crossing at right angles, some obliquely. Batonne paper was used for some of the stamps of Afghanistan, the Fiji Islands, Guadalajara, and the Indian State of Poonch. This paper may be laid or wove and the varieties are listed as laid batonne and wove batonne.

Quadrille Paper

This shows close-spaced batonne lines in two directions, making small squares or oblongs, the latter being found in some stamps of Guadalajara. The lines may sometimes cross obiquely, making small diamonds, as in the 1856 issue of Spain. Most of this paper used for stamps was manufactured without the lines and shows an effect produced by a paper converter—a pseudo-watermark. Some stamps of France and her colonies used such paper.

Wavy-Line Watermarks

These marks on Bavarian stamps were produced by the dandy roll. The absence of laid lines in some examples was an accident of manufacture. The paper showing horizontal wavy lines indicates that it was cut crosswise. No doubt the laid paper with wavy-line watermarks used for Russian stamps is similar.

Over-All and Spaced Watermarks

The first term indicates a continuous design. Segments of it may relate to the individual stamps later produced, or it may be that no relation was intended or possible. A spaced watermark appears on each stamp or pair or block. With careless press feeding a stamp may show parts of several spaced watermarks. This is particularly true of United States stamps, for the sheet used with the double-line "U S P S" contains only 81 watermarks and the single-line "U S P S" contains but 77.

U S P S

U S P S

FIG. 21–1. Single-Line and Double-Line Watermarks which Were in Paper Used for United States Stamps.

Reversed or Shaded Watermarks

These terms are applied to designs that are more opaque than the paper, an effect produced by using cutouts instead of solid bits. They are sometimes combined with normal watermarks and are well known on bank notes. This paper may have been used for some of the over-all watermarks such as the swastika design of Germany.

Marginal or Central Watermarks

Since watermarks hinder fine printing, the papermaker's name or identification is usually confined to the margins of the web or sheets, or placed where it will fall in the central gutter when the stamps are printed. Careless printing will cause letters to appear on some stamps, increasing their value to collectors.

Rubber-Ring Watermarks

More than seventy-five years ago, Mr. E. H. Behrend, president of the Hammermill Paper Company, designed a machine to impress machine-made paper on the under surface, thus leaving the printing surface smooth. A soft rubber roller bearing the letters or designs presses against the paper web as it leaves the wire bed, making an impression that is more legible than that of a dandy roll. The process approximates a true watermark and it is now in general use in American mills.

Stitch Watermarks

These marks occur on machine-made paper and are the impressions of the stitches where the ends of the wire mesh were sewn together to make a continuous belt for the pulp to ride on. Collectors recognize two varieties, the over-and-over stitch of ordinary sewing and the over-and-under stitch used on baseball covers. A minor stitch mark found in some paper is caused by the seam in the wire cover of the dandy roll. All stitch watermarks are slight and may be lost in finishing operations.

PSEUDOWATERMARKS

This term indicates marks pressed or printed on finished paper to imitate watermarks. The pressure method was used for the Swiss cross in oval, and for the crescent and star of Egypt from 1867 to 1879. The moistened paper is damaged to such an extent that the marks often fall out in later years.

Marks made by a phantom printing in Canada balsam or other chemical to render the paper semitransparent are a better imitation than those pressed in. However, in some cases the chemicals have damaged the paper. The 1935 Ostropa sheet of Germany and the 1936 Zeppelin issues had pseudowatermarks of this sort that fall out when the paper is soaked. This may have been due in part to a reaction with the inferior gum used.

A printed pseudowatermark is found on the backs of the New Zealand issue of 1925.

Much of the quadrille and batonne paper used for stamps was produced by phantom printing.

PAPER VARIETIES

Blueprint Paper

Ordinary blueprint (ferroprussiate) paper was used for local stamps when Mafeking was under siege in 1900.

Bluish Rag Paper

This is a philatelic term applied to paper used for an experimental printing of United States stamps in 1909. It contained a large percentage of rag pulp and was one of two or more mixtures tested in an effort to control shrinkage after the wet intaglio process. Its gray-blue color was a dye added for identification.

Bond

A strong, high-grade rag or sulphite paper, usually not calendered. It may be of any color, or granite, and in wove and laid types. One variety was used for some proofs of the United States 1847 issue.

Cardboard

Often used for proofs, cardboard was used for the Russian stamps of 1916-1917 that were to pass as money. When used for postal cards the paper is usually tinted.

Cartridge Paper

A hard, tough, normally colored paper designed originally for firearm cartridges and later used in the arts, cartridge paper was used for the 1853 issue of Trinidad.

Coated Paper

Paper was often coated with chalk or other substances to improve the printing quality, and some very inferior papers produced fine lithographic stamps. Certain stamps of Portugal and her colonies are examples. Their paper is now fragile and breaks easily if bent. Strictly speaking, the term applies only to white paper; loosely, it is extended to colored papers.

Colored Paper

The color is usually added in the pulp stage, but paper may also be dyed in a finishing operation. The term applies to colored-through paper, not surface-colored paper.

Enameled Paper

Strictly indicating a coated colored paper, in philatelic use the term is applied to any coated paper.

G.C. Paper

Grande consommation paper, usually called G.C., was used for French stamps during the final period of World War I. It is of inferior grade and varies in color from white to yellowish to dirty gray, the last probably due to pulp made from old newspapers. It appears to contain straw fibers or ground wood and these serve as an identification. Stamps printed on this paper were usually identified by a marginal inscription.

Glassine

A thin, hard, semitransparent paper made by treating a suitable paper with sulphuric acid. The product has five times the strength of the original paper and is not affected by hot water. It is used for envelopes, interleaves, and stamp hinges. A competing product is made with chloride of zinc.

Goldbeater's Skin

Listed for the 1866 issue of Prussia, this was a thin paper treated with collodion. The design was printed in reverse on the back and the gum was applied on top of the printing. In use on parcels the design was visible through the thin paper. The stamps were not sold to the public but were affixed by post-office clerks.

Granite

This paper is made by mixing quantities of unbleached fibers with the pulps. It may be any color, laid or wove, and may have silk threads in addition. It has been much used for stamps by Austria, Switzerland, and other countries.

Hard Paper

A rather thin, hard paper, this was specified for United States stamps printed by the National and Continental Bank Note Companies between 1870 and 1879. Similar paper, not so named, was used for the issues from 1861 to 1870. Similar paper for revenue issues is called "old paper." The wire marks are scarcely visible on a look-through examination.

India Proof Paper

This is a thin, absorbent paper used for the finest proof impressions from dies and plates. It is unsized and distintegrates when moistened. The name India is incorrectly applied to the thin paper used for Bibles, encyclopedias, and similar books.

Japanese Paper

Japan's first stamp paper is said to have been made from the inner bark of the mulberry tree with a sizing made of powdered hibiscus root or rice flour. It is extremely fragile and is injured by soaking.

Manila

A strong paper originally made from hemp and of natural color, but now usually made of wood pulp and dyed. May be wove or laid or watermarked and often is machine finished on one side and glazed on the other. The latter type is produced by a Yankee machine. Manila is much used for envelopes and wrappers.

Native Paper

A term applied to various papers used for the stamps of Indian states. Japanese paper is one of this group.

Paste-Up

Paste-ups occur where two sheets or webs of paper are joined. These sometimes are erroneously spoken of as "double paper." The first coil stamps were made by pasting sheets end to end, overlapping them about one-quarter inch. Some issues of Peru, 1868-1872, are found on strips made by joining two or more pieces of paper. In rotary web-fed printing a paste-up of some extent is made to connect the fresh roll to the one running out to avoid rethreading the press. All sheets with such paste-ups are supposed to be thrown out but some reach the public.

Pelure

The French word, meaning a peeling or skin, designates a paper like onionskin. Thin, hard, and somewhat transparent, it has been used for some stamps of the United States, the Dominican Republic, and New Zealand. May be wove, laid, batonne, quadrille, etc.

Rep Paper

A term applied to paper which is corrugated or ribbed, the ribs showing on both sides. In handmade laid paper the ribs roughen the paper on the wire side only, while in machine-made paper, on the surface or upper side only.

Rice Paper

An unusually delicate paper sized with rice-flour paste, this is not made of rice straw as some believe. It was used by El Salvador for a reissue of 1879 stamps which are overprinted "1889."

Ribbed Paper

Ribs are an unintentional effect produced in either machine- or handmade paper by contact with worn felts while in the pulp stage. The presence of ribbing in a lot, therefore, does not indicate a change in the paper. In 1892 or 1893, this ribbed paper was noticed on the 15-cent United States stamp of 1873. The reasons given for its presence by stamp and engraving experts were fantastic, but E. B. Sterling, an authority on revenue stamps, asserted that it was a paper variety well known on those stamps. He was upheld for soon duplicates were found and other values of the same issue appeared.

A pseudorib effect is produced by certain gumming methods, but this usually vanishes when the gum is removed.

Semipelure

Similar to pelure, this paper is softer and less transparent. It has been used for some stamps of the Transvaal.

Soft Paper

This term describes various papers used by the American Bank Note Company for stamp printing between 1879 and 1894. All were softer and more opaque than the paper used prior to that time, some being better and more adapted to the steam-driven presses. It may be slightly yellowish and a look through shows the wire marks more clearly than in hard paper. It lacks the snap or crackle of hard paper when flicked with a finger. The presence of ground wood in the pulp around 1890 accounts for the poor quality of stamps of that period, with their tendencies to thin and to break when folded.

Surface-Colored Paper

This is a paper colored on one side during finishing. It is much used for British colonial issues, some of which are referred to as "white backs." The term is not applicable to a coated paper.

Waterleaf

An unfilled, unsized, uncalendered paper, very absorbent and fragile, this was experimentally used in the United States under a patent of Charles F. Steel, and was designed to absorb cancelling ink to such an extent that removal would destroy the paper.

Wove Paper

This term includes handmade paper made on a mold covered with wire mesh, and all machine-made paper which has not been given a laid effect by the dandy roll. A look-through shows a sievelike effect. Nearly all current stamps are on this paper.

Writing Paper

A strong, well-sized paper, varying in finish in color, writing paper is much used for stamps.

SAFETY PAPERS

This term includes various papers, manufactured, finished, or printed in ways to discourage counterfeiting and fraudulent reuse. Watermarked papers, already described, are all, strictly speaking, safety papers.

Blue Safety Paper

This is an accidental variety found in the British fourpence stamp of 1855-1856. It was caused by prussiate of potash in the pulp. This sensitive chemical had been added to prevent cleaning but the presence of minute amounts of iron from the pulp engines caused the paper to turn blue prematurely.

Burelage

A burelage (or burele) is a printed network to render forgery or cleaning more difficult. Some may be invisible, some are in color. They have been used by Alsace and Lorraine, Denmark, the Dominican Republic, Hanover, Italy, Mexico, the North German Postal District, Prussia, Queensland, Russia, and other countries.

In the first issue of Denmark the colored network was printed on the paper in advance. On·Hanover stamps it was printed after the stamps were printed. Some stamp papers of the North German Postal District and of Prussia have a colorless network of carbonate of lead printed in advance of the stamps. This will turn black if an attempt is made to clean the stamps.

Some Russian papers were overprinted with lozenges of varnish to prevent photographic duplication of the design. The spaces covered with varnish appear blank in a negative. The bars of shellac or varnish on Austrian stamps may have had a similar purpose, and become quite prominent when soaked in hot water.

Mexico at one time used a stamp paper with a faint moire pattern printed on the back, and Queensland used a narrow band in a similar pattern for some of its issues.

Chalk-Surfaced Paper

The coating on this paper, much used for British colonial stamps, was added in the printing plant of De La Rue & Co. Although designed as a protective measure it provided a superior printing surface, for the full color was retained, none of it sinking below the surface. The paper was assigned to values largely used for revenue purposes, which would be cancelled with pen and ink. The stamps were printed in doubly fugitive ink to resist removal of pen marks, rubber-stamp impressions, and postal cancellations by water or acid or alkali and eradicators. The doubly fugitive colors were green, lilac, and black, and the chalk-surfaced paper prevented the colors from changing under high humidity. If soaked, the chalk washes off, carrying away some of the design in addition to changing the color. The stamps smudge and wear off easily in an album. Other colors than those mentioned are only singly fugitive in British issues and had only to resist attempts to remove the postal cancels.

Chameleon Paper

This was manufactured by James M. Willcox, of Glen Mills, Pennsylvania, for United States revenue stamps. While there is a question about the intended use of this paper, it actually was used for the second and third issues of revenue stamps beginning in 1871. The paper contained red and bue silk fibers and a violet coloring that would change color if cleaned with acid or alkali removers. For added safety the portraits in the first bicolored issue were printed in a fugitive black while the frames were in permanent blue. The third issue was identical except that the frames of several values were printed in other colors to avoid confusion.

Chemical Paper

A general term for any paper treated with a chemical to change color in the presence of another chemical. One variety was used by D. O. Blood & Co., of Philadelphia, for local stamps that were cancelled by touching them with a chemical which changed the colors of paper and ink. Other varieties are the chameleon and Francis papers.

Double Paper

This, the invention of Charles F. Steel, consisted of two layers of paper pasted together, the upper being thinner and softer than the lower, and designed to be damaged easily in cleaning. It was used experimentally for twenty million United States stamps of the 1873 and 1875 issues, all values of the former being included except the 7-, 12-, 15-, 24-, and 90-cent. The paper shows a peculiar mesh on a look-through examination and differs in general effect from ordinary thick-paper stamps. Some copies separate readily when soaked while others remain firmly attached. Copies may be found which are printed on the lower layer. The Fletcher punch was applied to some 3-cent stamps on double paper as an additional protection.

Douglas Patent

Another form of double paper, referred to as the Douglas patent, is similar to the last described except that the upper layer is punched with a ring of small round holes in each stamp position. Thus, the stamps would be printed partly on each layer, and likewise the cancellation. In any attempt to clean, the layers might separate or the upper would be damaged at the holes. Ten thousand copies each of the 1- and 3-cent stamps of 1881 were prepared and sold in Washington, D.C., but no further use was made of this paper.

Fletcher Cogwheel Punch

This was a treatment of stamp paper before printing in which dies equipped with eight U-shaped cutters punched a circular pattern in each stamp position. The cuts were designed to help the ink penetration and to be damaged easily in cleaning. C. A. Fletcher, the patentee, was able to obtain a test and ten thousand copies each of the 1- and 3-cent stamps were produced by the Continental Bank Note Company and sold in Washington, D.C., in 1877.

Francis Safety Paper

This chemical paper, invented by Dr. Samuel W. Francis and offered to the government, was treated with a simple chemical before the stamps were printed. Cancellation was effected by touching the stamp with another chemical that changed the paper color. It was used experimentally but none of the used copies known today were chemically cancelled. Today, some one hundred years later, the stamp paper is quite brown.

Russian Coated Paper

Early Russian stamps were printed on paper that had been surfaced with a weak glue size to reduce the curling of sheets after gumming. When these stamps are soaked some of the impression is lost and the stamps appear spotty. Later, white pigment was added to the glue size to improve the printing qualities. The stamps issued just after 1864 are damaged materially when soaked and are easily smudged. This second paper differs little from the British chalky paper in this action.

Security Paper

This term is applied to various papers with an over-all printed pattern which will change color when chemically cleaned. The paper was devised for checks, etc., but has been used for some stamps, such as the 1932 air-mail issue of Venezuela. The strong pattern detracts from the stamp designs.

Silk Paper

This stamp paper has scattered bits of colored silk thread in the pulp mixture. In some cases but one or two show on a stamp. It should not be confused with granite paper, which is filled with minute fibers.

Silk-Thread Paper

In 1839, just before the first stamps appeared, John Dickinson devised a process for placing continuous silk threads in a web of paper, near either surface or at the center. With various arrangements of colored threads, this paper was used for the Mulready envelopes and for the one-shilling and tenpence British stamps of 1847 and 1848.

Silk-thread paper for the stamps of Bavaria, Schleswig-Holstein, and Switzerland was made at Munich on a machine imported from England. The product was not equal to that made in England for in some cases the threads project from the surface.

Although considered counterfeit proof the use of silk-thread paper was abandoned when perforating was introduced, as the threads prevented the easy separation of the stamps.

MISTAKES IN THE USE OF PAPER

In all kinds of printing wrong paper may be used, and the collector should be on the watch for mistakes. Paper with a directional watermark may be fed to a press in eight positions, only one of which will be correct. The varieties resulting from careless press feeding are not especially important unless the country has a history devoid of such mistakes, or unless the position of the watermark indicates a special use of the paper, as for booklet panes or coils.

◆◦◦◦◆

PRINTING

The chief forms of printing that interest a stamp collector are typography, or printing from type and cuts; intaglio, printing from engraved metal plates; and lithography, or chemical printing.

Xylography, the art of wood engraving and printing, is of less importance, although many early stamp dies were engraved in wood for reproduction by typography or lithography. Many stamp cuts in early catalogs and albums were wood engravings, and even today there is no better method of picturing certain stamps. The only stamps actually produced from wood engravings were probably a few early issues of certain Indian states, printed in water color.

TYPOGRAPHY

In stamp printing, typography (also called letterpress and surface printing) includes all printing from designs raised above the surface of the block, whether it is of wood, metal, or other material. Blocks may be type-set, made by photoengraving processes, or by casting or coining from an engraved die. Stereotyping, electrotyping, and even typewriting have been used for producing stamps by the typographic method.

Stamp plates have been prepared by making sufficient clichés (or single stamp blocks) by any process, but this slow and expensive method has given way to the use of duplicate plates in nearly all cases.

Line Cuts

The usual procedure in making plates for a typographic issue is to reduce the design photographically to stamp size on a line block and then to duplicate it by stereotyping or electrotyping. The duplicate cuts may be set up as a plate for printing but it is common practice to make duplicate plates and to preserve the original.

In a modern plant much work is saved by using a step-and-repeat camera which makes one exposure after another in predetermined positions until the plate is filled. The process is further simplified if the exposure is made directly on a sensitized zinc plate. Since stamps usually are printed in vast quantities from several plates even the product of the step-and-repeat camera will be duplicated.

Line Color Plates

When a typographed stamp is in two or more colors separate cuts and plates are made for each color by routing out the parts of the design that do not show in the color in question. The cuts are then duplicated. Great care is needed in assembling the plates to ensure color register.

Ben Day Process

This method was devised to obtain tones other than black and white in line cuts. The tones are transferred from sheets of gelatin bearing patterns of raised lines or dots which are inked by a roller. The inked sheet is placed above the drawing to be toned and the pattern carefully transferred with a burnisher. The available patterns allow the user to select any shade from near white to near black. In a photoengraving plant the tones are transferred directly to the metal plate in a resist which prevents etching where the pattern occurs.

Half-Tone Process

This grew out of attempts to obtain the gradations of a photograph, a result not possible with the Ben Day process. A halftone breaks up the design into dots so fine that the eye perceives only the general effect. The first trials were made by photographing the subject through muslin and later through a grain screen, but the results were unsatisfactory. When Max Levy, of Philadelphia, perfected a machine which would rule lines as close as three hundred to an inch and when F. E. Ives devised the double screen the process was successful. Two sheets of glass were ruled with lines cutting through resist and then etched to preserve the lines. After filling the lines with an asphaltic compound the two sheets were cemented face to face with the lines crossing at right angles.

The halftone screen is placed in front of the plate in the camera and the exposure is made through it. The negative film is transferred to a copper plate and this is etched to become the printing plate. It is not possible to obtain brilliant whites without tooling away some of the dots and the margin of such tooled work is difficult to conceal.

When frames or solid lines are added to a halftone the cut is called a combination block and plate. An example of stamp printing combining line and halftone work from separate plates is found in the Greek air-mail issue of 1926 which has designs in line cuts and over-all color tints in halftone.

Color Process Plates

This is a development of the halftone process in which separate plates are used for each color. The halftone screens are set at a different angle for each color so that the dots of color will not superimpose or produce a moire effect. A stamp produced in this manner is the Mona Lisa issue of Germany of 1952.

Stereotype Process

This, the oldest method of duplicating blocks, was devised in 1725 by William Ged, a Scotsman, when he began to cast type metal in plaster molds of the work to be copied. This was laborious and not very practical until the paper matrix, or mat as it is called, was introduced in France in 1829. This was adopted at once and today nearly all book and newspaper printing is on stereotyped plates, as the paper mats can be curved to semi-circular form and the plates cast to fit the press cylinders.

Electrotype Process

This method of duplicating blocks and cuts was first used commercially about 1840. The original, which may be a wood-cut, a typeset form, or any relief, is coated with plumbago and pressed face down in a bed of fine wax. The plumbago prevents the wax from adhering to the design and provides the conductor for the electroplating action in a bath of sulphate of copper. The resulting copper shell is backed up with type metal to make the printing block. Nickel is used for electrotypes needing sharper definition, and these are not subject to corrosion from mercuric inks.

Typewritten Stamps

The first issues of Uganda in 1895-1896 were typewritten by the Rev. E. Miller of the Church Missionary Society. There are many types, due to the hand work, and the designs differ somewhat after a new machine with closer-spaced letters was purchased. A little later a purple ribbon was substituted for the black. These stamps could be plated if sufficient quantities were available.

Letterpress Printing Equipment

Every form of press used for letterpress printing has been employed to produce stamps, from a hand-operated screw press to high-speed web-fed newspaper presses. A single unit of the latter can deliver 170 million regular-size postage stamps per hour by threading it with a double web of paper to utilize the cylinder that prints the back of the news sheet.

INTAGLIO ENGRAVED PRINTING

This process, also known as recess printing, line engraving, and steel- or copperplate engraving, produces prints from designs below the surface of the plate. After the plate is covered with ink, the surface of the plate is cleaned, covered with a sheet of printing paper, and passed under the impression roll of an appropriate press. The ink on such a print projects above the surface of the paper and can be detected by touch.

The development of line engraving to produce identical stamps by the Perkins transfer process is described on pp. 258-9. With some recent changes this method has been used to produce the finest postage stamps from 1840 to the present.

Various means are used to replace hand engraving for the initial work in developing the master die, but handwork remains one of the essential features of the process. In one variation from handwork a piece of copperplate or steel-plate for a die may be coated with a resist and the design traced on it. The desired design lines can then be cut through the resist with a suitable tool after which the die is etched in acid to deepen the lines.

In the beginning, hand craftsmanship and artistry alone produced some stamp plates having subjects of the same design but unavoidably with each subject different in detail. The second issue of Mauritius provides an example of printing plates containing ten stamps, all directly hand engraved and all different from each other. The first issue of Japan provides a similar example.

Intaglio plates have been and are being made by electrotyping (electrolytic deposition). The design is faithfully duplicated but the plates originally did not have the strength to stand the pressure required in this type of printing. They would begin to crush at the edges of the lines and soon the stamps would show marked differences. These would have been corrected or the plate replaced. Formerly in making such a plate the engraved die was forced into sheet lead to make a mold. This was electrotyped to make a duplicate. Such duplicate electros were arranged to form a plate, or in some cases lead molds were put together in plate form and a single electro made of the entire plate. Copper was the electrically deposited metal and it is porous and soft. Plates so made would yield only about 500 perfect impressions while plates made by the Perkins process may produce from thousands to hundreds of thousands of impressions. The life of electrotype plates today, however, can be extended by electroplating; that is, by adding a surface coating of a tough metal such as chromium. The base metal also can be a strong metal other than copper so that many thousands of impressions can now be obtained. The Bomba heads of Sicily of 1859 and the engraved values of the "Standing Helvetia" stamps of Switzerland 1882-1920 were printed from early forms of electrotype plates.

Today in many printing establishments plates are reproduced electrolytically. A master plate made by the transfer method, or by soldering smaller units together, can be placed in an electrolyte bath and a suitable deposit or series of deposits built up thereon to the desired thickness of a strong metal such as iron or nickel. Once separated from the master this deposited replica in reverse is called an alto and it can then be used in turn to produce, in a repetition of the process, as many printing plates as desired.

Relatively few plates or cylinders are made today by the Perkins transfer process but our use of the word "cylinder" means that direct transfers can be made today in the flat or in the round and this has been done for some years though only recently applied in the United States.

Line-Engraved Printing Presses

Early intaglio printing was a hand operation. The plate printer inked the plate, wiped off the excess ink with a cloth, polished the plate with his hands with the help of whiting or

French chalk, and placed it face up on the press bed. Frequently the plate had been heated to facilitate inking. A sheet of dampened paper was then placed on the plate and pressure applied by pulling the assemblage between rollers by the use of a spoked wheel on the side of the press. When steam or electric power was added to the presses some or all of the operations were handled mechanically, except for the laying-on or taking-off of the paper. Thus, United States stamps of the mid-1880s and later were printed on steam-driven presses using five plates. In 1894 the Bureau of Engraving and Printing began to print most United States stamps on presses using four plates. The plates were fastened to moving units attached in turn to a continuous chain which traveled around the press, essentially in a square plane, without turning or changing the relations of the top of the plate to the starting position. The press operated continuously and used the services of a printer and two assistants. Because of the speed of the operation the assistants could not remove slight wrinkles or, until the addition of a pin feeder in the 1950s, place the sheets exactly. Any attempt to move the paper after it touched the plate could result in drags or possible kiss prints. When a fingerprint is found on a sheet in the color of the stamps it is likely that the printer either touched the plate after it was wiped, or touched the sheet of paper after printing and while examining it. The last version of this press used in stamp printing at the Bureau of Engraving and Printing in Washington utilized dry, pregummed paper. Prior to 1954 dampened paper was used almost exclusively.

The Stickney Rotary Press

Benjamin Stickney's contribution to the printing of engraved stamps has been described on pages 102-104. Although this web-fed rotary press was originally devised to print coil stamps, a larger model about 1920 permitted its extension to other forms of stamps—booklets and sheets—and in the 1930s Stickney replaced the flat-plate presses in the U.S. for almost all except bicolored issues and small printing runs.

The plates for the Stickney presses were made as for the flat-plate presses and then curved to fit the printing cylinder.

Two plates of 400 subjects each were required to cover the periphery of the cylinder in the case of ordinary small stamps (360-subject plates for booklets). The paper was moistened slightly before it reached the printing cylinder. After being printed it passed around electric heaters which set the ink before gumming and/or overprinting. The inking and wiping of the plates was automatic. After being gummed and dried again the web was coiled into rolls suitable for use on perforating machines. The web speed was about 60 feet per minute and one press could produce about 860,000 ordinary stamps per hour. Chromium plating, developed in the 1920s, prolonged the life of the plates so that some produced as many as $1\frac{1}{2}$-million impressions, or 600,000,000 stamps, before being retired after the equivalent of about a month's use over their lifetime.

The Stickney presses were replaced in the late 1950s by other presses at first designated as Huck-Cottrells. These are now called "web monocolor intaglio" presses. The first, or prototype press, was called the "Experimental Bi-Color Rotary Web-Fed Press", but only produced one postage stamp in that mode, the 3-cent bicolored International Red Cross stamp of 1952, and that by a combination of intaglio and letterpress similar to the way precancels and the 1959 postage-due series are produced. This press and the production models to follow have been used exclusively since in single-color production for coils, booklets, and sheet stamps; but still including the addition of phosphor-tagging inks, precanceling, or postage-due numerals when required.

The Serge Beaune Principle of Engraved Multicolor Printing

This principle, patented in the 1920s, and used on many line-engraved intaglio presses today (commonly in three-color versions), is simply that of cutting a series of inking rollers to apply ink only to desired areas of designs. *All inks* for a particular run, from one to three at any unit, will be applied to the printing base, be it a curved plate or a cylinder, *before* wiping or polishing. Then, after wiping and polishing, the print is taken and the whole procedure repeated with each revolution of the printing cylinder. Intaglio printing presses have been built using this principle and as many as seven different sets of inking rollers and inks in connection with one printing cylinder, but the three-color setup has proven to be the most practical without getting things overly large and complex.

Other Web-fed Intaglio Presses

There are a number of additional web-fed rotary presses made today. Goebel AG of Darmstadt, Germany developed a single-color model before WWII, and has since come out with a 3-color model utilizing the Serge Beaune principle as on many Giori presses. Winkler and Fallert (Wifag), Bern, Switzerland has built similar presses. Late in 1975 the first web-fed Giori 3-color press went into operation at the Bureau of Engraving and Printing in the production of coils. Other web-fed presses utilizing line-engraved intaglio include combination presses with rotogravure units—all the way from one gravure unit to as many as seven. These have all had only one engraved intaglio unit and these to begin with were monocolor but in recent years this unit has become a 3-color one using the Serge Beaune principle again.

Perhaps the press for this printing process showing the greatest departure from the common trend was the web-fed 9-color intaglio press built in the 1960s for the Bureau of Engraving and Printing, Washington, D.C. by the Huck Company, Montvale, N.J. The press is unique in the world of graphic arts and probably another will never be built because it has not completely worked out as hoped for. Within its 91-foot length this massive press of about 100 tons weight can print from a 5-mile roll of paper about 7 million stamps in 2 hours. The work can be produced in as many as nine separate colors or any combination thereof, can be phosphor-coated, gummed, perforated, and sheeted—ready for examination and processing into finished form. The press has been used to print both sheet and coil work and went into production with the U.S. Christmas stamp of 1968, using 90 small plates at a time.

This 9-color press has three printing stations, each handling three inks on the Serge Beaune principle, the first unit for in-direct intaglio, and the succeeding two for direct intaglio, with 30 plates needed at each unit. It has not yet been used for pro-duction at any one time to its maximum capability and it is not expected now that this will ever happen.

The German state printing office has used web-fed presses for some time. The presses use printing cylinders and the stamp designs are entered on the cylinder with a standard transfer roll. These presses have done double duty, for the lower values of issues are entered on other cylinders in relief with a negative transfer roll of the same design as the high values, and then are printed typographically (letterpress).

The French have used web-fed intaglio rotary presses built by Chambon. The first version was a small monocolor press, going into use about 1930. There was a 3-color Lambert Co. adaptation in 1939 followed by a larger press in the early 1960s with an added indirect mode, similar to the U.S. 9-color press which came later in that decade.

Sweden is using two Goebel rotary presses. One a mono-color intaglio that they've had since 1937 and the other a 3-color version acquired in 1964.

There are doubtless still other web-fed intaglio presses in use today besides those that have been mentioned.

The Giori Rotary Press

This press started out as a sheet-fed press but has now been made in a web-fed model. It utilizes the Serge Beaune principle, first developed in France and Italy in the building of other presses.

In the United States the first Giori press was put into pro-duction in 1957 for the flag stamp of that year and the usage and number of models has increased so that today the Bureau in Washington has two 2-plate sheet-fed 3-color examples, one with slipsheeting capability; two 4-plate sheet-fed 3-color models; and one cylinder web-fed 3-color example. There is also a combination web-fed press comprising a 5-unit gravure section and one 3-color Giori intaglio unit. This press was first used on part of the 1976 Currier Christmas stamp job. All of these presses are used for postage stamps but the Bureau also has eight monocolor 4-plate sheet-fed Giori's which they use for currency, and on a few occasions these have been used to print stamps.

ROTARY PHOTOGRAVURE

This engraving process goes under many names: rotogravure, rotoprint, rotaglyo, gravure, heliogravure, etc. Some of these are registered names used by a single company. In essence, the design is photographed, the photographic plate is etched, and engravings are taken from it. Out of this process, used only for reproducing works of art and very fine book illustrations, grew the modern rotary process in which a halftone screen in reverse produces the etching of little cups or depressions to hold the ink. By applying the etching to a cylinder instead of a plate it is possible to ink it by allowing it to revolve partly submerged in an ink trough. The paper, fed dry and pregummed, must be somewhat soft and elastic. A heavily coated or sized paper will not take up the ink in a satisfactory manner. The volatile nature of the ink allows it to dry very quickly, but since it is soluble, rotogravured stamps cannot be given the usual tests for watermarks in benzine and similar solvents.

The British stamps of Edward VIII, George VI, and Elizabeth II are rotogravured examples, and the process is now used for a large proportion of current stamp issues. Sheet-fed presses will handle up to thirty-five hundred sheets per hour, while a web-fed press might be expected to deliver four times that number.

The first gravure stamps of Egypt provide the only known example in which the etching was made through a grain of resin instead of the customary halftone screen.

Printing varieties are infrequently found showing flaws or blemishes caused by the tearing off of a bit of the chromium plating which usually is added to prolong the life of the soft copper plate.

LITHOGRAPHY

Lithography is based on the principle that oil and water do

not mix and in its original form consists of a drawing on stone in oily ink or crayon. If the stone is wet and a roller with oily ink passed across the surface the ink will adhere to the design and be repelled by the blank spots. A sheet of paper placed over the inked design will take up a copy. Normally there is no relief whatever in lithography but in some processes a light etch is given. In the finest work the artist draws directly on the stone. In work such as stamps, bank notes, borders, etc., the designs are usually made on small stones that can be filed for reuse.

Transfers are made from these original stones to the printing stone by means of transfer paper. Small repeating designs, such as postage stamps are usually transferred to a second stone to make a group of ten to fifteen subjects and this group in turn is transferred to the final stone. In the process small differences may appear in each of the ten or fifteen designs, and these are repeated throughout the plate on each of the transferred multiples. Other small differences may creep into some of the subjects so that there may be considerable variation in plates put together in this manner. The transfer paper is not strong and may be torn a little, or creased, or a spot may refuse the ink. Most of these variations were eliminated when photographic processes were introduced.

At some point it was discovered that a sheet of zinc could be substituted for the heavy stone and later it was found that aluminum also possesses the necessary qualities. Being light and flexible these metal plates can be bent to fit press cylinders. Designs may be transferred from any type of plates to lithographic plates. In postage stamp work dies often are line engraved or engraved in wood even though the stamps are to be printed by lithography.

Photolithography

This is simply the extension of photographic processes to lithography, widening the field of subjects available at low cost, since the designs may be enlarged or reduced to suit without expensive hand work, and broadening the effects to include the cuts and tone work devised for letterpress printing.

Offset Process

In this, the lithographic plate prints onto a rubber-covered blanket cylinder. From the blanket cylinder the impression is offset onto the paper. The impression is soft, and never harsh like much of the normal lithography from stone. The offset process allows lithographic plates of the least durable metals to give fairly long service. Unusual kinds of printing can be handled on an offset press for the soft rubber blanket roll will print on metal, enamelled sheets, and on rough surfaces that may be next to impossible to handle in any other manner. Color work is handled with ease and it is not unusual to have an eight- or ten-color job even though a separate plate is required for each.

Since the plate wear is very slight, it is possible for a photographic emulsion to act as the plate in some work. Using the principle that light-struck sensitized gelatin is insoluble in water, the designs are photographed on a sensitized plate. After a washing with hot water nothing remains but the lines of the design and these take the ink. This method was used in printing the offset 1-, 2-, and 3-cent United States stamps of 1918 to 1920.

The varieties in offset stamps are largely due to poor cleaning of the blanket roll between revolutions. Phantom images give the effect of light double impressions, and plate numbers and the like appear as phantoms along with the normal numbers.

The offset process is sometimes spoken of as surface printing, but this is incorrect. The printing is a form of lithography, even though the plate may have the raised lines of typography.

EMBOSSING

This process makes use of die and a counterpart die to impress a cameo-like design in the paper. In practice the counterpart is often omitted and a substitute provided by placing a sheet of lead, leather, or other yielding material on the press bed and striking it several blows with the embossing die to form a reverse.

A few stamps have been made by embossing only, without

color, but they are not very legible, especially after being moistened and pressed on mail matter. The stamps of Sardinia of 1853 and those of Natal of 1857-1858 are examples.

Embossed stamps were quite common in the early days and usually had an engraved or typographed frame in color with a colorless embossed central feature such as a portrait, a coat of arms, or numerals. The Sardinian stamps of 1855-1863, of Italy in 1862, Germany, 1872-1875, Portugal, 1853 and after, Portuguese India, 1885, and Heligoland, all issues, are examples with typographed frames and embossed central designs. The British higher values from 1847-1854 have engraved frames and embossed portraits. United States envelope stamps of all issues have been printed in color by typography with a colorless embossed portrait or design and in most cases have the lettering and value labels raised above the surface by embossing.

PHOTOGRAPHY

Photography in a simple form was used to print some stamps issued at Mafeking during the siege of 1900. These were blueprints made by sunlight through a negative design in contact with blueprint paper.

DETERMINING THE TYPE OF PRINTING

Stamps printed from engraved plates are not smooth for the ink projects above the paper and sometimes the paper projects slightly where it has been forced into the bolder lines of the engraving. The stamp backs may show indentations at the lines. This incuse effect is greater in the wet-paper flat-plate process than in rotary-press work where the paper is moistened only slightly.

The ordinary test for an engraved stamp is to press a piece of tinfoil or aluminum foil on the stamp with a finger or a soft eraser. This will cause the design to appear embossed in the foil.

Under ideal conditions typographed stamps should be perfectly smooth at the ink lines, or the ink may be very slightly raised. However, the printing pressure is nearly always a little greater than necessary with the result that the lines and inscriptions are pushed into the paper and may show slightly as an embossing on the back of the stamp. The tinfoil test of the face will show indentations at the printed lines. This embossed effect on the back is called a printer's squeeze. When the pressure is too great the printed lines may show in a pale shade with dark edges where the ink has been squeezed off the type faces. Few examples of this effect are found in modern stamps for presses are better designed and printing is done more carefully.

In a tinfoil test lithographed stamps should show nothing for there are no raised or depressed lines in this kind of printing.

Line-Engraved Stamps Made by the Perkins Process

Normal prints from line-engraved plates have clean, sharp lines even though the plate is much worn. Lines cut with a burin never appear ragged unless the plate is overinked or poorly wiped. The edges of etched lines show the irregular biting of the acid while those of electroplates begin to crumble soon after printing has started. The lines of engraving and etching become thinner as the plate wears. The lines of the electrodeposited design grow rougher and finally give a very irregular and blotched print.

When line-engraved designs are entered on a plate by the Perkins process all subjects are identical unless there are minor variations in the transfer roll reliefs in use, unless the plate has been finished by hand engraving as in the United States 3-cent stamp of 1851, or unless damage to the plate has required some hand engraving.

Engraved designs transferred to a plate by etching processes and finished by hand engraving have the same general appearance but all differ in small details when carefully examined. Those completely finished by etching more closely duplicate each other but all differ in detail for etching cannot be controlled carefully enough to make identical subjects.

Stamps which have been hand engraved on a plate without any copying process differ so much that varieties are apparent without a magnifying glass. Electrodeposited plates may be nearly identical in the first impressions before the plates start to break up under the pressure of printing.

To Separate Rotary-Press Stamps from Flat-Plate Stamps

In order to separate these issues a collector should obtain copies of stamps which have been printed by each process but not by both and study them carefully. The period of trouble lies between 1916 and 1926 for then both types of plates and presses were used in the production of ordinary postage stamps. All the difficult stamps, with a single very rare exception, are printed on unwatermarked paper.

In flat-plate printing, since the plates are wiped and polished by hand, it is unusual to find any tone or smears on the paper between the stamps. In the early stages of rotary-press printing, while the flat plates also were in use, the wiping mechanism was inefficient and more often than not diagonal ink smears show over the entire sheet. It may also be toned since there was no wiping corresponding to the French-chalk polishing of the plate.

Examine the backs of the stamps carefully. Any traces of ink here will identify flat-plate stamps. The traces are offset from one sheet to the next when the sheets pile up coming from the press. Rotary-press stamps cannot offset in this manner as the web of paper is gummed before it is rolled and any offset will be on the gum. Flat-plate stamps may also have traces of color on the gum when there is a slight sticking between sheets in a post-office book of stamps.

United States rotary-press plates are made flat and then curved to fit the printing roll after the designs have been entered. Before bending, they would produce stamps identical to those from other flat plates. After bending, the outer surface of the plate is stretched in the direction of the curve, affecting the stamps in one direction but not the other. The plates for ordinary small-size stamps in sheets have the subjects top up as one views the horizontal printing cylinder. Consequently, the stamp designs will be slightly taller than similar designs printed on flat plates. The same arrangement is used for plates for endwise coils, those in which the stamps are joined top and bottom with horizontal perforations between.

The only stamps that will be wider than normal are those for sidewise coils, those in which the stamps are joined side to side with vertical perforations between. These designs lie on their side as one views the printing cylinder.

Stamps which do not exceed 19¼ millimeters in width and 22¼ millimeters in height are printed on flat plates. Those that are about 23 millimeters in height come from rotary-press plates made for sheet stamps or for endwise coils, while those measuring 19½ to 20 millimeters in width come from similar plates intended for sidewise coils.

Since coiled stamps were put up in minimum rolls of 500 and had no paste-ups, any web ends of less than 500 stamps were cut up in sheets for economy reasons and perforated in the direction not already perforated. Perforating machines of various gauges were used, giving some compound varieties not occurring in the normal issues. The use of this coil waste was discontinued when collectors made inquiries concerning the many varieties produced.

During this period the United States produced the 1-, 2-, and 3-cent values by offset printing also, but the collector can separate these from the engraved issues by their flatness. The first 3-cent stamps produced by this process appear to be the same size as those printed on flat plates, but all succeeding plates had smaller subjects due to failure to maintain sizes when reproducing the subjects photographically. None of the offset stamps are larger than the flat-plate engraved issues.

Photogravure Stamps

A collector should have no difficulty in separating these stamps from all others. Under a strong glass the entire design is broken up into a pattern or screen of dots, except perhaps in the first gravure issue of Egypt where a grain was used, and there are no sharp or continuous lines. Since this is a form of intaglio engraving the dots of ink stand upon the surface of the paper, unlike those of a halftone.

Typographed and Lithographed Stamps

It has been mentioned that lithographed stamps should be perfectly smooth but it should be added that typographed stamps often are found in this condition after a soaking and thorough pressing. In such cases the identification must depend on the printing itself and on the paper used.

Lithographers use smooth paper wherever possible for the pressure necessary to flatten rough paper would spread the ink lines on the stone and ruin the printing if not the plate. Typographed stamps may also be printed on smooth paper and about all that can be determined is that the stamps on rough paper are generally typographed.

In lithographic plates made by paper transfers there usually are minute imperfections caused by tiny blank spots. Slight folds or cracks in the transfer paper appear as scratches without color or show as places where the lines of the design do not meet. Such little variations and soft or slightly irregular edges on lines and letters are the surest clues to lithographed stamps.

Typographed stamps seldom show any blank spots or missing lines unless the plate has been damaged, and the edges of lines and letters are usually sharp even though the plate is worn, except that rough paper should be recognized as altering the quality of a letter or line.

A careful lithographer will try to correct defects in a plate but nearly all repairs show clearly under a strong glass. Repair work on a typography plate is seldom attempted and usually is as apparent as the fault. In both types of printing little expense is involved in the substitution of new for damaged plates.

✦·✦

COLOR

Beginners and general collectors need not pay attention to all the shades and tints of a color that may appear during the long life a stamp. Unless a pronounced change is made, the color should not overshadow more important aspects for it will vary in every stamp issued. It is almost impossible to mix a new supply of ink so that a sharp eye cannot detect the change. In addition the slightest change in the tint or texture of the paper, or in the amount of ink used, will alter the apparent color of the stamp.

When plates are overinked or underinked the stamps may appear to be printed in different inks from those used for the normal issues. This is due mostly to the effect of the white paper for the color seen is a composite of the paper and ink. A carmine applied thinly has a decided bluish cast; applied too thickly it appears to be much redder.

No two stamp writers will agree on the names for stamp colors nor will they agree with the postal authorities' and printers' selection of names. Throughout philatelic history trade names associated with the sale of such merchandise as silks and paints have crept into the color names of stamps. Many have no connection with the color or the pigment, but are of such long standing that they are hard to change.

Elaborate color guides may be prepared for stamp collectors but they can show only a few of the shades and tints of the colors found on stamps. They are of some value when printed in stamp form with lines and ornamental details rather than in solid colors, but it is useless to match a typical stamp design with a spot of color. Unless the guides are protected against too much light some colors gradually bleach out and hinder rather than help a collector.

There are color publications in which the colors and the derived tints and shades include many thousands of examples, but there is no attempt to name any except the fundamental mixtures. Each of these is extended through eight or more tints by mixing with white until the result approximates white, and through the same number of shades by mixing with black until the result is near black. These tints and shades are differentiated by placing a modifier before the color name: pale, light, deep, dark, etc.

At one time *Stamps*, the weekly publication of H. L. Lindquist, carried a stamp form on its cover in a different color in each issue. This was not wholly successful because the cover paper differed from any stamp paper and the color named was not always matched, and at best the sample applied only to typography. It is peculiar but true that a single color of ink will give different effects and may have different names when used in engraving, lithography, and typography.

It is said that no two people see exactly the same color, and that a person's two eyes do not always see the same color, but unless color-blind anyone can distinguish all the primary and secondary colors, and many of the intermediate mixtures.

It is not possible to describe a color so that a person will recognize it, unless the description is in terms already known to him. When it comes to describing scarlet vermilion the average collector is completely lost unless he has a very definite idea of vermilion in its true color. If his eyes are pitched a little low on yellow he may see vermilion when the color is orange vermilion, but those who criticize his color judgment may be pitched a little high on red, so there can be no common meeting point except on blue.

In reds the greatest difficulty is found in the very light tints and the very dark shades, for the range extends from almost white to near black. The colors listed as pink, rose pink, and even light pink are near the top of the scale and only experience will enable a collector to identify them. At the other end are carmine lake, lake, and other darker shades which appear to be based on red.

The purple-violet colors, tints, and shades had a long run in United States commemorative issues when the letter rate was raised to three cents. Perhaps as many as a hundred issues have been printed in almost as many colors, shades, or tints. Correct names have not been assigned to many and the same name is often used for stamps which are nothing alike. There is a constant argument about the use of the names violet and purple, but like the weather, no one does anything about it.

Quite a number of the shades the collector finds unusual are changelings and faded colors. Some colors change under exposure to the atmosphere and others fade easily when exposed to full daylight. Many stamps are printed in fugitive colors and change when they are soaked in water or chemically treated to remove a pen cancellation.

In the 1860's a pigment used in the United States in printing lilac stamps was subject to great change. The 24-cent stamps of 1861-1866 are found in colors from violet to gray, and the 4-cent, 30-cent, $1.90, and $2.50 revenue issues of the same period and in the same color range are sometimes considered actual color mixes, but many appear to be only the remains of a violet color from which the basic pigment has vanished.

Certain inks darken when affected by the sulphuric acid in the atmosphere. In United States issues the 3-cent stamps of 1851-1857, the 6-cent stamps of 1908 and later years, and the 6-cent air-mail issue of 1918 are thus affected but may be restored to natural colors by immersion in hydrogen peroxide.

This chemical has no aftereffects if the stamp is rinsed in clean water but it removes gum as easily as does water.

These stamps would be classed as chemical changelings. There are many other effects that can be produced in stamps either accidentally or by intention. Some deep red shades in United States stamps have been explained by postal officials as an effect caused by mailing the stamps in recently fumigated mailbags. Some liquids considered harmless may be very active in changing colors. Grapefruit juice for example, had a remarkable effect on the 3-cent Stuart-type stamps of 1932.

An interesting color variety appears in some United States stamps printed during the First World War when certain pigments were no longer available from Germany. An analine red was tried as a substitute for the usual red used in mixing colors for the 2-, 3-, 12-, and 50-cent values of the ordinary series. Its presence became very evident as the backs of the stamps turned a light red. These "pink backs" were due to the bleeding effect of analine red, an effect known to everyone who has attempted to cover mahogany stain with a light-colored paint.

Chemists are able to change almost any stamp color, sometimes with a simple treatment but more often with a treatment so harsh that the paper is permanently changed. Examples have been shown of stamps with one-half changed to one color and the other half to another, or of bicolored stamps made out of a single color by changing the vignette only.

In this country the Secret Service, an agency of the Treasury Department, which is charged with the protection of postage stamps, frowns on the chemical changing of stamps, and although experiments have been allowed to show what a skillful forger might accomplish, the sale or distribution of such purposely changed stamps is forbidden.

Since these changes are possible by accident as well as design it is better for collectors not to buy unusual shades or color "errors" unless they are guaranteed. Stamps printed in a wrong color, generally in a color used for another value of the same set, are genuine errors. They are discussed in chapter 29.

❖•❖

GUM

Of all the components of postage stamps gum is the least important, yet its absence on an unused stamp has a more adverse effect on value than does a small cut or a pinhole in an otherwise superb used copy. Gum usually remains hidden in a collection and makes its presence known by curling or by sticking to the album page, or by cracking or staining the stamp.

Considering stamp collections alone it would have been an act of Providence if gum had never been used. Since it is applied to stamps we cling to the idea that it must be preserved. At intervals some outspoken collector brings up the question of whether or not to remove the gum from unused stamps. He may have an ax to grind—perhaps a stuck-down collection—but the outcome is always the same: a few collectors follow his lead and soak their stamps while most go on searching for mounting methods that will preserve the full gum without hinge marks.

The demand for gum is carried to such lengths that some collectors expect it on stamps issued without gum, and in some cases gum has been applied to such stamps to satisfy the demand. In the early period much of the gum was of dark color and abominable taste, and some of it dried out to the hardness of glass with the result that bending was almost certain to break the paper. Certain kinds of gum and paper appear to have been incompatible, the gum striking through the paper and appearing on the surface or staining the paper to a rich brown.

The rose-colored gum of the early stamps of Hanover and the obstinate gum on the Austrian stamps of 1890-1898 are mentioned in chapter 8.

Much as gum may be disliked it is important in early issues in helping to distinguish original stamps from reprints. In nearly all cases the early gum was coarse, rough, and somewhat colored, while that of the reprints is usually white or very light and is smooth and thin.

A harmful variety of gum was used by Germany for the Ostropa sheet of 1935 and for two 1936 air-post stamps showing the LZ 129—the Hindenburg. It has been stated that sulphuric acid in the gum turns it brown and eventually destroys the paper. The author witnessed an attempt to save some Ostropa sheets by soaking off the gum. When thoroughly wet the watermarks actually fell out of the paper. This suggests that there may have been a reaction between elements of the gum and watermarks, for the latter was a phantom printing, not a true watermark. It is possible that sulphuric acid, too concentrated for the purpose, was used.

Ever since gum was first applied, post offices have been bothered by the curling of sheets. The gum is applied in liquid form. As the paper dries, it starts to curl, giving the stamps a convex surface. If the paper is machine made, the convexity will be across the web direction. Under normal humidity the stamps will flatten out. As the moisture increases, the gum continues to expand until the stamps have a concave form.

While flat-plate stamps alone were in use in the United States this tendency to curl was not given much study even though the stamps would separate into strips as the sheets were alternately flattened and curled, but with the advent of web-fed rotary-press printing the curling was so pronounced that steps were taken to correct it. The flat-plate stamps were printed wet and dried under pressure, then gummed and dried and again pressed flat. The rotary-press stamps were printed from a small roll of paper so tightly coiled that it had an almost permanent curl. It was slightly moistened on the upper surface to assist the printing and this increased the tendency to curl. After a quick drying process the web of paper passed through the gumming machine, was dried again, then tightly wound in small rolls and seasoned a short time before going to the perforating machines.

Such paper resisted straightening out like a coiled spring. The perforating process did not reduce the curl tendency but merely divided the paper into strips separated by lines of weakness. When a postmaster opened a book of stamps, that is, a package of a hundred sheets, it was apt to spring into a series of rolls.

Experiments led to special gumming rolls and to spirally fluted gum-breaking rolls which cracked the gum film to prevent the continuity of shrinkage. By 1931 the breakers had been perfected and they are still in use. At one period during the experiments so much pressure was applied to the breakers that some stamps when soaked fell apart into small strips equal to the spacing of the flutes on the breakers. Since the breaker marks are visible on all rotary-press stamps a collector may find varieties in the breaker spacing in the period up to 1931.

Switzerland, Germany, and some other countries have applied gum with special rolls that deposit it in lines or dots so there is no continuous film. This, without doubt, is more effective than the use of a gum breaker. Since 1932 the Swiss stamps have been listed with grilled gum. The grilled effect shows on the paper even after soaking unless the stamp is thoroughly pressed.

Some 1932 stamps of Czechoslovakia were given a quadrille effect in the gum and each stamp shows a device containing the letters "C.S.P." on the back. This has the effect of a watermark on mint stamps but vanishes when the gum is removed. Some catalogs mention it as a brown printing on the surface of the gum but it is thought to have been made by the gumming roll and not at a later operation.

Tinted gum was used for the embossed stamps of Great Britain from 1847 to 1854 in order that the operator of the embossing machine could distinguish the upper from the under surface of the paper.

In many countries typographic and rotogravure stamps are now printed on pregummed paper. This does away with the shrinkage that took place when the gum was applied after printing.

Self-Adhesive Cement

An innovation in stamp gum is in the use of self-adhesive cement. The stamps of Sierra Leone of 1964, die-cut to the shape of that state, are provided with a pressure sensitive adhesive. The unused stamps are backed-up with a thin, tough paper which must be peeled off before the stamp is affixed to an envelope. Since this cement has no history in connection with stamps, it is not possible to forecast its effect on stamp paper or colors, or on covers bearing the stamps. Collectors must be cautious since some have had trouble with similar cements on some kinds of transparent tape.

❖❖❖

SEPARATION

This is a general term for any means provided for separating individual stamps. There was no provision at first and stamps were cut or torn apart. There is no handy term to describe this condition and today we use *imperforate* or *unperforated*, even though such terms obviously came into use only after the invention of perforation.

There are two forms of separation, perforation and rouletting. In the first, small bits of paper are punched out by pins operating against a counterpart die. In the second, sharp notched bars or toothed disks cut slits in the paper or pierce it with tapered pins. In rouletting no paper is removed.

Imperforate is used for three categories of stamps: those issued before separation was invented, those with the means of separation accidentally omitted, and those intentionally not separated—private coil stamps, for example. The second category includes stamps that normally are rouletted but have part or all of separation omitted.

THE INVENTION OF SEPARATION

When adhesive stamps appeared in 1840, no provision was considered for separating them: their advantages were so numerous that the inconvenience of cutting them apart was unimportant. But as their use increased this became a problem and ways were devised to reduce the work. Some sheets were torn along metal rulers. Others were punched with a tracing wheel and torn along the holes.

In England, about 1847, Henry Archer experimented with a machine that rouletted, and copies of the Penny Black with his little slit marks are prized items. The rouletting disks wore out so quickly that Archer turned to a hole-puncher, patenting such a machine in 1850.

The first stamps were perforated 16 and examples can be distinguished from the later issued stamps only by year dates on covers earlier than 1854. In 1851 these stamps were provided for the use of the House of Commons and the following year that body adopted the invention and paid Archer a substantial award.

Under the guidance of James N. Napier, a mechanical engineer, Archer's machine was improved and placed in general use. By 1854 all English stamps were perforated. Since Archer's original close perforation weakened the paper so that the stamps often fell apart, the new machines were built to punch fourteen holes in a two-centimeter space. This gauge was satisfactory and was used during the entire period of line-engraved stamps.

Archer called his machine a perforater to distinguish it from the rouletting machine. It operated as a punch press and had pins arranged on a long bar with short rows of pins projecting at one side like the teeth of a comb. It is now known as a comb-type perforator.

The first stamps of Sweden were issued July 1, 1855, and all were perforated. This appears to be the first use of separation outside England. Sweden produced Norway's stamps and they appeared perforated in November, 1856. The work was done with a harrow-type perforator that perforated full sheets at one stroke.

On February 6, 1857, the United States began to issue stamps perforated on a line machine operating on a rotary print ciple. Thus, in the first few attempts to solve the separation problem, three different types of machines were used, and since that time no new basic ideas have been developed.

The catalogs list some roulettes and roulette pin perforations for India and Victoria that may antedate some of the examples cited, but these are considered to be of private origin and not official.

PERFORATING MACHINES

Comb Perforators

The Archer-Napier machine perforates three sides of the stamps in a row at a single stroke. It then advances the sheet and perforates the next row. The pins enter a counterpart die after punching the holes. Since a separate comb and die are required for each stamp size these machines are less economical than line machines.

In comb perforation the stamps have regular perforations on three sides, there being one pin at the corner and a uniform pattern of holes for each stamp. Modern machines that automatically advance the sheet produce regular perforations throughout, but the early machines, in which the sheet was advanced by hand, often gave poor alignment between one row and the next. All comb perforators omit the starting margin but perforate the finishing margin. This peculiarity will identify comb perforation in a sheet.

Considerable pressure is required as there may be three or four hundred pins punching the paper at one time. It is possible that some machines have pins of two or more lengths in order to reduce the power requirement. In such a machine equipped with alternating long and short teeth, a failure to depress the comb fully might provide stamps perforated 6 when the normal gauge is 12, or a false start and quick release and subsequent completion of the stroke may be the reason for some of the half-gauge combinations that have been listed such as 5½ by 11 and 6 by 12.

Comb machines are used today in the original form and in types which will perforate two or three rows at one stroke. The latter are a combination of harrow and comb.

Harrow Perforators

In these the pins are set in horizontal and vertical rows to cover the entire sheet at one stroke; all perforations are regular and all corners are formed with one pin. In some cases the harrow perforators handle only a quarter-sheet and these are usually arranged with gutters between the quarters to avoid double perforations. The harrow perforator is not flexible and does a poor job on stamps printed by the wet-paper intaglio process as shrinkage may prevent any stamps from being perfectly centered.

There is every reason to assume that machines of this type had pins of varying lengths, for a harrow for a sheet of a hundred stamps might have several thousand pins and need great pressure to enter the paper. This machine is little used today except perhaps for miniature sheets with singles, pairs, or blocks of stamps. Here perfect centering can be obtained and the regular pattern of the holes improves the appearance of the little sheets.

Line Perforators

These machines are of two general types, the rotary and the guillotine, or single-line machine. Rotary machines may handle a single row or be equipped with multiple disks to perforate a sheet fully in one direction in one operation, in which case a different machine must be used for each stamp dimension.

Rotary Machines

The first line perforator was used for the United States stamps of 1857. Converted from a rouletting machine purchased in England, it was equipped with disks from which the pins projected like the spokes of a rimless wheel. The disks were mounted on a shaft and spaced to suit the width or height of the stamps. With this machine there is little regularity of perforation but the rows are parallel. When a sheet is started slightly askew all the stamps will be out of square. False starts and subsequent corrections give double perforations near the margin and there are examples of sheets reperforated throughout, giving double perforations on all sides of the stamps.

When rotary machines are used the perforations cross all margins. While two machines of this type are necessary to perforate oblong stamps without delay, it is a simple matter to re-space the disks to fit some other size. This is impossible in comb or harrow perforation. A complete new harrow or comb is necessary for each size of stamp. Until recently all United States stamps were perforated on multiple rotary line machines but when the sheets contained two hundred or four hundred subjects a cutting disk was placed at the center, except in the very early issue, to cut the large sheets into post-office panes as they were being perforated. When perforating standard sheets of four hundred small stamps the first machine punched the vertical lines and divided the sheet into two panes of two hundred stamps each. The second machine then perforated the horizontal lines and divided the half-sheet into two panes of 100 stamps. An analysis will show that there can be no imperforate sheets of less than four hundred stamps, or any part-perforate sheets of less than two hundred, except through the wrongdoing of an operator or from printers' waste.

In perforating two-hundred-subject panes of small stamps it is possible to obtain true part-perforates in hundred-subject panes if they miss passage through one machine. Plates as small as a hundred subjects have been used for some bicolored stamps, or after the first color has been printed the sheets have been cut to the small size to assist in color registration. In these it is possible to obtain hundred-subject sheets imperforate or part perforate in either direction.

The cutting disks are responsible for the straight edges that annoy collectors of United States stamps. An ordinary pane of a hundred contained nineteen straight-edged copies until the complaints of collectors brought the adoption of gutters between panes so that all stamps were fully perforated.

At present the rotary press printed stamps are handled by machines which perforate the continuous web of paper in both directions and cut it off in sheets of four hundred small or two hundred large stamps. The vertical lines are perforated by disks, the horizontal lines are punched by pins mounted on a transverse cylinder. The centering is maintained to a marked degree by "electric-eye perforation," using photoelectric cells that scan the margins and gutters, where short lines and dashes of color are provided, and move the perforating mechanism to line up with the marks.

The stamps leave the perforator in full sheets of four hundred subjects—two hundred if they are large commemoratives— and are piled in stacks of a hundred sheets with cardboard covers at top and bottom. Stapled at the sides, and cut into four post-office books, they are then shipped to postmasters.

In this process there is no stage where imperforate sheet stamps exist once the web, which is ordinarily twenty stamps wide, has entered the machine. Any peculiarities of perforation in the current rotary-press stamps are due to accidents in the machines and the damaged stamps should have been destroyed.

The so-called Farley Follies were made prior to the adoption of the latest type of perforation, and the sheets were taken from the press before reaching the gumming section. The two perforated varieties are readily distinguished from the normal stamps, if unused, by the appearance of the perforation holes. Holes punched in ungummed paper are not sharp and clean and may show pulled fibers. Good perforating depends to some extent on the stiffness the gum imparts to the paper.

Single-Line Rotary Machines

A rotary machine making a single line of perforations can punch stamps of any size in either direction. Though such machines have been used, the process is slow and inefficient, for a

sheet of a hundred stamps has to pass through the machine
twenty-two times to finish the task.

Guillotine Perforation

This line machine has pins on a horizontal bar operating
into a counterpart die below and is used in many job-printing
offices to perforate tear-off sheets in tablets, etc. Although used
to some extent for stamps, it is the slowest process unless several
sheets are handled at one time, as in France, where the first perforated stamps were from sheets stacked five high. There is no
regularity and the lines may not be parallel. The margins are
usually perforated.

ROULETTING MACHINES

Rotary Type

Rotary rouletting machines are nearly identical with rotary
line perforators except that the sharp edge of a notched disk re-
places the disk with pins. The spacing of the notches determines
the gauge of the rouletting. This machine may have a single
disk and roulette one line at a time or it may have multiple disks
to handle the entire sheet in one direction. As with perforators,
two machines are necessary unless the stamps are square. These
machines produce the same varieties as do the perforators.

Guillotine Roulettor

This machine contains a knife with a notched edge which
is forced through the paper. The process is slow but has been
speeded up by using multiple knives to roulette several lines in
one direction. In this case two machines are needed to finish
the work.

Roulette in Colored Lines

This work is performed as the stamps are printed and can
be used only when plates made up of individual clichés are set
up with the printer's "perforating rule" between the clinchés in

both directions. The rule projects slightly above the surface of the plate and slits the paper when the impression is made. It receives color when the plate is inked and the roulette shows as short colored lines around each stamp. The term "perforating rule" is a misnomer, for the effect it makes is a form of roulette. Stamps of Thurn and Taxis, 1867, had this rouletting.

PERFORATIONS AND GAUGES

The technical parts of the perforated edge of a stamp are the holes or slits and the teeth. Before separation the paper between the holes is sometimes called a bridge. In regular perforation the holes and bridges are about equal in width. There are narrow bridges between small holes and wide bridges between large holes. Otherwise the perforation is called "large" or "small," terms which are defined later.

The gauge of perforations and roulettes is determined by counting the number in a space of twenty millimeters. Counting is eliminated by the use of a cardboard gauge which shows markings to match with the holes in the stamp being examined. Per-

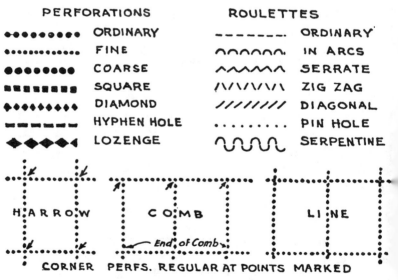

FIG. 25-1. Perforations and Roulettes.

forations are measured metrically in spite of the fact that many
perforating machines are built in countries not using the metric
system. Their stamps cannot be measured in the metric system
without decimals.

The perforation gauge is described further in chapter 6.

TERMS USED IN CONNECTION WITH SEPARATION

Blind Perforation

An American philatelic term for a condition in which the
perforations are marked in the paper but not fully punched out.

Clean-Cut Perforation

Clean-cut perforation is normal and the term seldom is used
except when regular perforating follows a period of rough perforations or when both kinds are found in one issue: for instance,
Queensland, 1860-1861, and St. Helena, 1861.

Coarse Perforations; Fine Perforations

These are general terms to describe a range of perforations
when actual gauge is not necessary. In the 1883 stamps of Austria, the perforations gauging 9 to 10½ are called coarse, while
the scarcer varieties gauging 11½ to 13 are called fine. Unless
collectors are specialists in these stamps they do not attempt
to secure examples showing all gauges but are content with
coarse and fine examples.

Compound Perforation

This term indicates that two gauges of perforations or roulettes are found on the stamp. In early days the mixing of gauges
probably was not intentional and occurred only because of inadequate equipment. In recent days varying gauges have been
used to equalize the separation of the stamps in both directions,
or to strengthen the paper in one direction. Since machine-made
paper is stronger across the web, United States stamps are now
perforated gauge 11 across the web and 10½ with the web. In

the case of some coils the gauge is modified across the web to keep the stamps from tearing prematurely in vending or affixing machines.

Compound perforations are fully described by listing both gauges, first the horizontal, then the vertical. The same method applies to roulettes but the term compound roulette is seldom used and such stamps are usually described by mentioning both gauges, as "roulette 7 by 10."

Defective Perforation

This term is applied to a perforation which is not clean cut, or is irregular in some respect.

Double Perforation

This term refers to doubled or partly doubled lines of perforations. Lines doubled for a short distance occur in rotary line perforation when the operator withdraws a sheet and starts it over in better position. In some cases the sheets have been fully perforated, perhaps at a slight angle or off center, and then reperforated throughout to improve them. They separate on any line.

Fine Perforations

See "Coarse Perforations; Fine Perforations."

Hyphen-Hole Perforation

This perforation of long narrow holes, sometimes mistaken for a roulette, was used for some of the Battleship revenue stamps of the United States in 1898. Ordinary rouletting also was used for this issue. Also called *oblong perforation*.

Imperforate

A negative term which collectors are forced to use for a normal sheet without means of separation. The term is synonymous with unperforated. The word *imperforated* is incorrect and should be avoided, unless in referring to trimmed stamps.

Imperforate Between

This term describes pairs or larger pieces which are perforated all around but lack a means of separation. This constitutes an error as a rule, but the omission of perforations between stamps and advertisements in various foreign stamp booklets is intentional to prevent the user from discarding the ad easily. The error results from the loss of a line of pins in a comb or harrow perforator, or a disk in a multiple rotary machine, or failure to perforate a line when using a guillotine or single-line rotary machine.

Imperforate Horizontally

This term refers to stamps lacking horizontal separation. Perhaps the condition occurs only as an error of perforation.

Imperforate Vertically

In this case the vertical separation is missing.

Interrupted, or Syncopated Perforation

To add strength between the stamps in the coils of the Netherlands, certain pins were removed to leave wide bridges. This prevented the premature separation of stamps in vending and affixing machines. Australia, for similar reasons, changed the gauge near each edge of her coils by substituting, for example, two pins for three.

Irregular Perforation

This term describes perforations that are unequally spaced or out of line due to bent pins or a poorly constructed machine.

Kansas City Roulette

Early in December, 1914, a quantity of unsalable imperforate sheets of the 1-cent and 2-cent stamps of 1912 were rouletted with a tracing wheel by postal employees in Kansas City, and sold at the regular stamp windows. On January 5, 1915, the postmaster was ordered to discontinue this private form of separation and to hold those in stock for stamp collectors. These were sold in lots of less than a hundred to collectors who called in person at the post office. A total of 93,600 1-cent and 69,200 2-cent stamps were rouletted, but only 7,900 1-cent stamps were on hand when the sale to collectors was ordered.

Large Perforations; Small Perforations

In general the diameter of pins is about equal to the space between pins. When holes are abnormally large with narrow bridges, they are called large perforations. When the pins are very small with wide bridges, the perforations are called small. Do not confuse these terms with coarse and fine perforations. The latter terms refer to the gauge, even though not actually measured. The terms large and small refer only to the size of the holes.

Lozenge Perforations

These are punched by diamond-shaped pins, or perhaps by diagonally set square pins. The Bulgarian due stamps of 1884 provide an example of true lozenge perforation. Often confused with lozenge roulette or coarse zigzag roulette.

Lozenge Roulette

These are lozenge- or diamond-shaped holes made by lancet-shaped pins that pierce the paper and enlarge the hole as they pass through. No paper is removed.

Mixed Separation or Mixed Perforation

Either term indicates the use of different forms of separations on the same stamp: for instance, perforation and rouletting. As in compound perforation the variety used at the top and bottom is mentioned first. More than two varieties are named around the stamp in clockwise direction starting at the top. The half-size stamps of South Africa of 1942-1944 were perforated and rouletted.

Oblique Roulette

A private roulette placed on the 1867 stamps of Tasmania by the postmaster at Deloraine. In these the cutting blades were parallel but set at an angle. The German term is herringbone roulette.

Oblong Holes

See "Hyphen-Hole Perforation."

Part Perforate

A general term applied to stamps lacking the means of separation in one direction.

Percé en Arc

A French term used by English, German, and American catalogers to define a roulette in which the cutting blades are in the form of tiny arcs. All blades face the same way and are set in line so that the roulette is a series of concave arcs on one stamp and convex arcs on the adjoining stamp. French lists use the term *percé en scie* for the Brunswick issue of 1863 though it was actually *en arcs*. Also called scalloped roulette.

Percé en Croix

This French term means pierced in cross form and refers to roulettes made by tapered cross-shaped pins that pierce the paper and expand the hole to a square shape as they penetrate deeper. No paper is removed and in a pair the holes may be closed by folding back the turned down corners. It is found on some Portuguese stamps of 1866 that were used in Madeira. The effect is similar to lozenge roulette.

Percé en Scie

A French term usually translated as saw-tooth roulette, this describes a form of roulette in which the cutting blades are set at an angle so that the projecting teeth on a stamp point toward one end and not directly outward. An example occurs in the

1861-1863 issue of Bremen. It is listed in the British and American catalogs as *Percé en scie,* but the French make it *percé en arcs* while the German catalog calls it *in Bogen durchstochen,* or roulette in arcs. It seems possible that the French and German catalogers have never examined one of the stamps.

Pin, or Sewing-Machine Perforation

This roulette can be made with a tracing wheel or with an unthreaded sewing machine. Examples are found in Mexico, issues of 1868 and 1872, New Zealand, 1856-1859, Colombia, 1902-1903, and Turkey, 1871.

Private Perforations

A general term for unofficial perforations or roulettes applied to stamps. Private perforations were added to imperforate sheets before machines for separation had been invented. The term also refers to punchings on stamps to be used in vending and affixing machines.

Regular Perforation

This is produced by harrow machines having a single pin at each corner and a uniform pattern of pins. Comb machines have the single pin at the intersections of the line of pins and the projecting short rows. The size of holes and the width of bridges are about equal, but there are exceptions to this requirement.

Rossbach Perforation

The H. F. Rossbach Company, of Benton Harbor, Michigan, built a perforating machine in 12½ gauge which was used experimentally in the Bureau of Engraving and Printing in 1919, and 1-cent offset-printed stamps, so perforated, were sold to the public.

Rough Perforation

In rough perforation the holes are ragged and not clean. This may be caused by worn counterpart dies or a poorly designed machine with loose-fitting pins. Queensland stamps of 1860-1861 and those of St. Helena, 1863, have rough perforations.

Serpentine Roulette

This roulette is made on a machine with curved cutters alternately faced opposite so that the finished roulette is in a sinuous or undulating line. When the cutters are semicircular the term half-circle-shaped may be added to the description. When the arc is much deeper the term tongue-shaped is applied. This roulette occurs in the stamps of Finland from 1860 to 1875.

Serrate Roulette

This term is used in Scott's *Standard Catalogue* but is not illustrated or described. In some stamp issues such as Greece, 1911, and in the high values of German inflation stamps of 1923, the minute cutting blades were set crosswise to the rouletting disk with adjoining blades tipped slightly with reference to each other, and not parallel, with the result that the stamps tear apart with a toothed margin hardly different from a perforation of the same gauge.

This use of the word *serrate* does not follow the dictionary, which states that the teeth should point slightly toward one end or the other and not point directly outward. Dentate roulette would be a more accurate name for this form.

Foreign lists seldom agree with Scott in the use of *serrate*. The British term this form *zigzag* and the French, *percé au zigzags*, although this term usually is reserved for coarser forms. German lists agree that there is some resemblance to a saw-tooth form, their terms meaning "saw-toothlike roulette" or "sawlike roulette."

Serrate Roulette in Colored Lines

The 1869 issue of Queensland provides an example of a printer's rule roulette in this form. The French term *dentelure indiquée par les zigzags noirs* is one of the longest in catalogs.

Square Perforations

These are formed by square pins set normal to the line and may be found in the stamps of Queensland, 1862-1866, and in Mexico, 1872. Some catalogers confuse these perforations with roulettes, one French list using the term *percés en carrés* (pierced in squares), while another which recognizes the punched holes uses *perforations carrés* (square perforations).

When the pins are set diagonally they produce diamond or lozenge perforations.

Syncopated Perforations

See "Interrupted Perforations."

Various Perforations

This term is used when stamps have more than two gauges or do not conform to the definition of compound perforation. The gauges are listed starting at the top and following around in a clockwise direction.

Walls of Troy Roulette

This term appears in many old catalogs but is not found in current philatelic dictionaries. It is not clear what form was meant or on what stamps it appeared. It would seem to indicate a form similar to serpentine roulette but made up of rectangular cuts instead of curved forms.

Zigzag Roulette

This term describes a form which is about the same as that used on the 1911 issue of Greece except coarser. Nearly all catalogs use the English term except the German lists which call it *zickzack*. It is found on stamps of Afghanistan, 1907.

❖❖

OVERPRINTS AND VARIETIES

An overprint may be defined as anything, numeral, inscription, or device, printed on a stamp or label, front or back, to alter its value, its place, purpose, or condition of use, to make it valid for postage or to restore validity after a previous demonetization, or adapt it to some special purpose. In this work the word *overprint* is synonymous with surcharge but the latter will be avoided since some writers attempt to limit its use to overprints that change the value of a stamp.

Collectors usually dislike overprints. They are easier to falsify than stamps, and in many cases the endless varieties appear to have been made for sale to collectors. However, overprinted stamps cannot be disregarded without losing what may be the most important philatelic history of a country.

The first few overprints were concerned with value, the very first being a large red "2" applied in 1846 to the 1843 3-cent carrier stamp of the United States City Despatch Post of New York City. Although not a national stamp issue it deserves mention on account of its primacy.

The next was a handwritten "5" applied to some 13-cent Hawaiian stamps in 1853 during a stamp shortage, and the third was the inscription "Four Pence" added to the green Mauritius stamps in 1854. This stamp, in common with some other British colonial stamps of the period, was without a value indication except as denoted by the color. The fourth overprint "Y¼" was applied to the 2-reales Spanish colonies stamp in 1855 to provide a new value for domestic use in Cuba and Puerto Rico.

Overprints have been used throughout stamp history to provide new values required by rate changes, to take care of temporary shortages, and to use up unneeded stocks of little-used values or remainders of previous issues. However, when a demonetized stamp is to be used it generally is necessary to include a revalidating inscription. In a number of cases stamps have been bisected by cutting or perforating and each half has received an overprint of the new value.

Many value overprints have been necessitated by currency changes made at a time when large stocks of stamps were on hand. In nearly all cases overprints to change the value in the same currency reduce the stamps' face value. This prevents forgers from producing overprinted stamps.

The second use of overprints was to provide stamps for a country which had none of its own. The first example came in 1867 when the stamps of India were overprinted "Straits Settlements." Prior to that time the Straits Settlements had been under India and used Indian stamps. When its administration was turned over to the Secretary of State for the Colonies, the stocks on hand were overprinted for temporary use.

This type of overprint is common and such entities as Cyprus, Gibraltar, and the Irish Free State were provided with provisional issues by overprinting the current British issues. Stamps for the mandated territory of South-West Africa were made by overprinting those of the Union of South Africa, and those for Aitutaki were overprinted on the stamps of New Zealand.

The first time that the use of a stamp was defined or altered by an overprint was in 1869 when the word "Postage" was added to the current stamps of Natal. It seems evident that the stamps had been used for both postage and revenue before that time and that it became desirable to separate the income from the two sources.

When official stamps were needed in Luxembourg in 1875, the word "Oficial" was overprinted on current issues. Newspaper stamps for the Portuguese colonies of Timor and Macao were made by overprinting regular issues with the word "Jornaes."

Almost all kinds of stamps have been provided by overprinting the stamps of other classifications, and nonpostal issues such as revenue and telegraph stamps have been pressed into postal use by overprinting in this manner. Some countries have resorted to this practice to provide commemorative stamps quickly or cheaply and the United States has been guilty with the Molly Pitcher and Hawaiian issues of 1928.

Changes in the form of government have been responsible for overprinted issues, prominent examples being the stamps of Portugal and her colonies overprinted "Republica" in 1910 and 1911, and Mexican issues overprinted "Gobierno Constitucionalista" in 1914-1916.

The Persian issues overprinted "Postes Iraniennes" in 1935 provide examples of the use of an overprint to show the change of a country's name.

Stamps for nations' foreign offices have usually been made by overprinting regular issues with the name of the office and if necessary a new value in the currency of the foreign office.

Although nearly all overprints are placed on the faces of stamps one unusual Nicaraguan issue of 1911 was intentionally overprinted on the back. These were nonpostage stamps in a heavy, dark design that previously had been overprinted for revenue use with a new value. Since any further overprinting would have made them completely illegible, the inscription "Vale—05 cts—Correo—de 1911" in four lines was placed on the backs.

The control numbering system used on the backs of Spanish stamps for many years and the value numerals found on the

backs of early Greek issues hardly fall into the category of overprints.

During the two World Wars overprinting came into extensive use to provide stamps for occupied areas. Local stamps were
overprinted if available; otherwise the issues of the occupying
power were placed in use with appropriate inscriptions and a
change in currency.

In the first 1895 issue of Salvador an overprint was used to
hide the vignette completely. A series of stamps had been prepared showing a portrait of Antonio Azeta, the brother of the
president, but a revolution took place before the stamps could
be issued and the succeeding administration caused the entire
issue to be overprinted with the arms of Salvador in a color dark
enough to hide the portrait. The second issue of that year bore
this coat of arms as the vignette design and not as an overprint.

Following the change in government of Egypt in 1953, an
overprint of three horizontal bars was placed on existing stocks
of stamps to deface the portrait of King Farouk.

Overprints have been applied by almost every printing
process but the usual method is typography, using typeset plates
or duplicate plates made by stereotyping or electrotyping. A
few overprints have been in manuscript, a few have been typewritten, as the ½-penny stamp of Tonga, 1896, and many have
been lithographed. In recent years photogravure has been used
and thus engraving is represented. Others have been handstamped and roller stamped, using rubber or metal stamps, and a
few have been given value overprints with numbering machines
set to repeat the numerals.

Overprints from typeset plates show more varieties than
any of the others for there may be misspelled words, wrong-font
type, missing letters, inverted letters, and every form of mistake
that the use of individual type can produce. It is practically impossible to set up a large overprint plate without some variation
in spacing between letters or lines or in the vertical relation of
multiple lines. Such a plate taxes the capacity of a print shop not

equipped with monotype or linotype machines and often the wrong fonts are used because there are no others.

The most satisfactory solution is to set a single unit and duplicate it by stereotyping or electrotyping.

Overprints are sometimes set up in a group of several subjects and then duplicated in sufficient numbers to form the plate. Mistakes made in the group will be repeated at intervals throughout the plate. When overprinting with a plate of smaller size than the stamp sheet there is a chance for unusual varieties, such as double overprints made by overlapping the printing jobs. This ordinarily leaves a row of stamps along the sheet edge without an overprint.

When extreme care is used there need be no varieties but under the conditions that must have prevailed in Nicaragua between 1904 and 1928, a collector finds such varieties as "double overprint—one in wrong color," "triple overprint—two reading up, one reading down," and perhaps even "triple overprint—one inverted and one on back." It is such varieties that make the collector shun overprinted issues of some countries and feel sorry that the idea ever was invented.

Overprints made with plates composed of nonidentical subjects have made it possible to plate some stamps which otherwise could not be reassembled in order, the overprint differences being sufficient to prove the plate positions.

The detection of fraudulent overprints involves a careful comparison with authentic overprints and accurate measurements of the type and spacing. The process is simplified by the use of a comparison microscope, or greatly enlarged photographs. The inks of suspected overprints may react differently from the genuine ink when viewed under ultraviolet light.

❖❖❖

GRILLS AND VARIETIES

At all times postal authorities have been concerned with stamp cleaning and fraudulent reuse. One preventative in use for many years in the United States involved the breaking of the paper fibers with an embossing grill somewhat like various check-protecting appliances in use today. The breaking of the paper surface permitted the cancelling ink to penetrate the fibers and attempts to remove it scuffed the paper and made the fraud apparent.

The idea was developed by Charles F. Steel, of Brooklyn, and was patented by him October 22, 1867, and sold or leased to the National Bank Note Company which was printing the United States stamps at that time. Experiments had been made before this date, however, for grilled stamps were issued some months previously, and a copy of the "all-over grill" exists with the date of August 13, 1867. This all-over grill was thought by John N. Luff, the American philatelic authority, to have been issued about August 8, 1867.

The machine used to grill the usual and most common varieties contained a large roll equipped with groups of tiny pyramidal bosses, the groups being spaced to correspond with the

354

stamps in the sheet. Some of the experimental grills of larger area, including the all-over type, were made with a roll having pyramid-shaped recesses into which the paper was forced. This caused the points of the grills to project above the surface of the stamps, just the reverse of the smaller and more common type of grills.

In the grilling process the sheets of gummed stamps pass between the grill roll and a flat yielding bed. In some cases it is probable that several sheets were grilled at once as the impressions are imperfect. Grills were applied to stamps by the National Bank Note Company from 1867 until some time in 1871 and after the experimental period ranged from 12 by 14 millimeters, through 11 by 13, down to 9 by 13.

When the small-size pictorial issue of 1869 appeared the grill was reduced to 9½ by 9½ millimeters and supposedly applied to all stamps issued. However, copies of all values except the 6-, 10-, 12-, and 15-cent, type II, exist with full original gum and no trace of grills. When the unsatisfactory issue of 1869 was withdrawn and replaced by the large portrait series of 1870-1871, the National Bank Note Company continued to grill the stamps, but there is the possibility that many were issued without grills at the start of this series in order to save time. The grill is found in two sizes, 10 by 12 millimeters and 8½ by 10, but in a majority of the stamps the impression is so faint that few collectors attempt to identify the two sizes. After the grilling process was discontinued in 1871, the company continued to print the stamps until the contract was lost to the Continental Bank Note Company in 1873. This company never placed the grill on regularly issued stamps but there are some examples embossed with a grill measuring 7¼ by 9½ millimeters. The purpose of this grill is unknown but it is said to have been used as an exhibit in a lawsuit over stamp cleaning operations, and to have been presented by the Continental company as a method of preventing stamp cleaning. Only a few sheets were grilled and as these were never issued at post offices they are not entitled to a catalog listing.

There are numerous grill varieties caused by careless feeding of sheets to the machine. These include double and triple grills, split grills, and quadruple splits in which the stamps show parts of four grills. There are marginal grills extending along the entire side of a stamp. These were caused by placing the sheet too near the end of the roll, where the embossing was continuous, to assist in feeding the sheets. Curious freak grills result from folded sheets. Inverted grills were caused by folded sheets or sheets fed upside down.

Peruvian stamps of 1874 to 1884 show the only foreign grills listed. These closely follow the pattern of the United States grills for the National Bank Note Company also printed the Peruvian stamps. This grill measures about 9 by 14 millimeters and was applied to the regular and postage due stamps. In this postage due series the National company used the same engraving of the S.S. *Adriatic* that appears on the 12-cent value of the United States pictorial issue of 1869.

❖❖

DESIGNS

At first stamp designs were limited to a very few subjects, with a majority showing a portrait of a sovereign, the arms of a country or its ruler, or a numeral of value. Today the subjects on stamps constitute a pictorial history of the world.

The shapes of stamps include triangles, quadrangles, octagons, circles, and ellipses. Many of these are modified by curved or irregular outlines. Occasionally the effect of the shape is altered by placing it in an unusual position; for example, a triangle on point, or a square standing on corner. All the shapes with unequal dimensions have been used both in horizontal and vertical format, but with the exception of one octagonal set and the triangular stamps, all shapes are on square or rectangular pieces of paper after perforating.

Sizes of stamps cover a wide range, with the extremes found in an 1863 stamp of the Colombian state of Bolivar, having an area of about one-sixth of a square inch, and the large four-part special-delivery stamp of China, 1905-1912, covering about twenty square inches. Souvenir sheets, which ordinarily include margins and inscriptions, are not included in this survey.

Generally the countries that use great numbers of stamps

produce them in vertical rectangular form about three-quarters of an inch wide and a little less than one inch high. In measuring stamps the horizontal dimension is stated first, and the sizes given are of the design and not of the paper, unless explicitly stated.

Commemorative, semi-postal, and special service stamps usually are larger than the regular issues of a country; in the case of the two first mentioned, to provide extra space for the subject, in the last, to call particular attention to the service to be rendered.

The stamp design consists of a central motif, which may be spoken of as the vignette, a surrounding frame, and appropriate inscriptions. As time goes on there is a tendency to eliminate the frame and allow the picture to cover the entire space allowed for the design. In a few cases the vignette groundwork has been omitted, leaving the portrait bust or other design motif free standing on the stamp paper except for the inscriptions.

At one time inscriptions were confined to the frames or borders, and in some instances formed the only frame. Today they are scattered about and placed in any space not otherwise occupied. At one period the frames were the one element the designer could treat according to his artistic ability, for there was little he could do with the portrait if the subject was to be recognizable.

If the designer had been trained in a classical school of art his borders contained traces of the orders of architecture, of the acanthus leaves, Greek frets, egg and dart moldings, and similar things. If his training had been in an early twentieth century school, the architectural elements were apt to disappear. Examples of the first are shown in the United States issue of 1902-1903, of the second in the Bosnian and Austrian issues beginning in 1906 and 1908, respectively.

The simplicity to be attained by subduing the frame to allow the vignette to fill the design is shown by the Edward VIII issue of Great Britain, 1936, and the 1938 presidential issue of the United States. Examples of designs without frame or groundwork are found in the William Penn and General Oglethorpe designs for the United States stamps issued in 1932 and 1933.

The design of a stamp should contain elements which will cause it to be recognized wherever it may travel as postage on a letter. It should indicate the intended use, the country of origin, and the face value in the currency of the country. The need for indicating the stamp's use is perhaps more important in the country of origin than elsewhere, for once the mail matter has entered the international mails, the stamp should be accepted as valid, whether it be regular postage, official, or of other category.

The need for the indication of the value is important. Some postal clerk was required to rate the letter and indicate whether it was fully paid or part paid. For many years part payment or even no payment at all was permissible in the international mails, and postal clerks were required to rate letters, indicating if they were fully or less than fully paid. After the Universal Postal Union was formed member nations were requested to show stamp values in Arabic (conventional) numerals, even though they might be meaningless in the country of origin. The request was generally carried out.

The simplest method of giving information on stamps is by the inscriptions, but this is not always done, and the only clue to the origin of some stamps may be in a portrait, or in the currency units. In a few cases there is no information in any language and the stamps must be identified by comparison with catalog pictures.

Great Britain introduced the idea of portrait design in 1840 and ever since this has remained the most popular design motif. It is not clear why the name of the country was omitted in this first portrait stamp, for the stamp was called upon to travel more widely than any other. It cannot be argued that the portrait of Queen Victoria would be recognized throughout the world in 1840, for she had then reigned only three years. At that time there were few international publications and no simple method of reproducing pictures for universal distribution. Very likely these stamps gave the world its first view of the queen, but once identified the portrait became the symbol of the country and served well for about sixty years.

The omission of the country name may have been done in a spirit of bravado or the designers may not have given any consideration to foreign use, but there is a suspicion that an appropriate name could not be selected. "Great Britain" might appear boastful on a postage stamp, while "United Kingdom" without the appendages would not be a very definite title.

Whatever the reason, the name has never appeared on English stamps, although a few recent commemoratives have given enough information to fix the location as the British Isles. These have inscriptions reading "British Empire Exhibition—1924," "Postal Union Congress—London—1929," "Victoria" and "George" on the centenary issue of 1940, and "Festival of Britain" on an issue of 1951.

The first British design and all successive ones until 1883 have the use indicated by the word "Postage," but after that date the values up to and including the one-shilling indicate the dual use with the words "Postage" and "Revenue." There are exceptions in which the double use is shown on 2-shilling, 6-pence values, and in all commemorative issues, for these bear the word "Postage" only.

The second national stamp issue came from a second continent when Brazil, in 1843, made use of the numerals of value as the subject of the design. It has been written that this issue was primarily made to enable German settlers to correspond with friends in the fatherland to stimulate further immigration, and that the rates on such letters were lower than the normal overseas charges.

These Brazilian stamps do not show the country or the use and the three values are printed in a single color, black. Other stamps with a numeral motif have been issued since that time but nearly all give some clue to the country of origin. In spite of faults, the Brazilian issue ranks high among desirable stamps. These "bull's eyes," as they are called, were succeeded during the following year by similar designs in a smaller size that added no more information. Finally, the set was increased to twelve values with four in color.

In 1866 the name "Brazil" and the portrait of Dom Pedro II appeared on the stamps but the use was not indicated until 1884. Since that time no changes of importance have been made except in the name of the country, following the establishment of the republic. This name, which has been given as "E.U. do Brazil," "Estados Unidos do Brazil," and "Brazil," was altered to "Brasil" in 1918 except on a few commemorative issues. The inscription "Correio," to indicate the use as postage, was added in 1884, and has been included on nearly all issues since that date.

The third stamp issue appeared on a third continent in 1847 when the United States brought out the famous five- and ten-cent stamps picturing Franklin and Washington. This issue has the first complete designs, since they show all pertinent information and give the value both in words and numerals. For an unexplained reason the inscription "Post Office" is used, although all succeeding issues have the word "Postage." This is not treated as a mistake, as it is in the 1847 stamps of Mauritius.

All of the useful information has appeared on all United States issues except the Pilgrim Tercentenary series of 1920, which lacks the name of the country. Several recent issue lack the word "Postage" and others lack the entire inscription which indicates the use and the name of the country.

On nearly all stamps up to 1933 the word *cents* has been spelled out, but in that year the N.R.A. issue appeared with the character "¢," and since that time about half the commemorative issues have the currency indicated in like manner. In the early part of 1940 the third group of the Famous Americans series, honoring five educators, appeared with a modified hammer and sickle instead of the usual character for cents. This was used throughout the remainder of the series, affecting five groups in all, and during the next six years on the Vermont, Kentucky, China, Railroad, Corregidor, Motion Picture, Florida, Toward United Nations, Iwo Jima, Roosevelt Memorial, Army,

Navy, Al Smith, and Texas issues, and finally was brought to a conclusion with the Merchant Marine issue of February 26, 1946.

Some complaints were made about a stubby star which appeared in the designs of a few stamps, but this so-called red star was public property before Soviet Russia appropriated it. Many foreign decorations showed it, and the annual encampment badges of the G.A.R. often used it. It appears that the original reason for its use was to obtain a larger field for decoration without increasing the over-all size. The stars shown on definitive Russian stamps show a conventional star more often than not, and only in the overprinted issues in 1922-1923, and in the stamps of the Transcaucasian Federated Republics, does the stubby star predominate.

Returning again to 1847, another continent was brought into philatelic prominence in that year when Mauritius was the fourth country to issue stamps, with her "Post Office" series. This British island colony used the portrait of Queen Victoria and included all necessary information. The two values, one penny and twopence, were engraved on a small copper plate by J. Bernard, a jeweler of Port Louis. The entire issue was made by taking five hundred impressions from this plate, a thousand stamps in all.

Since later Mauritius issues bear the inscription "Post Paid," the earlier inscription is treated as a mistake on the part of the engraver. These stamps are extremely rare and the story is told that nearly all were used to mail invitations to a local soiree. The prices of single copies range from $15,000 upward and stamps on cover are worth more than their weight in uranium.

In 1849, Mauritius brought out the design using Britannia or Minerva, and thus joins with France in being the first two countries to employ an allegorical figure as a stamp subject.

France used a head of Ceres on her first stamps in 1849 in a design including all needed elements. This country in 1852 set a precedent by showing the portrait of a president in office, Louis Napoleon. In the following year, as an empire, she pictured him as Napoleon III, but in 1870 she reverted to the Ceres type. In 1876 a new design, known as Type Sage, shows the allegory of Peace and Commerce, and in later years France has been consistent in the use of such subjects rather than national heroes. The Pasteur set of 1923-1926 is almost the only regular issue of France, not under occupation, which pictures an important Frenchman, and this set grew out of a commemorative issue of three values.

Stamps for the continent of Australia were first issued by New South Wales and Victoria in 1850. The designs were the view of Sydney for the first, and the half-length portrait of Victoria for the second. Each design represented a first use for a subject of that character. The Sydney view is actually taken from the arms of the colony but among topical collectors who have a copy of this stamp, it may be classified as the first scene to be used on a stamp.

The fifth continent, Asia, became known to stamp designers when postage issues were gotten ready for India and the Philippine Islands in 1854. The Indian stamps of that time were issued by the East Indian Company, while the Philippine issues, although without name, are identified by the portrait of Isabella II as a Spanish or Spanish colonial issue.

The first typeset stamp, which was also the first stamp in circular form, was issued by British Guiana in 1850, and showed only the name and denomination. A more workmanlike rectangular series of typeset designs was used in Hawaii in 1851. These contained all the necessary information. In 1852, a first of its kind was used in Hawaii, when a stamp with the inscription "H.I. & U.S. Postage" was issued, and again in the following year when another 13-cent stamp was itemized in the inscription "Hawaiian—5 cts.—Postage—United States 8 cts." Hawaii also may have been the first to use a bilingual stamp when she produced the 1859 issue with values expressed in the native language and in English.

Stamps using coats of arms were issued in 1851 by Austria, Hanover, Switzerland, and Schleswig-Holstein, and during the same year Canada and Tuscany made use of the principal element of their arms, the former showing the beaver, the latter, the Lion of Tuscany.

In 1850 the first tendency to break away from the few stereotyped forms of stamp design became apparent when Victoria issued the half-length portrait of the queen, and followed two years later with the enthroned figure. Canada, in 1851, placed the portrait of Prince Albert on a stamp, this being the first use of a portrait of a member of a royal family who was not the sovereign.

New Brunswick and Nova Scotia issued quite similar square stamps in 1851. These show the British crown and heraldic flowers, and both stamps are arranged to stand on corner. Newfoundland repeated this design in 1857 but in normal position. However, these were not the first square stamps as Bavaria had used that form in 1849.

In 1853 the Cape of Good Hope stamps were issued in a shape which has made them universally appealing. These "triangular Capes," each of which is half a perfect square, provide a stamp which may be collected in "blocks" of two, or blocks of eight, etc., in perfect squares. The stamp is one of four triangular forms that have been used in stamp designs.

The true octagon was introduced by Tasmania in 1853 and was copied by Victoria soon after. The latter was perforated as a square. It remained for Turkey to perforate octagonal stamps as octagons. This issue was to commemorate the annexation of Thessaly in 1898, and was for the use of the Turkish army in that district.

Other unusual forms are the diamond, lying horizontal for the Somali Coast stamps of 1894, and on end for stamps of Lithuania in 1923. The Brazilian "bull's eyes" were ellipses on side while the 1856 registration stamp of New South Wales is an ellipse on end.

The Roman States issue of 1852 was responsible for several new shapes which were regular in general form but modified by using concave or convex frame lines and by clipping the corners, etc. These forms and others were in use in Parma and Portugal during the following year. South America produced two new shapes when Colombia issued a registration stamp in 1856 in the shape of a six-pointed star, and Argentina issued regular postage stamps in a shield-shaped design in 1857.

Chile, in 1853, was the first country to honor a historic foreigner when she began to use the portrait of Columbus. Canada has been given this credit by some writers for her 1855 stamp showing the portrait of Jacques Cartier.

Some of the countries failing to show their names in their early issues were Austria, Hungary, Belgium, Spain, Portugal, Prussia, Persia, Cuba, and the Philippines. Switzerland was also in this class for several years but eventually her stamps were inscribed "Helvetia." The Latin name was chosen in order not to offend the French-, German-, or Italian-speaking citizens. In 1944, a three-value air-mail set used the three languages of Switzerland, one on each value, thus: "Schweiz Luftpost," "Posta Aerea Svizzera," and "Poste Aerienne Suisse."

Other instances of the first use of various stamp subjects are mentioned in chapter 10.

At first the language used on stamps was nearly always that of the issuing country, and the denominations were expressed in the characters in common use. The first Hawaiian inscriptions, exceptionally, were in a foreign language (English), but in this case stamps would not have been issued at the time except for the influence of the American missionaries.

After the organization of the General Postal Union, later the Universal Postal Union, many countries began showing their values in Arabic (conventional) numerals to assist postal clerks in other countries. Some countries also gave their names in Latin letters, usually in French or English, examples being China, Japan, Persia, among others.

Many countries have issued stamps with inscriptions in Latin letters and in native characters such as Arabic or Chinese, and there is at least one example of a design using four languages, three in Latin letters and one in Cyrillic, and the United Nations duplicates this and adds Chinese ideograms.

South Africa has issued stamps in bilingual pairs to avoid friction between sections of its population.

MISTAKES IN DESIGN

Mistakes in design are one of two kinds of errors which occur in stamps. Mistakes have little philatelic importance but they always are a source of publicity both in the general press and in stamp journals. Often the adverse publicity in such cases is the result of the critic's ignorance of what the stamp was intended to show.

Considering the many people who are concerned with a stamp issue and who have the opportunity to detect faults, it is surprising that any errors go undetected. When a slip occurs there are plenty of collectors and noncollectors waiting to spot it. Often this search for faults becomes an obsession, and sometimes is politically inspired in an effort to harass the administration in a small way. The practice is not limited to the United States but is prevalent wherever people can speak out.

Mistakes are the result of incorrect information or the inability of the designer to transfer correct information into a stamp design. Artists may take some liberty with a design for the sake of symmetry or style, but more often an error is analogous to a slip of the tongue, and there is no plausible explanation.

These mistakes are seldom the fault of the engraver, for he is usually a very efficient artist whose only concern is to transfer a design to a steel plate. Except for undetected slips his work is a faithful copy of the design, often more faithful than can be had by photography and zinc etching. In a few exceptional cases mistakes have been intentional and were initiated as political sabotage.

One mistake in United States stamps, due to incorrect information, occurred about 1912 when stamps were being prepared for the Panama-Pacific Exposition of 1913. The design of the 2-cent value had been approved, the die engraved, plates made and stamps printed, and the entire issue of twenty to thirty million was ready for distribution when someone noticed that the scene was at San Pedro Miguel Locks while the inscription read "Gatun Locks." The entire issue was destroyed except for a few copies for the archives and the question of error is purely academic as collectors cannot obtain the stamp. Should the archive copies come on the market, they would be valuable, but they should be classed as essays, since they were never issued. Had the issue been placed in circulation the stamps would be worth only as much as those in the replacement design with the inscription "Panama Canal." It was fortunate that the error was caught in time for there would have been plenty of caustic comment about it.

A similar example is found in the 18-centavos stamp in the 1932 issue of the Philippine Islands. The source material was provided by Philippine officials and the artist composed a striking design showing—he thought—Pagsanjan Falls. After the stamp had been in circulation some time an American collector called attention to the resemblance of the picture to the Vernal Falls in Yosemite National Park. This made good newspaper copy, especially as the stamps were printed in Washington, and criticism was directed at everyone except the individual who had furnished the mislabeled photograph. This stamp was withdrawn, but since much of the printing had been distributed it is in no sense a rarity, just a moderately scarce and desirable stamp.

Another example of the same character appears on the twopence Bermuda stamp of 1936 which was to show the cup-winning Bermudian yacht *Viking*. After the stamp had been placed in circulation the yacht was recognized as the *Lucie*, owned by Briggs Cunningham, an American of Southport, Connecticut. No change was made, and no withdrawal, and the stamp is no rarer for its mistake.

A mistake in caption occurs in the $5 United States stamp of the 1922-1923 series. The central motif is the upper portion of the statue which surmounts the United States Capitol and the caption reads "America." This statue was ordered from the sculptor under the name "Armed Freedom," and when the head was hoisted in place on December 2, 1863, all accounts gave it that name. The entire statue is shown on the 3-cent value of the National Sesquicentennial issue of 1950, with the caption "Freedom."

The three mistakes next described may be charged to the artists' lack of familiarity with the subjects. The first is in the design of the 5-paras Egyptian stamp of 1874. In this design an Arabic (conventional) "5" is placed at each corner, but all are inverted, indicating unfamiliarity with these numerals.

The second is found in a stamp issued in 1927 to honor Sir Edward Codrington, who was in command of a British squadron which with other foreign vessels assisted the Greek navy in the Battle of Navarino. This stamp was inscribed "Sir Codrington" by an artist who was not aware that the title is never used with the surname only. A corrected design was issued in 1928 but neither variety is scarce, although the first type is known in a scarce shade.

The third example appears in a 1951 issue of Korea to honor the twenty-one nations assisting the Republic of Korea army in the United Nations "police action." These were large stamps showing the flag of Korea at the left end and that of the honored nation at the right. The stamp for Italy bore the old royal flag with the arms of Savoy, but was soon altered by removing the crown above the arms. However it still was a mistake, for the flag of republican Italy has no device in the central panel.

The Cabot issue of Newfoundland in 1897 shows two examples of the use of wrong elements for unknown elements. The issue was to commemorate the 400th anniversary of the discovery of Newfoundland by John Cabot, but there was no picture of his vessel, the *Matthew*, and none of John Cabot. The American Bank Note Company, entrusted with this issue, substituted the *Santa Maria*, the flagship of Columbus, on the 10-

cent value, and the portrait of Sebastian Cabot, the discoverer's son, on the 2-cent value. The ship engraving had been used four years previously in the Columbian Exposition issue.

Since 1893 all stamp collectors have been aware of the fast-growing beard of Columbus, as indicated by stamps of the Columbian issue. He is beardless in the 1-cent value in the scene "Columbus in Sight of Land," but on the next day has a full beard in the scene "Landing of Columbus," on the 2-cent value. The engravers are criticized for this seeming error by people who should be able to recognize that these scenes are copies from paintings by different artists—neither of whom happened to make the voyage.

Another of these painter's mistakes is shown on the stamps of St. Kitt-Nevis in the subject "Columbus Looking for Land." The explorer is shown peering through a telescope, although that instrument had not yet been invented.

Criticism was directed against the United States for the design of the 5-cent value of the Norse American issue of 1925, for this pictured a Viking ship with the Stars and Stripes flying at the stern. This seeming anachronism vanished when it was explained that the stamp showed a reproduction of a Viking ship entering New York harbor in 1893 on its way to the Columbian Exposition.

Collectors sometimes call attention to the left-handed mail-catcher arm on the mail car shown on the 3-cent value of the Parcel Post issue of the United States, and attribute it to a reversed photograph. The explanation is that a car of the Chicago and North Western Railway is shown, and that this line not only uses the British word *railway* but is a left-handed railroad as well.

When the Mississippi Territory was organized the name placed on its great seal was spelled "Misissippi," but when this seal was reproduced on the commemorative stamp of 1948, collectors at once complained about the error.

Another stamp always mentioned when errors are discussed is the 12-pence stamp of Canada of 1851-1855. Since twelve pence equals one shilling, one is prone to call this a mistake in the indication of the value, and to blame it on the American engravers, Rawdon, Wright, Hatch and Edson. However, this is not a mistake at all. The Canadian currency was depreciated and it required fifteen pence to equal one shilling sterling. This 12-pence stamp represented about twenty cents in United States money. The 6-pence and 3-pence values were valued at about ten cents and five cents. This condition continued into the 1857 issue and both currencies were indicated on some stamps, as "10cy Ten Pence 10cy" and "8d Stg" and "6d Stg Six Pence Sterling 7½ Cy." The dual currency indications on the 1859 issue were for a different purpose and indicated the relation between the new Canadian cents and the English shilling on the values most used on foreign mail, as "Six Pence Sterling 12½c.," and "8d Stg 17 Cents," both of which were based on a shilling valued at twenty-five cents.

It seems unfortunate that a large share of the criticism directed toward trivial details could not be broadened to cover the entire subject of stamp design. Our search for the forest seems to be disrupted by the many trees we encounter.

❖❖❖

ERRORS

From a philatelic viewpoint errors are mistakes made during the actual production of stamps. These include the use of wrong materials or processes, and the incorrect use of proper things, none of which have prevented the issuance of the stamps, either because of lax inspection or considerations of economy. Also included as errors are stamps which have been issued in a partly finished state.

The important errors include stamps with inverted or missing colors in bicolor printing; inverts or missing portions in single-color printing; wrong value or wrong country clichés in any kind of printing; stamps in the color of another value, either by reason of a wrong cliché or the use of a wrong plate or wrong ink; double impressions, including impressions on the back of the stamps; use of paper of the wrong kind or color or with the wrong watermark; the omission or duplication of an overprint, the use of a wrong overprint, or the overprinting of the wrong stamps; and the omission or partial omission of the means of separation.

Some of the mistakes in the use of paper, in the means of separation, and in overprints may be classed as varieties rather than errors. The dividing line is not precise and may depend a great deal upon the general aptitude of the country producing the errors. Thus, an overprint variety might constitute a prized error if it occurred on a United States stamp, but be almost overlooked on a stamp of Nicaragua.

Mistakes in design are not classed as errors as they affect all stamps issued in that design. Where such a mistake requires correction the stamps issued in the altered design constitute a new major variety.

BICOLOR INVERTS

The most striking error is a bicolor stamp with inverted center, the product of sheet-fed work. Where two plates are used to print stamps in a single color, there also is the possibility of finding inverts but they may be long undetected unless an inscription or picture is involved.

It is surprising that any bicolor errors ever reach the public for inspectors always are alerted when a job of this kind is in progress. The printing processes are now perfected so that bicolor stamps may be printed on web-fed intaglio presses and now that that goal is reached there should be no more inverts.

India leads in having produced the first invert when the 4-anna blue-and-red stamp of the East India Company was issued in 1854. This is a rather rare stamp and very likely only one small sheet reached the public.

The United States has produced its share of inverted centers, starting with the issue of 1869, printed by the National Bank Note Company, in which the 15-, 24-, and 30-cent values, three out of the four printed in two colors, are found inverted.

Again in the series of 1901, three values of the bicolored Pan American issue appeared with inverted centers. The 1-cent and 2-cent values were sold through the post office but the 4-cent was printed at the order of a postal official. Part of this special printing was overprinted "Specimen" and allowed to reach stamp collectors. The remainder, without overprint, were placed in the government collection.

Not long after that time the collection was revised by the curator and various trades were made with stamp dealers and collectors to obtain needed varieties. In this exchange some 4-cent inverts without the "Specimen" overprint were traded off to favored collectors, and at the same time several United States issues previously unavailable in blocks were traded out of the government collection for the equivalent value in single copies of needed stamps. At that time there was no specialized listing to indicate the extreme rarity of the blocks traded away.

The 24-Cent Air-Mail Invert

After 1901 the United States made no bicolored stamps until the $2 and $5 values of the regular issue and the 24-cent air-mail stamp were issued in 1918. No errors of the first-mentioned stamps are known but a pane of a hundred of the air-mail issue with inverted blue airplanes was sold at the New York Avenue postal station in Washington, D.C.

The most reliable story, perhaps, is that written for *Weekly Philatelic Gossip* by W. T. Robey, the finder. He was a new collector and had agreed to exchange first-flight covers with a few collectors in Philadelphia and New York. Early on May 14, 1918, Robey went to the New York Avenue postal station to obtain the stamps. As all on hand were poorly centered, he left to return at noon, and at that time was shown a full pane. Robey said that his heart stopped for before him lay a sheet of inverts. He bought these and asked for more, but the others were normal and were handed back. He then showed the inverts to the clerk, who at once used the telephone. Robey then went to the Eleventh St. Station but all stamps there were normal, and a friend who visited other stations had no luck. Robey then called H. F. Colman, a Washington stamp dealer, but he was out and his assistant, Mrs. Catherine Manning, later curator of the philatelic collection in the Smithsonian, would not believe him.

Within an hour after the purchase, Mr. Robey was visited by postal inspectors who used every means short of force to obtain the stamps. Later Mr. Robey refused Mr. Colman's offer of $500 for the sheet, but that evening he showed it to him and Mr. Joseph B. Leavy, curator of the government stamp collection in the Smithsonian Institution.

Robey now sent word of his prize to Percy McGraw Mann, the Philadelphia correspondent of *Meekel's Weekly Stamp News*. Mr. Mann looked at the sheet and offered $10,000 for it. Meantime, it was learned that sale of the stamp had been halted in Philadelphia and New York until supplies could be checked.

Having declined Mann's offer, Robey took his sheet to New York, hoping to interest Colonel E. H. R. Green, but that collector was absent from the city. No offers worthy of mention being made, Robey started home. He stopped in Philadelphia and saw Eugene Klein who obtained an option on the sheet for $15,000. Next morning Colman bid $18,000, but Klein took up his option and received the inverts. Thus ends Robey's account.

Within a short time it was sold to Colonel Green, who agreed to break it up for the benefit of other collectors. Several blocks of four and a plate-number block of eight were kept by Colonel Green while the others were offered at $250 for fully perforated singles, and $175 for straight edge copies.

There are stories that 17 or 18 copies, mostly with straight edges, were blown from Colonel Green's desk and wound up in a vacuum cleaner and that Mrs. Green used one copy on a letter to her husband while he was in Washington. He is said to have removed this one from the cover and carried it in a locket.

In recent times fine singles have sold for many times the amount Robey received for the entire sheet. Numerous collectors regret that they did not take advantage of the $250 offer.

RECENT BUREAU OF ENGRAVING AND PRINTING ERRORS

The most publicized United States error is the Dag Hammarskjold invert of 1962. This Giori product was found at a few post offices with the yellow ground-tint inverted, It is not a striking error since the yellow tone is hardly noticeable. The elated finders rushed into print, and a chagrined postmaster-general hastily ordered the error reprinted, so that, as he said, each child might own a copy. These are listed as a special printing and have little premium value.

The error in the Canal Zone Thatcher Ferry Bridge stamp is mentioned since it occurred at the same time as the invert above, and almost met the same fate. It is a missing-color error produced just prior to the invert but not known until later. When its existence became known, the Canal Zone officials, following the Washington precedent, ordered reprints made. H. E. Harris, a Boston stamp dealer who discovered the error sheet, went to court to protect his property and obtained an injunction to halt the printing until the matter could be settled in court. Apparently the idea of reprinting later was dropped.

Revenue Inverts

In addition to postage issues the United States has had numerous inverted varieties among the bicolored revenue stamps of the second and third issues and the proprietary issues of 1871-1875. These stamps all had black vignettes with colored frames. Out of a total of 59 bicolored stamps, 21 are known inverted, nearly all being in the low-value items. One or two varieties are fairly common but others range from moderately rare up to extremely rare with the 5-cent proprietary issue in top rank with a catalog value in the upper 5-figures.

Which Is Inverted, the Center or the Frame?

In bicolored engraved stamps where this sort of error affects the entire sheet, it may be taken for granted that the plates are placed correctly and that the error is the result of inverting a sheet of paper after it has received the first color. This being the case, the color first printed is the one which is inverted in an error sheet.

Since all United States invert errors have been produced by the wet-paper intaglio process, it is customary to make the first printing in the color least liable to bleed when the paper is again wetted before the second printing operation. Thus, when one of the colors is black, it is printed first. In the Pan American issue with black vignettes or centers, the error stamps have inverted centers. The same is true of the revenue issues mentioned, and of the 15- and 24-cent values of the 1869 issue in which the blue or violet centers were considered more permanent than the brown or green frames. However the 30-cent value of the 1869 issue, printed in blue and red, has inverted flags, or frames, for the blue of the frames was printed in advance of the red center, showing a shield and eagle.

The 24-cent red and blue air-mail stamp had the blue vignette showing the airplane printed first and is correctly described as with "inverted center." Various other countries have inverted-center or frame varieties produced from intaglio plates, among the better known being three values of the 1881 issue of Guatemala which picture the quetzal in green with frames of various colors. These three values are correctly called "inverted centers."

One sheet of the 1-shilling stamp of Jamaica, 1919, was inverted and the stamps are described by Scott as with "inverted centers." Another authority describes this error as with "inverted frame," since it is on watermarked paper and the watermark is normal for the center. This reason is not logical, for the admission that the watermark is normal for the center proves that the sheet was inverted after the center was printed. Had the watermarked paper been fed to the press wrong end first, the second authority undoubtedly would have termed this error as with "center inverted," since he bases his description on the watermarks.

Other Bicolor Inverts

The early Russian issues from about 1866 to 1888 were typographed from two or three plates for each value depending on whether they were in a single color or bicolored. There were many inverts for at one time or another all except the 1- and 5-kopeck values have been noted with groundwork inverted, and nearly all the bicolored values were issued either with groundwork or center color inverted. The inverted groundwork varieties are not very noticeable but can be detected easily for they include small numerals of value, or have interlacing lines with a definite top and bottom.

A similar condition exists in the typographed issues of Denmark, 1870-1890, and in the similar stamps of the Danish West Indies. All the bicolored values are found with inverted frames, some being common while others are scarce, the difference in value being due to the two ways in which these inverts were produced.

The frame design probably was intended to be symmetrical but actually differs a little at some of the corners so that collectors are able to separate and list the varieties. The plates were made of individual clichés and the inverts were due in part to inverting sheets after the first color had been printed, and in part to inverted clichés in the frame plate. The latter are the scarcer varieties, but neither the scarce nor common varieties have the stature of errors and usually are classed as varieties.

Lithographed issues provide many examples of the inversion of one color in a single stamp in a sheet and are caused by placing one transfer upside down on the plate. Such an error can affect either the frame or the vignette and which element is inverted can be determined only by the relation of the stamp to one adjoining it.

One very rare example occurs in the 4-anna red and blue of the 1854 issue of India, which is listed as with "head inverted." Other examples are found in Spanish issues in the 12-curatos blue and rose of 1865, and the 25-milesimas de escudo blue and rose of 1867. Both of these have inverted frames.

An example of a true error in a typography plate assembly is found in the Brazilian 100-reis blue and red stamp of 1891, which is listed as with "inverted head," or center.

In order for any frame or center cliché, or lithographic transfer, to be placed upside down on a plate with small chance of detection it is almost necessary that the subject be symmetrical about a horizontal axis. The inverts mentioned thus far are all of this nature and the inversion of the sheet does not cause an overlapping of color to any extent, nor do the subjects appear far out of line in the plate or in the first printing.

When an unsymmetrical design is accidently inverted the resulting print is so misplaced that it is difficult to see how it could pass inspection. When such a design has inverted portraits or other vignettes centered in the frames it is evident that they were made to order, for it would require a different press setup to obtain this result.

OMISSION OF ONE COLOR

Another error occurring in bicolor or two-plate single-color printing is the failure to print the second color or plate. In commercial work this usually is caused by two sheets going together to the press. Unless detected such stamps may pass into circulation. They are much scarcer than color inverts for the absence of one printing makes them easy to detect. While of great philatelic interest they really are unfinished stamps and a second trip to the press would make them normal. A true printing error cannot be corrected in this way or otherwise restored to normal state.

ERRORS IN EMBOSSING

Sardinia provides an example of an error which is quite similar to those of bicolor printing. This occurs in the newspaper stamps of 1861 with frames in black and central colorless embossed numerals of value. Both values of the set, 1- and 2-centesimi, are found with inverted numerals, and both also with the wrong numeral. The list values would indicate that an entire sheet at least had been involved in each of the four errors. The frame design of each included the value in words.

CLICHÉS OF WRONG VALUE

The careless assembly of plates made up of individual clichés accounts for some very rare errors. In the 1851 issue of Spain one cliché of the 2-real value was placed in the 6-real plate and consequently is found in blue as a color error. The normal 2-real stamp in red is very rare while the normal 6-real blue stamp is much more common, and had the misplaced cliché remained throughout the printing there would have been a curious condition in which an error of color would have been more common than the normal color. Evidently it was discovered and removed after only a few sheets had been printed, for the 2-real blue is one of the great rarities.

In the Arthur Hind sale a se-tenant vertical pair with the 2-real stamp above the normal 6-real value sold for $11,000 and a single of the error brought $4750. Only one additional single copy is known and today singles are listed at 5-figure prices.

A like error in the 1858 issue of Uruguay comes from a cliché of the 180-centavo value in the 240-centavo plate. Only one copy of this dull vermilion stamp has been found and there is no basis on which to estimate its value.

When plates were locally made in the Cape of Good Hope, in 1861, for the issue generally misnamed "wood-block," one stereotype of each value was transposed. These remained throughout the limited printing and are not great rarities, but some used ones list at 5-figure prices. Naturally, unused stamps tend to bring higher prices than the used ones.

A study of the catalog will reveal that numerous errors of this kind were made in plates assembled from individual clichés.

WRONG VALUES IN INTAGLIO PLATES

While it is conceivable that a wrong value error might occur in an intaglio plate made by electrotyping or by etching, no stamp student would have admitted this to be possible in a plate laid down by the Perkins transfer process, yet early in 1917 United States collectors were combing post offices to locate sheets of 2-cent stamps containing 5-cent red errors. At the same time postal clerks were checking their stocks of 2-cent stamps to prevent the errors from reaching the public.

Collectors importuned the Bureau of Engraving and Printing for an explanation of this seemingly impossible condition.

It is well known that United States stamp plates are not made up of clichés but are integral steel plates to which the stamp subjects are transferred by a transfer roll under great pressure. Seemingly, only a conspiracy or magic could account for 5-cent stamps in a 2-cent plate.

However, the error was only the result of a little carelessness and lax inspection. When plate 7942 had been completely entered, proof sheets were taken for inspection before hardening. In this check three subjects were found to be defective and were marked with a colored pencil for correction. The nature of these defects is not now known but evidently it was more serious than a weak transfer for a re-entry would have corrected that. Perhaps the subjects were misplaced or showed some serious flaws for the order was given to erase them and to make new entries. The subjects involved were those printing stamps 74 and 84 in the upper left pane and stamp 18 in the lower right pane. Those are the fourth stamps in the eighth and ninth horizontal rows, and the eighth stamp in the second horizontal row of the panes mentioned.

Erasing a stamp subject on an engraved plate involves hammering the exact spot on the back of the plate to close up the lines of engraving and scraping and burnishing the face of the plate to provide a flat and true surface for a new entry. In spite of the greatest care there is no assurance that wear on the plate will not reveal some evidence or traces of the previous entry. Great care must be taken that the adjoining stamp subjects are not harmed and if any metal has been removed in the operation it is necessary to fill the cavity at the back of the plate or it will yield in printing and be indicated by darker, sly-wiped spots in the printed sheets.

When the plate was ready for the new transfers the operator applied to the custodian of dies and rolls for a roll to enter the 2-cent subjects. At this point the mistakes began for the custodian passed out a 5-cent transfer roll. Although the rolls are stored in numerical sequence it is possible that one was misplaced. It may be noticed that mixups may occur between the figures 2 and 5, for they are not unlike in some respects. That is, a normal 2 is almost identical with an inverted and reversed 5, and vice versa, and the confusion may have started there.

At any rate nothing was noticed from that time until the errors were discovered in post offices, for the designs were entered, the plate was approved and hardened, and printing was under way. The plate went to press March 17, 1917, and was in use when the errors were found on May 2. At that time 49,563 sheets had been printed, with a total of 148,689 single copies of the error.

When word reached the bureau the press was stopped and a search started. Many sheets were found in process, that is, printed, printed and gummed, or in the perforating department. Stocks ready for shipment were not opened but a notice was sent to every post office to search the stock on hand and all future shipments. The sheets and panes recovered in this search contained 41,537 copies of the error, leaving 107,152 at large and available to collectors.

The paper in use was unwatermarked but the perforating machines for sheet stamps were being changed from gauge 10 to gauge 11 and error sheets occur in both gauges. In addition a quantity had been shipped imperforate in sheets of 400 to be used in private coils for an affixing machine. About 700 of these sheets were located in Chicago but others reached the coil manufacturer and some of these reached collectors.

It has been estimated that about 50 imperforate sheets were available and that some sheets may have been punched with the Schermack Type III slots but none have been recorded, nor is it known whether or not they were precancelled.

CLICHÉS OF WRONG COUNTRY

In a few cases the error in plate assembly occurs through the use of a cliché of the wrong country. Of course this could occur only in a plant making stamps for another country, colonies, or for various countries.

In this manner, while the first Portuguese colonial stamps

were being printed at the government office in Lisbon in 1877 a cliché of the 40-reis value of Mozambique found its way into the plate of that value of Cape Verde. It remained in the plate throughout its life, being printed in blue from 1877 to 1881 and then in yellow buff until 1886. It is moderately scarce in the first color but easily obtainable in the second.

That stamps of different categories can also be mixed shows in the Icelandic error of 1902 where a cliché of the 20-aur. official stamp inscribed "Pjonusta" was inserted in the 20-aur. plate for regular postage. This was done at the Danish stamp printing office in Copenhagen.

INVERTED CLICHÉS

This is the error that produces the interesting "tête-bêche" or head to foot pairs. The stamp produced by an inverted cliché looks no different from other copies unless it is in a pair or larger piece with normal stamps. An inverted watermark on such a stamp is not sufficient to prove the error no matter how good a record the country has for keeping its stamps and watermarks in proper relation.

The present high values of these errors is the indication that many were discovered and corrected early in the printing. There are several tête-bêche errors in French stamps from 1849 through to the Type Sage issue of 1876 and some are extremely rare. It has been said that some of these were not accidental but purposely inverted by the printer to identify the work as of a certain period and to thwart any attempt to counterfeit the stamps in sheet form.

Other tête-bêche examples are those of Roumania, 1858, the Argentine Repubic, 1862, Buenos Aires, 1859, Spain, 1873, Austria, 1864, and Uruguay, 1858. One unusual example occurs in the ½-pie, 1898 issue, of Cochin, in which the square cliché is turned at an angle of ninety degrees.

Many recent stamps may be had in tête-bêche form and are not errors, but the result of special sheet arrangements used in printing booklet stamps. At various times these full sheets have been sold at post offices to provide collectors with tête-bêche stamps and with se-tenant varieties involving two values.

PARTIAL INVERSION IN A SINGLE COLOR

One example of the inversion of part of a design in single color where all other stamps in the sheet are normal occurs in the 1854 4-pence blue stamp of Western Australia. This pictures the famous black swan and for years the invert has been known as the "inverted swan" although actually the swan is in correct position and the frame is inverted.

This is a lithographed stamp and the error was caused by placing the transfer of one frame upside down. The transfers of these stamp subjects were made in two parts, the frames from one stone and the center designs, the swans, from another. The proof that the frame and not the swan is inverted is shown by the few multiple pieces containing the error. The error is fabulously priced and should be watched for in any lot of old Australian correspondence.

WRONG COLOR

In addition to color errors caused by wrong clichés, others occur when entire sheets are printed in a wrong color. These mistakes must happen at the start of the day's work, or at the start of printing with that plate. The most famous example is the 1855 3-skilling banco of Sweden, printed in the color of the 8-skilling banco. Only a single copy is known but one sheet, at least, must have been printed.

A similar error is found in the 1859 issue of Sicily, with two used copies known of the ½-grana value in the color of the 2-grana stamps. A well-known color error occurs in the United States Columbian issue in the 4-cent value, printed in the blue color of the 1-cent stamps. A more recent color error is the 2½-pence value of the British Silver Jubilee issue of 1935, printed in Prussian blue instead of ultramarine.

Minor variations of color should not excite much attention

as the range of shades of stamps in long use is remarkable. If collected at all they would be classed as varieties.

DOUBLE IMPRESSION

Errors of this kind are not as important as some other types and most of them should have been destroyed as printers' waste. Indeed many of those now on the market have been salvaged from material sold as waste paper. It is quite certain that no intaglio-printer could put a sheet of paper to press twice without being aware of it. However, many double impression errors affect only a few stamps in a sheet, for the sheet may have touched the plate at one end and then been placed in a slightly different position.

In printing from engraved plates such a kiss would produce only a light impression since much pressure is required in this process.

There is at least one well-known double print which should be classed as a variety rather than an error. A second impression in vermilion was made on sheets of the 20-öre stamp of Sweden, 1872, when it was found that the first impression in dull yellow was hardly visible. There was no attempt to register the colors but the yellow impression is seldom noticed except by a collector looking for it.

When a second impression is made on the back of a sheet it usually is done to save the sheet of paper after an unsatisfactory print has been made on the other side.

Double impressions are found in United States stamps in the 3-cent values of the 1851, 1857, and 1861 issues and in the 2- and 3-cent values of the 1870-1871 and 1873 issues. Examples printed on both sides include the 12-cent, 1851, the 5-cent, 1857, the 1-, 3-, and 30-cent values of 1861, and the 2- and 24-cent values of 1863. Nearly all of these errors are extremely rare.

Several similar errors are found in the United States issues between 1914 and 1920. The 1-, 2-, 3-, and 4-cent values are listed with double impressions in the engraved series, and the 1-, 2-, and 3-cent values in the offset printing are known with double impressions and the 3-cent value is found printed on both sides.

The beginner should not be confused by a reversed impression on the back of a stamp as this is an offset from another sheet not yet dry. Error impressions on the backs of stamps are positive like the impressions on the face.

WRONG PAPER

An important error of this class is found in the 1851 issue of Baden in the 9-kreutzer value on the green paper normally used for 6-kreutzer stamps. While this has long been classed as an error in the use of paper, Edwin Mueller recently stated that he believes it is the result of a misplaced 9-kreutzer cliché in the 6-kreutzer plate and used for only the earliest printings.

The 6- and 8-cent values of the United States issue of 1895 are known on paper watermarked double line U S I R instead of U S P S. These stamps and all higher values of the series were printed from plates of 200 subjects, on sheets of the same size as used for revenue stamps, and it is possible that other values on revenue paper may be found.

In 1950-1951 a similar error occurred in the $1 bicolored stamp of the 1938 presidential series, with stamps printed on U S I R paper instead of no watermark at all. A large number were found, as the printing was still in current post-office stocks.

Another type of wrong paper use occurs in the New South Wales issues of 1854-1855, in which all paper was watermarked with a numeral to correspond to the stamp value. At least eight errors occur in the use of the wrong value paper. The early Greek stamps with numerals on the backs of stamps include many errors in the use of wrong value paper, and Mexico has similar errors in the use of plain paper where moiré was intended.

ERRORS IN OVERPRINTING

It is not easy to draw a line between errors and varieties of overprints. When the stamp history of a country includes many mistakes in overprints, little consideration is given new examples, but in a country with a clean reputation an inverted or double overprint may be entitled to higher rank than a bicolored invert in another land.

When a stamp receives an overprint where none was intended, or an incorrect overprint, or when an intended overprint is omitted, it is listed as an error. An example of an overprint where none was intended is found in the 1886 issue of Dominica, in a sheet of 6-pence green stamps with a "ONE PENNY" overprint made during the revaluing of 1-shilling stamps. Missing overprints occur in many issues, such as the 2-cent value of Liberia, 1904, and in several values of the 1898-1899 issues of Brazil. Here it is necessary to have the error se-tenant with a normal stamp for when separated the error stamp is usually a common value of a previous issue.

An example of the last occurs in the 1880 issue of Cyprus, which was made by overprinting the regular British issue with the word "Cyprus." A se-tenant pair of the 1-penny value, one with overprint missing, is moderately scarce but the error stamp alone is a very cheap British stamp.

A more recent British overprint error occurs in the 1935 Silver Jubilee issue for the British office in the Spanish zone of Morocco. One stamp in the sheet is overprinted "10 centimes" instead of "10 centimos," but the two varieties must be se-tenant or the error becomes a common stamp of the French zone of Southern Morocco.

Occasionally the omission of an overprint produces a rare color error, for some stamps being overprinted are not taken from stock but are specially printed in a color not previously used for the value. When a change in postal rates made a 4-cent value necessary in the Straits Settlements in 1899, a supply was ordered, but without waiting for the plate to be finished, the printers ran off a quantity of 5-cent stamps in the new color selected for the 4-cent value, and overprinted them "Four Cents." This provided a quick stock of 4-cent stamps in the new rose color, but a part sheet without the overprint provides a listing as an error of the 5-cent value.

One of the most peculiar overprint errors occurs in the 1909 issue of the Indian state of Cochin, in a "2" overprint on a 3-pie value. According to Gibbons the No. 7 cliché in the 3-pie plate, of which no printing in red-violet without overprint is known, was inverted and to avoid an inverted overprint, the numeral "2" was inverted in the corresponding position. This produces tête-bêche pairs, with one stamp and its overprint inverted. The invert when detached would become a normal stamp without special value. Both Scott and Gibbons list this value as a single with inverted overprint but do not explain the variety. Perhaps an entire sheet was inverted in printing, which would provide a sheet with two normal copies, the others inverts.

ERRORS IN SEPARATION

Minor errors of separation, as of overprints, usually are treated as varieties, for in plants using perforating machines of various gauges there will sooner or later be cases of wrong use that are of little consequence. The principal errors in separation include the omission of all or part of the perforations in sheets which normally should be perforated. Such errors are chargeable to the machine operator. In harrow perforation the sheet may be misplaced and part of it may be imperforate but there can be no pairs imperforate between unless a row of pins is lost. In comb perforation any row of stamps may be missed and produce several peculiar situations. When the first row at the left, for example, is missed the row will be imperforate except at the right side. When an interior row is missed there will be two vertical rows imperforate between, the left row stamps will be perforated horizontally, and the right row will be perforated only at the right side.

With a single-line perforator of any kind any row or rows may be missed in either direction or the perforations in one direction may be omitted entirely.

The varieties produced with a multiple-line rotary machine are mentioned in chapter 25. In addition the operator may produce oversize panes, and perforate folded sheets to produce freaks with diagonal perforation and an occasional imperforate copy, but there can be no missing line of perforations unless a disk has been removed.

Few varieties are possible with electric-eye perforation. There is no stage when stamps imperforate between can be produced unless one of the two sets of perforators is temporarily out of use during a breakdown or adjustment. Unless partly finished sheets in the machine at the time of breakdown are thrown out by inspectors they may be bound in the books and delivered to post offices.

Sheets may be folded in the packaging operation and the result will be oversize and undersize panes but not errors of perforation. Many varieties of separation are unimportant but stamps with one or more sides perforated with a wrong gauge have considerable interest. The substitution of rouletting for perforating usually attracts more attention than a change in gauge, but such stamps usually are given a new catalog listing.

❖❖❖

VARIETIES

The word *variety* in philately is applied to a stamp differing in some respect from the normal stamp. Since we have an insufficient vocabulary we also use the word in another sense when we speak of a collection or packet of a thousand varieties and mean a thousand all-different stamps.

It is logical to assume that the stamp as first issued is the normal stamp, and that any subsequent deviation is a variety. However, some catalogers maintain the most common of the group is the normal issue and make the first issued stamp a variety of a stamp issued years later. It only causes confusion to find that a stamp which had a whole number in last year's catalog is relegated to a subnumber in this year's catalog and only because more copies of the later issue were printed. Scott's *Standard Catalogue* appears to give the whole number to the stamp first issued.

A collector working with a stamp that can be plated soon comes to the conclusion that all the copies are varieties and that the catalog listing applies only to unsorted stamps.

Varieties which affect a group of stamps are given designations such as "types" or "dies." This is further complicated in

389

some British colonies where "Die A" and "Die B" refer to the original die and a later refined die, while "Die I" and "Die II" differ in some details of the frame. There are two additional varieties of this Die I and in the stamps of Ceylon and other states we find two types of value inscriptions which may apply to any of the four dies.

The use of the word *type* is not restricted to varieties occurring in a number of stamps or issues but sometimes is applied to a single stamp in a sheet; for example, Type I of the 1-cent United States stamp of 1851.

Varieties may occur in any stage of stamp production and include those of design, plate making (covering all types of printing), printing, color and ink, paper, gum, overprintings, separation, and use.

DESIGN VARIETIES

Varieties affecting a plate or several plates, or only a part of a plate, are usually called types or dies and receive numbers or letters in the order of their use. The listing by types may be applied to designs which are identical except for some detail to

FIG. 30-1. How Types Result from Alterations to an Original Die. Two-cent United States stamps of 1894–1898, types I, II, and III.

identify the work of different printers. Examples of design types are found in the United States issue of 1894 with small triangles added in the upper corners to identify the work of the Bureau of Engraving and Printing. These small triangles were changed twice in the 2-cent value and are designated as Types I, II, and III, but remained unchanged in other denominations and are not identified by type.

In the same issue an engraving oversight in the $1 value and a similar oversight in the 10-cent value of 1898 produced a variety of each stamp listed as a second type. The change was not intentional but was due in each case to the omission on a new plate of a minor engraving operation which had been made when the stamp was first issued.

In the 1908-1920 issue of United States stamps changes were made in the dies of the 2-cent and 3-cent values which provide seven types of the 2-cent value and four of the 3-cent. These were premeditated design changes and are true types. Similarly the 2-cent value of the 1923 issue was strengthened at certain points and lines were added in the hair. This is given a type designation although a similar variety in another country might be listed as retouched.

PLATE VARIETIES IN INTAGLIO ENGRAVING

Varieties may originate in the die, the transfer roll, or the plate. Those originating in the die will affect all stamps unless corrected. Retouching or re-engraving a die usually provides a type designation but when the alterations are prominent the stamp may be given a new number in the lists.

Scratches and slight damages on a die may be corrected by erasing or by removal on the transfer roll. Damages on a transfer roll result in the loss or lightening of parts of the design and affect all stamp subjects entered with the damaged relief. When a slight movement occurs during the entering of a relief on a roll, all stamp subjects entered with that relief will show a slight shift. Erasures are sometimes made on a transfer roll to reduce the stamp size and provide more space between subjects. Thus, the United States 1-cent 1851 reliefs were trimmed individually and provide several types from a single die.

In making a plate there are intentional as well as accidental varieties. The intentional include layout lines, plate dots, recutting of frame lines, retouches at weak spots, abnormal engraving to conceal irregular spacing, re-entries to strengthen a weak design, general re-entry to restore a worn plate to serviceable condition, and others.

Unintentional varieties include short-rocked transfers, over-rocked transfers, shifted transfers, misalignment and poor spacing, accidental damages through careless handling of tools, flaws due to bits of metal lodging between transfer roll and plate, cracks developed during hardening of the plate, rolling-mill folds in the plate, rust spots, and others.

Intentional and unintentional varieties are constant and show in all stamps printed after the damage appears, but in varying strength, being affected by plate wear and wiping conditions. Some may be eliminated by erasing or burnishing while others grow stronger as the plate wears.

Some desirable plate varieties show no variation in the design but are important because of the position the subject occupies in the plate. These include the stamps with sheet margins, the corner margins, center lines, perhaps arrows, and imprints and plate numbers. When trimmed close these stamps lose their chief identification and become ordinary copies.

SPECIAL INTAGLIO TERMS AND VARIETIES

Cracked Plates

In steel plates cracks may be caused by too sudden cooling in the hardening process, by curling and straightening in the printing operation, by accidental damage, and by defective material in the plates. Some defects appearing to be cracks are actually roller-mill folds that open up in the printing process. These and genuine cracks print as colored lines in recess printing.

Guide Dots

Small dots on plates or transfer rolls to assist in the correct location of stamp subjects, these may show within the design or at one corner and are useful when plating the stamp position.

Guide Lines

Also called layout lines, these are faint lines drawn on a plate to assist in correct location of stamp subjects, or horizontal and vertical lines engraved to guide a workman when cutting the sheet into panes. Also called center lines, the latter usually end in dots or arrows in the sheet margins. Not all of the second group guide lines were located to show subdivision into panes and some seemingly served no purpose while others on plates for bicolored stamps may have aided in color registry.

Re-engraved

This term usually indicates a general touching-up, strengthening, or restoration of an original die, and the resultant printings are in a new type for stamp collectors. Re-engraving on a stamp plate would produce as many varieties as there are subjects on the plate. When only minor work is done on a die it may be spoken of as retouched, and the resultant stamps are a variety and not a new type.

Re-entry

This term indicates a second application of a transfer roll relief to a stamp subject on a plate. This may be done prior to printing to strengthen a weak subject, or after much printing to restore a worn one. Since it is almost impossible to place the transfer-roll relief in the exact lines of the original entry, the work produces many small shifts or double transfers.

Shift

A variety caused by a movement in position of the die, plate, or transfer roll, while stamp subjects are being transferred from die to roll, or from roll to plate, or are being re-entered.

Shifted Die

This term should apply only to a shift occurring while making a transfer-roll relief from an original die. All stamp subjects entered with such a relief would show identical shifts with thinned lines.

Shifted Transfers

These are caused by a movement in position between the transfer-roll relief and the plate, or by a re-entry, and result in doubled or thickened lines.

Triple Transfer

When three impressions of a line or portions of a design are visible it is an indication that three attempts have been made to locate the transfer-roll relief properly. The examples best known are from re-entered subjects where two attempts were made to fit the relief into a previous subject.

The terms shift, shifted die, shifted transfer, double transfer, and re-entry, are used in philatelic literature without discrimination.

PRINTING VARIETIES IN ENGRAVED STAMPS

Among the varieties noticed by specialists but of little interest to general collectors are stamps printed from plates with too little or too much ink. These may be called sly-wiped when there is too much ink and overwiped when there is too little. When an engraved design is ragged and not completely inked it may be spoken of as a "dry print." The explanation is that these prints were made at the start of the day's work before the plates had been heated enough to make good impressions.

When intaglio plates are not cleaned regularly there is a progressive deterioration in the impressions as the fine lines become filled with dried ink. These plates are warmed to increase the fluidity of the heavy ink, and any ink remaining in the lines bakes until it is almost as hard as the plate. Eventually some lines are filled and cease to print. These varieties are not constant and usually are designated as coming from dirty plates.

Spots and smears are due to defective wiping or to drops of ink that fell on the plate after wiping. An occasional fingerprint is found when the printer has touched the plate with an inky finger. Small bits of waste or paper adhering to the plate or to the paper usually fall off after printing, leaving a colorless spot.

When a plate is not inked completely a sheet may pass into circulation with incomplete stamps along one margin and cases have been noted where the imprint and plate number are missing from this cause.

When an operator placing the wet paper on the plate attempts to relocate a sheet which has already touched there may be light double printing, called "kiss prints."

Wetting and pressing the water out of the paper before printing may produce slight folds that become pleats under pressure. These may not be noticed and may open out later to produce the folded-paper varieties. One interesting copy of the 15-cent 1869 United States stamp shows a fold produced after the vignette was printed. When this stamp was straightened out the vignette became correct in width but the whole stamp was almost one-quarter inch too wide and had a colorless space across the frame design top and bottom.

GENERAL PRINTING VARIETIES

The more important printing varieties, double impressions, printed on the back, and the inverts and omissions of one-color in bicolor printing are classed as errors and were described in the previous chapter. Other varieties common to all types of printing include off-register work in bicolored issues, slight double impressions or kiss or slip prints, prints on folded paper and on paste-ups in web-fed printing. Collectors may like to look upon out-of-register bicolored stamps as errors, and if these are badly off register they may be desirable items for a specialized collection, but they truly belong in the same category as off-center stamps and should have been destroyed as printers' waste.

VARIETIES IN LITHOGRAPHED STAMPS

The section on lithographic printing in chapter 22 explains the transfer process which accounts for many of the minor varieties of lithography. Damages or faults in the original are repeated with each transfer and when the plate is made up of secondary transfers of groups of ten to fifteen subjects, the varieties appear at the same position in each group. Unequal spacing between subjects is very noticeable and often is the clue enabling a collector to determine the size of the secondary transfer.

The minor differences to look for are dots and spots, breaks and damages to lines and letters, misalignment of parts of the design, and similar things of no importance to a printer but valuable when plating. A careless workman often damages the transfers and may lose parts of a design, and when they are patched the workman must be careful to see that lines join correctly or stamps will be found which appear to come from a broken plate.

An example of such minor varieties is found in the 1-cent value of the Guy issue of Newfoundland, 1910. This stamp is listed as having one stamp with the inscription "NFW" instead of "NEW," but this is not the only variety, and it is doubtful if any stamp is completely normal.

Due to the fragile paper used in the transfer process there is always more chance for varieties in lithography than in intaglio work but with the advent of photographic processes the chances for mistakes and inferior work are greatly reduced.

VARIETIES IN TYPOGRAPHED STAMPS

In very early plates made up entirely of typeset clichés it would be remarkable if any two stamp subjects were exactly alike. Wrong-font letters and differences in spacing between letters and lines and border arrangements enable collectors to identify the various clichés. When a single typeset form was reproduced by stereotyping or electrotyping, the varieties were greatly reduced, but often the workman finishing the clichés was careless in trimming the cuts or in routing out the nonprinting spaces and so provided minor varieties.

Photoengraving has reduced the number of varieties still more but it is possible to find small differences between subjects due to a tiny flaw in the sensitized emulsion or to unequal etching at various places.

Although printing starts with a perfect plate it still is possible for varieties to appear. Careless handling will result in broken letters or lines, or flattened spaces, etc. After excessive use the impression will become coarser and coarser as the raised portions are worn down, for these are pyramidal in section, increasing in width in the downward direction. In typography the impressions from a worn plate become stronger as the plate wears, just the reverse of the condition in intaglio printing. In addition, in typography the lines and lettering lose their precise character and become irregular due to the acid etching.

No entire plate has ever been made up of typeset clichés without a few mistakes. It requires more than human accuracy to cut rules for the cliché frames that will join alike at all corners. Within the frame are various lines of type which should be identical in type, spaces, and in all measurements. Assuming that fifty to a hundred clichés have been set in identical form without any wrong-font letters or the like, it becomes a difficult task to lock these in a form so that the pressure is equally distributed throughout without bending any frames or pushing any corners out of line. Unless the form is locked up perfectly some of the very small type such as periods, commas, and small spaces will loosen and fall out when the form is cleaned between printings. If these characters and spaces are not restored to the proper places the entire form will lose its rigidity and all sorts of varieties will appear. In many cases the lost type is replaced inverted or sideways or even wrong end up, producing varieties that enable a collector to distinguish the original from a later printing.

Varieties Resulting from Careless Press Feeding

The use of wrong paper or the wrong use of special paper produces errors. (Page 385) Careless press feeding of paper with a directional watermark may produce eight varieties of the watermark, none very important unless they indicate a special use for the paper, as for booklets or coils.

❖❖

ESSAYS, PROOFS, SPECIAL PRINTINGS, FORGERIES

ESSAYS

Essays are printed designs in stamp size which have been submitted to postal authorities but not used, or have been prepared for use but never issued. The term does not include designs or models of large size or hand-drawn designs of stamp size.

Essays usually originate when a country asks for designs for a new stamp or series. The most useful are produced by engraving or photoengraving methods. Competing engraving companies may submit designs complete as to color, perforations, and gum. The selected design may go through the entire preparatory process and be rejected at the last minute, even after printing has started. Should an alteration be made, the rejected design becomes an essay although for a time it appeared to be the final design. In such a case there probably are die proofs and even plate proofs, but all are essay proofs.

Essays are of interest to specialists as they often show the sources of designs of issued stamps. Many of them embody ideas in design, use, and cancellation that have not been tried in any country. They are not included in any ordinary catalog of a

398

country's stamps but are found in special lists devoted to this and similar subjects. They may be very numerous and many cannot be tied in to any particular issue or series unless a record was made at the time.

ORIGINAL DRAWINGS AND MODELS

Although these seem to be outside the scope of a stamp collection numerous examples find their way out of official files and into one or more of the large specialized collections. These items are unique and their presence in a collection indicates laxity at some point.

Original drawings may be in any medium and may be in the size of the finished stamp but today it is common to make them at a larger size and reduce them by photography.

Models usually are designs made up of portions of photographs, original drawings, and the like. The designs for many values of the presidential issue of 1938 were prepared in model form using portions of some previous design with a photograph of the proper president and new hand-drawn value labels, etc. While some models may be in stamp size, many are several times larger.

PROOFS

Proofs are impressions taken from dies and plates during preparations for a stamp issue to check the work. Those taken at intervals while engraving a steel die or a wood block often are called progress proofs.

In intaglio engraving proofs may be taken from the die, the transfer roll, and the plate, at any time that seems desirable. Often a series of stamps has a common frame and various vignettes. After the dies of each have been approved from proofs, master dies will be made by transferring the frame and proper vignette to a new die block, and proofs will be taken for the final approval.

When designs are being transferred to a lithographic plate, proofs may be taken at various stages just as for engraved issues, and in letterpress or typography there will be proofs of line cuts or stereos or electros, as well as of the assembled portions.

Progress and finished die and plate proofs add interest to a specialized study of a stamp for they show an ideal picture of the design, a condition seldom realized in the issued stamps. The proofs of some countries are easy to obtain and it is evident that an edition is being printed for sale to collectors, but those of some other countries and private engraving firms are nonexistent for all practical purposes.

The paper used for engraved proofs is generally a fine un-sized variety made for the purpose, one being called India. It is a fragile waterleaf with remarkable qualities for taking a superior impression.

Die proofs are usually printed on sheets larger than the die block and unless trimmed will show a plate mark at the margins of the die just as do etchings and engravings. Some die proofs are mounted on cardboard and have an imprint or number or other identification.

Die proofs of bicolored issues should have the two colors printed in proper relation on the proof sheet but some are hybrid proofs made by pasting a trimmed proof of the vignette upon a proof of the frame. One group of United States proofs listed as small die proofs actually consists of reprint proofs struck off at a later date.

Die proofs may be made in various colors to aid in selecting one for the final printing and these are made from a finished die. Nearly all progress proofs are in black unless the stamp color has been selected in advance.

Transfer-roll proofs appear to be a recent addition to this group, and all seen have been impressed without color in a dark red fiberboard and exactly duplicate the original die. They have been rocked in on the fiber just as the finished transfer rocks in designs on a steel plate. The proofs may have been made to check the condition of the roll before hardening. Since a transfer to a steel plate could not be made with an unhardened roll, the fiberboard was substituted.

Plate proofs are prints taken from a plate or any part of it at any stage of manufacture or upon completion. Originally they were made to prove the correctness of the plate but now some are being made to sell to collectors. When a proof sheet shows faint impressions or defects, further work on the plate is indicated.

A plate proof of a scarce stamp printed in the actual color of the stamp may be a source of trouble, for the proof paper can be backed up to proper thickness and sold as a genuine stamp. This fraud can be detected with black light or an x-ray photograph for any added paper or glue will be evident.

Plate proofs are also printed on fine cardboard and these may be thinned down, gummed and perforated if required, and passed off as unused stamps.

Hybrid proofs are India plate proofs trimmed to the edge of the stamp design and mounted on cards to simulate large die proofs. A strong magnifier may be needed to detect the edges of the trimmed proof.

Plate proofs in colors other than those selected or approved are known as trial color proofs. Proofs are cataloged in specialized lists and in the case of United States proofs each is given the catalog number of the corresponding stamp followed by the suffix letter P.

SPECIMEN STAMPS

Stamps overprinted, handstamped, or punched with the word "Specimen" (or foreign equivalents: Spanish, "Muestra," Italian "Saggio," German, "Muster") are theoretically actual postage stamps marked for some reason to prevent their use for postage.

The earliest record of the overprint is on 1-penny and 2-pence British newspaper wrappers that replaced the Mulready envelopes in April 1841. Later the 1-shilling green stamp of Great Britain of 1847 was overprinted "Specimen" in red and in green.

The United States has placed "Specimen" overprints on

nearly all issues from 1851 until 1904, and on special delivery and postage due stamps. Those on the department stamps are in a special class and are described on page 404. They were not actual stamps overprinted for a special purpose, but special printings on which the word acted as a cancellation.

There was also a set of specimen stamps of the newspaper and periodical issues, and many revenue stamps from 1862 to 1898 received the overprint. When the Universal Postal Union met in Washington in 1897, the current postage, postage due, special delivery, and newspaper issues were overprinted "Universal Postal Union" in blue, and distributed to the delegates.

The second convention of the union in Paris in 1878 ruled that each country should send three copies of every stamp in use to every signatory country for reference purposes. In 1891 the number of copies was raised to five but in 1906 was again fixed at three. This regulation does not require a special marking on the stamps but some countries, particularly those of the British Commonwealth, mark their examples "Specimen."

Other specimen stamps have been made to compare the work of different printers or as examples on which a printer should submit a bid, or as samples submitted by printers for approval.

Specimen stamps are not plentiful but they sell at only a fraction of the price of unmarked stamps and this enables some collectors to complete their sets with high-denomination stamps. They suffer a loss in value for they are neither mint nor cancelled but simply invalidated.

Specimen stamps are highly desirable to a specialist as they usually are the first printing and show the original color. In at least one case a specimen stamp is the only visible reminder of a stamp printed but not placed on sale. When the universal color scheme was adopted for British colonies in 1912, a shipment of 5- and 10-shilling stamps was delivered to the Gold Coast, and specimen copies were delivered to the Universal Postal Union. These values were to be placed on sale in the Gold Coast as soon as existing stocks were used up. Meanwhile George V succeeded to the throne and new stamps were ordered for all colonies. The 5-shilling stamps were used up in the Gold Coast and the new universal color stamps went on sale, but almost at once the new George V stamps arrived and replaced all the old stamps. Thus, the 10-shilling value did not go on sale and exists in specimen form only.

Certain South Australian stamps of high value were over-printed "Specimen" to destroy their postal validity, and with reprinted obsolete stamps and cancelled-to-order low values were sold in sets to collectors. These and other specimen stamps are acceptable as space fillers only if they are genuine stamps which have been demonetized by the overprint. The United States department stamps mentioned earlier should not be used as space fillers because they differ from the stamps as issued.

SAMPLE, AND SAMPLE-A STAMPS

These overprints were placed on United States stamps in 1889 to identify suggested colors when the Post Office Department was soliciting bids on a new issue. Lists and sample stamps were furnished to all bidders. List A indicated the colors to be used if the current large stamps were continued and the sample stamps were marked "Sample." List B indicated the colors if smaller stamps were adopted and the accompanying stamps were marked "Sample A."

The smaller stamps were adopted and began to appear February 22, 1890, but not all values were in the colors suggested in List B.

SPECIAL PRINTINGS

The term *special printings* has been applied particularly to the stamps provided by the Post Office Department for the Centennial Exposition in Philadelphia, 1876. It was the intention to make all postage stamps of the United States available to stamp collectors, but this idea was followed for designs only, without regard for color variations, grills, gum, or perforations, or for any marks placed on dies for identification.

This was a most flagrant example of making stamps to sell to collectors and so few were sold that the government lost money, but the few purchasers ultimately owned a valuable asset. The stamps were placed on sale February 23, 1875, and with additional items remained available until July 15, 1884. The original notice listed the various items and explained their availability to pay postage. Included were the postage issues of 1847, 1851, 1861, 1869, and 1870, the official stamps of all departments, and the newspaper and periodical stamps of 1865 and 1874.

The notice stated that the first two issues were obsolete and not good for postage, but that other regular issues would be accepted. Since the official stamps were valid only on official mail these would be overprinted "Specimen" to prevent misuse. It stated also that the newspaper stamps of 1865 were obsolete and that the issue of 1874 could be used only by publishers and news vendors on bulk mail.

The stamps were to be sold without gum and in sets only, at face value, with the exception that the stamps of the State Department could be purchased as a set up to the 90-cent value, and that the dollar values could be purchased with the set or singly as desired.

These special printings were made by the Continental Bank Note Company, the current printer of stamps. The series of 1847 required new dies and the issue is listed as a "government imitation," that is, an official counterfeit. They are ungummed and on thin bluish paper.

New plates from the original dies were made for some values of the 1851 series and while these duplicate the originals in most respects, the spacing differs and the designs are complete, whereas in the original issue the designs of some values were trimmed. These stamps, which are listed as "reprints," are printed on hard white paper and are without gum. They are perforated 12, although the originals were imperforate or perforated 15.

The 1861 series, which in this printing includes all values

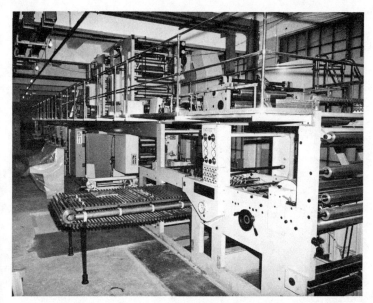

XXVI. Above, web 8-color gravure/intaglio press. This is a web-fed press but it sheets out the printed product at the end shown in this photo, with the sheet delivery being the small side segment at near left. First issued stamp produced on this press was the Currier scene, Christmas 1976. Below, a web-fed 3-color intaglio press, also seen from the delivery end but with printed roll rewind instead of sheet delivery. (Courtesy U. S. Bureau of Engraving and Printing.)

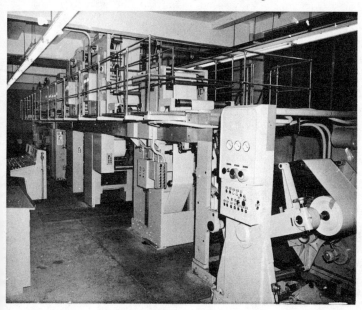

XXVII (above). Some designs in United Nations stamps. (U.N. Postal Administration.) XXVIII (below). The famous "Bull's Eye" of Brazil. First stamp of the Americas. (Newbury Collection.) Bottom: XXIX (left). Part perforate and imperforate errors of Canada, 1927-1928. (Marshall Field & Co. Stamp Section.) XXX (right). A rare used French error, printed on both sides. The used stamp is the 25 c. of the first issue. The stamps printed on the back are the 20 c. of the same issue which was not placed in use. Four of the stamps showing in part on the back are "tête-bêche" in both directions while the fifth impression is at a right angle to the others. Probably from a makeready sheet. (Courtesy Elmer Stuart.)

up to 1869, was made from the original plates but with little regard to matching colors. They are called "reissues" and contrary to the original notice, were issued with white crackly gum.

In the 1869 issue new plates were made for the 1-cent and 15-cent values, and for the latter value the new frame plate does not correspond to either of the types used for the issued stamps and provides Type III in this value. These stamps also are "reissues" and have white crackly gum.

The 1870 series was printed from the plates which were in current use for the general issue of stamps and they are listed as "special printings." The designs show the identifying marks by which we distinguish the work of the Continental company and are without gum.

The group of stamps as first offered for sale had a face value of $264.87 of which only $5.85 was in stamps that could be used by the public. Sales were so small that there was little excuse for expanding the series but all issues up to 1884 were eventually issued.

Soon after the official notice appeared the Eagle and Franklin carriers were added, the latter imperforate and the former both imperforate and perforated. A little later, in 1875, the 2-cent and 5-cent regular postage series, the former a new color and the latter a new value, were available as special printings almost at the time they appeared as regular stamps.

In 1879 the American Bank Note Company, into which the Continental company had been merged, issued the new postage due series as a special printing, and in the following year issued the current postage series as well and added the Registered Letter seal of 1872, which had been overlooked in the initial group. A special printing was also made of the 1-cent stamp of 1869 with and without gum, and of the 1-cent values of several department stamps without gum, the latter being overprinted "Specimen" for good measure.

From 1880 through 1883 special printings were made of all new designs, but the re-engraved values of 1881 were not included.

All special printings, except where noted, were perforated
12. Those printed by the Continental company were on hard
white paper and usually were separated for sale by cutting with
scissors, thus aiding in their identification but usually mutilating
the stamps to some extent. Those of the American company
were on soft porous paper and all were without gum except the
2-cent red-brown of 1883 and a part of the 1-cent 1869 issue.

The special printings of stamps in current use seem to have
had the least sale, probably because they were considered duplicates of ordinary stamps. The principal rarities are the 2- and
5-cent values of 1875 and 1880 and the 4- and 5-cent values
issued after 1880.

Although some of the special printings of the Continental
company must have been used for postage by design or accident,
only a single copy has been found on cover and that was discovered after 1952. The only copy a collector may have hopes
of finding in used condition is the 1880 special printing of the
1-cent 1869 on soft paper.

THE FARLEY FAVORS, OR FARLEY FOLLIES

At the initial printing of various commemorative stamps
issued during the time of Postmaster General James A. Farley,
that official presented full sheets of unfinished stamps to President Franklin D. Roosevelt and prominent officials.

These sheets had aroused considerable unfavorable comment in the philatelic press but when they began to appear on
the market the matter came to a head and members of Congress
were asked to investigate. An inquiry was stifled by the administration but the publicity was sufficient to cause postal authorities
to order a sale of similar items to collectors and others who
might desire them.

Twenty varieties were included in this special printing but
it has not been determined that the complete list of Farley gifts
was fully covered. Two items were issued without gum but
perforated, while all others were ungummed and imperforate.

Since considerable time had elapsed since some of the stamps were first printed the color matching was not perfect.

The announcement of the special printing was made February 7, 1935, with supplementary details February 12, and the stamps were placed on sale at the Philatelic Agency on March 15, in full sheets and in blocks of four, with the sale continuing until June 15, 1935.

Rumors were current that at least three additional stamps, the Byrd in imperforate form, the Maryland stamp, and the 50-cent Graf Zeppelin, should have been included. It also was rumored that some gift sheets of the Newburgh stamps had been perforated 11 by 11 instead of the 10½ by 11 gauge customarily used for rotary-press stamps. None of these questions has been resolved to this day. This matter was further complicated by the offer of the Bureau of Engraving and Printing to apply gum to any imperforate sheets which might be sent in for that purpose.

The special printing temporarily quieted the criticism but accomplished nothing more than to provide collectors with another series. Eventually most of the presentation sheets will reach the market and will be recognized by the autographs and salutations which they bear. If broken up into small lots the sellers will identify each by photography and provide affidavits of authenticity, as was the case when fragments of the Roosevelt collection were sold.

The Smithsonian Institution announced in January, 1956, that former Postmaster General James A. Farley had loaned his private collection to the philatelic section. This includes his set of the autographed presentation sheets which are said to be the second of five sets presented to President Roosevelt and others. Collectors will now have a chance to examine the stamps and not rely on reports.

A BRITISH SPECIAL PRINTING

The 1-penny red stamp of Great Britain, in the re-engraved type of 1854-1857, plate No. 66, was printed in black at the request of Queen Victoria it is said, since she was desirous of giving some "Penny Blacks" to the royal children. The type is not identical with the original Penny Black and should be called a special printing rather than a "royal reprint" as it has been dubbed.

REMAINDERS

These may be described as stocks of stamps on hand when a government decides to replace the current stamps with a new issue. There is little excuse for not using up the stamps unless the political administration of the country has changed to such an extent that the new regime will permit no reminder of the old to remain. A new government with any thought of economy will continue the use of the old stamps or overprint them in some cases, but some have profited by selling them to stamp dealers. When states have been absorbed it is usual to designate a period for the use of current stamps or even to allow them to be used until the supply is exhausted.

The remainders we know are those that have reached the stamp market but there are untold numbers of obsolete stamps in the postal vaults of many countries. Chances are, they will ultimately be destroyed. On several occasions early issues of various countries have been salvaged just as they were about to become waste paper.

Remainders are sold, as a rule, at some fixed price per thousand, or at a small fraction of face value, but in the case of old and more valuable issues the price may bear some relation to market values. When a country decides to sell remainders its first step is to demonetize the issue, preventing future use for postage. The sales often are advertised and sometimes are public auctions, and each time this has occurred the articulate collectors waste their time and energy bemoaning the low state to which philately has fallen.

When the number of remainders is moderate they will be absorbed within a short time and may benefit philately. It should always be remembered that they are actual original stamps and cannot be distinguished from those sold across the post-office counter one year or twenty years before.

In connection with a group of remainders which did not reach the stamp market, this story was told to the writer by Thomas G. Evans, a member of the Chicago Philatelic Society who had lived in the Cape of Good Hope for several years around 1890 before coming to America and Chicago. Mr. Evans worked in the Cape but had his evenings for recreation and, next to collecting stamps, one of his more pleasant avocations was walking with a clerk of the Cape Town post office. Mr. Evans collected under the theory that the labels did not become stamps until they had done postal duty and had received a good blow from some handstamp. When his friend learned that he saved stamps she invited him to look at some of the old triangular stamps at the office. Tom was not thinking clearly when he agreed to look at them and should have realized that they would be unused. When she brought out a package and opened it, he said, "But you know I don't collect that kind of stamps, for they are unused." She told him that there were other values and colors in addition to these 1-shilling green stamps, but Tom stuck to his collecting principles and the package went back into storage. By 1915 he was collecting unused stamps along with the used, and may have regretted his earlier action. But a sheet of 1-shilling stamps would have amounted to a lot of money and Tom was only a young Welsh laborer in the Cape.

Some remainders have been marked to indicate their true character. Among these are the St. Helena stamps with a cancellation in the form of a purple diamond grid, the Mauritius issues of 1863-1867 overprinted with the word "Cancelled," the Spanish issues overprinted with thick bars or perforated with a large hole, and the El Salvador stamps of 1899-1900 overprinted with a Catherine wheel rosette to distinguish bona fide stamps from remainders in the printers' hands.

REPRINTS

These are impressions of obsolete stamps printed from the original plates or lithographic stones. Loosely speaking, or perhaps through lack of a better term, the word is also applied to stamps printed from new plates made from the original dies.

Those made by government authority may be called "official," or "government reprints," while those made by persons who have acquired the plates, or by printers who have retained the plates after completing a contract, may be called "private reprints," or just "reprints."

In almost every case reprints differ from the originals in one or more or all of the elements of paper, color, gum, or perforation. In a very few cases these details have been followed so carefully or imitated so successfully that only an expert on the particular stamps can distinguish reprints from originals.

The Scott *Standard Catalogue* has a great many notes to describe the reprints of various issues, giving the characteristics as compared with those of the original stamps. These help an amateur very little for usually he has but a single stamp and cannot make a comparison. When the note states that the paper is whiter, or the color brighter, or the gum whiter, he is hardly helped. A difference in perforations or the lack of a watermark will help him more, but the presence or absence of gum is inconclusive.

Government reprints probably have not been made to deceive collectors, and while those made privately are for sale to collectors, they first were handled as reprints and not as original stamps. The danger lies in future sales, for all persons handling the stamps may not be ethical. When the reprints are found in old collections the new owners may honestly believe they are originals and sell them as such.

The stamp being obsolete and demonetized, its reprint's sale price should not be governed by the face value. Reprints have enabled some collectors to fill spaces at nominal cost that would remain vacant forever if original stamps had to be purchased, but today it is likely that the average collector would prefer a vacant space to such a substitute. Philately would be best served if all stamps reprinted from the original plates were indelibly marked to prevent confusion with the originals. Thus, when Bogert and Durbin reprinted the Providence, Rhode Island, postmaster's provisional, they printed the backs of the sheets with the firm name so that one letter appears upon each of the twelve stamps.

At one time South Australia operated an agency for the sale of stamps to collectors and practically all issues were available and on sale at a price of one pound per set. The obsolete issues were new prints on special watermarked paper and all were overprinted "Reprint." The current low-value stamps were cancelled to order and the current high-value stamps were overprinted "Specimen."

Unfortunately the word *reprint* is often applied to stamps which at best are imitations or counterfeits, but this misuse originates with stamp dealers and is a matter for them to correct.

SEEBECKS

In 1889, Nicholas Frederick Seebeck, president of the Hamilton Bank Note Company of New York, contracted with Nicaragua and El Salvador, and a little later with Honduras and Ecuador, to furnish each country with a complete supply of stamps each year in return for certain concessions. Each country agreed to demonetize the current issue and to return all unsold stamps to Seebeck upon receipt of the new annual issue, and to allow Seebeck to retain the plates and to make reprints for collectors.

The contracts with Nicaragua and El Salvador were for ten years and covered the stamps of the former from 1890-1899, those of the latter to 1898. Honduras received supplies until 1895, and Ecuador from 1892 until 1896. Official and postage due stamps were provided as well as the regular postage series.

At the end of each year Seebeck was in possession of remainders which were actual stamps although demonetized, and he had the authority to print additional copies for collectors. As long as the original paper stock lasted no one could distinguish between remainders and reprints. Only when new paper was used could they be easily detected, although as time passed the printings by him or the later owners of the plates showed variations in color.

This whole mixture of remainders and reprints received a bad reputation. The plates were in use over such a long period that the market was always glutted and the entire group of stamps was to be found in every 10,000-variety collection. Except for a few varieties which must have missed extensive reprinting, perhaps through loss or destruction of the plates, the values shrunk to the lowest figure allowed in a catalog, but in recent years there has been a tendency for the prices to advance.

In addition to remainders and reprints the Seebeck sets sometimes contain a few stamps which at best are essays. These include an 1895 issue of El Salvador showing the portrait of Antonio Ezeta, brother of the president, General Carlos Ezeta, which had been printed but not delivered when Ezeta was deposed. Rather than endure a year of stamps with an Ezeta portrait the printer was authorized to overprint the entire issue with the country's coat of arms. Occasionally copies are found showing the portrait. This condition may be charged to some new printer who neglected the overprint. These Ezeta stamps would be essays, perhaps, in a specialized collection of El Salvador.

In 1952 the Seebeck plates and other materials of the Nicaraguan stamps were discovered in the effects of the Security Bank Note Company of New York, successor to the Hamilton Bank Note Company. An official representing the government of Nicaragua was present at the cancellation or destruction of the plates, dies, and transfer rolls. The discovery makes it apparent that the stamps of Nicaragua were reprinted only by the bank-note companies and not by private firms. There have been rumors of Swiss reprintings, but it is probable that the great supplies made by Seebeck have lasted through these many years.

The Seebeck reprints usually appear on rather soft paper which shows a strong mesh or sieve effect on a look-through examination. However, some varieties are recorded on thin hard paper in shades varying from those of the original stamps.

PHANTOMS, OR BOGUS STAMPS

Every collector will acquire labels that appear to be postage stamps so far as inscriptions and value are concerned but cannot be located in catalogs or lists. Some believe that they have rarities too scarce to be listed. These are the phantoms of philately. They are bogus stamps of a phantom country, or in a few cases of an existing country, and nearly all were made to sell to collectors.

The old stand-bys of early collecting may be found even now and appear to outwear many genuine stamps. According to Fred Melville, phantoms were written up in 1862 when Dr. John Edward Gray, of the British Museum, exposed certain French, Turkish, and Chinese issues as being only pretended stamps.

His examples include a French stamp with the inscription "Essai 1858," portraying the head of Ceres, the symbol of the republic. This could not have been genuine as France was an empire under Napoleon III. The Turkish stamps must have been fraudulent for that country did not issue stamps until 1863, and the values shown as 6-truze and 3-mara are currency units which do not appear to have been used at any time. The so-called Chinese issues were only impressions of a mandarin's seal and in no sense postage stamps.

The well-known phantoms of the nineteenth century include those of Sedang, Trinidad, Franz Joseph Land, Brunei, the Torres-Straits Settlements of Australia, Moresnet, and others. Near the end of the century the Clipperton Island issues appeared and perhaps a little earlier collectors had the bogus newspaper stamps of Bolivia. Following the Civil War there were numerous bogus Confederate postmasters' provisionals and a blockade stamp which proved difficult to suppress.

Sedang

The stamps of Sedang were prepared about 1889 by M. O.
de Mayrena, a French officer of the Corps de Guides, who had
gone deep into Indo-China and after marrying the daughter of a
principal chief, soon announced that he had been crowned king.
His stamps were similar in design to those of Hong Kong, and
had a coat of arms crowned, in a rectangular panel, with the
word "Deh" at the left and "Sedang" at the right, with the value
at top and bottom in numerals and words. The set contained
½-, 1-, 2-, and 4-math, 1-monk, and ½- and 1-dollar values.
Mayrena issued several decrees under the title Marie, Roi de
Sedangs, and had a Paris postal agent through whom thousands
of sets of his stamps were sold.

Trinidad

The stamps of this minute "principality" were produced by
J. A. Harden-Hickey, a Frenchman who started round the
world in a British merchant vessel in 1885 and went ashore on
the island of Trinidad when the ship took shelter there during
a storm. He took possession of the island, located about 700
miles east-northeast of Rio de Janeiro, raised a flag, and pro-
claimed himself Prince of Trinidad. Later in Paris, he married
a wealthy American and addressed a proclamation concerning
his principality to the various world powers. In 1894 he issued
stamps in 5-, 10-, 25-, 50-, and 75-centime and 1- and 5-franc
values, and various items of postal stationery. The following
year the British took over the island as a cable station. The
stamps show a view of the island and have the inscription "Principaute de Trinidad" at the top.

Franz Joseph Land

This region enjoyed more than one phantom set and the designers favored one nation after another. One triangular set is
copied from the famous Cape design. This has "Cap Pest" at
the left, "1872-77" at the right, and "Franz Joseph Land" at

the bottom. Another set is rectangular and bears the portrait of Emperor Franz Josef of Austria, with "Franz Joseph Land" at the top, "Er.M.d.N.P.E. 1874" at the bottom, small armorial bearings in the upper corners and the letters "W" and "B" in the lower left and lower right corners respectively.

Brunei

These phantoms long preceded any genuine stamps from that land and certainly were made to sell to collectors.

Torres-Straits Settlements—Australia

The stamps bearing those inscriptions and showing two mountain peaks with value numerals above and value numerals and currency below were another set designed for the philatelic market.

Moresnet

One bogus issue was specifically prepared to trap a publisher. It appears to come from Moresnet, a bit of land four miles southwest of Aix-la-Chapelle, between Belgium and Prussia in early days, and known as neutral land. J. B. Moens, a Belgian stamp dealer and publisher of *Le Timbre Poste,* long desirous of getting even with a rival who used his news items without credit, prepared the Moresnet stamps and on April 1, 1867, broke the news story with illustrations of them. The printers of these stamps were identified as Messrs. De Visch and Lirva. The other publisher fell into the trap and built up the story of this new stamp-issuing country, and in May, 1867, Moens revealed that if the victim would translate De Visch into French and reverse the spelling of Lirva the result would be Poisson d'Avril, the French equivalent of April Fool.

Clipperton Island

Several designs were made for this island in the Pacific Ocean but all noted show a map and the date "1895," with birds and lobsters usually added as decorations. The Oceanic

Phosphate Company had a guano concession on the island and someone in that concern had the stamps made in San Francisco. Cancelled copies show part of the name of a San Francisco company. Collectors were warned against this bogus issue in the philatelic press of June, 1895, almost as soon as the stamps appeared.

Confederate Provisionals and Blockade Postage

The confusion which existed concerning the postmasters' provisionals and other Confederate stamps after the Civil War aided the bogus stamp-maker but eventually these issues were weeded out. In 1864 two stamps appeared which purported to be for use on letters to be sent through the Union blockade of southern ports. A 40-cent green stamp was inscribed "Blockade Postge to West Indies," and a $1 blue stamp, "Blockade Postge to Europe." Cancelled copies bear Mobile and Charleston postmarks. Within a short time the spelling error in "Postage" was corrected and the stamps appeared in five colors.

Other phantoms of the Confederacy include issues for Richmond, Virginia, the capital, and for Charleston, South Carolina.

Mormon Stamps

Some of the most controversial phantoms of the United States area were attributed to the Mormon colony in Utah Territory. One issue was in vertical rectangular form with clipped corners in 2-, 5-, and 8-cent denominations, with a portrait of Brigham Young inside a frame with the inscription "Utah" at the top, "Postage" at the bottom, the value in words at the left and the word "Cents" at the right.

Another Mormon design also shows the portrait of Brigham Young, with "Utah Terr." at the top, "Postage Five Cents" at the bottom, and a numeral in each lower corner, and is printed in black on yellow surface-colored paper. Many stories were written to prove the stamps genuine, and as many to show that they were bogus. The matter remained unsettled for years in spite of the fact that Brigham Young in 1864 wrote a letter denying that he had issued "nor so much as thought of issuing a postage stamp."

Spitzbergen

Stamps provided for service from Spitzbergen may merit a classification as a private local issue. The island hotel was patronized by invalids whose recovery was hastened by the extremely cold climate and the master of the vessel which plied between Norway and the island provided these stamps for letters mailed home by the hotel patrons. The two stamps pictured a hunter shooting a polar bear. Although they were suppressed as soon as seen by the postal authorities of Norway, they were available for years at the hotel as souvenirs.

North Pole Post

At the time of the Cook-Peary controversy over the discovery of the North Pole, some joker issued three stamps to cover the event. They were in large commemorative size in a format suggestive of the Hudson-Fulton celebration stamp. They are inscribed "North Pole Post" and have scenes of that region. The 1-tusk value is marked "Peary Land," the 2-bones value, "Cook Land," and the 5-skins value, "Nobody's Land."

BOGUS LOCALS AND CARRIERS

Local issues also have had their phantoms, among them the Bancroft City Express, of Montreal, and McGreely's Express—Dyea and Skagway. The latter was gotten out by S. C. Marcuse, owner of an express route, and pictured a dog-sled operation. It is said that Marcuse made no attempt to use the stamps on any letters which he carried, and that he did not operate any dog sleds.

KENYON'S ARMY FRANKS

About the time of the Spanish-American War three identical labels appeared printed in brown, blue, and red. The design is somewhat like that of the United States 10-cent stamp of

1869 with a shield topped by an eagle. The inscription "Army Frank" crosses the shield and "Official Business" appears below.

Major Brewster C. Kenyon of the United States Army produced these labels and seriously tried to have their use approved. However, on September 15, 1898, Third Assistant Postmaster General John A. Merritt refused to approve them, stating that they had been issued without permission and were wholly unnecessary as penalty envelopes were provided for all departments.

Major Kenyon is said to have been a stamp collector, and it has been told that he issued the labels to sell to collectors. On one occasion a set was offered at auction and through rigged bidding was run up to about twenty dollars before being knocked down to a venturesome collector.

MORE RECENT PHANTOMS

A spurious issue of Azerbaijan in values up to fifty rubles has "Republique d'Azerbaijan" at the right, an inscription in Cyrillic letters at the left, and a portrait of a bearded man. All genuine stamps of this country have inscriptions in French and Arabic, or in Arabic and Cyrillic.

Stamps which seem to be those of the Ukraine after 1919 are not genuine issues but were either of private origin or were never placed on sale in the country and cannot be better than essays.

A phantom issue for South Russia copies the ruble design of the Deniken issue except that small rosettes replace the numerals of value at the sides.

Recently a set of stamps inscribed "Gorny Slask" and listed for the Polish occupation of Upper Silesia was removed from the catalog as being of private origin. A large number of spurious stamps are now pictured in Scott's *Standard Catalogue*. They are in boxes with notations in many cases that they are not recognized as having been issued primarily for postal purposes.

Labels passing as stamps of Greenland show arctic scenes and bear the inscription "1910 Thule 1935," or "1936."

A more recent stamp which has come to be classed as a phantom is the $1 Wayzata air-mail issue of Newfoundland. This was printed in the United States for use on a 1932 flight from Wayzata, Minnesota, to Newfoundland and thence to Europe. When the flight was abandoned the Newfoundland post office notified purchasers of the stamps to return them for a full refund. Many were not returned. After Newfoundland united with Canada, April 1, 1949, her stamps became valid for postage throughout Canada for a limited period. Some holders of the Wayzata stamps then undertook to have them used on mail. Although they had no status, not every Canadian postal clerk was familiar with all Newfoundland issues, and a few slipped through and were delivered. Many were intercepted in the mail and sent to the dead-letter office. The accidental use of the stamps does not give them any official status.

Several sets of labels which have reached the market since World War II are not stamps at all. None have seen legitimate postal service in the countries they purport to serve, and all seem to have been made for collectors. One group passes for stamps of Free Croatia, having a set inscribed "N.D. Hrvatska 1874-1949 U.P.U.," with flowers and birds, and there are triangular sets, one showing flowers, for ordinary postal use, another with birds for air mail.

There are prolific issues for the Republic of the South Moluccas, inscribed "Republik Maluku Selatan." This region supposedly is in revolt against the Republic of Indonesia, and its agents in foreign lands made arrangements with a wholesale stamp dealer to prepare and market the stamps.

Numerous Spanish issues have been pronounced as bogus. These include Zaragoza charity labels, Iberian air-mail stamps, telegraph commemoratives, rural mail carriers, and others.

Stamps supposedly for Free India inscribed "Azud Hind" were not used in India and are phantoms. It has been said that they were prepared for use in the event of an Axis occupation of southern Asia.

CURRENT LOCALS

The local issues of Lundy Island and Herm Island originate in actual places but serve only the vanity of the islands' owners. There is no need for the issues and they are not honored except to carry the owners' mail to the English mainland, where regular British stamps must be affixed if the letters are to enter the post. Both of these locals reach the hands of stamp dealers in mint or cancelled form, in quantity, as soon as they are printed.

The three or more locals presently in use in the United States serve no purpose and the envelopes upon which they are affixed might as well be marked with an "X," for they must have United States stamps before they can be delivered.

FREE LABELS

An issue of Free labels during World War II may someday be classed as phantoms, for they were stopped by an arbitrary ruling of United States Postal authorities. The idea was suggested by Leon B. Noory, a cadet in the Advanced Flying School at Albuquerque, New Mexico, and taken to Babcock and Borough, printers of that city. Mr. Borough made a design and printed the labels in sheets of fifty, in blue and red. The blue portion shows tanks, destroyers, and airplanes with a soldier in the foreground. The red portion consists of the word "Free."

They were sold to army posts at seven cents per sheet, of which two cents was paid to Cadet Noory. Soldiers were glad to pay ten cents per sheet and their use spread throughout the nearby army posts. On April 25, 1942, the postal authorities denied a request for clearance to sell them throughout the army and navy camps, on the ground that they did not conform to Order No. 17352, regulating free mailing by members of the armed forces, and contemplating that the word "Free" should be written by the mailer. It was suggested that Babcock and Borough refrain from promoting the use of the labels.

The ruling was arbitrary, inasmuch as the act for free mail said nothing about writing the word by hand, and as a matter of fact it was printed on the envelopes provided by various welfare and social organizations. It is of interest that the officials did' not order the use of the stickers discontinued, but suggested that their use be not promoted.

NONPOSTAL LABELS

Some labels in packets or in older collections confuse beginners although there has been no attempt to sell them as postage stamps. One German set appears to be mourning labels, for the stamps show the flag at half-mast and each is inscribed with the name of a German colony. Another single stamp, bearing the word "Soumi" on the front and "1 Penni" on the back, shows the arms of Finland on a black ground, and may have been a label for charity or to support the underground work against the Russians who then ruled that country.

COUNTERFEITS

Counterfeiting, an established business long before postage stamps were invented, was usually directed against currency and revenue stamps. The first British postage stamps were designed to be counterfeit-proof. They were line engraved, with a portrait by the most skillful team of engravers in the country, the background was a reversed pattern made by the rose engine, and the paper was watermarked. Since photoengraving was then (1840) unknown, a counterfeit would have required hand engraving. It was certain that no engraver could duplicate the portrait and it was maintained that the background could not be reproduced even with another rose engine. Any passable imitations would have required woodcuts or lithographs and would have fooled very few postal clerks.

Although Great Britain began to use typographed stamps in 1855 she did not abandon engraving entirely until 1880. On the other hand, the United States has never stopped using this process and only as a temporary measure, issued three values printed by offset lithography in the 1918 to 1920 period.

It is doubtful that watermarked paper would be a major

deterrent to counterfeiting, for any person with the ability to make a new die or plate would not hesitate to copy watermarks. A forger who wished to do a first-class job might procure pulp and make the needed paper.

Another protection against fraud which Great Britain used for many years was a system of corner letters on the stamps. Just what this could accomplish has not been explained very clearly, but it has been stated that this prevented piecing together uncancelled parts of stamps to make a stamp that would pass as unused. This would not stop the practice but only slow it down for in the vast supply of used British stamps a forger could find copies with the proper letters.

Many kinds of paper were designed to prevent the reuse of stamps but only a few, such as the watermarked, laid with special watermarked lines, granite, silk, safety, and a few others were designed to prevent counterfeiting.

Only three of four United States stamps have been counterfeited to defraud the government. These were printed by typography or lithography and were expected to slip through the mails unnoticed but all were detected almost as soon as they were placed in use. Examples of the frauds are in greater demand by collectors than the original models.

A counterfeiter seldom fools a collector who is thoroughly familiar with the stamps of a country. Even when the advent of photoengraving made it possible to copy designs it was still difficult to obtain the exact size on account of the expansion and contraction in photography, especially when making stereotypes of drawings.

The most dangerous forgeries are the reprints from genuine plates in the possession of unauthorized persons. Thus, the first issue of Luxembourg appeared to plague collectors when someone obtained the cancelled plates, perhaps as scrap metal, and patched and re-engraved those with the fewest defects. To complicate matters, the forgeries were printed on a supply of genuine paper. The stamps can be detected only by the minute differences in the re-engraved copies.

Collectors need not worry much about counterfeits of medium-priced stamps for counterfeiting hardly pays when there is a good supply of genuine copies. Forgers concentrate on scarce items and a collector should be careful when these are offered below the market price. A general collector who makes no attempt to study his stamps should buy the high-priced items from a reputable dealer who will give an unconditional refund guarantee if the stamp proves fraudulent. The alternative is to have the stamp examined by a recognized expert.

Some countries have or have had curious laws about counterfeiting. In some cases counterfeits, usually called facsimiles, may be made and sold if they are not described as genuine. Others permit the sale of such items if an inscription is included in the design or overprinted to indicate their status. Such stamps may be found with the word "Falsch" or "Facsimile" in the design, preventing them from ever being dangerous frauds.

An extraordinary example of this practice existed in Japan for years in which the stamps had a tiny inscription of two characters meaning facsimile. American tourists often bought almost complete collections of Japanese stamps up to about 1900, all with the microscopic inscription. See Japanese inscriptions, fig. 33-14, in chapter 33.

Collectors must be alert to avoid stamps of the United States and other countries from which penmarks have been removed. When a good job has been done the stamps may be gummed and sold as unused, but if the removal is not quite satisfactory a handstamped postmark may be added to cover the cleaned spots. When these stamps are viewed under ultraviolet rays the penmarks show clearly, and if a postmarked copy is compared under the lamp with a similar stamp bearing a known genuine cancellation differences in appearance may expose the forgery.

One particular source of trouble lies in faked cancellations on remainders where the unused copies are cheap and the canceled copies very scarce.

Collectors of rare postal history items, such as covers with unusual cancellations or combinations of stamps, should learn that such things have been faked by using covers of the proper period to which cancellations or stamps may be added. When stampless covers were very common it was a favorite practice to select a cover with interesting markings and add a stamp to cover the rate mark, which was usually in the upper right corner.

When the stamp used had a nicely impressed marking, such as "PAID," which fell entirely on the stamp, the forger trusted to its simplicity to have it pass without being tied to the cover, but if it overlapped the stamp a little he would paint in the missing part and thus make it a more satisfactory cover for those who wanted their stamps tied on. Many packet covers sent along with shipments to enclose the waybills never entered the mail. Some later had stamps and postmarks added to take advantage of some unusual handstamp of the packet boat.

Sometimes an entire rare marking has been faked by making a metal or rubber handstamp. Such things were once hard to detect but now, with illustrated literature on the subject, and the improved methods of examining stamps, the frauds may be exposed quickly. Touched-up cancellations or those in new ink react differently under ultraviolet light, although they may appear perfect to the naked eye.

Early in the history of American stamp collecting the stamps of the independent and local posts became very scarce. Since they were not government issues, John Walter Scott, the philatelic publisher and dealer, arranged to make copies available at low cost. According to a notice in the 1874 edition of the combined album and catalog Scott would supply "good imitations, printed in the correct color only, of nearly all of the rare and unobtainable originals; these are offered at the uniform rate of 2 cents each." Towner K. Webster, Jr., who made this information available, says that the Scott company list also priced originals and reprints. Perhaps some of the locals today classed as counterfeits came from this stock of good imitations. Examples seen are in sheets of fifteen with an imprint of J. W. Scott & Co.

Half a century ago the stamp market was well acquainted with counterfeits made by François Fournier, of Geneva, Switzerland. He was not concerned with defrauding any government but only collectors and nearly every rare or classic issue and an untold number of cheap stamps received his attention. Eventually he was bought out by a Swiss philatelic society, which made up collections from his stock and from additional printings and sold these to stamp societies and dealers for reference purposes. It is said that Fournier's plates were then defaced so that no more printings could be made.

An almost parallel situation arose a few years ago when the British Philatelic Association bought out Jean de Sperati and prepared albums of his forgeries for sale to members of the association.

The Frenchman began his operations soon after the First World War and counterfeited about 550 different issues during a period of almost 40 years, many being counterfeited several times in his efforts to attain perfection. His work was greatly superior to that of earlier counterfeiters and he was able to avoid the mistakes and oversights usually relied upon to expose forgeries. This was due in part to his familiarity with such modern testing facilities as ultraviolet rays, comparison magnifiers, and micrometers.

De Sperati often removed the design completely from a cheap stamp to obtain paper with the proper characteristics and perforations. In this manner, beginning with a Swedish 4-skilling banco blue stamp of the 1855 series he produced a copy of the unique 3-skilling banco orange stamp.

De Sperati found that certain rare British colonial issues could be counterfeited best by removing the colony name or value from a genuine stamp and substituting the one desired. When forging bicolored inverts he was clever enough to remove the frame and print a new one upside down, knowing that the most careful examination would be given to the center, which had not been altered in any way.

When counterfeiting stamps with cancellations he avoided

any duplication of postmarks or similarity between them as he knew such items would be suspected if compared.

De Sperati was proud of his ability and struck proofs of many stamps bearing the usual French warning against reproduction. It is said that he never sold a stamp as genuine but always as a facsimile, and that he would become enraged if any were later declared genuine. Since French law permitted the sale of facsimilies as such, De Sperati was in the clear. It is said that he was exposed when he was accused of smuggling unused stamps out of France while currency restrictions were in force. In order to prove his innocence he found it necessary to demonstrate that his stamps were forgeries, and this soon became known to collectors. During the summer of 1952 he lost a court appeal, was fined, and paid a judgment to a French federation of collectors.

Now an old man with failing eyesight, he recently sold his stock of duplicates, plates, dies, proofs, and working secrets to the British Philatelic Association. Books containing a complete account of his work and numerous examples were made available to members of the association. It is probable that they will be scattered widely and be useful in making comparisons with suspected stamps.

PART V

Classification and Identification

CHAPTER THIRTY-TWO

❖❖

CLASSIFICATION

Many terms are used in describing and listing stamps, for they may be classified by the political status of the country; by the kind of issue with respect to its permanence; by the method of transmitting the mail bearing the stamps; by the type of stamps, whether a general issue or otherwise, and when other than general by the limitation of the use of the stamps to certain people, to certain districts, or on certain classes of mail matter; and by their use to collect nonpostal funds, to pay for special services, or to collect unpaid postage or other money handled by the post office.

In addition to the postage stamps thus covered there are other labels on covers, either alone or with postage stamps, which collectors should understand and describe when making a cover collection. These include tax stamps, used on mail on certain days in various countries, or on certain classes of mail at all times in other countries, and various stickers and labels, both postal and private, which are placed on mail for one reason or another.

The classification outlined below and subsequently described does not follow the grouping used in the Scott *Standard*

Postage Stamp Catalogue, but the identifying prefixes used in that work appear here and are also used in chapter 35.

Many subdivisions such as semi-postal air post, air post registration, etc., are not listed in detail since almost any combination is possible and the number is increasing daily. Various nonpostal stickers occasionally found on envelopes, such as revenue stamps unrelated to postage, Christmas seals, and charity labels, are not included but are mentioned elsewhere in this book. Private locals also are excluded even though they may be used legitimately on cover with government issues. They are also discussed elsewhere in this book.

CLASSIFICATION OF POSTAGE STAMPS, AND OTHER STAMPS AND LABELS FOUND ON COVERS

Note: The capital letters shown in many of the divisions are the prefixes used by Scott Publications, Inc. The letter *A* is enclosed in brackets inasmuch as it does not appear alone. For explanation of letters see page 543.

I		Political Aspect of Country.
	a	Autonomous state or colony. [A]
	b	Occupation issues. N
	c	Mandate issues. [A] or N
	d	Plebescite issues. [A]
	e	Revolutionary issues. Y
II		Temporary or Permanent Character of Issue.
	a	Forerunners.
	b	Provisional issues. X or [A]
	c	Definitive issues. [A], etc.
III		Method of Transmitting Mail.
	a	Normal or surface mail. [A], etc.
	b	Airmail. C
IV		General Issues.
	a	Ordinary issues. [A]
	ab	Postal-fiscal issues. AR
	b	Commemorative issues. [A]
V		Special User Issues.
	a	Official, governmental use. O

	b	Military use. M
	c	Franchise stamps. **S**
VI		Special Area Use.
	a	Local stamps. L
	ab	Carriers. LO and LB
	b	Offices abroad. K
VII		Stamps for Special Classes of Mail.
	a	Newspapers, periodicals. P
	b	Merchandise, parcel post. Q
VIII		Stamps to Collect Money in Addition to Postage.
	a	Semi-postal stamps, optional use. B
IX		Fiscal Stamps to Collect Funds on Mail; Obligatory, **No** Postal Value.
	a	Postal tax, charity or other funds. RA
	b	Postal tax, war funds. MR
	c	Newspaper tax. PR
	d	Authorized delivery, license for private delivery. EY
X		Special Service Stamps.
	a	Special delivery, regular. E
	b	Personal delivery, prepaid or collect. EX
	c	Special handling, parcel post. QE
	d	Late fee, special handling of letters. I
	e	Pneumatic post, special handling of letters and cards. D
	f	Registered letter stamps. F
	g	Insured letter stamps. G
	h	Acknowledgment of receipt, certified delivery. H
	i	Marine insurance, floating safe stamps. GY
XI		Unpaid Postage; Postage or Other Money to be Collected.
		All uses. J
XII		Labels without Postal Value.
	a	Post-office or official seals. OX (U.S. only)
	b	Registry and insured mail labels and endorsements.
	c	Air-mail etiquettes.
	d	Return letter labels and seals.
	e	Labels of the Good Samaritans.
	f	Labels of the Letter Return Association.
	g	Official explanatory labels.

    h   Routing labels.

    i   Censor labels and markings.

XIII   The Reason for the Issue, Postal or Philatelic.

I. POLITICAL ASPECT OF COUNTRY

1a. *Autonomous State or Colony*

The autonomous state is the most important of group I, and philatelically speaking the term includes any nations, states, colonies, dependencies, etc., which have stamp issues.

It is customary to speak of the stamps of autonomous states without such qualifying words as *occupation, revolutionary,* etc. Stamps of autonomous states account for most of the world's issues and include all categories.

1b. *Occupation Stamps*

These stamps are issued by one state while occupying another or portion of one by force of arms. The stamps may be used only in the region actually occupied while the national issues are used in the unoccupied parts. When the two groups of stamps are in concurrent use, catalogers differentiate them by adding a prefix letter (under the Scott system, N) to the numbers assigned the occupation stamps. When occupation stamps are the only ones in use, the prefix letter is not always used.

Should a country take over an island that did not previously issue stamps, there would be no need for a prefix letter, as a caption could indicate the status. When an occupation is complete and terminates the previous authority, all stamps are numbered consecutively without prefixes.

Occupation stamps may include all categories which the occupying authority requires to provide postal facilities.

1c. *Mandate Issues*

These stamps are a product of the First World War, and result from the attempt of the Treaty of Versailles to provide governments for all peoples. When an occupied region was held through the war and finally separated from its previous rulers, it usually was placed under the supervision of the occupying power, which was given a mandate by the treaty, or later by the League of Nations, to maintain order for a certain period while the region prepared for self-government.

Stamps for a mandated country usually are those of the supervising country overprinted with the region name and with new values in local currency. Mandate stamps may include all categories and all are given full catalog status without qualifying letters. If the mandated country issued stamps before the occupation, the mandate stamps follow the consecutive numbering with only a caption to explain the change.

The final status of a mandated region depends on several factors, for one may become an autonomous state while another may be absorbed by the supervisory state. Still another may be divided and absorbed by adjoining states, and others under mandates interrupted by the Second World War were occupied by the enemy, retaken by the original supervisor, and again mandated at the close of the war.

Id. Plebiscite Issues

In following out the principle of self-determination, lands with one nationality predominating were set up as autonomous states. Other regions with populations about equally divided between two nationalities were placed under a commission with power to hold an election to determine the country to which the region would be joined.

Thus, Poland became an autonomous state, since its population was largely Polish, while Upper Silesia, with German and Polish groups, held a plebiscite. The results, being nearly equal, caused the region to be divided and given to Poland and Germany. The regions which have held plebiscites had no definitive stamps before the war, and the plebiscite issues are given full catalog recognition without qualifying prefixes.

1e. *Revolutionary Issues*

Revolutionary issues do not always interrupt the consecutive numbering system in a catalog. When an existing government is overthrown in a *coup d'état*, the new regime usually overprints the existing stamps to indicate the change, and ultimately issues new definitive stamps, and all of these follow the old issues in consecutive numbering. Should a later reversal of government occur the same steps would be followed and none would be classed as revolutionary.

When a revolution is limited to a portion of a country or to some detached regions, the stamps of the country usually are overprinted by the rebellious group and are in use concurrently with the national stamps, although not in the same places. These revolutionary issues are listed with a prefix letter to indicate their character, and to avoid confusing them with the national stamps.

In the event that the rebellious region gains complete independence and establishes an autonomous government, the stamps first listed as revolutionary will be listed as the first issues of the new government and the prefix letter will be dropped.

The Aguinaldo issues of the Philippine Islands are an example of stamps with the prefix *Y*, and the 1936 revolutionary issues of portions of Spain are another. It may be that the stamps of the Confederate States of America should be classed revolutionary issues but catalogers have recognized the Confederacy as an autonomous state.

II. TEMPORARY OR PERMANENT CHARACTER OF ISSUE

11a. *Forerunners*

These are stamps used in a region before it has issued its own. They are the stamps of another country, usually the governing authority. But unless the region later issues stamps, the earlier stamps cannot be classed as forerunners. Such stamps must be used copies as the cancellation or postmark is the only proof of the forerunner status.

When ordinary United States stamps were used by the forces occupying Guam, a postmark of Agana indicates a forerunner use. The later issues overprinted "Guam" were provisionals. In this case definitive stamps were never issued as Guam was made a part of the United States and began using United States stamps.

British stamps cancelled with grid killers bearing certain numbers, letters, or combinations were used in various colonial possessions, consular offices, and elsewhere before any stamps were issued for those places. When one of those began to issue stamps, the British stamps previously used became forerunners. In a British collection these stamps are classified as "Used abroad," but in a collection of the stamps of a colony they are forerunners.

Stamps of Germany, Austria, and Russia, used in parts of Turkey and bearing the cancellations of Jerusalem, Jaffa, etc., are eagerly sought as forerunners by collectors of the stamps of Palestine-Israel.

IIb. Provisional Issues

These are the stamps made on short notice to provide issues for a country newly occupied, or to take care of a change in name or government or currency, or to provide stamps of needed values in short supply, or stamps of new values. Such stamps usually are made by overprinting other stamps with inscriptions of figures. Examples include the United States stamps overprinted for use in Cuba, Puerto Rico, the Philippine Islands, and Guam during the Spanish-American War.

Examples of value changes are very numerous. As a rule the value was reduced when overprinting, detering counterfeiting. Stamps bisected or fractioned to provide needed stamps of smaller value are provisionals but are a rather scarce form.

Unless the reason for the provisional issue disappears within a short time the stamp or stamps are replaced by definitive issues.

IIc. Definitive Issues

This is a recent name given to stamps intentionally designed for a country. The designs are definite, not temporary or provisional, and the group includes nearly all stamps in use. The term developed at the close of the First World War to indicate the new stamps which were made to replace the great number of overprinted and temporary issues of new countries.

III. METHOD OF TRANSMITTING MAIL

IIIa. Normal or Surface Mail

This group includes all stamps to prepay postage and special services on mail carried by ordinary means. These stamps are in the majority and include practically every issue prior to 1917.

IIIb. Air Mail

This group, including all special stamps to prepay air-mail postage, is growing in importance. While it does not include as many divisions at present as are listed for surface mail, it may be only a matter of time until its services exceed the latter.

Designs of these stamps often indicate their use and show such symbols of speed in the air as birds, winged horses, and rockets, in addition to aircraft of every character. Although considerable mail has been carried by pigeons, balloons, and rockets, no governmental stamps are listed for these services except the Zeppelin issues.

Ordinary and commemorative air-mail issues are combined in this classification just as in the regular issues for surface transmission.

The following are some foreign inscriptions which identify air-mail stamps. Though the forms given here are singular, many are used on stamps in plural form. Adjore, Aerea, Aereo, Aeriana, Aérien, Aérienne, Aero, Aerore, Ajrore, Aviao, Aviacion, Avion, Avionska, Flug, Flugpost, Hopflug, Idrovolante, Legi Posta, Luchtpost, Luchtposte, Luftpost, Lugpost, Ohupost, Oro Pastas, Repulo Posta, Ucak Postalari, Zeppelin.

XXXI (above). Part-perforate error of the 16-cent red-and-blue air-mail special-delivery stamp. (H. E. Harris & Co.) XXXII (left). The famous 24-cent air-mail invert in arrow block of eight with arrow and blue plate number. This exists now as a plate number block of four and an arrow pair.

XXXIII (above). Die proofs of a triangular bicolored stamp. Top center: Vignette. Left: Proof from a secondary die showing two vignettes in position to be transferred to the plate. Right: As last for two frames. Bottom center: Complete die proof. First three items trimmed in this cut to save space. (Courtesy Franklin Bruns.) Below: XXXIV (left). A shifted transfer variety in the 10-cent 1847 stamp of the United States. Note the inscription "Post Office," the letters "U" and "S," and the Roman numerals "X." (Philatelic Research Laboratories, Inc.) XXXV (right). Typical examples of the "special printings" of United States stamps, 1876, showing how scissors were used to separate the stamps.

XXXVI (top). Examples of the stamps of the Polish Government-in-Exile, overprinted to commemorate the capture of Monte Cassino in Italy in 1944. (Polish Embassy Financial Office, New York.) XXXVII (above). Swiss Pro Juventute semi-postals for aid of youth. (Swiss Post Office.) XXXVIII (below). (1-3) Regular postage stamps of Austria and (4) one of Lombardy-Venetia. (5-7) Austrian newspaper stamps. (8-9) First and second designs of Bosnian regular postage stamps.

IV. GENERAL ISSUES

General issues are the regular postage stamps which pay the charges on most of the mail carried. In some cases they are the only stamps used by a country and pay the charges of every character.

IVa. Ordinary Issues

These are the common stamps in use for long periods and usually are in a small size acceptable to business houses and others who use large numbers. Normally they are available concurrently with any commemorative issues which may be on sale. Since they constitute the largest group of stamps listed in the *Standard Catalogue*, the prefix letter, which would be *A*, is not used except in the next following subdivision.

IVab. Postal Fiscal Issues

Although a very large proportion of stamps of the British countries are used both for postage and revenue, there are certain stamps for revenue purposes only. Usually these are inscribed "Stamp Duty." In some instances revenue stamps are made available for postage during stamp shortages, but in other cases the use of high-value revenue stamps for postage avoids the necessity of providing such values in the postage set. This practice is not consistent throughout the commonwealth for some colonies or units provide very high values in the postage-revenue set, some of which cannot be used for postage in any event.

In 1881, New Zealand made available for postage all Stamp Duty issues having a face value above one shilling. On January 1, 1884, Victoria ruled that all revenue stamps inscribed "Stamp Duty," now on hand or hereafter issued, would be accepted in payment of postage. Victoria last used such stamps in 1896 and after that time included any needed high values in the postage set. Victoria became a part of the Commonwealth of Australia in 1901.

New Zealand has continued to issue the postal-fiscals since

1881, but has issued very few high values in the postage series. These postal-fiscals are in values to five pounds, as a general rule, but in one issue to ten pounds, with twelve denominations of two pounds or more. These are listed separately and are avoided by many collectors.

In earlier days the *Standard Catalogue* listed postal-fiscals from the British units of Great Britain, Hong Kong, India, Montserrat, Natal, Nevis, the Orange Free State, Queensland, St. Christopher, St. Lucia, South Australia, and Tasmania, and from Chile, Costa Rica, Guatemala, Venezuela, and Spain, but nearly all have been discontinued.

All postal-fiscals may be considered as collectible when unused, and definitely collectible when postally canceled. This provision of postal cancellation applies equally to all British issues of postage-revenue sets. Those with pen cancellations or bank marks should be avoided as these indicate revenue use.

In the case of scarcer stamps, collectors should watch for fraudulent cancellations on copies from which pen marks have been removed, as the temptation is great to change a cheap revenue use into a scarce postal use. The fraudulent marking may be located to cover any traces of the previous pen marks.

IVb. Commemorative Issues

These correspond in use to the ordinary issues, and they are listed with them in the *Standard Catalogue* without a prefix letter. Serving the same purposes as the ordinary stamps, they may replace them entirely during certain periods. They differ from ordinary issues only in that they call attention to some event or person, and supposedly are issued at a time and, in the United States at least, at a place having some connection with the issue. Designs usually relate to the reason for the issue and stamp sizes usually are larger than normal.

A collector will have no difficulty in arranging these stamps in groups, such as memorial stamps for the illustrious dead, stamps to honor living persons, those commemorating historical events, or important discoveries, inventions, and the like, and so on down to those advertising a current event or undertaking.

Although in a sense all portrait stamps honor the persons shown, those showing a ruler are not considered commemorative. Neither are the United States stamps of ordinary issues even though they show presidents, cabinet members, or military and naval heroes. Only when the stamps are so designated and issued at an appropriate time or place do they become commemorative and special inscriptions usually confirm the ideas involved.

Many collectors look upon the United States 15-cent black stamp of 1866 as a memorial to Abraham Lincoln for it bears his portrait and was the first stamp issued after his assassination. Although there is no proof, the stamp probably was designed with that thought in mind. Had it included the dates of Lincoln's birth and death there would have been no question.

The United States issue of 1869 also has been the subject of debate since its designs include methods of carrying the mail, and paintings connected with the discovery and formation of the nation, but it was intended to be a permanent regular issue.

The first commemoratives ever issued were the stamped envelopes of the Centennial Exposition in Philadelphia in 1876, and the next issue, which also included postal stationery, was made by Great Britain in 1887 for the 50th anniversary of the accession of Queen Victoria. The adhesives of this issue are not generally recognized as commemoratives as there are no pertinent inscriptions.

The first adhesive stamps with inscriptions identifying the issue as commemorative are those of New South Wales for its centenary in 1888, and the next was the single overprinted stamp issued by Hong Kong for its centenary in 1891. In the same year Roumania issued a five-value set to mark the 25th year of the reign of Carol I.

The 400th anniversary of the discovery of America saw the issuance of commemoratives in 1892 by Argentina and Paraguay, followed in 1893 by the long set of the United States and single stamps by Venezuela and Puerto Rico. Later Columbian issues were made by Grenada and Trinidad in 1898, and in 1898-1899 by Dominica to build a mausoleum for the explorer's remains. The Seebeck Columbian issues for Honduras and Nicaragua in 1892 are not given commemorative status as they were the regular issues for that year, and those of El Salvador of 1893 and 1894 are not known postally used.

In Europe, in 1893, Montenegro celebrated the 400th anniversary of book printing and France issued a postal card for a visit of a Russian squadron to Toulon, and a letter card for the centenary of Dunkirk. In 1894 she provided a letter card for an international and colonial exposition at Lyon. The same year Italy issued a special postal card for an international philatelic exhibition, the first honor ever paid to philately.

In the Far East, in 1894, Japan celebrated the 25th wedding anniversary of the emperor with stamps and China observed the 60th birthday of her empress. In Europe, Portugal provided an issue for Prince Henry the Navigator, and Belgium marked an exhibition in Antwerp. Of all the countries which tried commemoratives, Portugal seemed to be the most satisfied for she brought out the St. Anthony of Padua issue with Latin prayers on the backs of the stamps in 1895, and the Vasco da Gama issue in 1898. The former set was overprinted for some of the colonies but definitive issues of the latter were provided for the important overseas possessions.

During the remainder of the century the desire for special issues reached all parts of the globe, with several issues from South and Central America and such European countries as Bulgaria, Montenegro, Greece, and Switzerland. The issues best remembered are the Olympic Games set of Greece and the Universal Postal Union set of Switzerland. Canada provided an issue for the Jubilee of Queen Victoria; the issue was almost as long and costly as the Columbian set of 1893. Newfoundland brought out the Cabot issue, designed to combine the Victorian celebration with the anniversary of the discovery of that island. The United States Trans-Mississippi Exposition was the occasion for another large commemorative issue but postal authorities profited from the experience with the Columbian issue and curtailed the number of high-value stamps. Without question the ban of the Society for the Suppression of Speculative Stamps, the S.S.S.S., had the effect of reducing the number of stamps sold.

As a token of what might be expected in the years to come, Peru had an issue in 1901 to mark the arrival of the twentieth century. The stamps of 1895 and earlier are among those which caused collectors to form the S.S.S.S. and to issue a blacklist of stamps to be avoided. This first list was made up of issued stamps, among which were the 1895 issue of Peru and the St. Anthony of Padua set. Soon after the first list appeared the society published a list of proposed stamps which it was attempting to stop. Of the many issues listed only the Greek Olympic set ever appeared.

Actually the long-range effect of this society probably amounted to nothing at all. It may have accomplished a reduction in the size and cost of sets but not in the number of things to be commemorated. Nearly all the blacklisted stamps are in favor today. Bad publicity, it seems, won't harm a stamp.

V. SPECIAL USER ISSUES

Va. Official, Governmental Use

These stamps make up a rather large group but are not in great favor with collectors. Even those of the United States usually are missing in present-day collections of this country's stamps. The stamps are given to government departments and officials for use on official mail and may assist in auditing but hardly reduce the amount of free mail. The idea originated in England and the samples prepared were the same as the Penny Black but with the letters "V.R." instead of ornaments in the upper corners. They are listed in catalogs but were never placed in use.

Spain was first with official stamps, in 1854, and there were no others until Hyderabad, an Indian state, produced a set in 1866. Then South Australia followed in 1868, Ceylon in 1869, and Denmark in 1871.

In 1873 the United States, with a growing postal deficit due largely to the franked mail, brought out department stamps inscribed for use of the various executive departments, and abolished the franking privilege to that extent. Nothing appears to have been gained by the change and the stamps were discontinued after about seven years.

New Zealand issued special stamps in 1901 to prepay the mail of her Life Insurance Department. These are listed with the prefix OY, although there appears to be no reason for selecting this series of stamps for a special treatment.

Certain groups of countries, such as France, Portugal, Italy, and their colonies, have had little need for official stamps except in a few isolated cases in recent years.

The first South Australian officials were made by overprinting ordinary stamps with the initial letters of departments and minor sections so that 55 sets of initialed stamps were in use from 1866 until 1874, when they were superseded by stamps overprinted "O.S." or in some cases punched with those letters.

Stamps for official use nearly always bear an identifying inscription or overprint. The following list contains most of the important inscriptions.

O.Б. (Official Business), official in many languages, differing slightly in spelling. O.S. (On Service). O.H.M.S. (On His [or Her] Majesty's Service). D. Dienst. Dienstmarke. Dienstsache, Franco (not all such are officials), Franqueo. G. (for Government or Gobierno), G.B.F. Service, Servicio, S.P. (Service Publique). Dept., preceded or followed by the department name. M., followed by various letters, as M.A. for Ministry of Agriculture.

There are miscellaneous inscriptions, such as Govt. Parcels, Board of Education, and others followed by the word Official; Cour Inter-, etc.; Courrier du Bureau, etc.; Nations Unies Off-, etc.; S.d.N. Bureau, etc.; Société des Nations; Amtlicher Verkehr; Armenwet; Bezirksmarke; Francobollo di Stato; Frei Durch Ablosung; Hivatalos; Offentlig Sag; Pjonusta; Pjonustu-merki; Porto Pflichtice Dienst Sache; Przeslyka; Urzedowa; Regierungs; Resmi; Sarkari; Tjanste (or Tjenste) Frimarke; Tje-neste Frimaerke (or Frimerke).

Bavarian stamps overprinted with an "E" and Belgian stamps with a "B" in an oval are listed as officials as they are provided to frank the official correspondence of the national railways of those countries.

Vb. Military Use

This division includes stamps designed for military forces in camp, on the march, and while occupying foreign lands, but probably it does not include stamps for any war department use. They might have been classed as a division of official stamps but are listed separately with the prefix M in the *Standard Catalogue*.

Turkey issued the first military stamps in 1898 to commem-orate the annexation of Thessaly, after a war with Greece, and the stamps were used only by the occupying forces. They are octagonal and are perforated as octagons, a new shape for fin-ished stamps, and bear the sultan's tughra, with the Latin-letter word "paras" and conventional numerals.

In 1900, India overprinted regular stamps "C.E.F." (Chi-nese Expeditionary Force), for use by Indian troops sent to China during the Boxer Rebellion. In 1914 stamps were over-printed "I.E.F." (Indian Expeditionary Forces). Similar issues appeared until 1921.

The inscription "F.M." (Franchise Militaire) was over-printed on various current letter-rate stamps by France begin-ning in 1901. Later, definitive stamps were issued without stated value. These all were to give free postage to members of the military forces, and could be listed as franchise stamps except that the users were governmental employees.

Following the start of the First World War, Austria issued overprinted and definitive stamps with the "K.U.K. Feldpost" inscription for use in occupied territory. In 1912, four years after annexing the previously occupied Turkish provinces of Bosnia and Herzegovina, Austria placed the inscription "Militar K.U.K. Post" on all issues for that region to indicate military government.

From 1932 until 1936 the British military forces in Egypt enjoyed a special postage rate on letters to England when a special seal was affixed. In the latter year Egypt provided stamps for this purpose which have the inscription "Army Post."

During the Second World War, Belgium provided military parcel post stamps by overprinting parcel post issues with the letter "M." In 1941 Finland overprinted ordinary issues, and later issued definitive military stamps, with the inscription "Kentta-Posti Falt Post," or "Puolustusvoimat" and "Kentta Postia."

Under Free French administration in 1941, Syria issued provisional and later definitive military stamps including semi-postals and air-post semi-postals. Italy, in 1943, provided regular and special service military stamps by overprinting Italian issues "P.M." (Posta Militare). During a shortage of stamps in 1944-1945, these were placed on sale at all post offices.

The special military parcel post stamps of Germany of 1942 have the inscription "Zulassungsmarke Deutsche Feldpost" (German Fieldpost Permit Stamp). They served as postage on any package.

After the surrender of Japan, stamps for the Australian occupation troops were overprinted "B.C.O.F.-1946" (British Commonwealth Occupation Forces) to prevent their return to Australia, after having been obtained cheaply through currency manipulations.

Vc. Franchise Stamps

Stamps of this category have been issued only by Portugal, Spain, Switzerland, France, and Germany. In general they are supplied free to charitable, scientific, and military training organizations for use on institutional mail.

Portugal has provided stamps for the Red Cross, Civilian Rifle Clubs, the Geographical Society of Lisbon, the Congress of the International Colonial Institute, and the National Aid Society for Consumption. Those for the Red Cross in 1889 gave the first postal recognition to the society by any country. There is no indicated value on any of the franchise stamps.

The Red Cross issues appeared at intervals from 1889 to 1936, and have the inscriptions "Cruz Vermelha" and "Porte Franco." In 1916 they were overprinted "Comissao Portuguesa de Prisioneiros de Guerra" (Portuguese Commission for Prisoners of War). In 1926 and 1936 the issues for use in Lisbon were overprinted "Lisbao," while those for use elsewhere were overprinted "Delegações."

Stamps for the rifle clubs and the geographical society have the inscription "Porte Franco," and the name of the franchise holder. Rifle club stamps were issued from 1899 until 1910, the geographical society stamps at intervals from 1903 to 1927, and annually from 1929 until 1938. Stamps for the Colonial Institute have the inscriptions "C.I.C.I." and "Portugal–1933" overprinted on ordinary issues. The tuberculosis issue was made in 1904 and is inscribed "Assistencia Nacional Aos Tuberculosos."

Two Spanish franchise stamps are listed and both have interesting philatelic connotations. One pictures an envelope and has the inscription "Cartilla Postal de España" and was issued in 1869 to Diego Castel to frank a booklet on Spanish postal matters. In 1881 a similar privilege was granted Antonio Fernandez Duro for his *Reseña Historico-Descriptiva de los Sellos de Correo de España*, a treatise on Spanish postage stamps. His franchise stamp shows a book with the title inscribed on the open pages.

Spain granted a franchise to a third individual but since he provided the stamps they are not listed. The man, Mariano Pardo de Figueroa, a nobleman, wrote on many subjects under the nom de plume Dr. Thebussem, and on several occasions advocated postal reforms. Spain had authorized postal cards, and after waiting two years for them he had a million cards printed which read, "As the government objects to private postal cards, Dr. Thebussem has prepared the present issue for himself and his friends. It will be considered a mark of good taste to put a stamp in the upper right hand corner."

This brought no action so he had a second million printed. They read as before, except for the addition, "For the use of those who are not friends of Dr. Thebussem." It required four million cards to bring results but finally in December, 1873, the government cards appeared. Years later it was decided to reward Figueroa and he was offered the title *Jefe superior de administracion,* an honorary postmaster generalship. He declined, saying he would rather be the newest postman.

On April 4, 1880, he was certified as *Cartero mayor honorario,* or chief honorary postman of Madrid. This certification was later extended to cover all Spain and her colonies, and Figueroa had the privilege of sending and receiving letters free. His first stamps, prepared in May, 1880, are inscribed "Dr. Thebussem Kr T Ro Honorario," the central portion being a phonetic rendering of *cartero.* This stamp bore the word "Madrid," but his second issue, early in 1882, was inscribed "Habana," while a third, in May, 1882, reads "*España y de Sus Indias.*" A fourth, issued in July, reads "España," and the last, in October, 1890, shows his name only as "Doctor Thebussem," on a buckled strap enclosing a circle with a six-pointed star.

Figueroa enjoyed his franchise until February 11, 1918, when his death interrupted preparations for a national fete on his 90th birthday. In 1944 he was pictured on a commemorative air-mail stamp.

Switzerland issued franchise stamps from 1911 to 1935 in several designs but none have inscriptions to identify the user. All should have control numbers to identify the institution but entire sheets are known which escaped this overprinting. The stamps were given to a long list of institutions and charitable organizations.

German franchise stamps were issued in 1938 and in 1942 for the National Socialist German Workers' Party, as shown by the inscription "Nationalsozial Deutsche Arbeiterparte," reading around three sides of the design.

The lone franchise stamp of France was a 90-centime value overprinted "F" in 1939 to frank mail of Spanish refugee soldiers in that country.

VI. SPECIAL AREA USE

VIa. Local Stamps

The term *local stamps* is applied to two classes of issues: the official government issues, which should be called local postage stamps, and the issues of nongovernmental character which might be called private local issues. The second group is not a part of this classification of government issues. It is described in chapter 14.

Local postage stamps have restricted validity, with "franking power limited to a town, district, or route in any country or between seaports," according to a definition established at the Philatelic Congress of Great Britain, in 1937. While local stamps of many kinds are given the prefix L in the *Standard Catalogue*, others of equivalent character are listed without prefix, even though they have no franking value except in the country of origin. This listing of locals is arbitrary and many are ignored which appear to be as worthy as those included.

The first local postage stamps were issued by the Swiss cantons before the federal government provided stamps, and the use of the stamps generally was limited to the canton. They show various inscriptions such as "Local-Post," "Poste-Locale," "Local [or Cantonal] Taxe," "Port Cantonal," "Orts-Post," and "Stadt-Post." The federal stamps at first used the inscriptions "Orts-Post" and "Poste-Locale" but soon changed to "Rayon I" (or II or III) to indicate that the stamp was to be used within a radius of 30, 60, or 90 miles of the place of posting.

The Russian province of Wenden, or Livonia, which became a part of Latvia after the First World War, issued local stamps from 1862 until 1901. They are listed in the *Standard Catalogue*. Also listed are the stamps that Nicaragua issued for the province of Zelaya, which was on a silver basis while the rest of the country had inflated paper money. For these the regular issues were overprinted "B—Dpto Zelaya" or "Costa Atlantico—B." The final issue was used all along the Atlantic Coast.

Special stamps were issued for several Chinese provinces to prevent currency manipulations but these are listed as Chinese offices rather than as locals. They are not given a prefix letter.

Colombian stamps inscribed "Correos Departamentales" were for use in the states or provinces. There was an issue for the city of Bogotá with an inscription including the city name.

The Paraguayan locals of 1922 were issued to stimulate the use of the post in the interior and were sold to the natives at a reduced rate. They were overprinted "C" for Campaña (campaign) and were valid except in Asuncion, the capital, but could not be used on mail leaving the country.

Spain issued locals for use with the Lufthansa air service in the Canary Islands, and has had special stamps for the international city of Tangier since 1926. The most recent local postage stamps were those issued for the dependencies of the Falkland Islands. In 1944 a set was issued for each dependency, but later in 1946 the inscription was changed to the group title "Falkland Island Dependencies." The need for any stamps is not apparent for the entire population of the Falkland Islands and dependencies amounts to less than twenty-five hundred.

After the date of World War I a local status is given to the issues of the countries and states that were being united as Jugoslavia. The locals of Bosnia and Herzegovina and Croatia-Slavonia were in use in 1918, those of Slovenia in 1919. Some were overprinted, others were definitive, and their use continued until stamps were produced by Jugoslavia in 1921.

The Zemstvos, or stamps of the Russian rural posts, deserve listing as they were authorized by the imperial government to fill a need. In 1860 Russia had vast rural areas without postal service, for the imperial posts operated only along the railroads and highways connecting the cities. Following the liberation of the serfs in 1861, a decree of 1864 allowed limited local government in the rural districts of a majority of provinces. Elected assemblies could legislate on such local matters as roads, education, and health, and officers were elected to administer the acts. In each province a higher assembly representing all districts could settle complaints, but could be dissolved by the imperial governor if it went beyond the scope of the decree of 1864.

This limited self-government did not extend to Poland and Lithuania, nor to Siberia and the Caucasus and other sparsely settled districts. Postal systems were soon set up, with the first at Vetlonga in Kostroma at the beginning of 1865. The first to issue stamps was Schlusselburg, in the province of St. Petersburg.

In 1869 these postal systems were held to be an infringement of the imperial monopoly and several were suppressed. However, it had been apparent that they were beneficial and a proclamation of September 3, 1870, authorized their establishment and set up rules for their operation. Under the rules stamps were permitted if not similar to the national issues.

The need for the local posts gradually diminished as the imperial posts were extended, but 94 districts were still operating in 1896, and it was not until 1917 that the last was discontinued. During the height of the period the 91 provinces involved contained 762 districts. Most of these had rural posts but only 141 districts ever issued stamps. Several issues were suppressed because they resembled the imperial stamps, but the post continued to operate.

A single stamp of the required value prepaid a letter addressed within the district. More than one stamp was necessary if the letter had to cross the borders. When a letter had to be transported by the imperial post it was necessary to add a Russian stamp of the proper value, although in some cases this may have been paid by an equivalent value in local stamps.

VIab. Carriers

These stamps were used in the United States to pay a carrier fee which could be applied in several ways: (1) to carry a letter from a post office to an address, (2) to carry one to a post office or to another address in the same city, and (3) infrequently to pay the drop-letter rate.

Although carrier acts were passed in 1825 and 1836 no official service began until 1851. Prior to this time private local posts were engaged in the work without government sanction and often in competition with the official mail service. When the service seemed to be profitable, as in New York, the postal authorities took over its operation.

Many semiofficial carrier stamps were in use before 1851, issued in some cases by postmasters and in others by the carriers themselves, and in general the postal authorities encouraged their use. On August 16, 1842, the Post Office Department began to operate the United States City Despatch Post in New York. This had been Grieg's City Despatch Post, the first stamp-issuing authority in the United States, which had begun operations February 1, 1842.

In 1851 the Post Office Department issued the Franklin and Eagle carriers and both were used in limited areas, the former in New York, Philadelphia, and New Orleans, for the most part, and the latter in Philadelphia and nearby cities. With the introduction of free delivery service in 49 cities, July 1, 1863, and the removal of the carrier fee for such service, and its rapid extension to all cities, the need for carrier stamps was ended.

Nearly all properly used on cover are scarce and many are extremely rare. The history of the stamps is somewhat interwoven with that of the private local posts. See chapter 14.

VIb. Offices Abroad

This category includes stamps for use in offices outside the issuing country. Examples are the stamps issued by European countries for use in the Levant, China, Morocco, etc. The majority of these are treated as issues of an independent country, and appear without a prefix letter in the *Standard Catalogue*.

The few which are listed with the prefix K include the "Shanghai-China" overprints on United States stamps. These were sold at the United States Postal Agency in Shanghai, the overprinted value being twice the original value but in Chinese dollars. The stamps paid foreign postage from the agency at the original face value. The agency was established in 1868 and was in operation through 1922. It was under consular supervision until 1907 and in charge of an agent thereafter. When established there was no postal service from China to foreign lands except through such offices. A similar office was located at Tientsin, China, and in 1936 an office was established at Barranquilla, Colombia, to handle air mail.

United States Dispatch Agencies were established in some foreign countries to receive and forward mail addressed in their care. B. F. Stevens, London agent from 1866 to 1912, was the best known. The London office was discontinued in 1938.

VII. STAMPS FOR SPECIAL CLASSES OF MAIL

VIIa. Newspapers, Periodicals

This was the first kind of stamp issued for a special class of mail matter. The stamps were placed in use in Austria, January 1, 1851, and may have been for accounting or simply to indicate to postal clerks that the mail was secondary. Since that date about forty countries have used the stamps, with Portugal and her colonies accounting for sixteen and the remainder spread thin over the world. Only one British unit and two South American countries have ever required them.

The first Austrian stamps bore a Mercury head with the inscription "Zeitungs Stampel" (or an alternative spelling) until 1867 when the inscription was dropped. It next appeared in 1920 as "Zeitungs Marke," still with the Mercury head. Sardinia issued two values in 1861, inscribed "Giornali Stampe," with black frames and colorless embossed numerals "1" or "2." The same design was used for the buff Italian stamp of 1862. Several low-value Italian stamps once listed as newspaper stamps are now listed as regular postage, since their use was not confined to publications. In 1890 Italy converted parcel post remainders to newspaper stamps by overprinting them "Valevole per la

Stampe." These are not given the P catalog listing as they were used on all classes of mail.

The newspaper and periodical stamps of the United States, issued in 1865 and later, were not sold to the public or used in the mails, but were attached by publishers to a memorandum accompanying the shipment to the post office. The denominations were from one cent to a hundred dollars. When the final issue was demonetized in 1895 the Post Office Department sold the remainders, including some reprinted values at five dollars per set.

The French newspaper stamp of 1868, inscribed "Timbre Imperial—Journaux," were in use only a short time and some values actually were semi-postal as they included a tax. In 1919 France began to provide stamps for papers by overprinting various low-value stamps "½ centime." A little later the practice was extended to Algeria and Andorra.

Hungary's 1871 issue showed a crown and post horn but no stated value, but in 1874 the regular issue design was modified and issued imperforate in 1-kreutzer value in yellow or orange. In 1900 the inscription "Hirlapjegy" appeared in a new design.

The Spanish stamps of 1872, inscribed "Franqueo—Impresos," were not limited to newspaper postage and are listed with the regular issues. Her issues for Cuba and the Philippines at the end of the nineteenth century show the word "Impresos" at the top.

New Zealand, the only British unit with these stamps, issued half-penny values from 1873 to 1892, inscribed "Newspaper Postage."

Portugal added the category in 1876 with a 2½-reis value inscribed "Jornaes," and overprinted this for some colonies, while others used ordinary stamps overprinted "Jornaes." In 1893 all Portuguese colonial newspaper stamps appeared in a design with a diagonal band bearing the colony name but without special inscription. Brazilian newspaper stamps were introduced in 1889 and also are inscribed "Jornaes."

In 1879 Turkey provided stamps with the inscription "Imprimes" on a ribbon, and in 1891 added a Turkish word (in Arabic "Matbua"), but since 1897 has used the latter inscription only. The overprinted word "Imprimes" was also used by Persia in 1909.

Belgian issues were improvised by overprinting parcel post stamps "Journaux—Dagbladen," with or without a date. Belgian low-value stamps, once considered newspaper stamps, are now listed with the regular issues. Fiume's first issues were Hungarian newspaper stamps overprinted "Fiume," but later Fiume provided a definitive issue inscribed "Francobollo Postali per Giornali."

Other inscriptions on definitive stamps are "Avisporto-Maerke" for those of Denmark in 1907, and "Prensa" on the stamps of Uruguay in 1922. The remaining newspaper stamps may be distinguished by designs only. Czechoslovakia has used a windhover in vertical flight, a carrier pigeon, and a newsboy, the latter two designs being carried over into Bohemia and Moravia, while Slovakia overprinted the Czech stamps and produced a design showing a newspaper and a type block. Eastern Silesia used the first Czech design overprinted "S O—1920."

Poland's only newspaper issues were those of Austria overprinted "Poczta Polska." The issues of Bosnia show a Bosnian girl in an oval framed with floral ornament and are imperforate. These same stamps, overprinted with new values, and the same stamps perforated, were used by Jugoslavia for regular postage in 1918.

VIIb. Merchandise, Parcel Post

The first special stamps for merchandise were issued by Italy in 1884 and were inscribed "Pacchi Postali." After a short time these were overprinted for newspaper use but allowed to pay any postage. In 1914 that country devised the double stamp, half of which accompanied the parcel, the remainder being held at the sending office. Little care was given to which half was sent, and collectors are able to assemble full stamps. The distinctive words of the two-part stamps are "Pacchi" and "Bolle-tino" on one half and "Postali" and "Ricevuto" on the other.

Similar stamps were in use in the Italian colonies but those of Rhodes, at least, show the inscription "Pacchi Postali" on both halves.

Since 1879 labels have been used in Belgium to pay charges on parcels carried on the national railways. These are not post-age stamps and should be classed as express labels as the entire handling of the parcels is taken care of by railway employees, at least so far as domestic use is concerned. The first labels were inscribed "Chemins de Fer," French for railway, but later the Flemish equivalent "Spoorwegen" was added to please the non-French-speaking citizens.

These labels are not placed on parcels but upon waybills retained by the railroad for a period and then allowed to reach the stamp market. They show no wear but are rather heavily canceled. It is possible that the use of these stamps on parcels to the Belgian Congo brought them into contact with the postal system enough to account for their listing as postage stamps.

Belgium and the Belgian Congo had an agreement for par-cels which allowed the use of the railway labels from Belgium and ordinary postage stamps from the Congo. However, provi-sional parcel post stamps were locally made in the Congo by overprinting 5-franc stamps "Colis Postaux—Fr. 3.50" with rub-ber and metal handstamps. A definitive parcel post issue was provided in 1899, in 3.50- and 10-franc values, but as there were no qualifying inscriptions the stamps are listed as regular issues.

In 1928 Belgium began to issue actual parcel post stamps with inscriptions "Colis Postal—Post Collo" or "Colis Postaux—Postcolli." These and the express labels are listed in the *Standard Catalogue* in combined chronological order.

After years of debate the United States issued parcel post stamps late in 1912 to check the receipts from this new service. It was quickly determined that the service was self-supporting and June 26, 1913, an order discontinued the stamps and made existing stocks valid for the payment of any postage. This was a pictorial issue and the 20-cent value was the first stamp to show an airplane.

VIII. STAMPS TO COLLECT MONEY IN ADDITION TO POSTAGE

VIIIa. Semi-Postal Stamps, Optional Use

These stamps combine a postage value with a surtax for charity. They usually show two values separated by a plus sign, the first value being postal, the second the surtax. In a few cases the charity is mentioned on the stamp but more often not. When a symbol such as a red cross is included in the design the charity is obvious.

The stamps usually are sold at the sum of the two values, but in some cases at several times face value. The surtax is not always indicated on the face and such stamps may appear to be regular issues until the catalog is consulted. In recent years some sets have been issued which combine regular and semi-postal values, and these usually are listed with the regular issues to avoid breaking the set.

Although Great Britain seldom exploits stamp collectors she raised the lid of the Pandora's box of semi-postals by issuing a penny postal card in 1890 to commemorate the jubilee of penny postage. It was sold at sixpence with the excess going to a fund for postal employees.

The horde of stamps which has since been issued with surtaxes credited to a thousand and one charities has not been popular with some collectors, but others have been attracted by the stamps' variety and beauty of designs.

The first countries to follow Great Britain were New South Wales and Victoria, both issuing 1-penny and 2½-penny stamps for the diamond jubilee of Queen Victoria in 1897. These stamps were sold at twelve times face, by transferring the face value in pence into a sales value in shillings. The New South Wales stamps showed the postage value in words and the sale value in figures.

Both issues are noteworthy as being commemorative as well

as semi-postal, and that of New South Wales, inscribed "Consumptive Home," is the first postal issue for the purpose of fighting tuberculosis. The issue of Victoria was sold with the assurance that the money was for a charitable cause but it is not identified nor was the surtax indicated. The results were satisfactory and in 1900 Victoria and Queensland issued similar stamps in 1-penny and 2-pence values and sold them in shillings for funds in connection with the Boer War. The Queensland stamps read "Patriotic Fund—1900," while the Victoria stamps have no major inscriptions but the 1-penny value pictures a Victoria Cross with the legend "S. Africa—1900."

Since 1900 none of the Australian states nor the succeeding commonwealth has used semi-postal stamps to raise funds.

Russia was the next to try these stamps. Her purpose was to provide funds for the orphans of soldiers killed in the Russo-Japanese War. The issue in three colors consisted of 3-, 5-, 7-, and 10-kopeck values with 6-, 8-, 10-, and 13-kopeck surtaxes respectively.

In 1906 the Netherlands started an almost continuous line of semi-postals, at first to raise funds for charity, but later for such objects as the restoration of stained glass windows, meeting expenses of Olympic teams, and for aiding various societies.

Roumania also issued these stamps for charity in 1906 but has aided sports clubs, national defense, the air force, and various societies. She finally overstepped the bounds of decency with semi-postal souvenir sheets which have surtaxes up to five times the postage value. These were sold mainly to stamp collectors at prices up to six, and in one case ten, times the combined value.

The first semi-postal of the western hemisphere was issued by Barbados in 1907 to provide aid for earthquake sufferers in Kingston, Jamaica. In 1913 Switzerland started the "pro juventute" series, since 1915 issued annually. She now issues a second charity set each year and has occasional issues for special funds, but all follow a high standard of design and printing and the surtaxes are nominal.

In Europe during the First World War semi-postal issues

were used to raise funds for the Red Cross and other war work, and following the war this procedure was used for purposes which should have been taken care of by public subscription or general taxation rather than by the optional purchase of stamps.

France, in addition to rational subjects, has issued stamps for noncharity groups to build monuments, to aid music societies, and for such objectives as celebrating the 50th anniversary of the Eiffel Tower and the improvement of national highways. Belgium also has a varied list for charity, the restoration of Orval Abbey, and for monument dedications. She has offended collectors by her practice of placing a very high surtax on the high value of each set.

Germany's issues have followed the pattern of her neighbors, even through her changes in government, but there is little excuse for her semi-postal issue to raise a purse of a hundred thousand marks for a horse race.

On the whole, the stamps of this category are very interesting and their designs attract topical as well as ordinary collectors. When the surtax is greater than the postage value, collectors are being trapped into buying, particularly in those sets in which several values have normal surtaxes but one high-value item has a surtax of a thousand per cent.

La Fédération Internationale de Philatelie (F.I.P), a European organization of stamp clubs, has set up a boycott against semi-postal issues which have surtaxes greater than 50 per cent of postage values, on the theory that such stamps were made to exploit collectors.

The postal tax system used by some countries is a more equitable method of raising funds, for everyone who uses the post during certain periods must contribute to the cause, while in the semi-postal system no one is required to donate, and most of the funds are provided by stamp collectors who hesitate to break the consecutive numbers set down in the stamp catalogs.

IX. FISCAL STAMPS TO COLLECT FUNDS ON MAIL; OBLIGATORY, NO POSTAL VALUE

IXa. Postal Tax, Charity, or Similar Funds

These are stamps to collect funds for charity or other purposes by making their use obligatory on certain mail or at certain periods. Those we call postal tax issues usually are only the lower values of a fiscal issue to collect the funds desired, while the higher denominations pay a tax on telegrams, theater tickets, railway tickets, etc. All the values are of interest to a collector of revenue stamps, but only the values which may be found on cover belong in a postal history collection, and none of the stamps need be included in a general collection.

Many countries using these stamps also supplied postal tax dues to collect the tax from the addressee when the sender failed to pay it, and quite often this collection was double the deficiency.

Portugal started this system in 1911 when she overprinted her stamps and those of the Azores with the word "Assistencia," and made their use obligatory on certain days. Later she uséd definitive stamps on many occasions, with inscriptions such as "Lisboa–Festas da Cicade," "Para os Pobres," "Padroes da Grande Guerra," etc., and provided an issue, inscribed "Amsterdao," for funds to send her Olympic team to Amsterdam.

Greece began using the stamps in 1914 to provide health benefits to the employees of the postal, telegraph, and telephone service. One issue was a semi-postal tax set with the surtax for needy children and the postal tax for postal employees. Roumania has used the stamps since 1915 for purposes other than those associated with her semi-postal issues. In the "Timbru de Ajutor" stamps the tax was for aid to the families of soldiers, in the "Asistenta Sociala," for various charities, and in the "Timbrul Aviatiei" and "Fondul Aviatiei" issues the funds were for aviation. Roumanian tax stamps usually were required only on domestic mail.

In 1919 the idea crossed the Atlantic, took root in Guatemala as a tax to rebuild the General Post Office ("Timbre de Reconstruccion"), then spread over South and Central America and the West Indies. Since 1919 enough money has been raised to rebuild nearly all the post offices in that area, for it is customary to require the tax stamps on all mail. The post office rebuilding stamps usually are small and bear such inscriptions as "Sello de Construccion," "Casa de Correos," "R. de C.," "Resello de Construccion," "Reconstruccion Comunicaciones," and "Edificios Postales."

Turkey uses postal tax stamps to raise funds for the Red Crescent Society, the Moslem equivalent of the Red Cross, and for children's aid. The former bear a red crescent and the latter a five-pointed star with a superimposed crescent.

In general the postal tax stamps are confined to localities such as Latin America, the Balkan countries, a few Near East states, and to scattered countries such as Spain, Portugal, and Afghanistan.

IXb. Postal Tax, War Funds

Those values required on mail matter are postal tax issues of a special kind and have no postage value. They are usually the lowest values of a fiscal set to raise funds for the purpose.

The Canadian stamps with both postage and war tax values which are listed with the MR prefix actually should be listed as semi-postals, for the fact that they were the common postage stamps of the period makes it necessary to include them in a general collection. Other war tax stamps were obligatory during certain periods and will be found on covers, but general collectors need not pay attention to them.

War tax stamps were first issued in 1874-1879 by Spain and bear the words "Impuesta de Guerra," or "Impto de Guerra." During the Spanish-American War Spain again used stamps with the short inscription, or with the word "Recargo," and provided similar stamps for Puerto Rico by overprinting ordinary issues with the word "Impuesta de Guerra."

During the First World War many British colonies made

war tax stamps by overprinting low-value regular issues with such words as "War," "War Stamp," "War Tax," or "Tax." Portuguese colonies had similar stamps about 1919, made by overprinting regular issues "Taxa de Guerra." Only the colony of Mozambique provided a definitive issue.

IXc. Newspaper Tax

These stamps paid no postal charges but as a rule were a tax on foreign newspapers, or on all papers in some countries. They are included since they appear on mail and thus are a part of postal history.

Austria introduced the stamps in 1853 and provided another issue for her province of Lombardy-Venetia in 1858. Modena and Parma issued the stamps in 1853. Tuscany followed in 1854. Hungary, the last country to issue the stamps, started a long series in 1868. The Italian states issued no tax stamps after they were united into the Kingdom of Sardinia, or Italy, as it was called after 1862, and Lombardy-Venetia ceased when that province was relinquished to Italy in 1866. Austria and Hungary, however, continued the tax for many years.

The newspaper tax stamps of Parma are identified only by the values 6c and 9c (centesimi), which were not used for regular postage stamps.

IXd. Authorized Delivery, License for Private Delivery

Although these stamps are listed in the *Standard Catalogue* as a variety of special delivery, they actually are fiscal stamps and represent a fee paid for the privilege of delivering mail privately, the post office providing no service of any kind.

The prototype of authorized delivery service is found in the Sardinian letter sheets of the early nineteenth century, described in chapter 18.

Italy is the only country which has issued these stamps and they may be identified by the inscription "Recapito Autorizzato." Their use was extended to Trieste in 1947 by overprinting the Italian issues with "A.M.G.–F.T.T."

Authorized delivery is in use in the United States and under certain conditions letters may be delivered privately but generally the full postage must be paid as though the letters were regularly posted. Government stamped envelopes are preferred but higher rates must be in stamps. All must be cancelled in ink by the sender and each envelope must be dated by the sender or by the messenger when he receives it.

While this is considered a tax, since the post office gives no service, it differs from the Italian system by requiring the use of regular postage stamps. The regulations governing private delivery are published in *Restrictions on Transportation of Letters*, fourth edition; Government Printing Office, Washington, 1952.

X. SPECIAL SERVICE STAMPS

Xa. *Special Delivery, Regular*

Stamps of this class in all countries call for the rapid delivery of mail matter by special messenger to addressees within the area served by the post office. The United States was responsible for the category when it issued stamps for the special delivery of letters at designated post offices on October 1, 1885. In the following year the service was extended to all United States post offices.

In 1898, Canada provided these stamps and in 1899, during the Spanish-American War, this service accompanied the United States troops into Cuba and Guam, and in 1901, the Philippine Islands. In 1903, Mauritius, New Zealand, and Italy issued these stamps and since that time Italy has extended their use to her possessions.

The Bahama Islands is the only British unit which has provided special delivery stamps. They have never been issued in the French, German, or Portuguese spheres, nor in the Scandinavian countries. However, they are in general use in Spanish-speaking and a few other countries.

The usual foreign language inscription for special delivery contains the word *express* or other indication of urgency.

Special delivery service is available in many countries which do not provide special stamps, and this may be handled by the telegraph messengers. As an example, Belgium until 1903 used hexagonal telegraph stamps to indicate special delivery on local letters. The normal postage fee was paid in postage stamps and it was necessary to place the inscription "par express" or the Flemish equivalent on each letter.

Letters addressed to places reached by train or other conveyance usually were deposited at the post office and all charges were paid in postage stamps, but local letters and those directed to zones served by the local telegraph office, if fully prepaid, could be dropped in street letter boxes or placed in the letter box carried by every streetcar.

At the end of streetcar routes or at a central transfer point, telegraph messengers emptied the mailboxes, which were the customary place to deposit telegrams also. The contents were taken to the telegraph office, and local express letters and cards and telegrams were sent out for delivery as soon as the stamps were cancelled. This practice provided collectors with ordinary postage stamps with hexagonal telegraph postmarks.

Express letters directed to distant points and all regular letters picked up by telegraph messengers were delivered to the post office and dispatched after being postmarked. Here again there was an interchange and any local express letters picked up at street letter boxes or mailed at the post office were turned over to the telegraph messenger for delivery.

Express letters sent out of town, including those deposited at the post office and those picked up at street letter boxes and received from the telegraph office, were postmarked with the regular circular townmark. From these the collector may obtain hexagonal telegraph stamps with postal cancellations, but it should be remembered that these telegraph stamps never paid the regular postage fee, and that the express letters ultimately were delivered by telegraph messengers.

In the British Isles and in some other parts of the Commonwealth a vertical blue pencil line placed at the center of an envelope indicates that special delivery service is required for that piece of mail.

Xb. Personal Delivery, Prepaid or Collect

These stamps were introduced by Czechoslovakia in 1937, and are an indication to carriers that letters bearing them are to be delivered to the addressees only.

The Czechoslovakian stamps were in two varieties, one for prepayment, the other for use when the fee was to be collected on delivery, both triangular in form with point up, differing only in color and in small letters in the corners.

The variety to be placed on a letter by the sender has a small "V" in each corner, representing *vyplatni* (prepayment) and was printed in blue. The other variety, bearing a "D" in each corner for *doplatni* (postage due), was printed in red. When a letter was expected and instructions were given at the post office, the "D" stamp was affixed when the letter arrived and the fee was collected on delivery.

Upon the partition of Czechoslovakia, similar stamps were issued for Bohemia and Moravia in 1939, and for Slovakia in 1940. Following the end of the Second World War, a similar stamp without corner letters was issued by Czechoslovakia in 1946.

Xc. Special Handling, Parcel Post

These stamps were first issued in 1916, by Austria, where their use was limited to printed matter. The three designs used in that country between 1916 and 1921 have no identifying inscriptions but all have designs to indicate speed. The youthful Hermes or Mercury is pictured on the first two designs, in an equilateral triangle on point in one case and flanked by thunderbolts in a rectangular panel in the second case. The third design shows a post horn and arrow above a minute map of Austria.

The Bosnian issue of the same year is in a vertical rectangle and shows an adult Mercury in armor above clouds and bears the inscription "Militarpost Eilmarke."

In 1925 the United States issued a series of three green stamps bearing the inscription "Special Handling," which were for use on parcel post packages to secure the "same expeditious handling accorded to first-class matter." This is explained as meaning that the parcels will be dispatched at the first opportunity without waiting for other parcels. This service does not include special delivery at the destination.

Xd. Late Fee, Special Handling of Letters

Late fee stamps represent an extra charge for delivering letters to a boat after the regular mail has been dispatched, and thus are special handling stamps.

Victoria introduced this stamp category in 1855 and for many years there was no other example. Between 1886 and 1903 Colombia and three of its departments issued similar stamps, in 1923 Denmark, in 1936 Uruguay, and finally, in 1945, Ecuador provided stamps by overprinting postal tax issues.

Countries without special stamps often provide the service and usually endorse the mail with a handstamped "Too Late" or similar term.

In the United States late mail is called supplementary mail. In New York in the early days it was put on board vessels after the regular pouch had been sent, at a charge proportional to the normal postage. This fee was paid in cash and may have gone into the pocket of the postmaster. At first letters were marked "Supplementary Mail" in a box, but later the indication was placed in the townmark.

In Chicago, around 1860-1862, supplementary service was given to late letters taken to the office of the chief clerk. The service applied only to letters destined for east-bound trains scheduled to leave soon after the close of business. West-bound trains departed at an hour when all mail would be aboard. The indication "Supplementary Mail" was included in the townmark and there was no charge for the service.

Xe. Pneumatic Post, Special Handling of Letters and Cards

Stamps for use on mail carried by pneumatic tube systems have been provided only by Italy. This mail may be considered as a variety of special handling for, in the cities where used, it places the mail to be delivered into the hands of the carriers much sooner than if carried by wagons or truck, but no special delivery to patrons is involved.

Italy began issuing these stamps in 1913 with two values, perhaps for letters and cards, and in succeeding years increased the denominations in step with rising costs. These stamps are inscribed "Posta Pneumatica" and are in the general character of Italian special-delivery issues.

Collectors of postal stationery find many more items to collect in the cards, envelopes, and letter sheets provided where the tubes are in use. Paris, Berlin, Vienna, and Rome and perhaps other cities had the facilities but they provided stamped stationery. Some tube service was interrupted or destroyed during the Second World War and has not been restored.

Austria and France provided cards, envelopes, and letter sheets; Germany provided cards and envelopes, and there may be other special stationery for the service.

Pneumatic tubes were used in New York and Chicago for the quick transportation of mail between the main post office and postal stations or railway stations. The system in Chicago has long been out of service but collectors still find envelopes bearing the inscription "Chicago-N.W. Tube Sta." This was in the old Chicago and North Western Railway station at Kinzie and Wells Streets. No extra charge was made in the United States for mail carried by tube.

Xf. Registered Letter Stamps

These were used to indicate to postal clerks that the letters required particular attention. Victoria issued the first in 1854 and was followed by New South Wales in 1856, Queensland in

1861, Colombia in 1865, and in Canada and several other countries before 1900. The United States issued such a stamp December 1, 1911, but decided that it was useless and ceased to sell it May 28, 1913.

Since that date only China, Hungary, and the Western Ukraine have added registry stamps to their issues. None of these conform to the international code as the Chinese issues are without Latin-letter inscriptions, the Hungarian stamps show the "Ajanlos" or an abbreviation, and the Western Ukraine stamps show the Cyrillic letter for *P*, that is, a Greek *pi*.

Xg. Insured Letter Stamps

These differ little in use from registered letter stamps except that there is a clear indication that a value has been declared and is insured. The only listed stamps are those of the Dominican Republic, Mexico, and Panama, the last in 1942, the others in 1935. The inscription is "Primo Valores Declarados" on the Dominican Republic stamps, and "Seguro Postal," on those of Mexico and Panama. All Mexican stamps are definitive, the others include issues made by overprinting.

No story of these stamps should omit mention of the *cubiertas* (covers) of Colombia. Each was large enough to cover the back of an envelope so that the flaps could not be opened, and each was signed by postal officials. They were omitted from the *Standard Catalogue* more than fifty years ago as being of minor interest to general collectors.

Xh. Acknowledgment of Receipt, Certified Delivery

These stamps indicate that a receipt will be obtained from the addressee upon delivery of the letter. The receipt may be forwarded to the sender or in some cases retained by the post office.

With every registry system there is some provision to furnish the sender with proof of delivery. The service may be included in the registry fee or it may be separate. In some countries it is paid for in cash and does not appear in the postage paid. In others it is handled by an A.R. stamp.

In the United States the service charge becomes a part of the postage, and the letter is endorsed "Return receipt requested." In some countries letters are endorsed "A.R.," standing for the international French term *Avis de Reception*, the Spanish *Avis de Recepcion*, and *Acknowledgment of Receipt*.

Nearly every stamp for this purpose shows the "A.R." prominently but one stamp of El Salvador shows the Spanish term in full.

Acknowledgment of receipt stamps were introduced by Colombia in 1893, followed by Chile in 1894, Panama and El Salvador in 1897, and Antioquia and Bolivar in 1902 and 1903, respectively. The only stamps of this category outside of the Americas were issued by Montenegro, starting in 1895, and with a single exception these show the Latin letters "A.R." amidst the Cyrillic-letter inscriptions.

Nearly all the stamps are definitive but some of Colombia and its states were made by overprinting ordinary issues.

The certified mail stamp of the United States pays for a receipt of delivery. This is retained by the post office, but senders may obtain an official receipt for an additional fee. This service has eliminated letters without monetary value from the registered service, which now corresponds to the insured letter service.

Xi. *Marine Insurance, Floating Safe Stamps*

The stamps in this category were designed for a special form of insurance on letters passing between the Netherlands and the Netherlands East Indies.

Letters bearing these stamps were placed in a safe mounted on the deck of the vessel and designed to float off in case of shipwreck or the foundering of the vessel. The safe was equipped with automatic lighting and a bell-ringing apparatus.

The stamps were issued by the Netherlands in 1921, and by

the Netherlands East Indies in 1922, and are identified by the inscription "Drijvende Brandkast" (Floating Safe).

XI. UNPAID POSTAGE; POSTAGE OR OTHER MONEY TO BE COLLECTED

These stamps are to indicate that full postage has not been paid on mail matter, and to provide the patron with a receipt for the amount due. Five kinds are listed in the *Standard Catalogue*: ordinary postage due, local postage due, parcel post postage due, postal tax postage due, and occupation postage due.

The adoption of uniform rates and adhesive stamps made it unnecessary to take a letter to the post office. This easy mailing at a post box or letter slide was not an unmixed blessing to postal authorities for many persons did not fully prepay their letters.

Since partly paid letters could be sent on with the deficiency to be collected from the addressee, it became necessary to have some means of identifying short-paid matter which looked official to the person who had to pay the deficiency. A hand-written "Due 3 cents" did not carry much weight and postmen were suspected of adding such notations to increase their pocket money.

Postage due stamps were devised to cover this situation and were introduced by France in 1859, just ten years after that country adopted stamps. Great Britain, always conservative in issuing special stamps, did not find these labels necessary until 1914. The United States, with a population as adverse as any to the overpayment of postage, began using the labels in 1879, but they have now been discontinued and have been replaced by meter stamps applied at the post office in the necessary denomination.

It is strange that these stamps which seem so necessary in many countries have never been used in other countries of similar population and customs. Theoretically, at least, the stamps are a part of the accounting system of post office departments and there is no reason why unused stamps should reach the public.

For many years each piece of short-paid mail was marked and in countries using due stamps the proper stamps were affixed. The marking may have been added in the international service or in the railway mail service or in the post office where mailed or delivered, but all stamps were affixed in the delivery office.

In recent years, in the United States, for example, groups of short-paid mail addressed to one concern have been bundled and the total postage due marked on the package with the due stamps affixed to one letter. This system provides collectors with covers showing great amounts of postage due, and others short paid without any evidence that the shortage was collected.

Business houses using business reply envelopes or cards receive the replies in bundles with all due stamps affixed to the top item, another use for postage due stamps. In France, due stamps with a different inscription are used to collect money for various purposes such as magazine subscriptions. These operations are called *recouvrements* and stamps or postmarks contain this word as part of the design.

For years traveling men in the United States overworked the provision that first-class mail must be carried when one full rate is paid. This enabled them to mail daily reports of any size for two or three cents, and it was not necessary to weigh the package or to carry many stamps.

The postage due stamps of some countries have no inscriptions and it is evident that the postal officials do not expect them to leave the country. In almost every design the numeral of value is prominent and quite often is the principal feature. One colony, Hong Kong, has produced a due stamp which conveys the short-paid idea by showing a pair of scales with a letter depressing one pan.

The special types of due stamps are limited to a very few countries. Local dues were issued for Baden, Bosnia, and Herzegovina, and were used in certain restricted areas. Parcel post dues were used by the United States only and were placed in use with the parcel post series to keep an accurate account.

Both were discontinued when the system was found to be self-supporting.

Postal tax postage dues are mentioned under postal tax issues, group IX. Occupation dues do not differ from the ordinary dues except that the proceeds are taken by the occupying country.

XII. LABELS WITHOUT POSTAL VALUE

XIIa. Post-Office or Official Seals

Official seals are used in many countries to seal registered letters or reseal damaged letters or those opened by mistake. Although no longer listed in the *Standard Catalogue* they still appeal to some collectors.

In 1872 the United States issued a green seal with "Registered" in the inscriptions and a space for the sending office's postmark. This was used exclusively to cover the juncture of the flaps of the official envelopes in which registered letters were transmitted. In 1877 a smaller seal without the word "Registered" came into use to reseal dead letters. The inscription "Officially Sealed" is used and the seal, which first was in brown, appeared in succeeding years in smaller size in various designs and in several types of printing. These have been issued imperforate, perforated, rouletted, and with mixed separation.

One special official seal was issued for the Quartermaster General's office in 1949. During much of the period privately printed seals were in use in some offices and these often contain the post office name and some have the words "Opened by Mistake by" with space for a signature.

Several foreign countries use official seals for registered letters rather than to reseal opened mail. The early foreign seals were about the same size as the second type of United States seals and were often of better design than the country's stamps.

Official seals were placed in use in Denmark in 1878, Canada in 1879, Mexico, Chile, and Japan in 1885, New Zealand and El Salvador in 1890, Hong Kong in 1894, and Siam in 1895.

XIIb. Registry and Insured Mail Labels and Endorsements

These are small rectangular stickers used on much of the foreign registered and insured mail. The United States now uses only a handstamp of similar design but during the period between 1883 and 1911 used labels, at least on international registered mail.

Registered labels usually contain the letter "R," the name of the city and country, and space for the registry number. The design is enclosed in a frame and the "R" is red as a general rule. It usually is located at the left end of the label but examples from German offices in China have this letter at the right.

The labels used in New York under a convention of the Universal Postal Union show the word "City" or "Exchange" at the right end, perhaps to indicate local and transit letters, but the two types were used indiscriminately.

The number of varieties of labels seems unlimited. Australia since 1910 has used over 200 types, nearly all being available from each of 500 cities and towns. As with other nonpostage stickers these labels are of more importance on cover.

The handstamped rectangle with the word "Registered" and a number has counterparts in various languages. These endorsements may be written, handstamped, or in the form of stickers, but all show the letter "R" if a number is used.

Insured mail in the United States is handstamped with a rectangle showing the word "Insured" and a number. Foreign endorsements may be written, handstamped or in the form of labels, but the international symbol "V" or "VD" always accompanies an endorsement with serial number.

XIIc. Air-Mail Etiquettes

This is the name given to labels indicating that air service is required. They are provided free by most countries with air service and by many air lines. Private labels also are available at stationery stores. Few indicate the country of origin beyond what can be learned from the language or design. The labels are changed often and some are very scarce for more than half the varieties issued since 1918 are obsolete.

France provided the first examples August 17, 1918, for the Paris-St. Nazaire service starting that day. These imperforate labels were in black on red paper and show the inscription "Par Avion" within a heavy border. In 1919 private etiquettes appeared in the United States. In 1920 official etiquettes were provided by the post offices of Great Britain, Denmark, Norway, and the Netherlands.

The Universal Postal Union suggested certain standards in 1922. These were seldom followed but after about ten years some uniformity began to appear. The standard color is blue and the notice is usually bilingual at least, with one inscription in French, "Par Avion" and another in the native language. Some countries have labels in three or more languages, Colombia using one of the latter provided by the SCADTA operating company.

Czechoslovakia is the only country which has sold labels, so far as recorded. Four varieties were provided, showing destinations of London, Paris, Strasbourg, and Warsaw, and were sold in 1922 at ten hellers each.

While most etiquettes are in small sheets, some booklets have been issued by operating companies, and panes of labels have been included in stamp booklets by some countries. Errors and varieties are common but of little importance since the labels have no postage value.

XIId. Return Letter Labels and Seals

These are post-office labels or seals placed on letters returned to the writer. Some were used on any undeliverable mail returned according to the corner card while others were used as seals on letters opened at dead-letter offices to determine the writer's address. The labels of Bavaria, Norway, Spain, and Württemberg were once listed in the *Standard Catalogue*. While not actually stamps, return labels have a definite place in postal history.

Württemberg introduced the labels in 1857 with an inscription reading "Commission für Retourbriefe," but altered this to "Amtlich Eröffnet K.W. Post-direction" in 1875.

The Bavarian labels known as *retourmarken* were in use from 1865 until after 1878, and those of each of the seven postal administrations showed the district name. The first issue was inscribed "Commission für Retourbriefe," but in 1868 those of Regensburg were changed to read "Retourbriefe Kgl. Ober-postamt." A new design was supplied for all districts in 1870 and in 1872 the inscription was changed to "Retourbriefe Kgl. Oberamt," with a special issue in 1878 for Nuremberg reading "Commission für Ruckbriefe, Nuremberg."

Norway issued two return letter stamps in 1872, one reading "Som Ubesorget Aabnet af Post Departmentet," the other "Som Uindlost Aabnet at Post Departmentet." The first were attached to letters which could not be delivered according to direction and were being returned to sender; the second were attached to letters which were not called for, probably addressed to general delivery, or without a specific address.

The Spanish labels were issued in 1873 and bear the words "Correos Devolucion de Correspondencia Sobrante."

All return letter stamps are scarce on cover for it is probable that the original envelopes were destroyed and the letters re-mailed.

XIIe. Labels of the Good Samaritans

At various times in the United States individuals or organizations have undertaken to pay the postage on letters which reached the post office without stamps. The incentive may have been a hope that the receiver of such a letter would include a gratuity when he refunded the postage.

The earliest examples noted were the work of individuals, one in New Orleans in the 1860's and others in Mobile in 1868; St. Louis, 1869; Cincinnati, 1870; Baltimore, 1874. Around 1865 the YMCA's began to handle this work and examples have been noted from Richmond, Indiana, in 1865; Cleveland, 1868; San Francisco, 1870; and Worcester, Massachusetts, in 1874.

Other charitable and religious groups also took care of this lost mail in various cities but no later dates than 1874 have come to the author's attention. The letters given this service probably were selected from "Held for Postage" lists published in those days, but it would require the permission of the postmaster before the stickers could be placed on the envelopes.

The label usually states that the undersigned, thinking that the letter may be important, has paid the postage and will appreciate being reimbursed for his expense. The entire procedure may have been halted by the Post Office Department on the ground that it gave strangers too much access to the mail.

XIIf. Labels of the Letter Return Association

This Chicago organization, and there may have been others, seems to have been an agency to enable mailers to use envelopes without return cards and to recover undelivered letters without having them pass through the dead-letter office. None of the organization's labels has been found on "advertized" or "Held for Postage" letters. Examples are on envelopes of the middle 1880's.

Each mailer used small vertical labels bearing a serial number, the address of the Letter Return Association and instructions for return if not delivered. If returned the letter could be delivered to the holder of the serial number. It is probable that this service was discontinued by the postal authorities, as it could be subject to abuse.

XIIg. Official Explanatory Labels

This group includes the labels to explain the reason for the condition of the mail or its late delivery. They are placed on mail recovered from airplane crashes, train wrecks and shipwrecks, and train robberies; on mail damaged in a flying pickup, or accidentally run over when thrown from a moving train.

Included also are those explaining that the piece of mail was found in cleaning a mailbag or behind a cabinet, etc., in the post office. When only a few pieces of mail are involved the endorsement is made by hand or with a rubber stamp, in other cases by means of a printed label.

XIIh. Routing Labels

The only label of this nature known to the author reads "Exprès d'Orient" and was for use on letters originating at foreign post offices in Turkey which were to go by railroad rather than by steamer.

XIIi. Censor Labels and Markings

During World Wars I and II nearly all the participating nations established censorship of international mail. The notices indicating that the mail was opened were often printed on the tape or paper slips used to reseal the envelopes after the contents had been examined. The inscriptions on these and other labels often consisted of a number only, although the commoner types included advice that the letter had been examined.

In some instances it was required that letters be taken to the censoring office unsealed and in such cases only a handstamp was used to mark the envelopes after resealing.

Censorship of prisoner-of-war mail was customary in the United States during the Civil War. Letters were limited to a single note-size page and those sent out by the prisoners were examined before being placed in envelopes. This differed from the censorship of the recent wars for nothing was cut out or obscured. If the letter was not satisfactory it was returned to the prisoner. Approved letters were so marked on the envelope by means of an oval or circular handstamp.

XIII. THE REASON FOR THE ISSUE, POSTAL OR PHILATELIC

The many collectors who buy everything issued by their favorite countries seldom care to learn why certain stamps were issued, but there are occasions when it may be interesting to probe the thoughts of those responsible for stamp issues and learn whether they were for postage or for sale to collectors.

In the early days there was a need for each value in use and when a new rate was adopted it may have required a new denomination. Thus the 7-cent value was added by the United States in 1870 to pay the letter rate by direct mail to Denmark and Germany.

New designs sometimes were the result of popular demand and this caused the pictorial set of 1869 to be replaced by a new series of large stamps in 1870. Perhaps the small stamps were too effeminate for the hardy businessmen of that day.

Our ordinary stamps seldom are changed except by public demand or after a change in administration. Since 1900 there have been but seven issues, of which the overdecorated set of 1902-1903 was replaced within six years. Since 1908 each regular series of stamps has been in use for a long period, with changes made only in 1922, 1938, 1954, 1965 and 1970. This record refutes any claim that the United States exploits collectors in the long sets with high-value stamps.

Commemorative stamps can be charged to the event to be honored and this, at least, provides the published excuse for the issue. However it may be found that there are other reasons. There was ample excuse for the Columbian issue but not for the long sequence of high values. The next four or five commemorative issues also were for worthy events but might not have been issued except for the Columbian precedent. Fortunately some sanity prevailed and they were cut down in number and value as time went on.

In 1925 stamps were issued for the first time to honor immigrants, and in 1929 in compliment to an industry, and since that time many events have been commemorated, some appealing to one region or group but nearly all based on something important. The history of the country, its forty-eight states, and four territories, and the records of scientific, educational, and industrial achievements provide subjects without end, and in slack times scenic wonders can be shown and perhaps some institutions as well as their founders.

There is great doubt that any United States issue was intended to raise money at the expense of collectors although it has been so stated. Even the seven sets of Famous Americans cost only a little more than a dollar and a half at the post office and a used set could have been found in any wastebasket. The only persons exploited were the sheet collectors but now there is a handsome profit for those who had the nerve to buy seventy copies of each stamp.

Practically all commemorative issues have been requested by responsible organizations, not excluding stamp societies, but the moment collectors cease to buy first-day covers, blocks, and sheets, the special stamps will vanish except for the most important events. Perhaps each country can make the same claim and it cannot be contested if a large proportion of the stamps are used in that country. However, when the entire issue is sold to dealers and collectors with only a token sale at post offices it is certain that the issue was made for collectors.

The high values of the Columbian issue have been mentioned and the report of Postmaster General W. S. Bissel for the fiscal year ending June 30, 1893, implies that they were made for philatelic purposes. In 1893 the maximum rate on domestic first-class mail for an ordinary citizen was $1.28 plus registration and special delivery fees.

The report indicates that a great demand for the stamps had been anticipated and a profit—even as much as $2,500,000— had been expected. It goes on to state that this estimate was not correct and that Mr. Bissel became convinced by June, 1893, that the profits would hardly pay the extra cost of the stamps.

The Columbian issue cost the government 17 cents per thousand copies in comparison to 7.47 cents per thousand for the small stamps of 1890. The contract with the American Bank Note Company was renegotiated and the total printing was limited to two billion stamps with the second billion to be furnished at the lower rate.

On January 19, 1893, a joint resolution was introduced by
Senator Walcott, of Colorado, instructing the postmaster general to discontinue the sale of the "so-called Columbian issue."
When objected to, the resolution went over, but on January 21,
Senator Walcott asked that it be called up, remarking that the
issue savored more of a trick of a Central American state. He
stated that it was unjust to inflict punishment on sixty million
people in order to unload a cruel and unusual stamp issue on collectors, and urged the Senate to pass the resolution. Another
senator objected and it was referred to committee, and there
died.

Two other stamp issues were directly influenced by the
Columbian set as will be seen from the following notes gleaned
from publications of the time.

The 50th anniversary of the opening of Shanghai to for-
eigners fell on November 14, 1893, and the municipal authorities, having taken note of the Columbian issue, ordered a 2-cent
commemorative stamp to be placed on sale November 15. Of a
total issue of 300,000 copies, two-thirds were sold on the first
day and the remainder by noon of the second day. Sales were
limited to 250 copies to each person and only United States
dollar notes were accepted in payment.

The pleased authorities announced on December 1 that a
second commemorative would be made by overprinting current
stamps "1843—Jubilee—1893," and that 10,000 sets would be sold
by subscription. All had been taken by December 15, the date
for distribution, and the authorities produced a third issue consisting of the four low values of the previous set and all of the
current postal stationery similarly overprinted.

The local press accused the postal official of neglecting
their proper duties to make stamps for collectors but the repri-
mand was wasted for the municipal issues were replaced by the
imperial Chinese issues in 1897. These stamps are not in order
in the *Standard Catalogue* as the large 2-cent stamp was issued
prior to the overprinted set.

In connection with a projected festival in 1900 to observe

the 400th anniversary of the discovery of Brazil, the *Philatelic Journal of Brazil*, in the spring of 1897, contained this suggestion for raising money for the celebration:

"Worthy therefore . . . is the idea of celebrating . . . the discovery of Brazil . . . [with] a national exposition and other festivities.

" 'But where in such hard times as these are we to procure the money for this purpose?' is a question that will be asked by prudent and economical persons.

"The proposition for an issue of commemorative stamps furnished a satisfactory answer. . . . As has been shown . . . the World's Columbian Exposition issue, the . . . Prince Henry the Navigator issue of Portugal . . . etc., covered the expenses, and even left a large surplus [for] exhibitions, and magnificent festivals!

"In addition . . . an issue of artistic stamps . . . would . . . suffice to celebrate . . . the first appearance of Western civilization in Brazilian territory."

Then follows a list of 12 values from 10 reis to 10,000 reis with suggested subjects. The set as issued in 1900 was in four denominations from 100 to 700 reis, with a total of 1500 reis, and no doubt was better received than would have been the proposed issue with a face value of 19,880 reis.

❖✦❖

IDENTIFICATION OF STAMPS

Although most stamps have some inscriptions in Latin letters there are others with Cyrillic, Greek, or various Oriental letters, and still others which appear to have no inscriptions at all. Stamps with bi- or trilingual inscriptions usually have one in Latin letters. Since they are not hard to identify, they are not mentioned here except under unusual circumstances.

The Latin-letter inscriptions are given in chapter 36 and attributed to the country which uses them, but no attempt has been made to show all the inscriptions that appear on commemorative, semi-postal and postal tax issues. Currency units in Latin letters will be found in chapter 34.

Much of the difficulty of stamp identification lies in stamps with Oriental inscriptions or no inscriptions at all. The unusual languages and alphabets are explained to some extent in the following pages, and symbols and details that may identify stamps without inscriptions are shown in several of the illustrations.

CYRILLIC ALPHABET

This alphabet is used for part or all of the stamps of Azerbaijan; Batum; Bulgaria; Carpathia; the Far Eastern Republic;

Finland; Jugoslavia and its components; Bosnia and Herzegovina, and Slovenia; Latvia, under Russian occupation; Outer and Inner Mongolia; Roumania (Moldavia), and under Bulgarian occupation; Russia, with stamps for the Armies of the North, and Northwest, the Russian Soviet Republic, the Union of Soviet Socialist Republics, Wenden, Russian Offices in China and Turkey, and Wrangel issues; Serbia; Siberia; South Bulgaria; South Russia, the Don, the Crimea, and Denikin issues; the Transcaucasian Federated Republics, and the Ukraine and Western Ukraine.

Altogether 48 letters are in use, although the alphabet differs in various countries. The five basic alphabets are the Russian, White Russian, Ukrainian, Bulgarian, and Serbian. New members of the U.S.S.R. use the Russian letters and Jugoslavia follows the Serbian form, although a few stamps have been bilingual, using two Cyrillic alphabets.

When Slavic words are transliterated into Latin letters, many become understandable because they recall either English words or word roots with which we are familiar.

The alphabet shown in fig. 33-1 contains the 48 characters with the Latin equivalents used by the Library of Congress.

The letters are numbered for reference only. Column 2 shows a block form, column 3 a form with serifs, there being no significance when the letters are in a smaller size. Column 4 shows lower-case letters and a few script or italic forms, column 5 gives the Latin equivalents, and in the adjoining space symbols or letters indicate where the Cyrillic letters are used.

A dash indicates that the letter occurs in all five alphabets, the Russian (R), the White Russian (W), the Ukrainian (U), the Bulgarian (B), and the Serbian (S). In other cases two or three letters indicate the use, but where a letter occurs in four alphabets, the fifth letter is shown with a dash to cancel it.

In 1918 Russia dropped letters Nos. 14, 42, and 46, and substituted Nos. 13, 8, and 32, respectively. Character No. 39 was abolished at the end of words as it served only to harden the sound of the preceding consonant. Where No. 39 occurs in the

1	2	3	4	5				1	2	3	4	5
1	А	А	а	*a*	–		–	25	П	П	п *n*	*p*
2	Б	Б	б б	*b*	–		–	26	Р	Р	р	*r*
3	В	В	в в	*v*	–		–	27	С	С	с	*s*
4	Г	Г	г г	*g*	–		–	28	Т	Тт	т *m*	*t*
5	Г	Ѓ	г	*ġ*	∿U		S	29	Ћ	Ђ	ћ	*ć*
6	Д	Д△	д д	*d*	–		–	30	У	У ц	у	*u*
7	Ђ	Ђ	ђ	*d*	S		W	31	Ў	Ў	ў	*ŭ*
8	Е	Е	е	*e*	–		–	32	Ф	Ф	ф ф	*f*
9	Є	Є	є	*ē*	U		–	33	Х	Х	х	*kh*
10	Ё	Ё	ё	*ё*	RW		–	34	Ц	Ц	ц ц	*t͡s*
11	Ж	Ж Ӂ	ж ж	*zh*	–		–	35	Ч	Ч	ч	*ch*
12	З	З	з	*z*	–		S	36	Џ	Џ	џ	*dzh*
13	И	И	и и	*ī*	⩾		–	37	Ш	Ш	ш	*sh*
14	I	I	i	*i*	RWU		RUB	38	Щ	Щ	щ щ	*shch*
15	Ï	Ï	ï	*ï*	U		RBS	39	Ъ	Ъ	ъ	"
16	Й	Й	й й	*ĭ*	Ƽ		RW	40	Ы	Ы ь	ы	*y*
17	J	J	j	*y(j)*	S		–	41	Ь	Ь	ь	'
18	К	К	к	*k*	–		RB	42	Ѣ	Ѣ	ѣ	* i͡e*
19	Л	Л ᴧ	л л	*l*	–		RW	43	Э	Э	э	*ė*
20	Љ	Љ	љ	*ĺ*	S		Ƽ	44	Ю	Ю	ю	*i͡u*
21	М	М	м м	*m*	–		Ƽ	45	Я	Я	я	*i͡a*
22	Н	Н	н	*n*	–		R	46	Ѳ	Ѳ	ѳ	*f*
23	Њ	Њ	њ	*ń*	S		R	47	V	V	v	*ẏ*
24	О	О	о	*o*	–		B	48			ж	*u͡*

Fig. 33–1.

body of a word it may be retained but as a rule is replaced by an apostrophe.

Character No. 41 has no sound but softens the preceding consonant and may be considered similar to the sound between the *d* and *n* in the word *pardon*, which would sound the same if spelled *pard'n*.

The only variation in respelling is in character No. 38, which in Bulgarian is *sht* instead of *shch*.

The Cyrillic letters on many stamps, particularly those of Bulgaria, often are quite ornamental, but a little study will reveal the basic form of the letter.

The three plates of Cyrillic inscriptions, figs. 33-2, 33-3, and 33-4, show a selection from all countries and should enable a collector to identify stamps by comparison.

· SELECTED INSCRIPTIONS IN CYRILLIC LETTERS ·

АВNА ПОЧТА	%p Airpost	RUSSIA
АВNО ПОЧТОВАЯ or ПОЧТА	def. "	"
АЗЕРБАИДЖАНСКАЯ		AZERBAIJAN
АМУРСКАЯ ОБЛАСТНАЯ	Blagoveshchensk	FAR EASTERN REP.
БАНДЕРО ЛЬНОЕ ОТИРАВЛЕНIE НАВОСТОКЪ	Offices in Turkey	RUSSIA
БАКУ	Baku Province	AZERBAIJAN
БАКИНСКаГО Г.П.Т.О.Kо.	" "	" "
БАКИНСОИ П.К.	" "	" "
БАТУМ : БАТУМ ОБ. or ОБЛ.	%Russia, British Occ.	BATUM
БАТУМСКАЯ ПОЧТА		"
ВЕНДЕНСКАЯ ЧЫЬЗДНАЯ ПОЧТА	Wenden	RUSSIA
ВЕСПРИЗОРНЫМ ЛЕТЯМ	Semi-Postal	U.S.S.R
БИЉЕГА A·R at corners	Ack. of Receipt	MONTENEGRO
ВОСТОННАЯ КОРРЕСПОНДЕНЦIЯ	Offices in Turkey	RUSSIA
ВОСНА ХЕРЦЕГОВИНА	BOSNIA & HERZEGOVINA	
БЪЛГАРКА : БЪЛГАРСКА : БЪЛГАРИЯ		BULGARIA
БЬЗДЧЩНА ПОЩА БЬЛГАРИЯ	Airpost	"
БЬЗДЧЩНА ПОЩА ЦАРСТВО БЬЛГАРИЯ	"	"
БЬ ПОЛЬЗЧ	Semi-postal	RUSSIA
БЬРЗА ПОЩА	Special Delivery	BULGARIA
ГОЛОДАЮЩИМ Р.С.Ф.С.Р.	Semi-postal	SOVIET RUSSIA
D.B.P.= Д.В.Р.(Dalni Vostochini Respoublika)		VLADIVOSTOCK ISSUE
Д.В. коп. I коп. ЗОЛОТОМ	"	FAR EASTERN REP.
ДЕМОКРАТСКА -ФЕДЕРАТИВНА: JУГОСЛАВИJА		JUGOSLAV.
ДОПЛАТА (Numeral) ЗОЛОТОМ	Postage Due	RUSSIA
ДОПОМОГА ГОЛОДУЮЧИМ	Semi-Postal	UKRAINE
ДОПОМОГА and Donomora	"	"
ДОПЛАЩАНЕ and ДОПЛАЩАННЕ	Dues	BULGARIA
ДРЖАВА С.Х.С.	Slovenia	JUGOSLAVIA
ДРЖАВА С.Х.С. БОСНА ХЕРЦЕГОВИНА	Bosnia & Herzeg.	"
ЕДИНАЯ РОССIЯ	Denekin Issues	SOUTH RUSSIA
ЕРМАКЪ	Don Issue	" "
ЗА ДОПЛАЩАНЕ	Postage Due	BULGARIA
ЗА НАШИТѢ : ПЛѢННИЦИ	%p Semi-Postal	"
ЗА ЦРВЕНИ КРСТ	Postal Tax	JUGOSLAVIA
З.С.Ф.С.Р. in Star	%p Russia / Armenia	TRANSCAUCASIAN FED. REP.

Fig. 33–2.

З. С. Ф. С. Р. *and* Star, Crescent, Sickle TRANSCAUCASIAN FED. REP.

З. У. Н. Р. *and* Trident in Shield   o/p Austria WESTERN UKRAINE

ЈУГОСЛАВИЈА   JUGOSLAVIA

ЈА ЦРЕСНИ КРСТ *and* ✚   Postal Tax   "   "

КАРПАТСЬКА УКРАІНА   CARPATHO - UKRAINE

КОП - КОР. bil. in oval or vert. rect. with numeral   FINLAND

КОЛЕТНИ ПРАТКИ   Parcel Post   BULGARIA

КИТАИ   Offices in China   RUSSIA

КРАЉЕВИНА СРБИЈА c. ПАРА-ДИНАР   SERBIA

.   "   "   СРБА : ХРВАТАИ : СЛОВЕНАЦА   JUGOSLAVIA

КРАЉЕВСТВО С.Х.С. BOSNIA-HERZEGOVINA   "   "

КРЫМСКЛГО КРАЕВОГО ПРАВКТЕЛЬСТБА Crimea So. RUSSIA

КРСТ. А.   КРСТ   Postal Tax   JUGOSLAVIA

К. С. ПОЩТА *and* Coat of Arms   c ПАРА   SERBIA

К. СРБСКА ПОЩТА c. ПАРА   "

МАРКА *and* Double Head Eagle   RUSSIA

МОНГОЛ ЩУААН   OUTER MONGOLIA

Н. А. П. В. П. ."• %Russia, Nikolaevsk Issue   SIBERIA

НАРОДНА РЕПУБАИКА or H. P.   BULGARIA

Н. Р. БЪЛГАРИЯ Bulgarian Peoples Republic   BULGARIA

НЕЛЕЉА ЦРВЕНОГ КРСТА Postal Tax JUGOSLAVIA

ОБЩИНСКА ПОЩА   Officials   BULGARIA

ОДНА МАРКА ·· YKSIMARKKA   bilingual.   FINLAND

О. К. С. А. РОССІЯ   Army of the North 1919   RUSSIA

О. Ф. *and* Airplane , o/p on Regular Air Post   BULGARIA

П. В. 26. П. V. 1921-1922 in oval %p Far Eastern Republic PRIAMUR SIBERIA

ПЕН : PEN with numerals   Bilingual   FINLAND

ПОМОЩИА АКЦИЯ ЗА. П. Т. Т. СПУЖИТЕПИ Semi-Postal BULGARIA

ПОМОЩ. П. Т. Т.   "   "   "

ПОМОЩЪ. ГОЛОДАЮЩИМ НОВОЛЖЬЯ   " SOVIET RUSSIA

ПОРТО МАРКА   c. ПАРА   Postage Due   SERBIA

ПОРТО СКРИСОРИ Arms & Posthorn   MOLDAVIA   ROMANIA

ПОУТА with Portraits   c. КОП - РУБ   RUSSIA

ПОУТА · РУССНОИ · АРМІИ   WRANGEL ISSUE   "

ПОУТОВАЯ   МАРКА c. КОП-РУБ : Two Headed Eagle   "

"   "   as above with added circles   FINLAND

"   "   С. ПЕН - PEN : МАРОКЬ-MARKKAA FINLAND

FIG. 33-3.

ПОЩТА с. ПАРА - ДИНАР.   SERBIA
ПОЩТА УКР. Н.Р.РЕП   %р AUSTRIA   WESTERNUkraine
ПОШТЕ БИЉЕГА ЦР. ГОРЕ   MONTENEGRO
ПОШТЕ ЦРНЕГОРЕ or   ЦР. ГОРЕ   "   "
ПОЩЕНСКИ КОЛЕТНИ ПРАТКИ   Parcel Post   BULGARIA
ПОЩАВЬ РОМЖНИЯ %Bulgaria. BULGARIAN Occ. ROMANIA
ПРИЈМ . ЗЕЈНСКІЙ-КРАЙ   PRIAMUR ISSUE   SIBERIA
ПРНА ГОРА   MONTENEGRO
ПРТЬ ДЕСЯТЬ КОСЕЕКЬ   CRIMEA SOUTH RUSSIA
ПРТЬ РУБЛЕЙ   "   "   "
П. УКР. Н.Р. Registry stamp & label   WESTERN UKRAINE
РЕПУБЛИКА БЪЛГАРИЯ Bulgarian Republic BULGARIA
Р.О.П.и.Т. %р on Russian Offices in Turkey   UKRAINE
РОССІЯ   Sword Cutting Chain   1918   RUSSIA
РОССІЯ сЕВ AUMIЯ Army of the North 1920   "
РОССІИ %р Russia   CRIMEA   SOUTH RUSSIA
         Russian Soviet Federated
Р. С.Ф.С.Р. Socialist Republic   1921-23 SOVIET RUSSIA
РУССКАЯ ПОУТА   Wrangel issues in Turkey   RUSSIA
СПЕЩНАЯ ПОУТА   Special Delivery   "
СРБИЈА seated Figure. с. ПАРА Newspapers   SERBIA
      "   с. ДИНАРА or ДИН.   German Occ. of   "
Срба (СРБА) Хрвата и Словенаца %р BOSNIA S.P. JUGOSLAV.
С.С.С.Р.   Union of Soviet Socialist Republics 1923-   U.S.S.R
СЕв.Зап. ·АрмІЛ %р on RUSSIA . Army of Northwest 1919 RUSSIA
ТАКСА ДОПЛАЩАНКЕ   Postage Due   BULGARIA
ТАКСЕНА БИЉЕГА   "   "   MONTENEGRO
ЦАРСТВО БЪЛГАРИЯ   BULGARIA
ЦРНА ГОРА %р Italy   Italian Occupation MONTENEGRO
ЦР. ГОРЕ : ПОШТЕ UPHE ГОРЕ : UPHA ГОРЕ   "   "
ЦРНЕГОРЕ ТАКСЕНА БЕЉЕГЕ   Postage Due   "   "
УКРАІНСЬКА Р.О.П.й.Т. with trident   UKRAINE
УКР. Н.Р. : УКР. Н.РЕП %р Austria   WESTERN UKRAINE
ФИЛАТЕЛИЯ ДЕТЯМ Р.С.Ф.С.Р. semi-postal SOVIET RUSSIA
Ф.Н.Р. ЈУГОСЛАВИЈА   Official   JUGOSLAVIA
ФОНДЬ САНАТОРИУМЬ   Sunday Postal Tax   BULGARIA
ЮГО-ВОСТОК ГОЛОДАЮЩИМ Semi-Postal SOVIET RUSSIA
ЮЖНА БЪЛГАРИЯ and Lion Rampant SOUTH BULGARIA

FIG. 33-4.

GREEK ALPHABET

Greek letters are used on the definitive stamps of Greece, Crete, Epirus, the Ionian Islands, Samos, and on some stamps issued during the occupation of Dedeagatch by Turkey. They occur also as overprints on Greek issues and on Greek stamps during the occupation of Albania (North Epirus), Epirus, the Aegean Islands, Icaria, Lemnos, Thrace, and Turkey; on Bulgarian stamps during the occupation of Dedeagatch and Cavalle in Turkey, and on Turkish stamps during the Greek occupation of Thrace and Mytilene (Lesbos).

MODERN GREEK • TRANSLITERATION TO ENGLISH ••

A	α	A	a	I	ι	I	i	ʽP	ρ	Rh	rh
B	β	B	b	K	κ	K	k	Σ	σs	S	s
Γ	γ	G	g	Λ	λ	L	l	T	τ	T	t
Δ	δ	D	d	M	μ	M	m	Υ	υ	Y	y
E	ε	E	e	N	ν	N	n	Φ	φ	Ph	ph
Z	ζ	Z	z	Ξ	ξ	X	x	X	χ	Ch	ch
H	η	Ē	ē	O	ο	O	o	Ψ	ψ	Ps	ps
Θ	θ	Th	th	Π	π	P	p	Ω	ω	Ō	ō

Υ υ following Aα, Eε, Hη and Oo is "u" not "y"
Aü • Ay: ʽ • h: γ before γ, κ or χ is n: final s is "s" not "σ"

FIG. 33–5.

Fig. 33-5 shows the transliteration of Greek letters into Latin letters according to the standard of the Library of Congress, Greek capitals and small letters being followed by the Latin equivalents.

Fig. 33-6 shows examples of Greek inscriptions to help a collector identify the country of origin. No attempt has been made to include the many inscriptions on postal tax or semi-postal issues.

In some cases it is necessary to know the exact size of the inscription and the character of lettering to identify the stamps

SELECTED GREEK INSCRIPTIONS

Β.ΗΠΕΙΡΟΣ   o/p on Greek Occ.Stamps & Regular Greek   EPIRUS

ΔΕΔΕΑΓΑΤΣ (ΕΛΛΗΝΙΚΗ ΔΙΟΙΚΗΣΙΣ) greek occ. DEDEAGATCH

ΔΙΟΙΚΗΣΙΣ ΔΥΤΙΚΗΣ ΘΡΑΚΗΣ   o/p on Greek. Occ. of   THRACE

Διοίχησις Θραχης   o/p Greek. occup. WESTERN THRACE

Ε.Δ.   o/p Greek. Occ.Aegean Isl.   CILICIA

ΕΘΝΙΚΑ ΠΕΡΙΘΑΛΨΙΣ   POSTAL TAX   GREECE

ΕΚΘΕCΙC   SALONIKA   "   "   "

ΕΛΛΑΣ   "

ΕΛΛ. ΑΥΤΟΝ ΗΠΕΙΡΟΣ   o/p Turkey   EPIRUS

ΞΛΛ. ΔΙΟΙΚ.ΓΚΙΟΥΜΟΥ-ΑΤΖΙΝΑΣ   Greek Occ.   THRACE

ΕΛΛΗΝΙΚΗ -ΔΙΟΙΚΗCΙC   o/p Greek occ.No.EPIRUS ALBANIA

ΕΛΛΗΝΙΚΗ ΔΙΟΙΚΗΣΙΣ   "   Occ. of   TURKEY

Ελληνική - Κατοχή- Μυτιλήνής   o/p Turkey Greek Occ.MYTILENE   "

ΕΛΛΗΝΙΚΗ·ΧΕΙΜΑΡΡΑ   o/p Greek   Chimarra issue   EPIRUS

ΕΠΕΙΡΟΣ   o/p   "   and Def.   EPIRUS

ΙΚΑΡΙΑΣ·   ICARIA

ΙΟΝΙΚΟΝ ΚΡΑΤ.ΟΣ   IONIAN ISLANDS

ΚΟΙΝΩΝΙΚΗ ΠΡΟΝΟΙΑ   Postal Tax   GREECE

ΚΟΡΥΤΣΑ   Koritsa Issue   EPIRUS

Κ.Π.   o/p Greek. Postal Tax   GREECE

ΚΡΗΤΗ   CRETE

ΛΗΜΝΟΣ,   o/p Greek.·   Occ. of   LEMNOS

ΠΡΟΝΟΙΑ ΤΑΧ. ΥΠΑΛΛΗΛΩΝ   o/p   Postal Tax   GREECE

ΠΡΟΝΟΙΑ ΠΡΟΣΩΠΙΚΟΥ Τ.Τ.Τ.   o/p   "   "   "

ΠΡΟΝΟΙΑ   o/p   "   "   "

ΠΡΟΣΤΑΣΙΑ ΦΥΜΑΞΙΚΩΝ ΤΤΤ. Def.   "   "   "

ΠΡΟΣΩΡΙΝΟΝ· ΤΑΧΥΔΡΟΜ.(ΕΙΟΝ) ΗΡΑΚΛΕΙΟΥ   CRETE

ΠΡΟΣΩΡΙΝΟΝ and insc. in 2nd Line   DEDEAGATCH

ΣΑΜΟΥ   SAMOS

Σ.Δ.Δ.   o/p Greek. Occ. Dodecanese Isl.   AEGEAN ISLANDS

Υπάτη Αρμοστεια Θραχης o/p Turkey.Greek occ. WEST. THRACE

ΦΥΜΑΤΙΚΩΝ ΤΤΤ. or ΦΥΜ.ΤΤΤ o/p   o/p Postal Tax   GREECE

ΧΑΡΤΟΣΗΜΟΝ o/p Κ.Π.   "   "   "

Π.Ι.Π. o/p on Red Cross & Soldiers   "   "   "

FIG. 33–6.

of the Greek occupations of Icaria, Turkey, and Cavalle, and the *Standard Catalogue* will be needed.

A very few inscriptions show a substitution of the Cyrillic C *(S)* for the Greek *sigma*. One example occurs in overprints for the Greek occupation of Albania.

ORIENTAL ALPHABETS

Indian Native States, and Nepal and Pakistan

The native states of India may be difficult as all inscriptions may be in strange characters poorly drawn. It is fortunate that these issues have been discontinued and that all now use the stamps of India or Pakistan. There may have been little excuse for listing them in general catalogs for they were local stamps without franking power outside the state; except the reciprocal issues of Cochin and Travancore, which paid postage from either to points within the other.

Inscriptions in the various languages and dialects of India are in alphabets such as Devanagari and its derivatives, Oriya and Gujarati; in Malayalam and Dogra, as well as Arabic and native characters in the Moslem provinces of India and Pakistan. Through British influence English words or conventional numerals appear on a large proportion of the issues and all such are identified easily.

Many stamps use three or four languages with Devanagari predominating. This is easy to identify as the letters are written dangling from a line, but it is not so easy to transliterate as hundreds of ligatures or joined letters may be used or not according to the whim of the artist and some letters differ in the various states. Devanagari inscriptions were added to the Indian stamps when India became a dominion and they are now used by the Republic of India.

Oriya characters appear on the stamps of Bamra only, while Gujarati is used on all issues of Jasdan, Morvi, and Wadhwan, and on a single stamp of Nowanugger. Malayalam appears on the stamps of Cochin and Travancore, and on those of Burma, and of Ceylon since becoming a dominion. All the issues in this paragraph also have English inscriptions except the Jasdan and Nowanugger stamps. Typical forms of inscriptions are shown in fig. 33-7.

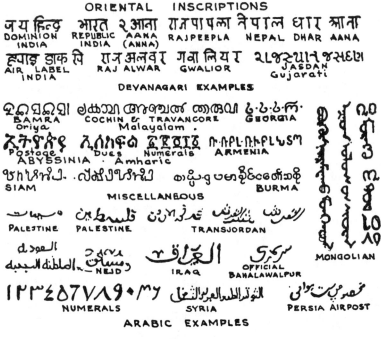

Fig. 33–7.

Devanagari Inscriptions

The following Indian states have some stamps with the principal inscriptions in Devanagari. There may be other languages but there is no English unless noted. The designs are shown in fig. 33-8 and are briefly mentioned below.

Alwar. Shows a well-drawn katar or arm dagger. No. 1.
Bhor. Two designs have inscriptions only, in frames. Nos. 2, 3.
Bundi. A poorly drawn katar in early issues; a seated raja with sacred cow supporters in issue of 1915. Nos. 6, 7.

FIG. 33–8.

Dhar. First issue has inscriptions only, with decorated frame. No. 5.

Duttia (Datia). The first type shows a seated figure of Ganesh, a god with an elephant head, within a decorated frame. English inscriptions were added for the second type. No. 8.

Gwalior. India stamps overprinted in English and Devanagari. Official stamps have only the latter. No. 9.

Indore. One design only is limited to Devanagari. No. 4.

Nandgaon. The second type is without English. No. 15.

Nepal. This is not a native state but uses Devanagari. Various designs, usually a seated figure with a background of mountains. Nos. 11, 12, 13.

Nowanugger. A type with curved dagger is not illustrated, another shows the arms of the state. No. 14.

Rajasthan. A frame and inscription overprinted on stamps of Bundi. No. 10.

Rajpeepla. All designs show a dagger or crossed daggers. Nos. 16, 17, 18.

Soruth. Two types show Devanagari. Nos. 20, 21.

DEVANAGARI VARIANTS

Jasdan. A sun with features within a central medallion, value at top in English "1 Anna 1," at bottom in Devanagari, inscriptions in Gujarati. Not illustrated.

Nowanugger. The second type shows a Gujarati inscription within a frame. No. 19.

Devanagari and Arabic Inscriptions

A few states have issued bilingual stamps in Devanagari and Arabic, and there may be other inscriptions in native characters such as Dogra but there are no English words or numerals.

Faridkot. Two similar designs. Fig. 33-8, No. 30.

Jammu and Kashmir. Circular and rectangular stamps with a narrow band of inscriptions are from Jammu and Kashmir. Rectangular stamps with a wide band of inscriptions with a star at top may be Jammu, or Kashmir. Nos. 26, 27, 28, 29.

Jhalawar. A dancing figure in oval or rectangle. Nos. 31, 32.

Poonch. Some divided horizontally with Arabic. Nos. 34, 35.

Others with Arabic in central panel and Devanagari all around. Not illustrated.

Arabic Inscriptions

Indian states that have issued stamps in Arabic only are Faridkot, Hyderabad, and Jhind, and Bahalawalpur (Pakistan) in its official stamps only. The Arabic design of Faridkot is shown in fig. 33-8, No. 25, and that of Hyderbad is No. 33. Examples of the Jhind are shown in Nos. 22, 23, 24, although all are identified by the letter "R." The Arabic overprint on the official issues of Bahalawalpur is indicated by name in fig. 33-7.

Since Pakistan was separated from India, none of its native states has issued stamps except Bahalawalpur. All stamps of Pakistan have the name in English except one set which bears the date "August 15, 1947."

ARABIC INSCRIPTIONS OUTSIDE INDIA

Countries that have issued stamps with Arabic inscriptions only include Afghanistan, Hejaz, Nejd, Persia, Saudi Arabia, Syria, Trans-Jordan (Jordan), Turkey, and Yemen. All issues of Egypt have some Latin-letter inscriptions and those of Azerbaijan have Cyrillic letters which will identify them.

Afghanistan

Stamps were circular until 1891 and all issues from 1871 to 1880 show a tiger head. Fig. 33-9, Nos. 2, 3, 6. Later issues show a small medallion with a mosque gate, Nos. 1, 4; a mosque with minaret (no illustration), or an eight-pointed star-shaped sunburst with the mosque and minaret (no illustration). Eventually the sunburst became a star with a crescent.

Conventional numerals of value were added in 1921, and the inscription "Afghan Postage" in 1927. Since 1928 this has read "Postes Afghanes" or "Postes Afghanistan." The tughra of the Amir, King Amanullah, appears on the 1928 issue commemorating the ninth year of his reign. This differs from the tughras on the stamps of other countries.

FIG. 33–9.

Hejaz

The first designs resemble oriental rugs, fig. 33-9, Nos. 14, 15, but all later issues are crude, see Nos. 13, 16, and overprints on old issues are more common than new designs. There has been no deviation from an all-Arabic design. After 1926 the stamps were of Hejaz-Nejd.

Nejd

The first issues were overprinted on Turkish stamps, as shown in fig. 33-10, Nos. 1, 2, and 3, and on Hejaz stamps as shown in fig. 33-7, "Nejd." Ibn Saud captured Hejaz in 1926 and governed both as Hejaz-Nejd, issuing stamps under that name. In 1928, Latin letters were in use and in 1934 the name was changed to the Kingdom of Saudi-Arabia.

Palestine and the Near East

The first issues were the "E.E.F." type under British military occupation, and one value change was made by overprinting "5 Milliemes," in that form and in Arabic as shown in fig. 33-7 at the first inscription above the caption *Palestine*.

These stamps were also used in various states of the Near East and in the adjoining districts of Egypt. In 1920, during the British mandate, the "E.E.F." stamps were overprinted with trilingual inscriptions in English, Hebrew, and Arabic, the latter being shown in fig. 33-7, at the second inscription above the caption *Palestine*.

Persia

Issues until 1881 were without Latin letters (see fig. 33-9, Nos. 17, 19), but in 1881 the words "Poste Persane" were added, changing to "Postes Persanes" in 1894. The country's name was changed to Iran in 1935, and the inscription became "Postes Iraniennes." The distinguishing elements of the first designs were the lion holding a sword with the sun rising behind, and next the full-face portrait of Shah Nasr-ed-Din wearing a plumed fez.

Syria

With one exception all stamps of Syria during the French mandate and the republic have Latin-letter inscriptions in addition to Arabic. The exception is shown in fig. 33-9, No. 22.

The 1920 issues of the Arabian government of Syria were overprinted Turkish stamps with the Arabic inscriptions shown in fig. 33-10, Nos. 17 to 20. Two definitive issues appeared in 1920, in horizontal rectangular form with the date "1920" at the left and the Arabic date at the right. Fig. 33-9, No. 21. A feature of the second design, not illustrated, is a seven-pointed star near the bottom center. Typical revenue stamps overprinted for postal use are shown in fig. 33-9, Nos. 20 and 23.

Thrace

This former Turkish province had several political changes following the Balkan disturbances and the First World War. Overprints and inscriptions of Greek occupation stamps are shown in fig. 33-6. Under Turkish rule, stamps were provided by overprinting Turkish issues with the inscription shown in fig. 33-10, No. 15, or Bulgarian and Greek stamps with that shown at No. 4.

There was a definitive issue in 1913 in two designs, both in Arabic except for the date "1913" in conventional numerals at the bottom center.

Trans-Jordan, Now Jordan

Under British mandate, 1920-1946, the first stamps were made by overprinting Palestine stamps with an Arabic inscription, fig. 33-10, No. 6, and until 1923 new values and issues were provided by handstamping the first issue with the inscriptions shown in fig. 33-10, Nos. 5, 7, and 9. From 1923 to 1927, Hejaz stamps generally were used, handstamped as in fig. 33-10, Nos. 10, 14, 12, 13, 16, and 11, in that order, the last being for postage dues. Palestine stamps also were used in 1923, handstamped as in fig. 33-10, No. 8.

In 1927 definitive issues show the name Trans-Jordan or Transjordan in English. In 1949 the name Jordan was adopted, the official name being "The Hashemite Kingdom of the Jordan."

Fig. 33–10.

Turkey

The design of 1863 shows a flat crescent with the tughra of the sultan above, fig. 33-9, No. 8. This design has a panel on a base which shows additional inscriptions. The design of 1865 shows a crescent and star on an oval center, fig. 33-9, No. 10, and was in use until September, 1876. Then the design began to show a crescent resting on a curved label with the inscription "Emp. Ottoman" in Latin letters and the value in conventional numerals with the word "paras" or "piastres." Within the horns of this crescent is a complicated inscription in Arabic.

In 1892 the stamps were enlarged in various designs but all have a central circular panel with the tughra surrounded by a display of arms. Fig. 33-9, No. 9. This and the succeeding issues have no Latin letters except in the values, which at first were in conventional numerals and repeated in French, as "Dix Paras" for "10 paras," etc. Later these French equivalents were omitted.

When Turkey became a republic in 1923, the tughra was omitted but the Moslem crescent and star were retained and the values were expressed in conventional numerals and Latin letters as well as in Arabic.

Following the language reform, the stamps of 1926 and later show the country name as Turkiye, usually followed by the word "Postalari" in full or abbreviated. The symbols will aid a collector in identifying Turkish stamps but the *Standard Catalogue* will be needed to separate all of the issues. The Red Star emblem of the Turkish Red Cross Society, as used on postal tax stamps, is shown in fig. 33-9, No. 11.

Turkey in Asia

This separate state, Anatolia, came into being in 1919 with the uprising of Mustafa Kemal Pasha, and included all of Turkey in Asia Minor. The first stamps were overprinted on Turkish revenue and regular postage issues showing the sultan's tughra. Definitive issues of 1922 and later show the crescent and star only and the inscriptions are in Arabic. With the formation of the Republic of Turkey and the expulsion of the sultan in 1923, Anatolia rejoined Turkey and later issues are listed for the Turkish Republic.

Yemen

Only the first issue is without the inscription "Yemen" in Latin letters. The crossed scimitar design is shown in fig. 33-9, No. 18.

OTHER ORIENTAL LANGUAGES

Aside from Chinese and Japanese the few remaining languages written in non-Latin letters usually are confined to a single country. Thus, Ethiopia, Armenia, Georgia, Burma, and Siam have their individual languages. The stamps of Outer Mongolia and Tannu Tuva have Mongolian inscriptions and those of Tibet are peculiar to that land. The plate of Oriental inscriptions, fig. 33-7, shows examples of the various alphabets.

Armenia

The first issues were provisionals made in 1920 by overprinting or handstamping Russian issues with a monogram, with or without frame. This is shown in fig. 33-11. In the same year a definitive design used the word "Armenia" but after becoming a socialist soviet republic in 1921 all inscriptions were given in Armenian. See fig. 33-7. The hammer and sickle show on some stamps, a five-pointed star on others, while some show neither and a few show both.

Armenian letters appear also on the quadrilingual stamps of the Trans-Caucasian Federated Republics, which included Armenia.

Burma

The first issues were overprinted on Indian stamps and from 1937 until the Japanese occupation were in English with bilingual value inscriptions. In 1942 stamps appeared with Japanese inscriptions, fig. 33-14, item *m*, and these were followed by ordinary Japanese stamps overprinted with new values in annas and rupees, and a little later these received a second overprinted value in cents, abbreviated *c.*

In 1943 a definitive issue used Burmese inscriptions only and later that year the first issue of 1942 appeared with values in cents, again abbreviated *c.* The final design of the Japanese oc-

EARLY   LATE
KOREA   **OUTER MONGOLIA**   **LATVIA**   **TANNU TUVA**

UKRAINE   **TRANSCAUC. FED. REP.**   **TURKEY**   **U.S.S.R.**   **ARMENIA**

AUSTRIA MERCURY HEADS   **EASTERN RUMELIA**   **SIBERIA**   **PUERTO RICO CHIFFRES**

FIG. 33–11.

cupation had Japanese inscriptions and was for use in a single district. This was soon attached to the Burma government and the stamps were overprinted in Burmese reading "Burma State."

Typical Burmese letters are shown in fig. 33-7. In 1945 the country was freed and the 1938 issue was overprinted "Mily Admn" (Military Administration). After becoming a republic in 1948 the first issue was in English but the next design and later issues are bilingual, Burmese and English.

Ethiopia

The stamps of this country from 1894 to 1909 have inscriptions entirely in Amharic, although the second issue was handstamped "Ethiope" and some later issues have overprinted values in conventional numerals. Only two designs were used, one for the lower values showing Menelik II with royal crown, facing right, the other showing the Lion of Judah facing left and holding the flag. The Amharic inscription and the overprint which identifies postage due stamps are shown in fig. 33-7.

Georgia

This part of the Russian empire first issued stamps in 1919, using the name "La Georgie" and the equivalent in Georgian letters. The second design uses the name "Republique Georgienne." In 1922 Georgia became a soviet republic. The first two issues show conventional numerals and a four-letter abbreviation of the new name. See fig. 33-7, Georgia. The third design of the republic has the inscriptions in full with the hammer and sickle emblem.

Stamps overprinted diagonally with Georgian letters are semi-postal issues. Georgian inscriptions appear also on the quadrilingual issues of the Trans-Caucasian Federated Republics.

Mongolia

The first issues of Outer Mongolia may be identified by the Scepter of Indra, the Yin and Yang, and other symbols of authority. Fig. 33-11. In 1926 the word "Mongolia" was added but two succeeding issues omit the English name and are overprinted with Mongol inscriptions and the word "Postage."

All following issues until 1945 are in Mongol and English, but in that year under Russian influence, the inscriptions became Cyrillic. See fig. 33-3, line "MOH." The stamps of Inner Mongolia are included with stamps using Chinese inscriptions.

Siam

The stamps of 1883 were entirely in Siamese but after that date have inscriptions in English and Siamese. In 1932 Siamese was used alone except for the highest value, but in 1939 the name "Siam" was restored, only to become "Thailand" in 1940. In

1941 Siamese only was used except in the value inscriptions, but in 1943 the English "Thai" or "Thailand" was restored. In 1947 the official name again became "Siam" but was changed back to "Thailand" in 1950. Typical inscriptions appear in fig. 33-7.

Before the English name was added three designs had been used, all showing a portrait facing left with different frames. One has a small circular value tablet near each corner with a Siamese numeral 1, which looks like this: ๐. The second type has a five-letter inscription on a ribbon near the bottom and the third has a six-letter inscription on a ribbon near the top.

One semi-postal issue has a cross in a circle in red, another has a tiger head with Siamese inscription, while others show the English "Scout's Fund" with the tiger head and Siamese words. Another Red Cross issue shows a stubby cross with Siamese lettering.

Tannu Tuva

The first issue, 1926, is in Mongol but may be identified by the Wheel of Life symbol at the center. Fig. 33-11. The next issue was made by overprinting the previous type with the inscription "Tovva K8K Postage," or with other numerals at the center, and succeeding issues bear the word "Touva" as a part of the design. In 1933 two values were made by overprinting "Posta 15" or "35" on revenue stamps with hammer and sickle at the center and Mongol letters below.

Tibet

These stamps have no franking power outside the country. The designs are bilingual in English and Tibetan, the first showing a lion head at the center, "Tibet" at the left, and "Postage" at the right. The second design is larger and has a less recognizable lion, and the inscription "Tibet Postage" on the lower half of a circular ring. The third design shows a lion of Chinese character in a square panel and the word "Tibet" at the bottom.

CHINESE IDEOGRAMS

Chinese ideograms are found on the stamps of China, including Shanghai and the treaty ports, and on those of Japan, Manchukuo, Inner Mongolia, Korea, the Ryukyu Islands, and Formosa. They have a minor part on the stamps of Hong Kong, Labuan, North Borneo, etc., principally in bilingual denominations.

SOME CHARACTERS FOUND ON CHINESE & JAPANESE STAMPS

	CHINESE	JAPANESE	ENGLISH EQUIVALENTS		
郵	YU	YU	PERTAINING TO POSTAL AFFAIRS		
政	CHENG	SEI	ADMINISTRATION, GOVERNMENT		
局	CHU	KYOKU	DEPARTMENT, BUREAU, OFFICE		
中	CHUNG	CHU [NAKA]	INSIDE, MIDDLE, CENTER		
華	HUA	HANAYAKA	SPLENDID, BRIGHT, FLOWERY		
民	MIN	MIN [TAMI]	PEOPLE	民國	A REPUBLIC
國	KUA	KOKU [KUNI]	COUNTRY	國民	A NATION
大	TA	DAI	GREAT		
軍	CHUN	GUN	MILITARY, ARMY		
便		BIN	FACILITY, MEANS		

FIG. 33–12.

They are found as overprints in countries occupied by Japan during the Second World War, and on definitive issues made for some of those countries when local stamps were exhausted. They appear also on stamps overprinted by China for the districts regained at the close of the war.

The inscriptions normally read from right to left or downward, but in recent Japanese issues and in the Japanese occupation stamps the form is reversed and they read from left to right.

The ideograms are found in several styles, some of which differ greatly from the ordinary characters and may be original with the stamp designer. The styles include seal script, a stylized form used on seals, medals, etc.; grass writing, a thin, cursive treatment of characters; type forms, as used in book printing;

and the ordinary brush characters as written by a scribe. Japan uses in addition the kana syllabary, a phonetic shorthand invented to simplify the written language.

Fig. 33-12 shows the Chinese characters commonly found on the stamps of more than one country, with the Chinese and Japanese names of the characters and their English equivalents. Although the Chinese and Japanese words seldom are the same, the meanings are identical.

STAMPS OF CHINA

The stamps of China give little trouble since all have English inscriptions until 1931. The name appears as China, then Imperial Chinese Post, Chinese Imperial Post, and finally Republic of China. After 1931 the Sven Hedin issue of 1932 alone has any inscription in English. All stamps prior to the formation of the republic show the name as "Ta Ch'ing" in ideograms; this is found in the corner tablets of the early issues and in the principal inscription after 1894. The original form of these characters is shown in fig. 33-13 item *a*. A later form with modified "Ch'ing," first used in 1897, is shown at *b*. Inscriptions read from right to left or downward and for purposes of symmetry the designer may vary the characters used. The inscription which at first was "ta ch'ing kuo" at the right, item *c*, and "yu cheng chu" at the left, item *d*, became "ta ch'ing kuo cheng," item *e*, and again but written in a single line, "ta ch'ing kuo yu cheng chu."

The currency change from candareens to dollars and cents in 1897 did not affect the stamps as the characters for cents and candareens are identical. The change to the republic brought a number of overprints reading downward "chung hua min kuo" (the Republic of China), fig. 33-13, item *f*. When the junk design appeared, the characters "yu cheng," item *g*, were added, making a six-part inscription.

Under the republic all issues with a postal inscription start with "chung hua" and end with "yu cheng." A few issues omit the "min kuo" leaving a four-part inscription as at item *h*. The twelve-pointed star, item *i*, was introduced on commemorative stamps in 1928 and made permanent with the definitive issue of

1931. It appears on all stamps through 1948, except a few commemorative issues, and its introduction coincides with the end of English inscriptions.

Two commemorative issues have no postal inscription or star. The Tan Yuan-chang set of 1933 shows a portrait, three-quarters right, with a tall inscription at the bottom and a numeral at upper left. The $5000 philatelic exhibition issue of 1948 shows facsimiles of previous Chinese stamps.

FIG. 33-13.

The inscriptions in fig. 33-13 include two varieties of the overprint "yu chan" (army post), item *j*, for military stamps. The overprint that the Chinese placed on the Japanese stamps of Formosa is shown at *k* and reads "tai wan sho" (Formosa Province).

The character "jin," meaning person or people, shown at *l*, is found on the stamps of Red China in the principal inscription to indicate the people's republic.

The remainder of the plate shows variations in characters, including some used on Japanese stamps which have little resemblance to the original brush-written ideograms.

JAPANESE STAMPS

Although the Japanese use Chinese characters, the stamps are not difficult to distinguish. From 1872 until 1947 all show the chrysanthemum "mon" or crest of the emperor, fig. 33-14, item

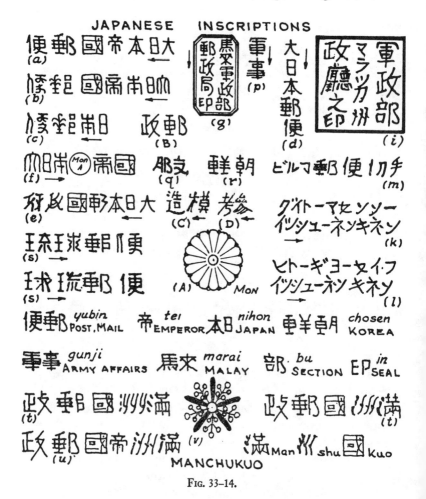

FIG. 33–14.

The inscriptions in fig. 33-14 are explained below. An arrow beside or beneath each of these inscriptions in the plate indicates the direction in which it is to be read. Three of the overprints, listed as items *j*, *n*, and *o*, are not illustrated.

a. "Dai Nihon tei koku yu bin," Greater Japanese Empire Postal Service, on definitive issues, 1876-1946, in ordinary characters.

b. Same, but in seal script, also on Japanese issues for Formosa.

b. Reversed, at top of stamp. Definitive issue with scenes, sen (cents) and rupees (gulden). Occupation of Java and Dutch East Indies. Same but with "cents" at right, occupation of Straits Settlements.

b. Reading down. Definitive issue with scenes, value in sen, for use in Java and Sumatra.

c. Four-character inscription "Nihon yu bin," Japanese Postal Service, in seal script, on definitive issue of 1946.

c. Reversed. Definitive issues of 1947 and later.

d. Reading down. "Dei Nihon tei yu bin," overprint on Straits Settlements, Johore, Negri Sembilan, Pahang, Perak, Selangor, and Trengganu during occupation.

e. Cursive writing overprint on stamps of occupied Brunei.

f. At top, flag in scenic design, occupation of Lesser Sunda Islands.

g. Handstamped overprint reading down at left "yu sei kyoku in," (Japanese Postal Bureau Seal), and at right "ma rai gun sei bu" (Malay Military Post Section), on Straits Settlements.

h. Same, handstamped overprint in line frame with rounded corners, on Straits Settlements, Kelantan, Negri Sembilan, Pahang, Perak, Selangor and Trengganu.

i. Handstamped overprint to cover four stamps of Malacca.

j. Overprint of black bars to cover all inscriptions, new values added. Philippine Commonwealth stamps during occupation. No illustration.

k and *l.* Two-line kana inscriptions on Philippine stamps.

m. At top of a definitive design showing a plowman, inscription in Chinese and kana, "yu bin," near center. Occupied Burma.

n. Regular Japanese issue overprinted in annas and rupees. Occupation of Burma. Not illustrated.

o. Same, with additional overprint in cents (c) and rupees. Not illustrated.

p. "Gun ji" on stamps for military use, overprint on regular Japanese issues.

q. "Shi na," offices in China, overprint on regular Japanese issues.

r. "Cho sen," offices in Korea, overprint on regular Japanese issues.

s. Left to right, two forms of "Ryu kyu yu bin," appearing on the definitive issues of the Ryukyu Islands.

t and *u.* See text for Manchukuo.

A. The chrysanthemum mon or crest of the Japanese Empire. This must have 16 petals. Facsimiles of stamps which have any other number of petals are not considered counterfeits by Japanese authorities.

B. The "yu sei" inscription for post office or postal service.

C. "Mo zo," meaning "make copy," placed on some facsimiles of Japanese stamps.

D. Another indication of forgery, "san ko," meaning "reference," placed on Japanese facsimiles.

The above inscriptions are followed by some inscriptions or overprints on Japanese stamps. These are defined in the plate.

A, and this is not used elsewhere except on one definitive issue for the Lesser Sunda Islands of the Dutch East Indies under Japanese occupation in 1945.

The first Japanese issue, 1871, is without the crest and has no English inscriptions. The square design is bordered with a Greek fret and shows a dragon at either side of a vertical value inscription. From 1872 to 1876, the crest indicates the country and below or beside it are the characters "yu sei" (post office), shown at *B*. The value is in conventional numerals with the currency "sen" in Latin letters.

From 1876 until 1896 nearly all designs have an inscription, item *a* or *b*, reading right to left, "dai Nihon tei koku yu bin" (Greater Japanese [Nipponese] Empire Postal Service), in regular or seal script, and an English inscription, "Imperial Japanese Post." After 1896 very few stamps have any Latin-letter inscriptions except the words "Sen," "Sn," or "Yen," following conventional numerals of value. After 1936 the currency designation is omitted except for yen values which are marked "En."

Prior to 1920 some designs have a short inscription, "Nihon yu bin," fig. 33-14, item *c*, using the crest instead of "Tei koku," and omitting "dai" entirely, but from 1920 until the fall of Japan in 1945 the "dai" was prominent. This had the same effect in the title as the word *Great* in Great Britain, but with the issue of 1946-1947 this character was discontinued. At about the same time the crest was dropped except on a few issues which had been designed earlier, and the inscriptions were reversed to read from left to right in Occidental style. These radical changes were in full effect by the end of 1947 but at present the only other concession to Western influence is in the conventional numerals of value for the sen values and the numbers and underscored decimals for the yen values.

None of these issues can be confused with Chinese or other stamps if the collector becomes familiar with the "Nihon yu bin" characters.

In addition to Chinese ideograms some Japanese issues show "kana" characters. Each indicates a sound in the language and they may be strung together like beads to form a word, thus reducing the memory task required for reading and writing. Chinese ideograms have no relation to sounds and must be memorized individually.

STAMPS OF MANCHUKUO

Manchukuo was a Japanese puppet state from 1932 until the fall of Japan in 1945, when it reverted to China. Its stamps after that date are Chinese issues overprinted for the Northeastern Provinces. The first stamps of the new country have a five-character inscription, "Manshu koku yu sei" (Manchu State Postal Administration), fig. 33-14, item *t*.

After the enthronement of Henry Pu-Yi in 1934 as Emperor Kang Teh, the inscription was expanded to "Manchu tei koku yu sei" (Manchu Empire Postal Administration), item *u*. In the following year the orchid crest, item *v*, was adopted and became prominent in stamp designs. The issue of 1936, for use to China, used the crest for the empire name and confined the Chinese characters to "yu sei" or postal administration. In the next definitive issue the full inscription was restored. Nearly all stamps show the denominations in "fen" and "yuan," or abbreviations.

The elements of the name Manchukuo are defined in fig. 33-14. It should be noted that this puppet state was former Chinese territory, ruled by a former Chinese prince, and it took its name from the Chinese names of the characters. The Japanese name would have been Man-chu-koku.

STAMPS WITHOUT COUNTRY NAMES

Fig. 33-15 shows early stamps which may be identified by the portrait and the language used for the word *postage*. The countries are: Spain, Nos. 1-5; Portugal, 6-8; Switzerland, 9-10; Hungary, 11; Finland, 12-15; the last two showing the small circles added to Russian stamps for use in Finland; Roman States,

F<small>IG</small>. 33–15.

16-18; Roumania, 19-20; Austria, 21-25; Bosnia, 26; Brazil, 27-29; France, 30.

Plate XXXVIII (facing page 437) duplicates some of the above but in halftone.

❖❖

MONETARY UNITS

In this list the currency make-up of each country is given after the particular unit most used on stamps. At one time there was a stable relative value for each foreign unit in terms of United States dollars but after many revaluations the units have little relation to an original value or to each other. Prior to 1900 the leu, drachma, lev, lira, marka, dinar, and the various francs were equivalent to a French franc. The tical and boliviano were equal to two French francs; the Straits dollar to three francs; The thalers of Bremen, Brunswick, and Hanover, to four francs; the scudo, toman, venzolano to the peso of the Spanish colonies prior to 1871; and the United States dollar to five French francs.

Similarly, the British shilling and German mark were of equivalent value, and the gulden of Austria-Hungary, the ruble, the florin of Bosnia, Montenegro, and Lombardy-Venetia, and the Japanese yen were equal to two shillings. The thalers of several German states and the North German Confederation were equal to three shillings and the five-franc equivalents were equal to four shillings.

Except in a few cases these equivalents were not absolute but the difference was slight and did not appear when comparing postal rates. Today values have little relation to those of fifty years ago, except those which have been devalued in direct proportion along with the United States dollar.

Under the Universal Postal Union the postage rates between countries by surface mail are quoted in terms of a gold franc of 100 gold centimes, which at this writing is equal to about 40 cents (U.S.). This gold franc is based on the original Swiss franc, then worth almost 20 cents but now higher in terms of the devalued United States cents.

In the following table the usual abbreviations of a unit follow the unit. Those which apply to a single country are placed with that country name. The abbreviations of the principal coinage unit of a country are capitalized in the inscriptions on stamps, those of the minor units are often in lower-case letters. Although some foreign words for units have diacritical marks, they do not appear consistently in the inscriptions. An asterisk indicates that the unit word or abbreviation does not show on stamps, or on the stamps of a country as marked in the listing. A double asterisk indicates that there are no Latin letters on the stamps having this currency.

Abasi (Abassi, abbasi).   See Shahi.

Adopengo(s), Ap.   See Filler (b).

Afghani (Afghan rupee), Af., Afg.   See Pul.

Agorot.   100 = 1 Israeli pound after 1960.

Angolar(s), Ag., Ags.   See Centavo (g).

Anna(s), A., An., As.

   (a)   16 = 1 rupee, 3 pies = 1 pice, 4 pice = 1 anna: Aden to 1951, Bahrain, Burma to 1953, India to 1956, Muscat, Pakistan, Zanzibar to 1908.

   (b)   16 = 1 rupee: British East Africa, British Occupation of Mesopotamia, East Africa and Uganda to 1907, French Offices in Zanzibar, Iraq to 1932, Kuwait, Somaliland Protectorate to 1951, Tibet to 1933, Uganda.

   (c)   16 = 1 rupee, 6 dokra = 1 anna: Indian state Nowanugger.

   (d)   16 = 1 rupee, 5 = 1 puttan, 12 pies = 1 anna: Indian state Cochin.

   (e)   1 = 2 chuckrams = 32 cash: Indian state Travancore.

(f) 1 = 4 folus or paisas: Indian states of Faridkot,** Rajpeepla.**

(g) 25 = 1 rupee Nepalese = 100 pice: Nepal.

(h) 16 = 1 rupie = 64 besa: Italian Somaliland to 1906.

Att(s). 64 = 1 tical: Siam 1883-1909. See Solot.

Auksinas, Auksinai, Auksinu, Auks. See Skatikas.

Aurar (singular Eyrir), A., Aur., Eyr. 100 = 1 krona: Iceland after 1876.

Avo(s), A. 100 = 1 pataca, 78 = 1 rupee*: Macao after 1894; Timor after 1895.

Baht. See Satang.

Baiza(s). 64 = 1 rypee: Omañ after 1966; 1000 = 1 rial saidi: Omañ after 1970.

Bajoccho(i). 100 = 1 scudo. Bai., Romagna; Baj., Roman States to 1867.

Balboa(s), B., B/. See Centesimo (d).

Ban(i), B. 100 = 1 leu: Roumania after 1868.

Banica.* 100 = 1 kuna: Croatia after 1921, inscription in kuna and decimals.

Besa. 100 = 1 rupie: Italian Somaliland 1922-1925. See Anna (h).

Bits(s). 100 = 1 franc: Danish West Indies 1905 and later.

Bogchah, bogaches, bogsha(s). 40 = 1 imadi: Yemen.

Bolivar(es), B., Bs., B/. See Centimo (c).

Boliviano(s), Bs. See Centavo (n).

Butut(s). 100 = 1 dalasy: Gambia 1971.

Cache(s), Ca. 24 = 1 fanon, 8 fanon = 1 rupia (roupie): French India 1923 on.

Candareen(s), Cand., Cands. 100 = 1 tael: Shanghai to 1877, also, 16 cash = 1 candareen 1877 to 1890.

Candarin(s), Cn. 100 = 1 tael: China to 1897.

Cash. See Candareen.

Caury. 100 = 1 syli: Guinea 1973.

Cedi. See Pesewa.

Cent(s), c., ct., cts., ¢.

(a) 100 = 1 dollar: United States; Bahamas after 1966; Bermuda after 1970; British Virgin Islands 1962; Canal Zone; Cayman Island after 1969; Cuba 1898-1905; Guam 1898; Hawaii; Liberia; Philippine Islands 1899-1906; Puerto Rico 1898; United Nations. U.S. equivalent: British Columbia 1865; Canada after 1859; New Brunswick 1860; Newfoundland 1866; Nova Scotia 1860; Prince Edward Island 1872; Danish West Indies to 1905.

(b) 100 = 1 dollar (British West Indian): Antigua after 1951; Barbados after 1950; British Guiana; Dominica after 1949; Grenada after 1949; Cruyana; Leeward Islands after 1951; Montserrat after 1951; St. Christopher, Nevis & Anguilla; St. Kitts-Nevis after 1951; St. Lucia after 1949; St. Vincent after 1949; Trinidad & Tobago after 1935; Virgin Islands (British) 1951-1962.

(c) 100 = 1 dollar (British Honduran): British Honduras; Belizē after 1972.

(d) 100 = 1 dollar (Malayan or Straits Settlements): Bangkok; Brunei; Fiji Islands 1872-1874; Johore; Labuan; North Borneo; Sarawak; Straits Settlements, the individual states, and the Federated Malay States; Malaya 1957, Malaysia 1963; Sabah.

(e) 100 = 1 dollar (Hong Kong): Hong Kong; China (dollar or yuan) 1897 on; Inner Mongolia; Outer Mongolia to 1926; Shanghai 1866 and after 1890; German and Italian Offices in China.

(f) 100 (abbr. c., ct., cnt.) = 1 gulden (also called florin): Netherlands and colonies.

(g) 100 (abbr. c.) = 1 rupee: British Indian Ocean Territory; Ceylon 1872; East Africa and Uganda 1907; German East Africa 1917; Maldive Islands to 1951; Mauritius 1878; Seychelles Island; Tanganyika to 1922, Zanzibar 1908.

(h) 100 = 1 shilling: Aden and states after 1951; Kenya, Uganda and Tanganyika 1922; Somaliland Protectorate 1951; Zanzibar 1935; Uganda 1962; So. Arabian Fed. 1963; United Republic of Tanganyika and Zanzibar, Tanzan, 1964.

(i) 100 = 1 piastre: Indo-China 1918-1950; Cambodia to 1955; Laos to 1955; Viet Nam; French Offices in China after 1907, various French offices in Chinese cities 1918.

(j) 100 = 1 kip: Laos 1955.

(k) 100 = 1 riel: Cambodia 1955.

(l) 100 = 1 leone: Sierra Leone 1964.

(m) 100 = 1 rand: So. Africa, S.W. Africa, Basutoland, Bechuanaland, Botswana, Swazieland, and Tristan Da Cunha, 1961.

(n) 100 = 1 lilangen: Swaziland 1975.

(o) 100 = 1 dollar: Australian or New Zealand; Aitutaki after 1972; Australia after 1966; Christmas Island, Cocos Islands after 1969; Cook Islands after 1967; Nauru after 1966; New Zealand after 1967; Niue after 1967; Norfolk Island after 1967; Papua New

Guinea after 1967; Penrhyn Island after 1967; Pitcairn Islands after 1967; Solomon Islands after 1966; Tokelay Islands after 1967; Tuvalu.

Centas, centai, centu, c., ct., cnt., cent.   100 = 1 litas: Lithuania after 1922; Lithuanian occupation of Memel 1923.

Centava(s).   100 = 1 conto: St. Thomas and Prince Islands 1975.

Centavo(s), c., ct., cto., ctv., ctvo., cv., cvo., co., cen., cent., cento., centav. (plurals add s), ¢. Some indicated as "centavos de peso" (or other unit) in full or by abbreviations.

(a)   100 = 8 reales = 1 peso: Costa Rica to 1900; Dominican Republic except in 1883; Guatemala to 1927; Paraguay to 1944; Salvador to 1879; Venezuela to 1879.

(b)   100 = 1 peso: Argentina; Canal Zone to 1906; Chile; Colombia; Cordoba; Cuba after 1905; Honduras 1878-1933; Marianas Islands 1899; Mexico after 1867; Nicaragua to 1913 (inv. ¢ also); Panama to 1906; Peru to 1874, Philippine Islands after 1906.

(c)   100 = 1 peso = 1000 milesimas (mils. not used on Cuban stamps after 1888): Cuba 1881-1898; Fernando Po after 1882; Philippine Islands 1890-1898; Puerto Rico 1881-1898.

(d)   100 = 10 dinero = 5 pesetas = 1 peso: Peru 1858-1874.

(e)   100 = 1 real: Uruguay to 1858.

(f)   100 = 1 escudo: Portugal 1912 and colonies 1912 or 1913.

(g)   100 = 1 angolar: (80 angolars 100 escudos): Angola 1932.

(h)   100 = 1 sucre: Ecuador after 1881 (abbr. C/. also).

(i)   100 = 1 lempira: Honduras after 1933.

(j)   100 = 1 cordoba: Nicaragua after 1913.

(k)   100 = 1 colón: Salvador after 1912.

(l)   100 = 1 sol: Peru after 1874.

(m)   100 = 1 cruzeiro: Brazil after 1942.

(n)   100 = 1 boliviano: Bolivia after 1897.

(o)   100 = 1 quetzal: Guatemala after 1927.

(p)   50 centavos M.C. = 1 real moneda corriente: Corrientes.

(q)   100 centavos fuertes = 1 peso fuerte: Corrientes.

Centesimo (i), c., cen., cent., centes., cente., centi., centmi., cmi.

(a)   100 = 1 lira: Italy; Italian colonies and offices except otherwise indicated; Fiume 1919; Italian Somaliland 1906-1916; Italian Offices in Crete 1906, in Tripoli 1910; Lombardy-Venetia to 1858; Modena; Parma; Roman States 1867; San Marino; Sardinia; Trieste Zone A; Trieste Zone B to 1949; Tuscany 1860; Vatican City.

(b)   100 = 1 somala: Italian Somaliland after 1950.

Centésimo(s). Abbrs. differ little from last except in plurals.

(c) 100 (cs., cmos.) = 1 escudo or 1 peseta (c.d. peseta): Cuba 1867-1881, Philippine Islands 1870-1895.

(d) 100 = 1 balboa: Panama 1906 and Canal Zone overprints.

(e) 100 (cent'mo) = 1 peso = 1000 milésimas: Uruguay 1858.

(f) 100 = 1 venezolano: Venezuela 1879-1880.

Centime(s), c., ct(s)., cent(s)., cme(s).

(a) 100 = 1 franc (prior to 1918 all francs were about equal): France and colonies and offices not otherwise mentioned; Albania 1917; Andorra (French); Austrian Offices in Crete; Bulgaria to 1881; Ethiopia 1905-1908; German East Africa 1916; Monaco; Persia (franc or khan) 1881-1933.

(b) 100 = 1 franc (metropolitan*): France; French colonies in Northwest Africa, South America, and West Indies; Morocco; Algiers; Tangier; Tunisia; Andorra (Fr.); Monaco; Saar.

(c) 100 = 1 franc (C.F.A.* = 2 francs metropolitan): French colonies in Africa not included in (b); St. Pierre & Miquelon; Central African Republic 1958; Chad; Congo (Fr.); Malagasy Republic; Mali Federation; Dahomey; Gabon.

(d) 100 = 1 franc (C.P.A.* 5 francs metropolitan): French colonies in the Pacific except (h).

(e) 100 = 1 franc (Belgian*): Belgium (centiemen in Flemish); Congo (centiemes); Belgian East Africa; Ruanda Urundi; Congo Rep. (Belg.); Katanga; Rwanda; Burundi.

(f) 100 = 1 franc (L.*): Luxembourg.

(g) 100 = 1 franc (Swiss*) (centimes or rappen): Switzerland, Liechtenstein.

(h) 100(c. or) = 1 franc or (gold): New Hebrides Condominium.

(i) 100 = 1 piaster: Alouites; Alexandretta; Fr. off. in China; Haiti; Indo-China; Latakia; Lebanon (centiemes); Syria.

(j) 25 = 1 piastre: Castellorizio 1920; Fr. off. in Turkey; Rouad.

(k) 12½ = 1 silbergroschen: Luxembourg 1852.

(l) 100 = 1 thaler (talari): Ethiopia after 1936.

(m) 100 centimes du piastre = 1 piastré: Haiti to 1898.

(n) 100 centimes du gourde = 1 gourde: Haiti after 1898.

(o) 100 = 1 dirhem. Morocco 1961.

Centimo(s), c., ct., co., cen., cent., cto. Plurals add s, and cms., ctms. Some inscriptions are indicated as centimos de peseta, or escudo.

(a) 100 = 1 peseta: Spain; Spanish colonies except as noted; French

Offices in Morocco to 1917; German Offices in Morocco; Andorra (Spanish); Fernando Po (escudas = pesetas) to 1894; Gibraltar 1889-1895; Puerto Rico to 1881.

(b)   100 = 1 escudo: Fernando Po (cen. de esc.) 1868; Spain 1866-1873, (cmos., cent. de esc.), also = 1000 milésimas (mila. de eo., mils de esco.).

(c)   100 = 1 bolivar: Venezuela after 1880.

(d)   100 = 1 colón: Costa Rica after 1900.

(e)   100 = 1 guarani: Paraguay after 1944.

(f)   500 = 5 francos = 1 peso: Dominican Republic 1883 only.

Cent. po. fe. (centesimo peseta fuerte). Value in coin, not paper money: Philippine Islands 1864-1874.

Chahi(s), Ch., chai., chais. 20 = 1 kran, 10 krans = 1 toman: Persia 1885-1932. See Shahi (b).

Chetrum(s) Ch.   100 = 1 ngultrum, Ng. (1 Indian rupee). Bhutan 1962.   See Trangka.

Cheun, Cn.   100 = 1 weun, 10 re = 1 cheun: Korea 1900-1953. For Korean cheun prior to 1900 see Poon; for cheun after 1953 see Weun.

Chuckram(s), Chs.   See Anna (e).

Colón(es), C., $, ¢, ₡.   See Centimo (d); Centavo (k).

Conto.   See Centava.

Cordoba(s), C.   See Centavo (j).

Corona.   Italian for krone in overprints for Ital. occ. of Austria.

Cowrie(s)*.   50 = 1 penny: Uganda to 1896.

Crazia(ie).   See Quattrino.

Cruzeiro(s), Cr., Crs.   See Centavo (m).

Cs. de Eo.   Centesimos de Escudo, Philippine Islands 1870-1874.

Cuarto(s), cs., ctos.   8 = 1 real: Spain to 1866; 8 = 1 real plata fuerte, Philippine Islands to 1864.

Cy.   Abbr. used by Canada, 1885, for stamps with values shown both in currency and sterling (stg).

D or d.   Abbr. for penny, pence, peni, pene.

Dala.   Dollar on stamps of Hawaii, native form of the word.

Dalasy.   See Butut.

Daler.   Word for thaler, or dollar, used in Denmark, Norway, Sweden, and Iceland.

d.cy.   Abbr. for pence in currency, Canada 1858-1859.

d.stg.   Abbr. for pence in sterling Canada 1855-1859.

Dinar(s), D., Di., Drs.   100 = 1 rial: Persia 1933-1934; Iran after

1935. See Fil; Para (d), (plural dinari), Millieme (c).

Dinero. See Centavo (d).

Dirham(s). 100 = 1 riyal: Dubai after 1966; Qatar after 1967; Umm al Qiwain after 1962; Libya after 1972.

Dirhem. See Centime (o).

Dokra**. See Anna (c).

Dollar(s), $. See Cent (a) to (e), Sen (c).

Drachma(ai)**. See Lepta.

Ducat*. See Grano.

Emilageni. See Lilangen.

En. Same as yen, see Sen (a).

Escudo(s), E., Eo., Eos., Ecs., $. See Centavo (f), (g), Centesimo (c), Centimo (b).

Eyrir, Eyr. See Aurar.

Fanon, Fa. See Cache.

Farthing. See Penny: Bil, insc. on Heligoland after 1875.

Fen, Fn. 100 = 1 yuan: Manchukuo; Inner Mongolia; People's Republic of China**.

Fenig, Fenigi, Fenigow, f., fen. 100 = 1 marka: Poland to 1918; Eastern Silesia overprints on Polish stamps.

Fil(s). 1000 = 1 dinar = 5 riyals: Bahrain after 1966; Iraq after 1932; Kuwait, 1961. South Arabia after 1967; Yemen (People's Democratic Republic) 1971. 1000 = 1 Kuwaiti dinar, Kuwait 1961.

Fillér.
(a) 100 = 1 korona: Hungary 1900-1926.
(b) f. 100 = 1 pengö: Hungary 1926-1946; = 1 adopengö (tax pengö), 1946 only.
(c) f. 100 = 1 forint: Hungary after 1946.
(d) 100 = 1 krone (corona): Fiume to 1919; Jugoslavia for Croatia-Slavonia.

Florin(s)*. See Cent (f), Novcica, Soldo.

Folus**. See Anna (f).

Forint, Ft. See Fillér (c).

Fraction. Labels with inscription "One Fraction" served as half-penny stamps in Trinidad on September 18, 1914, to carry Red Cross solicitations.

Franc(s), F., Fr., (Fcs. in Obock and Somali Coast). See Centime, Rappen, Bit.

Franc(s) (metropolitan*). See Centime (b).

Franc(s), Belgian*, and Congo*. See Centime (e).

Franc(s) (C.F.A.*) (Communauté Française d'Afrique) = 2 francs metropolitan, see Centime (c).

Franc(s) (C.F.P.*) Communauté Française du Pacifique) = 5 francs metropolitan. See Centime (d).

Franc(s) (Dj.*) (Djibouti) = about 1⅝ francs metropolitan. See Centime (c).

Franc(s) (L*) (Luxembourg). See Centime (f).

Franc(s) or. See Centime (h).

Franc(s) (Sw.*) (Swiss). See Centime (g).

Franco(s). See Centimo (f).

Franga, frank, Fr., Fr. Ar. See Qindar, Qintar.

Frank, franken. Flemish insc. for franc. See Centime (e).

Fuang*. See Solot.

Garch (piastre). 11 garch or garsh = 1 riyal: Hejaz**; Saudi Arabia 1929-1930.

Gourde(s). See Centime (n).

Grano(a), G., Gr., Gra. 100 = 200 tornesi = 1 ducat, Two Sicilies.

Grivna. See Shagiv (a), (b).

Groschen, Gr.

  (a) 30 groschen or silbergroschen = 1 thaler: Thurn and Taxis (north), North German Confederation, German Empire to 1874.

  (b) 100 = 1 schilling (abbr. G., S.): Austria 1925 on.

  See also Pfennig (c), Silbergroschen (b), (c).

Grosh, grossion (plural gurush). Albanian piastre 1913-1914. See Para (b).

Grosion**. See Metallick.

Grosz, grosze, groszy, Gr. 100 = 1 złoty: Poland after 1924.

Grote. 22 = 1 silbergroschen: Bremen.

Grush, ghurush, grouch. Turkish piastre, see Para (b), Kuruṣ.

Guarani, ₲. See Centimo (e).

Guerche(s). 16 = 1 thaler (Menelik or Maria Theresa dollar): Ethiopia to 1905.

Guerche, qirsh. 110 = 1 sovereign: Saudi Arabia 1931. See Garch.

Gulden, G., Gl., Gld. See Cent (f), Kreuzer (a), (b), Neukreuzer, Pfennig (b).

Gutegroschen, Gutegr., Ggr., gutengroschen. See Pfennig (f), Silbergroschen (a) to (e).

Halala(s). 100 = 1 riyal: Saudi Arabia after 1976.

Halerz, halerze, halerzy, H., Hal. 100 = 1 korona: Poland 1918-1924.

Haléř(ů), h. 100=1 koruna: Czechoslovakia; Bohemia and Moravia; Carpatho-Ukraine.

Halierov, h. 100=1 koruna: Slovakia.

Heleru(a), H. 100=1 kruna: Montenegro** 1902-1907.

Heller.
  (a) 100=1 krone: Austria 1899-1925; Jugoslavia for Bosnia, Liechtenstein to 1921; Western Ukraine.
  (b)* 100=1 krone: Bosnia 1900-1918; Eastern Silesia.
  (c) 100=1 rupie, German East Africa 1905-1906.

Hwan**. See Weun.

Imadi. See Bogchah.

Kapeika, kapeikas, kapeiku, kap. 100=1 rublis: Latvia to 1923.

Karbovanetz. See Shagiv.

Keneta. Hawaiian word for cents.

Kina. See Toe.

Kip. See Cent (j). New word for piastre in Laos, 1955.

Kobo(s). 100 = 1 naira: Nigeria after 1973.

Kopeck(s), k. 100 = 1 ruble: Russia and offices**; U.S.S.R. and component republics**; Estonia 1918; Finland to 1866 (abbr. kop. 1856-1860). See Shagiv.

Korona. See Fillér (a).

Korona, Korony, Koron, K. See Halerz.

Koruna, Koruny, Korun, K., Kč., Kčs. See Haléř; K., Ks., see Halierov.

Krajcár, Kr. 100=1 forint: Hungary to 1900. (Hungarian for Kreuzer.)

Kran(s), K., Kr. See Chahi, Shahi (a), (b).

Kreuzer.
  (a) 60 (kr.)=1 gulden: Austria to 1858, and see Neukreuzer; Baden to 1905; Bavaria to 1874; Thurn and Taxis (south); North German Confederation; southern parts of German Empire to 1874, Prussia.
  (b) 16=1 gulden*; Württemberg to 1875.

Króna, Kr. (plural kronur) see Aurar; (plural kronor) see Öre (c).

Krone. See Fillér (d). Plural kronen, K., see Heller (a). Plural kronor, Kr., see Øre (a).

Kroon(i). See Sent.

Kruna*. See Heleru, Para (e).

Kuna, kune, Kn. See Banica.

Kurus, Kurush, kurusiur, K., Krs., Krs. See Para (c), Santim (a).

Kwacha. See Tambala, Ngwee.

Kyat. See Pyas.

Laree(s). 100 = 1 rupee: Maldive Islands 1951.

Lats, lati, latu, Ls. See Santims.

Lek (Leke before 1948). See Qindar.

Lempira(s), L. See Centavo (i).

Leone. See Cent (1).

Lepton(ta)**. 100 = 1 drachma: Greece, Epirus, Corfu, Crete.

Leu, lei, L. See Ban.

Lev (a)**. See Stotinki.

Libra*. See Onza.

Li-Kuta. See Sengi.

Lilangen. See Cents (n). 2 = 1 emalageni: Swaziland 1975.

Lira, lire. See Centesimi (a), Quattrino, Para (c), where Lira appears on stamps after 1947.

Litas, litai, litu, L., Lt., Lit. See Centas.

Livre. £E or monogram. See Millieme (a).

Ma-Kyta. 100 = 1 zaire: Congo after 1967.

Maravedises, Md. Vd. 32 = 1 real: Spain 1874 on Carlist issue.

Maria Theresa dollar. See Guerche.

Mark(s), M. RM for Reichsmark: Germany 1931; DM, Deutsches-
   mark: Germany 1950; Mk., Heligoland. See Pfennig (a), Schilling (c).

Mark(a), M., Mk. See Penni (a).

Marka, Marki, Marek, M., Mk. See Fenig.

Markka(a), M., Mk.(bilingual with Mark to 1916). See Penni (b).

M.C. Moneda corriente.

Mehalek. 16=1 thaler (talari): Ethiopia 1928-1936.

Menelik dollar. See Guerche.

Menge. Variant of Mung: Outer Mongolia.

Metallik**. 4=1 grosion: Crete 1899-1900.

Milesima(s), Mila., mils. See Centavo (c), Centimo (b), Centesimo (a).

Milésimo(s). See Centésimo (e).

Millieme(s), Mill., Mills., Milmes.
   (a) 1000 = 100 piastres = 1 pound E: Egypt 1888 on; Sudan; Pal-
       estine to 1928; Fr. off. Egypt to 1921; 1000 = 1 pound: Libia 1952.
   (b) 10 = 1 piastre: Syria to 1920.
   (c) 1000 = 1 dinar: Tunisia 1959.

Milreis. $ between the milreis and reis, as $5000. See Rei (a).

Mils(s). 1000 = 1 Cyprus pound, 1955; 10 = 1 cent, 1000 = 1 Malta pound after 1972; 1000 = 1 Palestine pound: Palestine, Transjordan, Jordan; 1000 = 1 Israeli pound to 1949.

Mon, Mn. (a).

(a) 100 = 1 sen: Japan 1871 only.

(b) 100 = 1 tempo: Korea 1884-1885.

Moneda corriente, M.C. Currency.

Mung. 100 = 1 tuhrik. Also called menge. Outer Mongolia 1926.

Naira. See Kobo.

Naya Paisa. 100 = 1 rupee: India 1956-1964; Kuwait to 1957; Muscat & Oman 1957; Nepal 1958; Qatar 1957; Trucial States 1961; Dubai, sharjah, Umm al Qiwain 1963; Ajman, Abu Dhabi, Fujeira, Ras al Khaiman, 1964.

Neugroschen, Neu-grosch. See Pfennig (d).

Neukreuzer*. 100 = 1 gulden: Austria 1858-1899, insc. "Kreuzer."

New Cedi. See new pesewa.

New Pesewa. 100 = 1 new cedi: Ghana, 1972.

Ngultrum. See Chetrum.

Ngwee. 100 = 1 kwacha: Zambia after 1968.

Novcic(a). 100 = 1 florin: Montenegro**; Bosnia to 1900,* equals an Austrian Neukreuzer.

Obali.* 10 = 1 penny, 12-pence = 1 shilling: Ionian Islands.

Onza(s). 16 = 1 libra*: Sp. stamps in weights not currency.

Øre. 100 = 1 krone: Denmark 1874; Faroe Islands; Norway 1877; Schleswig 1920.

Öre.

(a) 100 = 1 riksdaler: Sweden 1858-1874.

(b) 100 = 1 króna: Sweden after 1874; Greenland.

Ouguiya. See Um.

Pa'anga. See Senit.

Paisa(s).**

(a) 60 = 1 rupee: Afghanistan 1921-1927. See Anna (f).

(b) 100 = 1 rupee: Bangladesh (= 1 taka 1972); Pakistan 1961; Nepal 1961; India 1964.

Para(s), P.

(a) 40 = 1 piastre: Albania 1913; Cilicia; Crete to 1899; Cyprus; Eastern Rumelia; Egypt to 1888; Ethiopia 1908-1928; Hejaz;

Saudi Arabia to 1929; Syria (Arab government); Thrace to 1919; Turkey to 1926; Turkey in Asia; Ukraine 1918; Austrian, Italian, Roumanian, and Russian offices in Turkey.

(b) 40 = 1 grush: Turkey 1926-1929; 40 = 1 grosh (or grossion): Albania 1913-1914.

(c) 40 (pa.) = 1 kurus (or kurush), 100 kuruṣ = 1 lira; Turkey after 1929; Hatay after 1939.

(d) 100 = 1 dinar: Croatia, Serbia, Jugoslavia, Trieste.

(e) 100 = 1 kruna: Montenegro 1907-1910**.

(f) 100 = perper: Montenegro after 1910**.

Parale(s), par.   40 = 1 piastre: Roumania to 1868.

Pataca, P.   See Avo.

Pene.   Early native word for penny or pence in overprints for Aitutaki; Cook Islands (Raratonga); Niue; Penrhyn Island.

Peni.   Later native word for penny or pence in overprints for Niue and Penrhyn Island, and in definitive issues of Tonga.

Penni(a).

(a) 100 (Pen.) = 1 mark: Estonia 1919-1928; Finland 1866-1916.

(b) P., Pen. (bilingual in Finland with Penni-Mark or with Cyrillic equivalents to 1916) 100 = 1 markka: Finland after 1866; North Ingermanland 1920.

Penny, Penny-pence, d.   12 = 1 shilling, 20 shillings = 1 pound, 100 pence = 1 pound 1970: British Commonwealth except as indicated; bil. insc. on Heligoland after 1875; Many former Br. col. now free. One penny = 4 farthings: Barbados; Bermuda; Malta. See Cowrie.

Perper**.   See Para (f).

Pesa.   60 = 1 rupie (plural rupien): German East Africa to 1905.

Peseta(s), P., Ps., Pt., Ptas., Pts.   See Centavo (d), Centesimo (c), Centimo (a).

Pesewa(s).   100 = 1 cedi: Ghana 1965, 1972.

Peso(s), $ (Ps. Buenos Aires).   See Centavo (a) to (d), Centesimo (e), Centimo (f), Real, Real plata fuerte.

Pfennig(s), pf. (Pfennige before 1880 in Germany, Pfenninge in Prussia).

(a) 100 = 1 mark: Baden official stamps to 1905; Bavaria 1874 on; Germany 1874 on; Prussia official stamps 1903*; Württemberg 1875 on; Heligoland after 1875; German offices and colonies not otherwise indicated; Danzig to 1923; Marienwerder; Memel to

1923; Saar to 1921; Schleswig plebescite.

(b) 100(P.)=1 gulden (G.): Danzig 1923; Memel after 1923.

(c) 10=1 silbergroschen: Brunswick; Hanover. See Silbergroschen (a).

(d) 10=1 neugroschen, 30 neugroschen=1 thaler: Saxony.

(e) 12(pfenninge)=1 silbergroschen: Prussia.

(f) 12=1 gutegroschen: Brunswick; Hanover. See Silbergroschen (a).

Piastre(s), Shown as P., P.T., piast., piaster, also piastra (Roumania). 9=1 shilling, Cyprus, and see Para (a) and Penny. See Cent (i), Centimes (i), (j), (m), Garch, Millieme (a), (b), Parale, Para (a).

Pice (Hindustani Paisa). See Anna (a), (g).

Pie(s), Ps. See Anna (a), (d).

Pinsin, pinsine p., d.p. Penny and pence on stamps of Ireland.

Piso(s). See Sentimo.

Plata fuerte. Silver coin, not paper.

Pond. Afrikaans for pound.

Poón. 5 = 1 cheun: Korea 1895-1900. See Cheun.

Pound(s). See Penny. (Value differs in dominions.) Shown as pound, £, and in some cases as "20 shillings." For Egyptian pound (£E or L.E.) see Millieme (a); for Palestine pound (£P), Cyprus pound, and Israeli pound (I£) to 1949, see Mil; for Israeli pound after 1949, see Pruta; after 1960, see Agorot; for East African pound, see Cent (h).

Pruta*. 1000=1 pound (I£): Israel after 1949.

Pul(s), R., Pol., Pool(s), Poul(s). 100=1 Afghani, or Afghan rupee: Afghanistan 1927.

Puttan(s). See Anna (d).

Pyas, P. 100=1 kyat: Burma 1953 on.

Pynung**. See Solot.

Qindar, Q., Qd., Qind. 100=1 frank: Albania 1923-1947; =1 leke 1947; =1 lek 1948.

Qintar, Qint., qind., qindar. 100=1 frank: Albania 1917-1923.

Quattrino(ni), Quattr. 60=20 soldi=12 crazie=1 lira (Italian): Tuscany to 1860.

Quetzal(es), Q. See Centavo (o).

Rand. R. See Cent (m).

Rappen, R., Rp. 100=1 franc: Switzerland; Liechtenstein 1921 on.

Re, Ri. See Cheun.

Real(es), Rs., Real^s. See Cuarto, Centavo (a), (e). 8 = 1 peso: Buenos Aires; Ecuador to 1881; Honduras to 1878; Mexico to 1867; Paraguay 1870; Peru 1857.

Real moneda corriente (currency), Real M.C. See Centavo (p).

Real plata fuerte, Rl. Plata F., Rl. Pta. F. 8 = 1 peso plata fuerte: Cuba to 1866-1867. Rl. Plata F., Rl. Fte.: Philippine Islands to 1864.

Real plata fuerte (coined silver), R^s. F^{tes}. See Cuarto.

Rei(s).

(a) R., Rs. 1000 = 1 milreis: Portugal and colonies to 1912-1916, Brazil to 1942.

(b) 12 = 1 tanga, 16 tangas = 1 rupia: Portuguese India after 1881.

Ri. Used for Re or Rin on Korean stamps 1903.

Rial(s), R., Ri., Rl. See Dinar, Halala.

Rial Saidi. See Baiza.

Riel. See Cent (k).

Rigsbank Daler (Rix-daler). See Rigsbank Skilling, Skilling (b).

Rigsbank Skilling R.B.S. Used only to 1953, see Skilling (b).

Rigsdaler. See Skilling (a).

Riksdaler. See Öre (b).

Riksdaler Banco. See Skilling Banco.

Rin, Rn. See Sen (a).

Riyal**. See Dirham, Garch, Fil.

Ruble(s), R. See Kopeck, Shagiv.

Rublis, Rubli, Rublu, Rub., Rbl. See Kapeika.

Rupee(s), R., Rs. See Anna (a) to (d), Avo, Cent (g), Laree, Naya Paisa, Paisa, Sen (b), Shahi.

Rupee (Afghan). See Pul.

Rupee (Kabuli). See Shahi.

Rupee (Nepalese). See Anna (g).

Rupia. See Rei (b), Sen (d).

Rupie(s), R., Ro., Roupie. See Pesa; Cache; plural Rupien, see Heller(c).

Salung(s)*. See Solot.

Sanar. See Shahi.

Sang**. See Trangka.

Santim(s). 100 = 1 kurush: Hatay 1939.

Santims, Santimi, Santimu, S., Sant. 100 = 1 lats: Latvia after 1923.

Satang, St., Stg. 100 = 1 tical: Siam 1909-1910, = 1 baht, 1912-1920 and after 1928.

Schagiw. Same as Shagiv.

Schilling, schillinge.

(a) 48 = 1 silbergroschen = 1 thaler: Mecklenburg-Strelitz.

(b) 48 = 1 thaler: Mecklenburg-Schwerin.

(c) 48 = 1 mark: Bergedorf; Hamburg; Heligoland; Schelswig-Holstein. See Groschen (b).

Schwaren, Schw. See Silbergroschen (c).

Scudo. See Bajoccho.

Sen, Sn.

(a) 100 = 1 yen: Japan 1872; 10 rin = 1 sen, Japan 1876-1899; Ryukyu Islands. Also see Mon (a).

(b) 100 sen (cents) = 1 rupee (gulden): Indonesia 1949.

(c) 100 sen = 1 dollar: Malaya, Fed. of Malaya, Malaysia.

(d) 100 sen = 1 rupia: West Irian (West New Guinea).

Sene. 100 = 1 tala: Samoa after 1967.

Sengi. 100 = 1 li-kuta: Zaire.

Senit(i). 100 = 1 pa'anaga: Tonga after 1967.

Sent(i), s. 100 = 1 kroon: Estonia after 1928.

Sentimo(s). Substituted for centavo (s), Philippines 1962. 100 = 1 piso.

Shagiv**, schagiw. 200 = 100 kopecks = 1 ruble (karbovanetz): Ukraine 1918. 100 shagiv or sotikiv = 1 ruble: Western Ukraine.

Shahi(s)**.

(a) 12 = 6 sanar = 3 abasi = 2 krans* = 1 rupee (Kabuli): Afghanistan to 1920.

(b) 20 = 1 kran, 10 kran = 1 toman: Persia 1870-1881, 1882-1884.

Shilling(s), s/, (Sh., Heligoland), (Shils., Great Britain), (Shills, Shilgs, British Central Africa). See Cent (h), Oboli, Penny, Piastre. Bil. insc. on Heligoland after 1875.

Silbergroschen, Silb. Gr., silbergr., silb. grosch., sgr. See Schilling.

(a) 30 = 1 thaler = 24 gutegroschen; 10 pfennige = 1 silbergroschen (foreign use); 12 pfennige = 1 gutegroschen (domestic use): Brunswick; Hanover.

(b) 30 = 1 thaler (silbergroschen or groschen): Thurn and Taxis

(North), North Ger. Confed.; German Empire (North) to 1875.
(c) 30 = 1 thaler = 72 grote; 12 schwaren = 1 silbergroschen: Oldenburg.
(d) 30 = 1 thaler* = 48 schillings*: Mecklenburg-Strelitz.
(e) 3 = 4 schillings: Schleswig-Holstein.

Sileni. Native word for shilling in overprints for Niue. See Pene.

Silini. Native word for shilling on stamps of Tonga. See Peni.

Silingi. Native word for shilling in overprints for Penrhyn Island. See Pene, Peni.

Skatikas, Skatikai, Skatiku, Sk. 100 = 1 auksinas: Lithuania to 1922.

Skilling, s., sk. for (a) and (b), skill for (c), also see Rigsbank Skilling.
(a) 96 = 1 rigsdaler: Iceland to 1876.
(b) 96 = 1 rigsbank daler: Denmark to 1874.
(c) 100 = 1 specie daler: Norway to 1877.

Skilling Banco, Skill. Bco., Sk. Bco. 48 = 1 riksdaler banco: Sweden to 1858.

S.L.M., Schilling Lauenburgische Münze (Lauenburg Minted Schilling). On one value of the 1864 issue of Holstein (Schleswig-Holstein).

Solot(s)**. 32 = 16 atts = 8 pynung = 4 songpy = 2 fuang* = 1 salung: Siam 1883. See Att.

Somala. See Centesimo (b).

Songpy. See Solot.

Sovereign. See Guerche.

Specie Daler. See Skilling (c).

S.R.M., Skilling Reichs Münze (State Minted Skilling). On 1864 issue of Holstein (Schleswig-Holstein). See S.L.M.

Stg. Abbr. for sterling: Canada 1855-1859. See Cy.

Stotinki**, Ctot., Ct. (Cyrillic). 100 = 1 lev: Bulgaria 1881 on; Thrace 1919.

Sucre(s), S/., $. See Centavo (h).

Syli. See Caury.

Tael*. See Candarin.

Talari. See Mehalek. Shows as Thaler(s) on Ethiopia issue of 1931.

Tambala(s). 100 = 1 kwacha: Malawa after 1971.

Tanga(s), T. See Rei (b).

Tempo. See Mon (b).

Thaler(s). See Centime (1), Groschen (a), Guerche, Mehalek, Pfennig (c), (d), Schilling (a), (b), Silbergroschen (a) to (d).

Tical(s), Tcl. See Att, Satang.

Tiringi. Native word for shilling in overprints for Aitutaki. See Pene.

Toe(a). 100 = 1 kina: Papua; New Guinea after 1975.

Toman, T. See Chahi, Shahi (b).

Tornese(si), T. See Grano.

Trangka*. 6 2/3 = 1 sang*, Tibet; Bhutan.

Tuhrik, Tugrog, Tug. See Mung.

Um. Also called Ouguiya, Mauritania after 1973.

Venezolano(s). See Centesimo (f).

Weun, Wn., Won in 1951. See Cheun, Korea 1900-1953; 100=1 hwan: Korea after 1953**.

Yuan. See Fen. Also the name of the Chinese dollar.

Zaire. See Ma-kuta.

Złoty, Złote, Złotych, Zł. See Grosz.

❖•❖

CHAPTER THIRTY-FIVE

TABLE OF THE WORLD'S STAMPS

This table gives the names of the countries in alphabetical order and shows the kinds of stamps issued by each, with dates of introduction of the important categories. The kinds of stamps are identified by the prefix letters (without periods) used by Scott Publications, Inc., and their use in this book is by permission of the company. The outline of the Scott classification follows this table on page 543.

The country name is that ordinarily used in the *Standard Catalogue*. A preceding dagger indicates that it no longer issues stamps. The abbreviation which follows gives the political status (see end of table, pages 543-544, for list of abbreviations).

The most common categories of stamps are in the columns marked [A], B, C, E, J, O, and P, A being placed in brackets as it is not used alone in the Scott classification. The date in a column indicates when the country first issued stamps in that category, and the absence of a date indicates that no such stamps have been issued. The table will thus serve as an easy reference when it is desired to know which countries have issued a certain kind of stamp.

The Remarks column contains the minor categories not

shown in the previous columns. When practical, information is included to show what followed when the country ceased to issue stamps. Thus, in the line "Confed. States," the abbreviation "U.S. 1865" indicates that United States stamps were used after the fall of the Confederacy. The notes in this column do not indicate a name change unless so stated. Some notes indicate the prior status of a country; thus Basutoland is followed by the note "From South Africa" to show that the stamps of that country were in use prior to the separation.

About 150 names listed as stamp issuing entities in catalogs are omitted from this index. They are not of great importance and in nearly all cases issued only regular postage stamps. One such group is the "Offices" in foreign lands. These are not the "Offices Abroad" of Scott's category "K," but are the offices of various countries in the Levant, in China, and elsewhere. They are indicated by a small "k" in the Remarks column. Italian offices in the individual Aegean Islands are not listed except for Rhodes, which has several issues and categories.

The Indian native states are omitted as their use appears to be local and their inclusion in a general catalog is questionable. Issues for provinces, departments, etc., also are omitted, but some mention is made to show that they exist. The cantonal stamps of Switzerland are included on account of their early dates and of their use in some cases beyond the limits of the canton.

SUPPLEMENTARY TABLE OF THE WORLD'S STAMPS

Country or State		[A]	B	C	E	J	O	P	Remarks
Afars & Isas	Fr.	1967	–	1967	–	1969	–	–	Formerly Somali
Bangladesh	A.	1971	–	–	–	–	1973	–	Formerly East Pakistan
Botswana	A.	1966	–	–	–	1967	–	–	Formerly Bechua
British Indian Ocean Territory	Br.	1968	–	–	–	–	–	–	Indian Ocean Isls group north of Mauritius
Christmas Island Australia took over island from Singapore		1958	–	–	–	–	–	–	In Indian Ocean, of Java
Equatorial Guinea	A.	1968	–	–	1971	–	–	–	Was Fernando P Rio Mundi (S₁ Provinces)
Faroe Islands	Den.	1919	–	–	–	–	–	–	Self-governing pⱥ Denmark
Guernsey	Br.	1969	–	–	–	1969	–	–	Islands in Englis Channel
Guinea-Bissau	A.	1974	–	–	–	–	–	–	Was Portuguese
Jersey	Br.	1969	–	–	–	1969	–	–	Island in Englisł Channel
Lesotho	A.	1966	–	–	–	1966	–	–	Enclave in Sout⊦ African Repuł Was Basutola
Malawi	A.	1964	–	–	–	1967	–	–	Was Nyasaland
Man, Isle of	Br.	1973	–	–	–	1973	–	–	In Irish Sea
Sri Lanka	A.	1972	–	–	–	–	–	–	Formerly knowr Ceylon
Trucial States	Br.	1961	–	–	–	–	–	–	Sheikdoms unde British Protec Persian Gulf
Tuvalu	Br.	1976	–	–	–	–	–	–	Formerly Ellice
United Arab Emirates	A.	1972	–	–	–	–	–	–	Union of Abu D Ajman, Duba Fujeira, Sharj Umm al Qiwⱥ al Khaima
West Irian and then Indonesia	U.N.	1962	–	–	–	1963	–	–	Was Neth. New
Zambia	A.	1964	–	–	–	1964	–	–	Was North. Rʰ

Country or State		[A]	B	C	E	J	O	P	Remarks
Abu Dhabi	B.P.	1964	-	-	-	-	-	-	Was Trucial State
†Aden	Br.	1937	-	-	-	-	-	-	
†Seiyun	Br.	1942	-	-	-	-	-	-	S. Arabian Fed. 1963
†Shihr &									East Aden prot.
Mukalla	Br.	1942	-	-	-	-	-	-	Ren. Hadhramaut
Hadhramaut		1955	-	-	-	-	-	-	East Aden prot.
Afghanistan	A.	1871	1953	1940	-	-	1909	-	F Q RA
†Aguera	Sp.	1920	-	-	-	-	-	-	Sp. Sahara 1964
†Aitutaki	Br.	1903	-	-	-	-	-	-	Cook Is. 1932
Ajman	B.P.	1964	-	-	-	-	-	-	Was Trucial State
Albania	A.	1913	1924	1925	1940	1914	-	-	RA
†Alexandretta	Fr.	1938	-	1938	-	1938	-	-	Ren. Hatay 1938
Algeria	Fr.	1924	1927	1946	-	1926	-	1924	CB
†Allenstein	Ger.	1920	-	-	-	-	-	-	Pleb. Ger. 1920
†Alouites	Fr.	1925	-	1925	-	1925	-	-	Ren. Latakia 1930
Andorra		1928	-	1950	1928	1931	-	1931	Spanish, French
Angola	Por.	1870	-	1938	-	1904	-	1893	RA RAJ
†Angra	Por.	1892	-	-	-	-	-	-	Azores 1906
†Anjouan	Fr.	1892	-	-	-	-	-	-	Madagascar ab. 1912
Annam &									
Tonkin	Fr.	1888	-	-	-	-	-	-	Indo-China 1892
Antigua	Br.	1862	-	-	-	-	-	-	MR
Argentina	A.	1858	1944	1928	-	-	1884	-	CB (Prov.)
Armenia	Sov.	1920	-	-	-	-	-	-	To T.C.F.R. 1923
Ascension	Br.	1922	-	-	-	-	-	-	
Australia	Br.	1913	-	1929	-	1902	1931	-	M
Aust. Ant.									
Terr.		1957	-	-	-	-	-	-	L for Aust. Exped.
Christmas Is.		1958	-	-	-	-	-	-	From Singapore
Austria	A.	1850	1914	1918	-	1894	-	1851	M MB N PR QE k MP
†Lombardy-									
Venetia	Aus.	1850	-	-	-	-	-	-	PR Italy 1859-66
†A.M.G.		1945	-	-	-	-	-	-	
Azerbaijan	Sov.	1919	1922	-	-	-	-	-	N (Baku). To T.C.F.R.
Azores	Por.	1868	-	-	-	1904	-	1876	Q RA RAJ Por. 1931
Baden	Ger.	1851	-	-	-	-	1905	-	LJ Ger. 1870, exc. Off.
Bahamas	Br.	1859	-	-	1916	-	-	-	MR
Bahrain	Br.	1933	-	-	-	-	-	-	
Bangkok	Br.	1882	-	-	-	-	-	-	Siam 1886
Barbados	Br.	1857	1907	-	-	1934	-	-	MR
Barbuda	Br.	1922	-	-	-	-	-	-	One issue only
Basutoland	Br.	1933	-	-	-	1933	1934	-	From South Africa
Batum	Sov.	1919	-	-	-	-	-	-	Georgia, July 1920
Bavaria	Ger.	1849	1919	-	-	1862	1908	-	Ger. 1920
Bechuanaland	Br.	1886	-	-	-	-	-	-	Cape Good Hope 1895
Bech. Prot.	Br.	1888	-	-	-	1926	-	-	
Belgian East									
Africa	Bel.	1922	-	-	-	-	-	-	Ruanda-Urundi 1924
Belgium	A.	1849	1910	1930	1929	1870	1929	1928	CB MQ N Q
Benin	Fr.	1892	-	-	-	1894	-	-	Dahomey 1895
Bergedorf	Ger.	1861	-	-	-	-	-	-	Hamburg 1867
Bermuda	Br.	1864	-	-	-	-	-	-	MR X
Bhutan	A.	1962	1964	-	-	-	-	-	L to Oct. 1963
Bolivia	A.	1866	-	1924	-	1931	-	-	RA
Bosnia &									
Herzeg.	Aus.	1879	1914	-	-	1904	1913	-	QE Jugoslavia 1918
Brazil	A.	1843	1934	1927	1930	1889	1906	1889	RAB RA
Bremen	Ger.	1855	-	-	-	-	-	-	N.G.P.D. 1868

Note: See pages 543-544 for lists of abbreviations. Abbreviations without periods are Scott classcation letters.

Country or State		[A]	B	C	E	J	O	P	Remarks
Br. Antar.									
Terr.	Br.	1963	-	-	-	-	-	-	Inc. Falkland Dep.
†Br. Central									
Afr.	Br.	1891	-	-	-	-	-	-	Ren. Nyasa. Prot. 1907
†Br. Col. &									
Vancouver	Br.	1861	-	-	-	-	-	-	Canada 1871
†Br. East Afr.	Br.	1890	-	-	-	-	-	-	E. Afr. & Uganda 1903
Br. Guiana	Br.	1850	-	-	-	1940	1875	-	MR
Br. Honduras	Br.	1865	1932	-	-	1923	-	-	MR
†Br. New Guinea	Br.	1901	-	-	-	-	-	-	Papua 1907
Br. Solomon	Br.	1907	-	-	-	1940	-	-	
Islands									
Brunei	Br.	1906	-	-	-	-	-	-	N
†Brunswick	Ger.	1852	-	-	-	-	-	-	N.G.P.D. 1868
Bulgaria	A.	1879	1920	1927	1939	1884	1942	-	Q RA CB
Burma	A.	1937	-	-	-	-	1937	-	N Br. to 1948
Burrundi	A.	1962	1963	1964	-	-	-	-	Part Ruandi-Urundi
Cambodia	A.	1952	-	1953	-	-	-	-	From Indo-China
Cameroons	Ger.	1897	1938	1942	-	1925	-	-	N Br. & Fr. man.
Cameroun	A.	1961	-	-	-	-	-	-	
Canada	Br.	1851	1916	1928	1898	1906	1949	-	CE CO EO F MR
Canal Zone	U.S.	1904	-	1929	-	1914	1941	-	CO
Cape Juby	Sp.	1916	1926	1938	1919	-	-	-	EB
†Cape Good									
Hope	Br.	1853	-	-	-	-	-	-	N South Africa 1910
Cape Verde	Por.	1877	-	1938	-	1904	-	1893	RA RAJ
†Caroline									
Islands	Ger.	1900	-	-	-	-	-	-	End at World War I
†Castellorizo	It.	1920	-	-	-	-	-	-	From Turkey
Cayman Islands	Br.	1900	-	-	-	-	-	-	MR
Cent. African									
Rep.	A.	1957	1962	1960	-	1962	-	-	Was Oubangi-Chari
†Central									
Lithuania	Sov.	1920	1921	-	-	1920	-	-	To Poland
Ceylon	A.	1857	-	-	-	-	-	1869	MR Rep. 1956
Chad	Fr.	1922	-	-	-	1928	-	-	Fr. Eq. Afr. 1934
Chile	A.	1853	1940	1927	-	1895	1907	-	H
China	A.	1878	1920	1921	1905	1904	-	-	F k M Q
China Peoples									
Rep.	A.	-	-	-	-	-	-	-	MD Listing
†Cilicia	F.O.	1919	-	1920	-	1919	-	-	To Turkey 1923
†Cochin China	Fr.	1886	-	-	-	-	-	-	Indo-China 1892
Cocos. Island	Br.	-	-	-	-	-	-	-	
Colombia	A.	1859	-	1919	1917	1866	1937	-	CF F H I L RA (Depts.)
Comoro Island	Fr.	1950	1962	1950	-	1950	-	-	Was Grand Comoro
†Confed. States	A.	1861	-	-	-	-	-	-	U.S. 1865
Congo (French)	A.	1959	-	1961	-	1961	-	-	Rep. 1959
Congo (Belgian)		1886	1918	1920	-	1923	-	-	Q; A. until 1907; Rep. 1960
Cook Islands	Br.	1892	-	-	-	-	-	-	
†Corfu	I.O.	1923	-	1941	-	1941	-	-	RA It. occ. 1923, 1941
Costa Rica	A.	1862	1922	1926	-	1903	1883	-	(Guanacaste also) CO R.
†Crete	Gr.	1898	-	-	-	1901	1908	-	N; to Greece 1913
†Croatia	Ju.	1941	1941	-	-	1941	1942	-	N RA Jugoslavia 1945
Cuba	A.	1855	1938	1927	1899	1899	-	1886	CE RA Sp. to 1902 CB
†Curacao	Net.	1873	1947	1929	-	1889	-	-	CB. Ren. Net. Antilles
Cyprus	A.	1880	-	-	-	-	-	-	
†Cyrenaica	It.	1923	1925	1932	-	1950	-	-	CB to Libia 1957
Czechoslovakia	S.D.	1918	1919	1920	1918	1918	1945	1918	EX
†Bohemia-									
Morav.	Cz.	1939	1940	-	-	1939	1941	1939	EX; to Cz. 1945
†Carp.									
Ukraine	Cz.	1939	-	-	-	-	-	-	One day only

Country or State		[A]	B	C	E	J	O	P	Remarks
†Slovakia	Cz.	1939	1939	1939	-	1939	-	1939	EX; to Cz. 1945
Dahomey	A.	1899	1915	1940	-	1906	-	-	Fr. W. Afr. 1945
†Dalmatia	I.O.	1921	-	-	1921	1922	-	-	To Italy 1923
†Danish W. Indies	Den.	1855	-	-	-	1902	-	-	To U.S. 1917
†Danzig	Pol.	1920	1921	1920	-	1921	1921	-	To Poland 1945
Denmark	A.	1851	1921	1925	-	1921	1871	1907	I M Q
†Diego Suarez	Fr.	1890	-	-	-	1891	1907	-	Madagascar 1896
Dominica	Br.	1874	-	-	-	-	-	-	MR
Dominican Rep.	A.	1865	-	1928	1920	1901	1902	-	CO G RA RAC CB
Dubai	B.P.	1963	-	1963	-	-	-	-	Was Trucial State
†Dutch East Indies	Net.	1864	1915	1928	-	1945	1911	-	CB GY N Indonesia 1948
Dutch New Guinea	Net.	1950	1953	-	-	-	-	-	Now West Irian
†E. Africa, Uganda	Br.	1903	-	-	-	-	-	-	Kenya & Uganda 1921
†Eastern Rumelia	Bul.	1880	-	-	-	-	-	-	Was Tur., to Bul. 1886
†Eastern Silesia	Aus.	1920	-	-	1920	1920	-	1920	Div. Pol. & Cz. 1920
Ecuador	A.	1865	-	1929	1928	1896	1886	-	CO I RA RAC L
Egypt	A.	1866	1940	1926	1926	1884	1892	-	M N NH See U.A.R.
†Elob. Ann & Coris.	Sp.	1903	-	-	-	-	-	-	Sp. Guinea 1909
†Epirus	1914	-	-	-	-	-	-	-	N Gr. & Albania 1916
†Eritrea	It.	1892	1915	1934	1907	1903	-	-	CB EY Q It. E. Afr. 1936
†Estonia	S.D.	1918	1920	1920	-	-	-	-	N U.S.S.R. 1940
Ethiopia	A.	1894	1935	1929	1947	1896	-	-	N It. occ. 1936-1942
Falkland Is.	Br.	1878	-	-	-	-	-	-	MR Now Brit. Ant. Terr.
Falkland Dep's.	Br.	1946	-	-	-	-	-	-	Separate issues 1944
†Far Eastern Rep.	Sov.	1920	-	-	-	-	-	-	N U.S.S.R. 1923
Fernando Po	Sp.	1868	-	1960	-	-	-	-	Sp. Guinea 1909-1960
†Fezzan	F.O.	1949	1950	1948	-	1950	-	-	Fr. occ. Libia
†Fezzan Ghad.	F.O.	1946	-	-	-	-	-	-	Fr. occ. Libia
†Ghadames	F.O.	1949	-	1949	-	-	-	-	Fr. occ. Libia
Fiji Islands	Br.	1870	1951	-	-	1917	-	-	MR
Finland	A.	1856	1922	1930	-	-	-	-	M
†Fiume	It.	1918	1918	-	1918	1918	-	1918	To Italy 1924
†Formosa		1945	-	1949	-	1948	-	-	Q Now Rep. China
France	A.	1849	1914	1927	-	1859	-	1868	CB M N S k
†Alsace Lorraine	G.O.	1870	-	-	-	-	-	-	Occ. 1870, 1916, 1940
†Morocco	F.P.	1891	1914	1922	-	1896	-	-	CB Q to Morocco
†A.M.G.		1944	-	-	-	-	-	-	Issues 1944
†Fr. Colonies	Fr.	1859	1944	-	-	1884	-	-	No issues 1906-1944
†Fr. Congo	Fr.	1891	-	-	-	-	-	-	To Gabon & Mid. Congo 1906
†Fr. Eq. Africa	Fr.	1936	1938	1937	-	1937	-	-	CB Div. 1958
Fr. Guiana	Fr.	1886	1915	1933	-	1925	-	-	CB
†Fr. Guinea	Fr.	1892	1915	1940	-	1905	-	-	Fr. W. Afr. 1943
†Fr. India	Fr.	1892	1915	1942	-	1923	-	-	To India 1955
†Fr. Oceanica	Fr.	1892	1915	1934	-	1926	-	-	CB Ren. Polynesia
Fr. Polynesia	Fr.	-	-	-	-	-	-	-	
Fr. So. & Ant. Terr.	Fr.	1955	1956	-	-	-	-	-	
†Fr. Sudan	Fr.	1894	1938	1940	-	1921	-	-	Fr. W. Afr. 1943
†Fr. W. Africa	Fr.	1943	1944	1945	-	1947	-	-	Divided 1958
Fujeira	B.P.	1964	-	-	-	-	-	-	Was Trucial State

Country or State		[A]	B	C	E	J	O	P	Remarks
†Funchal	Por.	1892	-	-	-	-	-	-	Madeira 1905
†Gabon	Fr.	1886	1916	-	-	1928	-	-	CB Fr. Eq. Afr. 1934
Galapagos Is.		1957	-	1957	-	-	-	-	Ecuador Dep.
Gambia	Br.	1869	-	-	-	-	-	-	Rep. 1963
†Georgia	Sov.	1919	1922	-	-	-	-	-	T.C.F.R. 1923
†Ger. E. Africa	Ger.	1893	-	-	-	-	-	-	N; Partitioned 1918
†Ger. N. Guinea	Ger.	1897	-	-	-	-	-	-	New Britain, Br. 1919
†Ger. S.W. Africa	Ger.	1897	-	-	-	-	-	-	S. W. Afr. 1920
Germany	A.	1872	1919	1919	-	-	1920	1939	MC MQ N S k
†Thurn & Taxis	Ger.	1852	-	-	-	-	-	-	Prussia 1867
†N.G.P.D.	Ger.	1868	-	-	-	-	-	-	Ger. 1870
†A.M.G.		1945	-	-	-	-	-	-	Issues 1945-46
†Fr. Zone		1945	-	-	-	-	-	-	Issues 1945, 1946
†Fr. Zone, Baden		1947	1949	-	-	-	-	-	Issues 1947-49
†Fr. Zone, Palat		1947	1948	-	-	-	-	-	Issues 1947-49
Fr. Zone, Wurtemberg		1947	1949	-	-	-	-	-	Issues 1947-49
†U.S. & Br. Zones Allied Sect.		1948	-	-	-	-	-	-	Issues 1948, 1949
Berlin		1948	1949	1949	-	-	-	-	
Ger.Dem.Rep.	A.	1948	1948	1957	-	-	1954	-	Was Soviet occ.
Ghana	A.	1957	-	1959	-	1958	-	-	Was Gold Coast
Gibraltar	Br.	1886	-	-	-	-	-	-	MR
Gilbert & Ellice Is.	Br.	1886	-	-	-	1940	-	-	MR
†Gold Coast	Br.	1875	-	-	-	1923	-	-	Now Ghana
†Grand Comoro Is.	Fr.	1897	-	1950	-	1950	-	-	To Comoro Is.
Great Britain	A.	1840	-	-	-	1914	1882	-	k
Greece	A.	1861	1944	1926	-	1875	-	-	CB N RA RAB
Greenland	Den.	1938	1958	-	-	-	-	-	Q
Grenada	Br.	1892	-	-	-	1892	-	-	MR
†Griqueland West	Br.	1874	-	-	-	-	-	-	Cape Good Hope 1880
Guadeloupe	Fr.	1884	1915	1945	-	1876	-	-	
†Guam	U.S.	1899	-	-	1899	-	-	-	U.S. 1900
Guatemala	A.	1871	1937	1929	1940	-	1902	-	CB CO RA
Guinea	Por.	1881	-	1938	-	1904	-	1893	MR RA RAJ
Haiti	A.	1881	1939	1929	1953	1898	-	-	CB RA RAC
†Hamburg	Ger.	1859	-	-	-	-	-	-	N.G.P.D. 1868
†Hanover	Ger.	1850	-	-	-	-	-	-	Prussia 1866
†Hatay	Tur.	1939	-	-	-	1939	-	-	To Turkey 1939
†Hawaii	U.S.	1851	-	-	-	-	1896	-	To U.S. 1898
†Hejaz	A.	1916	-	-	-	1917	-	-	Added to Nejd 1932
†Heligoland	Ger.	1867	-	-	-	-	-	-	Was Br. Ger. to 1890
Honduras	A.	1865	-	1925	-	-	1890	-	CO CE RA
Hong Kong	Br.	1862	-	-	-	1924	-	-	N UX
†Horta	Por.	1892	-	-	-	-	-	-	Portugal 1905
Hungary	A.	1871	1913	1918	1916	1903	1921	1871	CB F N PR Q
Iceland	A.	1873	1932	1928	-	-	1873	-	CO
Ifni	Sp.	1941	1950	1943	1943	-	-	-	
India	A.	1852	-	1929	-	1866	-	-	M (native states) k
†Indo-China	Fr.	1889	1914	1933	-	1904	1933	-	CB Q, ended 1949
Indonesia	A.	1950	1951	-	-	1950	-	-	Was Net. Indies to 1950
†Riouw Arch.	A.	1954	-	-	-	-	-	-	
†Inhambane	Por.	1895	-	-	-	-	-	-	Mozambique 1917
†Inini	Fr.	1932	1939	-	-	1932	-	-	From Fr. Guiana
†Ionian Is.	Br.	1859	-	-	-	-	-	-	To Greece 1864
†Ionian Is.	I.O.	1941	-	1941	-	1941	-	-	To Greece 1945
Iran	A.	1870	1945	1927	-	-	1881	1909	N Q was Persia

Country or State		[A]	B	C	E	J	O	P	Remarks
Iraq	A.	1918	1948	1949	-	-	1923	-	N RA
Ireland (Eire)	A.	1922	-	1948	-	1925	-	-	
Israel	A.	1948	-	1950	-	1948	1951	-	Was Palestine
†Ital. Colonies	It.	1932	-	1932	-	-	-	-	CE
†It. East Africa	It.	1938	-	1938	1938	1941	-	-	CE was Erit. & It. Som.
†It. Somaliland	It.	1903	1916	1934	1923	1907	-	-	CB EY Q It. E. Afr. 1936
Italy (was Sardinia)	A.	1862	1915	1917	1903	1863	1875	1862	CB CE CO D EY k M MC ME MCE N Q
†Aegean Is.	It.	1912	-	1930	-	-	-	-	CE; from Turkey 1924
†Rhodes	It.	1912	1943	-	1936	1934	-	-	BE CB Q
†A.M.G.		1943	-	-	-	-	-	-	
†A.M.G. Venezia Giulia		1945	-	1946	1946	-	-	-	Issues 1945-47
†Ital. Soc. Rep.		1944	-	-	1944	-	1944	-	EYQ
Ivory Coast	Fr.	1896	1915	1940	-	1906	-	-	Q; to Fr. W. Afr. 1944
Jamaica	A.	1860	1923	-	-	-	1890	-	MR
Japan	A.	1871	1937	1919	-	1921	1946	-	M k
Jordan	A.	1920	1930	1950	-	1923	-	-	N RA; was Transjordan
Jugoslavia	A.	1921	1921	1934	-	1921	1946	-	K KB N RA RAJ
†Bosnia & Herze.	Ju.	1918	1918	-	1918	1918	-	-	Jugoslavia 1921
†Croatia & Slav.	Ju.	1918	1918	-	1918	1918	-	1918	Jugoslavia 1921
†Slovenia	Ju.	1919	-	-	-	1919	-	1919	Jugoslavia 1921
†Carinthia	Ju.	-	1920	-	-	-	-	-	Jugoslavia 1921
†Istria, Zone B		1945	-	-	-	1945	-	-	Issues to 1947
†Karelia	Sov.	1922	-	-	-	-	-	-	N Russian province in rev.
†Katanga	A.	1960	-	1960	-	1960	-	-	To Congo 1960
Kenya	A.	-	-	-	-	-	-	-	Ind. 1963, Rep. 1964
†Kenya & Uganda	Br.	1921	-	-	-	1928	-	-	See next, 1935
†Kenya, Uganda, & Tanganyika	Br.	1935	-	-	-	1935	-	-	Tanganyika trusteeship
†Klauchau	Ger.	1900	-	-	-	-	-	-	Last issue 1910
†Kionga	Por.	1916	-	-	-	-	-	-	Mozambique, 1916
Korea	A.	1886	1953	1947	-	-	-	-	Japan 1905-45
Kuwait	Br.	1923	-	1933	-	-	1923	-	
†Labuan	Br.	1879	-	-	-	1901	-	-	Straits 1906
†Lagos	Br.	1874	-	-	-	-	-	-	Southern Nigeria 1906
Laos	A.	1951	1953	1952	-	1952	-	-	From Indo-China
†Latakia	F.M.	1931	-	1931	-	1931	-	-	Syria 1937
†Latvia	Sov.	1918	1920	1921	-	1924	-	-	U.S.S.R. 1940
Lebanon	A.	1924	1926	1924	-	1924	-	-	CB RA; orig. in Syria
Leeward Is.	Br.	1890	-	-	-	-	-	-	Ended July 1, 1956
Liberia	A.	1860	1915	1936	1941	1892	1892	-	CB CE CF F
Libia	A.	1912	1915	1929	1915	1915	1952	-	CE EB EY N Q; It. to 1952
Liechtenstein	A.	1912	1925	1930	-	1920	1932	-	
†Lithuania	Sov.	1918	1924	1921	-	-	-	-	CB N U.S.S.R. 1940
†Lourenco Marques	Por.	1894	1917	-	-	-	-	1894	Mozambique, ab. 1920
†Lubeck	Ger.	1859	-	-	-	-	-	-	N.G.P.D. 1868
Luxembourg	A.	1852	1921	1931	-	1907	1875	-	N
Macao	Por.	1884	-	1936	-	1904	-	1892	MR RA RAJ
†Madagascar	Fr.	1889	1915	1935	-	1896	-	-	CB Malagasy Rep.
†Madagascar	Br.	1884	-	-	-	-	-	-	To France, 1886
†Madeira	Por.	1868	-	-	-	-	-	1876	RA RAJ Por. 1898
Malagasy Rep.	A.	1958	-	1960	-	1962	-	-	Was Fr. Madagascar
†Malaya	A.	1957	-	-	-	-	-	-	To Malaysia
Malaysia	A.	1963	-	-	-	-	-	-	
Maldive Is.	A.	1906	-	-	-	-	-	-	Was Brit. col.

Country or State	[A]	B	C	E	J	O	P	Remarks
Mali, Fed. of	A.	1961	1962	-	-	1961	1961	-	Was Sudan, Senegal
Malta	A.	1860	-	1928	-	1925	--	-	MR Ind. 1964
†Manchukuo	Jap.	1932	-	1936	-	-	-	-	To China 1945
†Mariana Is.	Sp.	1898	-	-	-	-	-	-	To Germany 1899
†Marienwerder	Ger.	1920	-	-	-	-	-	-	Pleb. to Germany
†Marshall Islands	Ger.	1897	-	-	-	--	-	-	New Britain 1916
Martinique	Fr.	1886	1915	1945	-	1887	-	-	Q
Mauritania	A.	1906	1915	1940	-	1906	-	-	Fr. W. Afr. 1943
Mauritius	Br.	1847	-	-	1903	1933	-	-	
†Mayotte	Fr.	1892	-	-	-	-	-	-	Madagascar 1914
†Meckl'g-Schwerin	Ger.	1856	-	-	-	-	-	-	N.G.P.D. 1868
†Meckl'g-Strelitz	Ger.	1864	-	-	-	-	-	-	N.G.P.D. 1868
†Memel	Sov.	1920	-	1921	-	-	-	-	N; Lithuania 1924
†Mesopotamia	Br.	1918	-	-	-	-	1920	-	Became Iraq
Mexico	A.	1856	1918	1922	1919	1908	1884	-	CO G JX Q RA (Prov.)
†Middle Congo	Fr.	1907	1916	-	-	1928	-	-	To Fr. Eq. Afr. 1934
†Modena	It.	1852	-	-	-	-	-	(PR)	To Sardinia 1859
†Moheli	Fr.	1906	-	-	-	-	-	-	Madagascar, 1908
Monaco	A.	1885	1914	1933	-	1905	-	-	CB
†Mongolia, Outer	S.D.	1924	-	-	-	-	-	-	China to 1945
†Mongolia, inner	J.D.	1943	-	-	-	-	-	-	To China 1945
†Montenegro	A.	1874	-	-	-	1894	-	-	H N; Jugoslavia 1918
Montserrat	Br.	1876	-	-	-	-	-	-	MR
Mozambique	Por.	1877	1920	1938	-	1904	-	1893	MR RA RAJ
†Mozambique Company	Por.	1892	1917	1935	-	1906	-	1892	RA; Mozambique 1945
Muscat & Oman	B.P.	1944	-	-	-	-	1944	-	Sultinate of Oman
†Natal	Br.	1857	-	-	-	-	1904	-	To South Africa 1910
Nauru	Br.	1916	-	-	-	-	-	-	UN trusteeship
†Nejd	A.	1925	-	1949	-	1925	1939	-	Ren. Saudi Arabia 1932
Nepal	A.	1881	-	-	1958	-	1959	-	Valid also in India
Netherlands	A.	1852	1906	1921	-	1870	1913	-	GY
Net. Antilles	Net.	1949	1951	-	-	1953	-	-	Was Curacao
†Nevis	Br.	1861	-	-	-	-	-	-	Leewards 1890
†New Britain	Br.	1914	-	-	-	-	1915	-	New Guinea 1915
†New Brunswick	Br.	1851	-	-	-	-	-	-	Canada 1867
New Caledonia	Fr.	1859	1915	1938	-	1903	1959	-	CB Q
†Newfoundland	Br.	1857	-	1919	-	1939	-	-	Canada 1949
†New Guinea	Br.	1925	-	1931	-	-	1925	-	Papua & New Guinea
New Hebrides		1908	-	-	-	1925	-	-	Br. Fr. condominium
†New Republic	Br.	1886	-	-	-	-	-	-	Transvaal 1888
†New South Wales	Br.	1850	1897	-	-	1891	1879	-	F; Australia 1913
New Zealand	Br.	1855	1929	1931	1903	1900	1892	1873	AR MR OY
Nicaragua	A.	1862	-	1929	-	1896	1890	-	CO L RA (Prov.)
Niger	A.	1921	1938	1940	-	1921	-	-	From Fr. W. Afr.
†Niger Coast	Br.	1892	-	-	-	-	-	-	To S. Nigeria 1900
Nigeria	A.	1914	-	-	-	1959	-	-	Un. N. & S. Nigeria
Niue	Br.	1902	-	-	-	-	-	-	
Norfolk Is.	Br.	1947	-	-	-	-	-	-	
†North Borneo	Br.	1883	1916	-	-	1895	-	-	MR N Ren. Sabah
North Korea	A.	1946	-	-	-	-	-	-	No listing
†Northern Nigeria	Br.	1900	-	-	-	-	--	-	To Nigeria 1914
†Northern Rhodesia	Br.	1925	-	-	-	1929	-	-	Ren. Rhod. Nyasa. Fed.
†No. Ingerman-land	Sov.	1920	-	-	-	-	-	-	Rev. ended 1920

Country or State	[A]	B	C	E	J	O	P	Remarks
N. Viet Nam	C.D.	-	-	-	-	-	-	-	No listing
†No. West Pac.									
Is.	Br.	1915	-	-	-	-	-	-	Man. New Zealand 1922
Norway	A.	1854	1930	1927	-	1889	1925	-	
†Nossi Be	Fr.	1889	-	-	-	1891	-	-	Madagascar 1896
†Nova Scotia	Br.	1851	-	-	-	-	-	-	Canada 1867
†Nyasaland									
Prot.	Br.	1908	-	-	-	1951	-	-	Was Br. Cent. Afr.
†Nyassa	Por.	1897	-	-	-	1924	-	1897	RA RAJ; Mozambique 1925
†Obock	Fr.	1892	-	-	-	1892	-	-	Somali Coast 1902
†Oldenburg	Ger.	1852	-	-	-	-	-	-	To N.G.P.D. 1868
†Oltre Giuba	It.	1925	1926	-	1926	1925	-	-	Q; It. Somaliland 1926
†Orange R. Col.	Br.	1868	-	-	-	-	-	-	South Africa 1910
Pakistan	Br.	1947	-	-	-	-	1947	-	From India
†Palestine	B.M.	1918	-	-	-	1923	-	-	Became Israel 1948
Panama	A.	1878	-	1929	1926	1915	-	-	F G H I R A
†Papua	Br.	1907	-	1929	-	-	1931	-	See next
Papua & New									
Guinea	Br.	1952	-	-	-	1960	-	-	Aust. dep.
Paraguay	A.	1870	1930	1929	-	1904	1886	-	L
†Parma	It.	1852	-	-	-	-	-	(PR)	To Sardinia 1860
†Penrhyn Island	Br.	1902	-	-	-	-	-	-	Cook Is. 1932
Peru	A.	1857	-	1927	1908	1874	1884	-	N Q RA (Prov.) CB
Philippine Is.	A.	1854	1949	1933	1901	1899	1926	1886	EO N
Pitcairn Is.	Br.	1940	-	-	-	-	-	-	
Poland	S.D.	1918	1919	1925	-	1919	1920	1919	K KB N; CB N NB & NO
†Poland		1860	-	-	-	-	-	-	Russia 1865
†Poland, exile		1941	1944	-	-	-	-	-	Ceased 1944
†Ponta Delgada	Por.	1892	-	-	-	-	-	-	Azores 1905
Portugal	A.	1853	-	1937	-	1898	1938	1876	Q RA RAJ S
Por. Africa	Por.	1898	-	-	-	-	-	-	For any Afr. Colony
Por. Colonies	Por.	-	-	-	-	1945	-	-	MR Cent.-Esc. Col.
†Por. Congo	Por.	1894	-	-	-	-	-	1894	Angola 1915
†Por. India	Por.	1871	-	1938	-	1904	-	-	MR RA RAJ
†Prince Edward									
Is.	Br.	1861	-	-	-	-	-	-	Canada 1873
†Prussia	Ger.	1850	-	-	-	-	-	-	N.G.P.D. 1868
†Puerto Rico	U.S.	1855	-	-	-	1899	-	-	MR; to US 1898
Qatar	B.P.	1957	-	-	-	-	-	-	Was Trucial State
†Queensland	Br.	1860	1900	-	-	-	-	-	F; Australia 1913
†Quelimane	Por.	1913	-	-	-	-	-	-	Mozambique 1914
Ras al Khaimah	B.P.	1964	-	-	-	-	-	-	Was Trucial State
Reunion	Fr.	1852	1915	1937	-	1889	-	-	CB Q
†Rhodesia	Br.	1890	-	-	-	-	-	-	Div. N. & S. 1923
†Rhodesia &									
Nyasa.	Br.	1954	-	-	-	1961	-	-	Dis. 1963
†Rio de Oro	Sp.	1905	-	-	-	-	-	-	Sp. Sahara 1924
Rio Muni	Sp.	1960	1960	-	-	-	-	-	From Sp. Guinea
†Romagna	It.	1859	-	-	-	-	-	-	Sardinia 1860
Romania	A.	1858	1906	1928	-	1881	1929	-	CB k Q RA RAJ N NR NRAJ NJ
†Roman States	It.	1852	-	-	-	-	-	-	Italy 1870
Ross									
Dependency	Br.	1957	-	-	-	-	-	-	New Zealand, L only
†Rouad	F.M.	1916	-	-	-	-	-	-	1916 only
†Ruanda-									
Urundi	Bel.	1924	1925	-	-	1924	-	-	Was Ger. E. Afr.
Russia	A.	1858	1905	1922	1932	1924	-	-	k N L
Rwanda	A.	1962	-	-	-	-	-	-	From Ruanda-Urundi

Country or State	[A]	B	C	E	J	O	P	Remarks
Ryukyu Is. Man.	U.S.	1948	-	1950	1950	-	-	-	
†Saar	F.O.	1920	1926	1928	-	-	1922	-	CB to Germany
†Sabah	Br.	1964	-	-	-	-	-	-	Joined Malaysia
†St. Christopher	Br.	1870	-	-	-	-	-	-	Leeward Is. 1890
St. Thomas & Prince Is.	Por.	1869	-	1938	-	1904	-	1893	RA RAJ
St. Ch. Nevis Anguilla	Br.	1952	-	-	-	-	-	-	Anguilla added
St. Helena	Br.	1856	-	-	-	-	-	-	MR
†St. Kitts-Nevis	Br.	1903	-	-	-	-	-	-	MR; St. Ch. Nev. Ang.
St. Lucia	Br.	1860	-	-	-	1931	-	-	MR
St. Pierre & Miq.	Fr.	1885	1915	1942	-	1892	-	-	Q
St. Vincent	Br.	1861	-	-	-	-	-	-	MR
†Ste. Marie de Madagascar	Fr.	1894	-	-	-	-	-	-	Madagascar 1906
Salvador, El	A.	1867	-	1929	-	1895	1896	-	F H Q RA
†Samoa	Br.	1877	-	-	-	-	-	-	N; W. Samoa 1935
San Marino	A.	1877	1917	1931	1907	1897	-	-	CB EB Q
†Sarawak	Br.	1869	-	-	-	-	-	-	N; to Malaysia
†Sardinia	It.	1851	-	-	-	-	-	1861	Ren. Italy 1861
†Saseno	It.	1923	-	-	-	-	-	-	To Albania 1947
†Saxony	Ger.	1850	-	-	-	-	-	-	N.G.P.D. 1868
†Schleswig (pleb.)	Ger.	1920	-	-	-	-	-	-	To Ger. & Den.
†Schleswig-Holst.	Ger.	1850	-	-	-	-	-	-	Prussia 1866
Senegal	A.	1887	1915	1935	-	1903	-	-	CB; Fr. W. Afr. 1943
†Senegambia & Niger	Fr.	1903	-	-	-	-	-	-	Up. Senegal & Niger 1904
†Serbia	Ju.	1866	-	-	-	1895	-	1911	N; Jugoslavia 1921
Seychelles	Br.	1890	-	-	-	1951	-	-	
Sharjah	B.P.	1963	-	1963	-	-	-	-	Used Muscat to 1961
Khor Fakkan		1965	-	-	-	-	-	-	Dependency
†Shanghai	A.	1865	-	-	-	1892	-	-	China 1898
Siam (Thai)	A.	1883	1918	1925	-	-	1943	-	N
†Siberia	Sov.	1919	-	-	-	-	-	-	U.S.S.R. 1923
†Czech. Army Post		1918	-	-	-	-	-	-	Occ. to 1920
†Priamur Govt.		1921	-	-	-	-	-	-	Rev. 1922
Sierra Leone	A.	1860	-	1961	-	-	-	-	
†Singapore	Br.	1948	-	-	-	-	-	-	To Malaysia 1963
Somalia	A.	1960	-	1960	-	-	-	-	Was Br. Som. Prot.
Somali Coast	Fr.	1895	1915	1944	-	1915	-	-	CB
†Somaliland Prot.	Br.	1902	-	-	-	-	1902	-	To Somalia
S. Arabian Fed.	Br.	1963	-	-	-	-	-	-	Was Aden & W. dep.
†S. Australia	Br.	1855	-	-	-	-	1868	-	Australia 1913
S. George	Br.	1963	-	-	-	-	-	-	
S. Rhodesia	Br.	1924	-	-	-	1951	-	-	Was Fed. Rhod. & Nyasa.
†S. Nigeria	Br.	1901	-	-	-	-	-	-	Nigeria 1914
†S. Russia	Sov.	1918	-	-	-	-	-	-	Var. issues to 1920
S. W. Africa	BM.	1923	1935	1930	-	1923	1927	-	Was Ger. S.W. Afr.
Spain	A.	1850	1926	1920	1905	-	1854	-	CB CE CO E EB k L
(Rev. also)		-	-	-	-	-	-	-	MR RA RAB RAC S X
†Sp. Morocco	Sp.	1903	1926	1938	1914	-	-	-	CB EB RA L
†Sp. Guinea	Sp.	1902	1926	1941	1951	-	-	-	Bec. Rio Muni
Sp. W. Africa	Sp.	1949	-	1949	1951	-	-	-	
Sp. Sahara	Sp.	1924	1926	1943	1951	-	-	-	Sp. W. Sahara to 1941

Country or State		[A]	B	C	E	J	O	P	Remarks
†Stellaland	Br.	1884	-	-	-	-	-	-	To Br. Bech. 1885
†Straits									
Settl'mts	Br.	1867	1917	-	-	1924	-	-	N; end in 1946
†Fed. Malay									
St's.	Br.	1900	-	-	-	1924	-	-	Became Malaya
†Johore	Br.	1876	-	-	-	1938	-	-	N
†Kedah	Br.	1912	-	-	-	-	-	-	N
†Kelantan	Br.	1911	-	-	-	-	-	-	N
†Malacca	Br.	1948	-	-	-	-	-	-	N; joined Malaya
†Negri									
Sembiland	Br.	1891	-	-	-	-	-	-	N; federated 1900-35
†Pahang	Br.	1890	-	-	-	-	-	-	N; federated 1900-35
†Penang	Br.	1948	-	-	-	-	-	-	N
†Perak	Br.	1878	-	-.	-	-	1890	-	N; federated 1900-35
†Perlis	Br.	1948	-	-	-	-	-	-	
†Selangor	Br.	1878	-	-	-	-	-	-	N; federated 1900-35
†Singapore	Br.	1948	-	-	-	-	-	-	
†Sungei Ujong	Br.	1878	-	-	-	-	. -	-	To Negri Sembilan 1895
†Trengganu	Br.	1910	1917	-	-	1937	-	-	N
Sudan	A.	1897	-	1931	-	1897	1902	-	CO MO, was Anglo-Egypt
Surinam	Net.	1873	1927	1930	-	1886	-	-	CB
Swaziland	Br.	1889	-	-	-	1933	-	-	
Sweden	A.	1855	1916	1920	-	1874	1874	-	L Q
Switzerland	A.	1850	1913	1919	-	1878	1918	-	L S
†Basle	Sw.	1845	-	-	-	-	-	-	L; Switzerland 1850
†Geneva	Sw.	1843	-	-	-	-	-	-	L; Switzerland 1850
†Zurich	Sw.	1843	-	-	-	-	-	-	L; Switzerland 1850
†Syria	A.	1919	1926	1920	-	-	-	-	M MB MC MCB RA
†Arabian govt.	Tur.	1920	-	¬	-	1920	-	-	
Syrian Arab									
Rep.		1961	-	1961	-	-	-	-	
†Tahiti	Fr.	1882	1915	-	-	1893	-	-	Fr. Oceania 1903
†Tanganyika	Br.	1921	-	-	-	-	1959	-	Kenya &Uganda 1935
†Tangan. & Zanz.	A.	1964	-	-	-	-	-	-	Ren. Tanzan.
Tanzan.	A.	1964	-	-	-	-	-	-	
†Tannu Tuva	S.D.	1926	-	-	-	-	-	-	
†Tasmania	Br.	1853	-	-	-	-	-	-	Australia 1913
†Tete	Por.	1913	-	-	-	-	-	-	Mozambique 1914
†Thrace		1913	-	-	-	-	-	-	N; to Gr. Tur. Bul. 1920
†Tibet	A.	1913	-	-	-	-	1950	-	Local stamps
Timor	Por.	1885	-	1938	-	1904	-	1892	MR RA RAJ
†Tobago	Br.	1879	-	-	-	-	¬	-	Trinidad 1899
†Togo	Ger.	1897	1938	1940	-	1921	-	-	N; Fr. & Br. Man.
Togo	A.	1957	1959	1957	-	1957	-	-	
Tokelau Is.	Br.	1948	-	-	-	-	-	-	
Tonga	Br.	1886	-	1963	-	-	1893	-	CO
†Transcau.									
Fed. Rep.	Sov.	1923	-	-	-	-	-	-	U.S.S.R. 1936
†Transvaal	Br.	1869	-	-	-	1907	-	-	South Africa 1910
†Trieste Zone A		1947	-	1947	1947	1947	-	-	EYQ
†Trieste Zone B		1948	-	1948	-	1949	-	-	RA Jugoslavia 1921
†Trinidad	Br.	1851	-	-	-	1885	1893	-	Trin. & Tobago 1913
Trin. & Tobago	A.	1913	1914	-	-	1923	1913	-	MR
†Tripolitania	It.	1923	1924	1930	-	-	-	-	CB CE EB EY; Libia
Tristan-									
daCunha	Br.	1951	-	-	-	1957	-	-	
Tunisia	A.	1888	1915	1919	-	1901	-	-	CB Q 1901
Turkey	A.	1863	1915	1934	-	1863	1948	1879	M RA
†Turkey in									
Asia	A.	1920	-	-	-	1921	-	-	Became new Turkey 1923
†Turks Islands	Br.	1867	-	-	-	-	-	-	Turks & Caicos 1900
Turks &Caicos	Br.	1900	-	-	-	-	-	-	MR

Country or State		[A]	B	C.	E	J	O	P	Remarks
†Tuscany	It.	1851	–	–	–	–	–	–	PR; Sardinia 1860
†Two Sicilies	It.	1858	–	–	–	–	–	–	Italy 1862
†Ubangi	Fr.	1915	1916	–	–	1928	–	–	Fr. Eq. Afr. 1934
Uganda	A.	1895	–	–	–	–	–	–	E. Afr. & Uganda 1903
†Ukraine	Sov.	1918	1923	–	–	–	–	–	U.S.S.R. 1923
Union South Africa	A.	1910	1933	1925	–	1915	1926	–	
Umm al Qiwain		1964	–	–	–	–	–	–	From Trucial States
United Arab Rep.	A.	1958	1958	1958	–	–	1958	–	Was Egypt
†Syria U.A.R.		1958	1959	1958	–	–	–	–	Bec. Syrian Arab Rep.
United Nations		1951	–	1951	–	–	–	–	
United States	A.	1847	–	1918	1885	1879	1873	1865	CE F JQ K L Q QE X F.
†Up. Sen. & Niger	Fr.	1906	1915	–	–	1906	–	–	Ren. Fr. Sudan 1921
†Upper Silesia		1920	–	–	–	–	1920	–	Div. Ge. & Pol.
Upper Volta	A.	1920	–	–	–	1920	–	–	Divided in 1933
Uruguay	A.	1856	1930	1921	1921	1902	1880	1922	I Q
Vatican City	A.	1929	1933	1938	1929	1931	–	–	Q
Venezuela	A.	1859	1942	1930	1949	–	1898	–	CB F (Prov.)
†Victoria	Br.	1850	1897	–	–	1890	–	–	F I AR; Australia 1913
Viet Nam.	A.	1951	1952	1952	–	1952	–	–	From Indo-China
Virgin Is.	Br.	1866	–	–	–	–	–	–	MR
Wallis & Futuna	Fr.	1920	1939	1946	–	1920	–	–	
†West. Australia	Br.	1854	–	–	–	–	–	–	Australia 1913
West. Samoa	Br.	1935	–	–	–	–	–	–	
†Western Ukraine	Pol.	1918	–	–	–	–	–	–	F; Poland 1919
†Württemberg	Ger.	1851	–	–	–	–	1875	–	Ger. 1902, exc. Off.
Yemen	A.	1926	–	1947	–	1942	–	–	In U.A.R. 1958-1961
†Zambesia	Por.	1894	–	–	–	–	–	1894	Quelimane & Tete 1917
†Zanzibar	Br.	1895	–	–	–	1931	–	–	Became Tanzan.
†Zululand	Br.	1888	–	–	–	–	–	–	Natal 1897

Prefix Letters Used in the Scott Classification [1]

A   Regular Postage Issues, including Commemorative
  AR   Postal-Fiscal
B   Semi-Postal Issues
C   Air Post Issues
  CB   Semi-Postal; CE   Special Delivery; CF   Registration; CO   Official
D   Pneumatic Post Issues
E   Special Delivery Issues
  EB   Semi-Postal; ER   Delivery Tax; EY   Authorized Delivery; EO Official; EX   Personal Delivery
F   Registration Stamps
  FA   Certified Delivery
G   Insured Letter Stamps
  GY   Marine Insurance Stamps
H   Acknowledgment of Receipt Stamps
I   Late Fee Stamps
J   Postage Due Issues
  JQ   Parcel Post Dues; JX   Due Ships (Porte de Mar)
K   Issues for Offices Abroad
  KB   Semi-Postal Issues
L   Local Issues
M   Military or Army Issues
  MR   War Tax Issues
N   Occupation Issues
O   Official Issues
  OX   Post Office Seals, and Utility Stickers; OY   Life Insurance Stamps of New Zealand
P   Newspaper and Periodical Stamps
  PR   Fiscal Tax Stamps for Foreign Newspapers, also assigned to United States Newspaper and Periodical Stamps
Q   Parcel Post Stamps (see also JQ)
  QE   Special Handling
R   Revenue Issues
  RA   Postal Tax; RAB   Postal Tax, Semi-Postal; RAC   Postal Tax Air Post; RAJ   Postal Tax Due
S   Franchise Stamps
T   Telegraph Stamps (United States only)
U   Envelope Stamps
  UX   Postal Cards, and stamps for use on Postal Cards only, Hong Kong
X   Provisionals, as Postmasters' Provisionals
Y   Revolutionary Issues
The prefixes K, L, M, N, and Y may be used with any category.

---

[1] Reprinted from the *Scott's Standard Postage Stamp Catalogue*, by permission of Scott Publications, Inc.

*Abbreviations in the Table of the World's Stamps and
Table of Principal Latin-Letter Inscriptions*

A. autonomous
ab. about
adm. administration
Afr. Africa
A.M.G. Allied Military Govern-
  ment
Aus. Austria(n)
B.C. British controlled
B & H Bosnia and Herzegovina
Bel. Belgium, Belgian
bil. bilingual
B.M. British Mandate
B.P. British Protected
Br. Britain, British
Bul. Bulgaria(n)
c. currency
caps. capital letters
C.D. Chinese Com. Dom.
col. colony, colonies
Cz. Czechoslovakia(n)
Den. Denmark
dept., depts. department(s)
dom. domination, dominated
E. East, eastern
Eq. equatorial
fac. facing
F.M. French Mandate
F.O. French Occupation
F.P. French Protectorate
Fr. France, French
from separated from
G.O. German Occupation
govt. government
Gr. Greece, Greek
h/s handstamped
insc. inscription(s)
I.O. Italian Occupation
Is. Island(s)
It. Italy, Italian
Jap. Japan, Japanese
J.D. Japanese domination
Ju. Jugoslavia(n)
k. foreign offices

l.c. lower-case letters
man. mandate
mid. middle
mil. military
N. North, northern
Ne. Indies Netherlands East In-
  dies
Net. Netherlands
N.G.P.D. North German Con-
  federation
occ. occupation
off. offices
Off. Official stamps
o.p. overprint(s), overprinted
P-D postage due stamps
pleb. plebiscite
Pol. Poland, Polish
Por. Portugal, Portuguese
prot. protectorate
prov. provisional
Prov. provinces
P-T postal tax
ren. renamed
Rev. revolution(ary)
R-L registered letter stamps
S. South, southern
S-D special delivery stamps
S.D. U.S.S.R. dominated
semioff. semiofficial
Sov. U.S.S.R.
Sp. Spain, Spanish
S-P semi-postal stamps
Straits Straits Settlements
Sw. Switzerland, Swiss
S.W. Southwest
T.C.F.R. Transcaucasian Feder-
  ated Republic
Tur. Turkey, Turkish
Un. Union
U.S. United States
var. various
W. West, western

Addenda to Latin-Letter Inscriptions, etc. (see Chapter Thirty-Six)

AUSTRALIAN ANTARCTIC TERRITORY Insc. Polar regions.

BHUTAN Insc. local stamps for this Himalayan state, 1954.

CONSEIL DE L'EUROPE Insc. and o.p., France, for the Council of Europe, 1958.

CAMBODGE; ROYAUME DU CAMBODGE Inscs. Cambodia.

CHRISTMAS ISLAND O.p. on Australia for that dependency.

GHANA Insc. for State of Ghana, Mar. 6, 1957, was Gold Coast.

ISLAMIC REPUBLIC OF PAKISTAN Insc. one issue, 1956.

ISLAS GALAPAGOS Insc. for this Ecuadorean possession, 1957.

LIBYE; KINGDOM OF LIBYA; UNITED KINGDOM OF LIBYA Inscs. Libyan definitive issues.

MARRUECOS Insc. independent state formerly Spanish Morocco.

MAROC Insc. French Morocco and with ROYAUME DE MAROC Inscs. Kingdom of Morocco after Mar. 2, 1956.

NEDERLANDS (or NED.) NIEUW GUINEA Inscs. 1954; NIEUW GUINEA, inscs. 1950–1953, Netherland New Guinea.

POLYNESIE FRANCAISE Insc. French Oceania, 1958.

QATAR O.p. on Brit. for an oil region on Persian Gulf, 1957.

REPOEBLIK INDONESIA Insc. Republic of Indonesia (Java and Sumatra) prior to union with other parts of the Dutch East Indies in the United States of Indonesia.

REPUBLIC OF IRAQ Insc. after overthrow of ruler, 1958.

REPUBLIQUE ARABE UNIE– SYRIE Insc.; R.A.U. Insc. and o.p. Syria, in the United Arab Republic.

REPUBLIQUE AUTONOME DU TOGO Insc. 1956; REPUBLIQUE DU TOGO Inscs. after Dec. 1958, Togo.

REPUBLIQUE DE GUINEE Insc. Republic of Guinea, Oct. 2, 1958.

REPUBLIQUE LIBANAISE Insc. Lebanon after 1927.

REPUBLIQUE MALGACHE (Malagash Republic) Insc. Madagascar, 1958.

REPUBLIQUE TUNISENNE Insc. Tunisia after overthrow of ruler, 1958.

TERRES AUSTRALES ET ANTARCTIQUES FRANCAISES O.p. on Madagascar and insc. French Southern and Antarctic Territories, 1955.

TUNISIE Insc. Tunisia, French colony, kingdom and republic; TUNISIE AUTONOME, insc. one issue of kingdom, 1956.

UNITED ARAB REPUBLIC– EGYPT; THE UNITED ARAB REPUBLIC–SYRIA Inscs Mar. 22, 1958; U.A.R.– EGYPT, insc. Mar. 1, 1958; U.A.R., insc. after Oct. 14, 1958, and the last an o.p., 1959, Egypt and Syria, in the United Arab Republic; currency differs.

ZENTRALER KURIERDIENST Insc. Off. German Democratic Republic.

◆◆◆

CHAPTER THIRTY-SIX

PRINCIPAL LATIN-LETTER INSCRIPTIONS, OVERPRINTS, POSTAL MARKINGS, AND DESIGN SYMBOLS

A   O.p. on Colombia air-mail stamps for mail carried by Avianca, one of two competing airlines, the other being Lansa, which carried mail bearing stamps o.p. L. First used in 1950 and now replaced by ordinary air mail. Avianca absorbed Lansa in 1952, and the o.p. stamps were used without distinction, both types on some covers.

A   Preceding plate number on some plates of 1911-12, indicates that the stamp spacing is wider than usual. When this experimental spacing was adopted as standard the A was omitted.

A   Insc. on Colombia R-L. See ANOTACION.

Aangebragt per Land Mail.   Insc. on Dutch East Indies labels used about 1845-46. These appear to indicate how much postage should be collected on unpaid letters, prepayment not being obligatory, but are not P-D stamps in the ordinary sense.

A & T   With value, o.p. on French Colonies for Annam and Tonkin.

A (or At) BETALE-PORTOMAERKE   Insc. P-D, Norway.

Note: See page 544 for abbreviations used in this table. Because there is wide lack of accent marks in the inscriptions on foreign stamps, such marks have been omitted from the inscriptions in this list. For addenda, see page 545.

ACORES   Insc. and o.p. on Portugal for Azores Islands.

ADMIRALTY OFFICIAL   O.p. on British for Off.

Advertised   Postal marking to indicate that undeliverable mail matter has been advertised according to postal laws. If this brought no result, the mail was sent to the dead-letter office.

A.E.F.   The American Expeditonary Forces during World War I. Used in connection with mail, post offices, stamp booklets, etc.

A.E.F.   French Equatorial Africa (Afrique Equatoriale Française).

AEREA   O.p. on Ecuador for air mail.

AEREO   O.p. or insc. indicating air mail on the stamps of various Latin American countries, in some cases with dates or new values. Insc. on etiquettes also.

AEREO EXTERIOR   O.p. for air mail, Guatemala.

AEREO INTERIOR   O.p. on Off. for air mail, Honduras.

AEREO SEDTA   O.p. on P-T. for air mail, Ecuador.

AERO CORREO   O.p. for air mail, Honduras.

AERO O/Y   Insc. air mail, Finland.

AFFRANCHI AINSI FAUTE FIGURINE   H/s o.p. on Madagascar and Diego Suarez during a shortage of low values. Believed to be speculative.

AFFRANCH[ts]   O.p. as a precancellation in France, Morocco, Andorra, and Monaco. Also o.p. on some French stamps issued to officials for government mail.

AFF[t] O[c]   With Foreign Legion cross, O.p. for S-P, Tunisia, speculative.

AFRICA OCCIDENTAL ESPANOLA   Insc. for Sp. W. Africa. Sometimes preceded by TERRITORIOS DEL.

AFRICA ORIENTALE ITALIANA   Insc. It. E. Africa.

AFRIQUE EQUATORIALE FRANÇAISE   O.p. on Gabon and Middle Congo, and insc., Fr. Eq. Africa.

AFRIQUE FRANÇAISE COMBATTANTE   With cross and value, insc. S-P Fr. Eq. Africa.

AFRIQUE FRANÇAISE LIBRE   O.p. on Fr. Eq. Africa and Middle Congo, for Fr. Eq. Africa.

AFRIQUE OCCIDENTALE FRANÇAISE   Insc. Fr. W. Africa.

AGRICULTURE DEPT. OF.   Insc. Off., U. S.

AH PD   O.p. on 1896 Azores to make stamps valid in Angra, Horta, and Ponta Delgada, for which the letters stand.

AIDEZ LES TUBERCULEUX   With surtax o.p. on Tunisia for S-P.

AIR   Insc. air mail, Canada.

AIRMAIL, AIR MAIL   Insc. United States, Canal Zone, Philippines, Iraq, Liberia, India, Japan, Malta, New Guinea, New Zealand, Newfoundland, Papua, Sudan, South Africa, Southwest Africa, and United Nations. Also o.p. for Canal Zone and Philippines.

Airplane   A symbol o.p., with or without change in value, indicating air-mail stamps. In a few cases the o.p. includes a change in the country name. As stamp subjects, airplanes nearly always indicate air-mail issues.

AIRPOST   Insc. air mail, Newfoundland.

AJANLOS; Ajl.1; Ajl.2   Insc. R-L, Hungary.

ALCANCE Y.U.H.   Insc. late fee stamps, Uruguay.

ALFABETIZACION   O.p. on Ecuador (propaganda for adult education).

ALLEMAGNE–DUITSCHLAND.   Bil. o.p. on Belgium, Belg. occ. of Germany.

ALLIED MILITARY POSTAGE   Insc. Allied Mil. Govt. in Italy.

A.M.   O.p. on prov. Greek stamps, 1900, and insc. 1902. (Axia Metalliki, or value in coin.)

AMBULANTE LAQUINTINIE   With value in francs, o.p. for S-P, Cameroons.

A.M.G.   Insc. Mil. stamps, Allied occupation of Italy.

A.M.G. F.T.T.   Allied Mil. Govt.–Free Territory of Trieste, o.p. in various styles on Italy for Trieste.

A.M.G. V.G.   O.p. on Italy for Venezia Giulia.

A.M.POST and M in oval   Insc. Allied mil. occ. of Germany.

AMSTERDAO   Insc. Portugal, P-T to send Olympic team to Amsterdam.

AMTLICH EROFFNET BURCH DIE K.W. POSTDIRECTION   Insc. return letter stamps, Württemberg.

AMTLICKER VERKEHR   Insc. State Off. stamps, Württemberg.

ANCIENS COMBATTANTS and monogram RF.   O.p. on Tunisia for S-P.

ANOTACION   Insc. R-L stamps, Colombia.

A.O. Afrique Orientale, o.p. on Congo for S-P, Belgian occ. Ger. E. Africa.

A.O.F. O.p. on France for S-P, Fr. W. Africa.

A.O.I. O.p. on Italy for P-D, It. E. Africa.

A PAYER To be paid, insc. P-D, Luxembourg.

A PAYER / TE BETELEN Bil. insc. P-D, Belgium, Congo.

A PERCEVOIR To be collected, insc. P-D, France and var. col., Belgium, Egypt, Haiti. An insc. on bil. P-D, Canada, and o.p. on Monaco.

A.P.O. Army Post Office, used in postmarks with or without a number by the Army to simplify service addresses and conceal locations.

APURIMAC O.p. on prov. issues for Arequipa, Chilean occ. of Peru.

A RECEBER To be received, insc. P-D, Portugal and col.

AREQUIPA O.p. on fiscals, etc., of Peru, for prov. issues Chilean occ. Peru.

ARCHIPEL DES COMORES Insc. Grand Comoro Island.

ARMENWET Insc. Off. Netherlands.

ARMY OFFICIAL O.p. on British for Off.

ARMY POST Insc. mil. stamps of Egypt used by British army.

ARTS FESTIVAL ST. KITTS 1964 o.p. St. Kitts Nevis.

ARVIZKAROSULTAKNAK KULON For the flood sufferers, insc. 1913 S-P, Hungary.

ASEGURADO Insc. insured mail label, Spanish language.

ASISTENTA SOCIALA Insc. P-T, Roumania.

ASSICURATO Insc. insured mail labels, Italian-language countries.

ASSISTENCIA Insc. P-T, Portugal, Azores, Macao.

ASSISTENCIA–D.L. No. 72 O.p. on fiscal, Por. India, for P-T, Timor.

ASSISTENCIA NACIONAL AOS TUBERCULOSES–PORTE FRANCO Insc. Portugal franchise stamps, National Aid Society for Consumptives.

ASSISTENCIA PUBLICA Insc. P-T, Por. India and Mozambique Company.

ASUNCION O.p. on back 1886 Off., Paraguay, presumably to honor the founding of that city on Assumption Day, Aug. 15, 1536.

Aunus   O.p. on Finland for occ. of Russia.

Au profit de la Croix Rouge/ + 50 Fr. / Ten Voordeele van het Roode Kruis   Bil. o.p. on Belgian E. Africa for S-P (Ruanda Urundi).

AVIACON   Insc. air mail, Uruguay.

AVIAO   Insc. air mail, Macao.

AVION   Insc. air mail, Haiti; o.p. for air mail, on Alaouites, Lebanon, Syria; insc. on etiquettes of Colombia, etc.

AVION MESSRE TAFARI   Insc. air mail, Ethiopia.

AVIONSKA POSTA   O.p. on Jugoslavia, for air mail.

AVIS DE RECEPCION   Insc. acknowledgment of receipt stamps, El Salvador.

AVISPORTO MAERKE   Insc. newspaper issues, Denmark.

AYACUCHO   O.p. on prov. issues of Arequipa, Chilean occ. of Peru.

AYUDA EL ECUADOR   O.p. on Paraguay for S-P, for earthquake victims in Ecuador.

AYUNTAMIENTO DE BARCELONA   Insc. P-T, Spain.

B   O.p. on Straits for Bangkok; on Nicaragua, for Bluefields.

B in oval   O.p. and insc. Off. Belgium.

BADEN   Insc. for Baden, and in 1947-49 for the Fr. occ. zone of Germany.

B.A. ERITREA   With new value, o.p. on British for Middle East Forces.

BAGHDAD / IN BRITISH OCCUPATION   O.p. Turkey, Br. occ. Mesopotamia, Baghdad issue.

BAHRAIN   O.p. India; on India and British with value in new c., for Bahrain.

BAJAR PORTO   O.p. and insc. P-D, Indonesia.

Banat Bacska   O.p. on Hungary, Banat issues of 1919.

Baranya / 1919   O.p. Hungary, Serbian occ. first Baranya issue.

BARANYA   Ornamental capitals in an arc, with new values, second Baranya issue.

BARBERIA   O.p. Italy, off. in Tripoli.

B.A. SOMALIA   With new value, o.p. on British for Middle East Forces.

B.A.TRIPOLITANIA   With new value in M.A.L. (Military Authority Lire), o.p. on British for Middle East Forces.

BAYERN   Insc. Bavaria.

B.C.A.   O.p. with or without new value on Rhodesia for Br. Central Afr.

B.C.M.   With arms of Great Britain. Design for Madagascar British consular mail).

B.C.O.F. JAPAN 1946 (British Commonwealth Occupation Force) Insc. Australian Mil. stamps for occupation of Japan.

B. Dpto Zelaya   O.p. on Nicaragua, for province of Zelaya to prevent currency manipulation. May have period after Dpto.

BELGIE; BELGIQUE   Insc. Belgium.

BELGIEN   O.p. in Ger. text with value in centimes and francs, on German for Ger. occ. of Belgium.

BELIZE RELIEF FUND (plus 1, 2, 3, 4, or 5 cents)   O.p. on Br. Honduras, for S-P following a hurricane at Belize.

BENADIR   Insc. Italian Somaliland.

BENGASI   O.p. on Italy, off. in Tripoli.

BERLIN   O.p. on West German issues for use in West Berlin.

B.G.   Bollo gazzette, insc. newspaper tax, Modena.

BICENTENAIRE DE PORT-AU-PRINCE   Insc. P-T, Haiti.

BIJBELGENOOTSCHAP 1814-1964   Insc. Netherlands special issue for 150th anniversary of the Bible Society.

BIJZONDEREVLUCHTEN   Insc. air mail, Netherlands.

Bird   A windhover with spread wings, Czech. newpaper stamps.

BL CI   Corner letters, stamps of Bhopal, state, Central India.

B.L.P.   Bute lettere postali, o.p. on Italian stamps for use on envelopes with advertisements sold for the benefit of war invalids.

B M A   Br. Mil. Adm. o.p. on Sarawak, Br. occ.; same with MALAYA, o.p. on Straits following World War II.

B.M.A.   With ERITREA, SOMALIA, or TRIPOLITANIA and new value, o.p. on British for Br. mil. forces in those areas.

B.N.F. (Base Navale Française) **CASTELLORIZO**   O.p. on Fr. off. in the Levant, for Fr. occ. of Castellorizo.

BOARD OF EDUCATION   O.p. on British for Off.

BOHMEN UND MAHREN   Insc. Bohemia-Moravia, Czechoslovakia. Triangular stamps with this at left, CECHY a MORAVA at right, and a large 50 in center are personal delivery stamps.

BOLIVAR   Insc. Dept. of Bolivar, Colombia.

Bolivar, Sucre Miranda—Decreto (etc.)   O.p. in minute letters on Escuelas (school) stamps of Venezuela, in centavos and centesimos, to make them valid for postage. Similar stamps in centimos were not o.p.

BOLLO–DELLA POSTA NAPOLETANA (or DELLA POSTA DI SICILIA)   Insc. Naples and Sicily issues of Two Sicilies.

BOLLO STRAORDINARIA PER LE POSTE   Insc. newspaper tax on papers delivered by messenger. These may be a variety of authorized delivery stamps, Tuscany.

BOSNA I HERCEGOVINA; Bosna i Hercegovina   Insc. B & H issues of Jugoslavia.

BOSNIEN: HERZEGOWINA (or–VINA)   Insc. B & H under Austria.

BOYACA   Insc., Dept. of Boyaca, Colombia.

B.P.C.   Bureau de Poste de Campagne, insc. Belgian mil. postmark, also with V.P.K. (Veld Post Kantoor).

BRASIL   Insc. Brazil, used 1900, 1917, and after 1920.

BRAUNSCHWEIG   Insc. Brunswick.

BRITISH EAST AFRICA COMPANY   O.p. on British for Br. E. Africa.

BRITISH OCCUPATION   O.p. on Batum stamps during Br. occ.; same o.p. on Russia with Cyrillic word for Batum and new values, Batum.

BRITISH PROTECTORATE OIL RIVERS   O.p. on British for Niger Coast Prot.

BRITISH SOMALILAND   O.p. on India for Somaliland Prot.

BRITISH SOUTH AFRICA COMPANY   Insc. first issues of Rhodesia.

BRUNEI   O.p. on Labuan for Brunei.

BUCHANAN   Insc. R-L stamp for that city in Liberia.

BUENOS AIRES   Insc. for state of Buenos Aires before it joined Argentina when the latter gained its independence.

BUITEN BEZIT   Buiten Bezittingen (Outlying Possessions), o.p. on Dutch East Indies, 1908, for use throughout the colony except in Java and Madura, during a check of postal use. See Java.

BUREAU INTERNATIONALE du TRAVAIL   O.p. on Switzerland for Off.

BURMA   O.p. on Br. India, and insc. for Burma.

BURUNDI Insc., for. Urundi (Ruanda-Urundi) under Belgian adm.

BUSHIRE–Under British Occupation   O.p. on Persia.

BY AIR MAIL   Insc. various etiquettes.

C   Campana, o.p. on Paraguay for local use.

CABO   O.p. on Nicaragua for Cabo Gracias a Dios district to prevent currency manipulations.

CABO JUBI   O.p. on Rio de Oro for Cape Juby.

CACHES   O.p. in this c. on P-D of France or French Colonies, P-D, for Fr. India.

CADIZ VIVA ESPANA   O.p. on Spain for rev. issues of Cadiz.

CAISSE d'AMORTISSEMENT   With surtax, o.p. or insc. S-P, France.

CALCHI   O.p. on Italy for off. in Calchi, Aegean Islands.

CALIMNO (or CALINO)   O.p. on Italy for off. in Calino, Aegean Islands.

CAMEROŌNS U.K.T.T. (United Kingdom Trust Terri.)   O.p. on Nigeria.

CAMPANA CONTRA EL PALUDISMO   Insc. P-T, Mexico, for the abatement of malaria.

CAMPECHE   Insc. on prov. issue of Campeche, Mexico.

CANAL ZONE   O.p. on Panama and U.S. for Canal Zone.

CANARIAS   O.p. on Spain, rev. issues in the Canary Islands.

CANCELLED V-R-I   O.p. on South African Republic, Wolmaransstad issue, second Br. occ. of Transvaal.

CANTON   O.p. on Indo-China for Fr. off. in Canton.

CANTONAL TAXE   With numeral 6, insc. on Zurich cantonal issue.

CAPO VERDE   Insc. Cape Verde.

CARCHI   O.p. on Italy for off. in Calchi, Aegean Islands.

CARITAS   With surtax, o.p. on Luxembourg for S-P.

CARRIERS STAMP   Insc. on an official carrier delivery stamp. No value indicated, portrait of Franklin, 1851.

CARTILLA POSTAL de ESPANA   Insc. on a Spanish franchise stamp.

CARUPANA 1902 No hai estampillas PROVISORIO: (same with NO HAY ESTAMPILLAS Sello Provisorio)   Insc. on prov. typeset local stamps used at Carupano, Venezuela, during a shortage.

CASA DE CORREOS   O.p. on var. issues in several type faces and forms for Quito and Guayaquil, for P-T stamps to build a new general post office, Ecuador; also with additonal insc. Y TELEGRAFOS DE GUAYAQUIL.

CASO   O.p. on Italy for occ. of Caso, Aegean Islands.

CASTELROSSO   O.p. on Italy, It. dom. of Castellorizo.

CAUCA   Insc. Dept. of Cauca, Colombia.

Cavalle   O.p. on France, and insc. in caps., Fr. off. in ⌐avalle, Turkey.

C.C.C.P.   Cyrillic letters for U.S.S.R.

C. CH.   O.p. on French Colonies for Cochin China.

C Dpto Zelaya   O.p. on Nicaragua for Cabo Gracias a Dios district, to prevent currency manipulations.

CECHY A MORAVA   Insc. Bohemia and Moravia, Czechoslovakia.

C.E.F.   O.p. on India, mil. issues for the China Expeditionary Forces.

C.E.F.   O.p. on German Cameroons (c., pence, and shillings), for Br. occ. by Cameroons Expeditionary Forces, Cameroons.

centesimi di corona   With values 5 to 50, o.p. on Italy, It. occ. Dalmatia; 1 to 60, It. occ. Austria. These differ only in the type face.

Centime and franc values   O.p. on Austria, off. in Crete; o.p. on Germany, Ger. occ. France, Belgium; o.p. on Germany 1906, Ger. off. in Turkish Empire.

CENTIMES   O.p. on Ethiopia, with "5" to clarify value.

CENTIMOS   With value, o.p. on French P-D for Fr. off. in Morocco.

CENTURY OF PROGRESS FLIGHT, A   Insc. on 50-cent air mail for Zeppelin use.

CERRADO Y SELLADO   Insc. official seals, Mexico.

CERTIFICADA   Insc. R-L stamp, Bolivar, Colombia.

CERTIFICADO   Insc. R-L stamp, Salvador and Venezuela.

CERTIFIED MAIL   Insc. U.S. stamp to provide record of delivery.

CESKOSLOVENSKE ARMADY SIBIRSKE; CESKOSLOVENSKE VOJSKO NA RUSI   Insc. Cz. army post, Siberia.

CESKO SLOVENSKO (or one word)   Insc. Czechoslovakia.

C F A   Communauté Française d'Afrique, o.p. in ornamental type on France for Reunion.

C.G.H.S.   O.p. on German and Prussian Off. for Upper Silesia Off.

C.H.   Found in many early U.S. postmarks, county seats often using the county name with "C.H." (Court House) added, until a definite name could be selected.

CHALA   In circle, o.p. on Peru for prov. during Chilean occ.

CHAMBA STATE   O.p. on India, 1942 on, for Convention State of Chamba.

CHEMINS DE FER / SPOORWEGEN   With winged wheel, o.p. on Belg. for parcel post.

CHIFFRE TAXE   Insc. P-D, Haiti, and other countries.

CHINA   O.p. (sometimes in Ger. text) with new values, on Germany for off. in China; o.p. on Hong Kong, Br. off. in China.

CHINESE IMPERIAL POST   Insc. China 1898-1912.

CHRISTMAS ISLAND O.p. on Australia for that dependency.

CH. TAXE (value) O.M.F. SYRIE   O.p. on Fr. off. in Turkey for Syria P-D.

C.I.C.I.   Congress of the International Colonial Institute, o.p. on Portugal for a franchise stamp, 1933.

CIERRO OFICIAL   Insc. official seals, Chile, El Salvador.

C.I.H.S.   In circle, o.p. on Germany for Off., Upper Silesia.

CILICIE   O.p. on Turkey for Cilicia.

CINQUANTENAIRE 24 SEPTEMBRE 1853-1903   O.p. on French Colonies P-D, for P-D, New Caledonia.

CIRENAICA   O.p. on Italy for Cyrenaica.

C.I.S.   Commission Interallie Slesvig, o.p. on Schleswig for Off.

C.M.T.   With 60h in frame, o.p. on Austria, Roumanian occ. Western Ukraine.

COAMO   Insc. on a typeset prov. issue of Puerto Rico, U.S. occ., 1898.

CO. CI.   O.p. on Jugoslavia, It. occ. of Laibach (Ljubljana).

COLIS POSTEAU (Parcel Post)   Insc. and o.p. used by Belgium and colonies, Tunisia and some other French colonies and offices, and Persia.

COLOMBIA   Insc. above a map of Panama indicates a stamp of Panama, while a state of Colombia. These later were o.p. for the republic.

COLON   Insc. and portrait of Columbus on early stamps of Chile.

COLONIA DE RIO DE ORO   Insc. Rio de Oro.

COLONIA ERITREA   Insc., Eritrea; o.p. in arc, or in caps and l.c., Etritrea.

COLONIALI ITALIANE; COLONIE ITALIANE   First insc., second o.p. on Italy for Italian Colonies.

COMISSAO PORTUGUESA DE PRISIONEIROS DE GUERRA O.p. on Portugal Red Cross to provide franchise stamps for the prisoners' of war commission.

COMITE FRANCAIS   Insc. S-P, French col.

COMMISSARIATO GENLE DELL OLTRE GIUBA   Insc. Oltre Giuba, 1926.

COMMISSION D'ADMINISTRATION ET DE PLEBESCITE OLSZYTN ALLENSTEIN–TRAITE DE VERSAILLES   In oval, o.p. on Germany for Allenstein.

COMMISSION DE CONTROLE PROVISOIRE KORCA   Insc. Albania, 1914.

COMMISSION DE GOUVERNEMENT HAUTE SILESIE– OBER SCHLESIEN–GORNY SLASK   Pleb. insc. Upper Silesia.

COMMISSION FUR RETOURBRIEFE   Insc. return letter stamps, Bavaria and Wurttemberg.

COMMISSION INTERALLIEE MARIENWERDER   Insc. on Germany for Marienwerder pleb. Also in caps. and l.c.

COMMISSION FUR RUCKBRIEFE   Insc. return letter stamp, Nuremberg, Bavaria.

COMMUNICACIONES   With value, insc. var. Spanish, 1874-1909; same with ESP., ESPANA, or ESPANOLES, var. issues after 1870.

COMPANHIA DE MOCAMBIQUE   Insc. Mozambique Company.

COMPANHIA DE NYASSA   Insc. Nyassa.

COMPLEMENTARIO   Insc. P-D, Mexico.

CONFED. GRANADINA   Insc. early Colombia, Granadine Confederation.

CONFE'ON ARGENTINA   Insc. first issue, Argentina, 1858-60.

CONFOEDERATIO HELVETICA   Insc. National Fete day S-P, Switzerland, 1938 and later.

CONGO BELGE   Insc. Belgian Congo 1908-1910, bil. with BELGISCH CONGO after 1910.

CONGO FRANÇAIS   Insc. with new values on French Colonies for Fr. Congo. Also in caps. and l.c.

CONGRATULATIONS FALL OF BATAAN AND CORREGI-
DOR 1942   With new value, o.p. on Philippines, Jap. occ.

CONGRESO DE LOS DIPUTADOS   Off., Spain, 1896.

CON POSTA AEREA   Insc. etiquette, Italy.

CONSEIL DE L'EUROPE   Insc. and o.p., France for the
Council of Europe, 1958.

CONSTANTINOPLE   O.p. Italy, off. in Constantinople.

CONSTANTINOPOL–POSTA ROMANA and PTT   In circle, o.p. Roumania, off. in Turkey.

CONSTRUCCION   O.p. at sides or top for P-T, Guatemala.

CONSUMPTIVES HOME   Insc. S-P, New South Wales.

CONTRA LA FAIM (Against Hunger)   O.p. for Rwanda on
Ruanda-Urundi with inscs. obscured by overprinted silver panels.

CONTRASENA / Estampillas de Correo (or Estampilla de Correos)   O.p. in minute type on Escuelas (school) issues for prov.
use, Venezuela, 1874.

COO   O.p. on Italy, off. in Cos, Aegean Islands.

CORDOBA   Insc. Cordova, 1859, before joining the Argentine
Confederation.

COREAN POST; COREE, POSTES DE (or POSTES IMPERIA-
LES DE)   Insc. Korea.

CORFU   O.p. on Italy, It. occ. Corfu; on Greece, It. occ. Corfu
and Paxos.

corona, UNA (or 1)   O.p. Italy, It. occ. Austria; same with 1,
5, or 10, It. occ. Dalmatia.

Corps Expeditionnaire Franco-Anglais CAMEROUN   O.p. Gabon, Fr. occ. Cameroons.

CORREGIDOR MANILA   Small insc. on map of Manila Bay,
Jap. occ. Philippines.

CORREIO   C. reis, insc. Portugal.

CORREIO AEREO   Insc. air mail, Portugal and Brazil.

CORREIOS   With new value; CORREIOS DE ANGOLA 25
REIS in circle, o.p. on newspaper, for ordinary postage, Angola.

CORREO AEREO   O.p. on postal and nonpostal issues, var.
countries for air mail.

CORREO AEREO D.S.   O.p. Bolivia, air mail.

CORREO AEREO HABILITADO   O.p. Paraguay, air mail.

CORREO AEREO INTERIOR   O.p. Nicaragua; do INTERNO
o.p. Dominican Rep., domestic air mail.

CORREO AEREO NACIONAL   O.p. Cuba, air mail.
CORREO AEREO OFICIAL   O.p. or insc. air mail Off. Nicaragua.
CORREO INTERIOR   With arms design, c. cuartos, Insc. Spain.
CORREO OFICIAL   Insc. Off., Honduras, Nicaragua, Spain.
CORREO OFICIAL AEREO   Insc. air mail Off. Honduras.
CORREOS   Insc. Isabella fac. right, c.Rl. Plata F, blue paper, Cuba, Philippines. Needs postmark to identify fully. Same, white paper, design and paper varies for Cuba and Philippines. Same, c. cuartos-reales, Spain. Isabella, ¾ left, c.Cs de Eo Espana, Philippines. Same, c.Cs. 1870, Espana, Cuba. Isabella, fac. left, c. Rl. Plata F., Cuba and Puerto Rico. Same, c.cent. Po. Ft. Philippines. Same, c. Ctos. and date, Spain 1864-65. Same, c.Cmos. and date, Spain 1866, Cuba 1866.
CORREOS AEREO   Insc. air mail, Colombia.
CORREOS AEREOS   Insc. air mail, Mexico.
CORREOS DE LOS EE. UU. DE VENUZ   Insc. Venezuela, 1866 issue.
CORREOS DE OFICIO   O.p. on El Salvador, for Off.
CORREOS DEPARTAMENTALES (or DEPAMENTALES) H/s o.p. on Colombia for interior postage stamps to replace separate department issues.
CORREOS DEVOLUCION DE CORRESPONDENCIA SOBRANTE   Insc. return letter stamp, Spain.
CORREOS 1854 Y 1855 FRANCO   Insc. Isabella fac. right, c. Cs, Philippines.
CORREOS FONOPOSTAL   Insc. recorded message stamps, Argentina, 1939.
CORREOS FRANCO   Insc. c. Cs–Rls, Isabella, right or left, 1852-53, Spain. Same, arms type, with or without "1854," Spain.
CORREOS INTERIOR FRANCO   Insc. c. Cs–Rl Plata F., Philippines; c. Cs, octagonal vignette, Spain 1853.
CORREOS MEXICO   Insc. around three sides, typeset, Chiapas province, Mexico.
CORREOS NACIONALES   With value, some dated, o.p. on fiscals for postage, Guatemala.
CORREOS POSTAL MEXICANO   Insc. 1884-94, Mexico.
CORREOS [date] Vale   c. centavos, o.p. on fiscals for postage, Nicaragua.

CORREOS Y TELEGRAFOS   Insc. some issues, Argentina.

CORREO URBANO DE BOGOTA   Insc. Colombia locals for Bogotá.

CORREO URGENTE   Insc. S-D Spain, Andorra, Sp. Guinea.

CORREO URGENTE URBANO   Insc. city S-D, Colombia.

CORRESPONDANCE MILITAIRE; Correspond'ce M're   Insc. private mil. stamps, New Caledonia.

CORRESPONDENCIA A DEBE   Insc. P-D, Panama; same, o.p., Canal Zone.

CORRESPONDENCIA OFICIAL   Insc. Off., Chile, Dominican Rep., Mexico.

CORRESPONDENCIA URGENTE   Insc. S-D, Spain, Ifni, Andorra, Cape Juby.

CORRIENTES   Insc. Argentina, Corrientes province.

COS   O.p. on Italy, off. in Coo, Aegean Islands.

COSTA ATLANTICA–B   O.p. on Nicaragua, for Zelaya and coast.

COSTA ATLANTICA–C   Same, for Cape Gracias a Dios province.

Constituente Fiumana 24-IV-1921 (and with added 1922)   O.p. on Fiume S-P, for ordinary use.

COTE D'IVOIRE   Insc. Ivory Coast.

COTE FRANCAISE DES SOMALIS   Insc. Somali Coast.

COUR INTERNATIONALE DE JUSTICE   O.p. and insc. for Off., Netherlands.

COUR PERMANENTE DE JUSTICE INTERNATIONALE   O.p. for Off., Netherlands.

COURRIER DE LA SOCIETE DES NATIONS; COURRIER DU BUREAU INTERNATIONAL D'EDUCATION; COURRIER DU BUREAU INTERNATIONAL DU TRAVAIL   O.p. for Off., Switzerland.

C.P.   Colis postaux, o.p. Ivory Coast for parcel post.

Crescent   Red symbol on Turkey, equivalent to Red Cross, P-T, Turkey.

Crescent   White on red star, children's aid symbol, P-T, Turkey.

Crescent   White with star above, national defense, P-T, Turkey.

Crescent and Star   O.p. symbol on Straits, for Johore.

CROCE ROSSA ITALIANA   Italian Red Cross, insc. S-P, Italy, San Marino.

CROISSANT ROUGE TURC   Turkish Red Crescent, insc. S-P, Turkey.

CROIX ROUGE   Red Cross, insc. S-P, France; insc. Ethiopia, 1945, and o.p. with symbol, S-P, Ethiopia.

CROIX ROUGE HAITIENNE   Insc. 1945 air mail, Haiti.

Cross   In circle, o.p. on Siam for S-P.

Cross   Very short arms, with Siamese insc., o.p. on Siam for S-P.

Cross, Geneva   The Geneva cross with colors reversed is the symbol of the Red Cross Society. It is used as an o.p. to provide S-P issues for many countries. A surtax value and a date may be included. The cross also forms a part of the design of many S-P issues and of issues honoring the Red Cross Society.

Cross, Geneva   In outline, o.p. on Switzerland for officials.

Cross, Lorraine   Cross with two bars, symbol of Antituberculosis work, appears on P-T stamps of Cuba, Dominican Republic, and Spain, and on S-P of Jugoslavia, Fr. Eq. Africa, and others.

Cross, St. Andrew's   Three bars, one diagonal, encircled, alone, or with two Cyrillic letters, o.p. on Latvia; without a frame, but with "L P," o.p. on Russia for occ. Latvia.

Cross and Post Horn   No value stated, Hungary, newspaper stamps.

Crown   Symbol, c. cents, o.p. on India, for Straits.

CRUZ ROJA HONDURENA   Honduras Red Cross, insc. P-T.

CRUZ ROJA NACIONAL   Insc. P-T, Colombia.

CRUZ VERMELHA   Insc. Red Cross franchise stamps, Portugal; S-P Brazil.

CRVENI KRST   Plus surtax, Red Cross o.p. on Jugoslavia Offices Abroad, for S-P.

CRVENI KRST MONTENEGRO   With symbol and surtax, o.p. on Jugoslavia and Montenegro for S-P, Ger. occ. Montenegro.

C.S.; C.S.A.   Insc. on some issues, Confederate States of America.

CSOMAG (or CS)   Plus weight, o.p. on Hungary for parcel post.

CUNDINAMARCA   Insc. on Colombia for that department.

CUZCO   In var. forms, o.p. on Arequipa prov. and on Peru, for prov. use, Chilean occ. of Peru.

CYPRUS   O.p. on British for Cyprus.

D   Dienst, colorless on black disk, o.p. for Off., Dutch East Indies.

D   In three corners of triangular 50h personal delivery P-D, Czechoslovakia.

DAI NIPPON–2602–MALAYA   O.p. on Straits for Negri Sembilan, Pahang, Perak, Selangor, and Trengganu, during Jap. occ.

DAI NIPPON–2602–YUBIN   O.p. on Perak and Selangor, Jap. occ.

DANMARK   Insc. Denmark.

DANSK VESTINDIEN   Insc. Danish West Indies.

DANZIG   O.p. Ger. type, on Germany for Danzig.

DATIA   Insc. Duttia state, India.

D B P   Script monogram o.p. on Russia for Far Eastern Republic.

D. de A.   Insc. on prov. issues of Antioquia, Colombia.

DE   O.p. on Ecuador, Tunguragua prov. See LOJA FRANCA.

DECRETO DE 27 JANI'O 1870   O.p. in minute type on Escuelas design, 1879, Venezuela.

DEDEAGH   O.p. on France, off. Dedeagh, Turkey.

DEFENSA NACIONAL   Insc. P-T, Ecuador.

DEFICIENCIA DE FRANQUEO   O.p. and insc. P-D, Ecuador.

DEFICIENTE   Insc. P-D, Nicaragua and Paraguay.

DEFICIT   Arms design, no name, P-D, Peru 1874 1-cent. Insc. and o.p. for P-D, Peru.

DEFICIT O FRANQUEO   Insc. first issue P-D, Peru.

DELEGACOES   Insc. Portugal Red Cross franchise stamps, 1926, 1936, outside Lisbon.

DEL GOLFO DE GUINEA   Insc. Spanish Guinea.

DE OFICIO   Insc. El Salvador; o.p. El Salvador and Peru for Off.

DEPARTMENTO DEL TOLIMA   Insc. Tolima, Colombia.

DEPT. OF AGRICULTURE; OF THE INTERIOR; OF JUSTICE; OF STATE   Insc. on U.S. Off.

DEPT. OF FOREIGN AFFAIRS   Insc. Off. Hawaii.

DER BERLINER PHILHARMONIE   Insc. S-P, Germany.

DESMIT RBL; Desmit rubli   Ten rubles, new value o.p. on Latvia.

DEUTSCHE BUNDESPOST   Insc. Germany 1951 on.

DEUTSCHE DEMOKRATISCHE REPUBLIK   Insc. Soviet occ. zone (East Germany) 1949; Communist East Germany.

Deutsche Militaer-Verwaltung Montenegro   O.p. Jugoslavia Ger. occ. Montenegro.

DEUTSCHEPOST (or **DEUTSCHE POST**)   Insc. Allied sectors, Berlin; Germany 1946-50.

DEUTSCHE POST OSTEN   O.p. on Germany, for occ. Poland.

DEUTSCHE REICHSPOST   Insc. for Germany, 1872-89; o.p. on Danzig, Ger. occ. Danzig.

DEUTSCHES REICH   Insc. Germany 1902-44.

DEUTSCH-NEU-GUINEA   O.p. on German, and insc., Ger. New Guinea.

DEUTSCH OESTR. POSTVEREIN   German-Austrian Postal Union, insc. Thurn and Taxis and early Baden and Württemberg.

DEUTSCH OSTAFRIKA   O.p. on German, and insc. Ger. East Afrika.

DEUTSCH ÖSTERREICH   O.p. 1918, Ger. text and insc., Republic of Austria.

DEUTSCH SUD-WES-AFRIKA (or **SUDWESAFRIKA**) O.p. and insc., Ger. Southwest Africa.

Devastación de la Ciudad de Santo Domingo, etc.   Insc. P-T, Dominican Republic.

DIENST   O.p. on Dutch East Indies for Off.

DIENSTMARKE   Insc. Off. Germany, Bavaria, French Prot. of the Saar; o.p. for Off., Saar, Danzig, and Liechtenstein; with numeral 21, Off., Prussia.

DIENSTSACHE   Insc. Off. Liechtenstein.

DILIGENCIA   With sun, insc. carrier stamp, Uruguay.

DINERO   Insc. on arms design, Peru.

DIOS PATRIA LIBERTAD   Insc. Dominican Republic.

DIOS PATRIA REY—ESPANA (or **CATALUNA**)   Insc. Carlist issues, Spain.

DIWI RUBLI   Two rubles, o.p. to change value, Latvia.

DJIBOUTI (or **DJ**)   O.p. on Obock and insc., Djibouti.

D.L.O.   Dead Letter Office.

D M   Dienst marke, o.p. on Danzig for Off.

DOPLATA   Insc. P-D, Poland and Central Lithuania.

DOPLATIT (or DOPLATNE)   O.p. on Czechoslovakia for P-D.

DRIJVENDE BRANDKAST   Floating Safe, insc. marine insurance stamps, Netherlands and Dutch East Indies.

DRZAVA S.H.S.   Insc. on Jugoslavia for B & H.

DUC. DI PARMA   Insc. Parma.

DUITSCH OOST AFRIKA–BELGISCHE BEZETTING   O.p. on Congo for Belgian occ. Ger. E. Africa.

DURAZZO   O.p. on Italy, off. in Durazzo.

E   Eisenbahn (railway), o.p. for Off. Bavaria.

E.A.F.   East Africa Forces, o.p. on British for use in It. Somaliland.

Eagle on perch, distant airplane   Triangular air mail, Iceland.

EAST INDIA POSTAGE   Insc. India under East India Co., 1855-76

EDIFICIOS POSTALES   O.p. for P-T, El Salvador.

EDUCACION NACIONAL   Insc. P-T, Peru.

E.E.F. POSTAGE PAID   Egyptian Expeditionary Forces, with value, Br. occ. of Palestine. Used also in Trans-Jordan, Lebanon, Syria, and parts of Cilicia and Egypt.

EESTI VABARIK   Insc. Estonia.

EE. UU. DE COLOMBIA   Insc. Colombia, 1886.

EE. UU. DE VENEZUELA   Insc. Venezuela.

EFTERPORTO   Postage to pay, insc. P-D, Danish West Indies.

EGEO   O.p. on Italy, and insc. off. in Aegean Islands.

EGYKRAJCZAR   One kreutzer, insc. Hungary.

EINSCHREIBEN   Insc. R-L labels, German language.

EIRE   Insc. Ireland.

EJERCITO CONSTITUCIONALISTA TRANSITORIO MEXICO   Insc. Sonora rev., Mexico.

EJERCITO RENOVADOR   Insc. on a rev. issue of Sinaloa, Mexico, which was captured before being placed on sale.

EL PARLEMENTO A CERVANTES   O.p. for Off., Spain.

EL SALVADOR   The official name of Salvador.

ELSAS   Alsace, Ger. text o.p. on German, Ger. occ. Alsace.

EMP. OTTOMAN   First Latin-letter insc. on Turkish stamps.

ENCOMENDAS POSTAIS   Insc. Portugal, and o.p. on Azores, for parcel post.

ENCOMIENDA; ENCOMIENDAS; ENCOMIENDAS DE GRANJA   Insc. parcel post, Uruguay.

ENTREGA ESPECIAL   Insc. S-D Cuba and Dominican Rep.

ENTREGA INMEDIATA   Insc. S-D Panama, Cuba, Mexico. The first def. S-D stamps of the U.S. mil. occ. of Cuba used IM-MEDIATA in error.

Envelope   Feature of design with "l" between crown and post horn, newspaper stamps, Hungary.

E.R.I.   Edward Rex Imperator, o.p. on South African Republic, for Transvaal.

ERITREA   O.p. on Italy, and insc. Eritrea.

ESCUELAS   Schools, insc. on a fiscal issue of Venezuela used for postage. When o.p. were valid for postage 1871-80, and without o.p. for domestic postage until 1895.

E.S. de ANTIOQUIA   Estado Soberano (Sovereign State), insc. Antioquia, Colombia.

E.S. de PANAMA   Insc. Panama while state of Colombia.

ESPANA; ESPANOLA   Insc. for Spain and Spanish, the first being introduced in 1863, the second in 1929. The tilde may not show on the N in some inscriptions but does appear in typeset overprints. Spain and Spanish colonies.

ESPANA FRANQUEO; ESPANA VALENCIA   Insc. Carlist issues, Spain, portrait Carlos VII.

ESPANOLA   See ESPANA.

ESTADO DA INDIA   Insc. Por. India.

ESTADO DE NICARAGUA   Insc. Nicaragua.

ESTADO GUAYANA   Insc. locals, Guayana, Venezuela, ships or arms design.

ESTADO S. DEL TOLIMA   Insc. Tolima, Colombia.

ESTADO SOBERANO de SANTANDER (also BOLIVAR) Insc. for those depts., Colombia.

ESTADOS UNIDOS BRAZIL (or BRASIL)   Insc. Brazil.

ESTADOS UNIDOS DE COLOMBIA; Estados Unidos De Nueva Granada   Insc. Colombia.

EST AFRICAIN ALLEMAND OCCUPATION BELGE   O.p. on Congo, Belgian occ. Ger. E. Africa.

Estampillas de Correo—Contrasena   O.p. on Escuelas stamps for prov. issues, Venezuela. May have l.c. c in "correo."

ESTERO   O.p. on Italy for Offices Abroad.

ETABLISSEMENTS DE L'OCEANIE   Insc. French Oceania.

ETABLISSEMENTS DE L'INDE; ETABLISSEMENTS FRAN-
CAIS DANS L'INDE   Insc. French India.

ETAT DU INCHI YA KATANGA   Insc. Province of Katanga.

ETAT FRANCAISE   Insc. France, under Ger. occ., W.W. II.

ETAT INDEPENDANT DU CONGO   Insc. Congo 1886-1908.

Ethiopie   H/s o.p., 1901; ETHIOPIA, 1942-43, 1950 and later;
ETHIOPIE, 1919-50, except as above; with EMPIRE preced-
ing some values, 1931; ETHIOPIENNES, 1909 to 1917, with
POSTES; all insc. Ethiopia. ETIOPIA   O.p. Italy, occupation.

E.U. DE COLOMBIA   Insc. Colombia.

E.U. DO BRAZIL   Insc. Brazil.

Eupen   O.p. on Belgium, Eupen issue; EUPEN & MALMEDY,
o.p. on Belgium, general issue, for occ. of Germany.

EXECUTIVE   Insc. Off. U.S.

EXPERIMENTO POSTA AEREO, MAGGIO 1917, TORINO-
ROMA–ROMA-TORINO   O.p. Italy S-D.

EXPRES   Insc. S-D Canada, Egypt, Italy, Mexico, Russia.

EXPRESO   Insc. S-D Venezuela, Dominican Republic, Ecuador,
Guatemala; o.p. for S-D Peru, Panama, and Guatemala.

EXPRESS DELIVERY   O.p. for S-D Mauritius; insc. for same,
New Zealand.

EXPRESSO   Insc. S-D Italy and col., Fiume, San Marino, Vatican City, and Brazil.

EXTERIOR   With Mercury design, parcel post, insc. Uruguay.

FACTAJ   O.p. on Roumania for parcel post.

FARDOS POSTALES.   Insc. parcel post, El Salvador.

Fasces and ax over waves   O.p. on Italy, for It. Socialist Republic.

Fco Bollo   See FRANCO BOLLO POSTALE ITALIANO.

FEDERACION VENEZOLANO   Insc. Venezuela.

FEDERATION OF MALAYSIA   Insc. for Malaysia, a federation of Malaya, Singapore, Sarawak, and Sabah.

FEDERATION OF NIGERIA   Insc. for Nigeria, former Brit. col.

FEDERATION OF SOUTH ARABIA   Insc. for Aden and its
western protectorates 1963.

FELDPOST 2kg.   O.p. on Germany, MQ, 2 kg. being max. wt.

FESTAD DE CIDADE LISBOA   Insc. P-T, Portugal and Azores.

FEZZAN; FEZZAN-GHADAMES TERRITOIRE MILITAIRE
Insc. Fr. occ. Libya.

FIJI TIMES EXPRESS   Insc. on typeset design, Fiji Islands.

FILIPINAS; FILIP'AS   Insc. Philippines.

FIRST FOREIGN TRADE WEEK, etc.   O.p. on Philippines for a special issue.

FIUME   O.p. on Hungary for Fiume.

FLUGFRIMERKI   Insc. air mail, Iceland.

FLUGPOST   Insc. air mail, Germany, Austria, Danzig, Memel.

F.M.   Franchise militaire, o.p. on letter rate stamps; insc. on mil. stamps without stated value for soldiers' ordinary letters, France.

F.N.F.L.   Forces Navales Françaises Libres (Free French Naval Forces), o.p. on stamps of var. Fr. col.

FOMENTO-AERO-COMMUNICACIONES   O.p. and Insc. air mail P-T, Ecuador. Obligatory on domestic air mail.

FONDUL AVIATIEI   Insc. P-T, Roumania.

FONO FOU 1958 SAMOA I SISIFU   Insc. West. Samoa.

FORCES FRANCAISES LIBRES LEVANT   With two Lorraine crosses and new values, o.p. and insc. mil. stamps of the Free French in Syria.

FOREIGN AFFAIRS, DEPT. OF   Incs. Off. Hawaii.

F.P.O.   Fleet Post Office, used during World War II, at first with a number, to designate a mail unit in the U.S. Navy.

F.P.O.   Field Post Office, office of a Br. army unit in the field.

FRANCA   O.p. on Peru for a prov. issue, Chilean occ. of Peru.

FRANCAIS; FRANCAISE; FRANC; FR.   Insc. France.

FRANCO   Free, only insc. except c. on some Swiss stamps of Seated Helvetia type; o.p. on Uruguay for Off.

FRANCO BOLLO   Insc. Sardinia and first issue, Italy.

FRANCOBOLLO DI STATO   Insc. Off., Italy.

FRANCO BOLLO GIORNALI STAMPE   Insc. newspaper stamps, Sardinia and Italy.

FRANCO BOLLO POSTALE   Insc. Roman States.

FRANCO BOLLO POSTALE ITALIANO 1867 (or FCO for FRANCO)   Insc. second issue, Italy.

FRANCOBOLLO POSTALE PER GIORNALI   Insc. newspaper stamps, Fiume.

FRANCO BOLLO POSTALE ROMAGNE   Insc. Romagna.

FRANCOBOLLO POSTALE TOSCANO   Insc. Tuscany.

FRANCO BOLLO PROVINCIE MODONES   Insc. Modena.

FRANCO POSTE BOLLO   Insc. Naples, Two Sicilies.

FRANCO SCRISOREI   Insc. Moldavia-Walachia, Roumania.

FRANCO 6 Cts. CORREOS   Isabella II fac. left, insc. Spain.

FRANKEER ZEGEL 2½ CENT   O.p. on fiscals for postage, Surinam; same with var. values in cents o.p. on Netherlands marine insurance, for postage, Curaçao.

FRANQUEO DEFICIENTE   Insc. P-D, Ecuador, Nicaragua, Paraguay, El Salvador.

FRANQUEO ESPANA   Insc. Carlist issues, Spain.

FRANQUEO IMPRESOS   Insc. newspaper stamps, Spain.

FRANQUEO OFICIAL   Insc. or o.p. for Off., Ecuador, Dominican Republic, Guatemala, Nicaragua, El Salvador.

FRANQUICIA POSTAL   Design, a book with insc. SELLO DE CORREO, etc. Insc. franchise stamp, Spain.

FREI DURCH ABLOSUNG   Free through redemption, insc. Off., with NR.21, Prussia; Nr. 16, Baden.

FREIMARKE   Arms design, c. kreuzer, insc. Württemberg; portrait to right, c. pfenninge-silbergroschen, insc. Prussia.

FRIMAERKE   Lion on shield c. skilling, insc. Norway.

FRIMAERKE K.G.L. POST   C. rigsbank skilling, insc. Denmark.

FRIMARKE LOKALBREF   Insc. Stockholm local, Sweden.

FRIMERKI   Insc. Iceland.

FUERSTENTUM LIECHTENSTEIN (or FÜRSTENTUM)   Insc. Liechtenstein, national and Swiss postal adm's.

FÜR BERLINER WÄHRUNGSGESCHÄDIGTE   Insc. S-P, allied sector, Berlin.

FÜR KRIEGS-BESCHÄDIGTE   With surtax, o.p. on Germany for a S-P.

FÜR KRIEGSBESCHÄDIGTE FREISTAAT BAYERN.   O.p. on Bavaria for a S-P.

FUTURE DELIVERY   O.p. on U.S. documentary revenue stamps to show taxes paid on stock transactions involving future delivery.

G   O.p. on Canada for Off.; on Cape of Good Hope for Griqualand West.

GAB   O.p. on French Colonies for Gabon.

G C M   Gobierno Constitucionalista Mexico, in monograms. O.p. for Oaxaca and Sonora rev. issues, Mexico.

Gd Liban   With new values, o.p. on France, Fr. man. Lebanon.

GD–OT   O.p. on newspaper stamps, Bohemia and Moravia, Czechoslovakia for use by commercial firms.

G.E.A.   O.p. on East Africa and Uganda, Br. occ. Ger. E. Africa; o.p. on Kenya, 1921, for Tanganyika.

GEBYR; GEBYRMAERKE   First, o.p., second, insc. late fee, Denmark after 1923.

GENERAL GOUVERNEMENT   O.p. on Poland; Gen. Gouv. Warschau o.p. on Germany both in Ger. text; and GENERAL GOUVERNEMENT alone or with DEUTSCHES REICH or GROSSDEUTSCHES REICH. insc. Ger. occ. Poland.

GERUSALEMME   O.p. on Italy for off. in Jerusalem.

G et D; G & D   O.p. Guadeloupe.

G.F.B.   Gaue Faka Buleaga (On Govt. Service), o.p. Off., Tonga.

GHADAMES TERRITOIRES MILITAIRE   Insc. Fr. occ. Libya.

GHANA INDEPENDENCE 6th MARCH 1957   O.p. on Gold Coast for new Republic of Ghana.

GIBRALTAR   O.p. on Bermuda and insc. for Gibraltar.

GILBERT & ELLICE PROTECTORATE   O.p. on Fiji stamps.

GIORNALI STAMPE   Insc. stamps, Sardinia and Italy.

Girl with cap   Full face, numerals in lower corners. Imperforate issues are newspaper stamps of B & H under Austria; perforated issues are regular postage, B & H in Jugoslavia.

GOBIERNO   O.p. for Off., Peru.

GOBIERNO CONSTITUCIONALISTA MEXICO   Insc. Sonora rev. issues; o.p. on Mexico for Oaxaca rev. issues, Mexico.

GOBIERNO REVOLUCIONARIO   Insc. Yucatan rev. issues, Mexico.

GOVERNATORATO DEL MONTENEGRO   O.p. on Jugoslavia, It. occ. Montenegro.

GOVERNO MILITARE ALLEATO   Allied Mil. Govt. o.p. Italy, allied occ.

GOVT. PARCELS   O.p. on British for Off.

G.P. De M.; G.P.M.   First in ornate panel, second in monogram, o.p. Mexico, Oaxaca rev. issues.

GPE; G.P.E.   With value, o.p. on Fr. Col. for Guadeloupe.

GRAHAM LAND, DEPENDENCY OF   O.p. on Falkland Islands for Graham Land, 1944.

GRAND LIBAN; Grand Liban   Both with new values, o.p. on France, and insc. Fr. man. of Lebanon.

GRENVILLE   Insc. on R-L stamp for that city in Liberia.

G.R.I.   With new values, o.p. on Ger. New Guinea and Marshall Isls. for New Britain; o.p. on Ger. Samoa, for Samoa under Br. dom.

GROENEKRUIS   Green Cross, insc. S-P, Surinam.

GRØNLAND   Insc. Greenland.

GROSSDEUTSCHESREICH   Insc. Germany, 1944-45.

GUADALAJARA   Insc. for stamps of that city after the fall of Maximilian.

GUANACASTE   O.p. on Costa Rica, stamps being sold at a discount and use restricted to that province.

GUERNAVACA   H/s insc. for Cuernavaca. See GUADALAJARA.

GUINE   Insc. Portuguese Guinea.

GUINEA CONTI'AL ESPANOLA; GUINEA ESPANOLA Insc. Spanish Guinea.

GUINEE   Insc. French Guinea.

GULTIG 9. ARMEE   In frame, o.p. on German, for occ. of Roumania.

GUYANE; GUYANE FRANCAISE; GUY. FRANC.   Insc. and o.p. French Guiana.

G.W.   O.p. on Cape of Good Hope for Griqualand West.

HABILITADO   Qualified, o.p. to restore value to demonetized issues, Spanish-language.

HABILITADO AERO (or AEREO, or Aereo)   O.p. on Mexico for air mail.

HABILITADO PARA CORREO AEREO   O.p. on P-T, air mail P-T, Dominican Republic.

Habilitado para el Servicio Publico   O.p. on Off. to make valid for ordinary use, 1930; on air mail Off. for air mail, 1941, Honduras.

HABILITADO Servicio Aereo   O.p. on Honduras for air mail.

HABILITADO Servicio Oficial Aereo.   O.p. on Mexico for air mail Off.

HADI SEGÉLI ÖZVEGYEKNEK ÉS ÁRVÁKNAK KÉT (2) FILLÉR   O.p. Hungary, S-P.

HAGA PATRIA   Insc. P-T, Mexico.

HARPER   Insc. on R-L stamp for that city in Liberia.

HASHEMITE KINGDOM OF THE JORDAN   Insc. Jordan, 1949.

HATAY—DEVLETI   O.p. on Turkey for Hatay.

HAUTE SILESIE COMMISSION DE GOUVERNEMENT Insc. pleb. Upper Silesia.

HAUTE VOLTA   O.p. on Upper Senegal and Niger, and insc., Upper Volta.

HAUT SÉNÉGAL-NIGER (or HT)   Insc. Upper Senegal and Niger.

HEALTH   Insc. S-P, New Zealand.

H.E.H. THE NIZAM'S GOVERNMENT   Insc. Hyderabad state, India.

HELP STAMP OUT TUBERCULOSIS; HELP PROMOTE HEALTH   Insc. S-P, New Zealand.

HELVETIA   Insc. Switzerland.

HERZOGLICHE POST FRIMARKE   Insc. Holstein.

HERZOGTH HOLSTEIN (or SCHLESWIG)   Insc. for the Holstein and Schleswig issues, Schleswig-Holstein.

H. H. NAWABSUAH JAHAH BEGAM   Insc. Bhopal state, India.

H.I. & U.S. POSTAGE   Insc. on 13-cent stamp, 1851, Hawaii.

HIRLAP BELYEG   Insc. newspaper tax, Hungary.

HIRLAPJEGY   Insc. newspaper stamps, Hungary.

HIVATLOS   Insc. Norway Off.

HOCHWASSER 1920   High water, in German text; o.p. on Austria for S-P.

HOI HAO   O.p. on Indo-China for Fr. off. in Hoi Hao, China.

HOLKAR STATE POSTAGE   Insc. Indore state, India.

HOPFLUG   Insc. air mail, Iceland.

HOPFLUG ITALA 1933   O.p. on air mail for Balbo flight, Iceland.

H.P.N.   In oval frame, o.p. on Spain for Teruel province, rev. of 1868.

HRV; HRVATSKA   Insc. Croatia.

HRZGL POST FRM (or FRMRK)   Insc. Holstein, Schl.-Holstein.

HURRICANE HATTIE   O.p. on British Honduras for relief after hurricane, Oct. 31, 1961.

IDROVOLANTE   With hydroplane, o.p. Italy, air mail 1917.

I.E.F.   O.p. on India, mil. stamps, Indian Expeditionary Force.

I GILDA   In validity, o.p. on Iceland 1902, to restore validity.

Ile de la Reunion   Insc. Reunion, early issues.

ILE ROUAD   O.p. on French off. in the Levant for Rouad.

ILES WALLIS et FUTUNA   O.p. on New Caledonia, and insc., Wallis & Futuna.

IM FUERSTENTUM LIECHTENSTEIN   Insc. Liechtenstein, Austrian adm.

Immediata   A misspelling for *Inmediata* on S-D stamps of Cuba under U.S. mil. occ.

IMPERIO COLONIAL PORTUGUES   Insc. Portuguese African Colonies.

IMPERIO MEXICANO   Insc. Mexico, 1866.

Imper. reg posta austr   Insc., c. sld., Austrian off. in Turkey, 1883-86.

IMPRESOS   Preceded by name, insc. newspaper stamps, Cuba, Philippines.

Imprimatur   Let it be printed, endorsement on some proof impressions to indicate approval.

IMPRIME; IMPRIMES   First in box, second on scroll, o.p. on Turkey for newspaper stamps.

Imprimés   O.p. on Persia for newspaper stamps.

IMPUESTA DE GUERRA   O.p. on Puerto Rico for war tax, U.S. mil. adm.

IMPUESTO DE ENCOMIENDAS   O.p. and insc. Q Uruguay.

INCHI YA ETAT DU KATANGA   Insc. for Katanga in rebellion against Congo. (Belg.)

INDE F'ÇAISE; INDE FRANÇAISE   Insc. French India.

INDEPENDENCE and date   Insc. Trinidad and Tobago, o.p. Jamaica, Gambia to mark independence.

INDIA PORT; INDIA PORTUGUEZA   Insc. Portuguese India.

INDO-CHINE; INDOCHINE   O.p. on French Colonies, and insc. Indo-China. With surtax, o.p. on French S-P, for Indo-China S-P.

INDONESIA   O.p. on Dutch East Indies for Indonesia.

Industrielle-Kriegswirtschaaft   O.p. on Switzerland for Off.

INLAND   Only insc. except value, on 3-cent stamp, 1881, Liberia.

INLAND POSTAGE–3 CENTS   O.p. on Liberia.

Instrucao D.L. N° 7 de 3-2-1934   O.p. on Por. India war tax, for P-T, Timor.

INSTRUCCION   Insc. fiscal stamps, Venezuela. Some were valid for internal postage, 1893-95.

INSTRUCCION SELLO PROVISIONAL CARUPANO 1902 Insc. typeset local issue, Carupano, Venezuela.

INTERIOR Insc. parcel post stamps, Mercury design, Uruguay.

INTERIOR, DEPT. OF   Insc. Off. stamps, U.S.

I.O.V.R.   Insc. and o/p P-T, c. leu. Roumania.

I POLSKA WYSTAWA MAREK   With cross and surtax (White Cross Society), O.p. on Poland for S-P.

I.R.   Internal Revenue, o.p. on U.S. for revenue, 1898.

IRAN   Insc. Persia after 1949. No Latin letters 1939-1949.

IRAQ   Insc. Br. man. of Iraq; o.p., or insc., kingdom of Iraq.

IRAQ IN BRITISH OCCUPATION   O.p. on Turkey, (c. annas-rupees) Brit. occ. of Mesopotamia, Iraq issue.

IRIAN BARAT   O.p. on Indonesia to mark the acquisition of Dutch New Guinea.

I.R. OFFICIAL   O.p. on British for Off.

ISLAND   Insc. Iceland.

ISLAS GALAPAGOS   Insc. L Ecuador for Galapagos Isls.

ISOLE ITALIANE DELL'EGEO   O.p. on Italy, and insc. It. off., Aegean Islands.

ISOLE JONIE   O.p. on Italy, occ. Ionian Islands.

ISTRA SLOVENSKO PRIMORJE and ISTRIA LITTORALE SLOVENO Bil. insc. for Istria and Zone B, Jugoslavia.

ITA KARJALA   Insc. Karelia; o.p. on Finland, occ. of Karelia.

ITALIA Occupazione Militaire Italiana Isole, Cefalonia e Itaca O.p. on Greece in pairs, It. occ. Ionian Islands.

JAMHURI YA TANGANYIKA (Republic of Tanganyika) Insc. for the new republic in 1962.

JANINA   O.p. on Italy off. in Janina, Turkey.

JAVA   O.p. on Dutch East Indies, 1908, for Java and Madura, to check the use of mail. See BUITEN BEZIT.

JEEND; JHIND; JIND   O.p's. for Jind, a state of India.

JORNAES   Journals, insc. p stamps, Portugal and col., Brazil.

JOURNAUX   Journals, insc. newspaper stamps, France.

JOURNAUX DAGBLADEN   Bil. insc. p stamps, Belgium.

J.R.G. AEREO Vale 1946   With value, o.p. on ordinary and air mail, for air mail, Venezuela under the Junta Revolucionaria de Gobierno.

JUEGOS OLIMPICOS   Olympic Games, insc. S-P, Costa Rica.

JUSTICE, DEPT. OF   Insc. U.S. Off.

KAIS. KOENIGL. OESTERRPOST (or KAISERLICHEKON-IGLICHE OESTERREICHPOST) insc. Austria; same, c. paras-piastras, Austrian off. in Turkey.

KAIS. KON. ZEITUNGS STAMPLE (or STEMPLE)   Insc. newspaper tax, Austria, Lombardy-Venetia.

KALAYAAN NAM PILIPINAS   Insc. Jap. occ. Philippines.

KAMERUN   Insc. Cameroon.

Kans. To reduce post-office robberies the one- to ten-cent stamps, series 1923, were thus o.p. They were sold only in the state named and while this reduced theft, since the stamps could not be used in quantity elsewhere, the experiment soon was abandoned.

KAP   Kapeika (kopeck), Lettish.

KARJELA   Insc. Karelia.

KARKI   O.p. on Italy for off. in Calchi, Aegean Is.

KARNTEN UBSTIMMUNG   O.p. on Austria, Ger. text, for pleb. zone of Carinthia, used from Sept. 16 to Oct. 10, 1920.

KAROLINEN   Insc. Caroline Islands.

KATHIRI STATE OF SEIYUN   Insc. for that state in Aden.

KENTTA POSTIA PUOLUSTUSVOIMAT; KENTTA POSTI FALT POST   Insc. mil. stamps, Finland, 1941.

KENYA UHURU 1963   Insc. Kenya to mark independence.

K.G.C.A. 1920   With value, o.p. on Jugoslavia newspaper stamps for S-P, Carinthia. (Carinthian Govt., Commission Zone A.)

K.G.L. POST FRM   Insc. c. skilling, Denmark; c. cents, Danish West Indies.

KIBRIS CUMHURIYETI   Insc. for the Republic of Cyprus.

KINGSTON RELIEF FUND. 1d   O.p. on Barbados for S-P, for relief of Kingston, Jamaica, B.W.I.

K K K   As cancellation, refers to the Ku Klux Klan, a society active in the South after the Civil War; as insc. on Aguinaldo Philippine stamps, refers to Kataas-taasan Kagalanggalang Kati-punan, a political secret society.

K.K. Post Stemple   Insc. arms design, c. kreuzer, Austria; c. cen-tes, Lombardy-Venetia.

KLAIPEDA   Insc. Lithuanian occ. of Memel.

KONGELICT POST FRIMAERKE   Insc. Denmark.

KONGRESI K.K.F.S.   With red cross, date, and value, o.p. for P-T S-P, Albania.

KONTORET for Behandling af Ubesorgede Postsager   Insc. Off. seals, Denmark.

KOP With Cyrillic equivalent, arms in oval, insc. Finland.

KORCE; KORCA   Insc. Albania.

KOUANG-TCHEOU; KOUANG-TCHEOU-WAN   O.p. on Indo-China for Fr. off., China.

KOZTARSASAG   Republic, o.p. and insc. Republic of Hungary, 1918-1919.

K.P.   With Jap. insc., standing for Kagamitang Pampamahalaan, o.p. on Philippines for Off., Jap. occ.

Kr. 1.98; Kr. 2.12   O.p. on Sweden for parcel post.

KREIS   Insc. Wenden (Livonia), a Russian province.

K.u.K. FELDPOST   Insc. c. bani-lei, Austrian occ. Roumania; o.p. and insc. c. heller-krone, mil. stamps, Austria.

K.u.K. MILITARPOST   Insc. B & H under Austria.

K.u.K. MILIT.–VERWALTUNG MONTENEGRO   O.p. on Austria, occ. of Montenegro.

KUWAIT   O.p. on India; o.p. on British (c. annas-rupees); same with insc. SERVICE for Off. Kuwait.

K. WÜRTT. POST   Insc. Württemberg.

L   O.p. on Colombia air mail for mail to be carried by the Lansa company. See A (Avianca).

L A B   With wings, emblem of Lloyd Aereo Boliviano. Air mail, Bolivia.

LABUAN   O.p. on North Borneo for Labuan, 1894-1901. Labuan had definitive issues before and after.

LA CANEA   O.p. on Italy for off. in Crete.

LA CRUZ ROJA ESPANOL; LA CRUZ ROJA PARAGUAY Insc. Red Cross S-P Spain, Paraguay.

LA GEORGIE   Insc. Georgia.

LAND POST–PORTO–MARKE   Insc. rural post P-D, Baden, 1862.

L & S   Land and sea, o.p. on air mail, Newfoundland, for regular use.

LANDSTORMEN FRIMARKE   With value, surtax, and three crowns, o.p. for S-P, Sweden.

LATTAQUIE   O.p. on Syria for Latakia.

LATVIJA   Insc. Latvia; LATVIJA D.S.R., insc., Russian occ., LATWIJA PASTA, LATWIJA PASTY, inscs. Latvia.

LEGI POSTA   O.p. on Hungary for air mail.

LERO; LEROS   O.p. on Italy, off. in Lero, Aegean Is.

L'ETAT DU KATANGA   Insc. Katanga province in rebellion against the Republic of Congo (Belg.).

LEVANT   O.p. on British, Poland, off., Turkish Empire.

"LEY 8310"   Law 8310, o.p. on a P-T issue of Peru.

L F F   O.p. on Liberia for Off.

LIBAN; LIBANAISE   Insc. Lebanon.

LIBAU   O.p. on Germany, occ. of Latvia.

LIBIA   O.p. on Italy for Libia.

LIBIA–COLONIE ITALIANE POSTE   Insc. Libia.

LIBYA   O.p. on Cyrenaica, and insc., United Kingdom of Libia.

LIETUVA   With Cyrillic equivalent and value, o.p. on Russia, occ. of Lithuania.

LIETUVA; LIETUVOS PASTA[S]; LIETUVOS PASTO ZEN-KLAS; LIETUVOS PAS. ZENK   Insc. Lithuania.

LIFE INSURANCE   Insc. Life Insurance Dept. New Zealand.

LIGNES AERIENNES F.A.F.L.   With Lorraine crosses, o.p. on Syria air mail for mil. air mail.

LIGNES AERIENNES DE LA FRANCE LIBRE   Insc. mil. air mail. Free French Forces, Syria.

LINDBERGH ENERO 1928   O.p. on Costa Rica for Lindbergh issue.

LINEAS AEREA NACIONAL   Insc. air mail, Chile.

LINEAS AEREAS DEL ESTADO   Insc. air mail, Argentina.

Lion   Heraldic, rampant, crowned, fac. left, o.p. on Eastern Rumelia for South Bulgaria.

LIPSO   O.p. on Italy for off. in Lisso, Aegean Islands.

LIRE 1.20 DI CORONA   O.p. on Italian S-D for It. occ. Dalmatia.

LISBAO Insc. Red Cross franchise stamps, Portugal 1926 and 1936, for use in Lisbon.

LISSO   See LIPSO.

LITWA SRODKOWA   Insc. Central Lithuania.

LJUBLJANSKA POKRAJINA PROVINZ LAIBACH   Bil. o.p. on Italy, Ger. occ. Laibach.

L. MARQUES   O.p. on Mozambique newspaper stamps for Lourenço Marques.

L Mc L   In monogram, with ship. The packet LADY McLEOD on a phantom issue.

LOCAL-TAXE   Insc. Swiss cantonal stamp Zurich, 4-rappen 1843-1846.

LOCUST CAMPAIGN   With Arabic insc. o.p. on Trans-Jordan for S-P.

LOJA FRANCA   Control o.p. on stamps of Ecuador for the province of Loja, 1902-03. In a great fire at Guayaquil, July 1902, it was feared that stamps had been stolen and provincial governors were ordered to overprint all those on hand and to accept no others.

LOKALBREF   Insc. local letter stamp, Stockholm, Sweden.

LOSEN   Redemption money, insc. P-D, Sweden.

LOS RIOS; RIOS   Provincial control, Ecuador. See LOJA FRANCA.

LOTHRINGEN   In Ger. type, o.p. on Germany for occ. Lorraine.

LOTNICZA   O.p. and insc; air mail, Poland.

L.P.   Latvija Pawalda, with St. Andrew's cross, o.p. on Russia for occ. of Latvia.

L.T.S.R.   With date, o.p. on Lithuania to mark union with U.S.S.R.

LUCHA CONTRA EL CANCER   O.p. and insc. S-P, Panama.

LUCHTEPOSTE   Insc. air mail, Belgium.

LUCHTPOST   O.p. and insc. air mail, Netherlands and col.

LUCHTPOSTZEGEL   Insc. air mail, Netherlands.

LUFTFELDPOST   Insc. mil. air mail, Germany.

LUFTPOST   Insc. air mail, Danzig, Denmark, Germany, Norway, Saar, Sweden, Switzerland.

LUGPOS   Insc. air mail, bil. issues South Africa, S.W. Africa.

LUXEMBURG   In Ger. text, o.p. on Germany, occ. of Luxembourg.

M   O.p. on Belgian parcel post for mil. use.

M   In oval in Ger. text, Allied Mil. Govt., Germany.

M.A.   Ministry of Agriculture, o.p. for Off. Argentina.

MAFEKING BESIEGED   O.p. on Cape of Good Hope and

Bechuanaland for Mafeking under siege, 1899-1900, Cape of Good Hope.

MAGYAR KIR. HIRLAP BELYEG Insc. newspaper tax, Hungary.

MAGYAR KIR. (or KIRALYI) POSTA Hungarian Royal Post, insc. Hungary, last used in 1944.

MAGYAR NEMZETI KORMANY SZEGED 1919 Hungarian Peoples Govt. Szeged, o.p. on Hungary for the Komitat of Szegedin.

MAGYAR NEPKOZTARSASAG Peoples Popular Republic, insc. showing present full name was used only in 1949, Hungary.

MAGYARORSZAG Hungarian State, insc. Hungary, 1925.

MAGYAR POSTA Insc. recent issues Hungary.

MAGYAR TANACS KOZTARSASAG Hungarian Soviet Republic, insc. Hungary, 1919.

M.A.L. Military Authority lire, c. Br. forces in North and East Africa.

MALAGA ARRIBA ESPANA O.p. on Spain, rev. issue, Malaga.

MALAWI Insc. for new state, previously the Brit. Prot. of Nyasaland; **MALAWI UFULU** Insc. to mark independence.

MALAYA Insc. with state name for the Straits states joined in the Federation of Malaya.

MALAYAN POSTAL UNION Insc. Straits P-D, 1945.

MALAYSIA, FEDERATION OF Insc. for union of Malaya, Singapore, Sarawak, and Sabah (North Borneo).

Malmedy O.p. on Belgium, for occ. of Ger., Malmedy issue.

MANDAT Insc. money order stamps, Netherlands (Timbres pour Mandats).

MARIANAS ESPANOLAS In frame, o.p. on Spain, Mariana Is.

MARIENEN O.p. on German and insc. for Mariana Is.

MAROC Insc. French Morocco; Kingdom of Marocco.

MAROCCO C. centimes, O.p. on Germany, off. in Morocco.

MARRUECOS O.p. on Spain, off. in Morocco; insc. Morocco.

MARSHALL-ILSELN O.p. on German and insc. Marshall Isls.

MAURITANIE Insc. Mauritania.

M.B.D. In oval, o.p. on Nandgaon state, India, for Off.

MBRETNIJA SHQIPTARE Insc. It. occ. Albania.

MEDELLIN PROVISIONAL Insc. typeset prov. issue, Antioquia, Colombia.

MEDIA ONZA   Insc. on Off., Spain. See ONZA.

M.E.F.   Middle East Forces, o.p. on Br. for off. in Africa.

MEJICO   Insc. Mexico, 1856-1863.

MELAT-i-KAZERUN 1335   National Committee of Kazerun 1917, o.p. on Persia, 1911 issue, during a rebellion. Used only two weeks in Jan., 1917, unofficial.

MEMEL   O.p. on France for Memel.

MEMELGEBIET   In Ger. text, o.p. on Germany for Memel.

MENSAJERIAS   Messenger, o.p. and insc. S-D Uruguay.

Mercury   Head looking down, triangular or rectangular, special handling Austria; looking down to right, in armored cap with thunderbolt, special handling B & H.

Mercury   Figure, alone or inscribed EXTERIOR or INTERIOR, parcel post, Uruguay.

MEXICO TRANSITORIO   Insc. Sonora rev. issues, Mexico.

M.G.; M.H.; M.I.   Ministry of War, of Finance, of Interior, o.p. for Off., Argentina.

MILITAR K.u.K. POST   Insc. B & H, Austrian adm., 1912.

MILITAR POST EILMARKE   Insc. special handling B & H.

MILITARPOST PORTOMARKE   Insc. P-D, B & H.

MILY ADMN   O.p. on Burma, 1945, when freed from occ.

MIT FLUGPOST   Insc. etiquettes of Belgium, etc.

MIT LUFTPOST   Insc. etiquettes of Colombia, Switzerland, etc.

M.J.I.; M.M.   Ministry of Justice and Education, of Marine, o.p. for Off., Argentina.

M.O.B.   Money Order Business, insc. on handstamps often used for cancelling by careless postal clerks.

MOCAMBIQUE   O.p. and insc. Mozambique.

MONGOLIA   Insc. Outer Mongolia, 1926-1945.

MONGTZE; MONG-TSEU; MONGTSEU   O.p. on Indo-China, Fr. off. Mongtseu, China.

MONROVIA   Insc. on R-L for that city in Liberia.

Monster.   Dutch word appearing on specimen stamps.

MONTE CASSINO 18.V.1944   O.p. on Polish Offices Abroad, to honor the capture of Monte Cassino by Polish units of the Allied Forces.

MONTEREY   Insc. on prov. issues for Monterrey, Mexico.

MONTEVIDEO   With sun, insc. carrier and ordinary issues, 1858-60, Uruguay.

M.O.P. Ministry of Public Works, o.p. for Off., Argentina.

MOQUEA; MOQUEGUA O.p. on Arequipa prov. issues and ordinary Peru, Chilean occ.

MORELIA Insc. on prov. issues for state of Morelia, Mexico.

MOROCCO AGENCIES O.p. on British for Morocco.

MOYEN CONGO Insc. Middle Congo in Fr. Eq. Africa.

MQE; M.Q.E. O.p. on French Colonies for Martinique.

M.R.C. Ministry of Foreign Affairs and Religion, o.p. for Off., Argentina.

MULTA Fine, mulct; o.p. on Azores for P-D; insc. P-D, Bolivia, Costa Rica, Chile, Dominican Republic; o.p. on P-T, of var. Por. col. for P-T P-D.

MULTADA Fined, insc. P-D, Chile.

MULTAS Insc. P-D, Ecuador.

M.V.i.R. Militar Verwaltung in Rumanien (Mil. Adm. of Roumania), o.p. on Germany, in Roman or Ger. type, for ordinary and P-T P-D, and o.p. in script and script framed, on Roumania P-T, Ger. occ. of Roumania.

NACHMARKE With value, o.p. on Austria for P-D.

NACH PORTO After postage, insc. P-D, Liechtenstein.

NA OSWIATE For public instruction, insc. S-P, Poland.

NAPOLETANA Insc. Naples, part of Two Sicilies.

NA SKARB For national funds, insc. S-P, Poland.

NA SLASK For Silesia, with value, o.p. on Central Lithuania, for S-P.

NATIONALER VERWALTUNGS AUSSCHUSS O.p. on Jugoslavia and Montenegro, Ger. occ. of Montenegro.

NATIONALSOZIAL DEUTSCHE ARBEITERPARTE National Socialist German Workers' Party, insc. franchise issue, Germany.

NATIONAL VERSAMMLUNG National Assembly, insc. Germany, 1919 to honor the Weimar assembly.

NATIONS UNIES OFFICE EUROPÉEN O.p. on Switzerland for Off.

NAVY DEPT. Insc., on Off. U.S.

NCE; N.C.E. O.p. on French Colonies for New Caledonia.

N.D. HRVATSKA Nezavisna Drzava, insc. Croatia.

N.D. RATNI DOPRINOS Insc. Croatia.

Nebr. O.p. on U.S. stamps series 1923. See Kans.

NEDERLAND   Insc. Netherlands.

NEDERLANDS (or NED.) Nieuw Guinea, Nieuw Guinea. Inscs. Netherlands New Guinea. 1950-1962.

NEDERLANDSCH INDIE (or NEDER.INDIE, NED. INDIE) Insc. Dutch East Indies. Also on Jap. occ. Lesser Sunda Islands.

NEDERLANDSE ANTILLEN; NED. ANTILLEN   Insc. replacing Curaçao after 1949.

NEGRI SEMBILAN   O.P. on Straits. Definitive issue shows N. Sembilan, and N. Sembilan, Malaya.

Newsboy   Running left, square with round corners, p Czech.

NEW CONSTITUTION and year date.   Insc. Ceylon 1947, British Solomon Islands 1961, Cayman Islands 1959, Turks and Caicos Islands 1959; o.p. Gibraltar 1950, Dominica 1951, Grenada 1951, Bahamas 1964, to mark that event.

NEZAVISNA DRZAVA HRVATSKA   Insc. Croatia, with nurse or Red Cross, P-T.

N.F.   Nyasaland Force, o.p. on Nyasa. Prot., Br. occ. Ger. E. Afr.

NIEUWE REPUBLIEK ZUID AFRIKA   Insc. New Republic.

NISIRO; NISIROS   O.p. on Italy, occ. Nisiro, Aegean Islands.

NIVINY   O.p. on Czechoslovakia S-D for newspaper stamps.

NIWIN   With surtax, o.p. on S-P, Curaçao. The initials are of a relief society in Indonesia.

NLLE CALEDONIE   O.p. on Fr. Col. and insc. New Caledonia.

NO HAY ESTAMPILLAS   There are no stamps (and additional words) typeset prov. issues for var. depts. of Colombia.

NORDDEUTSCHER POSTBEZIRK   Insc. North Ger. Postal Dist. Germany.

NOREG   Insc. in ancient form on Garborg issue, 1951, Norway.

NORGE   Insc. Norway.

NOSSI-BE   O.p. on French Colonies and insc. Nossi-Be.

NOUVELLES HEBRIDES; same and CONDOMINIUM   Insc. Fr. adm. of New Hebrides Islands; the first also an o.p. on New Caledonia for New Hebrides.

NSB   With values, o.p. on French Colonies for Nossi-Be.

Numeral   Design feature, 30, 60, or 90 in large horizontal oval; 10 to 600 in small rectangle, early Brazil.

Numeral   In ring of star; or with colorless cross before mountains, P-D, Switzerland.

Numeral ½   O.p. on France, Algeria, and Andorra, for p.

N.W. PACIFIC ISLANDS O.p. on Australia for Northwest Pacific Islands.

OAXACA Insc. Oaxaca rev. issues, Mexico.

O.B. Official Business, o.p. on Philippines, for Off.

OBOCK O.p. on French Colonies, and insc. Obock.

OCCUPATION AZERBAYEDJAN O.p. on Russia by Entente officers, not official.

Occupation française O.p. on Hungary, Fr. occ., Arad issue.

Occupation Française CAMEROUN O.p. on Middle Congo, Fr. occ. of Cameroon.

OCEANIE Insc. French Oceania.

OCUPACION DE PASCUA Insc. S-P, Chile.

OESTERREICH; ÖSTERREICH Insc. Austria.

OEUVRES DE GUERRE Plus value, o.p. on Cameroon for S-P.

OEUVRES SOCIALES With thin cross and surtax, o.p. on St. Pierre and Miquelon for S-P.

O.F. CASTELLORISO Occ. Française, o.p. on France, occ. Castellorizo.

OFFENTLIG SAK Insc. Off., Norway.

OFFICIAL O.p. for Off. var. Br. col., Canal Zone, Phiippines, Brazil, and Liberia. Also insc. for Off., var. countries.

OFFICIAL AIRMAIL 1862 TAU'ATANIA EMANCIPATION 1962 O.p. on Tonga for airmail off. for the centenary.

OFFICIALLY SEALED Insc. official seals, Canada, Japan, Hong Kong, Siam, United States, and others.

OFFICIAL SERVICE O.p. on Liberia for Off.

OFFICIEL O.p. on Luxembourg and Switzerland for Off.

OFFISIEEL–OFFICIAL Bil. o.p. for Off., South Africa, S.W. Africa.

OFICIAL O.p. and insc. in Spanish and Portuguese for Off.

O.H.E.M.S. O.p., 1922; O.H.H.S. prior to 1922, Off., Egypt.

O.H.M.S. On His (or Her) Majesty's Service, o.p. on Canada for Off.

OHU POST Insc. air mail, Estonia.

OIL RIVERS O.p. on British for Niger Coast Prot.

O.L. Origine locale, a postal marking placed on letters of Monaco by French carriers who had been handed them or had found them in French letter boxes. This practice ended in 1908.

OLTRE GIUBA O.p. on Italy for Oltre Giuba.

O.M.F. CILICIE   O.p. on France, occ. of Cilicia.

O.M.F. SYRIE   Occ. Mil. Française, o.p. on France and Arabian during Fr. man. of Syria.

ON C.G.S.   O.p. on Cochin, India, for Off.

ONE ANNA   Only Latin-letter insc. on a Jasdan stamp with sun and human features.

ONE HUNDRED YEARS   Insc. centenary issue, New South Wales, 1888.

O.N.F. Castellorizo   Occupation Navale Française, o.p. on Fr. Levant, Fr. occ. Castellorizo.

ON H.M.S.   O.p. Somaliland Prot.; same, Chamba state, India, for Off.

ON K.D.S.   O.p. on Kishangarh state, India, for Off.

ON SERVICE   O.p. on Ceylon for Off.

ON S.S.   On State Service, o.p. on Travancore state, India, for Off.

ON S.S.S.   O.p. on Sirmoor state, India, for Off.

ON STATE SERVICE   O.p. on Br. man. of Iraq, and the kingdom for Off.

ONZA   Ounce. Spanish Off. stamps were marked to prepay one ounce or one-half ounce (MEDIA ONZA).

ORANJE VRIJ STAAT   Insc. Orange River Colony (Orange Free State).

ORCHA: ORCHHA   Insc. Orchha state, India.

ORDINARY   O.p. on Liberian Off. to make valid for ordinary postage.

ORGANISATION INTERNATIONALE POUR LES REFUGIES; ORGANISATION MONDIALE DE LA SANTE O.p.'s on Switzerland for Off.

ORO PASTAS   Insc. air mail, Lithuania.

ORPHELINS DE LA GUERRE   Insc. S-P, France.

ORTS POST   Local Post, insc. Zurich, cantonal stamps of 1850, and 2½-rappen stamps of Switzerland, 1850.

O.S.   On Service, o.p. on var. Br. states; on Liberia; in monogram on Liberia, for Off.

O.S.   Offentlig Sax, corner letters on recent Off., Norway.

O.S.G.S.   O.p. on Sudan for Off.

OSTLAND   O.p. on Germany, occ. of Russia.

O.T.   O.p. on Cz. newspaper stamps used by commercial firms.

Otvorenie slovenskeho snemu   18.1.1939   With shield, o.p. on Czechoslovakia for Slovakia.

OUBANGI-CHARI   O.p. on Middle Congo; same with additional o.p. AFRIQUE EQUITORIALE FRANCAISE; as first with A.E.F., o.p. on French P-D, Ubangi.

OUBANGI-CHARI-TCHAD   O.p. on Middle Congo for Ubangi.

O.W. OFFICIAL   Office of Works, o.p. on British for Off.

P   1   With Arabic between, o.p. on Turkey for Thrace.

P   Abbr. PORTO.

P   With crescent and star in oval, o.p. on Straits for Perak.

PACCHI POSTALI   Insc. parcel post, Italy; same with SUI BOLLETTINO and SULLA RICEVUTO in var. combinations on two-part parcel post issues of Italy and col., San Marino, etc.

PACKENMARKE   Parcel stamp, insc. 4-kopeck Wenden, 1863, for parcels.

PACKHOI; PAK-HOI; PAKHOI   O.p. on Indo-China, Fr. off. in Packhoi, China.

PAGO $0.−, EL AGENTE POSTAL MANUEL E. JIMINEZ   Typeset prov. Cauca, Colombia.

PAID   Written or h/s marking to show prepayment of postage.

PAITA   O.p. on Peru, for prov. issue during Chilean occ.

PALACIO DE COMMUNICACIONES   Insc. P-T, Colombia and Cuba.

PALESTINE   With Arabic insc. o.p. on Trans-Jordan for Palestine; same plus Hebrew insc., o.p. on E.E.F. issue, for Br. man. of Palestine; as first, o.p. on Egypt for occ. of Palestine.

PARA; PIASTRE   O.p. on Britain, France, Roumania, Russia, Italy, for off. in Turkey; insc. on stamps with a design of Arabic insc. or a Sphinx and pyramids, Egypt; numerals spelled out in French, as *Dix* for 10, *Vingt* for 20, etc., Turkey.

PARA OS POBRES   Insc. P-T, Portugal and Azores.

Paraph (or paraphe)   A flourish or signature of initials, o.p. on Cuba for use in Puerto Rico only. The tughra is an elaborate paraph.

PAR AVION   By airplane, universal insc. etiquettes; insc. var. air-mail issues.

PARDOES DA GRAND GUERRA   Insc. P-T, Portugal and Azores.

PAR POSTE AERIENNE   One insc. on etiquettes in Switzerland.

PARTICULAR   Op. on Nicaragua Off. to make valid for ordinary use.

PASCO   In lozenge frame, o.p. on Peru during occ. by Chile.

PATMO; PATMOS   O.p. on Italy, off. in Patmo, Aegean Is.

PATRIOTIC FUND   Insc. S-P, Queensland.

PATZCUARO   Insc. prov. issue for city of Patzcuaro, Mexico.

PE.   Abbr. of *piastre* as insc. early Egypt.

Peacock   O.p. on Burma during occ. by Burma Independence Army.

PECHINO   O.p. on Italy, off. in Pekin, China.

PELITA   With lamp and value, o.p. on Dutch East Indies for S-P.

PEN.   With Cyrillic equivalent above and below arms design, insc. Finland.

PER LUGPOS   Afrikaans, insc. etiquettes, South Africa and S.W. Africa.

PER PACCHI   O.p. on Vatican City for parcel post.

PER VLIEGTUIG   Insc. etiquettes, Belgium.

PESA   c. o.p. on Germany for Ger. E. Africa.

P.G.S.   O.p. on Straits for Off., Perak.

PHILIPPINE ISLANDS UNITED STATES OF AMERICA   Insc. Philippines under U.S. adm.

PHILIPPINES   O.p. on U.S. for prov. issues under U.S. mil. adm.

PIASTRE   See PARA.

PILGRIM TERCENTENARY   Insc. U.S. issue without country name.

PILIPINAS   O.p. and insc. Jap. occ; native insc. Philippines.

Pinsin; pinsine; p.   Erse insc. for penny on stamps of Eire.

PISCO   In oval, o.p. on Peru for prov. issues, Chilean occ.

PISCOPI   O.p. on Italy for off. in Piscopi, Aegean Islands.

PIURA   In various forms, o.p. on Peru for prov. issues, Chilean occ.

P.I.–U.S. INITIAL FLIGHT   O.p. on Philippines for air-mail issue.

PJON.FRIM; PJONUSTA; PJONUSTU; PJONUSTUMERKI   First three insc.; second and fourth o.p., Iceland Off.

PLEBESCITE OLSZTYN ALLENSTEIN   O.p. on Germany for Allenstein.

P.M.   Posta Militare, o.p. on Italy for mil. stamps; were used for ordinary purposes during a stamp shortage.

POBLACHT NA HEIREANN   Insc. Republic of Ireland.

POCZTA POLSKA   Polish post, o.p. on Austria for Poland; same in l.c. on Germany during Pol. occ; insc. for Pol. after 1919 except between 1944-45 and 1948, when the POCZTA was omitted.

POLAIRE INTERNATIONALE (1932); POLE DU NORD (1931)   Insc. air mail U.S.S.R.

POLYNESIE FRANÇAISE   Insc. French Oceanica 1955.

POMBAL   Insc. P-T, Portugal and Azores.

POR AVION   Insc. etiquettes, Venezuela.

POR CORREO AEREO   Insc. etiquettes, Colombia.

PORT CANTONAL   Insc. Geneva cantonal stamp, Switzerland.

PORTEADO   O.p. on Azores, insc. Portugal, for P-D.

PORTEADO A RECEBER; PORTEADO CORREIO   Insc. for P-D, Portugal and col.

PORTE DE CONDUCCION   With large numerals, insc. parcel post, Peru.

PORTE DE MAR   Sea postage, a Mexican label to indicate amount due the ship carrying the letter. The whole postage was paid by Mexican stamps.

PORT GDANSK   O.p. on Poland, off. in Danzig.

PORT LAGOS   O.p. on France, off. in Port Lagos, Turkey.

PORTO   Insc. P-D Denmark, Austria, Poland, Slovenia, Croatia, Jugoslavia, Liechtenstein. O.p. on Hungary, Denmark and others.

PORTO   With large numerals, c.hellers, P-D, Austria; c.piastres, Austrian off. in Turkey.

PORTO FRANCO   Postage Free, at top, CORREOS at sides, arms design, early Peru. Insc. labels are straight, or convex, or concave.

PORTO FRANCO   Insc. Portugal franchise stamps. Organization name appears but no denomination.

PORTO GAZETEI   Insc. Moldavia, Roumania, 1858.

PORTOMAERKE   Penalty stamp, insc. P-D, Norway, Danish West Indies.

PORTOMARKE   Insc. P-D, Austria, Baden, Croatia, B & H.

PORTO PFLICHTICE DIENST SACHE Insc. Communal Off. Württemberg.

PORTO RICO O.p. on U.S. for U.S. adm. of Puerto Rico.

POSESIONES ESPANOLES DEL SAHARA OCCIDENTAL Insc. Sp. W. Sahara.

POSSEEL Postage (Afrikaans), insc. on one stamp of a bil. pair. The other shows POSTAGE. South Africa, S.W. Africa.

POSTA O.p. on fiscals for ordinary postage, Tannu Tuva.

POSTA AEREA Insc. air mail, Italy and col., San Marino, Vatican City, Switzerland.

POSTA AERIANA Insc. air mail, Roumania.

POSTA AERORE (or AJRORE) Insc. air mail, Albania.

POSŤA ČESKOSLOVENSKÁ O.p. on Austria for S-P, Czechoslovakia.

POSTA FIUME Insc. on triangular stamp, newspaper issue, Fiume.

POSTAGE Insc. with Arabic, c. annas to rupees. Hyderabad state, India.

POSTAGE Insc. portrait Victoria, letters in lower or four corners, c.pence to pounds, early issues Great Britain.

POSTAGE Insc. view of city on bay, c.pence, insc. on ring "CAMP. AUST. SIGILLUM NOV.," New South Wales, Sydney views.

POSTAGE Reading down or diagonally, in l.c. o.p. on Outer Mongolia.

POSTAGE Portrait Andrew Jackson, C.S. in lower corners, Confederate States of America.

POSTAGE & REVENUE Insc. British and col. to indicate validity for both uses; c. annas, o.p. on Saurashtra, 1949-51, for the United State of Saurashtra, India.

POSTAGE DUE O.p. on var. countries for P-D; an insc. for same in English-speaking countries; c. pence–shillings, central numeral, general P-D series for Australian states, 1902.

POSTAGE I.E.F. 'D' O.p. on Turkish fiscals, Br. occ. Mesopotamia, Mosul.

POSTAGE TAX Insc. on P-D, Sudan.

POSTAL O.p. on fiscals, and var. special service stamps of Ecuador, to make valid for ordinary use.

POSTALARI Postage, insc. modern Turkish stamps.

POSTALE ITALIANO   Insc. Italy.

Postal-Frril Est. OTAVALO   With value, o.p. on consular fee stamp to honor a new railway service, Ecuador, 1928.

POSTAL SAVINGS U.S. OFFICIAL MAIL   Insc. U.S. Off.

POST & RECEIPT   Insc., c. annas, Hyderabad state, India.

POSTA PNEUMATICA   Insc. pneumatic post, Italy.

POSTAS LE NIOC   Insc. on bil. P-D, Ireland.

POSTAT AJRORE   Insc. air mail, Albania under It. dom. and later.

POSTAT E QEVERRIES SE PERKOHESHME–TE SHQIPO-NIES   With eagle and value, in double circle, h/s on white paper, Albania.

POSTAT EXPRES   Insc. S-D, Albania.

POSTAT SHQIPTARE   Insc. Albania.

POSTCOLLI; POSTCOLLO   Insc. the latter an o.p. also, parcel post, Belgium.

POSTE AERIENNE   Insc. air mail, France and col., Belgium, Egypt, Lebanon, Luxembourg, Monaco, Persia, Siam, Syria, Yemen, etc.; o.p. for France, Tunisia, etc.

POSTE AERIEO   O.p. on fiscals for air mail, Persia.

POSTE AVION   Insc. air mail, Haiti.

POSTE DE GENEVA (with Port Local or Port Cantonal)   Insc. Geneva, Switzerland.

POSTE ITALIANE   Insc. Italy.

POSTE LOCALE   With colorless cross, insc. Geneva, Switzer-land.

POSTE PAR AVION   O.p. on Lebanon, and h/s on Syria and Cilicia, air mail.

POSTE PERSANE; POSTES PERSANES   Insc. Persia.

POSTES   At top, value below portrait, c.centime-franc, Belgium, 1849-66; arms design, lion rampant to left, Belgium 1866-67; insc. at top, large numeral at center, centimes below, network over all, Alsace and Lorraine under Ger. occ. 1870.

POSTES AERIENNES   O.p. and insc. air mail, Persia, 1930.

POSTES AFGHANES   Insc. Afghanistan after 1928.

POSTES AVION   Insc. air mail, Haiti and Fr. off. in Morocco.

POSTES DE COREE   Insc. Korea, 1902.

POSTES DE YEMEN   Insc. low values, 1940 and P-D, 1942, Yemen.

POSTES EGYPTIENNES   Insc. Egypt, 1879-96.

POSTES EXPRES   Insc. S-D, Egypt.

POSTES HEDJAZ & NEDJDE   Insc. Hejaz and Nedj, 1930-32.

POSTES IMPERIALES DE COREE   Insc. Korea, 1903.

POSTES IRANIENNES   O.p. and insc. Iran (Persia), 1935.

POSTES OTTOMANES   Insc. Turkey, 1913.

POSTES PERSANES 1903   O.p. and insc. Persia 1903-1935.

POSTES SERBES   O.p. on France in pairs, for Corfu, 1916-18.

POSTES SYRIE   Insc. Syria, 1930-1936, 1945-1946.

POSTE VATICANE   Insc. Vatican City.

POSTFAERGE   O.p. on Denmark for parcel post.

POSTGEBIET OB. OST   O.p. on German for occ. Lithuania.

Post horn   Symbol of the post, used in designs, watermarks, etc.

Post horn and arrow   Over a map of Austria, special handling, Austria.

Post horn and crown   No stated value, newspaper stamps, Hungary.

POST LUCHTDIENST   Insc. air mail, Belgian Congo.

POST OBITUM   Insc. 1877 U.S. Post Office seals used by Dead Letter Office to seal letters opened to learn writer's name and address.

POST OFFICE   Insc. U.S. at top and 5's or X's at bottom, U.S. 1847 issue; insc. at left side, Mauritius 1847.

POST OFFICE DEPT.   Insc. on Off., U.S.

POST PAID (or one word)   A postal marking indicating prepayment of postage.

POST STAMP   Insc. c. annas, Hyderabad state, India.

POSTTAXE BAYER   Insc. P-D, Bavaria.

POSTZEGEL   Insc., c. in cents, as c., Netherlands.

POUR LA CROIX ROUGE   Insc. P-T, Jugoslavia.

POUR LE STADE MUNICIPAL DE PORT-AU-PRINCE   Insc. S-P; same with AVION, air-mail S-P, Haiti.

P.P.   In frame, o.p. on Fr. P-D, to make valid for ordinary postage, Fr. off. in Morocco.

PRENSA   O.p. in var. types on Uruguay, for newspaper use.

PRIMA VALORES DECLARADOS   Insc. insured letter stamp, o.p. same, and SERVICIO INTERIOR, same for domestic use, Dominican Republic.

PRIMER VUELO POSTAL–BARRIOS-MIAMI   O.p. for air mail, Guatemala.

PRIMO VOLO DIRETTO ROMA-BUENOS AIRES TRIMO-TORE "LOMBARDI–MAZZOTTI"   O.p. on Italy and Cyrenaica for air mail.

PRINCIPAUTE DE MONACO   Insc. Monaco.

PRINCIPAUTE DE TRINIDAD   Insc. on a phantom stamp issue.

PRO AERO   Insc. and o.p. Swiss air mail.

PRO AGRICULTURA Y CANADERIA   Insc. S.P, Paraguay.

PRO CARTERO   Insc. S-P, Argentina.

PRO CASA DE JUBILACIONES DE COMMUNICACIONES Insc. P-T, Bolivia.

PRO COMBATTENTI   Insc. and o.p. S-P, San Marino.

PRO DESOCUPADOS   For unemployed, insc. and o.p. P-T, Peru.

PRO EDUCACION FISICA   Physical education, Insc. P-T, Panama.

PRO FONDAZIONE STUDIO   Insc. S-P, Fiume.

PRO INFANCIA   Children's welfare, o.p. P-T, Mexico.

PRO JUVENTUTE   Youth, insc. S-P, Switzerland, Brazil 1939.

PRO PATRIA   Country, insc. Swiss S-P.

PRO PLEBISCITO TACNA Y (or &) ARICA   Insc. P-T, pleb. area, Peru.

PROTECCION A LA INFANCIA   O.p. for P-T, Mexico.

PROTECCION AL ANCIANO   For the aged, insc. S-P, Uruguay.

PROTECTORADO ESPANOL EN MARRUECOS   Insc. and o.p. on Spain, off. in Morocco.

PROTECTORAT COTE DES SOMALIS   Insc. Somali Coast.

PROTECTORATE   O.p. on Bechuanaland for Bechuanaland Prot.

PROTEJA A LA INFANCIA   Insc. P-T, Mexico.

PRO TUBERCULOSOS POBRES   Insc. P-T, Spain.

PROVINCE LAIBACH–LJUBLJANSKA POKRAJINA   With Ger. eagle, o.p. on Italy, and insc. for Ger. occ. of Laibach.

PROVISIONAL GOVT. 1893.   O.p. on Hawaii for Republic issues.

PROVISORIO   O.p. on demonetized Por. col. to make valid.

PRO VIVIENDA OBRARA   Insc. P-T, Bolivia.

PRZESLYKA URZEDOWA   Insc. Off. Poland.

P S   Monogram, design of Cauca, Colombia.

P.S.N.C.   Pacific Steam Navigation Co., corner letters, first issue, Peru.

PTO RICO 1898 Y 99; (or 1877, 78, or 79)   Insc. Puerto Rico.

PUNO   In double circle, o.p. on Peru and Arequipa, Chilean occ. Peru.

PUOLUSTUSVOIMAT KENTTA POSTIA   Insc. M Finland.

PUTTALIA STATE   O.p. on India for Patalia state.

QARKU POSTES I KORCES; Qarku I Korces   First, insc., second, o.p. Albania, 1918.

QU'AITI STATE OF SHIHR AND MUKALLA   Insc. on Aden for that sultanate in East Aden Protectorate.

QU'AITI STATE IN HADHRAMAUT   Insc. on Aden for that sultanate in East Aden Protectorate.

R   Insc. indicates registration, on R-L stamps, Colombia and Depts., Panama, etc.; same on registry labels.

R   Feature of stamps of Jhind state, India; o.p. on France for Reunion.

RAJASTHAN   O.p. on Jaipur and Kishengarh, for Rajasthan state, India.

RATNI DOPRINOS   Insc. S-P, Croatia.

RAYON I (II or III)   Insc. on early Swiss issues, indicating a zone system of rates.

R. COMMISSARIATE CIVILE TERRITORIO SLOVENI OC-CUPATI LUBLINA   O.p. Jugoslavia, It. occ. Laibach.

R. de C.   Reconstruction of communications, o.p. P-T, Nicaragua.

R. de C. Garzon 1894 No Hay Estampillas (etc.)   Typeset prov., Tolima, Colombia.

RECAPITO AUTORIZZATO   Authorized delivery, insc. Italy.

RECARGO   Extra charge, insc. Spanish war tax, 1898.

RECOMENDADA   Insc. R-L, Colombia.

RECOMMANDATA   Insc. registry labels, Italian language.

RECOMMANDE   Insc. registry labels, French language.

RECOUVREMENTS   Recoveries, P-D, to collect postage on returned C.O.D. parcels, or as next.

RECOUVREMENTS—TAXE A PERCEVOIR   Value to collect, insc. on stamps used to collect magazine subscriptions, etc. France, Algeria, Morocco, Monaco, and Andorra.

RECOUVREMENTS–VALEURS IMPAYEES   Values unpaid, same as preceding.

RED CROSS   With surtax, o.p. on Straits and Trengganu for S-P.

RED CROSS SOCIETY TRINIDAD ONE FRACTION   Insc. S-P, Trinidad & Tobago.

REGATUL PTT ROMANIEI in circle, also with BANI above, o.p. on Hungary for occupation of Romania.

REGENCY DE TUNIS   Insc. Tunisia.

REGIERUNGS DIENSTSACHE   O.p. Liechtenstein for Off.

REGISTERED   Insc. first U.S. Off. seal; same R-L stamps, of Canada, Queensland, New South Wales, Victoria, and Liberia.

REGISTRO   Insc. R-L stamps, Colombia and depts.

REGISTRY   Insc. R-L stamp, U.S.

REGNO D'ITALIA VENEZIA GIULIA or TRENTINO   O.p. Austria, Italian occupation of those provinces.

REHABILITADA PARA EL SERVICIO PUBLICO   O.p. on Honduras air mail to make valid for ordinary air mail.

REJISTRO   Insc. R-L, stamp, Colombia.

RELAIS   Insc. on Persian nonpostal labels attached to railroad tickets to permit the bearer to ride in the post wagon or mail coach between points not served by railroads.

REPOEBLIK INDONESIA (or REPUBLIK)   Insc. Indonesia, latter with SERIKAT, first issue United States of Indonesia.

REPRISE POSTE AERIENNE ETHIOPIENNE   O.p. on Ethiopia for air mail.

REPUBBLICA (or REPUB. or REPA. or REP. or R.) DI SAN (or S.) MARINO or RSM   Insc. San Marino.

REPUBBLICA ITALIANA   Insc. Italy, 1952. REPUBBLICA SOCIALE ITALIAN   Insc., o.p., Ital. Socialist Rep.

REPUBLICA MAYOR DE CENTRO AMERICA ESTADO DE EL SALVADOR   Insc. El Salvador.

REPUBLICA ORIENTAL DEL URUGUAY   Insc. Uruguay.

REPUBLICA (or R.) POPULARA (or P.) ROMANIA or ROMANA, or ROMINA   Inscs. Romania.

REPUBLIEK STELLALAND   Insc. Stellaland.

REPUBLIKA MALAGASY   Insc. Malagasy Rep. (Madagascar).

REPUBLIKA NG PILIPINAS   Insc. Jap. occ. Philippines.

REPUBLIKA POPULLORE E SHQIPERISE, REPUBLIKA SHQIPTARE   Insc. Albanian Republic.

REPUBLIQUE and state name.   Inscs. for states that once were French or Belgian colonies.

REPUBLIQUE ARABE UNIE–SYRIE (or R.A.U.)   Insc. Syria.

REPUBLIQUE GEORGIENNE   Insc. Georgia.

REPUBLIQUE LIBANAISE   Insc. Lebanon.

REPUBLIQUE MALGACHE   Insc. Malagasy Rep. (Madagascar).

REPUBLIQUE RWANDAISE   Insc. Rwanda, formerly Ruanda.

REPUBLIQUE SYRIENNE   Insc. Syria under French mandate.

REPUBLIQUE TUNISIENNE   Insc. Tunisia, 1958.

REPULA POSTA   O.p. on Hungary for air mail.

RESELLADO   Restamped, o.p. on var. Ecuador as a control mark. See LOJA FRANCO; o.p. on var. demonetized Venezuela to restore validity.

RESELLO   O.p. on demonetized Nicaragua to restore validity.

RESISTANCE   With surtax, o.p. on Syria mil. and mil. air mail to provide mil. S-P, and mil. air mail S-P.

RESMI   With star and crescent, o.p. and insc. Off., Turkey.

RETARDO   O.p. and insc. late fee stamps, Colombia, Panama.

RETOURBRIEF KGL OBERAMT   With district name, insc. return-letter stamp Bavaria; same but OBERPOSTAMT REGENSBURG return-letter stamp for Regensburg.

RETURN FROM NORFOLK ISLAND   Insc. Pitcairn Isl. to mark return of the former inhabitants.

RF; R.F.   Republique Française, insc. France.

RHEINLAND–PFALZ   Insc. Fr. occ. Ger., Rhine Palatinate.

RHEIN–RUHR–HILSE   With surtax, o.p. on Ger. for S.P.

R.H. OFFICIAL   Royal Household, o.p. on British for Off.

RIALTAR SEALDAC NA HEIREANN   Prov. Govt. of Ireland, o.p. on British for Ireland.

RIAU   O.p. on Indonesia for Riouw Archipelago.

RIO MUNI   Insc. 1960 for Rio Muni, formerly Sp. Guinea.

RIOS 19   Control o.p. on Ecuador. See LOJA FRANCO.

R I S   Republik Indonesia Serikat, o.p. on Dutch East Indies, for United States of Indonesia.

R.O.   Rumelie Orientale, o.p. on Turkey for Eastern Rumelia.

ROBERTSPORT   Insc. on R-L stamp for that city, Liberia.

RODI   O.p. on Italy for off. in Rhodes, Aegean Islands.

ROMANA; ROMANIA; ROMINA; ROUMANIA   Inscs. Romania.

ROMANIA–ZONA DE OCCUPATIE   O.p. on Hungary, during Romanian occupation.

ROODE KRUIS   Red Cross   Insc. S-P,   Netherlands.

ROSS DEPENDENCY   Insc. on New Zealand for Polar regions, 1957.

ROTARY INTERNATIONAL–CONVENTION WIEN 1932   O.p. on Austria for S-P.

ROUMELIE ORIENTALE   O.p. on Turkey for Eastern Rumelia.

ROYAUME DE BURUNDI   O.p. on Ruanda-Urundi and insc. for the Kingdom of Burundi.

ROYAUME DE CAMBODGE   Insc. Cambodia.

ROYAUME D'EGYPT   Insc. Egypt.

ROYAUME DE L'ARABE SOUDITE   Insc. Saudi Arabia.

ROYAUME DE MAROC   Insc. Kingdom of Morocco, 1956.

ROYAUME DE YEMEN   Insc. Yemen.

ROYAUME DU LAOS   Insc. Laos.

RPF   With preceding numerals, o.p. on Luxembourg in Reichspfennigs, Ger. occ.

RUANDA   O.p. on Congo, Belgian occ. of Ger. E. Africa.

RUE   Control o.p. on Ecuador. See LOJA FRANCO.

RUMANIEN   O.p. in Ger. type on German for occ. of Roumania.

RUSSISCH POLEN   O.p. in Ger. type on German for occ. Poland.

RWANDA   Insc. for Ruanda after 1962.

S   O.p. on Straits; same with crescent and star in oval, Selangor.

SAAR; SAARGEBEIT; SARRE   Insc. Saar; the last also o.p. on Germany.

SAARGEBEIT LUFTPOST   Insc. Saar air mail.

SAARGEBEIT VOLKSHILSE   Insc. S-P, Saar.

SABAH   O.p. on North Borneo, 1964 as new name for this state.

SACHEN   Insc. Saxony.

SAHARA ESPAÑOL   O.p. on Spain, and insc. Sp. W. Sahara.

SAHARA OCCIDENTAL   Insc. Sp. W. Sahara.

S.A.I.D.E.   Services Ariens Internationaux d'Egypte, o.p. for air mail, Egypt.

SAINT HELENA TRISTAN RELIEF   O.p. on St. Helena for relief of Tristan da Cunha, 1961.

St. PIERRE M—ON   O.p. on French Colonies, St. Pierre and Miquelon.

S. THOME E PRINCIPE   Insc. St. Thomas and Prince Islands to 1914; S. TOME etc., after 1914.

SALONICEO; SALONIKA   O.p. on Italy, off. in Salonika, Turkey.

SALVE HOSPES   Insc. S-P, Netherlands, for Natl. Tourist Assn.

SAMOA I SISIFU Insc. Western Samoa, 1958, for independence.

SANDJAK D'ALEXANDRETTE   O.p. on Syria for Alexandretta.

SANITORIUM   With cross of Lorraine, insc. P-T, Dominican Republic.

SAORSTAT EIREANN and date.   Free State of Ireland, o.p. on British.

SARKARI   O.p. Soruth state, India, for Off.

SARRE   O.p. on German, Saar.

SAURASHTRA   Insc. Soruth and o.p. on fiscals for United State of Saurashtra.

S.C.A.D.T.A.   Sociedad Colombia Allemana de Transports Aereos, a South American air line which issued private stamps.

SCARPANTO   O.p. on Italy, off. in Scarpanto, Aegean Islands.

SCINDE DISTRICT DAWK   Insc. first issue of India, Scinde District Post.

SCOUTS FUND   With tiger head, o.p. on Siam, S-P.

SCUTARI   O.p. on Italy, off. in Scutari, Albania.

S.d.N. BUREAU INTERNATIONALE DU TRAVAIL   O.p. Switzerland for Off.

SECOURS with Arabic insc. Insc. P-T, Saudi Arabia.

SECOURS AUX VICTIMES DE LA GUERRE   Insc. P-T, Haiti.

SECOURS AUX REFUGIES   With Arabic, o.p. for S-P, Syria.

SECOURS NATIONAL   With surtax, o.p. for S-P, var. Fr. col.

SEGNA TASSA   Insc. P-D, Italy 1863-69.

SEGNATASSE   With fan or lattice, o.p. on S-P, for P-D, Fiume.

SEGNETASSE   Insc. P-D, Italy and col., Vatican City, San Marino.

SEGURO POSTAL   Insc. insured letter stamps, Mexico.

SEGURO SOCIAL DEL CAMPESINO   O.p. for P-T, Ecuador.
SELLO POSTAL   O.p. on demonetized issues to revalidate, Nicaragua.
SERBIEN   O.p. on B & H for Austrian occ. Serbia; on Jugoslavia for Ger. occ. Serbia.
SERVICE   O.p. for Off., Burma, Ceylon, India, many Indian states, Pakistan, Somaliland Prot., Indo-China, and Persia; insc. for Off., India.
SERVICE DE LA SOCIETE DES NATIONS   O.p. for Off., Switzerland.
SERVICE DE L'ETAT   Insc. Off., Egypt, Saudi Arabia.
SERVICE DES POSTES PERSANES   Insc. Persia Off.
SERVICE FRANCO   Insc. Persia Off.
SERVICE POSTAL AERIEN   Insc. air mail, Belgian Congo.
SERVICE POSTAL AERIENNE   Insc. air mail, French Morocco.
SERVICIO AEREO   Insc. or o.p. air mail, generally used in Spanish countries.
SERVICIO AEREO HABILITADO   O.p. on Off. to make valid for air mail, Honduras.
SERVICIO AEREO INTERIOR (or EXTERIOR)   Indicates validity, domestic or foreign.
SERVICIO AEREO INTERNACIONAL   O.p. for air mail, Honduras.
SERVICIO AEREO SOBRETASA   Insc. air mail, Argentina.
SERVICIO CENTROAMERICANO   O.p. for air mail, Nicaragua.
SERVICIO DEL ESTADO   O.p. for Off., Chile.
SERVICIO OFICIAL   Insc. Off., Paraguay; o.p. for Off. Peru and Ecuador.
SERVICIO ORDINARIO   O.p. on air mail, Nicaragua, to make valid for ordinary postage.
SERVICIO POSTAL AEREO   Insc. Brazil; o.p. Colombia, Guatemala, Uruguay, air mail.
SERVICIO POSTAL DEL SALVADOR   Insc. El Salvador.
SERVIZIO DI STATO   O.p. on Balbo air mail for air mail Off., Italy; o.p. on air mail S-P, for air mail Off., It. Somaliland.
S F   Soldater Frimaerke (Soldiers' Stamp), o.p. for mil. stamp, Denmark.

S.G.   O.p. for Off., Sudan.

S H   At upper corners, an eagle with shield on breast, Schleswig-Holstein.

SHANGHAI CHINA   O.p. on U.S. (with value doubled) for off. in Shanghai to prevent currency manipulations.

SHANGHAI L.P.O.   Local Post Office, insc. Shanghai.

SHCO   On shield with Geneva cross, P-T, Mozambique.

SHQIPENIA; SHQIPENIE; SHQIPERIA; SHQIPERIJA; SHQIPERISE; SHQIPETARE; SHQIPNI; SHQIPONIES; SHQIPTARE; SHQYPNIS; SHQYPTARE   Insc. and o.p. on Albania.

S.H.S.   O.p. on Hungary, for Croatia-Slavonia in Jugoslavia.

SICILIA   Insc. Sicily, of Two Sicilies.

SIMI   O.p. on Italy, off. in Simi, Aegean Islands.

SLESVIG   Insc. pleb. issues, Schleswig.

SLOVENSKA   Insc. Slovakia.

SLOVENSKO   Triangular stamps with V or D in each corner are personal delivery stamps of Slovakia.

SLOVENSKY STAT   O.p. on Czechoslovakia for Slovakia.

SMIRNE   O.p. on Italy, off. in Smyrna, Turkey.

S.O.   Silesie Orientale, o.p. on Czechoslovakia, for Eastern Silesia.

SOBRE CLOTA PARA MULTOS POSTALES   Insc. parcel post, Mexico.

SOBREPORTO   Insc. P-D, Colombia; **SOBREPORTO AEREO** Insc. air mail, Colombia.

SOCIEDADE DE GEOGRAPHIA DE LISBON PORTE FRANCO   Insc. franchise stamps, Geographic Society, Portugal.

SOCIEDADE HUMANITARIA CRUZ DE ORIENTE   Insc. P-T, Mozambique.

SOCIEDADE PORTUGUEZA DA CRUZ VERMELHA PORTE FRANCO   Insc. franchise stamps, Red Cross, Portugal.

SOCIETE DES NATIONS   O.p. on Switzerland for Off.

SOLIDARITE 1947   Insc. S-P, Tunisia; **SOLIDARITE FRANCAISE**, insc. S-P, French Colonies, 1944.

SOMALILAND INDEPENDENCE 26 JUNE 1960   O.p. on Somaliland Protectorate when it became part of Somalia.

SOM UBESORGET [or UINDLOST] AABNET AF POST DEPARTMENTET   Insc. return letter stamp, Norway.

SONORA   Insc. rev. issues, Sonora, Mexico.

SOUDAN   With Arabic, o.p. on Egypt for Sudan.

SOUDAN FAIS; SOUDAN FRANÇAIS   Insc. French Sudan.
SOUTH AFRICA–SUID-AFRIKA   Insc. on alternate stamps in bil. pairs South Africa after 1926.
SOUTH GEORGIA, DEPENDENCY OF; SOUTH ORKNEYS, DEPENDENCY OF   O.p. on Falkland Islands for South Georgia and South Orkneys, 1944.
Sower   Design subject for French stamps 1903-37.
SOWJETISCHE BESATZUNGS ZONE   O.p. on Germany, Soviet occ. East Germany.
S.P.   Service Publique, o.p. for Off. Luxembourg.
SPECIAL DELIVERY   Insc. S-D, U.S., Cuba, Guam, Philippines, Liberia, Canada, and Bahamas.
SPECIAL EXPRES   Bil. insc. S-D, Canada.
SPECIAL HANDLING   Insc. for that service, U.S.
SPECIAL POSTAL DELIVERY   Insc. U.S. S-D, 1885-95.
SPITFIRE   Insc. S-P, Cameroons.
SPM   O.p. in caps, and h/s o.p. in Old English type on French Colonies for St. Pierre and Miquelon, 1885-86.
SPOORWEGEN CHEMINS DE FER   Bil. o.p. and insc. parcel post, Belgium.
SRBH HRVATA I SLOVENICA   Insc. Jugoslavia.
SRODKWA LITWA POCZTA   O.p. on Lithuania, and insc. Central Lithuania.
STAATS MARKE   Insc. State Off. Württemberg.
STADT BERLIN   Insc. Soviet occ. Germany, 1948-49.
STADT POST BASLE   Insc. Canton of Basle, Switzerland.
STAEMPLE; STAMPLE; STEMPLE   Insc. newspaper stamps, Austria.
STAMPALIA   O.p. on Italy for off. in Stampalia, Aegean Islands.
STAMP DUTY   Insc. postal-fiscals, New Zealand, Victoria.
Star   Bearing colorless crescent, P-T, Turkey.
Star and Crescent   With surtax, o.p. for S-P, Algeria.
STATE, DEPT. OF   Insc. U.S. Off.
STATE OF KUWAIT   Insc. for Kuwait, 1962 and after.
STATE OF SINGAPORE   Insc. 1959 and generally after.
STEAM; STEAMBOAT   Postal markings used on U.S. inland waterways.
STTVUJA or VUJNA   O.p. on Jugoslavia, and insc. for Ju. mil. govt. Zone B, Trieste.

SU; S.U.   Sometimes with crescent and star, o.p. on Straits for Sungei Ujong.

SUDAN POSTAGE TAX   Insc. P-D, Sudan.

SUID-AFRIKA or SUIDAFRIKA   Afrikaans insc. bil. pairs South Africa.

SUIDWES AFRIKA or SUID—WES   Insc. on bil. pairs, South-west Africa.

S. UJONG   Insc. Sungei Ujong, 1902.

SUOMI   Insc. Finland after 1917.

SURCHARGE POSTAGE   Insc. P-D, Grenada, Trinidad, and Trinidad and Tobago.

SURGOS   Insc. S-D, Hungary; o.p. on Hungary for Fiume.

SVERIGE   Insc. Sweden.

S.W.A.   O.p. on South Africa for Southwest Africa.

SYRIAN ARAB REPUBLIC   Insc. for Syria, 1961 and after.

SYRIE; Syrie—Grand Liban   O.p. on France; first, insc. also, Syria.

S Z   Insc. at sides of Off., Czechoslovakia.

T   Abbr. for tax in var. languages, the symbol for P-D in international mails. Used as an o.p. often framed, to provide P-D stamps; appears in the four corners of P-D, Dominican Rep.; with diagonal TAKSE or AXE as an o.p. for P-D, Albania.

T   In circle, o.p. on Peru for prov. issues of Huacho, Peru.

TAKCA   Cyrillic insc. P-D, Bulgaria.

TAKSE   O.p. and insc. P-D, Albania.

TANGER   O.p. on Morocco for the city of Tangier; o.p. on Fr. P-D, for P-D, Tangier; o.p. on Sp. Morocco, and insc. for Sp. Tangier.

TASA   Insc. P-D, Uruguay.

TASA POR COBRA   To recover by assessment, insc. P-D, Cuba.

TASSA GAZZETTE   Insc. newspaper tax, Modena.

TAXA   Insc. P-D, Uruguay.

TAXA DE FACTAGIU   Insc. parcel post, Roumania.

TAXA DE GUERRA   O.p. on ordinary or fiscal for war tax, Portugal and col.

TAXA de PLATA   Money fine, insc. P-D, Roumania.

TAXA RECEBIDA   Insc. air mail, Mozambique.

TAXE   Insc. on 6-rappen, Zurich, Switzerland (not a P-D).

TAXE   With post horn, o.p. for P-D, Albania.

TAXE A PERCEVOIR   Postage due to be collected, insc. P-D, France and col., Yemen, and others.

TAXE A PERCEVOIR T   O.p. for P-D, Ethiopia.

TAXE PERCUE   Insc. air mail, Mozambique. Under U.P.U. rules this insc. must be placed on mail prepared without stamps.

T.C.   O.p. on Cochin, for Travancore-Cochin state, India.

TCHAD   Insc. Chad.

TCHONGKING; TCH'ONG K'ING   O.p. on Indo-China for Fr. off. Chungking, China.

TE BETAAL; TE BETALEN   First, Afrikaans; second, Dutch; insc. P-D, South Africa, S.W. Africa.

TE BETALEN–A PAYER   Bil. insc. P-D, Belgium.

TE BETALEN PORT   Insc. P-D, Netherlands and col. stamps, blue for Netherlands, red for Dutch East Indies, lilac for Surinam, green for Curaçao.

TEN VOORDEELE VAN HET ROODE KRUIS [surtax] AU PROFIT DE LA CROIX ROUGE   Bil. o.p. for S-P, Belgian E. Africa (Ruanda Urundi).

T.E.O.   Territoires Ennemis Occupés, o.p. on France, Syria.

T.E.O. CILICIE   O.p. on Turkey for Cilicia.

TERRES AUSTRALES ET ANTARCTIQUES FRANÇAISE O.p. on Madagascar; insc. Fr. Southern Antarctic Territories.

TERRITOIRE DE L'ININI   O.p. on Fr. Guiana, for Inini.

TERRITOIRE DU FEZZAN   Insc. Fr. occ. Libya.

TERRITOIRE DU NIGER   Insc. Niger.

TERRITORIO DE IFNI   O.p. on Spain for Ifni.

TERRITORIOS DEL AFRICA OCCIDENTAL ESPANOLA Insc. Sp. W. Africa.

TERRITORIOS ESPANOLES DEL GOLFO DE GUINEA Insc. Sp. Guinea.

THAI; THAILAND   Insc. Siam, the latter after 1943.

THE UNITED ARAB REPUBLIC   Insc. Syria first issue, 1958.

THRACE INTERALLIEE; THRACE OCCIDENTALE   O.p. on Bulgaria for Thrace.

Thunderbolts and Mercury   Design for QE, Austria.

TICAL   First Latin-letter o.p. on Siam, 1885.

Tiger head   With Siamese insc., o.p. on Siam, S-P.; same with SCOUTS FUND.

TIMBRE COLIS POSTAUX   O.p. for parcel post, Indo-China.

TIMBRE DE RECONSTRUCCION   Insc. P-T, Guatemala.

TIMBRE DU SOUVENIR   Insc. S-P, Luxembourg.

TIMBRE FISCAL REPUBLIQUE SYRIENNE   And Arabic, o.p. for P-T, Syria.

TIMBRE IMPERIAL—JOURNAUX   Insc. p stamps, France.

TIMBRE PATRIOTICO   O.p. for P-T, var. Ecuador.

TIMBRE POSTE COLIS POSTAUX   O.p. for Q Martinique.

TIMBRE TAXE   Insc. P-D, France and col., Monaco.

TIMBRU DE AJUTOR   Insc. and o.p. for P-T, Roumania.

TIMBRU DE BINE-FACERE   Insc. S-P, Roumania.

TIMBRUL AVIATIEI   Insc. P-T, Roumania.

TIMBRU OFFICIAL   Insc. Off. Roumania.

TJANSTE FRIMARKE; TJENESTE FRIMARKE   First, insc., second, insc. and o.p. Off., Sweden.

TJENESTE FRIMAERKE   Insc. Off. Denmark; —FRIMARKE insc. Off. Norway; —POST FRIMAERKE insc. Off., Denmark.

TOGO   Insc. early Tonga Islands.

TOGO   O.p. on German Togo or on Gold Coast, Br.. occ.; o.p. on Germany for Togo; o.p. on Dahomey for Fr. occ. Togo.

TOGO ANGLO-FRENCH OCCUPATION   O.p. on German Togo for Br. occ. of Togo.

TOGO OCCUPATION FRANCO-ANGLAISE   O.p. on German Togo and Dahomey, Fr. occ. Togo.

TONGA FRIENDLY ISLANDS   Alternating multiple o.p. on back of round gold-coin stamps of 1963.

TOO LATE   Insc. late fee stamp, Victoria, 1855.

TO PAY   Insc. British P-D.

TOSCANO   Insc. Tuscany.

TOUVA; TOVVA K 8 K POSTAGE   Insc., o.p., Tannu Tuva.

TRAVANCORE ANCHAL (or ANCHEL)   Insc. Travancore state, India.

TREASURY DEPT.   Insc. U.S. Off.

TRIPOLI   Insc. Tripolitania.

TRIPOLI DI BARBERIA   O.p. on Italy, off. in Tripoli.

TRISTAN DA CUNHA RESETTLEMENT 1963   O.p. on St. Helena to mark the resettlement of those islands.

Tughra   Tura in modern Turkish. The cipher of the Sultan of Turkey in ornamental form. Used as symbol of the Ottoman Empire and contains the names of the sultan and his father, the title *Kahn*, and a laudatory phrase. It is said to have originated in a handprint of the sultan.

TURKIYE COCUK ESIRGEME KORUMU   Insc. P-T, Turkey.

TURKIYE CUMHURIYETI POSTALARI (Also T.C. POSTALARI, or POSTA)   Turkish Republic postage, insc. Turkey.

TURK POSTALARI   Insc. first issue of Turkey with Latinized words.

UCAK POSTALARI   Insc. air mail; UCAK ILT, etiquette, Turkey.

U.G.   Insc. typewritten stamps of Uganda.

U.H.   O.p. on P-T for late fee, Ecuador.

UHURU 9th DEC. 1961   Insc. Tanganyika; UHURU 1963 Insc. Zanzibar, for independence.

UKRAINE   O.p. on Germany for occ. of Russia.

ULTRAMAR   Beyond the sea, only insc. on some Sp. issues for Cuba; insc. on P-T, Macao and Guinea.

U.N.FORCE (INDIA) CONGO   O.p. India for U.N. Forces.

U.N.FORCE W.IRIAN   O.p. on Pakistan for troops in West New Guinea, 1963.

UNIAO DOS ATIRADORES CIVIS PORTO FRANCO   Insc. Rifle Club franchise stamps, Portugal.

UNION FRANCAIS   Insc. Laos.

UNION OF SOUTH AFRICA–UNIE VAN ZUID AFRIKA Bil. insc. South Africa 1910-1926. See South Africa.

UNION PANAMERICANA 1890-1940 CORREO AEREO   O.p. for air mail, Guatemala.

UNION POSTALE DEL SALVADOR   Insc. El Salvador.

UNITED ARAB REPUBLIC, U.A.R.   Insc. for Egypt, 1958.

UNITED STATES CITY DESPATCH POST   Insc. on first U.S. issue, the official carrier, New York City.

U.P.A.E. ADHESION VICTIMAS SAN JUAN Y PUEBLO ARGENTINO   Insc. S-P, Paraguay, for victims of an Argentine earthquake.

URGENCIA   Insc. S-D Spain; URGENTE same, Spain, Ifni.

URUNDI   O.p. on Congo for Belgian occ. Ger. E. Africa.

U.S.I.R.   U.S. Internal Revenue, insc. on some revenues. Without periods forms the watermark in paper used for revenue stamps.

U.S. PARCEL POST   Insc. U.S. parcel post.

USPS   These letters form the watermark used for U.S. stamps, 1895-1916, U.S. envelopes after 1915. Letters normally refer to the Postal Service, but may mean United States Postage Stamps.

U.S.T.C.   O.p. on Cochin, for the United State of Travancore-Cochin, India, 1949.

V   In corners of triangular 50-haleru Czechoslovakia personal delivery stamp.

Vale   O.p. on Nicaragua, meaning worth, or valid.

VALE UN CENTAVO R. de C.   O.p. for P-T, Nicaragua.

VALEUR DECLARE   Value declared, insured parcel label, French.

VALEUR DECLAREE   Value declared, insured parcel labels, Canada.

VALEVOLO PER LE STAMP   Available for printed matter, o.p. on Italy parcel post for newspaper stamps, but used for ordinary postage.

VALLEES D'ANDORRE   Insc. Fr. adm. Andorra.

VALMY   With surtax, o.p. for S-P, Cameroons.

VALONA   O.p. on Italy, off. in Valona, Turkish Empire.

VALOR DECLARADO   Insc. insured parcel labels, Spanish.

VALORE GLOBALE   Value in cent. or corona, o.p. to make valid for regular use, Fiume 1919-20.

VALPARAISO MULTADA   Typeset round or oval P-D, Chile.

VAN DIEMAN'S LAND   Insc. Tasmania 1853-58.

VATHY   O.p. on France, off. in Vathy, Turkish Empire.

VATICANE   Insc. Vatican City.

V.C.   Victor Castaigne, postmaster, feature of Meshad prov., Persia 1902.

VENEZIA GIULIA; VENEZIA TRIDENTIA   O.p. on Italy, occ. of Austria.

VIA AEREA   Insc. air mail, Paraguay and Brazil; o.p. for air mail, Ifni.

VICTORIA and large V   Insc. P-T, Cuba.

VIVA ESPANA   O.p. on Spain for rev. issues of Canary Islands.

VOJENSKA POSTA   Insc. Cz. army post in Siberia.

VOJNA UPRAVA JUGOSLAVENSKE ARMIJE   O.p. on Jugoslavia for use in Zone B, Istria and Slovene Coast.

VOJSKO NA RUSI   Insc. Cz. army post in Siberia.

VOLKSDIENST   Insc. S-P, Netherlands.

VOLKSSTAAT BAYERN; VOLKSSTAAT WÜRTTEMBERG
Insc. Off. Bavaria, Württemberg.

VOM EMPFANGER EINZUZIEHEN   From receiver to be
collected; insc. P-D, Bavaria.

VOM EMPFANGER ZAHLBAR   From receiver to be paid;
insc. P-D, Bavaria.

VOOR HET KIND   For the children, insc. S-P, Netherlands.

VOOR HET NATIONAL STEUNFONDS   Insc. S-P, Surinam.

VOOR KRIJGSGEVANGENEN (etc.)   O.p. on Curaçao air
mail for air mail S-P.

V.R.I.   Victoria Regina Imperatrix, o.p. Transvaal, Boer War,
1899-1902; o.p. on Orange Free State, for Br. occ. Orange River
Colony; o.p. on South African Republic for Transvaal.

V.R. SPECIAL POST   O.p. on Transvaal, Br. occ. Vryburg,
Cape of Good Hope.

V.R. TRANSVAAL   O.p. on South African Republic for
Transvaal.

VUJA [or VUJNA] STT   O.p. on Jugoslavia, mil. govt. Zone
B, Trieste.

WAR   O.p. for war tax, Br. Honduras.

WAR CHARITY 3.6.18   O.p. for S-P, Bahamas.

WAR DEPT.   Insc. U.S. Off.

WAR STAMP; WAR TAX   O.p. for war tax, var. Br. col. and
dominions.

**WENDEN; WENDEN [or WENDENSCHEN] KREISES
[KREIS]**   Insc. Wenden district (Livonia), Russia.

WERTAUGABE   Insc. insured parcel label, German.

WESTERN SAMOA   Insc. for Samoa under Br. dom. and o.p.
on New Zealand for same.

Wheat Sheaf   O.p. on Republic of Hungary when the kingdom
was restored.

W.H.W.   With value, Ger. type, o.p. for S-P, Danzig.

Winged propeller   O.p. for air mail, Switzerland.

Winged wheel   O.p. for Off. Belgium, Natl. Railways.

WINTERHILFE   With value, o.p. for S-P, Austria.

WINTERHULP   Insc. on S-P, Netherlands.

Y¼   O.p. on Cuba for a new value.

YCA; YCA VAPOR   First in oval, second in arc, o.p. on Peru, Chilean occ.

YUNNANSEN; YUNNAN FOU   O.p. on Indo-China, Fr. off. in Yunnan Fou.

Z. AFR REPUBLIEK   Insc. Transvaal.

ZA GRUENI KRST; ZA RDECI KRIZ   With cross, insc. P-T, Jugoslavia.

Z..A.R.   Value in pence, o.p. on Cape of Good Hope, Br. occ. Vryburg.

ZEITUNGS MARKE   Insc. newspaper stamps, Austria.

ZEITUNGS MARKE DEUTSCHES REICH   Insc. newspaper stamps, Germany.

ZEITUNGS STAEMPLE (or STAMPLE, STEMPLE)   Insc. newspaper stamps, Austria.

ZENTRALER KUBIERDIENST   Insc. off. German Democratic Republic.

ZEPPELIN 1930   O.p. for air mail, Iceland, Finland.

ZEPPELIN POST   Insc. air mail, Liechenstein.

ZOMERZEGEL   Insc. S-P, Netherlands.

ZONA DE OCCUPATIE P.T.T. 1919 ROMANA   In ellipse, o.p. on Hungary, Roumanian occ., first Debrecen issue; similar in circle, second Debrecen issue.

ZONA DE PROTECTORADO ESPANOL EN MARRUECOS   O.p. on Spain, and insc. Sp. off. in Morocco.

ZONA FRANCAIS BRIEFPOST   Insc. Fr. occ. Germany.

ZUID AFRIKA   Afrikaans insc. before 1926, South Africa.

Zuid-West [or Zuidwest] Africa   O.p. on South Africa for S.W. Africa. This spelling used only in 1923-25, in a bil. o.p. see SUID-WESAFRIKA.

ZULASSUNGSMARKE DEUTSCHE FELDPOST   Ger. field-post permit stamp, insc. mil. parcel stamp, 1942, without expressed value, to frank any parcel.

ZURICH   Insc. Swiss cantonal stamps, Zurich.

GLOSSARY OF SPECIAL TERMS

AMERICAN BANK NOTE CO. Incorporated by Rawdon, Wright, Hatch & Edson on May 1, 1858, the company printed Canadian stamps. It printed part of the reverses of the postage currency of 1862 for the United States as well as stamps for various countries. The National and Continental Bank Note Companies became a part of the company in 1879, which printed all United States postage stamps from 1879 until 1894. At present it is the parent company of the Canadian Bank Note Co. and of Bradbury Wilkinson & Co., of England.

AUGUST PRINTINGS. Term for the first designs of the United States issue of 1861, which are probably essays. Examples were submitted to postal authorities, and while not approved, a few values performed legitimate postal service.

BACKSTAMP. A postal marking placed on the back of United States first-class mail to indicate the time of arrival at office of delivery. Discontinued on ordinary mail May 8, 1913, on air mail March 23, 1934, but still used on special delivery, certified, and registered mail. Reinstated April 20, 1953, on all general-delivery mail at first-class offices, and on mail undelivered on the day of receipt at other offices, first-class mail to be backstamped and other classes front stamped to show the date. Backstamps are provided by special order on first flights, dedications of new air routes, H.P.O. routes, etc.

BANK NOTE ISSUES. Stamps printed by the National, Continental, and American Bank Note Companies between 1870 and 1890. Those printed by the National Company before 1870 and those of the American Company in 1890 and later are not included.

BATTLESHIP REVENUES. U.S. documentary and proprietary revenue stamps of the Spanish-American War period which show a view of a battleship.

BILINGUAL PAIRS. Stamps in different languages, alternately placed in the sheet. Stamps of South Africa and Southwest Africa have English and Afrikaans inscriptions on the adjoining stamps.

BLACK JACK. The two-cent black stamp of 1863 with portrait of Andrew Jackson.

BLACKOUT CANCELLATION. A term for cancellations (Canadian, for example) which are in ordinary form but without post-office name. Used to conceal locations of army camps, etc. Also called mute cancellations.

BLOCK. Term for four unseparated stamps, two by two. Triangular stamps may be in squares of two stamps, and in blocks of eight, etc., while fours are comparable in shape to pairs of ordinary stamps.

BOARDWALK MARGINS. Abnormally wide margins, as in a "jumbo" copy.

BORDEAUX PRINTS. French stamps lithographed in Bordeaux, November, 1870, to March, 1871, while the government was in that city during the siege of Paris.

BRADBURY WILKINSON & CO. Bank note engravers of London, a subsidiary of the American Bank Note Company.

BRANCH POST OFFICE. In the U.S. a subsidiary postal station located outside the corporate limits of the city to which attached. Cicero, Illinois, is a branch of the Chicago post office. During the 1860's the term was used for stations and Chicago had a West Branch and a North Branch within the city.

BRITISH-AMERICAN BANK NOTE CO. Stamp printers of Canadian stamps from 1868 to 1897, 1930 to 1934.

BUREAU ISSUES. Stamps produced by the Bureau of Engraving and Printing.

BUREAU OF ENGRAVING AND PRINTING. A division of the U.S. Treasury which has printed postage and revenue stamps, currency, bonds, etc., for many years. All U.S. postage stamps since 1894, except the Overrun Nations series, have been produced by the bureau.

BUREAU PRINTS. Precancelled stamps produced by the Bureau of Engraving and Printing by attaching a typographic unit to the rotary engraving press.

CAMEL MAIL, CAMEL POST. Camels were imported to the southwestern territory of the U.S. prior to the Civil War. They were undoubtedly used to transmit official dispatches between army posts, but there were no marks to identify such mail.

CANADIAN BANK NOTE CO. The name taken by the American Bank Note Company, in Canada, 1923. This company has printed all Canadian stamps from 1897 to the present time except the issues from 1930 to 1935.

CANCELED STAMPS. Postally canceled stamps, as opposed to canceled to order.

CANTONAL STAMPS. The local issues of Basle, Geneva, and Zurich cantons, prior to the federal issues.

CAPE TRIANGLES. The triangular stamps of the Cape of Good Hope.

CARRIER BACKSTAMP. A postal marking of 1870-1890 used in several large post offices to backstamp mail handled by carriers.

CENTER LINE. The horizontal or vertical line crossing the sheet of stamps to indicate where to divide the sheet into post-office panes. The line may occur where there is to be no division, particularly in bicolored stamps, and may serve some purpose in color registry. The center lines usually extend into the margins where they end in arrows or large dots.

CENTER LINE BLOCK. A block showing the crossed horizontal and vertical center lines.

CHALON HEAD. Stamps showing the head of Queen Victoria by Alfred Edward Chalon, R.A., as in the early New Zealand issues.

CHARITY LABELS. Stickers without postal value used to raise funds for various causes. Perhaps originated in the Sanitary Fair stamps of the Civil War and represented today by Christmas Seals. Most desirable when on cover with stamps of the period.

CHICAGO COUNTERFEIT. Counterfeits of the 2-cent U.S.

stamp of 1894, sold by the Canadian Novelty Co., of Hamilton, Ontario, and detected by Chicago Postal inspectors.

CHROMED, CHROME PLATED, CHROMIUM PLATED. An electroplated coat of this metal is often used to lengthen the life of steel or copper plates. A "C" appears in the margin of U.S. plates so treated.

CLIPPER POSTMARK. Incorrectly applied to an ocean mail mark used outbound from New York. Shows a small grid between the "New" and "York" in the townmark.

COLLATERAL MATERIAL. Maps, photographs, printed illustrations, autographs, etc., associated material mounted in an album.

COMBINATION COVERS. Those which bear the stamps of two postal administrations when such are required to carry the letter. This usage is found in some Confederate prisoner-of-war covers with United States and Confederate stamps, and in covers from Tibet with added Indian stamps.

CONSULAR FEE STAMPS. Fiscal stamps to show payment of consular service fees. First used by the U.S. in 1896.

CONTINENTAL BANK NOTE CO. Printed U.S. stamps 1873-1879; merged into American Bank Note Company, February, 1879.

CONTINENTALS. An old philatelic term for the common European stamps of the last century.

CONTROL NUMBERS, OR LETTERS. Also called *account numbers*. Numbers or letters printed on sheets to check quantities. Usually on margins.

CONTROLLED MAIL. For this the operator supplies selected stamps to large users with branch offices, and buys back the used stamps. He arranges for careful postmarking in some cases. The stamp user's postage bill is greatly reduced.

CONTROL OVERPRINTS. Inscriptions or devices printed on stamps to identify valid issues when identical stamps are in the hands of others through theft, remainders in printers' hands, etc.

CONVENTION STATES OF INDIA. These used Indian stamps overprinted with the state name. Valid throughout India, the stamps were discontinued January 1, 1951.

CORNER BLOCK. A block of stamps with margins on two adjoining sides.

CORNER CARD, RETURN CARD. Name and address of envelope user, usually placed in upper left corner. May include devices, illustrations, etc.

CUSTOMS STAMPS. United States fiscal stamps to collect customs duties at port of New York only.

CUT CANCELLATION. Some cancelling devices make cuts through revenue stamps and documents to prevent a second use of the stamps. May be hand cut also.

CUT TO SHAPE. Stamps of unusual shape which have been cut to the frame line of the design. This was customary when the first stamps were printed and many British octagonal stamps are found on cover or in old collections in this form. The value is greatly reduced by trimming.

CYLINDER NUMBERS. A British photogravure cylinder prints a number on the margin of each sheet, and if double-width, the same number on each of the two sheets but one is followed by a dot. These numbers are not consecutive for stamps of differing denominations.

DEMONETIZED STAMPS. Stamps declared not valid for postage. See *Obsolete Stamps*.

DENOMINATION. The face value indicated on the stamp.

DISTRICT. A U.S. political subdivision inferior to a territory. The Louisiana Purchase, excepting what is now the state of Louisiana, was once a district attached to the territory of Indiana. The district of Maine was attached to Massachusetts until Maine gained statehood.

DROP LETTER. A letter addressed to a person served by the office of cancellation where no carrier service is maintained.

DUPLEX HANDSTAMP. A cancelling handstamp combining townmark and killer on a single handle. Invented by Pearson Hill, of England.

DUTY PLATES. A term used in connection with stamp plates in a uniform design. The duty plate prints the variable denominations, colony names, etc. See *Key Plate* and *Head Plate*.

EN CREUX. In creases, gutters—French term for line engraving.

EPARGNE. French term used in connection with engraved relief dies for typography.

EXHIBITION LABELS. Poster stamps to advertise an exhibition or serve as souvenirs. Now issued for philatelic exhibitions.

Some are in sheet form, perforated like stamps, one to a sheet with inscriptions.

EXHIBITION SHEETS. Souvenir sheets containing a stamp or stamps with postal value.

EXPRESS COMPANY LABELS. Labels for letters and money parcels handled by private U.S. carriers, a new label being added when a parcel passed to another carrier. The government abolished this business.

F. This letter on a stamp plate indicates it has been hardened.

FANCY TYPE. Descriptive of overprints in ornamental type or details.

FLYSPECK PHILATELY. A derogatory term for the microscopic studies of some stamp collectors.

FORMAT. Refers to the shape and size of a stamp and the relative position of the form.

FRACTIONAL CURRENCY. Notes from three to fifty cents issued during the Civil War when metal money was scarce. The first issue pictured stamps and was called Postage Currency.

FRANK. A mark or label on a cover carried free on account of the official position of sender or receiver. Includes military personnel, wives of former presidents, etc. Also a term for imprints on express company envelopes indicating a payment for service. A postage stamp on the same envelope shows that postage has been paid for its transportation, even though it may never have entered the mail.

FREE MAIL. Franked mail.

GAP VARIETY. Term used by precancel collectors to indicate the gap or break in the lines of Bureau Print precancels at the joints between the electrotype plates.

GUAM GUARD MAIL. A local post of the army, using overprinted Philippines.

HAIR LINES. Colorless diagonal lines across the corners of the 4-, 6-, and 9-pence British stamps of 1862 to identify certain plates.

HAMILTON BANK NOTE CO. An engraving company best known for its connection with the Seebeck issue.

HANDSTRUCK STAMPS. A British term for postmarks, rate marks, etc., impressed on covers prior to postage stamps.

HARRISON AND SONS. British stamp printers, particularly of the George V issues.

HEAD PLATE. A special designation for the key plate when the design is a portrait. See *Key Plate, Duty Plate*.

IMPRINT. A marginal inscription on a sheet of stamps. An inscription below individual stamps to identify the printer.

IMPRINT BLOCK. A block of stamps showing the entire imprint.

INDICIA. The elements of a postage meter impression which show the meter number, the permit number if any, and the postage rate.

INSCRIPTION. The letters or numbers that are part of the definitive stamp design; to be distinguished from such a description as *overprint inscription*.

ISSUE. Term for a related group of stamps. The total number of stamps sold while current.

IVORY HEAD. A philatelic term for the 2-pence blue British stamps of 1847-1857, in which chemical action has blued the paper except under lightly inked portions. A similar effect is found in 1-penny red stamps.

JUBILEE LINES. A printing of lines or dashes on the margins of typographed stamps to receive the sharp blow struck by the impression roll as it crosses the gutter between plates on a cylinder. Before these were added the frame lines of marginal stamps were greatly damaged. They first appeared on the British issue of 1887, Queen Victoria's jubilee year.

KEY PLATE. In printing stamps for more than one colony, or several stamps in a set differing only in value, the basic design may be printed with a key plate while the variable country or colony names or denominations are added with the duty plate. The stamps produced may be bicolored or in a single color. The terms *key* and *duty* do not apply to ordinary plates for bicolor printing.

KNIFE. Term for the die that cuts paper blanks from which early envelopes were folded. Issues can be identified by the shape of flaps and points. So named to avoid confusion with the stamp-printing die.

LABEL. The first name for postage stamps as shown on the margins of the first sheets. Today Britain calls postage due stamps labels. Collectors use the word for various stickers without postage or revenue value.

LICENSE STAMPS.   Nonpostal stickers on items such as boots, shoes, collars, etc., to show that the article was manufactured under license.

LOCK SEALS.   Serially numbered engraved slips of paper to be inserted in padlocks on doors of bonded liquor warehouses. Opening the lock destroys the seal and indicates tampering. Collected with revenue issues.

MANUSCRIPT.   Handwritten, as early postal markings.

MANUSCRIPT PROVISIONALS.   Stamps with values altered by hand during stamp shortage, as Trinidad, 1882, 1d and 6d.

MASONIC CANCELLATION.   One showing a Masonic emblem or a device associated with that society.

MERRY WIDOW.   Term for the U.S. special delivery design of 1908, showing Mercury head with a very large hat.

MILLESIME.   Term for date figures on margins of French and colonial issues and on some stamps of Belgium; refers also to blocks with marginal dates.

MISSIONARY STAMPS.   Term for the first issues of Hawaii.

MISSTRIKE.   Term for misplaced stamps on postal stationery.

MOBILE POST OFFICES.   The name in some foreign countries for vehicular post offices that serve as temporary stations in an emergency, at large events such as exhibitions, or to visit isolated communities.

MOURNING STAMPS.   Black-bordered stamps issued in mourning for a ruler or famous person. The Belgian issues for King Albert (1934) and Queen Astrid (1935) are examples. There have been such stamps without borders, such as the 1882 Garfield of the U.S.

MUTE POSTMARK.   See *Blackout Cancellation.*

NAME TABLET.   The part of a duty plate that prints the country name.

NESBITT ENVELOPES.   Made by the George F. Nesbitt Co., of New York, in business from 1795 until 1912. The company produced U.S. envelopes from 1853 to 1870.

OBSOLETE STAMPS.   A term for stamps no longer on sale; does not imply demonetization.

ORIGINAL.   Term distinguishing an impression from a reprint; to distinguish between printings from original and altered dies.

PAID PERMITS. A system for mailing identical pieces in quantity without stamps, authorized in 1904.

PAIR. Two stamps attached at sides, or top and bottom.

PARIS PRINTS. Term for early Greek issues, identifying stamps printed locally and in Paris.

PATENT LINES. Heavy lines printed inside an envelope as a guide when writing name and address.

PHILATELIC STATION CANCELLATIONS. Special postmarks applied at postal stations set up at stamp conventions and exhibitions.

PLATE FLAW. An accidental blemish or damage on a plate, showing on the stamps.

PLATE NUMBER. A number assigned to a stamp printing plate. U.S. plates of the Bureau of Engraving and Printing are numbered consecutively. Some countries start each new type with No. 1, and in other cases each printing company numbers its plates consecutively. British stamps of 1858-1881 have small plate numbers within the design. In Japan, kana characters show on each stamp as plate numbers in the issues of 1874-1875. In both cases each new stamp starts with plate No. 1.

PLIMPTON ENVELOPES. The Plimpton Mfg. Co. and successors printed U.S. envelopes from 1874 until 1903.

POACHED EGG LABELS. Dummy stamps in coil form to test the operation of vending machines in England. Some copies left in machines reached the public and a few were. used to frank letters.

POSITION BLOCKS. Blocks from various portions of a sheet to show normal, center line, line, arrow, plate number, imprint, corner, register marks, and various margin blocks.

POSTAL NOTES. A postal method of transmitting money, adopted in the U.S. in 1883, and soon replaced by money orders. Revived in 1945 but soon discontinued.

POSTER STAMPS. Advertising or propaganda stickers in the shape of postage stamps.

POSTMASTERS' PROVISIONALS. Stamps issued by several postmasters in the U.S. and a few elsewhere prior to regular stamps. Also issued by Confederate postmasters before stamps were available.

PRINTING. An edition of stamps, as, first printing.

PRINTING FLAW.   A blemish on stamps due to some defect in printing, but not constant.

REAY ENVELOPES.   George H. Reay, noted for his fine engraving, produced U.S. envelopes, 1870-1874.

RECORDED MESSAGE STAMPS (CORREOS FONOPOSTAL). Argentine stamps, 1939, to prepay letters recorded on flexible records.

RECUT.   A minor strengthening of a line or part of a design, more extensive work would be called "re-engraving."

REDRAWN.   A design retaining the general features of a previous type but differing in detail.

REFERENCE NUMBERS.   British term for plate numbers on Empire stamps printed by De La Rue & Co. only. All plates have consecutive numbers, as customary in U.S.

REGISTER MARKINGS.   Lines, arrows, crosses, or dots placed on plates to aid in color registration in multicolor printing.

RESETTING.   A new arrangement of clichés in a plate. A resetting provides new combinations of varieties and may produce a tête-bêche variety.

REVALIDATED.   Restored to validity after being demonetized.

ROUND GUM.   The shape of the ends of the gum on flaps of U.S. envelopes. In 1876 the shape was changed from square to round.

ST. ANDREW'S CROSS LABELS.   Sheets of foreign stamps often had blank spaces to bring the sheet values to even amounts. In Austria these spaces had diagonal lines known as St. Andrew's crosses. In some stamp booklets similar blanks are used for advertisements.

ST. LOUIS BEARS.   Name for the postmaster's provisionals issued in St. Louis, Missouri, showing the arms of the city supported by bears.

SECRET MARKS.   Marks placed on the dies of U.S. stamps which the National Bank Note Co. turned over to its successor, the Continental Bank Note Co., in 1873. Plates later made from these dies could be identified by the marks on the stamps. They qualify as secret marks since they remained unknown for about twenty years.

SET.   A series of stamps as issued. The term, *Short set* refers to part of a series, usually the lower values.

SE TENANT.   Term for attached stamps which differ in a major respect: denomination, design, country, etc. This condition was an error in early issues but now occurs in sheets printed for stamp booklets in many countries.

SETTING.   The arrangement of clichés in a plate when they are movable and can be rearranged.

SHEET NUMBERS.   Consecutive numbers placed on sheets by a numbering machine to keep an accurate count of the number printed.

SLEEPER.   A stamp with a higher value than charged. Many varieties are underpriced because no dealer knows everything about all stamps. A collector may make a "find" in kiloware or in an attic, but "sleepers" come from dealers' stocks.

SPANDREL.   The triangular areas between a circle or ellipse and a circumscribed square or rectangle. At first applied only to the spaces at the sides of an arch between columns or piers. See U.S. issue of 1894 for triangles in the spandrels.

STAR DIES.   Term for second issue of U.S. envelopes with small star at each side between inscriptions.

STAR PLATES.   U.S. plates with a star in the imprint or near the plate number to indicate an experimental spacing of the subjects to obtain better-centered stamps.

STATION.   A subsidiary unit attached to a post office and within the corporate limits of a city.

STRIP.   More than two unsevered stamps in a row.

SUNDAY LABELS.   A small label at the bottom of Belgian stamps, 1893-1915, with inscription in French, *Ne pas livrer le Dimanche*, and Flemish, *Niet bestellen op Zondag*, meaning *Do not deliver on Sunday*. The Netherlands provided a separate label for this purpose which patrons could affix.

SUNDAY TAX STAMPS.   Bulgaria required a post tax stamp on letters to be delivered on Sundays and holidays, the proceeds providing sanitariums for postal and telegraph employees.

SURCHARGE.   A word given various meanings from overprint to additional charge. The only overprints this writer classes as requiring additional charges are those providing surtaxes on semipostal issues. The usual overprints affecting the face value are downward to prevent forgery, and this would not be an added charge. To avoid any conflict, this book confines its terminology in this respect to *overprint*.

TAB.   A sheet margin with an inscription, symbol, or device other than the plate number or imprint. Israel and Czechoslovakia provide many examples. Tabs are collected attached to single stamps or blocks.

TABLET.   A panel, framed or decorated, set apart for value numerals.

TERRITORIAL COVER, TERRITORIAL POSTMARK. Term refers to territories of the U.S. Some postmarks are rare because of the early period, or the shortness of their history. All are more desirable when "Ter." or "T" appears in the mark.

TIED ON.   Term indicating that the postal marking cancels the stamp and overlaps onto the envelope, making it more difficult to substitute a stamp, and proving that the stamp was on cover when it was cancelled.

TIN CAN MAIL.   Prior to its devastation by a volcano (1946) the Island of Niuafoou, in the Tonga or Friendly Islands, was reached at intervals by a vessel of the New Zealand Steamship Co., and mail sealed in a can was delivered to the vessel and that for the island taken off by a swimmer. Cachets were applied by the postmaster and the covers were popular.

TIN FOIL REVENUES.   These were tax-paid revenue stamps printed on the foil used to wrap tobacco.

TOPPAN, CARPENTER, CASILEAR & CO.   A bank note engraving company which printed the 1851-60 issue of U.S. stamps. Its successor, Butler & Carpenter, was the first printer of the Civil War revenue issues.

TURNED COVER.   Envelopes or letter sheets reversed for a second use. Common in the early days of the American post, especially in the South during the Civil War.

UNGUMMED.   When stamps of tropical countries are issued without gum it should be noted in the catalog. This term should not be used for stamps that have lost their gum.

UNLISTED.   A stamp not listed in a current catalog.

UNSEVERED.   Describing a pair or strip, as an "unsevered pair."

USED ABROAD.   Stamps used outside the issuing country, as U.S. used at foreign agencies, military stations, etc.

VIGNETTE.   An illustration shading off to an indefinite edge, much used in bicolor printing as color register is not so important as when the picture is framed. The word is erroneously applied by some writers to all pictures used in stamp designs.

WALLPAPER COVERS.   During the paper shortage of the Civil War many envelopes in the South were made of wallpaper.

WOODBLOCKS.   Philatelic term for the locally printed Cape triangles of 1861. They were printed from stereotypes mounted on small wooden blocks.

ZIP CODE TABS.   A postal service device printed on the side margins of United States stamp sheets to promote the use of Zip Code numbers.

INDEX